Literature for Today's Young Adults

NINTH EDITION

Alleen Pace Nilsen
Arizona State University

James Blasingame
Arizona State University

Kenneth L. Donelson
Arizona State University

Don L. F. Nilsen
Arizona State University

PEARSON

Boston   Columbus   Indianapolis   New York   San Francisco   Upper Saddle River
Amsterdam   Cape Town   Delhi   Dubai   Hong Kong   London   Madrid   Mexico City
Milan   Munich   Paris   Montreal   São Paulo   Seoul   Singapore   Sydney   Taipei   Tokyo   Toronto

Vice President and Editor-In-Chief: Aurora Martínez Ramos
Editor: Erin Grelak
Editorial Assistant: Michelle Hochberg
Executive Marketing Manager: Krista Clark
Production Editor: Mary Beth Finch
Editorial Production Service: S4Carlisle Publishing Services
Manufacturing Buyer: Megan Cochran
Electronic Composition: S4Carlisle Publishing Services
Interior Design: S4Carlisle Publishing Services
Cover Designer: Diane Lorenzo

Credits and acknowledgments borrowed from other sources and reproduced, with permission, in this textbook appear on appropriate page within text (or on page 449).

Many of the designations by manufacturers and sellers to distinguish their products are claimed as trademarks. Where those designations appear in this book, and the publisher was aware of a trademark claim, the designations have been printed in initial caps or all caps.

Library of Congress Cataloging-in-Publication Data
Nilsen, Alleen Pace.
  Literature for today's young adults / Alleen Pace Nilsen . . . [et al.]. —9th ed.
    p. cm.
  Alleen Pace Nilsen appears as the first author in 8th ed.
  ISBN-13: 978-0-13-268577-1—ISBN-10: 0-13-268577-9 1. Teenagers—Books and reading—United States. 2. Young adult literature—History and criticism. 3. Young adult fiction—History and criticism. 4. Young adult literature—Bibliography. 5. Young adult fiction—Bibliography. I. Title.
  Z1037.A1D578 2012
  028.5'35—dc23

                                                                      2011050181

10 9 8 7 6 5 4

ISBN-10:   0-13-268577-9
ISBN-13: 978-0-13-268577-1

From Don and Alleen to our grandchildren
who are reading many of the books we are discussing:
Taryn, Britton, Kami, Erich, David, Lauren,
Michael, Jenna, Avery, Jim, and Luke

From Jim
Dedicated to Margaret Blasingame (1927–1986) who
believed that all children were special and all children could learn

BRIEF CONTENTS

CONTENTS

part three
Adults and the Literature of Young Adults   319

SPECIAL FEATURES

Margaret A. Edwards Award

Winner

Honor List

Young Scholars Speak Out

Focus Boxes

Film Boxes

PREFACE

This is the first revision of *Literature for Today's Young Adults* that Ken Donelson has not worked on. He said it was time to pass the mantle to younger scholars, and so one of the things we did was to invite ten of our doctoral students, or recent graduates, to write "Young Scholars Speak Out" pages on subjects dear to their hearts. We hope you will enjoy reading their original ideas and opinions, which are scattered throughout the chapters. They range from questions on ethnicity and respect for people's names to the image of girls portrayed in teen magazines, and from what one student learned at chef's school about the teaching of young adult literature to what another student thinks is behind the new "darkness" in YA books. We hope their statements will inspire other students to realize that there are still many intriguing topics related to young adult literature that deserve further research and writing.

It took two hard-working and highly respected Arizona State University English department professors to jump in and do what had usually been Ken's half of each revision. They are James Blasingame and Don L. F. Nilsen. We want to assure readers that as the three of us worked on this edition, we felt Dr. Donelson's influence in every change we made. Back in the late 1970s, it was Ken Donelson's idea to write this book in such a way that it would help bring respectability to a field of study which, at the time, had more detractors than supporters. We are proud that, to a large extent, our book contributed to doing exactly that, as shown by the increasing number of colleges and universities where classes in young adult literature are taught either in Departments of English, Colleges of Education, or Schools of Library Science. We hope this ninth edition will continue to serve that purpose.

Besides formally thanking Dr. Donelson for his vision and hard work over many years, we want to thank the reviewers of this manuscript: Stanley E. Bochtle, Buena Vista University; Jacqueline N. Glasgow, Ohio University; Patricia Hauschildt, Youngstown State University; Karen Mae Lafferty, Morehead State University; and Ann K. Petersen, Buena Vista University. In response to suggestions made by these reviewers, we have added two new sections. In Chapter 10, we added a section on "Young Adult Books and English Language Learners," while in Chapter 11 we added a section on "Using Children's Picture Books with High School Students."

We also want to thank the students in one of Alleen's recent classes. She brought in folders holding page proofs from the eighth edition and let the students choose one of the chapters to critique for both money and extra credit. She explained how each edition of the book has gotten longer and that it was now time to go in the opposite direction, so they should give us advice on what to cut. Their comments were both thoughtful and thorough, and we have tried to follow their advice. We were especially impressed by their explanation that they understood why, when we made an observation about YA books in general, we would want to list several books to support whatever point we were making. But since they had not read the books that we were citing, it just confused and discouraged them. In light of their persuasive argument, we have tried to cut down on long lists of titles. Instead, we have placed the titles of the most important books, along with explanations and/or descriptions, in our Focus Boxes, which we hope readers will take seriously. It is fine with us if teachers copy and distribute some of the Focus Boxes to their own students if they happen to match a subject being studied. Encouraging students to take such lists with them to a library or bookstore will enable students to have some choice in what they read, while still being able to bring to class information on a common topic or theme.

New to This Edition

Chapter 3, which focuses on digital and other new literacies, is almost totally new thanks to Dr. Blasingame and the help he received from several teachers who are making good use of the ever-changing technology with which we are blessed. In Chapter 6, Dr. Blasingame also prepared new information on poetry for our time, and arranged for us to print poems from two contemporary poets: Myrlin Hepworth, a hip-hop artist, and Alberto Rios, a Regents Professor on our Creative Writing faculty as well as a finalist for the National Book Award. This addressed a weakness in previous editions in which we did not have permission to include actual poems, so we had to speak in generalities.

Also in Chapter 6, Dr. Don Nilsen, founder of the International Society for Humor Studies, provided information about positive uses of ethnic humor, as well as information about types and features of humor as illustrated not just in books but in films and on the Web. Among the types of humor he writes about are gallows humor, intentional ambiguity, incongruity resolution, irony, parody, role reversals, sarcasm, satire, understatement, and wordplay. We are also providing more information about the graphic novel and about crossovers between literature and video games.

In keeping with our desire to focus on high-quality materials, we have added a page on each of the recent winners of the Margaret A. Edwards Award (Laurie Halse Anderson, Jim Murphy, Terry Pratchett, and Susan Cooper). In addition, we have updated both our Honor List and our Focus Boxes. For all of those lists, we paid particular attention to the books that have gotten starred reviews or other strong recommendations in the professional journals. For example, in a new Focus Box we list the winners of the Edgar Award for "Best YA Mystery" from the year 2000 until the present. And of course, just as we have had to rearrange our bookshelves to give more space to fantasy and to all the books about vampires and other "undeads," we have rearranged our chapters so as to devote earlier and more focused attention to fantasy and the supernatural.

Although we still have the scholarly goal of proving to the world that the highest quality young adult literature deserves a place in academe and on the shelves of the world's best libraries, we are now willing to admit that, in light of the success of the Harry Potter and Twilight books, today's young adult literature not only reflects, but in many ways shapes, the popular culture. We are nevertheless proud to be a part of it. Please let us hear from any of you who have comments or questions.

Alleen.Nilsen@asu.edu; James.Blasingame@asu.edu; Don.Nilsen@asu.edu

Pearson's Children's and Young Adult Literature Database

Now available for purchase with this text, this searchable database of over **22,000 book annotations** makes it easy to:

- Search and create booklists by title, author, illustrator, grade level (preschool, K-2, 3-4, 5-6, 7+, and 10+), awards won, publisher, genre, or other special topic
- Special search topics include Literature with Characters with Disabilities, Literature for English Language Learners, Multicultural Literature, International Literature, and Literature with LGBT Characters
- Over 160 awards represented, including awards such as the Aesop Prize, Caldecott Medal, Edgar Allan Poe Award, Michael L. Printz Honor Award, and the Newbery Medal
- View a complete record for any book on the database
- Annotate books of interest with your own comments
- Add your own books to the database, without limit

To order this text with the *Children's and Young Adult Literature Database*, use ISBN 0-13-303434-8.

About the Authors

Since the year 2000, when James (usually called Jim) Blasingame joined the Nilsens as members of the English Department faculty at Arizona State University, the three scholars who are responsible for this ninth edition of Literature for Today's Young Adults discovered that in addition to their love of young adult literature, they had many things in common. First, they all have what they call "the Midwestern work ethic," maybe because of where they earned their Ph.D. degrees: Jim from the University of Kansas, Don from the University of Michigan, and Alleen from the University of Iowa. They were surprised to learn that Jim, who in the

early 1970s was an undergraduate student and an all-American wrestler, at the University of Northern Iowa in Cedar Falls, did his student teaching in the Malcolm Price Laboratory School at the same time that Alleen was teaching there. Jim even remembered watching Don, who was a UNI linguistics professor, play tennis with a colleague whose serve was as strange as Don's.

The three had an even bigger surprise, when in 2003, Jim proudly shared the good news that he had been appointed co-editor of *The ALAN Review*—a job he handled beautifully from 2004 to 2009. When he applied for the position, he had no idea that he would be bringing back to Arizona State University a publication that "was born" on the ASU campus nearly thirty years earlier when Alleen and Ken Donelson had started it as *The ALAN Newsletter*. To the Nilsens, it was like welcoming back a child who had left home as a toddler and returned all grown up as a sophisticated adult.

When Alleen came to Arizona State University in 1973 as "a trailing spouse" because her husband, Don, was being hired as a linguistics professor, one of the first people she visited was Ken Donelson. She had already read some of his work that had been assigned by her professor, G. Robert Carlsen, who ten years earlier had also been Ken Donelson's dissertation advisor. When Alleen came home from attending a National Council of Teachers of English conference where she had agreed to be the editor of a newsletter for the newly organized Assembly on Literature for Adolescents of NCTE, she immediately sought out Ken's help in hopes of getting him to negotiate using the English Department's bulk-mailing permit. The founders of ALAN were so eager to recruit members that they charged only two dollars for yearly dues. By the time the newsletter turned into a real publication, the dues had been raised to $5.00, but that still wasn't enough to pay for postage and printing. Then in what was clearly "an out-and-out case of nepotism," Alleen asked her husband, Don, if he would join the Newsletter staff as the humor editor. His job was to seek out and review humorous books, plus to help with the muscle work involved in the printing and mailing.

Three times a year, the Nilsens and the Donelsons would gather around the Nilsens' dining room table and sort by zip code (a requirement for bulk mailing) the new publication, which soon turned into a twelve-page folder, plus a couple of pages of card-sized reviews. This was the beginning of the Donelson/Nilsen partnership, which grew into their co-editing the *English Journal* from 1980 to 1987 and into co-authoring this textbook, whose first edition appeared in 1980 from Scott, Foresman and cost students less than $12.00.

From the beginning, Alleen's husband, Don, was an important part of the work, which means that getting his name on the cover of the ninth edition is an overdue honor. But because his name, *Don Nilsen,* is so similar to that of *Ken Donelson* (who at age 85 is now living in a nursing home) and because he nearly always attended NCTE and the ALAN workshops with Alleen, many people assumed he was Ken Donelson. It was always embarrassing to correct people who would come up to thank him for "the wonderful textbook." Now with both of their names on the cover, at least this one little problem in the world is solved.

In conclusion; here is a quick rundown of some of the professional activities of the three co-authors, all of whom have published extensively in such professional journals as *School Library Journal, English Journal, ALAN Review, and Journal of Adult and Adolescent Literacy*. Both Jim and Alleen have served as presidents and conference directors for ALAN, and they have both received the May Hill Arbuthnot Award as "Outstanding Professor of the Year in Children's or Young Adult Literature" from the International Reading Association. Jim has also been honored as the ASU 2008 Parents Association Professor of the Year and as the 2007 Dean's Distinguished Teacher for the Humanities. In his spare time, he co-directs the Central Arizona Writing Project and is Chair of the Kids Need to Read Board of Directors.

Alleen is the author of two editions of *Presenting M. E. Kerr* as part of the Twayne United States Authors Series (1986 and 1997) and of *Joan Bauer: Teen Reads: Student Companions to Young Adult Literature* (Greenwillow, 2007). She was the editor of *Living Language: Reading, Thinking, and Writing* (Allyn and Bacon, 1999).

Don L. F. Nilsen is the founder of the International Society for Humor Studies. He and Alleen have both served as presidents and conference directors of this organization which since 1987 has held annual conferences alternating between inside and outside of the United States. Together they wrote the *Encyclopedia of 20th-Century American Humor* (Greenwood Press), which was chosen by the American Library Association as an "Outstanding Academic Book for 2000." They also co-authored *Names and Naming in Young Adult Literature* (Scarecrow Studies in YA Literature, 2007) and have served as co-presidents of the American Name Society. Their book *Pronunciation Contrasts in English* recently came out in a new edition (Waveland Press, 2010) and in 2004 Pearson published the Nilsens' *Vocabulary Plus: A Source-Based Approach: K through 8* and *High School and Up*.

One of Jim Blasingame's greatest contributions to the field is that through his editing of both the *ALAN Review* and of the "Young Adult Literature" pages in the *Journal of Adult and Adolescent Literacy,* he has helped hundreds of individuals get their first professional publications, either as an article, a book review, or an interview with an author. Because he is so well known as a book reviewer and a supporter of YA authors, he is able to arrange for well-known authors to come for visits with our students. Among the famous authors who have publically expressed gratitude to him are Sherman Alexie, Stephenie Meyer, Laurie Halse Anderson, Jack Gantos, Nancy Farmer, and Ron Koertge. Gary Soto dedicated a book to him, while both Christopher Paul Curtis and Chris Crutcher have named characters in their novels after him.

In 2007, Scholastic published his *Books That Don't Bore 'Em: Young Adult Books That Speak to This Generation.* He is also a co-author with Ruth Culham and Raymond Coutu of *Using Mentor Texts to Teach Writing with the Traits* (Scholastic, 2010), and is a contributor to *Teaching Young Adult Literature Today: Insights, Considerations, and Perspectives for the Classroom Teacher* edited by Judith A. Hayn and Jeffrey S. Kaplan (Rowman & Littlefield, 2012). In 2007, he edited a series for Greenwood Press and wrote *Gary Paulsen: Teen Reads Student Companion to YA Literature.*

Young Adults
and Their Reading

chapter **1**

"Of all passages, coming of age, or reaching adolescence is the purest, in that it is the loneliest. In birth one is not truly conscious; in marriage one has a partner, even death is faced with a life's experience by one's side," wrote David Van Biema for a special issue of *Life* magazine devoted to *The Journey of Our Lives*. (October, 1991, p. 31)

He went on to explain that going from boy or girl to man or woman is "a huge leap on the slimmest of information." The person who fails grows older without growing wiser and faces ostracism, insanity, or profound sorrow. Because such a debilitated or warped individual is a "drag on the community," the community bands together with the young person to see that the journey is accomplished.

Life would go more smoothly if young people's aspirations were simply to step into the roles of their parents. The job of growing up, however, is more demanding because, at the same time that young people are trying to become adults, they are also trying to show that they are different from their parents. This leaves each generation scrambling to find its own way to be unique, which is one of the reasons that literature for young adults tends to be a contemporary medium. Each generation wants its own stories. See Film Box 1.1, "Films That Share Characteristics with Young Adult Books," on page 2 for some of these stories told on the screen.

What Is Young Adult Literature?

We have heard *young adults* defined as those who think they're too old to be children but who others think are too young to be adults. In this book, we use the term to include students in junior high as well as those graduating from high

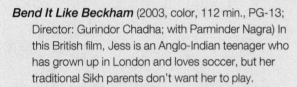

Film Box 1.1

Films That Share Characteristics with Young Adult Books

Bend It Like Beckham (2003, color, 112 min., PG-13; Director: Gurindor Chadha; with Parminder Nagra) In this British film, Jess is an Anglo-Indian teenager who has grown up in London and loves soccer, but her traditional Sikh parents don't want her to play.

Boyz n the Hood (1991, color, 112 min., Director: John Singleton with Cuba Gooding, Jr., Ice Cube, Laurence Fishburne, Morris Chestnut). This hard-hitting urban movie about inner-city teenaged boys won the New York Film Critics Circle Award in 1991 and was chosen for inclusion by the National Film Preservation Board in 2002.

The Breakfast Club (1985, color, 97 min., R; Director: John Hughes; with Emilio Estevez, Judd Nelson, Molly Ringwald, Anthony Michael Hall, and Ally Sheedy) Some critics credit Hughes with creating the genre of YA movies in this story about five rebellious teenagers assigned Saturday morning detention.

Diary of a Wimpy Kid (2010, color, 94 min., PG; Director: Thor Freudenthal; with Zachary Gordon, Robert Capren, and Rachael Harris) Wise-cracking Greg Heffley, who thinks middle school is the worst invention ever, records his grandiose plans (and failures) in his journal—which he insists is not a diary. The illustrated book was an immediate hit and so was the well-done film, soon followed by a sequel *Rodrick Rules*.

Ferris Bueller's Day Off (1986, color, 103 min. Director: John Hughes: with Matthew Broderick, Alack Ruck and Mia Sara) This hilarious film was so successful, it inspired a television show. It is an archetypal example of the conflict between authoritarian adults and playfully rebellious teenagers.

Finding Forrester (2001, color, 135 min., PG-13; Director: Gus Van Sant; with Sean Connery and Rob Brown) A reclusive writer serves as a friend and mentor to a basketball player on scholarship at an exclusive New York prep school.

It's Kind of a Funny Story (2010, color, 101 min., G; Director: Anna Boden and Ryan Fleck, with Keir Gilchrist, Zach Galifianakis, Emma Roberts, and Viola Davis) Adapted from Ned Vizzine's novel, this story about a suicidal teenager's journey of recovery in a mental institution and his quest for love is both lighthearted and dark, dramatic and funny, and essentially poignant.

Juno (2007, color, 92 min., PG-13; Director: Jason Reitman; with Ellen Page, Michael Cera, Jennifer Garner, Jason Bateman, Allison Janney, and J. K. Simmons) It wasn't the situation (a teen pregnancy) but the characterization that made Roger Ebert nominate *Juno* as the best film of 2007.

Napoleon Dynamite (2004, color, 90 min., PG-13; Director: Jared Hess; with Jon Heder, Jon Gries, and Elfren Ramirez) Part of the unexpected popularity of this indie film is its rural Idaho setting and the earnestness with which a geeky high school boy with the ironic name of Napoleon sets out to find success.

Nick and Norah's Infinite Playlist (2008, color, 90 min., PG-13; Director: Peter Sollett; with Michael Cera, Kat Dennings, Ari Graynor, Rafi Gavron, and Alexis Dziena) The student who recommended this "fun Friday night teen flick" said it has been described as "the best John Hughes film that John Hughes never made."

October Sky (1999, color, 107 min., PG; Director: Jake Gyllenhall; with Chris Cooper and Laura Dern) In this film adapted from Homer Hickam's *Rocket Boys*, a boy growing up in a West Virginia coal-mining town sees *Sputnik* streaking in the skies and determines to build his own rocket.

The Outsiders (1983, color, 91 min., PG; Director: Francis Ford Coppola; with Matt Dillon, Rob Lowe, and C. Thomas Howell) S. E. Hinton's novel is about two teenage groups in 1960s Oklahoma—the social superiors and the greasers.

Real Women Have Curves (2002, color, 86 min., PG-13; Director: Patricia Cardoso; with America Ferrera and Lupe Ontiveros) A bright young Hispanic girl in Los Angeles wants to go to college, but her mother wants her to work in a dress factory, lose some weight, and get married.

Rushmore (1998, color, 97 min., R; Director: Wes Anderson; with Jason Schwartzmann, Bill Murray, and Olivia Williams) A schoolboy is near expulsion because he is in almost every possible school activity and has no time for his studies. He falls in love with a first-grade teacher.

Slums of Beverly Hills (1998, color, 93 min., R; Director: Tamara Jenkins; with Alan Arkin and Natasha Lyonne) A father moves his motherless family first to this place and then that in Beverly Hills to give them a chance at a good education.

Whale Rider (2002, color, 101 min., PG-13; Director: Niki Caro; with Keisha Castle-Hughes) Filmed in Whangara and Auckland, New Zealand, this is a classic story of a young girl proving her worthiness to be a leader in modern Maori culture.

school and still finding their way into adult life. By *young adult literature*, we mean anything that readers between the approximate ages of twelve and eighteen choose to read either for leisure reading or to fill school assignments. When we talk about *children's literature*, we refer to books released by the juvenile or junior division of a publisher and intended for children from prekindergarten to about sixth grade.

Although our definition of *children's literature* is fairly standard, we should caution that not all educators define young adults the same way we do. The Educational Resources Information Clearinghouse (ERIC), for example, defines young adults as those between the ages of eighteen and twenty-two, whereas the National Assessment of Educational Progress (NAEP), administered by the Educational Testing Service, refers to "young adults, ages 21 through 25."

We confess to feeling pretentious when referring to a twelve- or thirteen-year-old as a *young adult*, but we shy away from using the term *adolescent literature* because as one librarian told us, "It has the ugly ring of pimples and puberty," and "it suggests *immature* in a derogatory sense." Still, many college courses in English departments are entitled Adolescent Literature, and because of our English teaching backgrounds, we find ourselves using the term for variety, along with *teenage books*, *teen fiction*, and *YA* or *young adult literature*. The terms *juvenile literature*, *junior novel*, *teen novel*, and *juvie* have been used in the past, but they became so weighed down with negative connotations that

Most libraries now separate their teen zone from the children's room. In some libraries it is as simple as putting up a sign, whereas in others the rooms are filled not only with books but with computers, games, and furniture for lounging.

they are seldom heard today. Even with the newer terms of *young adult* and *YA*, some teenagers feel condescended to, so librarians and teachers are looking for alternatives. David Spritz, writing in *Time* magazine July 19, 1999, used the term *teen fiction* for the genre that he said "used to be called" *young adult novels*. Although some librarians and bookstores have experimented with the term *popular literature*, at least in academic circles chances are that *young adult* is so firmly established that it will continue to be used for the near future. Anyone well acquainted with teenagers realizes that there is a tremendous difference between twelve-year-olds and seventeen-year-olds, or even between fourteen-year-olds and sixteen-year-olds. As teenagers are buying more books and publishers have become more interested in developing this market, a subcategory of young adult literature has developed. These are the books aimed primarily at students in junior high or middle school. Most Newbery Medal and Honor Book winners are written for the age level described as *tweeners*; see several examples in Focus Box 6.6, "Books to Make Readers Smile," in Chapter 6 (pp. 210–211).

Patty Campbell in her "The Sand in the Oyster" column in *Horn Book* (July–August, 2002) described tweener books as fiction "hanging on to the literary coattails" of young adult fiction. Tweener books sell better than "true" young adult fiction because in nearly every geographical area there are more middle school and junior high libraries than high school libraries. Also, the tween years are an age in which adults (parents, grandparents, teachers, and librarians) are still purchasing books for young readers or at least having an influence on what they read. The books are, of course, shorter and simpler, and because they are about younger protagonists, the love relationships—and the language—are fairly innocent. This means the books are less likely to be censored.

Tweener books also are better fitted to series books because at least in the old-fashioned kind of series books, the protagonists resemble those characters found in sitcoms. The story starts with the protagonist in a particular situation, then a complication occurs, which is solved as much through luck or help from outside as through the efforts of the protagonist. By the end, the situation is back to normal so that the protagonist is ready to be picked up and put into a similar, but slightly different, story. This differs from "true" YA fiction because, as Patty Campbell explained in her Horn Book column "The Sand in the Oyster: Middle Muddle" (July-August 2000, pp. 483–485):

> The central theme of most YA fiction is becoming an adult, finding the answer to the question "Who am I and what am I going to do about it?" No matter what events are going on in the book, accomplishing that task is really what the book is about, and in the climactic moment the resolution of the external conflict is linked to a realization for the protagonist that helps shape an adult identity.

She then cited a Richard Peck statement that "the last page of every YA novel should say not, 'The End' but 'The Beginning.'"

As you will learn in Chapter 2, young adult literature has a relatively brief and unsettled heritage, and there are many disagreements about its quality and the role that it should play in modern schools. On the positive side, however, such a changing field makes for a lively and interesting career for those of us working with books and young people. One thing that most people agree on is that those of us working in young adult literature should know and feel comfortable using the same literary terms that are used to talk about adult literature. We have, therefore, defined the main terms used throughout this textbook in Appendix A. Before going on to the other chapters, you might benefit from reviewing these terms to ensure that your understanding of them matches the way they are used throughout this textbook. Being comfortable using literary terms will:

- Give you terminology and techniques to use in sharing your insights with young readers.
- Help you gain insights into authors' working methods so that you get more out of your reading.
- Enable you to evaluate books and assist readers to move forward in developing the skills needed to further appreciate literature.
- Help you read reviews, articles, and critical analyses with greater understanding.

So many new books are published for young readers each year (nearly five thousand, with about one-fourth of them aimed at teenagers) that people who have preconceived ideas about what constitutes young adult literature can undoubtedly find examples to support whatever opinion they already hold. One illustration of the mixed feelings that people have is the argument that was waged in the Young Adult Library Services Association (YALSA), which is part of the American Library Association, prior to the 1998 establishment of the Alex Award, which each year honors ten titles published for a general adult audience but judged to have special appeal to young adults. The purpose of this honor is to help librarians encourage readers between the ages of twelve and eighteen "by introducing them to high-quality books written for adults." The award is named for Margaret Alexander Edwards, who, for her work during the 1940s and through the 1960s at the Enoch Pratt Free Library in Baltimore, is generally credited with being the first YA librarian.

This historical photo obtained from the Enoch Pratt Free Library in Baltimore, shows Margaret A. Edwards (in the plaid dress) taking the library's horse-drawn book cart out to neighborhoods in the 1940s.

A decade earlier, the Margaret A. Edwards Award had been established as a way to bring attention to an author who has made a significant and lasting contribution to literature for teenagers. The authors who have been so honored are each given a separate write-up in this textbook. See S. E. Hinton's and Madeleine L'Engle's in this chapter on pages 7 and 14, respectively. The winners are listed here in the order in which they received the award. (No award was given in 1989 when the ground rules were still being established.) Their write-ups are placed mostly in chapters related to the kind of writing they do.

- S. E. Hinton, 1988, see Ch. 1, page 7
- Richard Peck, 1990, see Ch. 8, page 271
- Robert Cormier, 1991, see Ch. 2, page 57
- Lois Duncan, 1992, see Ch. 7, page 253
- M. E. Kerr, 1993, see Ch. 10, page 354
- Walter Dean Myers, 1994, see Ch. 8, page 275
- Cynthia Voigt, 1995, see Ch. 4, page 107
- Judy Blume, 1996, see Ch. 2, page 61
- Gary Paulsen, 1997, see Ch. 7, page 231
- Madeleine L'Engle, 1998, see Ch. 1, page 14
- Anne McCaffrey, 1999, see Ch. 5, page 146
- Chris Crutcher, 2000, see Ch. 7, page 240
- Robert Lipsyte, 2001, see Ch. 7, page 241
- Paul Zindel, 2002, see Ch. 6, page 215
- Nancy Garden, 2003, see Ch. 9, page 311
- Ursula K. Le Guin, 2004, see Ch. 5, page 145
- Francesca Lia Block, 2005, Ch. 4, see page 139
- Jacqueline Woodson, 2006, see Ch. 11, page 386
- Lois Lowry, 2007, see Ch. 5, page 178
- Orson Scott Card, 2008, see Ch. 4, page 140
- Laurie Halse Anderson, 2009, see Ch. 12, page 402
- Jim Murphy, 2010, see Ch. 9, page 284
- Terry Pratchett, 2011, see Ch. 5, page 158
- Susan Cooper, 2012, see Ch. 6, page 224

A Word about Spoilers

Occasionally, people state that we have broken a cardinal rule by giving away the ending of a book and have therefore *spoiled* their desire to read the book. Of course we do not want to go around "spoiling" people's pleasure as they read some of the books we recommend. However, there is a difference between our goals in writing a textbook for professionals, the goals of teachers

Margaret A. Edwards Award

Winner (1988)
S. E. Hinton, The One Who Changed It All

S. E. Hinton loves horses and was able to get her own horse a starring role when *Tex* was filmed. The books that earned her the very first Margaret A. Edwards Award are *The Outsiders* (1967); *Rumblefish* (1976); *Tex* (1979); and *That Was Then, This Is Now* (1971). Admittedly, our subtitle is an exaggeration because no one person could have brought about all the changes that came to young adult literature in the late 1960s and early 1970s, but S. E. Hinton was at the right place at the right time to give the whole field a nudge that changed "the rules" about what was expected and what was possible in books published for teenagers.

After *The Outsiders* proved to be such a success, Hinton, who by the time it was published was nineteen, wrote in an August 27, 1967, article in the *New York Times Book Review:*

> Teen-agers know a lot today. Not just things out of a textbook, but about living. They know their parents aren't superhuman, they know that justice doesn't always win out, and that sometimes the bad guys win. They know that persons in high places aren't safe from corruption, . . . and that some people sell out. Writers needn't be afraid that they will shock their teen-age audience. But give them something to hang onto. Show that some people don't sell out, and that everyone can't be bought. Do it realistically. Earn respect by giving it.

The Outsiders spoke with such resonance to teenagers that, in the spring of 1980, Jo Ellen Misakian, a librarian at the Lone Star K–8 School library in Fresno, California, mailed a copy of the book, a cover letter asking that the book be turned into a movie, and a petition signed by seventh- and eighth-grade students to film director Francis Ford Coppola. Coppola turned the letter over to his producer, Fred Roos, with instructions to "check it out." Three years later, on March 17, 1983, Roos and five of the young stars—Darren Dalton, Leif Garrett, Patrick Swayze, C. Thomas Howell, and Ralph Macchio—paid an official visit to the Lone Star School library to thank the students for suggesting the book. Star Matt Dillon, along with seventy-five of those who signed the petition, arrived that night for the premier, where they cheered their own credit line given at the end of the movie.

Hinton was fortunate with the filming of her books. She was invited to work with the producers on three of them. In 1983, when *Tex* was released, Gene Siskel and Roger Ebert did a special TV program about movies with young male protagonists in which they cited *Tex* for being what the others only pretend to be—stories of growing up to be a man. They criticized the falseness of the male/female relationships shown in an epidemic of horny teenage movies in which the boys never risk a real relationship. Missing from these "lust/hate" relationships is affection, friendship, and honesty. They praised the honesty in the relationship between fifteen-year-old Tex and his big brother, Mace, and said it was worth all the other movies put together.

On September 29, 2007, the Associated Press carried a feature story about Susan Eloise Hinton (who since 1970 has also been Mrs. David Inhofe) in celebration of the publication of a fortieth-anniversary edition of *The Outsiders*. She toured Tulsa with reporter Hillel Italie, and at the Will Rogers High School library, where Hinton had written parts of *The Outsiders,* they found her picture sitting in a glass case. Librarian Carrie Fleharty laughingly explained that she knows the book is still popular because so many students "forget" to bring it back.

One of the things that Hinton told the Associated Press reporter, Hillel Italie, was that it would "be a piece of cake" to write another book about Ponyboy, but not with the same passion she felt as a teenager. Because she does not want to interfere with the place he holds in the high school canon, she is now writing different kinds of books, including two children's books, inspired by her son Nick, who is now off to college. In 2010 a new paperback edition of *Hawkes Harbor,* a paranormal suspense story for adults "definitely not for teens," was released as a TOR paperback, while in 2009 *Some of Tim's Stories,* originally published by the University of Oklahoma Press, came out as a Penguin paperback. ●

and librarians who give booktalks, and the goals of newspaper and magazine writers who write reviews. These latter groups are probably communicating about only five or six books in hopes of inspiring their listeners or readers to pick up one of the books and begin reading. We, in contrast, are writing about nearly one thousand books, many more than even the most ambitious of you will be able to read within the next year or so. One of the benefits of taking a class in young adult literature is that, based on both what we write in our textbook and on what you hear from your instructor and your fellow students, you will be able to give honest information to students about many more books than you have "personally" read. In order to do this, you sometimes need to know the ending.

We are not saying that you should *spoil* a book by telling a potential reader everything you know about the story; rather, as a responsible adult making recommendations to individual students, there are often things you need to know. So, yes, we do sometimes give away the endings. But in our own defense, we also want to say that the more you read, the more your pleasure will come not so much from being surprised at how a book ends but from your recognition of all the things the author did to bring you as the reader to the end of the story. As discussed in the following section, "Stages of Literary Appreciation," reading is similar to a journey where what you experience along the way is often as important as what you experience at your final destination.

In a July 2007 *Time* magazine article entitled "Harry Potter and the Sinister Spoilers," authors Lev Grossman and Andrea Sachs, hinted that the "Azkaban-level security" measures that were being taken to keep the plot of *Harry Potter and the Deathly Hallows* secret was more of a marketing ploy than an understanding of what reading is all about. If all readers care about is the ending, then "why would they turn out in such numbers to see the movie versions of the book?" They went on to explain:

> People read books for any number of reasons; finding out how the story ends is one among many and not even the most important. If it were otherwise, nobody would ever bother to read a book twice. Reading is about spending time with characters and entering a fictional world and playing with words and living through a story page by page. The idea that someone could ruin a novel by revealing its ending is like saying you could ruin the *Mona Lisa* by revealing that it's a picture of a woman with a center part. Spoilers are a myth; they don't spoil. No elaborate secrecy campaign is going to make *Harry Potter and the Deathly Hallows* any better than it already is, and no website could possibly make it useless and boring. (p. 52)

Stages of Literary Appreciation

The development of literary appreciation begins long before children learn to read. Table 1.1, "Stages of Literary Appreciation," presents an approximation of how individuals develop the personal attitudes and the reading, watching, and listening skills that are a necessary part of literary

TABLE 1.1　Stages of Literary Appreciation

Read this chart from the bottom up to trace the stages of development most commonly found in reading the autobiographies of adults who love to read.

Level	Optimal Age	Stage	Sample Literary Materials	Sample Actions
7	Adulthood to death	Aesthetic appreciation	• Classics • Significant contemporary books • Drama • Film	• Reads constantly • Dreams of writing the great American novel • Enjoys literary and film criticism • Reads many books a year • Sees plays • Revisits favorites
6	College	Reading widely	• Best-sellers • Acclaimed novels, poems, plays, films, magazines	• Talks about books and films with friends • Joins a book club • Gathers books to take on vacation
5	High school	Venturing beyond self	• Science fiction • Social issues fiction • Forbidden material • "Different" stories	• Begins buying own books • Sees movies with friends • Gets reading suggestions from friends • Reads beyond school assignments
4	Junior high	Finding oneself in literature	• Realistic fiction • Contemporary problem novels • Wish-fulfilling stories	• Hides novels inside textbooks to read during classes • Stays up at night reading • Uses reading as an escape from social pressures
3	Late elementary	Losing oneself in literature	• Series books • Fantasies • Animal stories • Anything one can disappear into • Comic books	• Reads while doing chores • Reads while traveling • Makes friends with a librarian • Checks books out regularly • Gets "into" reading a particular genre or author
2	Primary grades	Learning to decode Developing an attention span	• School reading texts • Easy-to-read books • Signs and other real-world messages	• Takes pride in reading to parents or others • Enjoys reading alone • Has favorite stories
1	Birth to kindergarten	Understanding of pleasure and profit from printed words and from visual and oral presentations	• Nursery rhymes • Folktales • Picture books • Television programs • Songs	• "Reads" signs for certain restaurants and food • Memorizes favorite stories and pretends to read • Enjoys singing and listening to stories

appreciation. The table should be read from the bottom up because each level is built on the one below it. We used to draw it as a fancy, stacked-up birthday cake, but this cut down on how much information we could put on the page. Our reason for the stacked-up cake was to illustrate that the levels get increasingly smaller. There are dropouts all the way along, with many people never rising to even the level of losing themselves in a good story, much less coming to appreciate the aesthetics of particularly well-done presentations of drama, film, or writing. People do not go through these stages of development; instead, they add on so that at each level they have all that they had before plus a new way to gain pleasure and understanding (see also the discussion of teaching literature in Chapter 11).

Level 1: Understanding That Pleasure and Profit Come from Literature

Children are fortunate if they have loving adults who share songs and nursery rhymes and who talk with them about the television shows and the movies they see together. They are also lucky if they get to go to bookstores and libraries to buy and borrow books and participate in group story hours. Researchers in reading education are discovering the social nature of reading. Children who seem to get the most from their reading are those who have had opportunities for "talking story" and for having "grand conversations" as in the title of Ralph Peterson and Maryann Eeds book, *Grand Conversations: Literature Groups in Action*.

If children are to put forth the intellectual energy required in learning to read, they need to be convinced that it is worthwhile—that pleasure awaits them—or that there are concrete benefits to be gained. In U.S. metropolitan areas, there's hardly a four-year-old who doesn't recognize the golden arches of a McDonald's restaurant. Toddlers too young to walk around grocery stores reach out from their seats in grocery carts to grab their favorite brands of cereal. We know one child who by the time he entered first grade had taught himself to read from *TV Guide*. Although its format breaks almost every rule any good textbook writer would follow in designing a primer for clear and easy reading, it had one overpowering advantage. The child could get immediate feedback. If he made a correct guess, he was rewarded by getting to watch the program he wanted. If he made a mistake, he knew immediately that he had to return to the printed page to try again. Today's equivalent is children who learn to read from the tiny screens on computerized games or from going online to find information, advertisements, or cartoons.

One of our students, Marlinda White-Kaulaity, who has now graduated with a Ph.D. and returned to be an educational leader in her Navajo community in northern Arizona, looked at our stages of literary appreciation and concluded that they were too specific and too limited. See her "Young Scholars Speak Out" statement on pp. 90–91 in Chapter 3. As you look at the chart, it might be a good idea for you to do what Marlinda did as she questioned the different levels and the specific examples, and thought about how they compared to her own development of literacy. For her culture, she thought we focused too heavily on print literacies; however, as we will show in Chapter 3, people living in today's world make use of many other kinds of literacy. Her earliest memories were of sitting on her grandfather's knee and being told stories and of participating in games and dances. She doesn't remember her parents ever reading a bedtime story to her, yet she grew up with a strong interest in stories and later in reading.

Level 2: Learning to Read

Learning the principles of phonics (i.e., to turn the squiggles on a page into meaningful sounds) is the second stage of development. It gets maximum attention during the primary grades, where as much as 70 percent of the school day is devoted to language arts. Developing literacy, however, is more than just decoding; it is a never-ending task for anyone who is intellectually active. Even at a mundane level, adults continue working to develop their reading skills. People tackling new computer programs or rereading tax guides in preparation for an audit exhibit the same symptoms of concentrated effort as do children first learning to read. They point with their fingers, move their lips, return to reread difficult parts, and in frustration slam the offending booklet to the floor. In each case, however, they are motivated by a vision of some benefit to be gained, so they increase their efforts.

Those of us who learned to read with ease may forget to help children who are struggling to find pleasure and enjoyment. Children who learn to read easily—the girl who sits in the backseat of the car and reads all through the family vacation and the boy who reads a book while delivering the neighborhood newspapers—find their own rewards for reading. For these children, the years between seven and twelve are golden. They can read the great body of literature that the world has saved for them: *Charlotte's Web*, the Little House books, *The Borrowers*, *The Chronicles of Narnia*, *The Wizard of Oz*, *Where the Red Fern Grows*, and books by Beverly Cleary, William Steig, Dr. Seuss, and hundreds of other good writers.

At this stage, children are undemanding. They are in what Margaret Early has described as a stage of unconscious enjoyment. With help, they may enjoy such classics as *Alice in Wonderland*, *The Wind in the Willows*, *Treasure Island*, and *Little Women*, but by themselves they are far more likely to turn to less-challenging material. Parents worry that their children are wasting time, but nearly 100 percent of our college students who say they love to read went through childhood stages of being addicted for months to one particular kind of book. Apparently, readers find comfort in knowing the characters in a book and what to expect, and this comfort helps them develop speed and skill.

Level 3: Losing Oneself in a Story

Children who read only during the time set aside in school and children who live in homes where the television set is constantly switched from channel to channel and where the exigencies of daily life leave little time for uninterrupted conversations and stories, probably have a hard time losing themselves in a good story. There are exceptions, of course, who are like Worm (short for bookworm), the eleven-year-old character in Rodman Philbrick's *Max the Mighty* who escapes the horrors of her everyday life by reading. She even uses a miner's helmet and headlight to read in the dark.

Because of life's complications, many children do not lose themselves in a good story until much later than the third or fourth grades, which is typical of good readers, or it may not happen at all. In this segment quoted from Theodore Weesner's *The Car Thief*, Alex Housman, who is being kept in a detention home, is seventeen years old when he first experiences losing himself in a story (i.e., finding what we refer to as "a good read"). Someone has donated a box of books to the detention home, and, because there's nothing else to do, Alex starts to read. He is initially intimidated by the words because he had never read anything before except school assignments; but because the book is straightforward and written in a style he can understand, he sits on the floor reading until he becomes sleepy. His eyelids droop, he lays over and rests his head on his arm, and he sleeps for a while, but soon he wakes up and carries the book with him to the bathroom.

> He became so involved in the story that his legs fell asleep. He kept reading, intending to get up at the end of this page, then at the end of this page, if only because he would feel more comfortable with his pants up and buttoned, but he read on. . . . Something was happening to him, something as pleasantly strange as the feeling he had had for Irene Sheaffer. By now, if he knew a way, he would prolong the book the distance his mind could see, and he rose again, quietly, to sustain the pleasant sensation, the escape he seemed already to have made from the scarred and unlighted corridor. Within this shadowed space there were now other things: war and food and worry over cigarettes and rations, leaving and returning, dying and escaping. The corridor itself, and his own life, was less present.

Level 4: Finding Oneself in a Story

The more experience children have with literature, whether through words or pictures, the more discriminating they become. To receive pleasure they have to respect the story. In reminiscing about his childhood fondness for both the Hardy Boys and motorcycles, the late John Gardner remarked that his development as a literary critic took a step forward when he lost patience with the leisurely conversations that the Hardy Boys were supposed to have as they roared down country roads side by side on their motorcycles.

Good readers begin developing this critical sense in literature at about the same time they develop it in real life at the end of childhood and the beginning of their teen years. They move away from a simple interest in what happened in a story to ask why. They want logical development and are no longer satisfied with stereotypes. They want characters controlled by believable human motives because now their reading has a real purpose to it. They are reading to find out about themselves, not simply to escape into someone else's experiences for a few pleasurable hours. They may read dozens of contemporary teenage novels, looking for lives as much like their own as possible. They read about real people in biographies, personal essays, and journalistic stories. They are also curious about other sides of life, and so they seek out books that present lives totally different from their own. They look for anything bizarre, unbelievable, weird, or grotesque: stories of occult happenings, trivia books, and horror stories. And, of course, for their leisure-time reading and viewing they may revert to level 3, escaping into a good story. When they are working at the highest level of their capability, however, their purpose is largely one of finding themselves and their places in society. Parents and teachers sometimes worry when children seem stuck at a particular level or with a particular kind of book. In most instances, as long as there are other choices available as well as time for reading, students sooner or later venture onward in a natural kind of progression.

Level 5: Venturing beyond Themselves

The next level in literary appreciation comes when people go beyond their ego-centrism and look at the larger circle of society. Senior high school English teachers have some of their best teaching experiences with books and stories by such writers as Ernest Hemingway, John Steinbeck, Harper Lee, F. Scott Fitzgerald, Carson McCullers, William Faulkner, Arthur Miller, and Flannery O'Connor. Students respond to the way these books raise questions about conformity, social pressures, justice, and other aspects of human frailties and strengths. Book discussions at this level can have real meat to them because readers make different interpretations as they bring their own experiences into play against those in the books.

Obviously, getting to this level of literary appreciation is more than a matter of developing an advanced set of decoding skills. It is closely tied to intellectual, physical, and emotional development. Teenagers face the tremendous responsibility of assessing the world around them and deciding where they fit in. Reading at this level allows teenagers to focus on their own psychological needs in relation to society. The more directly they can do this, the more efficient they feel, which probably explains the popularity of contemporary problem novels featuring young protagonists, as in the books by Will Hobbs, Brock Cole, M. E. Kerr, Robert Cormier, Jacqueline Woodson, Virginia Euwer Wolff, and Nancy Garden.

Although many people read fantasy and science fiction at the level of losing themselves in a good story, others may read such books as Nancy Farmer's *The House of the Scorpion*, Neal Shusterman's *The Dark Side of Nowhere*, Ursula K. Le Guin's *Tehanu*, and Philip Pullman's *The Golden Compass* and *The Subtle Knife* at a higher level of reflection. Such readers come back from spending a few hours in the imagined society with new ideas about their own society.

Levels 6 and 7: Aesthetic Appreciation

When people have developed the skills and attitudes necessary to enjoy imaginative literary experiences at all the levels described so far, they are ready to embark on a lifetime of aesthetic appreciation. This is the level at which producers, playwrights, authors, critics, talented performers, and literary scholars concentrate their efforts. Even they don't work at this level all the time, however, because it is as demanding as it is rewarding. The professor who teaches Shakespeare goes home at night and relaxes by watching *The Simpsons* or *The Office* or by scanning the Internet to see what might turn up on someone's blog or on YouTube. The author who writes for hours in the morning might put herself to sleep at night by listening to a mystery, while the producer of a new play may flip through magazines as a way of relaxing. Teenagers are much the same. Top students take a break from the seriousness of homework by watching *Glee,* skimming the sports page, listening to music, or playing video games.

In summary, the important points to learn from this discussion of stages of literary appreciation are that teachers, librarians, and parents should meet

Margaret A. Edwards Award

Winner (1998)
Madeleine L'Engle, A Writer Who Asks the Hard Questions

Madeleine L'Engle, who died on September 6, 2007, was back in the spotlight when the 2010 Newbery Award winner was announced. The book that won the award was *When You Reach Me* by Rebecca Stead. Stead's book is set in 1979 on the Upper West Side of New York and relies heavily for its plot on L'Engle's *A Wrinkle in Time.*

L'Engle was honored by the Edwards committee for two books from her series about the Austin family (*Meet the Austins* and *A Ring of Endless Light*) and for two books from her Time Quintet about the Murray family (*A Wrinkle in Time* and *A Swiftly Tilting Planet*). Although both sets were originally published as books for children, they have achieved a crossover audience partly because of the way L'Engle brings in philosophical and "other-world" considerations. The Time Quintet is about the intellectual Murray family and the disappearance of their physicist father, who is engaged in secret work for the government.

The introduction to the series, *A Wrinkle in Time*, which won the 1963 Newbery Medal, is still the most popular and, as far as we know, the earliest of all the books cited for the Edwards Award. L'Engle's next most popular book, *A Swiftly Tilting Planet*, won an American Book Award in 1980. In it, the "baby" of the family, Charles Wallace, is now a fourteen-year-old who, with help from his sister Meg, inherits the task of rescuing their father.

In May 2007, the Time Quintet was reissued with two different covers for each book, one for children and one for the adult market. The adult version included an interview with L'Engle and the text for her 1963 Newbery acceptance speech. In it, L'Engle noted that because she was born in 1918, she belonged to the first generation which grew up benefiting from the wisdom of librarians who chose to bring attention to particularly good books.

I learned about mankind from Hendrik Willem van Loon; I traveled with Dr. Dolittle, created by a man I called

Hug Lofting; Will James taught me about the West with Smoky; in boarding school I grabbed Invincible Louisa the moment it came into the library because Louisa May Alcott had the same birthday that I have, and the same ambitions.

L'Engle grew up in New York City, and then the family moved to Europe, but she came "home" for college. After college she moved to Greenwich Village to become an actress. She met and married actor Hugh Franklin. In 1952, they retired from the theater and moved to an old white farmhouse in northwestern Connecticut where they raised three children and L'Engle plugged away at her writing, with her own children being her first audience. It took two years of rejection letters before she had a book accepted.

L'Engle frequently explores questions of science, philosophy, and religious faith, sometimes in the same book. When *A Wrinkle in Time* won the 1963 Newbery Medal, critics in the field argued that it was a poor excuse for sci-fi. Thirty-five years later, in her acceptance speech for the Margaret A. Edwards Award, L'Engle said she knew she was breaking taboos, including the one that sci-fi protagonists had to be male. But, "I'm a female," she argued, "Why would I give all the best ideas to a male?"

Another "rule" was that fantasy and science fiction do not mix. "Why not?" she asked. "We live in a fantastic universe, and subatomic particles and quantum mechanics are even more fantastic than the macrocosm. Often the only way to look clearly at this extraordinary universe" is through imagination. She cited Erich Fromm's book *The Forgotten Language*, which makes the point that "fairy tales, fantasy, myths, and parables are the only universal language which crosses over barriers of race, culture, and time." ●

young people where they are and help them feel comfortable at that stage before trying to move them on. We also need to continue to provide for all the levels below the one on which we are focusing; for example, people at any stage need to experience pleasure and profit from their reading, viewing, and listening. This is especially true with reading, which requires an extra measure of intellectual effort. People who feel they are not being appropriately rewarded for their efforts may grow discouraged and join the millions of adults who no longer read, view, or listen to materials for personal fulfillment and pleasure. Their literary efforts focus entirely on acquiring the factual information that is needed to manage the daily requirements of modern living.

The Honor List

Some thirty years ago, when we, the authors, first started working on this textbook, out of pure selfishness, we began drawing up an annual Honor List of the books that reviewers and selection committees considered to be "the best" of each particular year. For the sources being used over the last few years, see Focus Box 1.1, "Pearls of Wisdom from Review Sources," which describes various "Best Book" lists and prizes that are given in young adult literature. Our reason for incorporating the work of many other book lovers is that we

The journals shown here are among those that regularly include information about prizes and awards as described in Focus Box 1.1 "Pearls of Wisdom from Review Sources."

Here are the sources that we consult each year to draw up our annual Honor List. We also look for prizes awarded by such newspapers as the *Los Angeles Times* and for the finalists and the winner of the youth division of the National Book Awards. In upcoming years, you might want to follow our procedure to make your own class reading list of the ten or twelve books that you find winning the most honors or being on the most "Best Book" lists. Once you have a reasonable list, you can divide up the reading; after two or three class members have read each book, you can hold a selection meeting where you talk, argue, and finally decide on a list of six or seven books you judge to be the most worthwhile—the ones that you think will last the longest—for the particular year you are working with.

Amelia Elizabeth Walden Award Established in 2008 to honor the wishes of its namesake, this award is administered by ALAN (Assembly on Literature for Adolescents, NCTE). The criteria include that the book takes a positive approach to life and has both widespread teen appeal and literary merit. Kristin Cashore's *Fire* was the 2010 winner. http://www.alan-ya.org/ as shown on this poster announcing a reception at the ALAN meeting to honor the winners.

American Indian Youth Services Literature Award
This fairly new award was first presented at the Joint Conference of Librarians of Color at Dallas, Texas, in October of 2006. Categories include Picture Book, Middle School, and Young Adult. YA winners have been Lurline Wallana McGregor's *Between the Deep Blue Sea and Me: A Novel,* Sherman Alexie's *The Absolutely True Diary of a Part-Time Indian,* and Joseph Bruchac's *Hidden Roots.* http://www.ailanet.org

American Library Association ALA gives more book awards than any other organization. Besides those listed separately here, the main ones of interest to us are the

Newbery Awards, which often go to books for young teens; the Pura Belpré Medals, which honor Latino/Latina writers and illustrators both for adults and children; and the Stonewall Children's & Young Adult Literature Awards for the best GLBT (Gay, Lesbian, Bisexual, Transsexual) books. http://www.ala.org

Booklist Each December, the editors of the official review journal of the American Library Association print their "Editors' Choice" selections. The categories we pay the most attention to are Youth Fiction, Youth Nonfiction, and Audio Books. The editors also compile a "Top of the List" (we give books two points for getting on this more restricted list), but we have to make our own distinctions between *children's* and *young adult.* http://americanlibrariesmagazine.org

Boston Globe—Horn Book Awards These awards have been presented since 1967, but they are not announced

knew we could not personally read the more than 1,200 YA books that are published each year, and even if we took one of those Evelyn Woods speed-reading classes that were fashionable at the time, we would not be able to wrap our minds around twenty books a week. And so we sought help from other trained readers, something we suggest all readers do if they want to make good use of both the money and the time that they have for reading young adult books.

until June; therefore, we usually use them as more of a backup because by then we are well into writing our reviews. However, throughout the year, we read the reviews and articles in the *Horn Book* magazine and pay close attention to their annual listing of best books, which is called the *Horn Book Fanfare*. The *Horn Book Guide Online* is also a good source for reviews. http://www.hbook.com

Coretta Scott King Book Awards for Authors and Illustrators The first of these awards was given some forty years ago; today, there are several categories including an Author Award, an Illustrator Award, a John Steptoe New Talent Award, and a Coretta Scott King—Virginia Hamilton Lifetime Achievement Award. Children's and young adult books compete with each other. The overall sponsor is the American Library Association. http://www.ala.org

Michael L. Printz Award *Booklist* magazine sponsors the Printz Award and up to four Honor Books. They can be fiction, nonfiction, poetry, or anthologies. The Young Adult Library Services Association (YALSA) administers the awards, which were first given in 2000. The idea was to have a book award for readers ages twelve through eighteen that would be somewhat equivalent to the Newbery Award for children. It is named for a school librarian from Topeka, Kansas, who before his untimely death was an active member of YALSA. http://www.ala.org

School Library Journal This monthly magazine tries to review all books published for children and young adults, with most of the reviews being written by volunteer librarians. Any book getting a starred review has to also be reviewed by one of the editors. Each December, the editors publish their long-awaited "Best Books" list for the year, which usually has around seventy books on it, with maybe one-third being for teens. The books are gleaned from the more than two thousand reviews published during the year. We give high priority to this list and are thankful that, besides giving the basic bibliographical information, readers are directed to the original reviews. http://.slj.com

VOYA (Voice of Youth Advocates) Published bi-monthly April through February, this journal for librarians is chock full of articles and reviews. The editors list their favorites in the last issue of each year, but fuller lists under genre categories are published in later issues. Their most useful all-around list appears in June under the title "Perfect Tens." The title comes from the fact that their reviewers give up to five points for quality and also up to five points for predicted popularity. For 2010, twenty-five books received "Perfect Tens," whereas in 2009 the honor went to eighteen books. This list arrives too late for us to use in making our initial decisions for the Honor List, but we do check their reviews to see which of our finalists have received "Perfect Ten" scores. VOYA, PO Box 958, Bowie MD 20718-0958 or subscriptions@voya.com

Young Adult Library Services Association (YALSA) YALSA is part of the American Library Association. Their large and hard-working committees made up of practicing librarians select the winners of the Michael L. Printz Award for the year's "best" YA book. They also give the Margaret A. Edwards Award for "significant and lasting" contributions to young adult literature, plus the fairly new YALSA Excellence in Nonfiction Award, the Odyssey Award (for best recorded books), and the William C. Morris YA Debut Award. They also produce several "Best Book" lists, which are announced every January at the ALA winter convention. We rely heavily on their "Best Fiction for Young Adults" list because it usually has something like sixty books on it. We give an extra point to the books placed in their "Top Ten" designation. We also look at their "Amazing Audio Books for Young Adults," "Fabulous Films for Young Adults," "Great Graphic Novels for Teens," and "Quick Picks." For further information, go online to the American Library Association, http://www.ala.org, and follow the links to YALSA "Book News & Book Awards."

As seen in Chapter 10, there is something to be said for allowing students to choose freely what to read, but for those of us who love YA books and want our colleagues in schools and libraries to appreciate them as we do, there is also something to be said for bringing the "very best" books to the attention of both teen and adult readers. This is why we keep reprinting the Honor List as on pp. 22 to 28. We have even told our students in a joking way that it will be fine with us if they choose all of their out-of-textbook reading from the Honor List because it includes every genre and gives a representative sampling of "the best" from the last thirty years.

A formal decision was never made about how many books would go on each year's Honor List, but it generally hovers around six to eight. We start with typing or running off one of the longest lists, and printing it out in table form with empty columns, as well as extra spaces to add books from the other sources listed in Focus Box 1.1, "Pearls of Wisdom from Review Sources." Once we make all the counts, we usually have a list of ten to fifteen books that have appeared on four or more sources (a book that wins the National Book Award, the Printz Award, or another notable award, gets double points for such a singular honor). Then we sit back for a month or so of wonderful catch-up reading of whatever books we missed during the year. We also involve student readers and whatever friends we can coerce into reading and offering opinions. When we finally have the list pared down to a reasonable number, we start writing the reviews, which for the last couple of decades have been published in the *English Journal*, usually in the November issue of the following year. The article always starts with a warning that no one should restrict their year's reading to just the books on the Honor List, because there are many more good books published each year than can make it to the Honor List. However, by reading the books that make the list, people can feel confident that the books they are reading are truly outstanding.

In the beginning, we paid almost as much attention to nonfiction as to fiction, but as the years went by we began noticing that nonfiction (except for the biographies and memoirs) had a shorter life-span. In later years, therefore, we have not included as much nonfiction. We have also dropped off a few books that have gone out-of-print or seem to have fallen off the radar screen. Also, we have occasionally gone back to second-guess ourselves and to add a few books that have grown in respect and popularity, such as Sandra Cisneros's *The House on Mango Street*, Orson Scott Card's *Ender's Game*, Laurie Halse Anderson's *Speak*, Ursula K. Le Guin's *Tehanu*, and Yann Martel's *Life of Pi*. In drawing up our original lists, we have stuck to books identified by the publishers as young adult mainly because most of our review sources and selection committees focus only on YA books. But as shown by Cisneros's and Martel's books, which were both published for general adult audiences even though the protagonists were teenagers, some "adult" books have been added as latecomers to the Honor List. The publishers listed with the books are the original publishers who first accepted the books and did the editorial work. However, a quick check online will show that many of the books now have different publishers, either because the rights were sold or the original publishers were bought out or were combined with other publishers. In its history, this textbook, for example, was first published by Scott, Foresman, then by HarperCollins, then by Allyn & Bacon, and now by Pearson.

Relevant Changes in the Honor List

After compiling the Honor List for thirty years, we decided it was time to take a retrospective look to see what changes have occurred in the books that are being chosen. Because there aren't the same numbers of books in each year or each decade, we will report our findings mostly through percentages by decades. The easiest thing to count was the average number of pages in the books.

Changes in the Length of YA Books

Decade	Number of Books	Average Number of Pages
1980–1989	52	218
1990–1999	63	189
2000–2009	70	284

We, along with most American publishers (as opposed to British publishers), had long assumed that books for teens needed to be fairly short. We remember pointing to books that were less than one hundred pages, such as Cynthia Rylant's 1992 *Missing May*, Berlie Doherty's 1990 *White Peak Farm*, and Francesca Lia Block's 1989 *Weetzie Bat*. But we can also remember pointing to occasional books that contained slightly over three hundred pages, such as Orson Scott Card's 1985 *Ender's Game*, Walter Dean Myers's 1988 *Fallen Angels*, and Robert Cormier's 1988 *Fade*. We don't know why the average length went down by thirty pages in the 1990s as compared to the 1980s, but we suspect the reason that it increased by nearly one hundred pages between 2000 and 2009 relates to our next finding, which is that there has been a steady decrease in modern, realistic books and an increase in fantasy, futuristic sci-fi, supernatural, and historical books.

Changes in the Genres of YA Books

Decade	Percentage of Realistic Books	Other Genres in Descending Order (actual numbers are given in parentheses)
1980–1989	67%	Fantasy (5), Supernatural/Occult (4), Sci-Fi Futuristic (4), Historical (2)
1990–1999	54%	Historical (12), Fantasy (5), Supernatural/Occult (4), Sci-Fi Futuristic (1), Other (4)
2000–2009	49%	Historical (16), Fantasy (10), Supernatural Occult (3), Sci-Fi Futuristic (4), Other (4)

As the historical (some of which also bordered on fantasy) and the fantasy novels grew in popularity, the length of the books chosen for the Honor List also increased. J. K. Rowling's 2007 *Harry Potter and the Deathly Hallows* contained 759 pages, while Jennifer Donnelly's 2010 *Revolution* contained 496 pages and Elizabeth Knox's 2007 *Dreamquake* contained 449 pages. Apparently, it takes longer for an author to set up a fantasy world; once it is set up, then there's more room for complicated plots and a full cast of characters. The same is true for such complicated historical books as M. T. Anderson's 2006 *The Astonishing Life of Octavian Nothing*, which contained 351 pages, and Mal Peet's 2007 *Tamar: A Novel of Espionage, Passion, and Betrayal*, which contained 431 pages.

Over the years, it has become increasingly hard for us to identify the books by genre because as more new authors have become attracted to writing for teenagers, they are getting braver about experimenting. After lulling their readers into one genre, they suddenly switch midstream into something like "magical realism," as Francesca Lia Block did with her 1993 *Missing Angel Juan* and Yann Martel with his 2001 *Life of Pi*. In 1997, when Annette Curtis Klause wrote *Blood and Chocolate,* we labelled it "supernatural." Today we would probably have just labelled it a "vampire book" or maybe a subdivision of such books. In 2005 we labelled Scott Westerfeld's *Peeps* as "vampire/science fiction," while we labelled Stephenie Meyer's *Twilight* as "vampire/romance."

Changes in Settings and Communities

Another change relates to the identity of the characters and their communities. Early on, we started by having a column marked "Ethnic Group," where we noted the inclusion of characters beyond the kind of white, middle-class figures featured in the old *Dick and Jane* readers of the 1940s and 1950s. But as books became more sophisticated and writers became more aware of matters related to inclusion, books became less segregated along racial lines. Also, authors began writing about other kinds of personal identity related to social class, politics, religion, and sexual orientations. Some psychologists say that the overwhelming job for all teenagers is the establishment of their own identity, separate from that of their parents, and so of course there are many novels relating to this

See Focus Box 1.2, "Going Beyond Dick and Jane," for descriptions of some of the Honor List books that demonstrate different ways in which protagonists are searching for their own identities.

Focus Box 1.2

Going Beyond Dick and Jane

These recent Honor List books illustrate the new freedoms that authors have to write about characters and themes previously thought to be inappropriate or of little interest to young readers.

The Absolutely True Diary of a Part-Time Indian by Sherman Alexie. **Little Brown, 2007** Although this wonderful book is Alexie's first to be published for teen readers, many of his earlier stories, along with the film *Smoke Signals,* can also be appreciated by teenagers of all ethnic groups.

American Born Chinese by Gene Luen Yang. **First Second Books, 2006** Yang's book has not only a different subject but a different format. It is a graphic novel which combines a legendary Chinese folktale ("The Monkey King") with stories of a second-generation immigrant from China and an American boy named Danny whose Chinese cousin visits each year. It won the 2007 Printz Award and was a finalist for the 2006 National Book Award.

The Astonishing Life of Octavian Nothing, Traitor to the Nation: Volume I: The Pox Party and *The Astonishing Life of Octavian Nothing, Traitor to the Nation, Volume II: The Kingdom on the Waves* by M. T. Anderson. **Candlewick Press, 2006 and 2008** Set in the years leading up to the American Revolution, these books are about an African American boy born to the daughter of a chief (and therefore viewed as royalty), who is taken in by a group of American scientists who are determined to see whether it is nature or nurture that makes the difference between blacks and whites. In the first book, the boy survives the madness of the Novanglian College of Lucidity, which includes holding grand parties to inoculate themselves with contaminated matter from the pox-sores of the dead in hopes of avoiding the disease. In the second book, the now almost-grown boy escapes with the help of Dr. Trefusis to British-occupied Boston and safety.

Chains by Laurie Halse Anderson. **Simon & Schuster, 2008** When Miss Mary Finch of Tew, Rhode Island, passes away in May of 1776, two young sisters who are owned as slaves by Miss Finch should have gotten their freedom, but Miss Finch's brother, Robert, who inherits her property, refuses to honor his sister's promise to the girls and instead sells them as slaves to the Lockton family in New York. This is the powerful story of how thirteen-year-old Isabel works to keep the promise she had made to their own mother that she would take care of her younger sister, Ruth, who suffers from epilepsy and related complications.

Chandra's Secrets by Allan Stratton. **Annick, 2004** Chandra, a sixteen-year-old girl who lives in sub-Saharan Africa, is faced with arranging for the burial of her baby brother and eventually for her mother, both of who succumb to AIDS. A film version titled *Life, Above All* premiered at the 2010 Cannes International Film Festival. However, we have also seen it advertised as *Chandra's Secrets.*

Charles and Emma: The Darwins' Leap of Faith by Deborah Heiligman. **Holt, 2009** Heiligman writes almost as much about Emma as about Charles so that readers come away with a new appreciation of the hardships faced by women in the 1800s, even those in well-to-do families. Emma's life differed from the lives of today's women more than did Charles's from the lives of today's men.

Claudette Colvin: Twice Toward Justice by Philip Hoose. **Farrar, Straus & Giroux, 2009** Hoose tells the true story of a teenaged African American girl who, on March 2, 1955, was forced off a city bus, arrested, and charged with violating segregations laws in Montgomery, Alabama. Desegregation leaders decided not to pursue her case but instead to ask the older, more respected Rosa Parks to repeat Claudette's action. The rest is history, but now thanks to Hoose, Claudette Colvin also has her place in history.

Marcello in the Real World by Francisco X. Stork. **Scholastic, 2009** Seventeen-year-old Marcello Sandoval is an autistic teen, whose condition is close to Asperger's Syndrome. He goes to a special school, but then his father thinks it will be good for him to come "into the real world" by working in his father's law firm for the summer. Marcello surprises everyone by understanding a lot more about "the real world" than anyone anticipated.

concept, but in ways that are far too sophisticated to be checked off in a box. A related point is that when we first began drawing up our Honor List, it was rare to have "imported" books on it. Teachers and librarians said that it was like pulling teeth to "sell" teens on books from other countries. But today, thanks to J. K. Rowling and Harry Potter, among others, this is no longer the case.

Characteristics of Young Adult Fiction as Shown Through the Honor List

In spite of changes made in the length of YA books, the blending of genres, and matters of inclusion, we still feel confident in listing almost the same characteristics of young adult books that we have worked with over the last several editions of this textbook. However, instead of listing a multitude of books to prove our point—which readers have told us was confusing—we will illustrate each characteristic by writing mainly about one book chosen as a prototypical example from recent Honor List books, occasionally supplemented by one or two other examples. Also, see Film Box 1.1, "Films that Share Characteristics with Young Adult Books," for films that illustrate many of the same characteristics that we are describing as belonging to young adult books.

Honor List The Best of the Best, 1980–2011

Year	Title	Author	Publisher	Genre	Protagonist		No. of Pages
					Sex	Age	
2011	Between Shades of Gray	Ruta Sepetys	Philomel	Realistic	M/F	Young Teens	341
	Chime	Franny Billingsley	Dial	Magical Realism	F	Young Teen	361
	Daughter of Smoke and Bone	Laini Taylor	Little/Brown	Supernatural	F	Teen	418
	Dead End in Norvelt	Jack Gantos	FSG	Realistic Humor	M	Young Teen	341
	A Monster Calls	Patrick Ness/ Siobhan Dowd	Candlewick	Magical Realism	M	Young Teen	205
	Okay for Now	Gary D. Schmidt	Clarion	Realistic	M	Young Teen	360
	The Scorpio Races	Maggie Stiefvater	Scholastic	Fantasy	F	Young Teen	407
	Where Things Come Back	John Corey Whaley	Atheneum	Realistic	M	17	240
2010	Nothing	Janne Teller	Atheneum	Realistic	M/F	Teens	217
	Please Ignore Sarah Dietz	A. S. King	Knopf	Real/Fantasy	M/F	Teens	336
	Revolution	Jennifer Donnelly	Delacorte	Hist/Fantasy	F	17	496
	Revolver	Marcus Sedgwick	Roaring Brook	Historical	M	14	201
	Ship Breaker	Paolo Bacigalupi	Little, Brown	Post Apocalyptic	M/F	Older teens	326
	The Things a Brother Knows	Dana Reinhardt	Random House	Realistic	M	17	245
2009	Charles and Emma: The Darwins' Leap of Faith	Deborah Heiligman	Holt	Biography	M/F	Adult life	268
	Claudette Colvin: Twice Toward Justice	Philip Hoose	Farrar, Straus & Giroux	Biography	F	15+	133

Year	Title	Author	Publisher	Genre	Protagonist		No. of Pages
					Sex	Age	
	Fire	Kristin Cashore	Dial	Fantasy	F	18	491
	Going Bovine	Libba Bray	Delacorte	Fantasy	M	16	496
	Marcello in the Real World	Francisco X. Stork	Scholastic	Realistic	M	17	320
	The Monstrumologist	Rick Yancey	Simon & Schuster	Horror/Fantasy	M	Teen	434
	Punkzilla	Adam Rapp	Candlewick	Realistic	M	14	244
	Wintergirls	Laurie Halse Anderson	Viking/Penguin	Realistic	F	17	278
2008	*The Astonishing Life of Octavian Nothing, Traitor to the Nation, Volume II. The Kingdom on the Waves*	M. T. Anderson	Candlewick	Historical	M	17	561
	Chains	Laurie Halse Anderson	Simon & Schuster	Historical	F	13	320
	The Disreputable History of Frankie Landau-Banks	E. Lockhart	Hyperion	Realistic	F	Teen	345
	The Graveyard Book	Neil Gaiman	HarperCollins	Gothic Fantasy	M	Child	307
	Graceling	Kristin Cashore	Harcourt	Fantasy	F	Teen	471
	The Hunger Games	Suzanne Collins	Scholastic	Fantasy	F	Teen	374
	Nation	Terry Pratchett	HarperCollins	Fantasy	M/F	Teen	471
	What I Saw and How I Lied	Judy Blundell	Scholastic	Realistic	F	17	284
2007	*The Absolutely True Diary of a Part-Time Indian*	Sherman Alexie	Little, Brown	Memoir	M	14	240
	Dreamquake: Book Two of the Dreamhunter Duet	Elizabeth Knox	FSG	Fantasy	F	Older teen	449
	Harry Potter and the Deathly Hallows	J. K. Rowling	Scholastic	Fantasy	M	19	759
	Tamar: A Novel of Espionage, Passion, and Betrayal	Mal Peet	Candlewick	Adventure Mystery/War	F	15	432
	Twisted	Laurie Halse Anderson	Penguin Viking	Realistic	M	16	272
	What They Found: Love on 145th Street	Walter Dean Myers	Random House	Short Stories	M/F	Mixed	256
	The White Darkness	Geraldine McCaughrean	HarperCollins	Adventure Mystery	F	14	384
2006	*American Born Chinese*	Gene Luen Yang	First Second Books	Graphic Novel	M	Young teen	233
	An Abundance of Katherines	John Green	Dutton/Penguin	Realistic	M	18	230
	Sold	Patricia McCormick	Hyperion	Realistic	F	13	263
	Surrender	Sonya Hartnett	Candlewick	Psychological Mystery	M	20	248
	The Astonishing Life of Octavian Nothing, Traitor to the Nation: Volume 1. The Pox Party	M. T. Anderson	Candlewick	Historical 1700s	M	Teens	351
	The Book Thief	Markus Zusak	Knopf	Young Teen	F	Childhood	550
	The Rules of Survival	Nancy Werlin	Dial/Penguin	Realistic Problem	M	13–18	260

(continued)

Year	Title	Author	Publisher	Genre	Protagonist		No. of Pages
					Sex	Age	
2005	Criss Cross	Lynne Rae Perkins	Greenwillow Books	Realistic	F	14	337
	Elsewhere	Gabrielle Zevin	Farrar, Straus & Giroux	Fantasy	F	16	277
	Inexcusable	Chris Lynch	Atheneum	Realistic Problem	M	17	165
	Looking for Alaska	John Green	Dutton	Realistic Problem	M	17	227
	Peeps	Scott Westerfeld	Pengiun/Razorbill	Vampire Science Fiction	M	19	320
	Twilight	Stephenie Meyer	Little, Brown	Vampire Fantasy	F	16	498
2004	Airborn	Kenneth Oppel	Harper	Adventure/Fantasy	M	15	368
	Chanda's Secrets	Allan Stratton	Annick Press	Realistic Problem	F	16	193
	Godless	Pete Hautman	Simon & Schuster	Realistic Problem	M	16	208
	How I Live Now	Meg Rosoff	Wendy Lamb	Realistic Dystopia	F	16	208
	Lizzie Bright and the Buckminster Boy	Gary D. Schmidt	Clarion	Historical Early 1900s	M/F	Early teens	224
	Private Peaceful	Michael Morpurgo	Scholastic	Historical War	M	18	195
2003	The Canning Season	Polly Horvath	Farrar	Realistic Humorous	F	13	208
	Fat Kid Rules the World	K. L. Going	Putnam	Realistic	M	Older teens	177
	The First Part Last	Angela Johnson	Simon & Schuster	Realistic	M	16	144
	A Northern Light	Jennifer Donnelly	Harcourt	Realistic Historical	F	16	396
	The River Between Us	Richard Peck	Dial	Realistic Historical	F	Older teens	164
	True Confessions of a Heartless Girl	Martha Brooks	Kroupa/Farrar	Realistic Problem	F	17	192
2002	Big Mouth and Ugly Girl	Joyce Carol Oates	HarperCollins	Realistic Problem Romance	F	17	226
	Feed	M. T. Anderson	Candlewick	Science Fiction Dystopia	M/F	Older teens	236
	The House of the Scorpion	Nancy Farmer	Atheneum	Science Fiction Dystopia	M	Young teens	380
	The Kite Rider	Geraldine McCaughrean	HarperCollins	Historical Adventure	M	Young teens	272
	My Heartbeat	Garret Freymann-Weyr	Houghton Mifflin	Romance Problem	F	14	154
	Postcards from No Man's Land	Aidan Chambers	Dutton	Problem Historical	M	17	312
2001	Damage	A. M. Jenkins	HarperCollins	Realistic Sports	M/F	17	186
	The Land	Mildred D. Taylor	Phyllis Fogelman	Historical	M	YA+	375
	Life of Pi: A Novel	Yann Martel	Harcourt	Magical Realism	M	16	319
	Lord of the Deep	Graham Salisbury	Delacorte	Realistic Romance	M	13	184
	The Rag and Bone Shop	Robert Cormier	Delacorte	Realistic Mystery	M	12	154

| Year | Title | Author | Publisher | Genre | Protagonist | | No. of Pages |
					Sex	Age	
	Seek	Paul Fleischman	Marcato/Cricket	Realistic Quest	M	17	167
	The Sisterhood of the Traveling Pants	Ann Brashares	Delacorte	Realistic Romance	F	16	304
	A Step from Heaven	An Na	Front Street	Realistic Romance	F	17	156
	True Believer	Virginia Euwer Wolff	Atheneum	Realistic Romance	F	15	264
	Zazoo	Richard Mosher	Houghton Mifflin	Realistic	F	13	248
2000	*The Amber Spyglass*	Philip Pullman	Knopf	Fantasy/Myth	M/F	Young teens	518
	The Beet Fields: Memories of a Sixteenth Summer	Gary Paulsen	Delacorte	Realistic Memoir	M	16	158
	Homeless Bird	Gloria Whelan	HarperCollins	Realistic Quest	F	13	216
	Hope Was Here	Joan Bauer	Putnam's	Realistic Quest	F	16	190
	Kit's Wilderness	David Almond	Delacorte	Historical Supernatural	M	13	229
	Many Stones	Carolyn Coman	Front Street	Realistic Quest	F	Mid-teens	158
	Stuck in Neutral	Terry Trueman	HarperCollins	Realistic Problem	M	14	114
	The Wanderer	Sharon Creech	HarperCollins	Realistic Quest	M/F	Young teens	305
	A Year Down Yonder	Richard Peck	Dial	Historical Realism	F	16	130
1999	*Anna of Byzantium*	Tracy Barrett	Delacorte	Historical Fiction	F	Older teens	209
	Frenchtown Summer	Robert Cormier	Delacorte	Realistic Poetry	M	12	113
	Hard Love	Ellen Wittlinger	Simon & Schuster	Realistic Quest	M/F	16	224
	Monster	Walter Dean Myers	HarperCollins	Realistic Problem	M	16	240
	Never Trust a Dead Man	Vivian Vande Velde	Harcourt	Mystery Supernatural	M	17	194
	Safe at Second	Scott Johnson	Philomel	Sports Problem	M	17	224
	The Smugglers	Iain Lawrence	Delacorte	Adventure	M	16	183
	Speak	Laurie Halse Anderson	Farrar, Straus & Giroux	Realistic Problem	F	13	197
	When Zachary Beaver Came to Town	Kimberly Willis Holt	Henry Holt	Realistic	M	13	231
1998	*Clockwork: Or All Wound Up*	Philip Pullman	Scholastic	Fantasy/Sci-Fi	M/F	Teens	112
	Go and Come Back	Joan Abelove	DK Ink	Realistic Historical	F	13	177
	Holes	Louis Sachar	Farrar, Straus & Giroux	Fanciful Adventure	M	14	233
	The Killer's Cousin	Nancy Werlin	Delacorte	Psychological Mystery	M	17	228
	Rules of the Road	Joan Bauer	Putnam's	Realistic Quest	F	16	201
	Soldier's Heart	Gary Paulsen	Delacorte	Historical	M	15	106
	Whirligig	Paul Fleischman	Holt	Realistic Quest	M	17	133
	The Wreckers	Iain Lawrence	Delacorte	Historical Adventure	M	14	191
1997	*Blood and Chocolate*	Annette Curtis Klause	Delacorte	Supernatural	F	18	288
	Buried Onions	Gary Soto	Harcourt Brace	Realistic	M	18	149
	Dancing on the Edge	Han Nolan	Harcourt Brace	Realistic	F	12	244

(continued)

Year	Title	Author	Publisher	Genre	Protagonist Sex	Protagonist Age	No. of Pages
	Ella Enchanted	Gail Carson Levine	HarperCollins	Cinderella Retelling	F	12	232
	The Facts Speak for Themselves	Brock Cole	Front Street	Realistic Abuse	F	13	184
	Out of the Dust	Karen Hesse	Scholastic	Narrative Poetry	F	13	227
	When She Was Good	Norma Fox Mazer	Scholastic	Realistic Mental Health	F	Early 20s	240
	Whistle Me Home	Barbara Wersba	Holt	Realistic Homophobia	M/F	17	108
1996	After the War	Carol Matas	Simon & Schuster	Historical Realistic	F	15	116
	A Girl Named Disaster	Nancy Farmer	Orchard	Realistic Quest	F	14	306
	The Golden Compass	Philip Pullman	Knopf	Fantasy/Sci-Fi	F	14	396
	Jip: His Story	Katherine Paterson	Lodestar	Realistic Historical	M	11	181
	Rats Saw God	Rob Thomas	Simon & Schuster	Realistic	M	17	219
1995	The Eagle Kite	Paula Fox	Orchard	Realistic Death	M	13	127
	Ironman	Chris Crutcher	Greenwillow	Realistic Sports	M	16	181
	Like Sisters on the Homefront	Rita Williams-Garcia	Lodestar/ Dutton	Realistic	F	14	165
	The Midwife's Apprentice	Karen Cushman	Clarion	Historical	F	13	122
	The War of Jenkins' Ear	Michael Morpurgo	Philomel	Realistic/ Religious	M	14	171
1994	Deliver Us from Evie	M. E. Kerr	HarperCollins	Realistic Homophobia	F	17	177
	Driver's Ed.	Caroline B. Cooney	Delacorte	Suspense	M/F	Teens	184
	Iceman	Chris Lynch	HarperCollins	Realistic Sports	M	14	181
	Letters from the Inside	John Marsden	Houghton Mifflin	Realistic	F	Teens	146
	When She Hollers	Cynthia Voigt	Scholastic	Realistic Abuse	F	17	177
1993	The Giver	Lois Lowry	Houghton Mifflin	Science Fiction Dystopia	M	Mixed	180
	Harris and Me	Gary Paulsen	Harcourt Brace	Realistic Humorous	M	Young teens	157
	Make Lemonade	Virginia Euwer Wolff	Holt	Realistic Single parent	F	14/17	200
	Missing Angel Juan	Francesca Lia Block	HarperCollins	Problem Occult	F	Teens	138
	Shadow Boxer	Chris Lynch	HarperCollins	Realistic Sports	M	Young teens	215
1992	Dear Nobody	Berlie Doherty	Orchard	Realistic Pregnancy	M/F	Older teens	192
	The Harmony Arms	Ron Koertge	Flare	Realistic Humorous	M	14	182
	Missing May	Cynthia Rylant	Orchard	Realistic Death	M/F	Mixed	89
	Somewhere in the Darkness	Walter Dean Myers	Scholastic	Realistic Family	M	14	224
1991	The Brave	Robert Lipsyte	HarperCollins	Realistic Sports	M	18	195
	Castle in the Air	Diana Wynne Jones	Greenwillow	Fantasy	M/F	Teens	199
	Lyddie	Katherine Paterson	Lodestar	Historical mid-1800s	F	13	183

Honor List continued

Year	Title	Author	Publisher	Genre	Protagonist Sex	Protagonist Age	No. of Pages
	The Man from the Other Side	Uri Orlev	Houghton Mifflin	Historical, War	M	14	186
	Nothing but the Truth	Avi	Orchard	Realistic	M	14	177
1990	The Shining Company	Rosemary Sutcliff	Farrar	Historical	M	Mixed	296
	The Silver Kiss	Annette Curtis Klause	Bradbury	Occult Romance	F	Teens	198
	Tehanu: The Last Book of Earthsea	Ursula K. Le Guin	Atheneum	Fantasy	F	Childhood	226
	The True Confessions of Charlotte Doyle	Avi	Orchard	Historical Adventure	F	13	215
	White Peak Farm	Berlie Doherty	Orchard	Realistic Family	F	Older teens	86
1989	Blitzcat	Robert Westall	Scholastic	Animal	M	–	230
	Celine	Brock Cole	Farrar	Realistic	F	16	216
	Eva	Peter Dickinson	Delacorte	Science Fiction	F	13	219
	No Kidding	Bruce Brooks	HarperCollins	Science Fiction	M	14	207
	Shabanu: Daughter of the Wind	Suzanne Fisher Staples	Knopf	Realistic Problem	F	12	140
	Weetzie Bat	Francesca Lia Block	HarperCollins	Realistic Spoof	M/F	Teens	88
1988	Fade	Robert Cormier	Delacorte	Occult	M/F	Mixed	320
	Fallen Angels	Walter Dean Myers	Scholastic	Realistic War	M	Older teens	309
	A Kindness	Cynthia Rylant	Orchard	Realistic Family	M	15	117
	Memory	Margaret Mahy	Macmillan	Realistic Disability	M/F	19 80+	240
	Probably Still Nick Swanson	Virginia Euwer Wolff	Holt	Realistic Disability	M	Teens	144
	Scorpions	Walter Dean Myers	HarperCollins	Realistic Crime	M	Teens	167
	Sex Education	Jenny Davis	Orchard	Realistic Death	F	Teens	150
1987	After the Rain	Norma Fox Mazer	Morrow	Realistic Death	F	Mid-teens	290
	The Crazy Horse Electric Game	Chris Crutcher	Greenwillow	Realistic Sports Disability	M	Teens	224
	The Goats	Brock Cole	Farrar	Realistic	M/F	Teens	184
	Hatchet	Gary Paulsen	Bradbury	Adventure Survival	M	12	195
	Permanent Connections	Sue Ellen Bridgers	HarperCollins	Realistic Family	M/F	Teens	164
	Sons from Afar	Cynthia Voigt	Atheneum	Realistic	M	Mid-teens	224
	The Tricksters	Margaret Mahy	Macmillan	Occult	F	17	266
1986	The Catalogue of the Universe	Margaret Mahy	Macmillan	Realistic	F	17	185
	Izzy, Willy-Nilly	Cynthia Voigt	Atheneum	Realistic Disability	F	15	288
	Midnight Hour Encores	Bruce Brooks	HarperCollins	Realistic	F	16	288
1985	Beyond the Chocolate War	Robert Cormier	Knopf	Realistic	M	17	234
	Dogsong	Gary Paulsen	Bradbury	Adventure Occult	M	13	177
	Ender's Game	Orson Scott Card	Tor	Science Fiction	M	Young boy	357
	In Country	Bobbie Ann Mason	HarperCollins	Realistic	F	Teens	247

(continued)

Year	Title	Author	Publisher	Genre	Protagonist		No. of Pages
					Sex	Age	
	The Moonlight Man	Paula Fox	Bradbury	Realistic Alcoholism	F	Teens	192
	Remembering the Good Times	Richard Peck	Delacorte	Realistic Suicide	M/F	Teens	192
1984	*The Changeover: A Supernatural Romance*	Margaret Mahy	Macmillan	Fantasy	M/F	Teens	214
	Cold Sassy Tree	Olive Ann Burns	Ticknor & Fields	Realistic Historical	M/F	Mixed	391
	Downtown	Norma Fox Mazer	Morrow	Realistic	M/F	Young teens	216
	Interstellar Pig	William Sleator	Dutton	Science Fiction	M	16	197
	The Moves Make the Man	Bruce Brooks	HarperCollins	Realistic	M	Young teens	280
	One-Eyed Cat	Paula Fox	Bradbury	Realistic	M	Young teens	216
1983	*Beyond the Divide*	Kathryn Lasky	Macmillan	Historical Fiction	F	Teens	254
	The Bumblebee Flies Anyway	Robert Cormier	Pantheon	Futuristic	M	Teens	211
	The House on Mango Street	Sandra Cisneros	Arte Publico	Realistic	F	Young teens	134
	A Solitary Blue	Cynthia Voigt	Atheneum	Realistic Family	M	Early teens	182
1982	*Annie on My Mind*	Nancy Garden	Farrar	Realistic Homophobia	F	Teens	233
	The Blue Sword	Robin McKinley	Greenwillow	Fantasy	F	Late teens	272
	A Formal Feeling	Zibby Oneal	Viking	Realistic Death	F	Teens	162
	A Midnight Clear	William Wharton	Knopf	Realistic War	M	Early 20s	241
	Sweet Whispers, Brother Rush	Virginia Hamilton	Philomel	Occult	F	Teens	224
1981	*Let the Circle Be Unbroken*	Mildred D. Taylor	Dial	Historical U.S. South	F	Early teens	166
	Notes for Another Life	Sue Ellen Bridgers	Knopf	Realistic Family	M/F	Teens	252
	Rainbow Jordan	Alice Childress	Coward McCann	Realistic	F	14	142
	Stranger with My Face	Lois Duncan	Laurel Leaf	Occult	F	17	250
	Tiger Eyes	Judy Blume	Bradbury	Realistic	F	15	206
	Westmark	Lloyd Alexander	Dutton	Historical Fantasy	M	16	184
1980	*The Beginning Place*	Ursula K. Le Guin	HarperCollins	Fantasy	M/F	Early 20s	183
	The Hitchhiker's Guide to the Galaxy	Douglas Adams	Crown	Fantasy	M	Adults	224
	Jacob Have I Loved	Katherine Paterson	Crowell	Realistic	F	Teens	216

Characteristic 1: Young Adult Authors Write from the Viewpoint of Young People A prerequisite to attracting young readers is to write through the eyes of a young person, and one of the ways to do this is to write in first person. First-person narration gives an immediacy to a story and serves as a narrative hook to grab readers' attention. It is so common in YA fiction that we have heard people discuss it as a prerequisite for the genre. But writing totally in first person has its limitations because the author isn't free to tell the thoughts of any character except the narrator. However, some authors let their characters take turns in telling various parts of the story, or they do a combination of first-person and omniscient narration, or they use omniscient narration so skillfully that readers go away with the feeling that the main character was speaking personally to them.

An important aspect of this characteristic is that the emotions being explored are important to young people. Often the difference in the life span between two books that are equally well written from a literary standpoint is that the ephemeral book fails to touch kids where they live, whereas the long-lasting book treats experiences that are psychologically important to young people. It's not that good authors peruse psychology books searching for case histories or symptoms of teenage problems that they can envision making into good stories. This would be as unlikely and as unproductive as it would be for a writer to study a book on literary devices and make a list: "First, I will use a metaphor and then a bit of alliteration and some imagery, followed by personification." Rather, in the best books, both the literary devices and the psychological insights emerge from the honest telling of a story.

A book on the 2010 Honor List that does a good job of illustrating how a skilled author can reveal the unique thinking of several young characters is Janne Teller's *Nothing*, translated from Danish by Martin Aitken. In some ways it resembles William Golding's 1955 *Lord of the Flies*. However, Golding's book was about a group of boys being forced by circumstances to develop their own society and customs, whereas Teller's book is about a group of thirteen- and fourteen-year-old boys and girls who have been together in a village school for their whole lives. The story begins in the fall of their last year before they will graduate and be spread around to specialized schools. The only person in the class who is not involved is a boy whose father is a teacher, and the students instinctively know that adults have no place in what they are doing.

The catalyst for the events, which develop over a period of several months, is the leaving of school by Pierre Anthon, a boy who lives with his father in an old farmhouse that has been turned into a commune. Adults in the town refer to the residents of the commune as hippies, "still stuck in '68." Although they have no idea what this means, the kids repeat the saying, which shows that they had not accepted Pierre Anthon as a full fledged member of their group. What bothers the students now is that every day Pierre Anthon parks himself in a plum tree that the other students pass on their way to school. He refuses to engage in conversation with them, but recites his daily mantra which, in a spacious three-page layout, makes up Chapter 1 of the book:

Nothing matters.

I have known that for a long time.

So nothing is worth doing.

I just realized that.

Day after day, this message grinds itself into the heads of the dutiful students as they make their way to school. They resolve to make Pierre Anthon admit that he is wrong. As the days and weeks go by, the students engage in a kind of group-think, which cycles way out of control. They do terrible things to each other and finally to Pierre, all in the name of convincing Pierre that he is wrong. However, readers will find themselves wondering just who is getting convinced of what.

The book was originally published in Denmark in 2000, where it won the "Best Children's Book Prize" from the Danish Cultural Ministry, and later won a prize for the best children's novel published in the French-speaking world. It took ten years for *Nothing* to make its way to America, but it is most likely here to stay. Martin Aitken, who translated *Nothing* into English, explained that he altered a few of the children's names so they would be easier for English speakers to pronounce, but he chose to leave the name of the town, *Tæring,* which is the author's creation rather than the name of a real town, because it "allows the reader an important sense of being somewhere foreign." The word comes from a Danish verb meaning "to gradually consume, corrode, or eat through" as when rust corrodes metal. This is a powerful bit of foreshadowing for Danish readers. English readers will get the same message; it will just take them longer.

Laurie Halse Anderson's 2009 *Wintergirls* and Jennifer Donnelly's 2010 *Revolution* (both of which will be discussed elsewhere in this text) are other good examples of books that do a powerful job of revealing the viewpoints and the emotions of the teenaged protagonists.

Characteristic 2: "Please, Mother, I Want the Credit!"   With formula fiction for young readers, one of the first things an author does is to figure out how to get rid of the parents so that the young person is free to take credit for his or her own accomplishments. Although the Honor List is not made up of formula fiction, authors have nevertheless devised a multitude of ways for young characters to be the ones who solve the problem or who in some other way become the heroes of the story. The title of Judy Blondell's 2008 *What I Saw and How I Lied* foreshadows the confidence of fifteen-year-old Evie in this winner of the National Book Award. The story opens with a scene that fits into the plot much later, but is printed on page one because it is crucial that readers understand both the mother in the story and the relationship between Evie and her mother. Evie is the narrator who explains

> The match snapped, then sizzled, and I woke up fast. I heard my mother inhale as she took a long pull on a cigarette. Her lips stuck on the filter, so I knew she was still wearing lipstick. She'd been up all night.

The year is 1947, just after World War II, when Evie's stepfather, Joe, comes home to reunite with Evie and her mother, as well as his own mother. These three unhappy women had been living together in a house in Queens belonging to Joe's mother. Shortly after Joe comes home, he opens a couple of appliance stores and, in the postwar housing boom, the money begins to roll in. Evie and her mother are happily looking forward to moving with Joe to a house of their own. But then just before school starts, Joe comes home from work with the surprising announcement that they are taking a family trip to Florida.

This is a strange trip, especially after Peter, a young soldier who served under Sergeant Joe in Germany, shows up in Florida. The sudden trip to Florida had actually been Joe's way of running away from Peter, who claims that Joe owes him a lot of money. Peter, not to be thwarted by the family's disappearance, steals a car and follows Joe to Florida. Money—how people get it and what they do with it—is a big part of the story, and so is the postwar prejudice that many people felt against Jews. However, the part of the story that is probably going to resonate most strongly with girl readers is Evie's developing sexuality and the niggling feeling of competition—combined with a strong loyalty from the days before Joe entered their lives—that Evie feels toward her mother. The events of the trip are complicated and even though there are storm warnings, the three of them, plus Peter, go out on a boat trip. Peter ends up dead. Evie is a witness to the events and her court testimony is crucial. What she does in court is way too sophisticated to have been plotted either by her parents or by their lawyer, and certainly not by an ordinary fifteen-year-old girl. However, Evie is not an ordinary fifteen-year-old girl, and it speaks well for Blundell's writing that the court accepts Evie's testimony and so do we—the readers—at the same time that we sit up and pay more attention to the second part of the title: *How I Lied*.

Stanley Yelnats in Louis Sachar's *Holes* obviously deserves the credit for the story's happy ending because he had been separated from home and family when he was sentenced to Camp Green Lake. Another teen protagonist who obviously deserves a lot of credit is Sig, a fourteen-year-old boy in Marcus Sedgwick's 2010 *Revolver*, which is an adventure story from the early 1900s set in the gold rush area of the Arctic. The story opens with Sig and his sister having just dragged the frozen body of their father into their cabin. The sister and their stepmother go to the nearby village for help when Sig looks up and sees a giant of a man standing in the doorway. This man tells Sig that he is now responsible for a debt that the man claims Sig's father owes him.

Characteristic 3: Young Adult Books Are Basically Optimistic with Characters Making Worthy Accomplishments   For teenagers to feel proud of their accomplishments, they have to have felt truly challenged and to feel that they have made progress in their own right. YA editor Stephen Roxburgh talked about this at the 2004 NCTE/ALAN workshop. He said that the defining literary characteristic of young adult books is that the first-person narrator starts out as unreliable and then by the end of the book evolves into a reliable narrator, which means that he or she has truly learned something.

A good illustration of this is the story of Levi Katznelson in Dana Reinhardt's 2010 *The Things a Brother Knows*. Seventeen-year-old Levi is telling the story, which he begins with "I USED TO LOVE MY BROTHER. Now, I'm not so sure." The main characters are Levi's mom, Abba (Levi's father), Dov (Levi's grandfather), and Boaz (his older brother). Three years before the story begins, Boaz had left home to join the Marines. He served in the Middle East and has now returned to a modest local hero's welcome. He looks like his old self, except stronger and a little more "high and tight," as befitting a marine. However, he is not the same brother who went away. Rather than letting anyone meet him at the airport, he walks home and simply knocks on the door. He refuses to get into any kind of a vehicle, and except for joining the family for tense dinners, he spends all of his time in his room, or taking long, hot showers. He has been accepted to at least three high prestige colleges, but he doesn't make any plans.

After a few weeks of living in the same house, but not really communicating, Boaz announces that he wants to take a walking tour along the Appalachian Trail—something the family once did for a vacation. The boys' parents are supportive, but Levi doubts Boaz's intentions. While Boaz takes his long showers, Levi sneaks into his room and, by looking into his brother's computer searches, finds detailed maps of the northeastern United States. He has marked pedestrian-accessible highways and bridges, along with cheap motels and camp-sites. He has also written in abbreviated names, addresses, and telephone numbers.

Levi makes note of all this information and decides that he's going to accom-pany Boaz. Of course he doesn't tell Boaz, and he even waits a day before he lies to his parents and tells them that Boaz called and wants him to come along. Mom rushes out and buys Levi the same high-quality camping gear that she had bought for Boaz. Levi arranges for two friends to drive him to the first town where he expected Boaz to stop. As Levi predicted, it is a challenge, but not impossible to catch up with someone who is walking. When Levi eventually finds his brother, Boaz is less than thrilled. Nevertheless, Levi ends up following along behind Boaz, much like he did when they were both kids, but this time Levi is relieved that when they were walking, he didn't "have to look someone in the eye."

Levi makes sacrifice after sacrifice to keep up with Boaz. Finally, at the Walter Reed Hospital, which is where Boaz was heading all along so that he could visit his badly injured friend, Levi slips into the bathroom and cuts off his long hair in a symbolic gesture of solidarity with Boaz and his friend, Jack. Levi calls the fam-ily to let them know where they are and invites them to come and meet that night at a big patriotic rally, which is where he thinks Boaz is going. However, Boaz didn't come to Washington to attend the rally. Instead, he had come to take his in-jured friend to a much quieter ceremony at the Vietnam Memorial. Thanks to cell phones, Levi manages to get the family to this smaller ceremony just in time to see Boaz go to the podium and pull out a bloody T-shirt, which he leaves in memory of three Afghan brothers who were killed in the same fight that injured Jack.

Levi still does not feel totally comfortable around Boaz, but at least he now understands him better than does the rest of the family. Abba (the father), in his usual take-charge manner, is telling Boaz to get in the car so they can all drive home. Levi interrupts Abba—something he never would have done in the past—and says, "Let him finish." In the awkward silence that follows, Boaz explains that after he gets Jack back to the hospital, "I might stick around there myself for a while. Maybe try and get some help with all my pieces." Levi knows that Boaz is "finally beginning the task of coming home again," so he throws his arms around his brother and says, "I'll walk you there."

Characteristic 4: Young Adult Literature Is Fast-Paced, Containing Narrative Hooks, Secrecy, Surprise, and Tension   In 1999, *Time* magazine reporter David Spritz wrote that, "Teen fiction may, in fact, be the first literary genre born of the Internet. Its fast-paced narratives draw upon the target demographic's kin-ship with MTV . . . and with the Internet and kids' ease in processing information in unconventional formats." In reality, teen fiction, which Spritz called "edgy," was around long before the Internet, but his point is well taken that many of the most popular books tell their stories at almost the same frantic pace and with the same emphasis on powerful images that viewers have come to expect from MTV.

There could hardly be a better book to illustrate these characteristics than Libba Bray's *Going Bovine,* which won the 2009 Printz Award. Besides being available in print, it can also be downloaded to a Kindle or listened to on CD discs as beautifully read by Erik Davies. It took more than the estimated sixteen hours to listen to it on CDs because we kept going back to re-listen to parts that

In the 1970s when scholars first began to look seriously at what was then called "adolescent literature," they were so eager to encourage teachers to bring this "new" kind of literature into English classrooms, that they stressed the seriousness and the high quality of the writing. It was almost an insult to consider the books as "pop culture." But today when such YA books as the Harry Potter series and the Twilight series, not only reflect, but in many ways determine, the popular culture, most of us have quit denying that our field of study is part of the pop culture.

we didn't understand. We finally decided that it was a *surbook* (like a *surtax* or a *surcharge*) because of the way it was "way out there" going "above and beyond" in ways that were *surreal*. The protagonist and narrator is sixteen-year-old Cameron (or Cam) who begins the book with "The best day of my life happened when I was five and almost died at Disney World." When Cam rescues a yard gnome, it turns out to be the Norse God Balder who, despite being trapped in a body that he cannot move, is perfectly capable of thinking and talking to those characters he happens to like. And when Cameron gets sick, he doesn't come down with an ordinary illness such as mononucleosis or diabetes. He is diagnosed with Creutzfeldt-Jacob, *aka* the incurable "Mad Cow" disease, which inevitably turns brains into something like sponges.

But going back to his memorable day at Disney World, he is on the *Small-Small-World* ride, floating with his parents and his sister through a darkened tunnel when he suddenly has a dystopian vision that they are all being ferried toward certain destruction. He spies a little door on the side of the passage and flings himself out of the boat and into the water with the intention of escaping through the door and turning off the machinery to save his family. Of course the boat is stopped and Cameron and his family—along with all the other ticket holders—are "rescued."

We suspect that author Libba Bray started with this incident as a way of introducing readers to Cameron's fertile imagination, which soon shows up in full bloom. One good thing about Cameron's illness is that he doesn't have to finish reading *Don Quixote* for his English class, but yet he launches himself on a journey that even casual readers can't help but recognize as having similarities to the picaresque wanderings of Don Quixote and his faithful Sancho Panza. Cameron's sidekick is Gonzo, a boy he knew only casually at school but who turns out to be Cam's hospital roommate. Gonzo is a dwarf, suffering from asthma and an overprotective mother. Cameron has a hard-sell in convincing Gonzo that the two of them are destined to go on a journey to find Dr. X, a man who will not only be able to save Cameron from his disease, but also to save the world from a disaster that is already on the horizon.

Cameron is told to go on this journey by Dulcie—undoubtedly a shortened form of *Dulcinea,* who was Don Quixote's heartthrob. In Cameron's case, she is a punk fairy with pink hair who throughout the story serves as a guide and helper, but who occasionally needs protection from villains wanting to get her back into one of those globes with falling snowflakes. The quest that Cameron and Gonzo take is not just an ordinary trip. It takes them from the hospital in Texas to the jazz clubs of New Orleans and eventually to spring break in Florida, where they join college kids vying to get on television and create new reality shows.

The success of this kind of dark humor is that readers' emotions are stretched from the tragedy of Cameron's real-life situation to the comedy of his hallucinations. And because readers' emotions are stretched taut, they become even more involved with the challenge of figuring out what is real and what is imagined. As we neared the end of the book, we began suspecting that the few moments that Cameron thinks he is hallucinating might really be the times when he is getting glimpses of the real world. But either way we felt fortunate to become a part of Cameron's fascinating, surreal world in which he freely explores the kinds of life and death questions that most of us try not to think about.

A couple of other recent Honor List books that are filled with secrecy and tension are Rick Yancey's 2009 *The Monstrumologist,* a horror story told in an old journal kept by a man who lived way longer than natural, probably because of what was done to him when he was an assistant to a nineteenth-century American scientist studying creatures from the underground. The other one is Andy Mulligan's 2010 *Trash,* which is a story that resembles the film, *Slumdog Millionaire,* about three garbage-picker boys who find something accidentally thrown away. Mulligan, the author, has been a teacher in different poverty-stricken areas of the world. In the acknowledgements, he said he based his fictional Behala on a dumpsite village he visited in the Philippines where "there really are children who will crawl through trash forever."

Characteristic 5: Young Adult Literature Includes a Variety of Genres, Subjects, and Levels of Sophistication   Perhaps in reaction to all of the religious books that were published for teens in the late 1800s and early 1900s, mainstream publishers have for the most part avoided creating books that deal with religion. One reason they shy away from the topic is the fear of offending the religious beliefs of some teens or of sounding as though they are trying to recruit teens to a particular religion, something that most people think should be handled in the home. This is why Pete Hautman's 2004 *Godless* attracted lots of attention. Hautman does a good job of probing sixteen-year-old Jason Bock's psyche. Jason is bullied, threatened, coerced, degraded, ridiculed, manipulated, and generally pinballed through life. The local tough guy scares the crap out of him, whereas his mother keeps scheduling him for doctors' appointments to see what's wrong with him. His father, who is an attorney accustomed to getting problems solved, enrolls Jason in a church youth group called TPO (Teen Power Outreach).

In a moment of rebellion, Jason mockingly tells the TPO group that instead of being a practicing Catholic he is founding a new religion, one that will worship the town water tower and will be called *Chutengodianism.* To Jason's surprise, several of the teens join his new religion. They find it fun to be doing something so different, but Shin, a younger boy who, when the story starts, was Jason's only friend, takes the whole thing seriously.

A playful night spent "worshipping" the water tower (which really means climbing up and accidently going swimming in the "holy water") ends badly and Jason is branded as a lost soul, a weirdo, a troublemaker, and a bad influence. Readers know differently and so does Jason, but still the book leaves readers, as well as Jason, pondering several questions of the kind that are often on kids' minds but not very often brought out for open discussion.

A couple of other sophisticated books that will further demonstrate the strength and the variety in current YA books are Neil Gaiman's 2008 *The Graveyard Book* and Laurie Halse Anderson's 2007 *Twisted,* both of which will be further discussed in later chapters.

Characteristic 6: The Body of Work Includes Stories about Characters from Many Different Ethnic and Cultural Groups Not Often Found in the Literary Canon Fifty years ago, the novels written specifically for teenagers and sold to schools and public libraries presented the same kind of middle-class, white picket fence neighborhoods as the ones featured in the *Dick and Jane* books from which most U.S. children were taught to read. But the mid- and late-1960s witnessed a striking change in attitudes. One by one, taboos on profanity, divorce, sexuality, drinking, racial unrest, abortion, pregnancy, and drugs disappeared. With this change, writers were freed to set their stories in realistic, rather than romanticized, neighborhoods and to explore the experiences of characters whose stories had not been told before.

This freedom was a primary factor in the coming of age of adolescent literature. Probably because there was such a lack of good books about non-middle-class protagonists, and because this was where interesting things were happening, many writers during the late 1960s and the 1970s focused on minorities and on the kinds of kids that S. E. Hinton called *The Outsiders.* With the conservative swing that the United States took in the 1980s, not as much attention was paid to minority experiences, but with more globalization and instant communication, the trend is reversing so that there are many appealing new books that will be read by large numbers of teenagers of all races. And with some of the books, race is being downplayed. For example, in Virginia Euwer Wolff's 1993 *Make Lemonade,* there is no overt mention of skin color, but as one reviewer stated, Jolly and LaVaughn are held together by "the race of poverty."

One of the most unusual 2010 books was *Ship Breaker,* the first book for teens by the acclaimed science fiction and mystery writer Paola Bacigalupi, which won the Printz Award. It is a post-apocalyptic story that may not be as far in the future as we would hope. The setting is the Gulf Coast, with some of the events taking place in sections of *The Orleans,* a spread-out area divided by waterways and differing levels of destruction caused by greed and mismanagement, as well as by flooding. References are made to "the flooded cities up north," so readers know that since Hurricane Katrina worse things have happened to the United States.

The book opens with a claustrophobia-inducing scene featuring the lead character, a teen named Nailer, who is squeezing himself through the ventilation ducts of a grounded ship. Nailer's mother is dead and his father is the epitome of a bad parent: "sober he was scary but drunk he was a demon." Nailer is on the *light crew,* meaning that he can gather only the wire and small items like staples and screws, while a gang higher up in status gets to take the heavier pipes, and the bosses get to take any oil that is found. Readers meet a whole host of characters with such names as *Tick-tock, Jackson Boy, Moon Girl, Gorgeon, Lucky Strike, Li, Rain, Glack Ling, Chen,* and *Teela.*

Nailer's boss, Bapi, comes aboard to tell him to pull as much wire as possible because a bad storm is coming and they'll have to be off the boat for probably two days. Nailer has to go back down in the dark—his only light coming from some phosphor LED paint splashed on his forehead—and pull out every last piece of wire in the belly of the ship. Bapi wants him to hurry, first, so that his crew can get the wire before someone else sneaks on board during the storm, and second, so that Nailer will be able to keep working during the storm by sitting on the beach and pulling the coating off from the copper to make it ready to sell.

Such planning goes awry when Nailer falls through a collapsing vent into a room filled with oil. His partner, appropriately named *Sloth,* abandons him, a sin for which she is beaten and expelled from the crew. Nailer's struggle to escape from the room full of oil matches up against any survival or adventure story we've read. He finally discovers a wheel that he manages to turn so that he is "vomited" out of the ship in a gush of oil. Luckily the tide has come in and he lands in water rather than on the rocky beach. He is nevertheless bleeding profusely and Pima, a fellow crew member, takes him to her mother for a rough kind of patching up.

After the storm a beautiful girl turns up almost drowned in a luxurious yacht that the storm washed up on a nearby island. Nailer and Pima are at first tempted to leave the girl to die and to scavenge as much as they can from her ship. But then she regains consciousness and convinces them that her wealthy father will soon come to rescue her. They finally agree to team up with her because in the back of their minds they see that she looks clean and healthy enough that at the least they could sell her as an organ donor. However, she proves to be much more valuable as a friend and partner. The ending of the book is at least somewhat more optimistic than was the beginning.

Most readers would probably identify the book as being "ethnic," but they would be hard pressed to identify just what ethnic groups were involved because the groups were identified as "crews," "partners," and "bosses." By putting the story in an imagined setting, Bacigalupi was able to treat racism and prejudice without pinning particular attitudes and actions onto particular groups. It reminded us of the way that the authors and artists of picture books for children often tell stories about personified animals with the idea that children can identify with the characters regardless of race or ethnicity.

See Focus Box 1.2, "Going Beyond Dick and Jane," on page 21 for other books that treat characters and ideas fairly new to books for teen readers.

In the early 1900s when the market was flooded with Bobbsey Twins, Hardy Boys, Tom Swift, and Nancy Drew books, teachers and librarians gave lots of attention to series books, but it was mostly negative. Educators worried about the quality of these "short-order" books; however, the fact that no one ever accused Anne McCaffrey, Lloyd Alexander, J. R. R. Tolkien, or Ursula K. Le Guin of carelessly writing "quickie" books, shows that it is not the publication details, but the skill and dedication of the author that determines quality. And, in fact, several of the books on our Honor List were written as parts of series or sets including Ann Brashare's *The Sisterhood of the Traveling Pants,* Philip Pullman's *The Amber Spyglass* and *The Golden Compass,* Virginia Euwer Wolff's *Make Lemonade,* Francesca Lia Block's *Weetzie Bat,* Ursula K. Le Guin's *Tehanu: The Last Book of Earthsea,* and Gary Paulsen's *Hatchet.*

While these books were mostly promoted as individual titles, thanks to the success of J. K. Rowling's Harry Potter series, Stephenie Meyers' Twilight books, Suzanne Collins's Hunger Games, and Rick Riordan's myth-based books, series books now have a new kind of prestige. In the February 2012 issue of *VOYA,* the editors printed excerpts from the reviews of the 24 books that in 2011 received "Perfect Tens." Because *VOYA* reviewers give a maximum of five points for quality and five points for predicted popularity, these 24 books could be considered the "best of the best." Ten of these new books were parts of series or sets. They include Cassandra Clare's *Clockwork Prince: The Infernal Devices, Book Two;* Janet Evanovich and Alex Evanovich's *Troublemaker, Book 1* and *Troublemaker Book 2;* Gayle Forman's *Where She Went* (sequel to *If I Stay*); Alexander Gordon Smith's *Death Sentence: Escape from Furnace 3;* Scott Kieran's *He's So Not Worth It* (sequel to *She's So Dead to Us*); Michael Grant's *Fear: A Gone Novel* (fifth entry in the Fear series); Ellen Hopkins' *Perfect* (companion to *Impulse*); Marissa Meyer's *Cinder: The Lunar Chronicles;* and Laurence Yep's *City of Ice* (sequel to *City of Fire*).

A second indicator of the rising importance of series books is an article, "What Teens Are Really Reading," published in the January 2012 *School Library Journal.* The author, Karen McCoy, engaged the help of one hundred media specialists from around the country to explore teen reading preferences by identifying the books that are "flying off the shelves." In her article, she posted the "Top Twenty" series above her list of the "Top Twenty" individual titles. This is more evidence that all of us working with young readers need to learn not just the names of individual books, but also the series they belong to, which can be challenging.

For example, McCoy found that Maggie Stiefvater's "Wolves of Mercy Falls" series was fourth in overall popularity, but when *Shiver, Linger,* and *Forever* were marketed in a 2011 boxed set, they were identified not with the series name but by their individual titles. Cassandra Clare's Mortal Instruments series would be easier to remember if it were called the "City of . . ." series because her titles are *City of Bones, City of Ashes, City of Glass, City of Fallen Angels,* and *City of Lost Souls.* Other series from McCoy's top twenty list that you might want to look up through the publishers or the authors' websites include P. C. Cast and Kristin Cast's House of Night, Michael Scott's The Secrets of the Immortal Nicholas Flamel, Gabrielle Lord's Conspiracy 365, James Patterson's Maximum Ride, Angie Sage's Septimus Heap, and L. J. Smith's Dark Visions and The Vampire Diaries.

Concluding Comments

Psychological aspects of well-written novels are a natural part of stories as protagonists face the same kinds of challenges readers are experiencing, such as the developmental tasks outlined three generations ago by Robert J. Havighurst in his *Developmental Tasks and Education:*

1. Acquiring more mature social skills.
2. Achieving a masculine or feminine sex role.
3. Accepting the changes in one's body, using the body effectively, and accepting one's physique.
4. Achieving emotional independence from parents and other adults.
5. Preparing for sex, marriage, and parenthood.
6. Selecting and preparing for an occupation.
7. Developing a personal ideology and ethical standards.
8. Assuming membership in the larger community.

Some psychologists gather all developmental tasks under the umbrella heading of "achieving an identity," which they describe as *the* task of adolescence. Some aspect of this is in practically any piece of fiction, poetry, drama, informative nonfiction, biographies, and self-help books that are written and published specifically for teenagers.

Close connections exist between adolescent literature and adolescent psychology, with psychology providing the overall picture and literature providing individual portraits. Because space in this text is too limited to include more than a hint of what you need to know about adolescent psychology, we suggest that professionals working with young people find a good book to read on adolescent psychology. Three recent books recommended in library journals are Angela Browne-Miller's *Raising Thinking Children and Teens: Guiding Mental and Moral Development*, Patricia Hoolihan's *Launching Your Teen into Adulthood: Parenting Through the Transition*, and *A Family of Readers: The Book Lover's Guide to Children's and Young Adult Literature*, edited by Roger Sutton and Martha Parravanno. And as a reminder of the fact that teenagers face many different problems from those of adults, you might also want to view some of the films recommended in Focus Box 1.1, "Films that Share Characteristics with Young Adult Books."

The more that you know, not only about the individual teen readers that you work with, but also about the emotional challenges and the interests that are common to most—if not all—young adults, the better able you will be to

- Judge the soundness of the books teens read.
- Decide which ones are worthy of promotion.
- Predict which ones will last and which will be transitory.
- Make better recommendations to individuals.
- Discuss books with students from their viewpoints.
- Gain more understanding and pleasure from personal reading.

A Brief History of Young Adult Literature

chapter *2*

200 Years of Young Adult Literature: 1800 to 1999

We feel the best way to learn about young adult literature is to read widely in current books, but you will get more from that reading if you also know something about the history and the background of these new books. Knowing our common background gives us a sense of the past and insights into the values that our society wants to pass on to its young people. Being familiar with what came earlier will also help you realize why certain kinds of books have consistently proven popular while providing deeper understanding of current events and trends in the world of books and modern entertainment.

When we went to our local theater to see Judd Apatow's 2007 comedy *Knocked Up*, starring Katherine Heigl and Seth Rogen, we smiled at the poster featuring an enlarged quote from reviewer Joe Leydon. What he wrote reminded us of the differences between the domestic and the dime novels of the 1800s. Leydon praised the film as a balance of "the madcap swagger and uninhibited bawdiness of a high testosterone farce" (that is, a dime novel) with "the unabashed sweetness and romantic yearning of a chick flick" (that is, a domestic novel).

In another example, we thought of the Stratemeyer Syndicate of the early 1900s when we read a *USA Today* story, "A Double Scoop of Patterson," published in our local *Arizona Republic* (June 28, 2011). It told how the prolific writer of murder thrillers was setting a new record, even for himself, by releasing two books on the same day—one for adults and one for kids. Patterson writes with a multitude of coauthors, and he includes their names on the covers of his books, which is something Edward Stratemeyer never did. Patterson was listed as the main author for eight out of the one hundred best-selling books of 2006, but it's too early to tell how he will fare in the young teen market. On June 27, 2011, when his adult murder story *Now You See Her* (written with Michael Ledwidge) was released, it came encased in a narrow wrapper showing a picture of Patterson's first kid's book, *Middle School: The Worst Years of My Life,* written with Chris Tebbetts and illustrated by Laura Park. Patterson admitted that the book, for readers ages eight to twelve, was similar to Jeff Kinney's *Diary of a Wimpy Kid,* but he said what really got him going with the idea of doing a book for young readers was Brian Selznick's *The Invention of Hugo Cabret: A Novel,* which "took the ceiling off for how the visual stuff can enhance the text." His future plans include a "Middle School" series with a girl detective, written with Maxine Paetro. In May of 2011, Patterson joined Rick Riordan, the author of *Percy Jackson and the Olympians,* at a sold-out reading for kids in New York's Lincoln Center. When a young girl asked Patterson why he didn't write more books by "himself," he said that his ideas come faster than he can write them, but that "There is nothing that I put my name on that I don't put through several drafts."

This kind of statement makes librarians and teachers wonder if they are supporting *Literature with a capital L* or *Business with a capital B.* Their suspicions were further aroused by the news story in the spring of 2011 about Greg Mortenson, the author of the highly acclaimed *Three Cups of Tea.* Fellow author Jon Krakauer, as reported on CBS's *60 Minutes* television show, accused Mortenson of "making up" some of the incidents in his supposedly "true" account of his mountain-climbing experiences, followed by his establishment of a foundation to build schools in Pakistan and Afghanistan. David Oliver Relin is listed on the cover of *Three Cups of Tea* as a coauthor; however, the coauthor was not mentioned in the news stories that we saw about the controversy. Krakauer published his findings in a 2011 book *Three Cups of Deceit: How Greg Mortenson, Humanitarian Hero, Lost His Way,* which was given a starred review by *Publishers Weekly,* whose editors praised it as a "stunning example of investigative journalism."

If you know something about the history of publishing, you probably will not be so surprised by these stories, or at least you will be able to put them in perspective. A more important reason for getting acquainted with the history of young adult literature, however, is that teachers and librarians may profit from discovering that many of the books are well worth hunting up and reading. To get ideas, look at the books listed in Focus Box 2.1, "Golden Oldies: A Sampling of Books Appreciated by Young Adults 1864–1959," on pp. 42–43, as well as Focus Box 2.2, "A Sampling of Good Books from the 1960s," on p. 54 and Focus Box 2.3, "A Sampling of Good Books from the 1970s," on p. 59, which provide bibliographies of good books from the 1960s and 1970s. Exceptionally good books from the 1980s are included in the Honor List (see Chapter 1) and also in many other chapters. Also included in this chapter are write-ups on two of the most influential winners of the Margaret A. Edwards Award: Robert Cormier on p. 57 and Judy Blume on p. 61. Both authors left indelible marks on the development of young adult literature as a unique branch of publishing.

In response to suggestions from previous users of this text, we are condensing this chapter and putting most of it in a timeline, which we hope will be easier for readers to absorb. We also devised some art work to assist readers in connecting the events in the world of books and libraries with what was going on in the world at large.

1800: Early in the 1800s, the books being read by teens and preteens were heavily influenced by religion. Many children, like young Abe Lincoln, grew up reading the Bible, which is said to have been a major influence on his speaking and writing style. Young readers were also given John Bunyan's *The Pilgrim's Progress* (1678) with the expectation that they would learn moral lessons from it, although most readers actually focused on the adventure.

1823: Brooklyn's Apprentice Library Association established a Youth Library where boys and girls over age twelve were allowed to check out one book during a designated hour each week. Thirty years later, Milwaukee School Commissioner Increase A. Laphnam provided for the library to be open Saturday afternoons and recommended that schools spend $10 a year for books. Children over ten, along with their parents and teachers, could withdraw one book each between 2:00 PM and sunset. Fines were assessed for overdue or damaged books.

1824: The American Sunday School Union was formed under the direction of a board representing six major religions. Over the next sixty years it produced millions of books designed to educate young people not only in religious values, but also in mathematics, grammar, history, and all sorts of practical skills. In cities and towns throughout America, the organization offered two hours of school on Sunday mornings and then two hours again from 4:00 to 6:00 in the late afternoons. The idea was to provide schooling for young people in towns and cities who had already entered the country's workforce and therefore could not attend weekday schools. Titles ranged from *Wild Flowers: or the May Day Walk* to *The History of Patriarchs* and *The Sin of Cruelty Exposed and Rebuked*. The Union was best known, however, for its heavily moralistic fiction. A common theme was first of a child near death reminding readers of the virtues they should cultivate in this life before going on to the next. Another formula was for good children to get a come-uppance because they had temporarily forgotten their duties to parents and siblings.

1835: New York was the first state to pass legislation permitting voters in any school district to levy a tax for libraries. The idea that books—especially those for young people—should teach some kind of a lesson is a holdover from the days before the invention of the printing press when the only books available for reading were those that had been considered worthy enough by religious leaders to have been copied by monks laboring in monasteries. Deep in our cultural subconscious, many people still believe this. As evidence, note that books are quicker to be censored than is pop culture music treating similar themes. In the 1800s, even commercial publishers felt it was necessary to produce books that taught moral lessons. Oliver Optic (pen name of Boston writer William T. Adams) was one of the first to succeed in producing books that were entertaining to young readers, but preachy enough that adults felt good about buying them for youngsters. Optic also produced a popular goody-good magazine, *Student and Schoolmate.* In 1867, he accepted a

Focus Box 2.1

Golden Oldies: A Sampling of Books Appreciated by Young Adults 1864–1959

1868: *Little Women: Meg, Jo, Beth, and Amy. The Story of Their Lives. A Girl's Book* by Louisa May Alcott is so honest that it is still loved today.

1870: *The Story of a Bad Boy* by Thomas Bailey Aldrich launched a new kind of literature about boys who were imperfect and tough—a refreshing counterbalance to the good-little-boy figures prevalent in too many unrealistic books of the time.

1883: *Treasure Island* by Robert Louis Stevenson is filled with the kind of adventure and derring-do that still appeals to boys.

1888: *Derrick Sterling* by Kirk Munroe tells the story of the title character. When Derrick's father dies, Derrick must leave school and work eleven-hour shifts in the mines. In this early, realistic picture of the mines and child labor, he becomes a hero when disaster strikes.

1897: *Master Skylark: A Story of Shakespeare's Time* by John Bennett is the witty account of young Nick Attwood, a golden-voiced boy singer involved in more than his share of adventure.

1899: *The Half-Back* by Ralph Henry Barbour was the first of many popular sports books, including *The Crimson Sweater* (1906), in which boys at school learn who and what they might become through sports.

1904: *Rebecca of Sunnybrook Farm* by Kate Douglas Wiggin sold more than 1.25 million copies and launched a formula in which a young child (usually a girl) makes life happy for apathetic or depressed adults.

1908: *Anne of Green Gables* by Lucy Maud Montgomery continued the Wiggin formula when an orphan girl is sent by mistake to a childless couple who wanted a boy to help on the farm.

manuscript, *Ragged Dick; or, Street Life in New York*, sent to him by Horatio Alger, Jr., a young writer living in New York City. Alger had graduated from Harvard at age eighteen and taken a position as a Unitarian minister in Brewster, Massachusetts, but within two years was forced out under a cloud of scandal. Today, Horatio Alger stories are mocked for their sentimentality and their unrealistic plots. Nevertheless, his popular stories set a model for many later books in which an irresponsible boy takes his first steps toward maturity, respectability, and affluence. Many contemporary books rely on this theme, except that writers are less apt to focus on the idea of affluence. This is probably because, even with the economic downturn, few families live in the kind of poverty that was typical for many people in the late 1800s.

1850: Susan Warner's 1850 *The Wide Wide World*, which Warner wrote under the pen name of Elizabeth Wetherell, immediately became a best seller. It is the story of a girl whose mother died early and whose father put her in the care of her Aunt Fortune Emerson. She very soon became close

1913: *Pollyanna* by Eleanor Porter, the climax (or the finishing blow) to the child-as-savior formula, was a popular adult novel, eighth among best sellers in 1913 and second in 1914.

1936: *Tangled Waters,* about a Navajo girl on an Arizona reservation; *Shuttered Windows* (1938), about an African American girl who leaves Minneapolis to live with her grandmother in South Carolina; and *The Moved Outers* (1945), about Japanese Americans forced into a relocation camp during World War II, all by Florence Crannell Means, were the first sympathetic and rich portraits of young protagonists from minority cultures.

1936: *Peggy Covers the News* by Emma Bugbee, a reporter for the *New York Times*, launched a deluge of career books for girls that included Helen Boylston's books about nurse Sue Barton and Helen Wells's books about nurse Cherry Ames and flight attendant Vicki Barr.

1937: *Bright Island* by Mabel Robinson is the story of spunky Thankful Curtis, who was raised on a small island off the coast of Maine and later attends school on the mainland.

1938: *Iron Duke* by John Tunis was the first of several popular books written by an amateur athlete and sports reporter. Other Tunis titles, some of which have been recently reprinted, include *All-American* (1942), *Yea Wildcats* (1944), and *Go, Team, Go!* (1954).

1942: *Seventeenth Summer* by Maureen Daly is the story of shy and innocent Angie Morrow and her love for Jack Duluth during the summer between high school and college.

1942: *Adam of the Road* by Elizabeth Janet Gray reveals the color and music of the Middle Ages as young Adam Quartermain becomes a minstrel.

1945: *Pray Love, Remember* by Mary Stolz is one of the earliest and one of the best of Stolz's many quiet, introspective books; it is a remarkable story of Dody Jenks, a popular but cold young woman who likes neither her family nor herself.

1950: *Swiftwater* by Paul Annixter (really Howard A. Sturzel) mixes animals, ecology, symbolism, and some stereotyped characters into a rousing tale that remains a better than respectable book.

1952: *Two and the Town* by Henry Gregor Felsen. A young girl is pregnant and a marriage is forced on two teenagers, something that at the time was taboo for YA books. Felsen is better known for *Hot Rod* (1950) and *Crash Club* (1958).

1957: *Ring Around Her Finger* and *The Limit of Love* (1959) by James Summers were effective delineations of young people's sexual feelings and actions told from the boys' points of view. Critics feared readers were too young to handle such emotional intricacies.

1959: *Jennifer* by Zoa Sherburne is an enduring portrait of the effects of alcoholism, but it is not as good as Sherburne's *Too Bad about the Haines Girl* (1967), a superb novel about teenage pregnancy that is honest and straightforward without being preachy.

friends of her aunt's fiancée and of the daughter of the local minister, who was doomed to die soon. Amidst all the tears, the book taught submission, the dangers of self-righteousness, and the virtues of a steadfast religion. In the 1890s, it was said to be one of the four most widely read books in the United States, along with the Bible, *The Pilgrim's Progress,* and *Uncle Tom's Cabin.* There was actually no way to keep young people from reading books published for adults because many of the popular books were first serialized in newspapers and magazines. Since the majority of teens were not in school, they read whatever was available. Much of the pop culture reading was gender specific with females reading what were called *domestic novels.*

1855: Nathaniel Hawthorne bitterly lamented to his publisher that "America is now wholly given over to a d—d mob of scribbling women, and I should have no chance of success while the public taste is occupied with their trash—and should be ashamed of myself if I did succeed."

1860: Erastus and Irwin Beadle published Ann S. Stephens's *Malaeksa: The Indian Wife of the White Hunter,* which had both the melodrama and the tears of a domestic novel, but also the chills and thrills of a dime novel. It was originally serialized in 1839 in *The Ladies Companion,* and when Erastus and Beadle decided to publish it as a book they launched a huge advertising campaign:

BOOKS FOR THE MILLIONS

A DOLLAR Book for a dime!

128 pages complete, only ten cents!!!

MALAESKA

The

Indian Wife of the White Hunter

By Mrs. Ann Stephens

Irwin P. Beadle and Co., Publishers

The book was set during the Revolutionary War days in upper New York State. It was 128 pages long, printed in the six-by-four-inch format of the dime novels, and sold out its first printing of 65,000 copies in record time.

1863: Robert Louis Stevenson's 1863 *Treasure Island* was published and immediately became popular with both adult and young readers. Noah Brooks's 1876 *The Boy Emigrants* and Kirk Munroe's 1888 *Derrick Sterling* brought in more male readers.

1866: Edward Stratemeyer took his first step toward founding the most successful industry ever built around adolescent reading. He wrote on brown wrapping paper an 18,000-word serial, *Victor Horton's Idea,* and mailed it to a Philadelphia weekly boys' magazine, which promptly sent him a check for $75.00.

1867: Augusta Jane Evans Wilson's *St. Elmo* became wildly popular with a special edition being advertised as "limited to 100,000 copies." An orphaned girl befriends a wealthy woman whose dissolute son is immediately enamored of the young woman. He is rejected by her, leaves home for several years, returns to plead for her love, is again rejected, and eventually becomes a minister in order to win the young woman's hand. Towns were named or renamed St. Elmo, as were hotels, railroad coaches, steamboats, one kind of punch, and a brand of cigars. Part of the book's charm was the satisfying idea that another wicked man had been reformed by the power of a good woman.

1868: Although today few people read either Oliver Optic's or Horatio Alger's books, we may never have had Louisa May Alcott's *Little Women* if Roberts Publishers had not set out to find an author who could write a book for girls that would be as popular as the Optic and Alger books were for boys. They approached Alcott, who had been writing and selling stories to popular magazines, to see if she would attempt writing a book for girls. She agreed

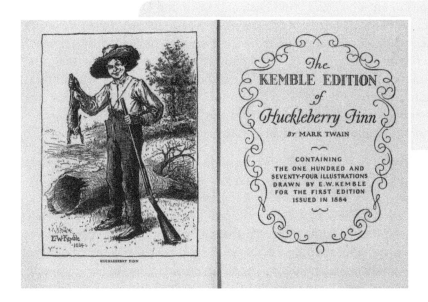

Who would have dreamed that this 1884 book would still be causing trouble in the twenty-first century?

to "try" and *Little Women: Meg, Jo, Beth, and Amy. The Story of Their Lives, A Girl's Book* was published in November of 1868. Part of the reason for its success was Alcott's refreshing glimpses into a life that was probably more like the life she dreamed of, rather than the one she actually lived. Today we look at the book as a nostalgic reliving of American life at the time of the Civil War. But actually, Alcott's book was in many ways radical for its time. With the sisters, Alcott provided alternative roles for women at a time when very few women imagined themselves as doing anything other than marrying a man and raising his family.

1870: Thomas Bailey Aldrich published *The Story of a Bad Boy,* which was a refreshing counterbalance to the good-little-boy figures prevalent in most of the contemporary books. In some ways it laid the groundwork for Mark Twain's 1876 *The Adventures of Tom Sawyer* and his 1884 *Adventures of Huckleberry Finn.* Twain's books were published for adult audiences, but in the introduction to *Huckleberry Finn,* he mentions young readers, which some people think contributed to the book's immediate—and long-lasting—problems with censorship.

1887: The *Publishers' Trade List* contained sixteen pages listing 440 authors and 900 books produced for young readers under the Lee and Shepard logo. Especially popular were series books written mainly by Harry Castlemon, Oliver Optic, Martha Finley, and Susan Coolidge. Castlemon's approach was pragmatic, as shown by this quote: "Boys don't like fine writing. What they want is adventure, and the more of it you can get into 250 pages of manuscript, the better fellow you are."

1890s: Because so many boys were reading dime novels and boys had little money, the price of the books dropped to a nickel. The first and most popular books were set in Colorado and points west, where there was plenty of room and opportunity for adventure. Leading characters were such wondrous he-men as Deadwood Dick and Diamond Dick; however, as the romance of the west began to fade, writers began adapting their formulas and their stock characters to detective stories and then to early forms of science fiction. Librarians hated dime novels and campaigned against their "immorality." But in truth, most of these books represented sound moral values, and what really offended the librarians was nothing more than the unrealistic and melodramatic plots and the stereotyped characters, which were more typical of the time than of just the dime (or half-dime) novel.

1892: The New York State Legislature passed landmark legislation authorizing the development of school libraries. Four years later the American Library Association appointed a Committee on Cooperation with the National Education Association to work together for the promotion of school libraries. While librarians and other educators agreed that libraries presented opportunities for pleasure and education of the masses, arguments about their purposes rose almost as fast as the buildings. The three big objections to libraries were:

- The normal dread of taxes.
- The philosophical belief that government had no rights except to protect people and property.
- Concerns over the kinds of books that libraries might buy and circulate.

1893: By now, Edward Stratemeyer was editing *Good News,* Street and Smith's boys' weekly with a circulation of nearly 200,000. This brought his name in front of the public; in 1894, he published his first book under his own name. By 1897, he had six series and sixteen hardcover books in print. A major breakthrough came in 1898, when an editor suggested that he change a war story he had just written to tie it in with real life. He rewrote it and returned it as *Under Dewey at Manila: or, The War Fortunes of a Castaway.* His career was off and running, and he evolved the idea of a literary syndicate. He would devise the plots for stories, assign them to anonymous writers, give them a few weeks to fill in the details, pay them with a check for $50 to $75, and publish their stories under the names of fictional authors. Among the most famous were the Nancy Drew books by Carolyn Keene, the Tom Swift books by Victor Appleton, and The Bobbsey Twin books by Laura Lee Hope.

1897: In a March issue of the *Library Journal,* William S. Stevenson made a case for "Weeding Out Fiction in the Carnegie Free Library of Allegheny, Pennsylvania." He maintained that "If the public library is not first and foremost an educational institution, it has no right to exist. If it exists for mere pleasure, and for a low order of entertainment at that, it is simply a socialistic institution." In spite of such objections, newly published fiction that was finding its way into the hands of young readers included John Bennett's 1897 *Master Skylark: A Story of Shakespeare's Time* (a witty account of young Nick Attwood, a golden-voiced boy singer involved in more than his share of adventure), Ralph Henry Barbour's 1899 *The Half-Back* (the first of many popular sports books meant to illustrate how boys at school can learn who and what they might become through sports), and Laura Elizabeth Howe Richards's 1899 *Peggy* (a sports book about a poor girl going to school and becoming a basketball hero).

LATE 1800's
ADVENTURES OF HUCKLEBERRY FINN

SERIES BOOKS BY
Harry Castelmon
Martha Finley
Susan Coolidge

Edward Stratemeyer connects a fictional story to Admiral Dewey's 1898 victory in Manila Bay.

1904: *Rebecca of Sunnybrook Farm* by Kate Douglas Wiggin sold more than 1.25 million copies and launched a formula in which a young child (usually a girl) makes life happy for apathetic or depressed adults. In 1908, *Anne of Green Gables* by Lucy Maud Montgomery continued the Wiggin formula in a story about an orphan girl sent by mistake to a childless couple who wanted a boy to help on the farm. Five years later, Eleanor Porter's *Pollyanna* was published as an adult novel and was eighth among best sellers in 1914 and second in 1915. Some people think that it was so over the top that it was the climax (or the finishing blow) to the child-as-savior book.

EARLY 1900'S
REBECCA OF SUNNYBROOK FARM
ANNE OF GREEN GABLES
POLLYANNA

Books are divided by gender.

Study and criticism begin.

Paperbacks and "junior novels" are invented.

1908: Psychologist G. Stanley Hall encouraged the division of "books for boys" and "books for girls" in an article for the April 1908 *Library Journal,* "Children's Reading: As a Factor in Their Education." He wrote "Boys love adventure, girls sentiment. . . . Girls love to read stories about girls which boys eschew." He added that girls are the only ones reading books "dealing with domestic life and with young children. . . . Boys, on the other hand, excel in love of humor, rollicking fun, abandon, rough horse-play, and tales of wild escapades." He concluded with, "A book popular with boys would attract some girls, while one read by most girls would repel a boy in the middle teens. The reading interests of high school girls are far more humanistic, cultural and general, and that of boys is more practical, vocational, and even special." In this same year, Franklin T. Baker wrote in an introduction to *A Bibliography of Children's Reading* published by Teachers College, Columbia University, that with the exception of Alcott, girls' books were "painfully weak" because they lacked "invention, action, and humor." Over the next several decades, many parents, teachers, publishers, and librarians began to reject Stanley Hall's strict classification because they thought that boys' books were simply more interesting than girls' books, not because of the sexual or psychological nature of boys and girls, but rather because of the way the authors treated their audiences. For example, Julia Carter wrote in an article for the April 1935 *Wilson Bulletin for Librarians,* "Will someone please tell me why we expect the boys to know these things and still plan for the girls to be mid-Victorian, and consider them hoydens beyond reclaiming, when instead of shrieking and running like daughters of Eve, they are interested in snakes and can light a fire with two matches?"

1911: The National Council of Teachers of English was established, mainly because English teachers wanted to organize themselves to protest effectively against the way that a few elite colleges were determining what books should be taught in high schools. In the 1890s when the prestigious Committee of Ten on Secondary School Studies decided to make English an accepted discipline in high schools to be studied in place of Latin, the committee also decided that uniform college entrance examinations should be established throughout the United States. Elite eastern colleges published lists of such classics as Shakespeare's *Twelfth Night* and *As You Like It,* Milton's Book I and II from *Paradise Lost,* Scott's *The Abbot and Marmion,* and Irving's *Bracebridge Hall* as the basis for their entrance exams. This was at a time when the majority of young people did not graduate from high school, and of those who did, only a small percentage went on to attend college.

High school educators thought it was presumptuous of a few eastern colleges to dictate a national high school curriculum under the guise of preparing students to pass entrance exams. They agreed with John M. Coulter, who wrote "What the University Expects of the Secondary School" for the February 1909 *School Review*. He maintained that "The high school exists primarily for its own sake; and secondarily as a preparatory school for college. This means that when the high school interest and the college interest come into conflict, the college interest must yield. It also means that the function of a preparatory school must be performed only in so far as it does not interfere with the more fundamental purpose of the high school itself."

1926: Enough books were being published that people began to ask for help in choosing what they wanted to read. The Book-of-the-Month Club was founded in 1926, and the Literary Guild was founded one year later. Arguments over what students should read in high school were reflected in the lengthy *Winnetka Graded Book List* compiled by Carleton Washburne and Mabel Vogel. However, readers were more curious about the many books that the two educators left off because of judging them to be "definitely trashy or unsuitable for children." In response to popular request, the authors added two supplements listing the books they objected to Martha Finley's. *Elsie Dinsmore* was among the damned, and so were Edgar Rice Burroughs's *Tarzan of the Apes,* Eleanor Porter's *Pollyanna,* Zane Grey's westerns, books from the Ruth Fielding and Tom Swift series, Mark Twain's *Tom Sawyer Abroad,* and Arthur Conan Doyle's *The Hound of the Baskervilles.* However, *The Adventures of Sherlock Holmes* was considered worthy of inclusion.

1927: In an article in the January 1927 issue of *English Journal,* William Lyon Phelps published "The Virtues of the Second-Rate," and argued, "I do not believe the majority of these very school teachers and other cultivated mature readers began in early youth by reading great books exclusively; I think they read *Jack Harkaway, an Old Sleuth,* and the works of Oliver Optic and Horatio Alger. From these enchanters they learned a thing of tremendous importance—the delight of reading. Once a taste for reading is formed, it can be improved. But it is improbable that boys and girls who have never cared to read a good story will later enjoy stories by good artists."

1929: Dr. G. O. Ireland coined the term *bibliotherapy* when he wrote about using books as part of his treatment for psychiatric patients. By the late 1930s and early 1940s, articles about bibliotherapy became almost commonplace in education journals. The idea of using books to help readers come to terms with their psychological problems was supposedly justified by Aristotle's *Poetics* and the theory of emotional release through catharsis. However, it soon became apparent that making such connections was sometimes beyond the realm of what an *English-teacher-turned-psychologist* should be doing. In a March 1951 *English Journal* article, "Diversifying the Matter," Lou LaBrant explained that certainly she could make a much wiser selection of offerings when she knew and understood the potential reader. But this "does not mean as some have interpreted" that young readers will enjoy only literature which answers their specific questions or tells them what to do. "It is true, however, that young and old tend to choose literature,

In the decades before the 1929 stock market crash, U.S. high schools developed in their present form, including the establishment of athletics teams as a way of "bribing" boys into reading and writing. Shown here is the 1917 Tempe Public Schools baseball team.

whether they seek solutions or escape, which offers characters or situations with which they can find a degree of identification."

1930: Professor Dora V. Smith, who taught children's literature at the University of Minnesota, began to promote the idea that books for teenagers were different from books for children. She is generally thought to be the first teacher to separate YA books from children's literature and to teach classes specifically in *adolescent* literature. Among her students were G. Robert Carlsen, Dwight L. Burton, and Stanley B. Kegler, who carried her message out to other scholars who also went on to teach a new generation of professors of young adult literature. In a January 2000 issue of *English Journal*, Chris Crowe wrote "Starting with Dora V.: A Genealogy of YA Literature Specialists," in which he traced his own academic ancestry back to Dora V. He was amused to learn that he had not only inherited her attitudes, but also her housekeeping skills. Her office was a jumble filled with stacks of books and note cards, and she was frequently seen trundling a cart full of books to class, just as he does and just as his own professors did when he took his college classes in adolescent literature.

1933: The term *junior* or *juvenile novel* was first applied to *Let the Hurricane Roar,* a believable and moving story of a young pioneer couple written by Rose Wilder Lane. Rose was a journalist and the daughter of Laura Ingalls Wilder, author of the well-known *Little House on the Prairie* books. It is now known that Rose gave her mother considerable editorial help with the Little House books. Between 1933 and 1958, the book went through twenty-six printings; in 1976, it was made into a television movie and reissued under the title *Young Pioneers.*

1936: Lou LaBrant at the Ohio State University Laboratory School began working with the idea of free reading in which students are encouraged to choose whatever they want to read and then to talk about it with a teacher. LaBrant is one of the few scholars who managed to do a long-term study, which years later showed that the students who had participated in free reading classes enjoyed reading as adults and brought significantly more reading activities to their children than did comparable students at the Laboratory School who had studied reading and literature in a more traditional manner.

1936: Over the next few years, several books that appealed to young teens, as well as to children, were published, including Helen Dore Boylston's *Sue Barton: Student Nurse* (1936), Florence Crannell Means's *Shuttered Windows* (1938), Marjorie Kinnan Rawlings's *The Yearling* (1938), and John R. Tunis's sports books: *The Kid from Tompkinsville* (1940), *All-American* (1942), and *Yea, Wildcats!* (1944).

1937: John Steinbeck's 1937 *Of Mice and Men* and his 1939 *The Grapes of Wrath* both reflected and promoted the awareness that American society was changing with deeply disturbing consequences. The books were highly censored, but as censorship lessened somewhat, young people began reading books that showed them all was not well.

1938: Louise Rosenblatt published the first edition of her *Literature as Exploration,* which gave high school teachers a legitimate and effective way to work with students in free reading classes with the kinds of books that Dora V. Smith was bringing to the attention of teachers and, in turn, to their students. In a later edition of Rosenblatt's book, she made the point that "No one else can read a literary work for us. The benefits of literature can emerge only from creative activity." We as readers must respond to the little black marks on the page, or to the sound of the words in our ears, and "make something out of them."

1938: Paperbacks as we know them today entered the mass market when Pocket Books offered Pearl S. Buck's *The Good Earth* as a sample volume in mail order tests. A year later, a staff artist created the trademark sketch of Gertrude the Kangaroo with a book in her paws and another in her pouch. A few months later, the company issued ten titles in 10,000 copy editions, most of which became long-term best sellers. Avon began publishing in 1941; Penguin entered the U.S. market in 1942, and Bantam, New American Library, Ballantine, Dell, and Popular Library began publishing in 1943. Paperbacks were frowned upon by teachers and librarians, partly because of their lurid covers and partly because they were hard to catalogue and keep track of. Some teachers forbade the reading of paperbacks. One of us remembers teaching in a school where the students read paperbacks and then would come to us to see if we could provide a hardback copy of the same book that they could carry to class for their book report. However, by the mid-1960s, paperbacks had become a fully accepted part of teenagers' lives. Early on, paperback publishers purchased rights for books that had already proven popular as hardbacks, but today some books are published only in paperback editions, and some hardback publishers have taken it upon themselves to publish both the hardback and the paperback editions.

1942: Nonfiction was not as popular as it would later become, but true stories about battles and survivors included Robert Trumbull's 1942 *The Raft,* Richard Tregaskis's 1943 *Guadalcanal Diary,* Ernie Pyle's 1943 *Here Is Your War* and his 1944 *Brave Men,* and Quentin Reynolds's 1946 *70,000 to One.*

1944: Perhaps as a reaction to the realities of war, both adult and teen readers turned to exaggerated romances and adventure stories. When Kathleen Winsor's *Forever Amber* was published in 1944, parents worried, censors paled, and young adults smiled as they ignored the fuss and read the book. The uproar was much the same as that awaiting Grace Metalious with her 1956 *Peyton Place.* A few years later, Ian Fleming's James Bond, Agent 007 series caught the mood of the time with escapist excitement tinted with what appeared to be realities.

1946: George W. Norvell wrote "Some Results of a Twelve-Year Study of Children's Reading Interests" in the December 1946 *English Journal.* His data showed that much of the library and classroom material being used in schools was "too mature, too subtle, and too erudite to permit its enjoyment by the majority of secondary-school pupils." He concluded that three-fourths of the selections currently being read in school were uninteresting, especially to boys, and that to increase reading skills while producing a generation of book-lovers, teachers needed to give students at least some choice because "there is no factor so powerful as interest."

1947: Marie Rankin reported in the Teachers College, Columbia University *Contributions to Education* (1947, No. 906) that, when she surveyed eight public libraries in Illinois, Ohio, and New York, she found that Helen Boylston's *Sue Barton: Student Nurse* was the most consistently popular book. Her study ushered in a raft of reading interest surveys in which young people were asked what they preferred to read. For example, Stephen Dunning in the December 15, 1959, issue of *Junior Librarian* surveyed fourteen school and public libraries and concluded that the ten most popular books were Maureen Daly's *Seventeenth Summer,* Henry Gregor Felsen's *Hot Rod,* Betty Cavanna's *Going on Sixteen,* Rosamond Du Jardin's *Double Date,* Walter Farley's *Black Stallion,* Sally Benson's *Junior Miss,* Mary Stolz's *The Sea Gulls Woke Me,* Rosamond Du Jardin's *Wait for Marcy,* James Summer's *Prom Trouble,* and John Tunis's *All-American.* Critics pointed out that reading interest surveys were fairly limited because they were nearly always conducted on whatever sample was convenient to the reviewer and so could not predict what would be the favorites in a different setting. However, the fact that so many people conducted such surveys helped to get the message out that it was important to give students a choice in what they read.

1948: With encouragement from teachers, some teens read Alan Paton's 1948 *Cry, the Beloved Country* and later his 1953 *Too Late the Phalarope* about racial struggles in South Africa. In ways it was easier for students to read about racial struggles in South Africa than in the United States, but some young people read Richard Wright's 1940 *Native Son* and 1945 *Black Boy.*

1950s: By now, the *bildungsroman,* a novel about the initiation, maturation, and education of a young person, had developed as a genre. Although the

MID 1900'S

Hot Rod
All American
Seventeenth Summer
Black Stallion
To Kill a Mockingbird

Comic books are popular.

Interests grow to include problems here and abroad.

Scholars take notice.

These "good girls" of the 1950s, who are pretending to be "bad girls" as they strut in their crinoline petticoats and carry fake cigarettes, were more likely to be reading fiction published in women's magazines and such books as Mrs. Mike, Forever Amber, *and* Peyton Place *than books published specifically for teenagers.*

books were about young people, they were written for adult audiences. However, several of them, including Dan Wickenden's 1940 *Walk Like a Mortal*, Betty Smith's 1943 *A Tree Grows in Brooklyn*, J. D. Salinger's 1951 *The Catcher in the Rye*, and William Golding's 1955 *Lord of the Flies*, found their way into the hands of teenagers.

1951: Dwight L. Burton wrote the first literary criticism of young adult novels in the *English Journal* 40 (September 1951, pp. 363–369). He injected judgments along with appreciation as he commented on works by Dan Wickenden, Maureen Daly, Paul Annixter, Betty Cavanna, and Madeleine L'Engle. He wrote that the attributes of a good novel for young readers were "no different from any good novel."

> It must be technically masterful, and it must present a significant synthesis of human experience. Because of the nature of adolescence itself, the good novel for the adolescent should be full in true invention and imagination. It must free itself of Pollyannaism or the Tarkington–Henry Aldrich–Corliss Archer tradition and maintain a clear vision of the adolescent as a person of complexity, individuality, and dignity. The novel for the adolescent presents a ready field for the mature artist.
>
> Other scholars who began looking seriously at this relatively new field of literature included Richard S. Alm and Emma L. Patterson.

1957: Russia's successful launching of Sputnik struck fear into the hearts of Americans who were afraid that the United States would be unable to compete with the technological sophistication of the Soviet Union. The general public, along with government agencies and educators, scrambled to focus attention on education in high-tech fields. Funds were first set aside to support science and math, but very soon it became apparent that students could not learn math and science if they did not know how to read, and so the educational focus was broadened to include the language arts and libraries.

1960: Many adults and teenagers were genuinely touched by Harper Lee's 1960 *To Kill a Mockingbird*. The American Library Association began paying more attention to teenagers, as shown by the Young Adult Services Division establishing a committee on Standards for Work with Young Adults and sending delegates, along with copies of the newly published *Youth in a Changing World in Fiction and Fact*, to the Golden Anniversary White House Conference on Children and Youth.

1960s: Questions related to civil rights for African Americans came to the forefront. In Danville, Virginia, thirteen African American high school students entered the main library and refused to leave. During the 1960s, books by three African American nonfiction writers were appreciated by many young adults: Claude Brown's stark picture of African American ghetto life in *Manchild in the Promised Land* (1965), Malcolm X and Alex Haley's (the latter better known for *Roots*) *The Autobiography of Malcolm X* (1965), and Eldridge Cleaver's *Soul on Ice* (1968), an impassioned plea by an African American man in prison who wrote to save himself. In 1974, James Baldwin's novel, *If Beale Street Could Talk*, resonated with many young readers.

1962: In what was almost a repeat of the kinds of arguments that resulted in the founding of the National Council of Teachers of English in 1912, the Modern Language Association criticized how high school students were, or were not, being prepared for college. High school English teachers were not amused, but they nevertheless participated in a series of Basic Issues conferences and in twenty Project English summer institutes held in 1962. Many of these institutes focused on what should be included in the high school English curriculum. Nearly everyone agreed on the holy tripod of literature, language, and composition, but from there opinions varied widely. Marjorie Smiley's center at Hunter College was exceptional in the way the participants focused on student involvement and interest and on finding personal and social significance in literature.

1963: The Knapp Foundation sponsored a School Libraries Project to set up model media centers throughout the country. This new focus on media contributed to the alternative name of media centers for school libraries. Alfred E. Bestor published the first edition of *Educational Wastelands: The Retreat from Learning in Our Public Schools* (Univ. of Illinois Press), which sang what would become a national anthem of complaints about how U.S. schools were not preparing our country to compete against the Soviet Union.

1964: The International Reading Association, which was founded in 1956 as a professional organization for those involved in teaching reading, began publishing the *Journal of Reading*, renamed in 1985 to the *Journal of Adolescent and Adult Literacy (JAAL)*. It presently goes to 15,000 subscribers

Focus Box 2.2

A Sampling of Good Books from the 1960s

Across Five Aprils by Irene Hunt. Follett, 1965. In this historical novel, the Civil War comes to a farm family.

A Blues I Can Whistle by A. E. Johnson. Four Winds, 1969. A boy who failed at suicide explains how he got there.

The Book of Three by Lloyd Alexander. Holt, 1964. This was the first of the Prydain series that came to include *The Black Cauldron* (1965), *The Castle of the Llyr* (1966), *Taran Wanderer* (1967), and *The High King* (1968).

The Chosen by Chaim Potok. Simon & Schuster, 1967. Through *The Chosen* and *My Name Is Asher Lev* (1972), Potok introduced a whole generation of high school students to a young man's life in a Hasidic Jewish community.

The Face of Abraham Candle by Bruce Clements. Farrar, Straus & Giroux, 1969. In silver-mining-era Colorado, a boy helps plunder treasures from Mesa Verde.

Jamie by Jack Bennett. Little, Brown, 1963. A young boy has one mission, to avenge his father's death by one of Africa's most dangerous animals, a water buffalo. See also Bennett's *The Hawk Alone* (1965).

Jazz Country by Nat Hentoff. HarperCollins, 1965. In this superb story, a white boy tries to break into the African American world of jazz.

The King's Fifth by Scott O'Dell. Houghton Mifflin, 1966. Conquistadors plunder and ravage the New World in search of gold.

A Love or a Season by Mary Stolz. HarperCollins, 1964. Stolz treated young love and sexual tension with both affection and dignity.

Mr. and Mrs. Bo Jo Jones by Ann Head. Putnam, 1967. Head was one of the first to treat a premarital pregnancy with respect and understanding.

The Owl Service by Alan Garner. Walck, 1968. Three young people replay a Welsh myth from the *Mabinogion*.

The Pushcart War by Jean Merrill. Scott, 1964. In this wonderful satire, war erupts between New York City pushcart owners and the drivers of those mammoth trucks that hog city streets.

Red Sky at Morning by Richard Bradford. Lippincott, 1968. A boy and his mother go to live in New Mexico while their father is at war and the experience brings the boy to examine his values.

A Separate Peace by John Knowles. Macmillan, 1961. The story of two boys whose friendship ends in tragedy, was predicted to be a novel that would be taught in high school English classes for generations.

A Single Light by Maia Wojciechowska. Harper & Row, 1968. An unloved Spanish girl finds someone to love, a white marble statue of the Christ Child.

Sounder by William Armstrong. HarperCollins, 1969. An Academy Award–winning film brought even more readers to this sad story of a 1920s African American family that loses both its father and its dog.

and represents the interests of reading teachers at the secondary level. In all, IRA has 85,000 members in over one hundred countries, and nearly forty Special Interest Groups (SIGs) including a Network on Adolescent Literature. Especially in recent years, *JAAL* has devoted several pages to articles and to reviews of new YA books. And at both national and regional conferences, awards are given and sessions are devoted to authors and scholars working with young adult literature.

1965: Congress passed the Elementary and Secondary Education Act (ESEA), which provides money for the purchase of library materials and textbooks. Many schools established their first libraries in order to qualify for these funds, which were available for almost a decade. The National Defense Education Act (NDEA) also provided funding for teachers' institutes throughout the country. Out of these came new ideas for teaching English and working with nonprint media (especially film); multicultural literature; adolescent literature, as it was then called; team teaching, linguistics, and performing rather than just reading Shakespeare.

1965: The College Entrance Examination Board turned its attention to the teaching of literature in its widely read *Freedom and Discipline in English*. It rejected the idea that "so-called junior books" might ease young readers into a frame of mind in which they will be ready "to tackle something stronger, harder and more adult," by writing, "The Commission has serious doubts that it does anything of the sort. For classes in remedial reading a resort to such books may be necessary, but to make them a considerable part of the curriculum for most students is to subvert the purposes for which literature is included in the first place. In the high school years, the aim should be not to find the students' level so much as to raise it, and such books rarely elevate. For college-bound students, particularly, no such concessions as they imply are justified. Maturity of thought, vocabulary, syntax, and construction is the criterion of excellence in literature, and that criterion must not be abandoned for apparent expediency." High school teachers resented such criticism coming from college professors who had clearly not read such good books as Marjorie Hill Allee's 1937 *The Great Tradition*, Esther Forbes's 1943 *Johnny Tremain*, Paul Annixter's 1950 *Swiftwater*, Mary Stolz's 1954 *Pray Love, Remember*, Rosemary Sutcliff's 1954 *The Eagle of the Ninth*, and Nat Hentoff's 1965 *Jazz Country*. Such negative criticism galvanized the resolve of knowledgeable teachers to change the public's opinion about books written for teenagers.

1966: Daniel Fader published *Hooked on Books: Program and Proof* (Berkley). The book grew out of one of the 1962 Project English Centers in Michigan where participants worked with the W. J. Maxey Boys' Training School (a euphemism for *reform school*). Each boy was allowed to choose and keep two paperback books from the library, a paperback dictionary, and a spiral notebook (a journal) in which he was to write at least two pages a week. While railing against current practices in the teaching of reading, Fader used paperbacks of all sorts to get the boys to read—and read they did. His techniques were so successful that his book was revised and republished several times and quoted almost as if it were holy writ.

1967: The Young Adult Services Division of the American Library Association combined forces with ALA's Intellectual Freedom Committee to cosponsor a conference on "Intellectual Freedom and the Teenager." Five years later, ALA adopted "Free Access to Minors: An Interpretation of the Library Bill of Rights."

1967: G. Robert Carlsen published *Books and the Teenage Reader* (Harper & Row). While bringing national attention and a degree of respect to adolescent literature, his work also attracted several doctoral students to his English Education program at the University of Iowa, including two of the authors of this textbook and such scholars as Ben Nelms, Terry C. Ley, Richard Abrahamson, and Ruth Cline, all of whom have gone on to train other doctoral students now working in the field. Carlsen earned his own Ph.D. at the University of Minnesota where he studied with Dora V. Smith, who is usually cited as doing for adolescent literature in English Education what Margaret A. Edwards did for it in libraries.

1967: S. E. Hinton published *The Outsiders* and Robert Lipsyte published *The Contender*. See pages 7 and 241 for statements about them as winners of the Margaret A. Edwards award. Other authors who published outstanding books in the 1960s and 1970s and were subsequently chosen as winners of the Margaret A. Edwards award include Paul Zindel (see p. 215), M. E. Kerr (p. 354), Robert Cormier (p. 57), Judy Blume (p. 61), Orson Scott Card (p. 140), Richard Peck (p. 271), Anne McCaffrey (p. 146), Lois Duncan (p. 253), and Ursula K. Le Guin (p. 145).

1969: Margaret A. Edwards published *The Fair Garden and the Swarm of Beasts* (Hawthorne). The title comes from an essay in *The Old Librarian's Almanac*, in which Jared Bean advised his fellow librarians that the Treasure House of Literature "is no more to be thrown open to the ravages of the unreasoning mob [the general public, especially the young] than is a Fair Garden to be laid unprotected at the Mercy of a Swarm of Beasts." Six years later, at the ALAN breakfast in San Diego, two hundred English teachers applauded the choice of Margaret A. Edwards as the recipient of the second ALAN Award for her contribution to the promotion of books for young readers. Thirteen years later, YALSA, in cooperation with the *School Library Journal*, established the Margaret A. Edwards Award to honor a living author whose books have spoken to young adults over a period of time. Winners of that award are featured on special pages throughout this text. See Edwards' photo on page 5.

1971: Prentice Hall published *Go Ask Alice,* a book purported to be the diary of an anonymous teenager who dies of a drug overdose. By 1979, it had been translated into sixteen languages, reprinted forty-three times as an Avon paperback, and made into a popular TV movie, all of which increased sales and library check-outs. The book's anonymity lent it a certain air of mystery and made it more or less exempt from regular literary criticism because it was supposedly the diary of a deceased young woman. However, censors did not shy away from criticizing the book. Then in 1978, Beatrice Sparks identified herself on the cover of a new book, *Voices* (Time Books, 1978), as "The author who brought you *Go Ask Alice.*" Critics, who had already been questioning how much of the diary was really that of a young girl as opposed to the imaginings of an adult "editor," suspected that Sparks waited seven years to identify herself so that the statute of limitations would have expired and the girl's parents could not sue her for releasing their daughter's story without their permission. Once she identified herself,

Margaret A. Edwards Award

Winner (1991)

Robert Cormier, **Who Took It to the Top**

The Chocolate War, *I Am the Cheese*, and *After the First Death* are the books Robert Cormier was honored for in 1991. Other exceptionally good books by Cormier include *The Bumblebee Flies Anyway*, *Beyond the Chocolate War*, *Fade*, *We All Fall Down*, and *Heroes*.

When in 1974, Cormier's *The Chocolate War* was published to critical acclaim, readers soon followed the critics. Censors, never willing to let a fine novel pass unnoticed and uncensored, also took note. The book was attacked from almost every imaginable viewpoint and for almost every imaginable sin. When Cormier's next two novels, *I Am the Cheese* and *After the First Death* were published, again to the approval of critics and readers, censors trailed not far behind.

What were Cormier's sins? One was the fact that Archie in *The Chocolate War* had taken a picture of Emile in a restroom stall with his "pants dropping on the floor, one hand furiously at work between his legs." Masturbation, as decent people knew, was not to be mentioned. Cormier did not shy away from crude language. His books were also filled with pessimism and, as one censor told us, the books were "unnecessarily realistic." Immorality prevailed, terror and evil abounded, corruption was everywhere, and worse yet, *I Am the Cheese* and *After the First Death* were unpatriotic, implying that the Witness Relocation Program was dishonest and that our government could not be trusted.

What were Cormier's virtues? He was honest, and he told readers what they already knew but were often afraid to admit—that corruption existed around them, not in some far-off place, and that bad guys and evil sometimes won and good guys and innocence could lose even at the end of a book.

Although Robert Cormier passed away on November 2, 2000, he and his works are still very much a part of the literary scene. British scholar Adrienne E. Gavin has just finished editing *Robert Cormier: A New Casebook* coming out from Palgrave Macmillin (2012). And in 2006, Delacorte published a new edition of Patty Campbell's *Robert Cormier: Daring to Disturb the Universe*. From the beginning, Campbell has been a supporter of Cormier's work. In her *Horn Book Magazine* column for March/April 2003, she

remembered what it was like in the 1970s to hope for real maturity in the YA novel and then to read Cormier's first YA book, which was "something else again—a book that shook us profoundly, a book that nobody could ignore."

From that first simple sentence in *The Chocolate War*, "They murdered him," readers knew Cormier was different. And from the first inklings of the plot, readers had the essentials before them. Jerry Renault was not superhuman, Archie and the Vigils were in charge of Trinity High School, and Brother Leon, who was nominally the assistant headmaster of the school but who "served as a flunky for the Head," was evil and enjoyed manipulating and corrupting others.

For the first edition of this textbook, Cormier told us,

I have always been interested in the plight of the individual versus the system, whether the system is the family, the school, the government or society in general. I hope to pursue this theme on an increasingly broader and more penetrating level. However, I am really more interested in creating credible human beings in situations that provide shocks of recognition for the reader. And I'm willing to let these characters take me where they will, even if I have to abandon preconceived notions about a particular theme. What's beautiful about this is that I can deal with character and theme in a manner that satisfies me as an author and have my work accepted in the field of adolescent literature.

Robert Cormier had never thought of himself as a writer for young people, but when his agent submitted *The Chocolate War* to Pantheon, the editor convinced Cormier that, as good as the book was, it would be simply one more in a catalogue of adult books. If it were published for teenagers, however, it might sell well, and it certainly would not be just one more in a long string of available adolescent novels. The editor's predictions came true and Cormier later acknowledged that although his initial reaction to becoming a *young adult* author was one of shock followed by a month long writer's block, he was grateful for the editorial help, which led not only to considerable attention from reviewers but also to his first financial success as an author. ●

Sparks went into business, almost like a modern day Stratemeyer Syndicate, focusing on "anonymous teenager" stories including *It Happened to Nancy, Almost Lost, Treacherous Love, Kim: Empty Inside, Annie's Baby,* and *Jay's Journal.*

1972: Francelia Butler, a faculty member in the English department at the University of Connecticut, established the Children's Literature Association as a Division of the Modern Language Association. In these early years, she referred to children's literature as "the great excluded," because of the low status that most academics gave it. As the years have gone by, ChLA members no longer use the phrase and they have also begun to interpret *children's literature* as including books for young adults.

1973: A group of about a dozen English teachers gathered at the National Council of Teachers of English annual conference and formed an Assembly on Literature for Adolescents of NCTE (ALAN). In keeping with their goal to promote the reading and teaching of young adult literature, they wrote their constitution to allow people to belong to the Assembly without having to pay dues to the National Council because they wanted to encourage membership from authors, publishers, reading teachers, and librarians, as well as English teachers. They planned a preconference workshop to be held at the 1974 convention in New Orleans. These workshops have been held every year since and have now been expanded to two full days. At the 2011 conference in Chicago, over sixty authors and over seventy members had parts on the two-day program attended by five hundred participants, all of whom went home with boxes of books provided by the authors' publishers.

1974: The Young Adult Services Division (YASD) of the American Library Association tactfully changed the name of its annual listing of recommended books that were of high interest but with a low reading level from "Books for Slow High School Readers" to the more positive sounding "Quick Picks." This was only one of many changes reflecting an increased respect for the viewpoints of young readers and a desire to involve teenagers as members of library advisory boards and "Best Book" selection committees.

Beauty: A Retelling of the Story of Beauty and the Beast by Robin McKinley. HarperCollins, 1978. Funny and surrealistic, McKinley's excellent writing undoubtedly inspired many of the more recent retellings of old stories.

The Bell Jar by Sylvia Plath. HarperCollins, 1971. Although not published as a YA book, Plath's own story of her emotional problems still attracts mature young adult readers.

Bless the Beasts and Children by Glendon Swarthout. Doubleday, 1970. Boys at a summer camp are appalled to see a government-sponsored slaughter of penned-up buffalo. Swarthout presented the first copy of his book to the governor of Arizona, where the slaughter was held.

The Book of the Dun Cow by Walter Wangerin, Jr. HarperCollins, 1978. Wangerin told his story as a beast fable, in which one of the beasts plays the role of the biblical Job.

A Day No Pigs Would Die by Robert Newton Peck. Knopf, 1972. On this Depression-era farm, Rob has to become the man of the family after the death of his father, whose job was slaughtering pigs.

Dragonwings by Laurence Yep. HarperCollins, 1975. When Yep found a historical allusion to a Chinese kite maker who succeeded in flying years before the Wright Brothers, he wrote a story of how it might have happened.

Happy Endings Are All Alike by Sandra Scoppettone. HarperCollins, 1978. Two lesbian girls are stalked by a dangerous young man interested only in rape.

A Hero Ain't Nothin' but a Sandwich by Alice Childress. Coward, McCann, and Geoghegan, 1973. A family tries to save a young drug user from himself.

Home Before Dark by Sue Ellen Bridgers. Knopf, 1976. A girl in a family of migrant workers manages to come to terms with a new life. In Bridger's 1979 *All Together Now*, a young girl comes to a small Southern town during the Korean War and becomes friends with the retarded but delightful Dwayne.

House of Stairs by William Sleator. Dutton, 1974. Six young people are placed in a strange house with stairs going everywhere and nowhere at all.

The Last Mission by Harry Mazer. Delacorte, 1979. Mazer tells at least part of his own story in this book about a young Jewish boy who enlists during World War II to destroy Hitler.

The Man Without a Face by Isabelle Holland. Lippincott, 1972. A boy learns some hard lessons from the disfigured man who agrees to tutor him for a summer.

Ordinary People by Judith Guest. Viking, 1976. When two brothers are boating and one of them drowns, the surviving brother and his parents have a hard time moving on.

Run Softly, Go Fast by Barbara Wersba. Atheneum, 1970. In this haunting novel, a boy's father dies and his angry son is left trying to figure out why he hates the man he used to love.

The Slave Dancer by Paula Fox. Bradbury, 1973. A fife-playing boy is kidnapped and brought to a ship where he is to play exercise music to help keep the cargo (slaves) in good health until they can be sold.

The Strange Affair of Adalaide Harris by Leon Garfield. Pantheon, 1971. A comedy of errors begins when two schoolboys leave a baby sister outdoors to see if wild animals will rescue her.

A String in the Harp by Nancy Bond. Atheneum, 1976. A dysfunctional family, transplanted to Wales, learns how to become a family again when one of the children finds an ancient harp-tuning key that opens the door to the sixth century.

A Wild Thing by Jean Renvoize. Little, Brown, 1971. In this tragedy, a fifteen-year-old outcast and runaway girl is living in a cave and wanting one thing—a baby.

Z for Zachariah by Robert C. O'Brien. Atheneum, 1975. A girl in an isolated valley that had been protected from a nuclear blast thinks she is the last person on Earth—but then she discovers another survivor who makes it worse than being alone.

1975: *School Library Journal* began publication separate from *Library Journal*. While *SLJ* started out with the idea of reviewing all books published for young readers, the burgeoning of the publishing business forced it to modify such an ambitious goal. Still, in its twelve issues per year, it manages to review over four thousand books. It also publishes four or five feature articles and a half-dozen regular columns in each monthly issue. Readers especially await the December issue in which the editors list their choices of sixty to seventy books identified as the year's best.

1975: In "Reason, Not Emotion," published in the April 1975 *Top of the News*, Elaine Simpson expressed the frustration that many were feeling about the way new YA books were being received. She complained about how for years librarians criticized junior novels for being written to formulas and for having "pat, sweetness and light resolutions" that instilled false conceptions of life and failed to deal with fundamental problems of personal and societal adjustments. But "then juvenile authors and editors began giving us such books as *Go Ask Alice*; *Run Softly, Go Fast*; *Admission to the Feast*; *Run, Shelley, Run*; *The Chocolate War* . . . And what happened? All too many of those same people who had been asking for an honest story about teenage problems began protesting." They didn't like the language and questioned whether young readers were ready for such realistic topics as "rape, abortion, homosexuality, unwed mothers, suicide, drugs, unsympathetic portrayal of parents, and violence." The mood of the times was shown by the fact that Bradbury Press, Judy Blume's publisher, which had always specialized in children's books, felt it necessary to create an adult division before they published her "mature" teen novel, *Forever*. By today's standards, the novel is mild, indeed, but at the time it was considered revolutionary because two teens "do it," and were not "punished" nor "forced" to try living together for the rest of their lives.

1978: *VOYA* (*Voice of Youth Advocates*) was established by Dorothy Broderick and Mary K. Chelton as a library publication focusing on young adult, as separate from children's, literature. The bimonthly journal has become a major force in reviewing and promoting young adult books and media. Scarecrow Press published it for many years; it is now published by E. J. Kurdyla Publishing in Bowie, Maryland, with RoseMary Honnold serving as editor. Although it is directed toward librarians, reading and English teachers have learned to rely on its feature articles, its help in drawing together thematically related units, and its columns to keep up with websites, computer games, and graphic novels.

1978: Patty Campbell, former YA librarian for the Los Angeles Public Library, began writing "The Young Adult Perplex" column in *Wilson Library Bulletin*. She brought a refreshing level of aesthetic as well as pedagogical criticism to the field. When the *Wilson Library Bulletin* ceased publication, she moved as a columnist to the *Horn Book Magazine*, where she wrote her "Sand in the Oyster" columns. She also served as series editor for Twayne's Young Adult Authors series and later for the Scarecrow Studies in Young Adult Literature.

Margaret A. Edwards Award
Winner (1996)
Judy Blume, Who Endures

The Edwards committee honored Blume for her 1975 *Forever*, but her other excellent books that young teens love include *Are You There God? It's Me, Margaret* (1970); *Then Again, Maybe I Won't* (1971); *Deenie* (1973); and our favorite, *Tiger Eyes* (1981), all published by Bradbury.

Judy recently co-authored the script for a film based on her book *Tiger Eyes,* which she is producing. She wrote to say now that the work has been completed on the film, she is returning to her writing and is working on a novel set in the 1950s in her hometown of Elizabeth, New Jersey.

In December of 2004, when Judy Blume was the first author of young people's literature to be honored by the National Book Foundation for her "distinguished contribution to American letters," readers all over the country—in fact, all over the world—cheered because they owned one or more of the 75 million Judy Blume books purchased by readers within the past thirty-five years. Blume was a young housewife and mother living in a New Jersey suburb when she began writing. On the morning after she received the award, she explained in a PBS interview with Jeffrey Brown that she chose to make Margaret age twelve because she had such vivid memories and warm feelings toward the thoughts and emotions she remembers from that time in her life. She loves the optimism and the faith that young readers have, as reflected in a letter she quoted in her acceptance speech: "Please send me the facts of life, in number order." She was still pondering on just how to answer that letter, but in general she says that her approach to writing is to go from deep inside herself and to be as truthful and honest as possible.

From the beginning, young readers loved the books and loved talking to Blume, either in person or by mail. Increasingly, college teachers of YA lit began recommending Blume's books and assigning them for class reading, and Blume became a welcome speaker at meetings of teachers and librarians. But the more successful Blume's books became, the more censors paid attention to them.

Everyone knows that sexuality sometimes comes into Blume's books, but as Faith McNulty observed in the *New Yorker* (December 5, 1983), "only to the degree that it enters most young minds." And sex isn't Blume's sole topic. In *Are You There God? It's Me, Margaret*, twelve-year-old Margaret is perplexed about what religion she should belong to. In *Then Again, Maybe I Won't*, Blume draws a devastating portrait of a family moving up in social class only to discover that the move may not have been a good thing. In *Tiger Eyes*, Davey has to accept the death of her father in a senseless act of violence. And in the most feared of all of Blume's books, *Forever*, Katherine struggles through the excitement of first sex only to learn that a first love may not endure. For the seventh edition of this textbook, Blume wrote that:

> *Fear has always made people anxious, and we are living in fearful times. . . . Book banning satisfies a need for parents to feel in control of their children's lives. This fear is often disguised as moral outrage. They want to believe that if their children don't read about something, their children won't know about it. And if they don't know about it, it won't happen.*

Blume is encouraged, though, by how many children and their parents and teachers are speaking out and defending children's right to read. Her message is that parents have the right to decide on books for their own child, but not for all children. ●

1980: Scott Foresman published the first edition of this textbook, *Literature for Today's Young Adults,* by Ken Donelson and Alleen Nilsen. They were the publishers of several textbooks written by May Hill Arbuthnot on various aspects of children's literature, and decided that it was time for a comprehensive textbook appropriate for use in English departments as well as in colleges of education and schools of library science. Previous books had focused mostly on realistic, problem novels. It was fortuitous that, at the last minute, an editor happened to notice that *young adult* was a term coming into fashion and so *adolescent,* which now sounds old fashioned was dropped from the title.

1980: Scholastic publishers discovered through their school book fair sales that the most popular books for girls ages twelve-and-up included elements of love or romance. They set to work developing a romance line of original paperbacks: *Wildfire* for young teens and later *Wishing Star* for the older girls. Bantam soon followed with a *Sweet Dreams* series, and Simon & Schuster with a *First Love* series. Feminist critics were indignant and labeled the books "training bras for Harlequin romances." Because of such criticism, Scholastic cancelled plans, after only one issue, of a *Wildfire* magazine, which they had intended to distribute as a marketing tool. Instead, the companies began advertising directly through teen magazines and placing their books on the shelves of newsstands and chain bookstores, especially those located in shopping malls. At the time, romance novels accounted for 30 percent of mass market paperback sales to adults, and the publishers for young people soon found something similar. In fact, 1980 was the first year that Scholastic made more than half of its money through commercial sales rather than through school book clubs.

Early 1980s: Many highly acclaimed new books reflected changing attitudes toward social issues. See the write-up on Nancy Garden (p. 311) whose 1982 *Annie on My Mind* introduced lesbian characters into a mainstream book. Books by African American authors that reached large audiences included Mildred D. Taylor's *Let the Circle Be Unbroken* and Alice Childress's *Rainbow Jordan,* both published in 1981. Virginia Hamilton's *Sweet Whispers, Brother Rush,* a book that introduced supernatural elements into what at first appeared to be realistic fiction, came a year later as did Sandra Cisneros's *The House on Mango Street,* a powerful exploration of a Mexican-American neighborhood. It was published for a general audience, but soon found its way into the hands and hearts of many teenage readers—and their teachers.

1981: Librarians and teachers were surprised when a *New York Times* story quoted in the August 1981 *School Library Journal* said that Paul Zindel had paid a ghost writer $10,000 for working with him on *The Pigman's Legacy,* a kind of autobiographical follow-up to Zindel's groundbreaking *The Pigman,* which was published in 1968. The man was suing Zindel for $250,000 plus one million dollars in damages. He also asked to be listed as a coauthor. The matter was settled out-of-court.

1983: Lillian N. Gerhardt, editor of *School Library Journal,* brought up questions about the future of young adult literature in her August 1983 editorial entitled "Selectors vs. Cheerleaders." She criticized "the fan-club mentality" among teachers and librarians, which she said "is nurtured by their professional associations, whose leaders continue to choose programs for conferences larded with popular authors present at their publishers' expense." The result was meetings that were "too seldom more than just pleasant, ladies' club fare" that "produces claques, not critics" and "sales not selectivity."

1984: Don Gallo edited and published *Sixteen: Short Stories by Outstanding Writers for Young Adults* with Delacorte. This was the first collection of short stories written specifically for a teenage audience by authors whose skill in writing for young adults was already recognized. Over the next few years, Gallo also edited similar collections under such titles as *Visions, Connections, Join In: Multiethnic Short Stories, Ultimate Sports,* and *Within Reach.* The success of these books inspired several other YA writers to publish their own collections of short stories.

1990s: Realistic fiction was still the dominant genre, with authors and publishers continuing to push the envelope. Walter Dean Myers's 1992 *Somewhere in the Darkness* is about a boy who "runs-away" with his father, an escaped convict he recognizes only after examining the one photo he has of the long-absent father. Virginia Euwer Wolff's 1993 *Make Lemonade* shows some of the complications of being a young, single mother living in "the projects." Cynthia Voigt's 1994 *When She Hollers* is about a girl being sexually abused by her step-father, while Rita Williams-Garcia's 1995 *Like Sisters on the Homefront* is about a teenage mother whose own mother took her in for an abortion to keep her from having a second child. The book opens as the girl and her toddler are on their way from Queens to live with relatives in the South in hopes that they will help her change her lifestyle. Gary Soto's 1997 *Buried Onions* shows some of the misery suffered by young Hispanics in California, while Walter Dean Myers's 1999 *Monster* is about a boy who was arrested for being at the scene of a crime and who during the trial has to figure out whether he really is a monster or just an "accidental" criminal.

1990s: During this decade, if we look carefully, we can see that squeezed in-between the realistic problem novels are some forerunners of the sci-fi and fantasy books that became the dominant genre in the following decade. Annette Curtis Klause's 1990 *The Silver Kiss* and her 1997 *Blood and Chocolate* are "vampire" love stories. Lois Lowry's 1993 *The Giver* is one of the few YA books that we can count on having already been read by our college students. They remember reading it when they were in junior high school and are still arguing over whether Jonas dies in the snow or is saved to live another day. Philip Pullman's *The Golden Compass* and its sequels were forerunners to the Harry Potter books, while Vivian Vande Velde's 1999 *Never Trust a Dead Man* is a supernatural novel that includes fun as well as fantasy.

Concluding Comments

We feel a little strange including the 1990s in a "historical" chapter because, to us, that time period seems like "just yesterday." This means you can expect to see much more about the 1990s throughout the remainder of this textbook. But for now, we will simply mention a few of the ideas we hope you have gleaned from reading this timeline.

The Publishing of Books: Historically, books have a mixed parentage. On one side is the publisher, who is in business to make money. On the other side is the much older parent, the one who promoted the making of books by religious scribes painstakingly copying each word at a time. These carefully prepared pages were made to preserve the history and the rules of the realm, along with religious teachings. From this heritage comes the idea that books have a moral obligation to "teach" the values that will be best for society. Of course there have always been disagreements over just what these values should be, which is why there are continuing problems between the people who are interested in making money and the people who are more interested in instilling positive attributes in the young, a subject that will be discussed further throughout this book, especially in Chapter 12 on censorship.

The Development of Libraries: Librarians started out as keepers or guardians of the books, but over the last two hundred years their jobs have changed more than have the jobs of teachers. As Madeleine L'Engle said in her acceptance speech for the Edwards Award, having been born in 1918 she was a member of the first generation who grew up benefiting from the wisdom of librarians, who by the 1930s considered it their job to encourage reading by all children. Of course, librarians still consider this one of their jobs, but especially in school libraries, they took on the additional responsibility of encouraging teachers to use films and other media; hence the changing of the names of some *school libraries* to *school media centers*. Today, their jobs have changed even more, which is why some *schools of library science* have changed their names to *schools of information management*.

The Study of Young Adult Literature: Another area that has changed considerably is that of literary criticism and the academic study of young adult literature. There have always been adults who scoff at the idea that teens need a literature of their own. In the early years, people who appreciated what was then called *adolescent literature* were mostly on the defensive and focused their speaking and writing on the benefits of such books to young readers. But by the end of the 1900s, the field had grown so much that it could support strong and healthy criticism focusing on the literature itself, rather than just on how it could be used to initiate young readers into "real" literature.

Many of the concepts and books that are mentioned here will be written about in later chapters, so please check the index if you wish to learn more about some of the books, authors, or concepts noted in this chapter. Also, see the pages throughout this textbook about the Margaret A. Edwards Award winners, many of whom began writing in the last few decades of the twentieth century. We will close by quoting from five of these authors who back in the 1970s, when we were preparing the first edition of this textbook, were kind enough to answer our question about what they predicted for the future of young adult literature. They all included disclaimers about being unable to tell the future; nevertheless, as you read the rest of this textbook, you will see that these authors from the 1970s were more prescient than they thought.

Where Is YA Lit Going from Here?

Lois Duncan: I think we have come about as far as we can in the direction of "let-it-all-hang-out" realism. My reader-mail indicates that kids are beginning to feel bogged down with so much depressing slice-of-life. . . . My prediction is that the next few years will show an increase in the demand for escape literature. There may even be a swing back toward fantasy, which to my way of thinking would be wonderful. The most valuable thing an author can do for today's teenagers is to help them realize that it's as much fun to read a book as to turn on the television.

S. E. Hinton: The reason I wrote *The Outsiders* was that I had read all the horse stories and there wasn't anything else to read because I didn't want to read *Jeannie Goes to the Prom*. With the new trends in adolescent literature, I don't think kids will ever again have that experience. More and more good writers are realizing that teenagers make up a reading audience that in many ways is preferable to the adult audience. There's room in young adult books for all kinds of writing—nonfiction as well as fiction and fantasy.

Harry Mazer: What I would like to see in young adult literature is more direct contact between reader and writer, and the books of interest to young adults made widely and easily available. Paperbacks, of course, are the way. We need libraries with the widest selection of what's available and paperback bookstores at the school's doorsteps, where the young congregate. I have a vision of an open market where the goods (the good books) are colorfully and abundantly displayed like fruit in season, and where pleasure (why else should anyone read?) is the first and foremost rule.

Richard Peck: A second generation of [YA] books might do well to include a dimension now missing. We might continue plumbing the coming-of-age theme and then follow our young characters into adult life. That way we could depict not only actions, but their ultimate consequences. And I'm not talking about cautionary tales that warn young unwed mothers and fathers that they've blighted their entire lives. Such a message might not even be true. But it would be pleasantly expansive to indicate to the young that all of life need not be as cruelly conformist and conservative as adolescence—unless you want it to be—and that the most truly successful men and women were not high-school hotshots, beauty queens, super jocks, or manipulative gang leaders.

Paul Zindel: What I'm trying to say is that a YA book in particular is a grand opportunity to take full advantage of word and phrase configuration as a take-off point from which a boy and girl can enter into *performance* of life. Jung knew a single alien letter from an unknown alphabet was enough to trigger endless thoughts in the human mind. Imagine the power of a whole book in the hands of a teacher and class. Right now in America we are just beginning to dream of turning away from fact bombardment and opening up our ears to listen to the kids. So many children in schools are denied expressing their experiences, and hearing of the experiences of others. So many never had a chance to think of goals, success paths, or, simply, opportunities to practice showing their emotions.

Digital and Other New Literacies for Teachers and Librarians

It is indeed a new world for some of us. We remember in elementary school when our teachers would lead discussions about the future, which mostly centered on transportation. We were promised there would be no more traffic jams because we would all go to work either on those high-speed trains—like the Jetsons had—or we would step out the door and lift off through the air, thanks to personal jet-propelled backpacks. A teacher once mentioned the possibility of having telephones where we could see the person we were calling, and we all gasped at such a possible embarrassment. However, it never occurred to any of us that reading and writing were important enough that scientists would go to the trouble of figuring out new ways of communication. And not until we became connected to "machines" designed to help us speak with our fingers did we realize how much our lives revolve around reading and writing.

In this chapter, we are first discussing some of the new literacies connected to the digital revolution, without which we could not possibly be writing this book in its present form. In the second part of the chapter, we will then talk about other kinds of literacies still connected to writing and reading books and communicating, although they are more social than technological.

Digital Immigrants Teaching Digital Natives

A look of frustration crosses Mrs. McGillicuddy's face as she turns away from her computer screen toward her sophomore English class:

"Can someone help me with this darned new computer attendance program, please?"

As usual, Juan rises from his desk in the front row and takes charge of the mouse. Also as usual, Mrs. McGillicuddy strains to follow his clicks and screens but to no avail.

In the time it takes Mrs. McGillicuddy and Juan to post today's attendance online, Gianna uses her iPhone to shoot a video of her best friend, Aliyah, modeling her new *Twilight Breaking Dawn Part 1* T-shirt. She edits the video, posts it on YouTube, advertises it on Facebook, and also posts links to the movie trailer, to an *Entertainment Weekly* interview with the actors, and to a fansite, *Twilight Lexicon*. Following along in cyberspace, several young women with faces turned toward Androids and iPhones nod in approval until Juan starts back toward his seat and Mrs. McGillicuddy addresses the class again:

"Put those phones away, please, and we'll continue our cooperative learning technology projects from yesterday."

The irony of students expertly using technology to access and dispense information in seconds while connecting with peers—both across the aisle and across the planet—as their teacher flounders with a simple computer program for sending attendance to the main office isn't lost on anyone who has spent much time in a classroom lately. Nor is a curriculum designed and implemented to teach the use of technology to young people who are what Marc Prensky, in his book *"Don't Bother Me Mom—I'm Learning,"* termed *digital natives* in the hands of teachers who themselves may be, at best, *digital immigrants*. Such teachers often have what Prensky calls *thick accents,* meaning actions or language that reveal one foot still firmly planted in the pre-digital world (Mrs. McGillicuddy, for example, prints out the attendance for every period and puts it in a binder).

Students access and interact with the world, including each other, in ways as different from the previous millennium as the automobile was from the horse and buggy. In his 2001 treatise on the technological chasm between the generations, Prensky explains, "It is now clear that as a result of this ubiquitous environment and the sheer volume of their interaction with it, today's students *think and process information fundamentally differently* from their predecessors."

Where Are We Going and How Do We Get There?

In terms of facility with technology, we teachers may indeed lag far behind our students; nevertheless, we need to design thoughtful curriculum and employ instructional approaches that focus on what we want students to

This sign in front of our local library reflects the changing roles of all of us involved with books and public education.

know and be able to do with technology. They need to understand that "how" and "why" are as important as "what" in the realm of technology use. In other words, we need to provide them with an array of learning experiences which include an intelligent and ethical framework for employing technology, regardless of what new developments become available to them in the future.

The National Council of Teachers of English (NCTE) has carefully assessed the needs of schools and teachers in the twenty-first century and created helpful guidelines and resources. On November 19, 2008, the NCTE Executive Committee adopted their *21st Century Literacy and Assessment Framework Position Statement*, which can be found on the NCTE website at http://www.ncte.org/positions/statements/21stcentframework. An important point is that "Because technology has increased the intensity and complexity of literate environments, the twenty-first century demands that a literate person possess a wide range of abilities and competencies, many literacies." The Executive Committee also makes it clear that "proficiency with the tools of technology" is only a small part of the curriculum. It is how and why the technology is used that provides the majority of the framework, such as collaborative problem solving, working globally, analyzing data, "evaluat[ing] multimedia texts," and addressing "the ethical responsibilities."

In addition, in their *Supplemental Resource for NCTE Policy Brief on 21st Century Literacies* at http://www.ncte.org/library/NCTEFiles/Resources/

PolicyResearch/21stCenturyClips.pdf they state the imperative for K–12 education:

- We live in a technology-driven, global, diverse, and quickly changing world.
- New literacy skills that attend to these changes are a necessary part of English/language arts curricula.

They go on in paragraph 4 to expound on what our students should experience at a macro level as a result of curriculum and instruction:

- Develop proficiency with the tools of technology
- Build relationships with others to pose and solve problems collaboratively and cross-culturally
- Design and share information for global communities to meet a variety of purposes
- Manage, analyze, and synthesize multiple streams of simultaneous information
- Create, critique, analyze, and evaluate multimedia texts
- Attend to the ethical responsibilities required by these complex environments

Specifics at a more micro level are addressed with these suggestions for instructional approaches:

- Encouraging students to reflect regularly about the role of technology in their learning.
- Creating a website and inviting students to use it to continue class discussions and bring in outside voices.
- Giving students strategies for evaluating the quality of information they find on the Internet.
- Being open about your own strengths and limitations with technology and inviting students to help you.
- Exploring technologies students are using outside of class and finding ways to incorporate them into your teaching.
- Using a wiki to develop a multimodal reader's guide to a class text.
- Including a broad variety of media and genres in class texts.
- Asking students to create a podcast to share with an authentic audience.
- Giving students explicit instruction about how to avoid plagiarism in a digital environment.

Another important document to consider in the pursuit of teaching with technology comes from the International Society for Technology Education (ISTE). The ISTE NETS (National Educational Technology Standards) are carefully considered learning and teaching goals and outcomes designed by a consortium of professionals and reviewed by their peers. The NETS include the following, which we have adapted from the ISTE website

(http://www.iste.org/standards/nets-for-students/nets-student-standards-2007
.aspx). Each of these six standards has additional bullet point details which
can be found on the website.

1. *Creativity and innovation:* Students demonstrate creative thinking, construct knowledge, and develop innovative products and processes using technology.

2. *Communication and collaboration:* Students use digital media and environments to communicate and work collaboratively, including at a distance, to support individual learning and contribute to the learning of others.

3. *Research and information fluency:* Students apply digital tools to gather, evaluate, and use information.

4. *Critical thinking, problem solving, and decision making:* Students use critical thinking skills to plan and conduct research, manage projects, solve problems, and make informed decisions using appropriate digital tools and resources.

5. *Digital citizenship:* Students understand human, cultural, and societal issues related to technology and practice legal and ethical behavior.

6. *Technology operations and concepts:* Students demonstrate a sound understanding of technology concepts, systems, and operations.

Although the "what," such as students' "understanding of technology concepts, systems, and operations," and their ability to "apply digital tools to gather . . . information" is present, the "how" and "why" are greatly emphasized by both ISTE and NCTE, in such outcomes as "think creatively," "work collaboratively . . . contribute to the learning of others," "evaluate and use information," "solve problems and make informed decisions," "understand human, cultural, and societal issues related to technology," and perhaps most importantly, "practice legal and ethical behavior." In order to prepare students for the workplace and for higher education, we must help them to move beyond the bells and whistles of technology, which change from moment to moment, and attain a level of mastery of the underpinnings of ethics and efficiency whether they are providing information, accessing information, or participating as a member of a group. As students use technology for multiple purposes, they must understand that just because they CAN do something, it doesn't mean they SHOULD do it, and just because something is on the Internet does not mean that it should be accepted without intellectual or social filtering. With these caveats, we'll look at some ways for using technology to help students engage with young adult literature in meaningful ways.

Out in the Real World of Teaching

To get an idea of what teachers in the field are using as instructional approaches, we sent out a "Call for Help" and here are some of the replies categorized according to the individual teacher's approach.

While communicating online is wonderfully efficient, in-person communication also has its advantages. Mary Wong, a librarian in the Phoenix area, has for years hosted dinner parties for visiting authors and artists. In the last few years, she has been bringing out marker pens and inviting the guest of honor to leave an autograph or a picture on the archway of her dining area. They are wonderful conversational topics; the only problem is that it is going to be a challenge to move the wall to a museum.

Skype

Dr. Denise Roth, reading teacher and literacy coach at Washington Technology Magnet School in St. Paul, Minnesota, makes use of one of the simplest but most impressive tools for engaging young readers with young adult literature: Skype. Skype (http://www.skype.com/intl/en-us/welcomepage) can be quickly downloaded, and has become a mainstay for authors who want to connect with their young readers without always engaging in the difficulty of long travel to author appearances. Skype allows the author to come right into the classroom and visit with students. They can see each other and interact spontaneously. A computer camera and microphone are the primary tools needed. The majority of authors give notice on their websites about their availability to Skype into K–12 classrooms and indicate if this can be done at no cost or if there is a charge. At the appointed time, the author and the teacher log on to the Internet and one of them opens the Skype program and clicks on the other's Skype name and then on "Video Call." Both are then visible on the computer screen and a conversation can take place. Practicing beforehand with a colleague or with the actual author, is a good idea. Dr. Roth connected with *Softwire* science fiction author PJ Haarsma from his home in Irvine, California, to her classroom in St. Paul, Minnesota, as the opening activity for her summer school class. In this email (reprinted with permission), she thanks him for providing her students with a great learning and motivational experience:

> Good Morning P.J.! Skyping with you was a perfect beginning to our summer session, and I want to tell you thank you again for taking that time! Do take care and let me know of your progress on *Witches*, it sounds terrific!
>
> Thank you!
>
> Denise

Obviously, Skyping makes for exciting engagement between students and their reading, especially if they play a role in preparing the questions for the Skype session and speak with the author themselves, face to face on the computer screen.

WebQuest

Sarah Sacco, seventh grade English language arts teacher at Santan Junior High, in Chandler, Arizona, has made extensive use of WebQuests. Credit for the development of this model for educational websites that have been dubbed WebQuests most often goes to Dr. Bernie Dodge at San Diego State University. The ultimate website on how to create, find, and/or use WebQuests is Dr. Dodge's, hosted at San Diego State University (http://webquest.org/index.php). This is the best resource on every aspect of WebQuests from pedagogical considerations to technical construction methods. He defines a WebQuest as "an inquiry-oriented lesson format in which most or all the information that learners work with comes from the web." In Ms. Sacco's case, students read *Nothing But the Truth*, by Avi, and turned to the WebQuest she designed for a "quest" of reading and writing activities that led to a much greater understanding of, and engagement with, the book. As she explains:

> As a language arts teacher, technology has really opened up the realm of possibilities for going beyond a book. With web-based activities, and WebQuests in particular, the opportunities for extension are limitless. Students can utilize literature as a springboard for investigation into more complex social and political issues. On a more personal level, they can use technology to discover infinite connections between the literature they read and the world around them.
>
> (personal communication, July 25, 2011)

WebQuests about books provide students with tasks that involve making text-to-self, text-to-world, and text-to-other text connections. The WebQuest provides the task (i.e., the quest) and a starting point of links to websites where students may find additional information and/or an explanation of how to use the web to research the topic on their own. These links deal with ways in which the topics in the book they have read play out in the real world. It is the students' role to reflect upon the book, their lives, and what they find on the Internet as they move from link to link and make sense or meaning of it all, and, perhaps, even attempt to make sense of the world and their own lives as related to the book's topic. This goes far beyond traditional K–12 literature study in which students read, are asked questions to which the teacher has correct answers, and are graded according to their degree of alignment with the teacher's answers. Instead, students learn how to make meaning of their reading, of the world, of their lives, and of themselves.

As Ms. Sacco goes on to explain:

> The benefits of using this WebQuest over any traditional pen and paper activity were countless. Not only was the activity personalized and self-paced for students, the investigative portion of the activity had this quality of authenticity that so many activities lack. True, students were completing a classroom assignment, but they were also conducting research that many adults will do for pleasure when selecting a new novel. The WebQuest, by nature, served as a starting line for students by leading them in a controlled fashion to other areas of the Internet that would hold valuable information. Students were the ones who had the power to discover this information, and the subsequent standards-based writing assignment fit in seamlessly with the tasks they were asked to do in the WebQuest. Without technology, it would not have been possible for students to complete such a meaningful activity with such ownership.

Ms. Sacco's WebQuest presented students with this challenge:

> In *Nothing But the Truth*, Phillip Malloy does not enjoy his English class or his English teacher, Miss Narwin. He particularly dislikes the book *Call of the Wild*, which he is reading as part of class. However, he is reading the novel *The Outsiders* at home and he enjoys that book. What if Phillip were allowed to read *The Outsiders* instead of *Call of the Wild*? Or how about another book entirely? Would that have changed his attitude toward English class?
>
> Your task is to first evaluate the two books Phillip reads during *Nothing But the Truth*. You will research more about these books and analyze what aspects of them would make Phillip like or dislike them. You will need to think about Phillip's personality, background, and interests.
>
> You will then use what you have learned about the two books to find two additional books that you think Phillip would rather read. You will use this information to create a book proposal in the form of a typed business letter addressed to the Harrison School District Board of Education.
>
> (http://questgarden.com/80/28/7/090413085350/evaluation.htm)

The WebQuest goes on to provide fifteen website links on specific topics, such as professional analyses of the books and templates for writing business letters, and two general search engines for investigating topics they think of themselves.

A scoring rubric is included so that students know what they are intended to be learning and how they will be graded on meeting the desired outcomes. For example, a perfect score in the category of persuasive writing on the rubric is described as: "Letter is written with clear intent to persuade the audience. Letter used at least one of the six persuasive techniques taught in class." (screen 4)

WebQuests can be hosted at any number of free sites, sometimes including space on the school district's server. Usually, however, teachers choose to use resources such as:

1. Angel Fire: http://www.angelfire.lycos.com/
2. Google Sites: http://www.google.com/sites/help/intl/en/overview.html
3. PBWorks Basic Edition: http://pbworks.com/content/edu-classroom-teachers
4. Tripod: http://www.tripod.lycos.com/
5. Wiki Wetpaint: http://wikisineducation.wetpaint.com/
6. Wikispaces: http://www.wikispaces.com/

Website hosting that requires a monthly fee is also available at a wide range of pricing, but free sites, such as Google Sites, are more than adequate.

Blogging

Another technology offered by Google is blogging, available through Blogger at http://www.blogger.com/create-blog.g, also known as Blogspot. Users will have to sign up for a Google account, but this is easily done and free of cost at https://www.google.com/accounts/NewAccount. Google is only one of many companies providing what is known as *blogspace,* meaning a website that can be personalized and secured according to who the operator wants reading and posting on the site. The term *blog* is short for *web log,* and according to Andy Carvin, writing for the Public Broadcasting Service website *learning.now,* the modern web log we see today evolved from simple travel diary websites in the mid-1990s when programmers saw a demand for prepackaged websites with fill-in-the-blank templates so that people could share their experiences, thoughts, and opinions online without having to know programming. According to http://www.blogpulse.com/ (August 13, 2011) this resulted in "167,727,918" "Total identified blogs" and "186,308" "New blogs in last 24 hours."

Jennifer Prince at Jac-Cen-Del Junior/Senior High School in Osgood, Indiana, employs blogs on a regular basis, using Blogger/Blogspot as her location. Ms. Prince sets up her class blog as the school year begins and assigns students to make entries introducing themselves. The class members continue the blog conversation as the year progresses, centering on literature. Students can provide links to related items on the web, providing the catalyst for text-to-world connections as the conversation snowballs in breadth and students bring in their own experiences, other books they have read, and events taking place locally and globally. It is important to note that the individual who sets up the blog online has the power to dictate who can access it and who can post on it, a necessity for Internet safety.

As needed, Ms. Prince provides fodder for opening a discussion, such as in the blog discussion on Sherman Alexie's *The Absolutely True Diary of a Part-Time Indian,* for which she asked students to fill in the blank in The Absolutely True Diary of _____ and explain "why the title was apt for them" (personal communication July 25, 2011).

Ms. Prince is a strong proponent of this instructional approach:

The use of blogs in my classroom gives students a voice, especially those who are typically too shy or too underconfident to speak up. And, it gives ownership of the work to the entire class, not just one or two students. I find that students are more honest, more open, and more willing to discuss issues if they can have time to formulate their responses in an electronic format like a blog. Wikis are another great tool to get students to do the same thing, but it limits the interaction to only the students in that class. I currently teach English 9 and 11, creative writing, mythology, etymology, dual-credit composition, and dual-credit speech in Southeastern Indiana. I use technology in every one of those classes.

Glogging, Google Docs, Prezi, and Animoto

One limitation of blogging may be that it is mostly restricted to linear text. In other words, it's mostly writing. An even newer and more innovative means for students to express their views is Glogster, which first began on December 10, 2007, and is explained at http://glogster.glogster.com/glogster-story/.

Glogster is committed to bringing the best Multimedia Tool & Expression Space for young people, students, educators, and all creative people through its innovative Glog format and the new online phenomenon, Glogging.

This "Multimedia Tool & Expression Space" allows students and teachers to create multimodal collages. After signing up for a free account, users are presented with a blank poster and given tools to insert graphics, images, text, sound, and video on a background wall of their choosing.

Tracy Weaver, at Mountain View High School in Mesa, Arizona, facilitates her students in the use of Glogster for class presentations. In addition to Glogster, Ms. Weaver's students have their own personal Ning sites for class, and use Prezi, which is an online presentation application (http://prezi.com/) that allows students to move beyond the individual slides in linear arrangement provided in PowerPoint. Instead, Prezi provides a complete "canvas" on which all the topics for the presentation are arranged in a schematic the presenter designs to fit the subject matter. Prezi allows the presenter to show the entire schematic or to zoom in on any portion of it to any level of detail. This zooming in and out provides the viewer with a visual representation of the relationship among all components of the topic, and allows the presenter to move among and across the components to help display these relationships. As in PowerPoint, Prezi allows the presenter to embed videos in the presentation. Ms. Weaver puts all course materials on a Ning site for students to access and assigns students to collaborate with each other on writing projects at Google Docs.

While Glogster provides a canvas for students to make multimedia posters, Animoto http://animoto.com/ provides a canvas for students and teachers to create videos. Thirty-second videos are free to make, and Animoto has a sliding cost scale for videos of longer length. 21st Middle school teachers Virginia Koppel

TALKING BOOKS

In these rapidly changing times, some of the "older" technologies are also better than ever. Recorded books have become increasingly well performed, and many of them are released simultaneously with the books. And as shown by the PowerPoint that Dr. Blasingame is presenting on Laurie Halse Anderson, it is getting easier to make exciting slides.

and Lisa Spangenthal, at Valley View Elementary School in Phoenix, Arizona, have a grant from the 21st Century Real Estate Company, which pays for all of their students to have netbooks (mini-laptop computers). Animoto is one of their favorite tools.

TumbleBooks, MyOn, and XtraNormal

The Florence Unified School District in San Tan Valley, Arizona, emphasizes educational technology because it can be an effective tool in differentiating instruction among students with diverse learning styles and abilities. Erinn Holloway, a middle school resource room teacher who works with fourth through eighth grade students with autism uses *Beyond Textbooks*, a curriculum designed in Vail, Colorado, which includes a wiki on which teachers share lessons and resources across the Vail School District and twenty-three schools in Arizona. Ms. Holloway explains the value of technology for autistic students in her classroom:

> The pen and paper approach to learning is often a struggle for students with autism. They require differentiated instruction that suits their unique communication and sensory needs. The use of technology not only meets their specialized demands, but it prepares them for a future in the real world and fosters independence.

(personal communication July 25, 2011)

Ms. Holloway keeps all assignments and course materials on a class website available to students and parents. She scans in assignment sheets for the benefit of students who miss school or lose the assignment. She uses Google Docs and Google Forms to create WebQuests for students to surf the Internet looking for answers to questions. One advantage of Google Docs is that Ms. Holloway can create a printout of all responses across the class, providing a helpful set of data for identifying problem topics. She uses a bank of mp3 players for students who read below grade level to listen to young adult novels which are popular with their age group peers. The Florence School District also subscribes to Tumble Books (http://www.tumblebooks.com/library/asp/about_tumblebooks .asp), animated books for young readers that display the print text as the words are highlighted and spoken online. The district also provides MyOn (http:// www.thefutureinreading.com/about-myon/myon-reader.html), a digital library of books which allows young readers to create a profile of their interests and reading ability, from which the program creates a suggested reading list. MyOn also aids students as they read by highlighting words and providing definitions. Ms. Holloway also facilitates students in the use of XtraNormal, a video-making program available free online at http://www.xtranormal.com/. Students can make their own video versions of important passages from young adult novels, helping them to internalize their analysis of plot, characterization, dialogue, theme, and setting.

YouTube, Digital Stories, and Movie Maker

Deborah O'Dowd, an English language arts teacher in the night school program at Metro Tech High School in Phoenix, Arizona, also uses videos with her students, in this case, for the creation of digital stories. The night school program at Metro Tech includes a high percentage of second language learners and students who have not done well in traditional academic settings. According to Ms. O'Dowd:

> Vocational students who are more likely to be found in an alternative night school program and who are focused on graduating so that they can begin their careers immediately are bothered by doing "pointless busywork" but find lessons in digital

story making to be RELEVANT because the connection to reality is CLEAR and can be translated into profit. Business people are using this for advertising with no cost!

(personal communication July 25, 2011)

The students in the Metro Tech night school program become the directors of their own movies based on themes from their favorite books. These students have been especially successful with scenes from *If I Die in Juarez* by Stella Pope Duarte; *Hatchet* by Gary Paulsen, which has been especially popular with second language learners; *Twilight* by Stephenie Meyer; *The Kite Runner* by Khaled Hosseini; *The Lovely Bones* by Alice Sebold; *My Sister's Keeper* by Jodi Picoult; *The Absolutely True Diary of a Part-Time Indian* by Sherman Alexie; and *Bless Me, Ultima* by Rudolfo Anaya.

The students are assigned to complete a two-part response to their chosen books, including expository writing in which they write about their book in much the same style as the traditional book report, paying close attention to the elements of organization and content, and especially to "inference and evidence," as found in the National Common Core Curriculum.

The second part of their response depends upon technology and the students' intuitive understanding of story as they move from their reading of the novel to a video based on the theme of their novel, for which they must create a visual "script" without dialogue, work with camera angles, determine a point of view, and consider all the elements a visual and audio story requires. Students use the computer video editing program Movie Maker for this project. Ms. O'Dowd explains the procedure:

Students determine one theme that stands out in their selected book. They then data mine on the Internet about that theme. For example, if a student is reading *Night*, potential themes might be racism, the Holocaust, Judaism, human frailty, human resilience, death, or whatever else most stood out for the student. They are to use pictures, Movie Maker clips, transitions, effects, graphs, etc., to create a thematic "movie trailer." NO VOICE NARRATION is allowed on this part. When they have a visual product, they are to add music from a bank of classical music in my outbox folder. The videos are then uploaded to YouTube.

(personal communication July 25, 2011)

One of the most popular forms of literature, including young adult literature, around the world is Manga, and Ms. O'Dowd remembers one video project with which she was especially pleased:

One of the greatest success stories I can think of is that of an 18-year-old autistic girl in a self-contained class that I tutor. I showed her a few steps in the movie making process and she "took off" creating Manga digital stories, and even learning how to time the slides like cartoons. She learned to upload her Manga pieces to YouTube and now communicates worldwide. (Of course she is also using Paint and Audacity programs, etc.) She is now writing words on these stories and even adding music and her own voice.

Focus Box 3.1

Help for Adults in Developing New Literacies

Adolescents' Online Literacies: Connecting Classrooms, Digital Media, and Popular Culture **edited by Donna E. Alverman. Peter Lang, 2010.** The ten chapters written by multiple authors include such topics as hip hop, video games, redefining literacy boundaries, ethnic influences, and a look at teachers' culture vs. students' culture.

Building Literary Connections with Graphic Novels: Page by Page, Panel by Panel **edited by James Bucky Carter. NCTE, 2007.** Contributors who wrote the chapters each take a traditional text and pair it with one or more graphic novels; for example, Dante's *Inferno* is taught alongside an *X-Men* story, while Dickens's *Oliver Twist* is taught alongside Will Eisner's *Fagin the Jew.*

Bullying Beyond the Schoolyard: Preventing and Responding to Cyberbullying **by Isameer Hinduja and Justin W. Patchin. Corwin Sage, 2009.** Admittedly it is going to take more than teachers and librarians to solve this problem, but still it is good to know that there are things we can do in our own bailiwicks.

Everything Bad Is Good for You: How Today's Popular Culture Is Actually Making Us Smarter **by Steven Johnson. Penguin/Riverside, 2005.** Johnson makes a persuasive case for the idea that popular culture entertainment ranging from *The Simpsons* to *The Lord of the Rings* and video games is growing more sophisticated and posing cognitive challenges that make us better thinkers.

Fame Junkies: The Hidden Truths behind America's Favorite Addiction **by Jake Halpern. Houghton Mifflin, 2007.** Halpern speaks out for moderation and for guiding teens into areas where they can feel fulfilled from developing skills and interests rather than longing for instant fame, which is something dependent on many factors outside of any young person's control.

From Digital Natives to Digital Wisdom: Hopeful Essays for 21st Century Learning **by Marc Prensky. Corwin, 2012.** Earlier Prensky books that have been well-received include *Teaching Digital Natives—Partnering for Real Learning* (Corwin, 2010), and *"Don't Bother Me Mom—I'm Learning"* (Paragon House, 2006). More than any other writer, Prensky has shown that a new generation has grown up "surrounded by and using computers, video games, DVD players, videocams, eBay, cell phones, iPods, and all the other tools of a digital age," and consequently has different thinking patterns and approaches to life than do those of us coming to the digital world as immigrants and still waiting for someone to explain and "teach us about each new device."

Graphic Novels: A Genre Guide to Comic Books, Manga, and More **by Michael Pawuk (Genreflecting Advisory Series). Libraries Unlimited, 2006.** Written for both adults and young adults, this 663-page book is a good source for both skimming and answering specific questions.

The Tech Imperative

Ms. O'Dowd's memory of this young woman's tremendous leap in school and her ability to express herself, connect with peers worldwide, and disperse her work is not only touching but also a great example of the power of technology in education, and especially in the teaching of young adult literature. The power of this venue bears a return to the chapter's opening contention from Marc Prensky. See his books listed in Focus Box 3.1 "Help for Adults in Developing New Literacies." Prensky' claim is that because of the new technologies and the sheer volume of teen's interactions with these technologies, today's students think and process information in ways that are fundamentally different from the ways of learning engaged in by most of their parents and their teachers. Another helpful source is Mark Bernstein's article "10 Tips on Writing the Living Web," *A List Apart: For People Who Make Websites.* A List Apart Magazine 16 August, 2002, Web 4 May, 2009.

Language and Learning in the Digital Age by James Paul Gee and Elizabeth Hayes. Routledge, 2011. Gee and Hayes show how language is a social convention and how digital media is "powering up" that convention, much like the invention of writing gave more power to language hundreds of years ago. They have also written an interesting book, *Women and Gaming: The Sims and 21st Century Learning* (Palgrave Macmillan, 2010).

Lesson Plans for Developing Digital Literacies edited by Mary T. Christel and Scott Sullivan. National Council of Teachers of English, 2010. This is a continuation and enrichment of the editors' 2007 *Lesson Plans for Creating Media-Rich Classrooms*. While there is plenty of how-to information, the authors start with lessons to help students evaluate what they find online and to understand voice, audience, and purpose in social networking sites.

ReadWriteThink is an online partnership between the National Council of Teachers of English and the International Reading Association, along with the MarcoPolo Education Foundation. It was established in 2002 and is open and free to users, who can access it through either of the organizations or just by typing the name into any search engine. It provides classroom lessons and background material relating to many aspects of literacy.

Secondary School Literacy: What Research Reveals for Classroom Practice edited by Leslie S. Rush, A. Jonathan Eakle, and Allen Berger. NCTE, 2007. Reviewers are praising this research book for the way the different chapters come together to show similar trends across different kinds of literacy education.

Understanding Manga and Anime by Robin E. Brenner. Libraries Unlimited, 2007. Chapter topics include the history of manga and anime, plus its specialized vocabulary, cultural differences, favorite topics for male and female readers, fan culture, and what librarians can do to build and promote their own collections.

un.Spun: Finding Facts in a World of Disinformation by Brooks Jackson and Kathleen Hall Jamieson. Random House Trade Paperback Original, 2007. The authors' website, FactCheck.org, was listed by *Time* as one of the "25 websites you can't live without." The premise of their book is that "*Spin* is a polite word for deception," and that being able to recognize deception is a necessary literacy for our time.

Words That Work: It's Not What You Say, It's What People Hear by Frank Luntz. Hyperion, 2007. Luntz writes about the power of framing and how much more successful politicians are if they can learn to use phrases that will make them sound active and on task. For example, it is less effective for a politician to go on "a listening tour" than on a "getting it done" tour.

The World Is Flat: A Brief History of the Twenty-First Century, Updated and Expanded, Release 2.0 by Thomas L. Friedman. Farrar, Straus & Giroux, 2006. *School Library Journal* recommended Friedman's book not only to adults but also to sophisticated teenagers who are interested in the many ways that people from different countries are interacting with each other.

Other "New" Literacies

When Professor Brian V. Street from King's College in London came to speak at Arizona State University (April, 2007) on "New Literacies: New Times: Ethnographic Perspectives," one of the points he made is that Western culture has overemphasized writing and the written language as a means of communication. He also argued that some of the practices that we currently view as "new" literacies are very old. Going back to prehistory, cultures have had religious ceremonies and customs and have communicated not only through speech but through gestures and drawings. In addition, they have had means of trading goods and of establishing respect and consideration for people besides oneself. Even in the modern world, people who are described as *illiterate* often understand such concepts as tickets, taxes, and maps.

The Astonishing Adventures of Fanboy and Goth Girl
by Barry Lyga. Houghton, 2006. Fanboy loves comics and dreams of being "discovered" at a comic-book convention because of his in-progress *Schemata* graphic novel, but his real life is far from such success. Then Goth Girl Kyra, herself a loner, reaches out to him through an Instant Message.

The Body of Christopher Creed **by Carol Plum-Ucci. Harcourt, 2000.** Popular Torey Adams, age sixteen, is thrown into a whole new life and a new way of looking at people when an unpopular classmate disappears after posting a cryptic email message that mentioned Torey.

Evil Genius **by Catherine Jinks. Harcourt, 2007.** A boy who hacked into computers when he was only seven and then more or less tests out of high school launches himself into a grown-up career at age fourteen by enrolling in the Axis Institute and taking classes in Misinformation, Disguise, Basic Lying, Embezzlement, and Explosives.

The Invention of Hugo Cabret **by Brian Selznick. Scholastic, 2007.** In this original novel, which was a finalist for the National Book Award, Selznick created 272 full-page drawings plus over 250 pages of text, all deliciously fitted onto black bordered pages that give readers the feeling of stepping into an old fashioned film or more mysteriously into the back rooms of a museum that once housed the predecessors of today's robots,

known as *automata.* The book got a big boost in 2011 when the film *Hugo,* directed by Martin Scorsese, was released and people realized that part of the story was based on a real pioneer in the history of film.

The Last Days **by Scott Westerfeld. Penguin/Razorbill, 2006.** *The Last Days* is a continuation of Westerfeld's *Peeps*, but rock music plays a big part in this story, and in fact is the medium that calls up and helps to defeat the mysterious forces that almost destroy New York City.

Little Brother **by Cory Doctorow. Tor, 2008.** Marcus is a computer whiz who develops a replacement for the Internet after terrorists attack San Francisco. He is organizing rebels against the Department of Homeland Security's clampdown on the city. His friends have been wrongfully incarcerated and tortured for information. It's a high-tech adventure.

Lugalbanda: The Boy Who Got Caught Up in a War **by Kathy Henderson, illustrated by Jane Ray. Candlewick, 2006.** Excavators in the 1800s found the cuneiform tablets on which this Sumerian legend was recorded, but the tablets were not transcribed until the 1970s. And now readers can enjoy what is perhaps the oldest written story in the world. It is about a boy left behind by a marching army, but who becomes a hero anyway.

Memories of Survival **illustrated by Esther Nisenthal Krinitz and told by Bernice Steinhardt. Hyperion,**

Nonreaders are also skilled in trading and in interpreting such symbols as the internationally agreed-upon highway markers and such commercial logos as the golden arches for a McDonald's restaurant and the classic red and white design of Campbell's soup cans. That design isn't quite as "classic" as it was when Andy Warhol painted it back in the 1960s because the company now includes a picture on the front of each can to show what kind of soup is inside. The Nilsen family was quick to notice this change because when they lived in Afghanistan between 1967 and 1969, they would bring home cans of soup from the American Commissary. Siddiq, their Afghan cook, knew that the family was big enough to require two cans of soup, but since he could not read he would open and mix together any two cans: Creamy Mushroom with Tomato, Chicken Noodle with Vegetable, and so on.

Professor Street's speech reminded us of some of the new books we've recently seen in which authors are exploring alternative kinds of communication strategies. See Focus Box 3.1, "Help for Adults in Developing New Literacies," and Focus Box 3.2, "YA Books with Plots Involving New (and Old) Communication

2005. Thirty-four hand-stitched, embroidered, fabric panels tell in great detail the story of Esther's early childhood in a Polish village, then the Nazi invasion followed by a labor camp and death.

A Monster Calls **by Patrick Ness, illustrated by Jim Kay. Candlewick, 2011.** A thirteen-year-old boy has to cope not only with bullying at school and an absentee father, but also a mother who is undergoing cancer treatments. An ancient monster comes to him in the night and tells him three stories and then demands that the boy tell a story of his own. The boy's own story helps him accept the truth about his mother's upcoming death. Shadow illustrations along the borders of the pages set the mood of what reviewers call "a brilliantly executed, powerful tale."

Princess Academy **by Shannon Hale. Bloomsbury, 2005.** Petite fourteen-year-old Miri feels left out because she does not get to work in the quarry with the other girls. Hoping to prove her worth, she goes away to a special school—far different from a typical "princess" school—but while there she discovers her special talent for "quarry speech," which is a silent way of communicating.

The Road of the Dead **by Kevin Brooks. Scholastic/The Chicken House, 2006.** Two brothers are trying to solve the murder of their sister on the English moors. It is a grisly and violent story, and the most interesting part is how fourteen-year-old Ruben has the psychic power to see what his older, more impetuous brother, Cole, is doing and thinking even when they are miles apart.

Thirteen Reasons Why: A Novel **by Jay Asher. Razorbill, Penguin, 2007.** See the fuller discussion of this book in Chapter Four, but the part that relates to telling a story through different strategies is that the main part of the story is told through thirteen audio tapes made by a teenager before she commits suicide. She cleverly figured out how to have the set of tapes delivered in sequence to each of the thirteen "friends" who played a part in her sad story. In order to get the full impact, they are instructed to listen to each tape in the place that it happened.

Voices **by Ursula K. Le Guin. Harcourt, 2006.** Seventeen-year-old Memer and her mentor, the Waylord, are protectors of a secret library in a country where the written word has been declared demonic and books are outlawed. But then the stage is set for change when Orrec, a poet and storyteller, and his wife, Gry, come for a visit.

Why We Broke Up **by Daniel Handler, illus. by Maira Kalman. Little Brown, 2011.** Handler is the author of the Lemony Snicket books, and so we wouldn't expect him to write a typical romance. While the story is not as sad as Asher's *Thirteen Reasons Why,* it is similar in that a girl documents her romance. When she breaks up with her popular boyfriend, she dumps a box of mementos on his doorstep, accompanied by a long letter (which makes up the text of the book) explaining why their romance couldn't have worked. Each chapter is introduced with a full-color painting of one of the mementos that range from movie tickets to condom wrappers.

Strategies," some of which are as old as the hills and some of which are so new that society has not yet agreed on what to call them. Street gave such examples as *low-rider literacy,* which means being able to "read" the stories told in the artwork drawn by Hispanic-American youths. He also mentioned *palpatory literacy,* to refer to the knowledge of masseuses about the feelings associated with particular kinds of touching. For himself, he restricts literacy to ideas that somehow relate to communicating through visible or auditory symbols, but this is not as simple as it sounds because of all the different ways people either send or receive messages.

At least until fairly recently, the most common kind of literacy talked about in educational circles has been *critical literacy,* whose advocates believe in questioning the social, political, and economic conditions that underlie the creation of stories, novels, books, films, essays, advertisements, and other kinds of communication. Some advocates of critical literacy have as their first goal simply training people to look beyond the obvious and to become aware of the conditions under which they live and how these conditions are reflected

Young Scholars Speak Out

Meredith DeCosta-Smith on Tech Time in the English Language Arts Classroom

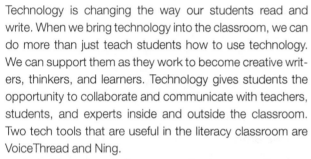

Technology is changing the way our students read and write. When we bring technology into the classroom, we can do more than just teach students how to use technology. We can support them as they work to become creative writers, thinkers, and learners. Technology gives students the opportunity to collaborate and communicate with teachers, students, and experts inside and outside the classroom. Two tech tools that are useful in the literacy classroom are VoiceThread and Ning.

VoiceThread, an online space where conversations are collected and shared, is as easy as *create*, *upload*, *comment*, and *share* (http://www.voicethread.com). VoiceThread is a free web-based application, and all an individual needs is an email address and Internet access to sign up for an account.

VoiceThread allows its users to create interactive, multimedia slideshows that feature pictures, documents, and videos. Students can comment on their own slideshow by adding voice, text, audio, or video files. They can then share their slideshow with others, so their classmates can comment too, sparking a discussion about the slideshow's content.

One of the primary benefits of using VoiceThread is that it gives students the chance to collaborate and communicate. Unlike other presentation programs that are static and created by a single user, VoiceThread allows multiple users to get involved and make comments on the slideshow. This means that students can use VoiceThread to respond to young adult literature in a number of ways, including:

- Reviewing a young adult novel.
- Generating a slideshow featuring a character or characters in a text.
- Creating a presentation depicting important social issues in a book.
- Exploring themes within a single text or across texts.

Once students have created a slideshow, all they have to do is click "share" and other students can respond by posting their thoughts on the book.

in daily communications. Other advocates want to inspire people to transform the world in humane ways to make it a more just place to live. None of us could argue with such lofty goals, nor with asking thoughtful questions, but we need to strive for balance lest we raise a generation of students who will be as pessimistic and gloomy as is Eeyore, the doleful donkey in *Winnie the Pooh*.

The term *literacy* obviously implies deep knowledge of a particular field. To demonstrate how young adult literature ties into many different kinds of literacy, we asked four of our doctoral students to write short pieces related to a particular kind of literacy that they feel strongly about. Of course in a couple of pages, they cannot communicate everything they know and feel about their chosen "literacy," but they have also included suggestions for further reading. Besides, by introducing some of the subcategories of critical literacy that are important to those of us working with young adults and their reading, we hope their statements will inspire other young scholars to further research and writing.

There are three ways to sign a class up for a Voice-Thread account. First, students can sign up using their own email address. Students can also log in using one teacher-generated email address and password. Lastly, teachers, schools, and districts can purchase larger subscriptions to create a secure, collaborative VoiceThread network.

Another useful multimedia platform for teaching young adult literature is a Ning site (http://www.ning.com/). Ning is an online platform where groups can create and customize their own social network. With a Ning site, users can post blogs or pictures, inform the group of upcoming events, and take part in dialogue in the discussion forum. While these sites are not free, there are discounts available for educators who want to sign their class up for an account. In order to sign up, teachers need to visit the site, sign up for an account, create a group name, and begin to play around with the format of the site. Like VoiceThread, students need an email account and Internet access to create and access a Ning account and will need to log in to the site each time with this information.

Students can use the Ning site to:

- Take part in a book club on a book or set of books.
- Blog about a text, giving reading updates or sharing their feeling toward the book.
- Hold discussions revolving around the social issues in a novel.
- Post pictures connected to a book.
- Share links to outside resources related to a novel or its content (including fan fiction sites or YouTube videos).
- Post poetry or other creative pieces that emerge from their reading of a text.

Unlike traditional websites, Ning sites allow students to interact and network in a variety of ways, all of which can be customized according to the teacher's preferences.

While there are a number of educational tech tools on the market, it is important that we select tools that best meet our students' needs and best facilitate the kinds of collaboration expected of individuals in the twenty-first century. Above all, we can use tech tools like VoiceThread and Ning to help students draw on their own and others' strengths and intelligences to improve.

Meredith DeCosta-Smith is a Ph.D. candidate in English Education at Arizona State University. Her work focuses on language, literacy, and equity in urban, multicultural contexts. She serves as technology liaison for the Central Arizona Writing Project and works with English teachers to bring new media into the classroom. Before becoming a Ph.D. student, she taught high school English for four years in Indiana, where in her school she was named Teacher of the Year. Meredith has written several articles and book chapters and has presented at regional, national, and international conferences.

Different Kinds of Literacy

As this sampling of statements about different kinds of literacy shows, while the world in some ways is getting smaller or "flatter," it is also getting larger because to understand our immediate environments we all need to know more than we do. This is especially true in relation to appreciating the values and the attitudes of whatever groups we happen to belong to, as well as the values and attitudes of the young people we meet through our work.

At the 1991 National Council of Teachers of English convention in Seattle, Washington, Rudolfo Anaya, author of *Bless Me, Ultima* and a professor of creative writing at the University of New Mexico, talked about the incorporation of minority literature into the mainstream. He did not mean just the inclusion on book lists of the names of authors who are members of minority groups

Young Scholars Speak Out

Art Valdespino on **Multicultural Texts:**
The Uniqueness of Reading
to My Two-Year-Old Son

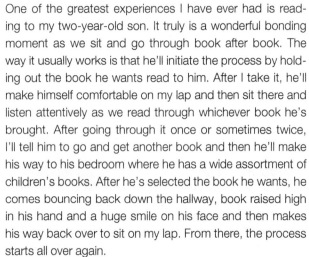

One of the greatest experiences I have ever had is reading to my two-year-old son. It truly is a wonderful bonding moment as we sit and go through book after book. The way it usually works is that he'll initiate the process by holding out the book he wants read to him. After I take it, he'll make himself comfortable on my lap and then sit there and listen attentively as we read through whichever book he's brought. After going through it once or sometimes twice, I'll tell him to go and get another book and then he'll make his way to his bedroom where he has a wide assortment of children's books. After he's selected the book he wants, he comes bouncing back down the hallway, book raised high in his hand and a huge smile on his face and then makes his way back over to sit on my lap. From there, the process starts all over again.

In reading to my son, what has struck me as unique is that every now and then my son will bring a book written either in Spanish or written in English, but with Spanish translations. The uniqueness that I feel does not come from the fact that the books we are reading are in Spanish, but from my knowing that I didn't read my first book written in Spanish until I was in college. I realize that saying this may not sound all that unique, but you need to consider my background. To begin with, I grew up along the U.S./Mexico border in El Paso, a city that is over 80 percent Latino. Secondly, I was raised in a bilingual home where my parents spoke to my sister and me as much in Spanish as they did in English. Still, with as much exposure as I was getting to Spanish at home, I was not getting that same kind of attention at school. Even in a city as culturally rich as my own, the curriculum at the schools I attended was founded on the belief that all teaching should be done in English. That's just the way it was. At least I can say I had it better than some of my older family members who had attended school in the 1940s and 1950s and who told stories of being hit by their teachers for speaking Spanish. Although this was never my experience, the books I read at school never had a Spanish speaking character or even one with a Spanish first or last name. Instead, my literary exposure came from books like *Where the Red Fern Grows* and some highly enjoyable books in the Encyclopedia Brown series. I will admit that I have some fond memories of these books, and of many others, but the truth is I never found myself relating to them in any sort of cultural or linguistic way.

Once I began teaching in 1999, I noticed a shift in education in regards to the use of multicultural texts, at least in comparison to how little they were used when I was going through school. Works by minority authors are far more

but also the incorporation of new styles and ideas into the writing of nonminority authors. One example is the incorporation into mainstream literature of the kinds of magical realism that for a long time have been common in Hispanic literature. Another way is through the desegregation of characters as seen in several of the books listed in Focus Box 4.6, "Looking through Different Lenses" (p. 132).

Anaya went on to explain that Mexican Americans have a different worldview. When he was in college, he loved literature and read the standard literary canon with enthusiasm and respect, but when he went to write his own stories, he couldn't use Hemingway or Milton as models. He could create plots like commonplace than they ever were when I was growing up, or at least that's how it seems. Still, introducing students to multicultural works is a process that faces two major obstacles. The first is that school budgets rarely allow for the purchase of new, or even used, class sets of multicultural texts. This was certainly the case at the high school where I taught and at many other schools in our district. Yes, budget constraints can hinder the educational process, but the real problem lies in the perception that even as rich and powerful as these stories are, they are not generally included in the supposed "Classical Canon" of texts that are still part of the day-to-day curriculum of a vast majority of schools.

Consequently, there are still several Latino students who have never read or even heard of writers such as Gary Soto (*The Afterlife, Buried Onions*) or Ben Saenz (*Last Night I Sang to the Monster, He Forgot to Say Goodbye*), and who have never been introduced to the rich, poetic verses of Pat Mora (*Dizzy in Your Eyes: Poems About Love, Abuelos, Book Fiesta!*). Worse still, these same students have no idea about the existence of the new wave of Latino authors like Matt de la Peña (*Mexican Whiteboy, We Were Here),* whose YA book *Ball Don't Lie* tells a tale that transcends cultural lines and touches on universal experiences.

When it comes to my son, he's got a huge jump start in the reading of multicultural texts. Because my wife and I are both educators and avid readers who want our son exposed to texts written in both English and Spanish, he'll always have access to stories filled with characters and experiences to which he'll be able to relate. But his situation is unique, and the fact is that for every Latino student who is like my son, there are far more who do not have his advantages. Multicultural texts, regardless of the language in which they are written, touch upon many of the exact same issues as their supposed "Classic" counterparts, only they

do so from a perspective that has largely gone unrecognized within the classroom. Furthermore, the introduction of multicultural texts doesn't mean that students shouldn't read "Classics" after all, they are considered classics for a reason. But mixed in with these should be stories told from a minority perspective, if for no other reason than to allow students to relate to a story filled with characters who are "just like" the readers.

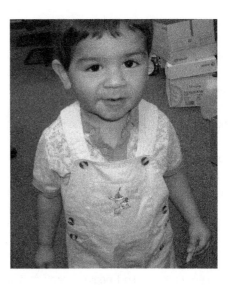

- Art Valdespino is a Ph. D. candidate in English Education at Arizona State University. He is now completing his dissertation, which is based on work he did at an Arizona high school over the past two years. He is doing a study of secondary Latino/a writers and their narrative stories of immigration. After being advanced to candidacy, he returned to his home town of El Paso, Texas, where he is working as the Instructional Coordinator in the Da Vinci School for Science and the Arts, which is part of the Burnham Wood Charter School District.

theirs, but then he was at a standstill because nowhere in the literary canon did he find people like the ones he knew. His Spanish-speaking family has lived in eastern New Mexico for more than one hundred years. The harsh but strangely beautiful landscape and the spirit of the Pecos River had permeated his life, as had stories of La Grande, the wise old woman who had safely pulled him from his mother's body even though the umbilical cord was wrapped around his neck.

Anaya worked on *Bless Me, Ultima* for seven years, during which he felt he was "writing in a vacuum. I had no Chicano models to read and follow, no

Young Scholars Speak Out

Cynthia S. Nicholson on "That's Not My Name!" What YA Authors Can Teach about the Names of African American Students

One of my surprises when I first began teaching was that there was no *right* way to spell even such simple names as *Amy,* which appeared on my rolls as *Aimee, Amiee,* and *Aimé*. My initial instinct was to minimize the idea that names were a means of ethnic identity and pride. Yet it became more and more obvious that the names of my African American students were likely to differ in spelling from the names of Caucasian students. I wanted to believe that ethnicity did not play a major role in the choice of name spelling, even though as a child I had refused to be called *Cindy* instead of *Cynthia* because I thought *Cindy* was a "white girl" name.

Only after years of seeing common names like *Michael* and *Kayla* take on such new spellings as *Mychal* and *Kaela, Kaylah,* or *Kaila* did I begin to look at such names as *DeShonna*, *Dameon*, *Turquoise*, and *Seven* as reflections of ethnic pride. Almost every ethnic group has its own naming practices, but African Americans—more than most groups—are especially interested in creative naming patterns. One reason is the history of my people which includes slavery, Jim Crow laws, and segregation. It stands to reason that some of us would develop naming practices that defy those of the mainstream society.

But on the other side of the argument are people like my grandmother who explained, "I named your father and aunts names that would be easy for others to pronounce. The color of their skin was enough to cause problems. I didn't need their names to bring them more attention." My parents were raised during the era of *Brown vs. the Board of Education* and I am empathetic to my grandmother's decision because fearing for the safety of one's child must be a gripping feeling.

Yet today, fifty-six years after the Supreme Court decision to provide quality education for all children regardless of race, children's names can still cause them to face injustice when they are in a classroom and the teacher fails to pronounce their name correctly or in some other way shows that the name is "inferior." As a secondary English teacher in urban and rural high schools, I have been included in conversations with colleagues who expressed negative sentiments about children's names. Since I was a fellow educator, with a "normal" name, the assumption was that I, too would feel the same way they felt about how a name was spelled. The fact that I am African American was trumped by my educational status. Nevertheless, I often found myself as a confidante for children, who could not defend themselves from the attitudes of their teachers. It was not their fault that mom or dad took the liberty to give them a special identity through their name.

In Chapter 16 of *I Know Why the Caged Bird Sings,* Maya Angelou records an abbreviated history acknowledging the psychological impact that name-calling had upon Blacks in the 1930s. She explained that every person she knew "had a hellish horror" of being "called out of his name" because of centuries of "having been called *niggers, jigs, dinges, blackbirds, crows, boots*, and *spooks."* Then she tells a wonderful story (short enough to read aloud) of how as a preteen she was sent to the home of a white neighbor, Mrs. Cullinan, to work as an apprentice housemaid. The fun in the story comes when Mrs. Cullinan decides to change Margaret's name to *Mary,* and feisty Margaret decides to get even with her.

In a 1989 article "What's in a Name? Some Meanings of Blackness," published in *Dissent* 36:4 (pp. 487–494), Henry Louis Gates wrote about naming practices during his childhood in West Virginia. He remembers hearing a familiar white acquaintance address his father as *George*. After the man left, Henry asked his father, "Doesn't he know your name, Daddy? Why don't you tell him your name? Your name isn't George!"

Gates's father explained that an easy-to-say name like *George* was commonly used by white speakers to refer to black men in "polite or reverential discourse" in contrast to such labels as *nigger* or *jigaboo*. Even as a young child, Henry realized that intentionally calling someone "outside of his name" was a matter of disrespect. The man was ignoring his father's true identity.

In connection with the 2008 Olympics, David Zax on *Salon Online* (viewed March 2009) wrote about the names of participating athletes and pointed out: "It is the black names that disproportionately stand out: Tayshaun, Dreon, Rau'shee, Raynell, Deontay, Tarajae, Jozy, Kerron, Hyleas, Chaunte, Bershawn, Lashawn, Sanya, Trevell, Sheena, Ogonna, Dremiel." Zax lamented that the subject of black names regularly manages to make its way into the one-liners of comedians and satirists alike. In spite of this token acknowledgement about it being a problem, he was actually contributing to the problem by listing these names in isolation, not even connected to the individuals' surnames or to the sport they were competing in. The reason I want students to read about many different African American characters is that they will learn their names at the same time that they get to know the characters as individuals. People do not make fun of the names of people they know and like. This was a point that Robert Cormier understood in his book, *I Am the Cheese*. When Adam meets Amy Hertz, he vows that he will never make a joke about her name because she must have been hearing such jokes all her life. Cormier used this little detail to show us that Adam likes Amy and feels a sense of companionship with her.

Part of being an educator requires that we create a safe learning environment for all students to achieve. An unfamiliar spelling or pronunciation of someone's name should not make him or her an outsider. Acknowledging students' understanding of Standard American English by accepting their names as additions to the language opens doors for learners to appreciate the beauty of words. While this may appear to be a trivial matter, it means a great deal to our students. It behooves each of us to reflect on the interaction that we have with each person who enters our classrooms or our library. We must seize every moment to encourage a love for words. Why not start with students' names.

This approach was vividly demonstrated on the April 3, 2011, CBS *60 Minutes* program, which dedicated two segments to a "Gospel for Teens" choir in Harlem. The program began with a lively performance of a "My Name Is . . ." number in which the more than forty members sang out their names. Later, when Lesley Stahl interviewed Director Yolanda Howard, she explained that she had created that part of the show because when the kids came in to audition she was shocked at how shy they were. They mumbled and looked down at the floor "as if they were ashamed of their names—or of themselves," and so making them proud of their names was the first thing she worked on.

Over the past seventeen years, Cynthia Nicholson has been a high school English teacher in South Carolina and Virginia. In Arizona, she worked as a district Literacy Specialist, and after completing her doctorate, returned to the southeast to continue her leadership role in professional learning communities. For her dissertation, she investigated how students' community literacy practices can be utilized in language arts classrooms, a topic she will continue to work on in her new position as Instructional Coach for Griffin High School in Georgia. Her greatest contentment comes from spending time with her husband, Lewis Nicholson, and with their children, Ava 14, and Gregory, 11.

Cynthia recommends that teachers read Valerie Kinloch's *Harlem on Our Minds: Place, Race, and the Literacies of Urban Youth* (Teachers College Press, 2010) because the text highlights the journey that students travel to acquire voice and critical agency as they struggle with the changes that surround them. She also acknowledges that while unusual naming is most often recognized as an African American trait, immigrants from many parts of the world also face decisions about what they want to be called. For example, a *School Library Journal* reviewer of Carlos Eire's *Learning to Die in Miami: Confessions of a Refugee Boy* (Free Press S&S, 2010) wrote that "Eager for acceptance, Carlos becomes Charles then Chuck then Charlie, until finally Carlos is reborn." We recently saw an article in a journal, "Why Are Chinese Names Funny?" which explained Chinese names in children's books, but if you open a search engine asking the question, you will find several sites making fun of the English names that Chinese people choose for themselves. To help students of all ethnic groups feel comfortable with a veriety of naming patterns, encourage the reading of the prize-winning books in Focus Box 10.3, "Names and Naming in Multicultural Books," pp. 356–357, which provide a chance for readers to learn about multi-cultural naming as part of the bigger picture.

Young Scholars Speak Out

Marlinda White-Kaulaity
on Building a Circle of Influence with Native American Teens

Part of teaching kids that reading is important is to *be* a reader and to model it. My high school students often saw me reading, and when I asked them to read, I read with them. I often talked with them about what I was reading at the time and I told stories about my reading. Sometimes a student would curiously ask me, "What are you reading now? What is it about?" Many times I read aloud to my high school students, and they enjoyed it, although this method is often presumed to be more for elementary students. Older kids like to *hear* writing, and it is necessary that they hear and *feel* the sound and movement of words and language.

Some time ago I read Sherman Alexie's *The Absolutely True Diary of a Part-Time Indian,* which I knew my high school son would enjoy. As he lay in his room listening to music, I would enter every now and then and say, "Listen to this part" and then I would read a humorous segment of the book to him. He smiled. With each different part I read, his reactions grew more animated and he became more hooked. Eventually amusement brought laughter, and he finally asked, "What book is that?" I showed the book cover and said, "You can read it if you want."

In the days that followed, he would put away his earphones and read the book. Then he told his friends about Alexie's novel and some of them read it as well. Later he came and asked if I had any other Sherman Alexie books. I provided my copies of *Flight, Indian Killer,* and *Reservation Blues*. He read them all, and his friend read some of them too.

Then his English teacher "caught him" reading a non-assigned book and asked what he was reading. She had not heard of Sherman Alexie. Too often teacher education programs do not require that preservice teachers read multicultural literature, specifically. If it occurs, they often choose books from African American young adult writers. This is fine, but they could cross over to the field of Native American Literature which is comprised of several Native writers from different tribal nations. Often their work is not written specifically for young adults, that is, they don't have young protagonists or deal with issues related to young adult life. Alexie's novel is an exception. However, as English teachers often do with other literature, they can find ways to adapt literature so it can be read by high school students.

My son's English teacher eventually read *The Absolutely True Diary of a Part-Time Indian* and recommended it to other interested English teachers. She also asked if Alexie

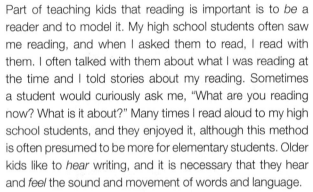

fellow writers to turn to for help. Even Faulkner, with his penchant for the fantastic world of the South, could not help me in Mexican/Indian New Mexico. I would have to build from what I knew best." In his *Autobiography: As Written in 1985* (TQS Publications, 1991), he explained:

> I began to discover that the lyric talent I possessed, as the poet I once aspired to be, could be used in writing fiction. The oral tradition which so enriched my imagination as a child could lend its rhythm to my narrative. Plot techniques learned in Saturday afternoon movies and comic books could help as much as the grand design of the classics I had read. Everything was valuable, nothing was lost. (pp. 16–17)

had written any poetry; thus, my son's next question to me was, "Did Sherman Alexie write any poetry?" Alexie's work certainly had grabbed my son's attention and that of his English teacher as well. Language Arts teachers have much power to influence students about literacy, and about school in general, but it depends on the choices they make for how they carry out the curriculum.

I pulled from my shelf Alexie's book, *The Business of Fancydancing*, and read aloud one of my favorite poems, "Giving Blood" (p. 78). I talked to my son about how I connected to this, also giving him a few lessons about Indian history (which is often excluded from school curriculum). The talking aspect of my reading is a method I did with my own students in the English classroom, and it's important that kids *hear* teachers talk genuinely about what they read and what it means to them. This helps students learn that reading is about making connections, making meaning, and taking words and ideas beyond the printed page and bringing them to life.

The English teacher read some of Alexie's poems and then shared them with my son's class, and no doubt shared them with other English classes as well. This year I was delighted to hear that another English teacher in the department had purchased a copy of *The Absolutely True Diary of a Part-Time Indian* for every student to keep.

Dialogue and stories are meaningful when working with literacy. When kids *hear* their teacher talk about reading or how they are challenged with writing, teachers give to kids the opportunity to feel part of the "community" when kids join and relate to such conversations and experiences. "The community of readers" and "the community of writers" are special groups of which we want all students to be a part.

Most importantly, we educators have to teach them to "naturally" be a part of these groups, almost as though they "came into" the group never having known they were applying for admission. This phenomenon occurs with teacher and adult guidance, when students feel comfortable with reading (and writing) and see its value and relevance for them. It then becomes part of their identity, and such connectedness to literacy is a primary goal toward creating lifelong readers.

> Dr. White-Kaulaity is a long-time Language Arts educator having taught English courses at high school, community college, and university levels. She is a strong supporter of using Native American literature in all Language Arts classes.
>
> After completing her doctorate at Arizona State University, she returned to her home community and works with her local school district on the Navajo Indian Reservation in northeastern Arizona. She first worked as a school improvement specialist in professional development, and presently, coordinates programs for students that involve college readiness and career awareness. She started a dual enrollment program in which Native American high school students can get a jumpstart on college coursework and graduate with both high school and college credits. Her heart and energy are dedicated to helping move Native American education forward and to inform people about minority education in general.
>
> Native American literature that she recommends includes Linda Hogan's 1998 *Power* and 1990 *Mean Spirit*, James Welch's 1986 *Fools Crow*, and Leslie Marmon Silko's 1977 *Ceremony*. She also suggests that teachers consult the website of the American Indian Library Association for its Youth Literature Award http://www.ailanet .org/activities/youthlitaward.htm.

Anaya's observations about not having models to follow and being forced to create a new narrative style to tell a story coming from his own experience relates to the frustration that teachers and librarians often express when they go to look for young adult novels about minority characters. They look for the same kinds of coming-of-age stories that are typical in mainstream young adult literature except they want the characters to have brown skin and "different" names. The absence of such books, especially such books written by Native American authors, is in itself part of the cultural difference. We've noticed that the more closely a book with a Native American protagonist resembles what we described in Chapter 1 as a typical young adult book, the greater the chance that the author is not a Native American and that the protagonist is of mixed parentage or is living apart from the native culture.

Being in the blood line of a particular group does not guarantee acceptance by the group. Most high school teachers think they are contributing to an awareness of cultural diversity and the enlargement of the literary canon by leading students to read Maxine Hong Kingston's *Woman Warrior*. But some sinologists have criticized Kingston's versions of the old stories. They think she has made mistakes about such matters as gender and religion. When her books are illegally translated and printed in Taiwan and China, "experts" change the stories back to make them conform to more traditional versions. Kingston's reaction is that these people do not understand that myths have to change to be useful. In a personal statement printed on p. 24 of Shirley Geok-lin Lim's *Approaches to Teaching Kingston's* The Woman Warrior (Modern Language Association, 1991), Kingston explained that these people do not understand that myths have to change to be useful. She wrote:

> Like the people who carry them across oceans, the myths become American. The myths I write are new, American. That's why they often appear as cartoons and Kung Fu movies. I take the power I need from whatever myth. Thus Fa Mu Lan has the words cut into her back; in traditional story, it is the man, Ngak Fei the Patriot, whose parents cut vows on his back. I mean to take his power for women.

Knowledge of these opposing viewpoints should not frighten teachers back into the comforts of the established canon; instead, it should help teachers prepare for meeting the challenges involved in going beyond the "tried and true."

Thomas L. Friedman's *The World Is Flat: A Brief History of the Twenty-First Century* is a book that the *School Library Journal* recommends to teens as well as adults. Friedman is not using "flat" in a negative sense as we might talk about a "flat drink" or a "flat tire." He is talking about the lowering of borders and dividers between countries, and how it is now possible to "innovate without having to emigrate." He makes a persuasive argument that today more people than ever before from all parts of the world can collaborate and compete in real time on a huge variety of tasks. He focuses on three contributing factors: the collapse of Communism, the worldwide Y2K gearing up for adjusting the world's computers to the new century, and the dot-com bubble, which resulted in heavy investments in fiber-optic telecommunications. When the bubble burst, the fiber optics were still in place and available below cost, which is what enabled Delta Airlines, for example, to hire reservation clerks who are living in India and Jet Blue Airlines to hire retirees and housewives to take its reservations from their homes in Utah.

The Friedman anecdote that is most likely to interest teenagers is the one about an owner of several McDonald's restaurants in Colorado who decided to consolidate the way his customers order their hamburgers at the drive-through window. In fast-food restaurants, nothing slows things down more than for a customer to get to the window and have the wrong order so that the whole line of cars has to wait while the new order is prepared. This owner managed to cut his restaurants' average wait time significantly by having all orders taken by someone in a sound-proof room trained to "get it right" and to send the correct order via computer to the kitchens in the originating restaurant. Although he set up his order system in his home state of Colorado, he could have as easily set it up in a different country or a different part of the United States.

We thought about Friedman's observations when we recently visited with Shannon Hale, author of the Newbery Honor Book *Princess Academy*. She is a young mother living in Utah, who flew into Phoenix to make a presentation and do a book signing at Changing Hands Bookstore. She was coming to promote her new book *Austenland: A Novel*, which is officially an adult book but which we are sure teen lovers of Jane Austen will be reading. Hale had brought her four-month-old baby with her and right after eating with us, then being interviewed by a newspaper reporter, making her presentation, and autographing books, she was flying back to Salt Lake to spend the night at home with the rest of her family. When someone asked if it was hard being both famous and a mother, she gave a disclaimer to the fame part, but then laughingly confessed that one of her relatives had figured out that today she is known by more people than was the Pope in the 1300s.

The Internet, especially author websites and blogs, makes a huge difference in connecting writers and readers. For an illustration, see Cynthia Leitich Smith's website (http://www.cynthialeitichsmith.com). We first got acquainted with it when we read in *School Library Journal* that if someone wanted to keep up with only one website in YA or children's literature, Cynthia's was the one. As soon as we found it and spent a few minutes investigating we could understand the reason for the recommendation and also why the site is listed among the American Library Association's "Great Web Sites for Kids" and why *Writer's Digest* chose it as one of the top-ten author sites on the Internet. When we asked Cynthia to describe her site, the first thing she said was that, from the beginning,

Cynthia Leitich Smith is a New York Times best-selling author, who is generous with her time and talents. With help from her husband, Greg, she hosts Cynthia Leitich Smith's Children's & Young Adult Literature Resources, which is available at http://www.cynthialeitichsmith.com.

she has received considerable help from her husband, Greg, who, besides keeping his day job as a lawyer, also writes books for kids. But even with Greg's help, we wondered how Cynthia could possibly squeeze out the two or three hours a day she devotes to the site, and she smilingly said, "Some people garden. I link!" Cynthia also finds time for her own writing. Her latest book is *Blessed*, which is the third in her Dark Universe series (following *Tantalyze* and *Eternal*), an updated retelling of Bram Stoker's *Dracula*. Cynthia went on to say that all the work is possible because their "commitment is to the body of literature as a whole, not just our own—though we couldn't be more passionate about it."

Another difference today is the speed with which popular new books are being translated and sold in other countries. Within less than two years, Stephenie Meyer's 2005 *Twilight*, the first of four books about star-crossed lovers, had already been translated into over thirty languages. Readers can go online to amazon.com and buy Spanish, Dutch, and German versions as easily as the English one. Stephenie lives in metropolitan Phoenix, and here at ASU we agreed to help host a spring "prom" on May 10, 2007. The main event at the prom was Stephenie reading a chapter from the third book, *Eclipse*, which was not going to be released for three more months; however, attendees could buy an edition of the second book (*New Moon*) that would include the forthcoming chapter. The $8.00 tickets, which Meyer offered on her website, sold out so fast that the organizers quickly set up both a matinee and an evening event. Girls, mostly accompanied by a parent (a small number came with boyfriends), flew in from all over the country, with one girl coming from London. Just prior to the big event on our campus, Stephenie and her husband had been on a book signing trip to Rome. They had also been invited to go to South America, but had turned down the invitation, at least for the time being, because such a trip would keep them away from their three young sons as well as from the rigorous writing schedule that Stephenie was committed to.

Other evidence of a flat world in relation to young adult books is how many YA books from other countries (some of which have had to be translated) are being distributed by American publishers. See Focus Box 3.3, "Highly Acclaimed

One of the biggest changes that we have seen since we started writing this textbook is how much more enthused today's teenagers are to read books from other countries.

NEW BOOKS FROM THE WORLD-AT-LARGE

The Crow-Girl: The Children of Crow Cove by Bodil Bredsdorff, translated from Danish by Faith Ingwersen. Farrar, 2004. Young teens will be the ones to appreciate this historical tale set in a remote coastal area of Denmark. A young girl lives with her grandmother, who does everything she can to prepare the girl to survive when she dies, and with the help of the crows the girl manages.

The Door of No Return by Sarah Mussi. Simon & Schuster, 2008. Zac's grandfather is murdered and as Zack tries to find out why, he uncovers an amazing family history in Ghana, where his royal ancestors were betrayed by the British government. It's a gripping historical mystery.

Emil and Karl by Yankev Glatshteyn, translated from Yiddish by Jeffrey Shandler. Roaring Brook/A Neal Porter Book, 2006. Middle school students studying the Holocaust will be the ones to appreciate this novel written about two boys growing up in prewar Vienna. Glatshteyn wrote it after returning to America from a 1934 visit to Poland where he saw how Nazi persecution was changing all of Europe.

Jasper Jones by Craig Silvey. Knopf/Borzoi, 2011. Older teens are the appropriate audience for this rough-and-tumble Australian story about 14-year-old Charlie Bucktin, who is awakened one night by the town outcast, Jasper Jones, knocking on his window. An *SLJ* reviewer compared the book to both Harper Lee's *To Kill a Mockingbird* and to J. D. Salinger's *Catcher in the Rye.*

Out of Shadows by Jason Wallace. Holiday House, 2011. Thirteen-year-old Robert Jacklin is a student at a mostly white boys' school in 1980s Zimbabwe. The author based the story on his personal experience when he played all three roles: victim, bully, and bystander as students re-enact the hostilities they have witnessed from their parents as the country tries to adjust from its civil war and to Robert Mugabe's term as Prime Minister in a country undergoing tremendous changes.

Outlaw by Stephen Davies. Clarion, 2011. In this thriller appropriate for middle school readers, Jake Knight is left behind in a British boarding school, while his parents and sisters go off to Burkina Faso, where his father is the British ambassador. When Jake gets expelled for playing a dangerous game involving a GPS, he is sent to be with his parents. He thinks it is going to be an interesting vacation, but then he and his sister are kidnapped and he—along with readers—get some insights into the political issues facing many African countries.

Inkheart by Cornelia Funke, translated from German by Anthea Bell. Scholastic, 2003. Twelve-year-old Meggie has a loving father, whom she calls Mo. He is a book mender, but unknown to her he has the accidental, and sometimes dangerous, talent of making characters come right out of a book into real life. Middle school readers especially like this charming fantasy, which is continued in *Inkspell.*

Over a Thousand Hills I Walk with You by Hanna Jansen, translated from German by Elizabeth D. Crawford. Carolrhoda Books, 2006. For mature students, this painful book was written by the author as she tried over and over to help her adopted daughter, Jeanne d'Arc Umubyeyi, recover from the sadness and the anger she felt toward the Hutu neighbors in Rwanda who participated in the 1994 genocide killing of Jeanne's family, destroying her home and life as she knew it.

The Pull of the Ocean by Jean-Claude Mourlevat, translated from French by Y. Maudet. Delacorte, 2006. Middle school readers who like mysteries and stories set in the past are likely to be charmed by this mysterious story of three sets of twins and their dwarf-sized little brother. When they learn that their father intends to kill them, they set off to sea.

The Queen of Water by Laura Resau and Maria Virginia Farinango. Delacorte, 2011. A seven-year-old girl is taken from her family in the rural Ecuadoran Andes and sold to a middle class family. This moving coming-of-age story will make readers take a second look at how young girls are exploited around the world.

Secrets in the Fire by Henning Mankell, translated from Swedish by Anne Connie Stuksrud. Annick, distributed by Firefly, 2003. This fictional account is based on the true story of Sofia Alface, a friend of the author who survived the civil war in Mozambique (1975–1992), only to lose both of her legs when she stepped on a landmine.

The Water Mirror by Kai Meyer, translated from German by Elizabeth D. Crawford. S&S/Margaret K. McElderry Books, 2005. Part of the Reflections series, this fantasy is set in medieval Venice. Protagonists are two orphans apprenticed to a maker of mirrors. One of them is blind. The adventure starts when the Egyptian Army invades and the survival of Venice is in doubt.

Books from Around the World," for examples. Some of the credit for American teenagers developing more of a worldview must also go to the Harry Potter books, which are now a worldwide phenomenon. When we attended an International Society for Humor Studies meeting, we talked with a woman from Spain whose research project was comparing the humor in the German, Spanish, and Portuguese translations of the Harry Potter books with the original English version. Because we have studied J. K. Rowling's clever invention of names, we asked her about how the names were translated. For the most part, she said the names have stayed the same. This means that non-English readers would miss some of the jokes, but many of them are still understandable because Rowling based most of her names on Latin roots which have carried over into many other languages, especially the Romance languages of French, Spanish, and Portuguese, as well as other languages, like English, which have been heavily influenced by the Romance languages.

We wrote a letter to Scholastic, the American publishers of Harry Potter, to ask about the level of changes that were made to accommodate American readers. We knew that several changes had been made in the first book, with fewer in the second one, which Scholastic decided to publish sooner than they planned because people were going online and buying the British version rather than waiting for the American one. Editor Arthur A. Levine responded that as the series moved on, fewer changes were being made between the British and the American versions, not because of Scholastic's fear of losing sales, but because by now American readers are so well acquainted with the setting and the vocabulary that they feel comfortable with "Britishisms."

At a 2006 meeting of the Children's Literature Association, we heard Cornelia Funke's name included in a list of celebrities who had suddenly begun to publish children's books just because they had name recognition. Actually, Cornelia Funke did not belong in that list because she had written some forty books in German before *The Thief Lord* was translated into English and into nearly thirty other languages. She compared seeing her books in other languages (she reads Italian, German, and English) to seeing them in a new dress. For the seventh edition of this textbook she wrote:

> So, with the help of many translators and publishers my stories have started traveling to places I've never been. They find their way to people I've never met who choose to spend some of their time walking in my imagination. In a world where borders still cut the world into artificial pieces, where differences are thought to be more important than the things that people share, it is wonderful that writers and readers can travel together for a while in their imaginations. It still feels like a miracle.

We were surprised to read on the back of Listening Library's boxed set of CDs for *Inkspell* that "Funke lives in California, with her husband and children." When we received this statement from Funke for the 2005 edition of the text, we communicated through international mail, and she was still excited about her first trip to the United States in 2002.

We wrote to several publishers asking them if they now sponsor their writers on overseas visits or if they pay to have "foreign" writers come to the

United States. They mostly said they were not the ones sponsoring such visits, but that they were always happy when visits were arranged and they would be supportive in furnishing publicity handouts, and so forth. On rare occasions, for example, if an author were invited to appear on the *Today* show or to accept an award and speak at a big convention, they might help with expenses, but usually the bookstores or the host school or conference handled the finances.

We chatted with Linda Sue Park (author of *A Single Shard*) when she came to Phoenix to participate in our state library convention. She told us about feeling fortunate to be invited to a large conference in Hong Kong connected with the Man Booker Awards. She was invited as the Asian American children's writer, while Amy Tan was the Asian American general writer. Another international tidbit that we happened to hear about was that the Fitchburg State College in Massachusetts, whose library houses the Robert E. Cormier collection, holds an annual memorial service in which attendees stand and read a favorite portion of one of his books. A highlight of the program is when foreign students read some of Cormier's writing in their native languages.

A flat earth does not mean that the world is free from dangers and fears, but there is something comforting in knowing that young people around the world are reading many of the same books and being exposed to many of the same ideas and values. Even dictators are known to warm up to children's stories. As one author confided when he was invited for a two-week visit to a totalitarian country, the people who invited him tactfully explained that in order to get his visa approved, he should identify himself not as an "author," but as a "children's storyteller."

Teaching Ethnic Literature

Most educators feel a duty to bring ethnic-based literature to young people in hopes of increasing their general understanding. Besides that lofty goal, here are some additional reasons for making special efforts to bring ethnic books to young people:

- Young readers can identify with characters who straddle two worlds because they have similar experiences in going between the worlds of adulthood and childhood.

- Motifs that commonly appear in ethnic-based stories—including loneliness, fear of rejection, generational differences, and troubles fitting into the larger society—are meaningful to teenagers.

- Nearly all teenagers feel that their families are somehow different, and so they can identify with the theme of family "differentness" that often finds its way into stories about immigrant families.

- Living in harmony with nature is a common theme, especially in Native American literature, and this theme appeals to today's ecology-minded youth.

- As movies, television programs, mass media books, and magazines inundate teens with stories and photos of people who are "all alike," readers find it refreshing to read about people who have their own individuality.
- Myths and legends that are often brought into ethnic-based literature satisfy some deep-down psychological and aesthetic needs that are not met with contemporary realism or with the romanticism masked as realism that currently makes up the main body of fiction provided for young adults.

One of the most important concepts that needs to be taught is that there are large differences among people typically identified as a group. When Europeans first came to the American continent, there were more than thirty distinct nations speaking perhaps a thousand different languages. During the past five hundred years, these people have had such common experiences as losing their lands, being forced to move to reservations, and having to adapt their beliefs and lifestyles to a technological society. These experiences may have affected their attitudes in similar ways, but still it is a gross overgeneralization to write about Native Americans as if they were one people holding the same religious and cultural views. Although in a single class it would be impossible to study dozens of different Native American tribes, a compromise solution might be to study the history and folklore of those tribes who lived, or are living, in the same geographical area as the students. With this approach, it is important for students to realize that they are looking at only one small part of a bigger group, and that if they studied a different group they would learn equally interesting but different facts.

Similar points could be made about the thoughtlessness of talking about Africa as if it were one country and as if one set of folktales could represent a continent that contains nearly twelve million square miles and over forty independent countries. Asian Americans also resent being lumped together. The Chinese and Japanese, the two groups who have been in the United States the longest, come from countries with a long history of hostility toward each other. A refugee from Vietnam or Cambodia has very little in common with someone whose ancestors came to California in the 1850s. Likewise, Puerto Ricans in New York have a different background from Mexican Americans. Even in the Southwest, people whose families have lived there from the days before Anglo settlers arrived resent being grouped with people who just came over the border from Mexico.

We need to teach about the histories of groups whose literature is being read to help readers understand the bitterness that finds its way into some ethnic literature. Readers who get impatient with Hispanic authors for including words and phrases in Spanish will probably be a little more tolerant if they realize that today's generation of Mexican American authors went to school in the days before bilingual education. In their childhoods, many of them heard nothing but Spanish and were amazed to arrive at English-speaking schools where they would be punished for speaking the only language they had ever known.

While Rudolfo Anaya broke new literary ground with his *Bless Me, Ultima*, many other minority writers are breaking new ground by changing the format of stories and translating them from an oral tradition into a written form. Before printing presses, typewriters, word processors, movies, radio, and television, people had more of an incentive to remember and tell the stories that communicated the traditions and values of a society. Even today, oral traditions play an important role, as seen on television talk shows as well as with kids telling stories and workers and travelers whiling away long, boring hours. Because minority writers are translating oral stories into written and printed formats, some of the first publications to come from particular groups are more likely to be poetry and short stories than novels.

There are many beautifully designed collections presenting art, poetry, photographs, essays, observations, interviews, and short stories. Besides the obvious advantage that anthologies present a variety of pieces short enough for classroom and library use, the differences in the statements demonstrate that members of groups are first and foremost individuals. They have their own thoughts, feelings, and values, just as do the members of one's own family, one's own church, and one's own neighborhood. A helpful new book is *Integrating Multicultural Literature in Libraries and Classrooms in Secondary Schools* by KaaVonia Hinton and Gail K. Dickinson. The authors include specific examples of fiction, nonfiction, poetry, screenplays, and picture books with suggestions of how to use them alongside the more standard offerings found in most textbooks.

This is probably a lesson that works better through demonstration than through lecturing. Jim Burke, on p. 252 of *The English Teacher's Companion*, gives two examples of ways that teachers might introduce Sandra Cisneros's *The House on Mango Street*.

Scenario One

Okay guys, today we're going to be getting a new book called *The House on Mango Street* by a Latina author. I thought it was really important that we read an author from a different culture since so many students here are Latino.

Scenario Two

[*after reading a brief section from Cisneros's book*] So, we've been talking about this whole idea of growing up, about creating an identity for oneself, what it means, how and when it happens. Huck Finn allowed us to talk about some important aspects of that whole experience. And Nathan McCall's book told us what it was like for him to grow up as a young black man in the sixties. I thought it would be interesting to see what this other book has to say about the experience since unlike Huck she didn't take off but stayed on Mango Street. I love this book a lot. It took her five years to write this 120-page book. It's like a poem almost, the language and images are so intense.

As Burke explains, the second scenario is clearly better in that the teacher grabbed students' interest by reading an excerpt and then linked the book to what the class had been doing. By emphasizing the book's literary quality, the teacher helped students see why they were reading the book while the teacher in the first scenario left students with the idea that they were reading *The House on Mango Street* to be politically correct.

Those of us working with books and young adults need to continue seeking out and promoting the use of minority literature. Some of us shy away from working with minority literature because:

- We didn't study it when we were in school and so we feel less prepared than when teaching mainstream literature.
- We fear censorship both because of prejudice against minorities and because of the fact that some minority writers use language considered inappropriate for schoolbooks.
- Minority literature is harder to find, especially minority literature that has been given a "seal of approval" by the education establishment (i.e., positive reviews and suggestions for teaching).
- Ethnic identification is such a sensitive topic that teachers fear that when they are discussing a piece of literature either they, or their students, may say something that will offend some students or hurt their feelings.

Closely connected to developing literacies about different cultural groups is becoming literate about different religions, or even one's own religion. Many high schools are now offering classes in the Bible as Literature, but not so many are offering classes in religions other than Christianity. Nevertheless, people are becoming more aware of the need for greater understanding. See the well-recommended books listed in Focus Box 3.4, "Books to Help Educators and Students Develop Religious Literacies."

As shown by the daily news, there is indeed a need for all of us to know more about not just our own, but also other people's religious beliefs. See the October 2010 issue of VOYA, for an update of their World Religion Resource List, which includes both fiction and nonfiction related to Buddhism, Christianity (Protestant, Catholic, and Orthodox), Hinduism, Islam, Judaism, and other world religions. Also see Focus Box 3.4 on p. 101, "Books to Help Educators and Students Develop Religious Literacies" for earlier recommendations made by the VOYA editors.

Books to Help Educators and Students Develop Religious Literacies

The Bookseller of Kabul by Asne Seierstad. Little, Brown, 2003. A Norwegian journalist tells about her three-month stay with a bookseller in Kabul. Her book reveals some of the engaging and horrifying details of Muslim life and is considered to be one of the best accounts of Afghan life after the fall of the Taliban.

Daughters of the Desert by Claire Rudolf Murphy, et al. Skylight Paths Publishing, 2003. Murphy tells the stories of Eve, Mary Magdalene, Fatima, and many other significant women in the Christian, Jewish, and Muslim faiths. An important point is that these three major religions share a common genesis in the Middle East, and that the women are more similar than different.

The Encyclopedia of Native American Religions by Arlene Hirschfelder and Paulette Molin. Facts on File, 1999. This book tells about the spiritual traditions of the Native Americans of the United States and Canada both before and after contact with Europeans. There is a listing of sacred sites, biographies of Native American religious leaders, influential Christian missionaries, and information about sacred ceremonies and sacred medicine.

For this Land edited by Vine Deloria, Jr. Routledge, 1998. This volume documents the clash between Christianity and Native American religious beliefs. A *VOYA* reviewer said, "It is an excellent resource for high school student research, particularly in the context of Christianity's influence upon Native American religious practices."

God Is Not One: The Eight Rival Religions That Run the World by Stephen Prothero. Harper One, 2011. This recent book follows Prothero's well received *Religious Literacy: What Every American Needs to Know and Doesn't* (Harper SanFrancisco, 2007). Prothero, who is a professor of religion at Harvard University, has explained that biblical illiteracy is not just a religious problem, it is a civic problem. "How," he asks, "can citizens participate in biblically inflected debates on abortion, capital punishment, or the environment without knowing something about the Bible?"

Islam edited by William Dudley. Greenhaven, 2004. This book, which is part of the "Opposing Viewpoints" series, presents articles which debate such controversial questions as whether or not the values of Islam and the West are in conflict, whether or not Islam promotes terrorism and violence, the status of women under Islam, and some of the factors that will have an impact on the future of Islam.

Islam in World Cultures: Comparative Perspectives edited by R. Michael Feener. ABC-CLIO, 2004. Ten international scholars give insights on how Islam interacts with other religions in global and local cultures; a good reference book for advanced high school students.

The Many Faces of Biblical Humor by David A. Peters. Hamilton Books, 2007. Advanced students might enjoy bringing some of these observations to their classmates; although they shouldn't be expecting the kind of laughs that comedians aim for. Similar books include William E. Phipps *The Wisdom and Wit of Rabbi Jesus* (Knox, 1993) and *The Humor of Jesus: Sources of Laughter in the Bible* (Regent College, 2001).

Rainbow Tribe: Ordinary People Journeying on the Red Road by Ed McGaa. HarperCollins, 1992. The author encourages readers to help restore the harmonious balance between nature and man by experiencing the spirituality of Mother Earth. McGaa tells about the "Path of the Rainbow," a philosophy that employs religion in such spiritual practices as the vision quest and the spirit-calling ceremony.

Sacred Doorways: A Beginner's Guide to Icons by Linette Martin. Paraclete Press, 2002. This book discusses the histories and meanings (both straightforward and symbolic) of sacred icons. It also tells how to use icons at prayer time. It could be considered a companion volume with *The Meaning of Icons* by Vladimir Lossky and Leonid Ouspensky (St. Vladimir's Seminary Press, 1982).

Same God, Different Churches by Katie Meier. Tommy Nelson Publishers, 2005. This book tells about the major beliefs and statements of faith of different Christian denominations in the United States. It's perfect not only for teens who want to know more about how their friends worship, but it can also be used for "church-shopping."

A Time to Love: Stories from the Old Testament by Walter Dean Myers. Scholastic, 2003. This is a family collaboration in which Walter Dean Myers, his young son Christopher, and his older son Michael Dean (a captain and a chaplain) retell and re-illustrate the stories of "Samson and Delilah" "Reuben and Joseph," "Ruth and Naomi," and three other stories from a young-adult narrator's point of view. The stories range from passionate to heartrending to tender.

We were amused during the 2008 presidential campaign when Mike Huckabee developed a reputation as part of the religious right by frequently bringing biblical allusions into his speeches. A reporter for National Public Radio went to one of his speeches and after his speech interviewed people in the audience. Less than 30 percent could identify the stories that Huckabee was alluding to.

Concluding Comments

Back in 1970, when the National Council of Teachers of English passed a Resolution on Media Literacy and endorsed a "Summary Statement on Multimodal Literacies," few members realized the responsibility they would soon have in teaching their students to think critically about still images, photos, movies, animations, drama, art, alphabetic and non-alphabetic text, music, speech, sound, physical movement, gaming, and whatever else might come down the road or over the airwaves. But being a professional does not include shying away from responsibilities just because they are challenging. Instead, you prepare so that you can be successful—at least, most of the time. The fact that we are working in an exciting and changing field where we have to keep learning new things is something to be grateful for rather than afraid of. Pablo Casals, the great cellist, was still practicing three hours a day when he was ninety-four years old. When someone asked him why he was still practicing, he answered, "I'm beginning to notice some improvement."

Contemporary Realistic Fiction: From Romances to Tragedies to Magical Realism

chapter **4**

E ven though respected authors and critics argue against realism as a literary concept, we are using the term mainly because we can't think of a better one. Also, because people commonly use *realism* to describe the books in this chapter we would be at a communication disadvantage if we invented a new term. We are writing about young adult fiction with real-world settings in historical periods not far removed from our own. The books feature young protagonists solving problems without the help of magic. Marc Aronson in his book, *Exploding the Myths: The Truth about Teenage Reading* says that what makes realistic novels succeed is their level of intimacy. "Does a book have the potential to touch readers deeply so that, in the struggle with it, they begin to see and to shape themselves?" (p. 20)

The Romantic Quest

The archetypal story of "The Journey" or "The Quest" as outlined by Joseph Campbell in his 1968 *A Hero with a Thousand Faces* is well illustrated in Cynthia Voigt's Homecoming series (see her write-up on p. 107), as well as in some of the books discussed in Chapter 8 where we write about the experiences of young soldiers. These stories are especially appealing to young readers because many romantic symbols relate to youthfulness and hope, and many of the protagonists in traditional and classic tales are in their teens. They have reached the age at which they anticipate leaving home to embark on a new way of life. Today, this is more likely to be called "moving out" than going on a romantic quest, but the results are much the same.

Seeking and securing a "true love" usually, but not always, takes up a greater proportion of the time and energy of young adults than of middle-aged adults. And the exaggeration that is part of the romantic mode is quite honestly felt by teenagers. Robert Cormier once said that he began writing about young protagonists when he observed that in one afternoon at the beach his own children could go through what to an adult would be a whole month of emotional experiences.

A distinguishing feature of such romances is the happy ending, achieved only after the hero's worth is proven through a crisis or an ordeal. The suffering nearly always purchases some kind of wisdom, even though wisdom is not what the hero set out to find. Authors like to send young people on trips, not just for the symbolism of a quest, but because the trip provides the protagonists with a new environment, new challenges, and new acquaintances, all of which add interest. More than any other author, Sharon Creech has worked with journeys. For the seventh edition of this text, she wrote

> I love the way that each book—any book—is its own journey. You open the book, and off you go. You don't know who you're going to meet along the way, nor where you will go, and when you finish a book, you feel as if you've been on a journey. You are changed in some way—large or small—by having traveled with those characters, by having walked in their moccasins a while, by having seen what they've seen, heard what they've heard, felt what they've felt. These journeys echo all of our daily journeys: not knowing who we will meet today, tomorrow; who will affect our lives in small ways and profound ways; where we will go; what we will feel; what will happen to us. (p. 149)

As you read the stories in Focus Box 4.1, "Literal Journeys/Figurative Quests," notice the different ways that creative authors have figured out how to adapt ancient literary customs into modern life. For example, in traditional romances the protagonist usually receives the vision or insight in a high or isolated place like a mountain top, an island, or a tower. In Virginia Hamilton's *M. C. Higgins, the Great*, the boy,

Of all the archetypes, the one about going on a quest or a journey is most fitting to teen readers because it is a metaphor for their own stage of life as they journey into adulthood. See Focus Box 4.1, "Literal Journeys/Figurative Quests," on p. 105 for recommended examples.

Focus Box 4.1

Literal Journeys/Figurative Quests

An Abundance of Katherines by John Green. Dutton, 2006. Colin Singleton is a budding genius. However, when he graduates from high school, he feels as though he's already wilting. So far he's had way too many girls—all named Katherine—give him the heave-ho, but as he and his buddy drive across the country, he finally meets a girl whose name is not Katherine.

Circle of Secrets by Kimberley Little. Scholastic, 2011. Middle school readers are most likely to identify with ten-year-old Shelby who has been living with her father and grandmother, but then her father's job takes him out of the country and her grandmother's health puts her in a hospital. Shelby is sent to live with her mother in the Louisiana bayou. It takes a long time for Shelby to warm up to the mother, but she gets help from the mysteries of the bayou and from people she meets.

Defining Dulcie by Paul Acampora. Dial, 2006. When Dulcie's father dies, she and her mother move from Connecticut to California as a way of starting over. When it doesn't work for Dulcie, she takes the truck and in a somewhat madcap adventure drives back home. Although she learns that she cannot pick up the pieces of her old life, she nevertheless begins to heal.

Gingerbread by Rachel Cohn. Simon & Schuster, 2002. Gingerbread is the rag doll that Cyd's biological father, who was almost a stranger, gave her when she was five. Now as a teenaged "recovering hellion," she is sent from her San Francisco home to New York City to get acquainted with him and his family.

Homeless Bird by Gloria Whelan. HarperCollins, 2000. This winner of the National Book Award is set in India and is about thirteen-year-old Koly. Through an arranged marriage that turns out badly, she is forced on a journey toward making a life for herself.

Hope Was Here by Joan Bauer. Putnam, 2000. Sixteen-year-old Hope and her Aunt Addie leave New York City for promised jobs in Wisconsin—Addie as a cook and Hope as a waitress. They find their jobs—and much more. *Rules of the Road* (1998), along with its companion book, *Best Foot Forward* (2005), and *Backwater* (1999), all from Putnam, are also highly recommended Bauer books in which journeys play a role.

Many Stones by Carolyn Coman. Front Street, 2000. Berry and her father travel to South Africa to attend a memorial service for Berry's older sister, who was killed while working at a church school in Cape Town. The title comes from the stones that Berry places on her chest each night, one at a time, to calm her troubled mind.

Shift by Jennifer Bradbury. Atheneum, 2008. After graduation, Chris and Win go on a cross-country bicycle trip. Chris is both angry and disappointed as he tries to find Win, who has disappeared and is being hunted by the FBI as a "Person of Interest."

True Confessions of a Heartless Girl by Martha Brooks. Farrar/Melanie Kroupa Books, 2003. A plot summary would make this book seem grimmer than it is. Brooks's main point is to demonstrate the power of community in the process of healing.

Whirligig by Paul Fleischman. Holt, 1998. This is a perfect story to show how a journey provides time for reflection and growth. A boy who in a fit of rage causes an automobile accident that kills a girl sets out on a journey to memorialize her in each corner of the United States.

M. C., comes to his realization about his family and his role while he contemplates the surrounding countryside from a special bicycle seat affixed to the top of a tall steel pole standing in the yard of his mountain home. The unique pole was given to M. C. by his father as a reward for having swum across the Ohio River. Another characteristic of the heroic quest is that the young person is shown to be "special," something that Robert Lipsyte communicated in *The Contender* by starting with Mr. Donatelli, the manager of a boxing gym, listening to the confident sound of young Alfred Brooks climbing the steps to his gym. Donatelli says he can tell who has what it takes to be a contender (readers are to interpret this as meaning a contender in life as well as in the boxing ring) by how they climb those stairs.

The idea of a sacrifice is shown in Jean George's *Julie of the Wolves* when Julie learns that her father still lives and that she has arrived at his village. When she learns that he has married a "gussack" and now pilots planes for hunters, the disillusioned Julie grieves for the wolves and the other hunted animals and vows to return and live on the tundra. However, the temperature falls far below zero and the "ice thundered and boomed, roaring like drumbeats across the Arctic." Despite all that Julie does to save him, Tornait, Julie's golden plover, who has been her faithful companion, dies from the cold. Tornait is the last symbol of Julie's innocence, and as she mourns his death, she comes to accept the fact that the lives of both the wolves and her people are changing, and she points her boots toward her father and the life he now leads.

Success is demonstrated in Chris Crutcher's *The Crazy Horse Electric Game*, in which pitching star Willie Weaver is seriously injured in a water skiing accident. He runs away from home when it appears that he is also losing his girlfriend. At first he is only concerned with surviving, but then he gets involved with other people and attends an alternative school where, with help, he recovers many of his motor skills. He returns home strong enough to cope with all the changes that have occurred.

Some critics fear that when authors use such physical changes as Willie Weaver's almost miraculous recovery as a tangible or metaphorical way to communicate emotional or mental accomplishment, young readers interpret the physical achievement literally rather than figuratively. Teenagers are already overly concerned about their bodies and any defects they might have. Many physical challenges, including the common motif of obesity, cannot be totally overcome, so these critics prefer stories in which the protagonist comes to terms with the problem as does Izzy in Cynthia Voigt's *Izzy, Willy-Nilly*, about a young girl who loses her leg, and the young Native American boy in Anne Eliot Crompton's historical *The Sorcerer*. The boy is named Lefthand because he was injured by a bear and cannot hunt. In his tribe, this is a serious problem, because hunting is what the men do. There is no miraculous cure for his disability, but he gains both his own and his tribe's respect when he develops enough skill as an artist to draw the pictures of animals needed for the tribe's hunting rituals.

A book from the 2009 Honor List that illustrates a quest and a compromised dream is Adam Rapp's *Punkzilla*, which is the story of fourteen-year-old Jamie Wyckoff, called Punkzilla or Punk because of his love for punk music. He is a runaway trying to get across the country to Memphis, Tennessee, in time to say goodbye to his dying brother, Peter, or P as Jamie calls him. The story is told through the letters that Jamie writes and reads as he alternates between hitchhiking and riding buses. On the trip, he is both helped and harmed by strangers, and he is so young, innocent, and confused that when he is sexually molested, he simply shakes it off and looks for another ride.

His brother, P, is an intelligent and successful playwright who has always had a good relationship with Jamie. P was pretty much expelled from the family because the boys' father, a military man, is horrified at the idea of having a gay son. And probably because Jamie has a small build and "dainty" features, the father fears that he too will be gay. His reaction is to send Jamie to Buckner Military Academy in Missouri, allegedly because he believes that a good military lifestyle will straighten him out and keep him away from the "bad crowd" and the drugs and alcohol he had been experimenting with.

Jamie goes AWOL from Buckner and hitchhikes to Portland, Oregon, where he falls in with a much worse crowd than he could ever have found at

Margaret A. Edwards Award

Winner (1995)

Cynthia Voigt, **A Writer Who Keeps on Learning**

Cynthia Voigt is unusual in being honored for a total of seven books: *Homecoming*; *Dicey's Song*; *A Solitary Blue*; *Building Blocks*; *The Runner*; *Jackaroo*; and *Izzy, Willy-Nilly*. A surprising fact is that these seven are fewer than one-third of the books that Voigt has published. Besides having written more than a dozen independent novels, between 1973 and 1989 Voigt wrote six books about the Tillermans and their associates; one of which (*Dicey's Song*) won the 1983 Newbery Medal. Between 1985 and 1999, she wrote four fantasy stories in the Kingdom series, and between 1996 and 2006, she wrote the Bad Girl series about Mikey and Margolo, who are really more "inconvenient" than "bad." They are based on some of the students Voigt remembers from the years that she taught middle school.

Another surprising fact about Voigt's books was noted by Jaime Hylton in "Exploring the 'Academic Side' of Cynthia Voigt" in *The ALAN Review* (Fall 2005, pp. 50–55). Hylton wrote that "After nearly a quarter of a century, every book that Voigt has published is still in print." She went on to give credit for this happy event to the fact that Voigt does all that we expect from an excellent writer; plus, she provides a richness that "transcends topical stories with teen-oriented, identity-focused themes." Hylton's thesis is that Voigt achieves this kind of transcendency by suffusing her books "with allegory, literary allusion, classical mythology, and traditional folk and fairy tales."

Hylton's observation sent us back to check out a Focus Box statement that Voigt wrote for the third edition of this textbook under the title of "Learning and Knowing." In it she explored "a central and an essential difference" between adults and young people. She said that the real difference between the two is that kids expect themselves to *be learning* while adults expect themselves *to know*. For herself, Voigt chooses to be in the kid category so that her "attitude towards experiences, people, the whole side show, is characterized by questions and curiosity," which will guarantee that she will keep changing and adding to herself—"perpetually growing up with no end in sight to the arduous and uneasy occupation."

At the beginning of *Izzy, Willy-Nilly*, which is the story of a young girl who has been in an automobile accident and lost a leg, Voigt acknowledges learning a great deal from medical personnel who taught her about physical and mental aspects of amputation. And it is obvious that while writing *Come a Stranger* and *Building Blocks*, Voigt had to learn a lot about slavery and the Underground Railroad, and that while writing *David and Jonathan* she learned new things about the Holocaust. But as Hylton points out, the real power of Voigt's learning is in the uses she makes of her deep knowledge of the world as revealed through its great thinkers and writers. This is what keeps Voigt's books fresh and interesting year after year.

David and Jonathan is an allegorical story filled with biblical and Talmudic parables. In *Homecoming*, Voigt uses sailing as an extended metaphor, while in *The Runner*, she uses cross-country track. In *A Solitary Blue*, she builds the whole story around a glimpse of a blue heron that her protagonist, Jeff, gets. The heron, who is half-hidden in the marsh, seems to be all by herself, but as Jeff works his way toward an understanding of his two very different parents, he realizes that each of them has a place in his life. One of the things that helps him begin to accept both of his parents is his realization that the heron was not really solitary; herons build their nests in colonies, "all of them together."

The literary allusions that Voigt uses to help put across her points range from Shakespeare's *Macbeth*, *The Tempest*, and *Hamlet* to Hemingway's *The Old Man and the Sea* and de Saint Exupéry's *The Little Prince*. In her later books, she includes pop culture references. Both Emily Dickinson and Judy Blume are alluded to in *Izzy, Willy-Nilly*, while one of Virginia Hamilton's books makes it into *Bad Girls*. Voigt's *Orfe* is a modern telling of the myth of Orpheus and Eurydice, while *Homecoming* has many similarities to the Greek myth of Odysseus. In an interesting reversal, Voigt puts females in the place of the traditional male heroes. ●

home. He supports himself by selling stolen iPods to a man named Fat Larkin. He gets them through conning people or through hiding in a park and waiting for vulnerable runners to come through. He then knocks the runners unconscious with a heavy alarm clock. When Jamie hears that his brother is dying of cancer, he starts on a cross-country trip and manages to get to Memphis while P is still alive but unconscious. When P dies and the brothers' parents come to attend the funeral, Jamie watches from afar, never letting his parents know he is there. The book ends on a positive note when P's partner, Jorge, agrees to take Jamie in and give him a new start.

This new start will still require hard work—both physically and emotionally—from Jamie, but certainly it is a step-up from living in a park and stealing iPods from runners. The compromised dream is an element of the romantic quest particularly meaningful to teenagers who are just beginning to achieve some of their goals and to discover the illusory nature of the end of the rainbow, which is a symbolic way of saying such things as, "When I graduate," "When we get married," "When I'm eighteen," or "When I have my own apartment." Like the characters in the romances, they are not sorry they have ventured, for they have indeed found something worthwhile, but it is seldom the pot of gold they had imagined.

Stories of Friendship and Love

When people hear the term *romance*, their first thought is usually of a love story, which for young readers probably includes friendship as well as love. This is because in the old romances, which were stories coming from such romance languages as Latin, Italian, Spanish, and especially French, the climax of the story was often the uniting of a young couple. A common motif was for successful adventurers to be rewarded with the love of a beautiful maiden. While

Friendships seem simpler the younger people are, but maybe they are all complicated. See Focus Box 4.2, "Love and Friendship," on p. 109 for stories that explore teen friendship.

FRIENDS

***Blink & Caution* by Tim Wynne-Jones. Candlewick, 2011.** Caution is a girl trying to recover from the death of her brother, while at the same time hiding from her old boyfriend who is a drug dealer. She comes in contact with Blink, a street kid with even more troubles than Caution. The two "doomed" kids decide to work together to save themselves.

***Heart on My Sleeve* by Ellen Wittlinger. Simon & Schuster, 2004.** The author of the Printz Honor Book *Hard Love* uses emails, postcards, IMs, and regular old letters to tell the story of Chloe and Julian's spring and summer relationship after they meet when Chloe is on a trip to scout out a college.

***If You Come Softly* by Jacqueline Woodson. Putnam, 1998.** This story of love between a white girl and a black boy was chosen as one of the top-ten books of the year by the Young Adult Library Services Association.

***My Heartbeat* by Garret Freymann-Weyr. Houghton, 2002.** Fourteen-year-old Ellen has a crush on her brother's best friend, but things get complicated when she finds out that her brother and his friend are more than friends. Nevertheless, she and the friend go ahead with their own sexual relationship and readers are left to ponder the difficulties of trying to put people in boxes.

***The Plain Janes* by Cecil Castellucci, illus. by Jim Rugg. Minx, 2007.** This amusing and quirky graphic novel is about the friendship of four girls who all feel like misfits until they form their secret club, the Plain Janes. This may be just the book to convince regular readers of realistic YA fiction that graphic novels can have their own kind of power.

***Planet Middle School* by Nikki Grimes. Bloomsbury, 2011.** The strength of this warm story about Joylin and her best girlfriend Kaylee, is Grimes's beautifully poetic way of relating Joylin's feeling that she is an alien who accidentally arrived in "Planet Middle School" and is "searching for that spaceship//that's gonna take me home."

***Prom* by Laurie Halse Anderson. Viking, 2005.** Readers were happily surprised to learn that the author of such a serious book as *Speak* could also write a lighthearted and humorous book about Ashley and what she does to save the prom after a dishonest teacher steals the funds.

***Son of the Mob* by Gordon Korman. Hyperion, 2002.** Seventeen-year-old Vince Luca, whose father could easily be part of the Sopranos, usually manages to stay out of his father's business ventures, but then he falls in love with the daughter of an FBI agent.

***Sweet Hereafter* by Angela Johnson. Simon & Schuster, 2010.** This is the final volume of Johnson's *Heaven* trilogy. Shoogy and her boyfriend, Curtis, live in a cabin near Heaven, Ohio, and Shoogy goes to school part-time and also works. Curtis is in the Reserves and has served one tour in Iraq and is now AWOL because he doesn't want to go back.

***When Zachary Beaver Came to Town* by Kimberly Willis Holt. Henry Holt, 1999.** It is the 1970s and the world is thinking about Vietnam, but thirteen-year-old Toby is much more interested in Zachary Beaver, a boy billed as the fattest boy in the world, who gets left by his manager in the parking lot of the neighborhood bowling alley.

***Who Am I without Him? Short Stories about Girls and the Boys in Their Lives* by Sharon G. Flake. Hyperion, 2004.** Flake's stories aren't all wish-fulfilling; instead, she makes girls take a second look at what they are willing to give up to please the boys.

few of us have the ability or the means to go on a grand adventure or to compete and win against incredible odds, most of us can imagine finding a true love. Because of the universality of this wish to love and be loved, this element of adventure stories became the feature that many readers, especially females, came to identify with the term *romance*. The challenge or problem is invariably the successful pairing of a likable young couple. An old definition of the love-romance pattern is, "Boy meets girl, boy loses girl, boy wins girl." But with teenage love, the pattern is often reversed because most of the romances are told from the girl's point of view. She is the one who meets, loses, and finally wins a boyfriend.

The tone of most love romances, as shown by the works listed in Focus Box 4.2, "Love and Friendship," is lighter than that of the adventure romance.

Its power lies in its wish fulfillment, although critics worry that we may be setting young girls up for disappointment when we consistently reward girls who have had a disappointment or who have worked their way through a difficult time with a boyfriend who appears out of nowhere. They also worry about the stories in which an ugly duckling girl is suddenly transformed by the love of a boy into a swan. In her new role as swan, she is not only popular but also happy.

For the writer of a love story, probably no talent is more important than the ability to create believable characters. If readers do not feel that they know the boy and girl or the man and woman, or maybe two males or two females, as individuals, they cannot identify with them, and consequently will not care whether they make it. Another characteristic of the good love story is that it provides something beyond the simple pairing of two individuals. This something extra may be interesting historical facts, an introduction to a social issue, glimpses into the complexity of human nature, or any of the understandings and concepts that might be found in quality books or movies.

Although most formula romances are aimed at a female audience, comparable to the way that most pornography is aimed at a male audience, some writers are trying to write romances that will also be read by boys. The most obvious difference between these boy-oriented romances and the larger body of love stories written from a girl's point of view is that their authors, who are mostly men, tend to put less emphasis on courtship and romance and more on sexuality. Rather than relying on discreet fade-outs, they allow their readers to know what happens, which sometimes means sexual intercourse. For the most part, the descriptions are neither pornographic nor lovingly romantic, but in such books as Chris Crutcher's *Running Loose*, Robert Lehrman's *Juggling*, Terry Davis's *Vision Quest*, and Aidan Chambers's *The Toll Bridge*, there is little doubt about the abundance of sexual feelings that the characters experience.

As an antidote to the lopsidedness of books that are either overly romantic or overly sexy, some adult critics suggest offering books in which boys and girls are as much friends as lovers. This is especially true in lighter books read by tweeners where the romantic relationship is only part of a bigger story. Also, neither partner exploits or manipulates the other, as often happens in exaggerated romances or in pornographic or sex-oriented stories. As a ploy to attract male readers (publishers already feel confident that girls will read romances), authors often tell the story through the boy's eyes or perhaps through chapters that alternate back and forth between the boy and the girl, as Paul Zindel did in *The Pigman* and M. E. Kerr did in *I'll Love You When You're More Like Me*. Zindel told us that he wrote his books for girls to read, but he always kept in mind the fact that girls recommend books to their boyfriends, and he did not want those girls to be disappointed when their boyfriends didn't like the book. He therefore tried to avoid including things that would be an automatic turn-off to boys. If more authors followed his example, we would probably have more "love stories" that could be appreciated by readers of both sexes.

Wish-Fulfilling Stories

The most wish-fulfilling stories for males are most likely to be the sports and adventure stories found in Chapter 7, while for females wish-fulfilling stories are usually about friendship or love. Especially for young teens, friendship books are more appealing than love stories because they are free from the complications of sex. It was the friendships that a decade ago kept many girls reading the Babysitters Club and the Sweet Valley High series. A few years ago in one of our classes, Ann Brashares's *The Sisterhood of the Traveling Pants* turned into "The Sisterhood of the Traveling Book." While no males borrowed it, the women passed it from friend to friend, even to roommates not taking the class. When we asked for it back, there was always one more student wanting to read it. The book is a coming-of-age story in four parts. Lena, Tibby, Bridget, and Carmen have been "best friends" ever since their mothers took the same aerobics class for pregnant women. By the time the mothers begin drifting apart, the girls are old enough to maintain their own close friendship, and the book opens with them being in high school and getting ready for the first summer they will be apart. Carmen had purchased a pair of jeans at a thrift shop, and as the girls gather to help Carmen pack (she's the first to leave, going to South Carolina to spend the summer with her divorced father), each one playfully tries on the pants. Even though the four friends have different body builds, they are happily surprised to find that the pants "fit" and, in fact, make each girl feel elegantly fashionable. Carmen had offered to give the pants to whoever wanted them, but now everybody wants them and so the girls come up with the idea of taking turns. Each one will have the pants for a few weeks.

Part of the charm of the book is Brashares's writing, which lends credibility and interest to the four stories, but more important are the wish-fulfilling aspects of the supportive friendship. The girls experience rough times, especially their first summer apart when Lena goes to Greece to visit her grandparents and Bridget goes to soccer camp in California. The supportive friendship of the girls, as symbolized through the traveling pants and shown through their letters, notes, and candid observations, helps them survive and, in some ways, thrive.

Ever since the biblical story of David and Jonathan, we have had stories about boys' friendships. It is a refreshing change to read about girls helping each other. And because readers came to know and like the girls, it was to be expected that Brashares would continue their story, which she did in 2003 with *The Second Summer of the Sisterhood,* in 2005 with *Girls in Pants: The Third Summer of the Sisterhood,* and in 2007 with the final book, *Forever in Blue: The Fourth Summer of the Sisterhood.* The success of the 2005 film also helped to garner readers, but in relation to the third and fourth books we did hear some worries from junior high teachers who felt uncomfortable about twelve- and thirteen-year-old girls racing through the series, which ends with the girls being away at college and having mature sexual experiences.

Author Meg Cabot came up with the ultimate in wish-fulfilling stories when she created The Princess Diaries series about five-foot-nine, flat-chested Mia

Thermopolis, who suddenly learns that she is a real princess and is heir to the throne of the small but wealthy European country of Genovia. The books are frivolous and fun "diaries" of Meg's experiences as she trains to be a princess. The books have been best sellers and led Cabot to also write *All-American Girl*, the story of how Samantha (aka Sam) Madison, the awkward middle daughter in an upper-class family, happens to save the life of the president of the United States and then have his son fall in love with her.

As a side note, it is interesting to see that by July of 2011, Meg Cabot had changed from writing innocent and wish-fulfilling romances to writing dark fantasy. Her book *Abandon* is about a girl named Pierce, who was advised by a *Publishers Weekly* reviewer to "Bag the tiara and get the gun!" Her book *Overbite*, which came out two months earlier, is about a girl named Meena hired by the Palatine Guard to protect the Vatican from demons.

One of the points we made in Chapter 1, where we outlined the stages of developing literary appreciation, is that throughout life people keep reading at all the different levels. No one wants to read seriously taxing material all the time. It is our job to surround young readers with many books of different types and to give them time and encouragement to read a wide variety. Virtually all of the studies that have been made of people who read widely and with pleasure and understanding shows that in their lives they have done a fair amount of "pleasure reading."

Moving Toward Serious Problem Novels

In one sense, all novels are problem stories because the problems provide the tension and the interest; without a problem, there would be no plot. The difference in the books we will mention in this section as opposed to the romances in the earlier section is that when books are described as "problem novels," the problems are severe enough to be the main feature of the story. Oftentimes, there is some force or some individual in the story who will help the young person, as does Jorge, P's partner, in *Punkzilla*.

Authors frequently use nature or animals as the helper or the catalyst. Many children come to high school already familiar with this technique because they saw it in such stories as Frances Hodgson Burnett's *The Secret Garden* and Kenneth Grahame's *The Wind in the Willows*. Animals play major roles in Allan Eckert's *Incident at Hawk's Hill*, Fred Gipson's *Old Yeller*, Sterling North's *Rascal*, Marjorie Rawlings's *The Yearling*, and Wilson Rawls's *Where the Red Fern Grows*. In many such stories, the animals are sacrificed as a symbol of the loss the young person undergoes in exchange for wisdom. Gordon Korman makes fun of this literary custom in his *No More Dead Dogs*, written for middle school readers, but fortunately some animals in stories live long, happy lives, providing companionship and even inspiration to the humans with whom they share the planet.

A different kind of story is the one in which a young person is helped through a religious experience, as in Cynthia Rylant's *A Fine White Dust*. The book's title comes from the chalklike dust that gets on Pete's fingers when he handles the "little bitty pieces of broken ceramic" that used to be a cross he had painted in Vacation Bible School—back before he got so old that it was not cool to go any more. His best friend is a confirmed atheist, and he has "half-washed Christians for parents." Nevertheless, the summer that Preacher Man comes to town, "something religious" begins itching Pete, something that going to church could not cure.

Rylant's skill in developing Pete's character and revealing the depths of his emotions when he is saved and wooed, and then betrayed, by the Preacher Man led to a well-deserved Newbery Honor Award. The twelve short chapters are almost an outline for a traditional quest story beginning with "Dust" and a sense of ennui, moving through "The Joy," "The Wait," and "Hell," and ending with "The Light" and "Amen." In the end, Pete decides that "The Preacher Man is behind me. But God is still right there, in front."

Books that unabashedly explore religious themes are relatively rare, which is one reason that Pete Hautman's *Godless*, discussed in Chapter 1 as an Honor List book, attracted such immediate attention. One reason for their rarity is that public schools and librarians fear spending taxpayers' money on religious material. Also, mainstream publishers fear cutting into potential sales by printing books with protagonists whose religious beliefs may offend or make readers uncomfortable. It has been easier for schools to include religious books with historical settings, such as Lloyd Douglas's *The Robe*, Scott O'Dell's *The Hawk That Dare Not Hunt by Day*, Elizabeth George Speare's *The Bronze Bow*, and Jessamyn West's *Friendly Persuasion*. Accepted also are books with contemporary settings that have proved themselves with adult readers—for example, Margaret Craven's *I Heard the Owl Call My Name*, Catherine Marshall's *A Man Called Peter*, and William Barrett's *Lilies of the Field*. In lamenting the shortage of young adult books treating religious themes, author Dean Hughes wrote in an *English Journal* bait/rebate page, Dec. 1981:

> We need to be careful that, in effect, we do not say to young people that they should be most concerned about pimples and clothes and dates and football games—or even sex. Part of being human is addressing oneself to questions about justice, creation, morality, and the existence of divinity. (p. 14)

In many ways, the negative portrayal of religion in books for teenagers is similar to the negative portrayal of parents and other authority figures. Such presentations serve as a foil to make the good qualities of the young protagonists shine all the brighter. Authors rely on the general assumption that religious people are good to provide contrast, as when the evil in Robert Cormier's *The Chocolate War* is all the heavier because of the book's setting in a religious school.

Another reason that books for teenagers appear to have so many religious characters portrayed in a negative light is that the good characters go unnoticed. For example, in M. E. Kerr's *Little Little*, one of Little Little's suitors is a dishonest evangelical preacher. When Kerr was criticized for this negative portrayal, she pointed out that Little Little's grandfather—the only person in the whole book who approached Little Little's dwarfism with common sense—was also a minister, but few readers noticed because he did his work in the manner expected from a competent clergyman in a mainstream church.

Although there are some good books focusing on broad religious themes and questions about whether there is a God and an afterlife (e.g., Aidan Chambers's *NIK: Now I Know*, Iris Rosofsky's *Miriam*, and Phyllis Reynolds Naylor's *A String of Chances*), what is more common is for an author to bring in religion as a small part of a bigger story. In Jim Naughton's *My Brother Stealing Second*, Bobby reminisces about his family's church experiences before his brother was killed, and in Sue Ellen Bridgers's *Permanent Connections*, Rob finds comfort by visiting a little country church. Katherine Paterson, who has attended theological school and served as a missionary in China, includes both implicit and explicit religious references in her books, most directly in *Jacob Have I Loved* and *Bridge to Terabithia*. Her *Preacher's Boy* is set in rural Vermont between May 1899 and January 1900 when the excitement of a new century was being felt. But this excitement includes worries about Darwin's theory of evolution and what is predicted to be the end of the world.

Madeleine L'Engle was devout and, along with some other writers of fantasy and science fiction, included religious overtones in her books; for example, the struggle between good and evil in *A Wrinkle in Time* and Vicky's hard-won acceptance of her grandfather's dying of leukemia in *A Ring of Endless Light*. Other books that include casual references to religious people and beliefs are Alice Childress's *Rainbow Jordan*, J. D. Salinger's *Franny and Zooey: Two Novellas*, Mary Stolz's *Land's End*, and Jill Paton Walsh's *Unleaving*. Chaim Potok's *The Chosen, My Name Is Asher Lev*, and *In the Beginning* show what it is to come of age in a Hasidic Jewish community. Cynthia Voigt's *David and Jonathan* asks questions about religious and cultural differences; Marc Talbert's *A Sunburned Prayer* is about eleven-year-old Eloy making a seventeen-mile pilgrimage on Good Friday to pray for his grandmother, who is dying of cancer.

Of course, religious publishing houses provide books focusing on religious themes, but these are seldom useful in schools because they are aimed directly at believers of a particular faith, and sometimes in their zeal to convert potential believers, the authors write polemics against other groups. Nevertheless, teachers and librarians are advised to visit religious bookstores to see the upscale marketing techniques currently in fashion. An especially troublesome group of books about religion are the books in which a misguided life is set right by an end-of-the-book conversion. Teachers hesitate to discuss the credibility of such stories because they fear that in the process of building up literary sophistication, they may tear down religious faith. Because so many people turn a blind eye, it is all the more important that educators seek out and support those authors and publishers who treat religious motifs with honesty as well as with respect for literary quality. We also need to help parents and other critics realize that strong religious feelings, including doubts, are part of the maturation process and that reading about the doubts that others have or about imperfections in organized religion will not necessarily destroy readers' faith.

The Modern Problem Novel

The general public seems to have an almost subconscious belief that children will model their lives after what they read. Since all of us want our children to be happy, we feel more comfortable when they are reading "happy" books. The problem novel, however, is based on the philosophy that young people will have a better chance to be happy if they have realistic expectations and if they know both the bad and the good about the society in which they live. This changed attitude is what opened the door to writers of irony and even tragedy for young people. Irony is the feeling good tennis players get when they are served a ball they can't return. They can admire its perfection, its appropriateness, and even the inevitability of the outcome, but they just can't cope with it and so are left feeling at least momentarily defeated.

Actually, there is a refreshing honesty in stories that show readers they are not the only ones who get served that kind of ball and that the human spirit, although totally devastated in this particular set, may rise again to play another match.

When, in the late 1960s, publishers began feeling comfortable in encouraging writers to create serious coming-of-age stories to be read by teenagers themselves, they identified the books as new realism or as problem novels rather than as the more literary term of *bildungsroman*, which is formally defined as "novels dealing with the development of a young person usually from adolescence to maturity." The books are often autobiographical and are sometimes called "apprenticeship novels."

In addition to their candor and the selection of subject matter, these new problem novels differ from earlier books in four basic ways. The first difference lies in the choice of characters. The protagonists come from a variety of social and economic levels, which ties in with the second major difference—that of setting. Instead of living in idyllic, pleasant suburban homes, the characters come from settings that are harsh and difficult places to live. To get the point across about the characters and where and how they live, authors use colloquial language, which is the third difference. Many

Although the complications written about in Focus Box 4.3, "Challenges: Physical and Mental," on pp. 118–119 and in Focus Box 4.4, "Buddies and Bullies," on p. 127 are not "chosen" by the protagonists, protagonists still have many choices to make as they deal with such challenges.

of today's authors write the way people really talk, including profanity and ungrammatical constructions. That the public has generally allowed these changes shows that people are drawing away from the idea that the main purpose of fiction for young readers is to set an example of proper middle-class behavior.

The fourth difference also relates to this change in attitude, and that is the change in mode. As it became acceptable to provide readers with more vicarious experiences than would be either desirable or possible in real life, the mode of YA novels changed. Most of the books for young readers—at least those endorsed by parents and educators—used to be written in the comic and romantic modes. Statistically, this may still be true, but several of the books currently getting critical attention are written in the ironic or tragic modes.

For example, John Green's *Looking for Alaska*, which won a Printz Award, is far from a happy story. It is told by sixteen-year-old Miles Halter, who leaves his family home in Florida to attend the Culver Creek Boarding School in suburban Alabama. His roommate, Chip, is a poor but brilliant scholarship student who delights in "getting even" with the rich kids at Culver Creek. Both Chip and Miles—and most of the other boys in school—fall madly in love with Alaska Young, a beautiful and full of life—and death—young woman who chooses to hang out with Chip and Miles. There is no happy ending for Alaska and the whole book is organized around the number of days before and after the tragedy that befalls her.

When the problem novel was first developing as *the* genre in young adult literature, it played a relatively unique role in openly acknowledging that many young people's lives are far removed from the happy-go-lucky images shown in television commercials and sitcoms. The best-known books from the 1960s and 1970s were new and interesting because they vividly demonstrated that young people worried about sex, drugs, money, peer pressure, and health problems. Such information does not come as news today because the mass media does a thorough job of communicating that many adults are less than perfect and that many young people are facing problems ranging from minor to severe. In fact, talk shows, reality shows, courtroom TV, soap operas, and even news programs and magazines make us privy to so many people's problems that we simply do not have the energy to empathize with all the sad stories that we hear. We shrug our shoulders and turn off our tear ducts, which leaves us feeling alienated and dehumanized. Also, most media treatments present a one-shot portrait chosen to tug at the emotions of viewers or readers. To increase the drama, they make a virtue of suffering and pain by portraying people as victims unable to move beyond their pain. In contrast, in the best of the problem novels authors take the space to develop various strands of their stories and to show differing viewpoints and alternate solutions. This differs from television sitcoms as well as from most series books, which preserve the status quo so that at the end the producer or the author can start all over again with a similar story.

In relation to the term *realism*, it is only fair to mention that some critics have justifiably pointed out that the large majority of high school readers are more likely to experience something akin to a wish-fulfilling romance than to the experiences described in many of the so-called realistic novels shown in this sampling of recent books and in those described in Focus Box 4.3, "Challenges: Physical and Mental."

- Meg Rosoff's *How I Live Now* (winner of the 2005 Printz Award) is about a futuristic war that breaks out in England where Daisy has been sent in hopes that with the help of her aunt and her cousins and the fresh country air, she will recover from her eating disorder. She says her food problem started when she was afraid that her father's new wife was trying to poison her, but then she confesses it became very satisfying to see both parents worrying about her. When she arrives at the old family farm, her aunt, who is active in a peace movement, is just rushing off to Oslo to give a speech and Daisy is left with her cousins. A strange kind of war breaks out and the teenage children are left to fend for themselves, which they do but only with some terrible consequences. An interesting technique is the way that Rasoff uses vague language when talking about the enemy so that readers are left to fill in their own images with whoever or whatever they fear the most.

- One of our students who read E. R. Frank's *America* responded with "grim, grim, grim." A fifteen-year-old boy named America was born to a drug-addicted woman who abandoned him, but nevertheless reappears for terrifying episodes. The boy's best memories are of living with Mrs. Harper and her half-brother. However, the half-brother introduces the preteen America to vodka and sex; in guilt and rage, America sets the man's blanket on fire and escapes. Years later, a capable therapist is coaxing America's story from the reluctant fifteen-year-old, who is living in a residential treatment center and trying to gain control over his suicidal depression. Readers are left with hope for a boy who, so far, has been a survivor against incredible odds.

- In *Hush*, Jacqueline Woodson uses a similar situation to the one that Robert Cormier used in *I Am the Cheese*, in which a family is uprooted and put into the Federal Witness Protection Program. In Woodson's story, the family is African American, and the protagonist, Evie Thomas (née Toswiah Green), is twelve years old when her father testifies against other African Americans in a racially motivated murder. Instead of creating the kind of dramatic situation that Cormier created, Woodson shows the tedium and the depression that sets in when a family is torn from its past and has yet to build a future. Evie's mother finds a kind of solace in the Seventh Day Adventist Church, but her father spends his days staring out the front window, while her older sister plots how she can escape from this nonlife. Rather than being left with a happy ending, readers are left pondering what is a less-than-perfect solution to a very real family problem.

Adam Rapp is known for writing "downer" books. *Little Chicago* is the grim story of eleven-year-old Blacky, who is sexually abused by his mother's boyfriend. Although he is brave enough to tell "all the right people," no one helps him. His best friend makes it even worse by telling kids at school, who cruelly taunt him. He gets a gun and, with no money for ammunition, performs

Accidents of Nature **by Harriet McBryde Johnson. Holt, 2006.** A summer at Camp Courage, which is designed for teenagers with disabilities, proves to be life-changing for seventeen-year-old Jean. She has cerebral palsy and is assigned to share a cabin with the intelligent and thoughtful Sara, who is in a wheelchair and has a different "take" on the matter of disability.

Boy Toy **by Barry Lyga. Houghton, 2007.** Seventeen-year-old Joshua Mendel is almost ready to graduate from high school, but he is still struggling emotionally with the fall-out from being sexually abused by Eve, the woman who was his seventh-grade history teacher. Older teens will be fascinated at how their relationship developed and its long-term effects.

Crank **by Ellen Hopkins. Margaret K. McElderry, 2004.** When Kristina Snow flies to New Mexico for a court-ordered visit with her father, who she hasn't seen for six years, she meets a boy who introduces her to drugs. When the visit is over and she flies back home, she finds a new side to her personality and new popularity with a crowd of "enablers." The book is in free-form verse, so it reads smoothly. Readers of *Crank,* will probably appreciate the two sequels, *Glass* in 2007 and *Fallout* in 2010. In *Fallout,* the focus shifts to Kristina's three teen-aged children, whose lives have been affected by their mother's addiction.

The Dark Days of Hamburger Halpin **by Josh Berk. Knopf/Random, 2010.** Will Halpin is deaf and for the first time enrolls in a regular high school. He makes friends with Devon Smiley and they team up to do some detective work, helped out by Will's ability to read lips and his computer skills.

Dope Sick **by Walter Dean Myers. HarperCollins, 2009.** Lil Jay is hiding out in an abandoned building. He is still high and on the run from a drug deal that went bad.

Every Time a Rainbow Dies **by Rita Williams-Garcia. HarperCollins, 2001.** Thulani's mother died three years ago, and he is a relatively unwelcome "guest" in the apartment of his older brother and the brother's wife. Thulani spends hours with the pigeons he raises on the roof of their apartment house. When he witnesses a brutal rape, he rushes down to "rescue" the girl and takes an important first step toward reentering life.

Invisible **by Pete Hautman. Simon & Schuster, 2005.** Seventeen-year-old Dougie has one good friend, and readers hope that will be enough to help him maintain his focus. When he hides his medication and resists help from his psychiatrist, readers begin to realize that Dougie has a secret too awful to reveal.

Memoirs of a Teenage Amnesiac **by Gabrielle Zevin. FSG, 2007.** Naomi is recovering from a serious head injury and is in a way having to make a new life for herself. Changing friendship, touches of romance, and family problems all contribute to a powerful story.

Messed Up **by Janet Lynch. Holiday House, 2009.** RD, who lives with his grandmother and her boyfriend, Earl, is repeating eighth grade. But then his grandmother runs away with a new boyfriend, leaving RD and Earl to struggle along. Then Earl dies and RD is

a sexual act to get bullets. His one friend, who suffers almost as much as he does, has told him that if you follow a deer long enough it will lead you to paradise. The book ends with Blacky following a deer into a forest, but only the most optimistic of readers can believe that this is going to make Blacky's life better. Tyrrell Burns closed her *School Library Journal* review with, "The sense of hopelessness in this disturbing novel is almost physically painful." For *VOYA,* Kathleen Beck wrote that Rapp's books are valuable because of their honest recognition that young people can suffer and face really difficult questions, but "Forget using them as bibliotherapy.... There are no solutions here."

left to manage on his own and decide what kind of a life he will have.

Saving Francesca by Melina Marchetta. Knopf/Borzoi, 2004. Francesca's mother, who used to be strong and successful, is so depressed that she cannot function and so Francesca has little help from home when she changes schools and experiences her first romance. Nevertheless, readers come away feeling positive for Francesca.

Shooting Star by Frederick L. McKissack, Jr. Atheneum, 2009. Not all addictions are for recreational purposes. Jomo Rogers is an undersized football player, who takes the game so seriously that he decides to also take steroids. The book could be a good tie-in to current news stories about athletes on trial for suspected steroid use.

Slam by Nick Hornby. Putnam, 2007. A sixteen-year-old skateboarder gets slammed with something new—he's about to become a father. Hornby is being praised for treating such a serious subject with warmth as well as respectful humor.

A Small White Scar by K. A. Nuzum. HarperCollins/Joanna Cotler Books, 2006. Besides being responsible for his disabled twin brother, fifteen-year-old Will wants to be free to ride in a rodeo and to work like a man on his father's 1940s Colorado ranch.

The Spectacular Now by Tim Tharp. Knopf, 2008. We had a hard time deciding whether this finalist for the National Book Award should go here as a problem story or later in a focus box on love and romance. But since Sutter Keely avoids paying attention to his senior year of high school, including Aimee's sincere interest in him, by staying drunk and cracking jokes, we decided to put it here as a problem novel.

Story of a Girl by Sara Zarr. Little, Brown, 2007. Older teens will be touched by this story of a girl whose life is drastically changed when her father catches her at age thirteen having sex in a car, and she is immediately "branded" by her own family as well as by the school community as a slut.

Stuck in Neutral by Terry Trueman. HarperCollins, 2000. Fourteen-year-old Shawn McDaniel thinks his father is planning to kill him, a suspicion that readers gradually grow to share in this story of a boy who is born with cerebral palsy. The story is continued in *Cruise Control* (HarperCollins, 2004), told from the viewpoint of older brother Paul, who hates his father and is striving to learn to control his own violent behavior both on and off the basketball court.

Surrender by Sonya Hartnett. Candlewick, 2006. Fire and a haunting secret from the past play a part in this powerful story, which is on the Honor List. A major character is a dog named *Surrender*, and readers are left wondering whether the book is named after the dog or after the mental attitude of the twenty-year-old protagonist who lies dying.

Total Constant Order by Chrissa-Jean Chappell. HarperTeen, 2007. Numbers continually pound inside Fin's head and treatments for her condition are not working, but maybe help is on the way when she meets a mysterious graffiti artist.

The Very Ordered Existence of Merilee Marvelous by Suzanne Crowley. HarperCollins/Greenwillow, 2007. Thirteen-year-old Merilee Monroe has her life in order, but then all kinds of troubles start intruding and readers get glimpses into the condition known as Asperger's Syndrome (not identified by name), alcoholism, senility, and plain old meanness.

In the February issue of *VOYA* when the "Top-Shelf Fiction for Middle School Readers 2002" (a list of twenty-four "Best Books") was published, *Little Chicago* received twice as much space as the other books, but its annotation was in a gray box under the unusual heading, "Adult Reader Recommendation." The committee's idea was that adults should read the book to keep such a story from ever happening. Their closing line was, "This book is not to be handed to young readers without forethought—not because it is unrealistic but precisely because it shows how heartlessly unprotected they might find themselves to be" (*VOYA* 25:6, p. 437).

Rapp's *33 Snowfish* is about four kids on the run. One of them has killed his parents and stolen their car. One is a prostitute; one has recently escaped from a pedophile, while the youngest is just a baby, whom the others think they might sell. Reviewer Joel Shoemaker in the April 2003 *School Library Journal* said that the book is bound to be controversial: "The fearsome elements escape the pages like nightmares loosed into daylight, . . . but for those readers who are ready to be challenged by a serious work of shockingly realistic fiction, it invites both an emotional and intellectual response, and begs to be discussed" (p. 166).

Young Adult Novels as Tragedies

In traditional literary criticism, tragedies have three distinct elements. First, there is a noble character who, no matter what happens, maintains the qualities that the society considers praiseworthy; second, there is an inevitable force that works against the character; and third, there is a struggle and an outcome. The reader of a tragedy is usually filled with pity and fear—pity for the hero and fear for oneself that the same thing might happen. The intensity of this involvement causes the reader to undergo an emotional release as the outcome of the story unfolds. This release, or catharsis, has the effect of draining away dangerous human emotions and filling the reader with a sense of exaltation or amazed pride in what the human spirit is called on to endure.

But rather than writing pure tragedies, most young adult authors used to soften their stories with hopeful endings. Even the books that include death, as with those listed in Focus Box 4.7, "Death and Grieving" (pp. 136–137), in some way focus on recovery and the future. The feeling has been that young readers deserve books with happy endings. Virginia Hamilton illustrated this belief when she was awarded the Newbery Medal for *M. C. Higgins, the Great*, and a reporter asked her if she really thought that the retaining wall that M. C. was building on the mountain above the house would keep the mine tailings from sliding down and ruining the family's home. She responded with something to the effect that, "Probably not, but this is a book for kids. They have to have hope."

Her statement illustrates a long-cherished belief that young readers deserve books with happy endings. These are the kinds of books that serve as a counterbalance to the depressing realism of the "true" problem novel. There is nothing magical in the books, so they are "real" in that sense, but as Richard Peck has observed, teenagers' favorite books are "romances disguised as realism." He was not saying this as a negative, because he was describing his own books along with those of many other well-respected writers. It is understandable that teenagers want both the happy endings and the assurance that happy endings are possible. Actually, most readers prefer happy endings, but it is assumed that adults have had more experience in coping with difficult life experiences so that they might be "turned off" by endings that come across as falsely hopeful. See Table 4.1 for suggestions of how to evaluate problem novels.

Three popular stories about young protagonists that were published as somber adult novels are J. D. Salinger's *The Catcher in the Rye*, Hannah Green's *I Never Promised You a Rose Garden*, and Judith Guest's *Ordinary People*.

TABLE 4.1 Suggestions for Evaluating the Problem Novel

A Good Problem Novel Usually Has	A Poor Problem Novel May Have
A strong, interesting, and believable plot centering around a problem that a young person might really have.	A totally predictable plot with nothing new and interesting to entice the reader.
The power to transport the reader into another person's thoughts and feelings.	Characters who are cardboardlike exaggerations of people and are too good or too bad to be believed.
Rich characterization. The characters "come alive" as believable with a balance of good and negative qualities.	More characters than the reader can keep straight comfortably.
A setting that enhances the story and is described so that the reader can get the intended picture.	Many stereotypes.
A worthwhile theme. The reader is left with something to think about.	Lengthy chapters or descriptive paragraphs that add bulk but not substance to the book.
A smoothness of style that flows steadily and easily, carrying the reader along.	A preachy message. The author spells out the attitudes and conclusions with which he or she wants each reader to leave the book.
A universal appeal so that it speaks to more than a single group of readers.	Nothing that stays with the reader after the book has been put down.
A subtlety that stimulates the reader to think about the various aspects of the story.	A subject that is of interest only because it is topical or trendy.
A way of dealing with the problems so that the reader is left with insights into either society or individuals or both.	Inconsistent points of view. The author's sympathies change with no justification.
	Dialogue that sounds forced or inappropriate to the characters.
	"Facts" that do not jibe with those of the real world.
	Unlikely coincidences or changes in characters' personalities for the sake of the plot.
	Exaggerations that result in sensationalism.

In all three, worthy young heroes set out to find wisdom and understanding. They make physical sacrifices, including suicide attempts, and even though they receive help from wise and kindly psychiatrists (today's counterpart to the white witches, the wizards, and the helpful gods and goddesses of traditional romances), they must prove their worthiness through hard, painstaking work. This is what Deborah Blau's psychiatrist communicates in the sentence used for the book's title, *I Never Promised You a Rose Garden*. If Green had intended her book for teenagers, she would have been more likely to have ended the book with Deborah leaving the mental institution to "live happily ever after."

A relatively new award being given through the American Library Association is the Schneider Family Book Award designed to "honor an author or illustrator for a book that embodies an artistic expression of the disability experience for child and adolescent audiences." Three awards are given each year: one for children, one for middle school readers, and one for teens. The 2011 winner for middle school readers was *After Ever After* by Jordan Sonneblick. It is about Jeffrey and Tad, two eighth-grade boys who survived cancer, and are now coping with the after-effects. The teen winner was *Five Flavors of Dumb* by Antony John, in which Piper, a high school senior who is deaf, volunteers to manage an amateur band, even though she would have preferred they had chosen a different name.

Young Scholars Speak Out

Laura Walsh on How the Commercialization of Teen Magazines Is Bad for Girls

Expectations for women with regard to beauty and body image are not new. Many women, including myself, have encountered the increasing pressures from the media to look young and to focus all our energies on somehow reversing the aging cycle, as if growing old is a disease. However, in writing my dissertation, I was horrified at the discovery that these same pressures are now being placed upon adolescent girls, most of whom are just beginning to develop their identities, through teen magazines. The three magazines analyzed in my study—one issue each of *Seventeen*, *Teen Vogue*, and *Girl's Life*—paint a grim picture of what girls have to look forward to as they advance into the world of female adulthood.

Teen magazines for girls are both focused and formidable. Advertisements—which make up the majority of the magazines—gleam from every page, offering young customers a chance to "buy" their way to beauty. Whether through concrete objects, such as clothing and cosmetics, or through abstract concepts, such as the dream of a glamorous lifestyle, these ads are what keep the magazines running and keep the readers spending. Yet if teen girls believe what they read and what they see in the advertisements, then many of them are in for great disappointments, for the magazines create an impossible aspiration: to become the "ideal girl." Over 70 percent of the visuals in the magazines I studied implied that to become the "ideal girl," one must be Caucasian. In addition, she should have long, straight hair, small features, a perfect white-toothed smile, and, of course, be thin. In fact, only one photo in *Girl's Life* depicted

a girl with a "normal" body size. The rest were pictures of perfection, and as they peeked out from every page, they seemed to be repeatedly asking girl readers, "Don't you wish you were me?"

For girls who do not meet the ideal as specified in the teen magazines, there is still hope, as they can purchase numerous products that claim to help them achieve perfection through modification. This idea of "change" is a common theme in each magazine with regard to beauty and body image. Teen girls have to be the "best," or "perfect," as emphasized in the repeated language of the magazines, and these magazines do not just ask girls to make this happen; they command them. Teen readers are told to "*Glisten* up!" "*Flaunt* your favorite feature!" "*Update* your hair!" and "*Transform* your body." Exclamation points often follow these commands, emphasizing the urgency and excitement in making these changes, for these changes are portrayed as a necessity if girls wish to reach the ideal.

To further promote this idea of change, numerous advertisements focus on perceived "flaws" and offer ways to fix them. In this way, girls' insecurities are created or reinforced and then put on display and analyzed, so that the proper treatment or solution can be applied to eradicate them. If their bodies or makeup or clothes are not just right, girls are encouraged to modify them in some way. If a girl has large breasts, she is shown how to play them down. If a girl has short legs, she is taught how to make them look longer. It doesn't matter how it's done, through clothing or exercise, as long as the girl comes out looking the part.

In 2012 the committee did not choose a children's book, which disappointed our local bookstore manager because she said that practically every day someone comes in and requests a children's book related to disability. However they did choose two books for middle school readers. One of the winners, *Close to Famous* by Joan Bauer is about an interracial girl, 12-year-old Foster, and her mother, who leave Memphis in the middle of the night to escape from her mother's abusive

In emphasizing these supposed problems, teen girls are taught to judge themselves and judge themselves harshly by constantly being reminded of who they are not and what they do not have. Good is never good enough.

Occasionally an editor publishes an article that does not promote the ideal image of young beauty, but sending such mixed messages could easily create confusion and frustration for young female readers. For example, one *Seventeen* (2009) article, "My Body Peace Breakthrough," contradicts everything else in the magazine (pp. 102–103). In this article, girls are told to appreciate and be happy with their bodies no matter their shape or size. Television reality star Kim Kardashian, one of several celebrities featured in the article, states, "No matter your size, as long as you're confident and feel comfortable in your own skin, it's okay to be who you are" (p. 103). The piece appears as a tiny glimmer of hope for all those readers who are "different," yet when all the other pictures and advertisements are telling teen girls to change because they are not good enough, the hope gained from one article like this is quickly dashed. And if there were more articles of this type, the magazine would likely be in danger of losing its advertisers.

For educators like myself, keeping hope alive for teen girls is of primary importance, and the antidote I want to offer them can be found in YA literature. Authors like Laurie Halse Anderson take this idea of perfection for girls and turn it in on itself as the female protagonists in such novels as *Speak*, *Prom*, *Catalyst*, and *Wintergirls* strive to be the ideal perfect girl and fail. In this failure, however, the girls come to realize their own potential. As the characters slowly begin to discard their negative images of themselves, they grow empowered, which facilitates positive changes in their lives. While some of the changes are surface level, these are never the ones that bring them happiness; it is the inner transformations that prove most important. Anderson's female protagonists come to believe in who they are, not how others see them, and, in the end, this is what ultimately defines them.

Teen girls need YA literature to help them see beyond the gender roles and expectations exemplified in teen magazines. They need texts that show them possibilities instead of limitations and texts that celebrate uniqueness over conformity. From such readings, a new generation of young women may no longer be afraid of growing up and growing old. They will see the ideal girl for who she really is: a piece of fiction.

Laura Walsh was a high school English teacher for eight years, working in Yigo, Guam, and Mesa, Arizona. She spent an additional six years as the Secondary Language Arts Specialist for the Mesa Public School District. After codirecting several writing projects in the Mesa area and having multiple opportunities to interact with young adult authors, Laura was inspired to obtain her Ph.D., and in 2010 she completed her dissertation entitled, "Get Real, Girl! You'll Never Be Perfect: An Analysis and Comparison of Feminine Identity Construction in Popular Teen Magazines and the Novels of Laurie Halse Anderson." She is currently an Assistant Professor of Secondary Education at the State University of New York in Potsdam.

Laura added in a note that Laurie Halse Anderson is not alone in her development of young adult fiction featuring strong female characters. The following list highlights other YA books with a feminist edge, all of which have been honored in various ways by YALSA (Young Adult Library Services Association) of the American Library Association. Go get 'em, girl!

Ash by Malinda Lo. Little Brown, 2009.

Climbing the Stairs by Padma Venkatraman. Penguin, 2008.

Crossing Stones by Helen Frost. FSG, 2009.

The Disreputable History of Frankie Landau-Banks by E. Lockhart. Hyperion, 2008.

A Great and Terrible Beauty by Libba Bray. Delacorte, 2003.

Magic or Madness by Justine Larbalestier. Razorbill, 2005.

Mare's War by Tanita Davis. Knopf, 2009.

A Northern Light by Jennifer Donnelly. Harcourt, 2003.

The Plain Janes by Cecil Castellucci and Jim Ruggs. DC Comics, 2007.

A Step from Heaven by An Na. Front Street, 2001.

boyfriend. They end up in the small, friendly town of Culpepper, where they find friends and help—even someone who teaches Foster to read. This is the same disability that Doug Swieteck has in *Okay for Now*, one of the 2011 Honor List books.

Wonderstruck: A Novel in Words and Pictures by Brian Selznick was the other winner for middle school readers. It is a magical book, with one of the characters being deaf, and is written and illustrated in the style of Selznik's prize-winning

The Invention of Hugo Cabret. The 2012 winner for the teen category is Wendelin Van Draanen's *The Running Dream,* about a girl named Jessica whose passion in life is running. But then she is in an accident and one of her legs has to be amputated. She almost wishes she had been killed in the accident, but gradually changes her mind.

Devising happy, or at least hopeful, endings for tragic stories is a challenge for authors. Even a good book such as Laurie Halse Anderson's 1999 *Speak,* which was a finalist for the National Book Award and a Printz Honor Book, has a coincidence at the very end that for some readers stretched believability. Thirteen-year-old Melinda is raped at a summer party. When she calls the police, who come and break up the party, she becomes a social outcast. No one knows why she called the police, and out of shame she hides behind silence for almost a whole year. Finally, a wonderful art teacher helps her not only to "speak," but to speak about the incident. The boy who raped her is furious and vengeful. He stalks her and after school one day pulls her into a janitor's closet and slams the door. She is saved from a severe beating or another rape—if not death—by her own efforts, including cries for help, and the arrival of the girls' lacrosse team. They are coming in from the field and when they hear Melinda, they pound with their sticks on the closet door, calling for additional help.

Another challenge for writers of problem novels is that they most often write the books in first person. Thoughtful readers must surely question how these malfunctioning and troubled kids can write so well. In A. M. Jenkins's *Out of Order,* Colt, who is a star baseball player, tells the story of his senior year in high school. The story is beautifully written, but Colt's main problem is that he has little interest and little aptitude for academics. Readers have to enter into a willing suspension of disbelief when they compare the pitiful essay he wrote for his English class with the rest of the beautifully written book.

What Are the Problems?

The best authors treat candidly and with respect problems that belong specifically to young adults in today's world. Many of the problems that go along with modern adolescence did not exist in the nineteenth century, so at least in this one area there is ample justification for books directed specifically to youthful audiences, as in several of the new books mentioned in Chapter 1, such as Patricia McCormick's *Sold* about sexual trafficking of young girls in India, Allan Stratton's *Chanda's Secrets* about the tragedies connected to AIDS in Africa, and Pete Hautman's *Godless* about questions connected to organized religion.

If authors have a teaching goal when they are creating problem novels, it is probably to help young readers develop an internal locus of control through which they assume that their own actions and characteristics will shape their lives. They ask the question, "What am I going to do with my life?" while people with an external locus of control depend on luck, chance, or what others do. Their major life question is "What will happen to me?"

Although we all know adults who blame others for whatever happens to them, most of us would agree that we want to help young people feel responsible for their own lives. Books cannot substitute for real-life experiences, and one or two books, no matter how well written, are not enough to change a teenager's view of life. Skilled authors, however, can show what is going on in characters' minds, whereas cameras can show only what is externally visible. The title of Laurie Halse Anderson's *Catalyst* hints at the idea that what happens from outside can trigger changes, but the changes actually come from within. *Catalyst* is the story of Kate Malone, who, through her minister father, becomes involved with Terri, a classmate who has been touched by the severe problems of incest, pregnancy, abuse, and mental illness. Kate is on the track team and the honor roll, and when the book opens her main concern is whether she will be admitted to MIT, the only college she has applied to. Anderson's thought-provoking character study shows how experiences can trigger changes, but it is Kate who is responsible for the growth that allows those changes.

Other examples include Janet McDonald's *Spellbound*, in which a teenage mother who lives in the projects decides to turn her life around by studying for a spelling bee and getting in line for a program that might lead to a college scholarship. Ruth White's *Tadpole* is set in Appalachia in the 1950s. It is the story of a thirteen-year-old orphan and the effect he has on his four cousins and their mother when he seeks them out as a refuge from an uncle who beats him and uses him as free labor. Sometimes, in spite of all the protagonist does, help is still needed, as in Kimberly Willis Holt's *Keeper of the Night*. When thirteen-year-old Isabel Moreno's mother commits suicide, Isabel struggles to care for her seven-year-old sister and her twelve-year-old brother. The story is set in Guam and there are some interesting cultural differences, one of which is Aunt Bernadette, who is a traditional healer. Isabel does not take as much help from her as she might because she is determined to prove that she is stronger than her mother. Isabel's grief-stricken father avoids the family problems by spending long hours on his fishing boat, but after the brother collapses, Isabel and her family get some of the help they need.

Peer Groups

Peer groups become increasingly important to teenagers as they move beyond social and emotional dependence on their parents. By becoming part of a group, clique, or gang, teenagers take a step toward emotional independence. Even though they are not making truly independent decisions, as parts of different groups they try out various roles, ranging from conformist to nonconformist and from follower to leader. Young adult literature can extend the peer group by giving teenagers a chance to participate vicariously in more personal relationships than are possible for most youngsters in the relatively short time that they spend in high school. When they were children, parents were responsible for locating in the "right" neighborhood near "good schools," so that children had no reason to give particular thoughts to differences in social and economic classes or ethnic backgrounds. Then quite suddenly their environments are expanded, not only through larger, more diverse schools but also through jobs, extracurricular activities, public entertainment, shopping in malls, and church or community activities.

While high school students have always known that some of their fellow students were truly scary, the Columbine tragedy forced adults to pay attention to a problem that many of us had preferred to ignore. Tackling the problem in 1974 of school bullies and peer pressure was what made Robert Cormier's *The Chocolate War* so unusual for its time. When Cormier was asked at a meeting of English teachers about the changing nature of school violence now that kids were bringing guns to school, he sadly admitted that he was as troubled as everyone else. However, one of the teachers in the group pointed out that it is actually the beginnings of the alienation and the hostility that are interesting. The simplest of video games can show people getting shot, but it takes great literature to help people understand the intensity of the emotions that might trigger such actions.

Today, virtually everyone is aware that tough kids, mean kids, frightened kids, and plain old nutty kids are "out there," but we are still unsure about what to do. The increased awareness of the problem and the formation of school policies and procedures to deal with incidents may help. Recommended books include Meline Kevorkian's *Preventing Bullying: Helping Kids Form Positive Relationships* (Rowman & Littlefield, 2006). *Bullying Prevention and Intervention: Realistic Strategies for Schools* by Susan M. Swearer, Dorothey L. Esrelage, and Scott A. Napoli (The Guilford Practical Intervention in Schools Series, 2009), and for teachers working with younger students, *No Kidding about Bullying: 125 Ready-to-Use Activities to Help Kids Manage Anger, Resolve Conflicts, Build Empathy and Get Along* by Naomi Drew (Free Spirits Press, 2010).

Although Louis Sachar's 2006 *Small Steps* is not the great book that *Holes* is, it nevertheless does a good job of illustrating different kids in different situations taking on the responsibility of making their own decisions. It is a follow-up or companion book to *Holes* with the focus being on Armpit and X-Ray, two of the boys from Camp Green Lake, who are back home living in Austin, Texas. Armpit has a job (putting in irrigation pipes for a lawn service company) and is going to school and being friends with a ten-year-old disabled

Few areas of teen culture have changed as much as has the concept of family and what it means. See Focus Box 4.5 on p. 128 for explorations of contemporary "Family Ties."

Focus Box 4.4

Buddies and Bullies

Big Mouth and Ugly Girl by Joyce Carol Oates. HarperCollins, 2002. Popular Matt Donaghy says something in the school cafeteria that is interpreted as a threat to school safety. He is ostracized, except by Ugly Girl Ursula Riggs, who knows a thing or two about being on the outside.

Bluefish by Pat Schmatz. Candlewick, 2011. Middle school readers are most likely to appreciate this story that has a hint of romance, but starts with the new boy in school helping a student who is being bullied and thereby adding to his own problems.

Boys Lie by John Neufeld. DK, Ink, 1999. Gina is traumatized by being sexually assaulted in a New York swimming pool. Rumors follow her to California where her family moves to help her start over.

Buddha Boy by Kathe Koja. Farrar, Straus & Giroux, 2003. This book would be way too grim if not for the friendship that develops between Justin and the very different Jinsen, the Buddha Boy of the title, who is victimized by most kids at school.

Fat Kid Rules the World by K. L. Going. Putnam, 2003. Troy Billings weighs nearly three hundred pounds and is contemplating jumping off a subway platform. To his surprise, he is stopped by a punk-rock guitarist and occasional fellow student from W. T. Watson High School. And so begins a strange friendship.

Freak Show by James St. James. Dutton, 2007. Billy calls himself a "Gender Obscurist," even though other people at the Eisenhower Academy are more direct. Reviewers used such adjectives as "fast-paced," "snarky," and "playfully naughty" for this story about a queen who turns things upside down by running for Homecoming Queen.

Friction by E. R. Frank. Simon & Schuster, 2003. Stacy enters the eighth grade at Forest Alternative School and disproves the stereotype that it is always the newcomer who gets bullied. She also demonstrates that bullying can be done through words as well as actions.

Hate List by Jennifer Brown. Little Brown, 2009. Two teens, who have been bullied decide to compose lists of their enemies. Valerie makes the list almost as a game just going along with her boyfriend, Nick, but he is deadly serious. Readers come away with a new appreciation for the ripple effect of bullying.

Leap of Faith by Kimberly Brubaker Bradley. Dial, 2007. An extra bonus to this story about a sixth-grade girl who pulls a pocketknife on a boy who has been sexually harassing her is that the author follows the girl into a Catholic school and an exploration of both the comfort and the questions that this new experience brings to a girl who has been raised in a nonreligious family.

The Nine Lives of Travis Keating by Jill MacLean. Fitzhenry and Whiteside, 2008. When Travis moves to a small town, he becomes the latest victim of the school bully; nevertheless, he takes on the difficult task of caring for a group of feral cats.

Touching Spirit Bear by Ben Mikaelsen. HarperCollins, 2001. Cole Matthews is a street-wise bully who permanently damages a classmate in a beating. He chooses to participate in Circle Justice, an alternative program for Native American offenders, because he mistakenly thinks he can outsmart the system.

Who the Man by Chris Lynch. HarperCollins, 2002. An alternate title might be *A Week in the Life of a Thirteen-Year-Old Bully*. Lynch does an excellent job of characterization, and by the end even Earl (the thirteen-year-old bully) has a bit more understanding of what drives him.

girl who lives next door. X-Ray hangs around trying to involve Armpit in a get-rich-quick scheme photocopying and selling concert tickets. Through some rather unlikely events, Armpit becomes friends with singer Kaira DeLeon and through his experiences with her learns that not even the rich and talented are immune from bullies and frauds. Focus Box 4.4, "Buddies and Bullies," has other examples as well.

Between Mom and Jo **by Julie Anne Peters. Little, Brown, 2006.** A boy has two mothers and when they decide to separate, the boy (Nicholas Nathaniel Thomas Tyler) goes through all the pain normally associated with a family breakup. However, since he is biologically related to only one of his mothers, there are extra problems.

Confessions of the Sullivan Sisters **by Natalie Standiford. Scholastic, 2010.** A family hopes for an inheritance from their wealthy grandmother, but she has been offended by someone in the family. Each of the sisters writes a confessional letter telling about something they need to be forgiven for. There is an unexpected ending.

How to Save a Life **by Sara Zarr. Little, Brown, 2011.** How would most teenage girls feel if their widowed mother unexpectedly takes in an abused, pregnant, and confused teen, with the idea of adopting the girl's baby. This is all too much for high school senior Jill, who is still grieving the loss of her father.

King of the Screwups **by K. L. Going. Houghton Mifflin, 2009.** Liam is kicked out of his house by his father and goes to live upstate with his uncle, who is gay, and his partner. Liam has always called his uncle "Aunt Pete" and is not exactly thrilled at his new living situation, but some good things come out of it.

Looking for JJ **by Anne Cassidy. Harcourt, 2007.** Alice Tully is seventeen and has been given a new identity and a new chance in life. Her troubles started in her childhood when she alternated between living with a resentful grandmother and following her emotionally disconnected and transient mother. Even with all the new chances, her old life when she was Jennifer Jones, or JJ, keeps intruding.

One Crazy Summer **by Rita Williams-Garcia. HarperCollins, 2010.** Set in the late 1960s, three sisters are sent to spend a month with their "hippie" mother in Oakland, California, where she's involved with the Black Panthers and their protests. As one reviewer predicted, "Readers will fall in love with these self-possessed siblings, even if their mother doesn't."

Pregnant Pause **by Han Nolan. Houghton Harcourt, 2011.** Sixteen-year-old Eleanor hastily marries her boyfriend because she is seven months pregnant. Her own parents go off to Kenya to do missionary work and she is left living with her unsympathetic inlaws who run a camp for overweight kids. Eleanor's spunky personality saves the story from being overly grim, while still presenting a picture of the complications of teen motherhood.

Saving Francesca **by Melina Marchetta. Knopf/ Borzoi, 2004.** Francesca's mother, who used to be strong and successful, is so depressed that she cannot function and so Francesca has little help from home when she changes schools and experiences her first romance. Nevertheless, readers come away feeling optimistic for Francesca.

Street Pharm **by Allison Van Diepen. Simon Pulse, 2011.** When seventeen-year-old Ty Johnson's father is arrested, Ty is expected to carry on the family business of selling drugs in Brooklyn, a job that he succeeds at. A *VOYA* reviewer liked the way the book shows that using drugs is a choice, but the choice is lots more complicated for some teens than for others.

Sucker Punch **by David Hernandez. HarperTeen, 2008.** In this edgy novel, Marcus wants to get even with his father for beating on his little brother, Enrique. A *VOYA* reviewer warned that "Marcus's loyalty to Enrique is admirable, but we fear he's going about it the wrong way." She adds that it is "raw and profane."

Tyrell **by Coe Booth. Scholastic/Push, 2006.** Booth said that she wrote this book in a language that she thought would resonate with her younger brother and his friends. Booth used to be a New York City social worker often called in for emergencies so she knows the kinds of situations that she writes about in this vibrant problem novel.

Waiting for Normal **by Leslie Connor. HarperCollins, 2008.** Addie is left alone to cope with an increasingly problematic mother. Addie misses her caring stepfather when he goes off with her half-sisters, but thanks to his help and her own resilience, she manages.

Family Relationships

Michael Cart says, in the introduction to his book *Necessary Noise*, that what is needed is something that will help "kids who are living outside the mainstream in radically nontraditional families deal with their circumstances—circumstances that often result in their being marginalized, rendered invisible, regarded as unacceptably different, or even being persecuted by peers." And equally important is helping "mainstream kids begin to comprehend—intellectually and emotionally—the dramatic differences that now define the daily lives of so many other teens. Kids need to learn empathy. They need to learn how the other can become us." One approach, he thinks, "is through reading fiction that captures—artfully, authentically, and unsparingly—the circumstances of kids" whose lives are different. See Focus Box 4.5, "Family Ties," for books whose authors are trying to do this.

For his *Necessary Noise* collection of short stories, Cart asked leading YA authors to contribute stories that would illustrate the importance of dialogue and discussion, of talking about our circumstances, of leaving room, in short, "for some necessary noise." In his introduction, he comments on all the changes in "family" that have come about since he grew up in the 1950s' world of *Ozzie and Harriet*, *Father Knows Best*, and *Leave It to Beaver*. Well into the 1970s, 45 percent of American households were headed by a husband and a wife living together with their offspring. Today that is true for only 24 percent of U.S. households. Some of the reasons include changing attitudes toward same-sex parents, less restrictive rules on who can be foster parents, and new immigration patterns that have resulted in many partial families or people with different ideas of "family" coming to the United States.

A look at mythology, folklore, and classical and religious literature shows that stories featuring inadequate or absent parents appeal to young readers because they provide opportunities for the protagonists to assert their independence and prove that they can take care of themselves. Nevertheless, in real life, most kids want to be closer to their parents than they are. A news story in July 2003 reported that 75 percent of the nearly 1,500 teenagers contacted in a national survey really liked their parents and wanted to have more to do with them. Still, in many young adult novels, good relationships between teenagers and their parents are the exception. If they are there, the focus is more likely to be on one than on both parents, as in Virginia Euwer Wolff's *Make Lemonade* and *True Believer*, in which LaVaughn's mother is a pillar of common sense. In Paul Fleischman's *Seek*, Rob puts tremendous importance on the family he has grown up in while still wanting to find the father he has never known. In Carolyn Coman's *Many Stones*, Berry's father is wise and generous as he plans a trip to help both himself and Berry come to terms with the death of older daughter/sister Laura. The emphasis on relating mainly to one parent is not so much a reflection of real life as of the literary limitations of not crowding stories with more characters than readers can relate to.

Of course, with the problem novel, just as with today's news stories, the focus is going to be on the more dramatic stories about family relationships, as in

Will Weaver's *Claws*. The story starts with a description of the "perfect" life of Jed Berg, the top player on the school's tennis team. He has a popular girlfriend, is an honors student, and is the son of adoring and successful parents. His father is an architect and his mother an attorney. Then Jed receives an email from a girl asking Jed to confront his father about the affair he is having with the girl's mother. This is the beginning of what a caustic classmate describes as the fun of watching a preppie "in a downward spiral." See Focus Box 4.5, "Family Ties," for other examples that support the old saying that troubled families are all dysfunctional in their own ways.

One of the freshest books about family relationships is Christopher Paul Curtis's *Bucking the Sarge*. Fifteen-year-old Luther T. Farrell is stuck working for his mother, "The Sarge." She is a scheming, huckster-type landlady in Flint, Michigan. She runs Happy Neighbor Group Homes where she cheats on the food and the clothes she is supposed to buy for the residents, several of whom are elderly men that Luther has to take care of, including driving them around in a pretty cool van. He doesn't get much pleasure from the van since it's always for "business," and his driver's license is a fake, so he's nervous.

Living in a Multicultural World

Kids are probably more aware than are their parents of changing demographics. During the 1970s when the parents of today's teenagers were in school, 4.7 percent of Americans were foreign born. A *Wall Street Journal* article on "Immigrant Impact" said that in 1990 the figure was 8.6 percent, while in 2040 it is predicted to be 14.2 percent. Today's immigrants are primarily Asian or Hispanic, with increasing numbers coming from the Middle East. By the year 2020, the fastest-growing segment of the population will be the very old—those over age eighty. Marriage is being postponed or not even considered, and over 25 percent of new births are occurring outside of marriage. The population is being divided into extremes, with the middle class

A big change in recent YA books is that they are no longer as segregated as they used to be. Authors are writing about protagonists interacting from a wide spectrum of ethnic and cultural backgrounds. See Focus Box 4.6, "Looking through Different Lenses," on p. 132 for some recommended examples.

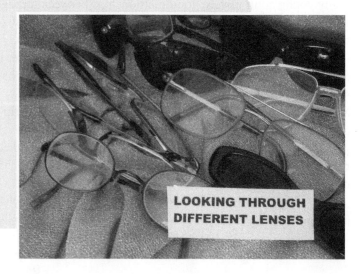

LOOKING THROUGH DIFFERENT LENSES

shrinking and the numbers growing for those in "permanent" poverty and "permanent" affluence.

Many people find these changes threatening. One result has been an increase in incidents of racism on high school and college campuses. While those are the incidents that grab public attention, there have also been many incidents showing the development of friendship and understanding across cultural and ethnic lines. See Focus Box 4.6, "Looking through Different Lenses." These are powerful books because they explore the edges where young people brush up against values and practices different from their own.

Gary Schmidt's *Trouble* tells the story of how Henry's older brother is critically injured in a hit-and-run accident. After he dies, Henry is embittered, but sets out to climb Mt. Karahdin in Maine, just as he and his brother had planned to do. The driver of the pick-up truck that was hit in the accident was a Cambodian classmate, a fact that Schmidt weaves into Henry's grieving process as he asks himself many different questions about race relations and family secrets.

Among the most critically acclaimed books of the 1960s and 1970s were Eldridge Cleaver's *Soul on Ice*, William H. Armstrong's *Sounder*, Maya Angelou's *I Know Why the Caged Bird Sings*, Sharon Bell Mathis's *Teacup Full of Roses*, Alice Childress's *A Hero Ain't Nothin' but a Sandwich*, and Rosa Guy's *The Friends*. As powerful as these books were, they had a grimness to them, and the protagonists were mostly segregated from mainstream culture. It is refreshing today to have books in which a variety of characters from different backgrounds face problems by working together.

Cynthia Kadohata's *Weedflower* reveals a three-way relationship among Japanese families being sent to internment camps just before World War II, their "American" neighbors, and the Native Americans who manage the Poston Internment Camp where Sumiko's family is sent. This is the camp where Kadohata's father was sent and so she relates to it in a special way even though her story is fictional. Several internment camps were placed on Indian reservations, but only at Poston were the Indians in charge.

Within a few days of being at the camp, Sumiko makes friends with a girl named Sachi, and together they go to look at the bean fields, which have been planted by people who arrived at the camp earlier. The green foliage is like a miracle in the dry desert. Suddenly Sachi hisses, "Shh! Hide!" Three Indian boys are also exploring the bean field, and Sachi explains that "they're not supposed to be in our camp. If they catch us, we'll get scalped. . . . After they scalp us, they'll cut off our fingers and boil them."

Then, the girls hear a rattlesnake. Sachi screams and runs, but Sumiko trips on the vines and finds herself sitting "on her rear end a foot from the snake," which rises into the air and hisses. A calm voice says, "Walk back slowly. *Slowly.* It doesn't want to hurt you," and someone from behind lifts her onto her feet and partly walks/drags her backward.

This is Sumiko's introduction to a boy called Frank. Over the months that Sumiko is in the camp, she and Frank slowly develop a kind of respectful friendship, which on the day she leaves he acknowledges by sharing with her his "Indian" name of "Huulus, which means 'lightning.'"

A multicultural book that older teens are reading is Khaled Hosseini's *The Kite Runner*, a book written by a young American immigrant from Afghanistan. It was

The Arrival by Shaun Tan. Scholastic, 2007. In this unusual graphic novel, which is wordless except for an invented alphabet, Tan uses sepia drawings to depict the emotions and the challenges faced by a man bringing his family to a new country. While there is a sense of fear, there is also a sense of warmth and caring for others.

Bat 6 by Virginia Euwer Wolff. Scholastic, 1998. World War II has been over for nearly four years, but pockets of prejudice are very much alive in the towns of Barlow and Bear Creek Ridge in rural Oregon. People choose not to notice until the prejudice erupts during the annual Bat 6 girls' softball championship.

Bone by Bone by Bone by Tony Johnston. Roaring Brook, 2007. Set in the 1950s in small-town Tennessee, this haunting novel tells about the friendship of two boys, white David, age nine, and black Malcolm, age eight. Readers will be left with a deeper understanding of how far we've come.

Draw the Dark by Ilsa J. Bick. Carolrhoda, 2010. Perhaps this should go in fantasy because of the way that Christian is able to draw out the collective bad memories of his town and its Nazi past.

Esperanza Rising by Pam Muñoz Ryan. Scholastic, 2000. Ryan's engaging novel about how her Mexican family became Americans is both joyous and lyrical. A *Publisher's Weekly* reviewer noted that only by the end of the story do readers recognize how carefully "Abuelita's pearls of wisdom" have been strung.

Long Powwow Nights by David Bouchard and Pam Aleekuk. Red Deer Press, 2009. This is more of an informational book than one with a fictional plot, but it does a good job of showing intergenerational and group connections through music, poetry, and art.

Mister Pip by Lloyd Jones. Dial, 2007. In the early 1990s there's a civil war on the island community of Bougainville. Thanks to one white teacher who stays because he's married to one of the natives,

thirteen-year-old Matilda is in love with Charles Dickens's *Great Expectations,* but even this contributes to misunderstandings.

Paper Covers Rock by Jenny Hubbard. Delacorte, 2011. Two boys at boarding school in the 1980s witness the drowning of a friend. The three had been drinking and jumping into a dangerous river. When the boys are questioned, they fear they will be expelled and so they lie about the situation, and negatively involve a teacher who has befriended them. This might be a good book to read alongside John Knowles's 1961 *A Separate Peace.*

Seedfolks by Paul Fleischman. HarperCollins, 1997. Fleischman traces the sprouting of the Bigg Street community garden in inner city Cleveland through the voices of thirteen young and old neighbors—Mexican, Haitian, Black, Vietnamese, Korean, British, Guatemalan, Rumanian, Indian, and Polish.

Tasting the Sky: A Palestinian Childhood by Ibtisam Barakat. Farrar, 2007. Barakat was three years old in 1967 when her family fled their home as the six-day war broke out. She now lives in the United States and tells her story through childhood memories, which are being praised for their power and at the same time for their lack of sentimentality and exploitation.

When the Black Girl Sings by Bill Wright. Simon & Schuster, 2007. Lahni is African American and has been adopted by white parents. She feels awkward being the only African American girl in her exclusive girl's school, but then her mother takes her to an interracial church where she learns to make her own music.

You Against Me by Jenny Downham. Random/David Fickling, 2011. The story of two star-crossed lovers is almost hidden behind the terrible problems of their respective families. Nevertheless, the honesty of the story is so touching that readers will come away feeling as though they want to jump in and help Mikey and Ellie.

published in 2003 as a book for general audiences. Even though it is fiction, readers can't help but believe that much of it is autobiographical as Hosseini writes about a young boy living in Kabul during the 1960s and 1970s and watching and adjusting to the changes that came to his country. The Nilsen family lived in Afghanistan between 1967 and 1969 and so, of course, we found the book especially meaningful because it was set at about the same time we were there. But Hosseini is such a good writer that as we listened to a recorded version of the book, we had in our minds vivid mental images from both California and Afghanistan. That the book was made into a movie also helped promote its reading by young adults.

It is expecting too much from any one book to think that its reading will change a bigoted bully into a sensitive and loving individual. However, for the majority of young readers such books can serve as conversation starters and as ways to focus needed attention on matters of hostility related to racial, ethnic, and class differences. It is good that some authors prefer to focus on the similarities among all people rather than on differences between particular groups. For example, African American author Lorenz Graham is quoted in Anne Commire's *Something about the Author* Vol. 1 as saying

> My personal problem with publishers has been the difference between my image and theirs. Publishers have told me that my characters, African and Negro, are "too much like white people." And I say, "If you look closely, you will see that people are people." (p. 123)

Jamake Highwater expresses a counterbalancing view in his book *Many Smokes, Many Moons*:

> In the process of trying to unify the world we must be exceedingly careful not to destroy the diversity of the many cultures of man that give human life meaning, focus, and vitality. . . . Today we are beginning to look into the ideas of groups outside the dominant culture, and we are finding different kinds of "truth" that make the world we live in far bigger than we ever dreamed it could be—for the greatest distance between people is not geographical space but culture.

Teachers, librarians, and reviewers should not present and discuss any single book as if it represents the African American point of view or the Asian American point of view. Adults need to help young readers realize that there are many points of view. This concept is further discussed in Chapter 10, along with the increased willingness of today's teenagers to read about protagonists in countries other than the United States.

The Physical Body

Among the books listed in Focus Box 4.3, "Challenges: Physical and Mental," are several relating to sex, but we do not wish to imply that we consider the whole matter of sex to be a problem. We realize that sex also has something to do with the books in Focus Box 4.2, "Love and Friendship" (on p. 109). In trying to satisfy their curiosity, teenagers seek out and read vivid descriptions of sexual activities, as was hinted at when we took a survey for the last edition of this textbook. When we asked what students looked for in picking out magazines, many girls said they picked magazines for the "fine boys," while the boys said they picked their magazines to "learn about and talk about girls."

In the first edition of this textbook, we wrote that the three sexual issues treated in problem novels were rape, pregnancy, and homosexuality. We stand corrected by a reader who wrote to us and made the persuasive point that homosexuality is not a problem. The problem is homophobia. (See the discussion on this matter in Chapter 9, p. 307.) In addition to these concerns, we now see problem novels treating disease, incest, and child abuse, and, in a big change, we also see teen protagonists being written about as parents. In the earlier books, pregnant girls had an abortion, as in Paul Zindel's *My Darling, My Hamburger*; the baby died, as in Ann Head's *Mr. and Mrs. Bo Jo Jones*; or the baby was given up for adoption, as in Richard Peck's *Don't Look and It Won't Hurt*. In today's books the babies actually appear, as in the highly acclaimed *Make Lemonade* by Virginia Euwer Wolff, *Gypsy Davey* by Chris Lynch, and *Like Sisters on the Homefront* by Rita Williams-Garcia. In *Hanging on to Max* by Margaret Bechard, seventeen-year-old Sam is a single parent struggling to keep his infant son. A May 2007 *School Library Journal* reviewer praised the book because "In a world where much of YA literature is fraught with noir plots peopled with dysfunctional characters caught in tragic situations, *Hanging on to Max* is a breath of fresh air." It is a book "peopled with human beings all struggling to make their lives work." One of these people is Sam's father who agrees to support Sam and Max for one year if Sam will stay in high school and graduate.

One reason that we refer to the problems that are the topics of the books in Focus Box 4.3 as both physical and mental is that the two usually go together. In any area of life, it is hardly possible for someone to have a severe physical problem without also having an accompanying emotional problem. A vivid example is Priscilla Cummings's *A Face First*. It tells the story of twelve-year-old Kelley waking up from her affluent and "beautiful people" world to a Baltimore hospital's burn unit. She has been in a horrific automobile accident and fire, and experts are working to peel off the skin that melted, along with her earrings. Even worse than the pain and the physical therapy is the day when a clear mask is strapped onto her ruined face. In shock and depression, she ceases all human communication. But finally, she starts her long road to emotional recovery when she empathizes with a crying baby who is brought into the burn unit.

We had a different kind of illustration of the connections between physical and emotional problems several years ago when Paul Zindel visited us in Arizona. He commented on how surprised he was that next to *The Pigman*, his most popular book was *My Darling, My Hamburger*, which is about pregnancy and abortion. Soon after the book was published in 1969, a Supreme Court decision made most abortions legal, and Zindel thought that would be the end of all sales because his book would seem terribly old-fashioned. It did not turn out that way, however, because rather than settling the issue, the legalization of abortions increased interest in the moral and psychological aspects of the problem. Decision making was passed from the courts to every female with an unwanted pregnancy. It is not only the girl herself who is involved in making a decision, but also the woman's parents, the father of the baby, the teachers and counselors at school, and anyone else closely connected to the father, the grandparents, and the friends.

To introduce a thematic unit dealing with physical challenges, teachers might want to read aloud a couple of the short stories from Don Gallo's 2010 edited collection *Owning It: Stories about Teens with Disabilities*. The disabilities range from asthma to Tourette's syndrome and cancer. Ron Koertge's *Stoner and Spaz,* winner of the 2003 Pen Center Literary Award, might also be good to bring into class because of the way it asks questions about the language we use when talking about disabilities. On the first page the protagonist, Ben Bancroft, who has cerebral palsy, goes up to buy a movie ticket and "jokes," "Since it's Monster Week, do I get a discount?" The book was reissued with a new cover in 2011, along with a sequel, *Now Playing: Stoner & Spaz II.*

Modern Tragedies and Magical Realism

A truly tragic story is Laurie Halse Anderson's 2009 *Wintergirls.* When best-friends-for-life Cassie and Lia first meet in third grade, Cassie shows Lia her most treasured possession, a round disc of green sea-glass. Cassie claims it is not *sea-glass* but *see-glass* because it had not been formed in the sea but forged inside a volcano. If they look through it at the right time and study the stars they can see their futures: "Poet, Acrobat, Engineer, Friend, Guardian, Avenging Whirlwind." The possibilities are limitless and wonderful. Little do they know that by their senior year, Cassie's self-destructive behavior will lead to her death, and Lia will be on the verge of meeting the same fate, both victims of anorexia.

As the story opens, Cassie has been found dead in a motel room. The confidential autopsy determines her cause of death as kidney failure and a ruptured esophagus, probably from years of forced vomiting and an inadequate intake of healing nutrients. There are flashbacks to eighth grade, and to fifth grade, and to the first time the girls were left to their own devices on a New Year's Eve. They get drunk on nonalcoholic champagne laced with vodka and swear a blood oath to become the skinniest girls in school.

Anderson's writing surpasses anything she's done before, and that is no small feat. She experiments with writing techniques such as inserting the number of calories in parentheses whenever a piece of food is mentioned and by having Lia write what she really thinks and then crossing it out in favor of what she actually

People have always read sad books about people dying, but the difference today is that these books are written specifically for young readers, rather than for adults. See Focus Box 4.7, "Death and Grieving," on p. 136 for good examples.

***Beautiful Malice* by Rebecca James. Random House, 2010.** Katherine's sister is brutally murdered and Katherine tries to get away from the awfulness of the event by changing schools and using her mother's maiden name. Katherine isn't really connecting until she meets Alice, a charismatic girl whose attitudes and behaviors will worry readers, who by now are cheering for Katherine's recovery.

***Before I Die* by Jenny Downham. Random/David Fickling, 2007.** Sixteen-year-old Tessa has only a few months to live and she sorrowfully tries to cram in all the life experiences that she's not going to have. Except for the plot, this touching book has little in common with the 2007 *Bucket List* film starring Jack Nicholson and Morgan Freeman.

***A Brief Chapter in My Impossible Life* by Dana Reinhardt. Random, 2006.** A sixteen-year-old girl has always known she was adopted, but hasn't thought much about it. Then her birth mother calls and wants to meet her. Everything changes when she learns that the woman is dying.

***Cures for Heartbreak* by Margo Rabb. Delacorte, 2007.** A bonus for readers is the touching afterword that tells how closely this sad story follows the real events of the author's teenage years when she lost her mother to cancer and her father developed heart trouble. A vibrant New York City setting, flashes of dark humor, and beautiful characterization make this a wonderful read for older teens.

***Double Helix: A Novel* by Nancy Werlin. Dial, 2004.** Eli Samuels is about to lose his mother to Huntington's Disease, but this is just the background for Werlin's mystery. Eli goes to work for Wyatt Transgenics Lab and gradually discovers why his father doesn't want him to work there. Werlin brings up some intriguing bioethical issues.

***Ghost Girl: A Blue Ridge Mountain Story* by Delia Ray. Clarion, 2003.** It's the 1930s and pale April Sloane with her white-blonde hair and her light blue eyes feels like a ghost, especially since the death of her younger brother a year ago. Her mother has fallen into a deep depression and it's pretty much up to April to pull herself out of her problems.

***Green Angel* by Alice Hoffman. Scholastic, 2003.** Mature readers will grieve with the fifteen-year-old girl who is now ashamed of her sullen behavior when she didn't get to go with her parents and sister to the city. They never came back.

***Hothouse* by Chris Lynch. HarperTeen, 2010.** Two firemen are killed while fighting a blaze. Their sons bond over the tragedy and join the community in honoring their fathers as heroes, but then an investigation indicates that the men had been drinking alcohol and using drugs, and suddenly the town's emotions change. The boys are left to cope with this awful news.

***The Key to the Golden Firebird: A Novel* by Maureen Johnson. HarperCollins, 2004.** After their father's death, three sisters—sensible May, frightened Palmer, and rebellious Brooks—are left pretty much on their own while their mother works to provide financial support. Their father's Pontiac Firebird helps each one heal in her own way.

***The Probability of Miracles* by Wendy Wunder. Penguin/Razorbill, 2011.** A high school senior has been battling cancer for seven years and during spring break is told that the doctors have done all they can do. An *SLJ* reviewer wrote that Wunder's book is not "your typical teenage fatal disease, let's make-the-most-of-my-last-summer novel." Instead it's playful and a little bit kooky.

***Strays* by Ron Koertge. Candlewick, 2007.** Fifteen-year-old Ted O'Connor would rather communicate with animals than people. His situation is understandable in that he worked in his parents' pet store until they were killed in an accident and he was placed in an inappropriate foster home. But in a basically optimistic book, Ted gradually learns that he doesn't have to be a "stray."

***Under the Mesquite* by Guadalup Garcia McCall. Lee & Low, 2011.** In this winner of the Pura Belpré Award, fourteen-year-old Lupita is the oldest child in a Mexican American family when her mother dies from cancer. The autobiographical story is beautifully told in free verse poetry.

***White Crow* by Marcus Sedgwick. Roaring Brook, 2011.** Unlike most of the books in this list, *White Crow* is a mysterious and chilling adventure tale exploring the age-old question of what awaits us after death.

says. Readers get both versions because the crossed-out text stays in the book. Just before Cassie died, she had phoned Lia but Lia had not picked up. Instead she had turned off her phone and gone back to sleep. In the morning she checks her phone and finds thirty-three calls from Cassie, who by now is dead. The number thirty-three haunts Lia as does her long-ago promise to Cassie that they will do everything together.

This is where magical realism comes into the story with Cassie appearing to Lia and the two of them arguing over what Cassie should do. Death, and survivors' reactions to death, are prominently featured in the works in Focus Box 4.7, "Death and Grieving."

Magical Realism

Magical realism is what it says it is. It is *realism,* but it is also *magical.* It has been a common device in Spanish novels at least since the 1500s when Cervantes used it in *Don Quixote.* It is one of the techniques from his Spanish heritage that Rudolfo Anaya used when he wrote *Bless Me, Ultima.* John Nichols used it in *The Milagro Beanfield War* (*milagro* is the Spanish word for "miracle"). It is also commonly used in both Native American and African American literature when animals take on speaking roles and when characters find themselves consulting with ancestors.

One of the reasons that contemporary writers incorporate magical realism in some of their saddest or grimmest stories is that they need a way to pull the reader out of the depression caused by the tragedy of the story. A. S. King's 2010 *Please Ignore Vera Dietz* is such a sad story that we mentally classified it as a "Worst Case" scenario. Yet it is softened—at least a bit—by the fact that some of the necessary back stories are told by the pagoda in the local park, a structure surviving from more prosperous and supposedly happier times.

Jewell Parker Rhodes's realistic book for middle-school readers, *Ninth Ward,* is a moving retelling of the experience of one New Orleans family during Hurricane Katrina. Laneshsa has lived with Mama Ya-Ya (her grandmother) her whole life. When the hurricane comes, Laneshsa and Mama Ya-Ya remain in their home, but are forced to move higher and higher as the water rises. They are joined by a young neighbor, TaShon, who got separated from his family. One of the beautiful descriptions in the book is of Grandma Ya-Ya's voodoo offering sitting on her dresser, right beside her Catholic rosary. This is in the upstairs bedroom, where elderly Grandma Ya-Ya goes to bed and stays as it becomes apparent that they are all going to drown. As the water fills the upstairs and the attic, Lanesha and TaShon climb out onto the roof and receive magical help to get into an empty boat that floats into their vicinity. Lanesha believes the help came from the ghost of her mother, someone she knew only through what Grandma Ya-Ya had told her. Readers agree that a miracle has occurred, but Rhodes leaves it to her readers to decide just who or what should get the credit.

Many of the most respected authors of the *new realism* that made such big news in the 1970s were also among the earliest writers to dabble in magical realism. Robert Cormier in his 1988 *Fade* wrote about the struggles of young Paul Moreaux,

In 1994 when Joan Bauer and Paul Zindel were on a panel about creating humor, Bauer was shocked when Zindel pulled out a very real looking—but actually fake—rat which he used as a visual aid to explain connections between humor, shock, and fear. At the same time, Zindel was just beginning to write his scary science fiction books, including Rats *and* Reef of Death. *They were never as popular as his realistic books, but when Hyperion re-issued them in paperback in 2000, they helped to usher in a new kind of YA book.*

who through his inherited ability to be invisible begins to understand the differences between good and evil. During the 1990s, Paul Zindel, who gets lots of credit for being one of the founders of *realism* for teens, wrote fantasy including *Rats, Loch, Doom Stone,* and *Reef of Death,* which never gained the kind of popularity that came to his realism. Nevertheless, he was laying the groundwork for what we have today.

Annette Curtis Klause, in her 1990 *The Silver Kiss*, created a vampire ghost to help Zoë adjust to her mother's death. While Francesca Lia Block focuses on such problems as loneliness, alienation, sexual confusion, and love, she accepts wholeheartedly the deconstructionist idea of creating her own world, which she carefully ties to the real world, and then works within it. Readers who are puzzled or troubled by her books are usually those accustomed to looking for a kind of "realism" that can be tested against their own observations or against statistics of probability.

This does not work for the many writers who are now experimenting with stretching their readers' imaginations by writing in the style of everyday realism and then slipping over to fantasy elements as does Stephenie Meyer. At least in *Twilight,* readers had time to get to know Bella first as a person. For readers here in Arizona she was literally "the girl next door." *Twilight* had all the characteristics of the modern, realistic problem novel, but then along came Edward the Vampire and several other "real" vampires and werewolves, which is why her books are fully classified as fantasy.

Margaret A. Edwards Award

Winner (2005)
Francesca Lia Block, The Bringer of Magical Realism

The five Weetzie books published between 1989 and 1995 (*Weetzie Bat*; *Witch Baby*; *Cherokee Bat and the Goat Guys*; *Missing Angel Juan*; and *Baby Be-Bop*) are the ones that the Edwards Committee cited when they chose to honor Francesca Lia Block. Her selection was a surprise because the Margaret A. Edwards Award is for lifetime accomplishment and Block is the youngest person to have been so honored. Everyone expects her to continue writing for many more years.

A second reason for the surprise is that her books are so controversial. Block says that she writes urban fairy tales, but critics point out that her fairy tales start where the traditional ones end, and rather than implying that as soon as young people step into adulthood they can walk off into the sunset and live happily ever after, Block encourages her characters to seek happiness and fulfillment wherever in life's journey they happen to be.

Having grown up in Hollywood and lived all her life in California, Block makes her Los Angeles setting as important as any of her characters. Actual names taken from the Los Angeles area include Hollywood Boulevard, Tick Tock Tea Room, Fredericks of Hollywood, Loves, Shangri-la, Shangri Los Angeles, Shangri-L.A., and Hollywood. She also uses the way Weetzie's father, Charlie Bat, describes Hollywood as an illusion and an imitation and a mirage, to help prepare her readers for the magical realism that she incorporates into the plots of her books.

Most readers think of the stories as lighthearted and fun, even while her characters take in stride such heavy issues as drug overdoses, broken families, sexual experimentation, and abandoned children left on their own. We remember reading *The Hanged Man* when it came out in 1994 and conjecturing with our students on whether Block had studied the *Newsletter on Intellectual Freedom* and made a list of all the reasons censors give for wanting to keep particular books away from kids and then concocted a story to include 90 percent of the actions and words that fundamentalist critics abhor.

When Block won the Margaret A. Edwards Award, even she was surprised. She told David Levithan, who interviewed her for the June 2005 issue of *School Library Journal*, that she suspected in this conservative political climate that the committee members said something like, "In defiance of what's happening now, we're going to do this."

Block's books appeal to older teens and to what Michael Cart describes as a "crossover" audience of readers between the ages of sixteen and twenty-five. In 2005, HarperCollins published a follow-up adult book about Weetzie Bat entitled *Necklace of Kisses*. In this book, written almost twenty years after the first one, Weetzie's relationship with My Secret Agent Lover Man has withered and so Weetzie leaves the man who now goes by the more ordinary name of Max. Even though HarperCollins published the book in its adult division, a bookseller who brought the Weetzie Bat books to the 2006 convention of the Children's Literature Association in Mission Beach, California, laughingly assured customers that teen readers were going right through the original Weetzie books, now published in a single volume entitled *Dangerous Angels: The Weetzie Bat Books*, and then happily buying *Necklace of Kisses* to see what happens to the adult Weetzie and her uniquely named pals and children.

In the *School Library Journal* interview, she told David Levithan that when she was in college she started writing "short, odd, little punk-influenced stories." The creation of her most famous character was inspired by a WEETZIE license plate on a little "cartoon-looking car" being happily driven down the road by a bleached-blond girl. Block told Levithan that she still remembers "the moment—the time of day, the way the sky looked kind of smoggy—everything."

That was all it took—one name and one flashing image—for a character now loved worldwide to move into Block's creative mind and to make herself at home for at least the next twenty-five years. Only the future will tell if Weetzie is going to stay through middle and old age. Many readers hope she does, and while they wait they will be only too happy to read Block's other books including *The Rose and the Beast Fairy Tales*; *Roses and Bones: Myths, Tales, and Secrets*; *How to (Un)Cage a Girl* (poetry), *The Frenzy* (a werewolf novel), and *Pretty Dead* (a vampire book). ●

Margaret A. Edwards Award

Winner (2008)

Orson Scott Card, A Writer with Talent and Versatility

When the American Library Association announced that it was honoring Orson Scott Card with the 2008 Award, specifically for *Ender's Game* and *Ender's Shadow,* the committee praised him for writing two books that "continually capture the imagination and interest of teens." Tor published *Ender's Game* in 1985 and *Ender's Shadow* in 1999, with the later book being not a sequel but a companion book because it tells the same story except from the perspective of Bean, a boy who becomes Ender's friend and helper.

Card's most recent books include *Shadows in Flight, Pathfinder,* and *Ender in Exile.* In 2008, *Ender's Game, Speaker for the Dead, Xenocide,* and *Children of the Mind* were sold as a boxed set. Readers are especially interested in *Pathfinder,* which introduces a boy named Rigg and his relationship with his father. Rigg's "birthright" enables him to see into people's pasts, but not into his own.

Ender's Game is set in a somewhat vague future time when humans fear another attack from the insect-like buggers. Seventy years earlier, a military genius in Earth's army saved the world, and military leaders are now looking for one more child genius who can be trained to repeat the act. Peter and Valentine Wiggin have the military genius but the wrong temperament to be the proper choice. However, their little brother Andrew, who is called Ender because that's how his two-year-old sister pronounces his name, has both the temperament and the genius. Government officials take him to Battle School in hopes that he will be the one to prevent the attack that seems imminent.

The announcement that the American Library Association had chosen Card as the 2008 winner was made on January 14, which coincided with the first day of our young adult literature class in the spring semester. We always start a new semester with students introducing themselves by telling about a favorite book, one that has meant something in their lives. This year one of the first students spoke lovingly about how much she, along with the rest of her family, loved *Ender's Game* and *Ender's Shadow.* Her concluding comment was that her older brother had just come back from two years in Poland and the only souvenirs—the only thing Polish—that he brought back were *Ender's Game* and *Ender's Shadow* translated into Polish.

It was fun to tell the class that just that morning the American Library Association, which was meeting in Philadelphia, had announced that Card was being honored for the very books that the student's brother had brought home from Poland.

Card is a man of many talents and many ambitions. To get a hint of his wide-ranging interests, check out his website at www.hatrack.com/osc/about-more.shtml. He has written nearly three dozen plays, and if not for his love of drama, we might never have had his science fiction. One reason is that by writing plays and hearing his words spoken on stage he developed an awareness of how careful he had to be to keep his words from being misinterpreted by the reader. The other reason is more mundane. After college, he took a job as a copy editor, but in his spare time he established a theater company that performed on an outdoor, public stage that had been built during the Depression in Provo, Utah. The company did fine during the summer when they did not have to pay rent, but when winter came their expenses increased and debts piled up. Card knew he could never pay the debts from his modest salary and so he gave himself another part-time job of writing and selling science fiction.

When the short story that eventually turned into *Ender's Game* was accepted, the editor wanted to use the title "Professional Soldier," but even though Card was desperate to sell the story he insisted on keeping the title of "Ender's Game." He had devised the boy's name and the story title so as to make readers think about the "endgame" in chess. Fortunately the name also works for people who play more football than chess because it is reminiscent of an "end run," and as one of the boys says when he first meets Ender at school, "Not a bad name here. Ender. Finisher. Hey," which is exactly what Ender turns out to be when he plays the all-important video game named *The End of the World.* ●

Today's authors are incorporating multiple genres in their pieces as they lead readers circuitously from the consideration of serious everyday problems into magical realism. They do not make it obvious because they want the reader caught up in the whole story and believing all of it. When (or if) they begin to grow skeptical, they can look around in the story and find some kind of an explanation. For example, in Jennifer Donnelly's complicated *Revolution* (see Melissa Williamson's related essay on pp. 268–269) they can believe that Andi Alpers might have been fantasizing her experiences during the French Revolution because she took an overdose of her anti-depressant or drank alcohol when she was already overly medicated. In Libba Bray's *Going Bovine,* readers can, of course, figure out that Cameron's experiences are related to the heavy medication he is taking for his disease.

With most of Terry Pratchett's books, readers know immediately that they are in one of his fantasy worlds, but with *Nation,* it pretty much appears to be historical fiction, but he sets the record straight in a two-page "Author's Note" which he labels "The great big multiple-universes get-out-of-jail-free card." In it he writes

> This might look like a book set in the Pacific Ocean. *Nothing could be further from the truth!!!!!* It is in fact, set in a parallel universe, a phenomenon known only to advanced physicists and anyone who has ever watched any episode of any SF series, anywhere.

Then by listing some of the key items that played a part in the plot and warning readers that they must not depend on shooting cannons with cracked barrels, even if they mended them with layers of vines, or escaping from bullets by jumping in the ocean, he is pointing out some of the places where he used magical realism.

Yann Martel's *Life of Pi* starts out as a serious story about a young boy whose father ran a big-city zoo in India. The family is immigrating to Canada and is traveling by ship so that they can bring many of the animals to new homes in a Canadian zoo. The ship sinks in the middle of the night (and the middle of the ocean), and still readers think of it as a true story. Only gradually do they begin to wonder about the ever increasing fantastic things that happen to Pi. At the end of the story, Martel plays further with his readers' imaginations because the ship that had sunk was owned by Japanese businessmen. When Pi is eventually rescued, two of the company officials come to the hospital to hear his story. They think it is way too fantastic to be believed. So Pi offers them a less-fantastic story—and then somberly asks which version they prefer.

Jay Asher's *Thirteen Reasons Why* is among the most surprising of the serious problem novels that have the power of magical realism. Although Asher contrived a realistic way to get the effect of "hearing a voice from the grave," the book can still be viewed as absolutely straightforward. Because of its immediacy, it is being used all over the country to start discussions on bullying and suicide. The reason we say it is part magical realism is that the story is told through audio tapes, made by a girl before she commits suicide. She arranges for the thirteen tapes to be delivered after her death and passed sequentially to each of the individuals whose contributing actions are described on one of the tapes.

Asher got the idea for writing his epistolary novel in this format while he was on a museum tour listening to a taped discourse from a disembodied voice in his ear phones. It was an eerie feeling for this voice to know exactly where he was and what questions he would likely want answered. We listened to Asher's book on a CD, so the experience of hearing the voice of Hannah Baker (the girl who committed suicide) may have been more powerful than if we were reading it silently, but we have heard from many teachers that their students have loved reading and talking about Hannah's tapes.

Besides its message, the book is a good demonstration of a well-structured argument, with each of the thirteen tapes relying on the earlier arguments and forming a foundation for arguments to come. Readers get the story from the viewpoint of Clay Jensen, a sympathetic character, who was the fourth person on the list to receive the package. Clay does not know who else has received it. He dutifully follows Hannah's directions of going to the places where she tells him to listen to each tape. Through interior monologues, readers get to see inside Clay's mind and agree with him that surely he was not responsible for Hannah's suicide. One of the strengths of the book is that each tape tells a different story, giving readers a chance to understand the cumulative nature of bullying. On the final tape, Hannah alludes to a Valentine Day's activity at her school. She changes the lyrics to the song, "Oh my darling, Clementine," to the following:

Oh my dollar . . .

Oh my dollar . . .

Oh my dollar . . . , Valentine

And then she sings the next line of the song, changing only two words:

Thou art lost and gone forever, Oh my dollar . . . , Valentine!

Concluding Comments

The books written about in this chapter make up the large body of what, at least until recently, the general public viewed as young adult literature. Realistic "problem novels" will undoubtedly continue to be published, but young adult literature does not exist in a vacuum separate from the literature of the rest of the world. This is one of the reasons that the creators of the Printz Award did not specify criteria other than "The Best" book of each year. They did not want to limit the creativity of authors for young adults. As producers of realistic books try not to repeat themselves while at the same time plucking psychic strings that remain untouched by superficial media stories, they are pulled in the same directions as writers for adults. The reason we added a few comments about magical realism is that we wanted to illustrate how the lines between genres are fading. And while we, along with many readers, continue to appreciate well-done realistic books, we are at the same time pleased to realize that the field is not standing still. Many of today's writers are finding new ways to treat old stories, which is why we had so many more new books to consider for Chapter 5, "Fantasy, Supernatural, Science Fiction, Utopias, and Dystopias," than we had for this chapter on realistic books.

Fantasy, Supernatural, Science Fiction, Utopias, and Dystopias

"Move over, Holden Caulfield. There's a new breed of teen heroes in town," wrote Anita Silvey in a feature article in the October 2006 issue of *School Library Journal*. She went on to explain:

> In fact, there's been such a shift in young adults' reading tastes that all of us are scrambling to figure out what truly appeals to teens. Of one thing I'm certain: instead of craving realistic stories about people like themselves, today's teens are crazy about characters (and scenarios) that have little in common with their own everyday lives. As one young reader put it, his peers are hunting for novels that will "take them away to another world, not like this one." ("The Unreal Deal," pp. 44–47)

Although Silvey was writing about suspense and mystery as well as fantasy, it is fantasy that has forced us, as well as many school librarians, to rearrange our bookshelves to make more room for that particular genre. Certainly, the success of J. K. Rowling's Harry Potter books has something to do with it, but as Tamora Pierce told us at the 2006 ALAN meeting in Nashville, it is not so much that writers suddenly climbed onto the Harry Potter bandwagon. Instead, what happened is that Rowling's success made publishers, especially the publishers of children's books, look at fantasy with new respect and give more serious readings to the kinds of manuscripts they had been receiving all along.

Fantasy and science fiction are related to each other and to humankind's deepest desires, but it is not easy to draw a clear-cut line between the two. In 1983, Walter Wangerin, Jr., told an audience at Bowling Green University that "Fantasy deals with the *immeasurable* while science fiction deals with the *measurable*." As a follow-up to the audio recording of Orson Scott Card's *Ender's Game,* which was released in 2005 as part of a twentieth-year celebration of the book's publication, Card laughingly gave his own definition. He said it was a matter of rivets versus trees. If the cover of a book shows trees, it is a fantasy, but if it shows rivets holding pieces of metal together, then it is science fiction.

Anyone who is around young people knows that in this area books cross genre lines and age lines. Young adults read what adults read, and books that may have been published for young readers are now also read by adults. *Fantasy* comes from a Greek word meaning "a making visible." Perhaps more than any other form of literature, fantasy refuses to accept the world as it is, so readers can see what could have been (and still might be), rather than merely what was or must be. The appeal of fantasy may be, simply, that it is so elemental. Writers sing their lighter tales through stories about Beauty and the Beast, the happier and younger life of Arthur, and many of the old folktales and legends that are childhood favorites.

Fantasy allows us—even forces us—to become greater than we are, greater than we could hope to be by confronting us with the major ambiguities and dualities of life—good and evil, light and dark, innocence and guilt, reality and appearance, heroism and cowardice, hard work and indolence, determination and vacillation, and order and anarchy. Fantasy presents all these, and it provides the means through which readers can consider both the polarities and the shadings in between.

Conventions of Fantasy

Jo-Anne Goodwin, in an article titled "In Defense of Fantasy" published in London's *Independent Magazine* (July 25, 1993, p. 32), commented about the nature of fantasy. Her view is worth repeating for its accuracy and succinctness.

> Classic fantasy is centered around quests. The quest may have any number of different motives—spiritual, political, sexual, material—but its presence in the text is essential. The quest expresses the desire to accomplish a thing fraught with difficulty and danger, and seemingly doomed to failure. It also enables fantasy writers to deal with rites of passage; the central figure grows in stature as the quest evolves.

Goodwin went on to say that magical, symbolic, and allegorical events help authors externalize the internal struggles of the heroes. Plus, the fact that the hero is in a different world opens the door for the author to give the hero enormous responsibilities. And while the responsibilities may affect a whole world,

Margaret A. Edwards Award
Winner (2004)
Ursula K. Le Guin, **A Definer of Fantasy**

Le Guin was honored for *A Wizard of Earthsea, The Farthest Shore, The Tombs of Atuan, Tehanu, The Left Hand of Darkness,* and *The Beginning Place.* The books were praised for having helped adolescents address questions about their role and their importance in society and in the world. If we had been making the list we would have also added Le Guin's realistic *Very Far Away from Anywhere Else* and her two later books, *Tales of Earthsea, The Other Wind,* and *The Telling.*

In a 1974 article in the Winter 1974 issue of *Pacific Northwest Library Association Quarterly,* Vol. 38, p. 18, entitled "Why Are Americans So Afraid of Dragons?" Le Guin pondered the question of why people are made uncomfortable by fantasy.

> For fantasy is true, of course. It isn't factual, but it is true. Children know that. Adults know it too, and that is precisely why many of them are afraid of fantasy. They know that its truth challenges, even threatens, all that is false, phony, unnecessary, and trivial in the life they have let themselves be forced into living. They are afraid of dragons because they are afraid of freedom.

> So I believe we should trust our children. Normal children do not confuse reality with fantasy—they confuse them much less often than we adults do (as a certain great fantasist pointed out in a story called "The Emperor's New Clothes"). Children know perfectly well that unicorns aren't real, but they also know that books about unicorns, if they are good books are true books.

A few years later, she offered an often-repeated definition of fantasy in an essay in *Teaching Science Fiction: Education for Tomorrow,* edited by Jack Williamson, Oswick Press, 1980, p. 22.

> The basic concept of fantasy, of course, is this; you get to make up the rules, but then you've got to follow them. Science fiction refines the canon: You get to make up the rules, but within limits. A science-fiction story must not flout the evidence of science, must not, as Chip Delaney puts it, deny what is known to be known.

Le Guin's six books in the Earthsea series make up an amazing myth. For readers, Tenar and Ged are real people, not mere characters in books. Though aimed at young adults, the books make no apologies for posing difficult and unanswerable and universal questions and dilemmas. When Francisca Goldsmith asked Le Guin what she wanted to teach in the Earthsea books for the June 2004 *School Library Journal,* Le Guin explained that she sees herself as a storyteller, but that in a sense the story tells itself.

> I am responsible for telling it right. The words that I work in are the words of the story. I'm not a philosopher. I'm not a moralist. If my story seems to begin preaching, I make it stop, if I notice it. I'm not a preacher either. My responsibility is to my art and to the people who perceive it, the readers. That's an aesthetic responsibility and if it's aesthetically right, then it will probably also be morally right.

In 2004, Le Guin began her Annals of the Western Shore with *Gifts,* followed in 2006 with *Voices,* and in 2007 with *Powers,* which all received positive reviews. In praising *Powers,* which features a dark-skinned and hook-nosed slave boy named Gav, a *Publishers Weekly* reviewer wrote that Le Guin's fans have ample reason to hope that her new saga is building toward a fantasy cycle as ambitious and as satisfying as are the beloved Chronicles of Earthsea.

Besides receiving the Edwards Award in 2004, Le Guin was asked to give the May Hill Arbuthnot memorial lecture. We were fortunate at ASU to get to sponsor an all-day symposium on Le Guin and her books. In getting ready for the symposium, we developed a whole new appreciation for the amount and the variety in Le Guin's books, which include short stories, poetry, translations, criticism, and fiction for all three age groups: children, teens, and adults. When author Nancy Farmer introduced Le Guin, she described her as writing "stealth bestsellers" which she defined as books that slowly develop large and dependable audiences. A look at how many of Le Guin's books are still in print and at how regularly they are repackaged and released in new formats lends strong support to Farmer's thoughtful description. ●

Margaret A. Edwards Award

Winner (1999)
Anne McCaffrey, **The Dragon Lady**

On November 21, 2011, Anne McCaffrey passed away at the age of 85. She was at her home in County Wicklow, Ireland, which she had designed for herself when she moved to Ireland from the United States in 1970. She was born in Cambridge, Massachusetts and graduated from Radcliffe College in 1947. Although she has some Irish ancestry, she was actually wooed to move to Ireland because of a government promise that authors would not have to pay income taxes on the money they made from their books. McCaffrey would laughingly explain to visitors that she named her self-designed home, which is south of Dublin, *Dragonhold* because it was the "dragons who paid for it."

Before turning to writing, McCaffrey had tried her hand at singing and acting, skills that she told the science fiction magazine *Locus,* in a 2004 interview, directly influenced her writing because in all these fields the important thing is emotion. The writer has to have a strong enough feel for her story to go through all that it takes to write and publish a book. And unless the emotion is genuine, it won't be strong enough to carry over to the readers.

The novels that the YALSA committee honored in 1999 were *Dragonflight*, *The White Dragon*, *The Ship Who Sang*, *Dragonquest*, *Dragonsong*, *Dragonsinger*, and *Dragondrums*. At the time of her death, there were 23 related novels in print with one more ready for publication in 2012. Over the last decade as her health failed, she began working closely with her son, Todd. They co-authored five of the books, including the twenty-third novel, and Todd wrote three others under just his own name.

It all started in the late 1960s when Anne McCaffrey created a fictional world, which she named PERN (Parallel Earth Resources Negligible). It was created for a short story, and that supposedly was that, but history proved differently. Every two hundred years PERN is threatened by shimmering spores—organisms that devour all organic matter. The only protection is the dragons, who are able to destroy the threads as they fall. Beginning with *Dragonflight* in 1968, followed by *Dragonsong,* the books were ahead of their time in having a mixture of science fiction and fantasy. When she was interviewed for the June 1999 *School Library Journal* in relation to winning the Edwards Award, Michael Cart asked her in which genre she wrote. She answered,

they are carried out in a global village because fantasy is a "deeply social genre" where every decision taken by the hero affects someone else.

Heroes must prove worthy of their quest, although early in the story they may be fumbling or unsure about both themselves and their quests. The quests in fantasy are analogies for the readers' own lives. We all begin our quest, that long journey, seeking the good and being tempted by the evil that we know we must ultimately fight. We face obstacles and barriers throughout, hoping that we will find satisfaction and meaning during and after the quest. Our quests may not be as earthshaking as those of fantasy heroes, but our emotional and intellectual wrestling can shake our own personal worlds.

Attacks on fantasy are common and predictable. It is said to be childishly simple reading, a claim that most readers will reject after having struggled to understand strange beings and even stranger lands filled with mystical and moral overtones and ambiguities. Fantasy has been labeled escapist literature because it allows readers to escape the mundane and to revel in glorious adventures. For some readers (perhaps occasionally for all readers), escape is all

We keep having to settle that question. I write science fiction. It may seem like fantasy because I use dragons, but mine were biogenetically engineered; ergo, the story is science fiction.

Perhaps one of the reasons that she wanted to be known as a science fiction writer is that she enjoyed coming into a field that had been dominated by male writers. We read several obituaries and they all included something about her being the first woman to win both of the top two prizes in science fiction: the Hugo and the Nebula. But actually in the online descriptions of each of these awards they are now defined as including both science fiction and fantasy.

Dragonsong is a favorite of many McCaffrey fans because of its especially intriguing heroine, which Mc-Caffrey modeled after two of her youthful friends. Her name is Menolly and she wants nothing more than to become a musician on PERN, but only men are allowed to become harpers. As punishment for her ambitions, her father beats Menolly, but she is rescued by a dragonrider. When the Master Harper of PERN listens to her music, he invites Menolly to become the first female harper. It's not surprising that Menolly, with her talents and her obstacles and her bravery, is a model for female readers. She deserves to be.

McCaffrey's dragons are almost as attractive to readers as are her characters. While dragons may have universal appeal, they have had bad press for years. So McCaffrey created dragons that are attractive to readers and gentle and devoted to their riders. Given McCaffrey's fascination with dragons, she said she didn't mind being called "the Dragon Lady," even though the original Dragon Lady was a bewitching but dangerous woman in *Terry and the Pirates*, a comic strip of the 1940s.

McCaffrey says that *The Ship That Sang* is her favorite because her father had fought in three wars and then died at age sixty-three. In grieving for the death of a character in *The Ship That Sang*, she was actually grieving for her father's death and for the lost chance to prove to him that she would amount to something. In this novel, shell persons—crippled females—and their brawns—males chosen to aid them in their jobs—give up their lives to run ships with their minds. Heroism and devoting one's life to the good of others is a theme that runs through her books, and no place is that better illustrated than in *The Ship That Sang*.

For the second edition (1985) of this textbook, she told us that she writes love stories that are "xenophilic, rather than xenophobic since I do feel that we shall, one day or another, encounter other sentient beings. I can devoutly hope that our species will greet them with tolerance and an overwhelming desire to understand alien minds and mores."

Perhaps this is the proof people have been looking for that Anne McCaffrey was a writer of science fiction. ●

that is demanded. But for other readers, venturing on those seemingly endless quests and encountering all those incredible obstacles sends them back to their own limited and literal worlds to face many of the same problems they found in fantasy.

In spite of fears and objections, fantasy has moved to the center of YA interest. Tolkien has virtually been awarded sainthood, and given the steady or growing popularity of such writers as Ursula K. Le Guin (see p. 145) and Anne McCaffrey (see p. 146), along with two more recent winners of the Margaret A. Edwards Award: Orson Scott Card (see p. 140) and Terry Pratchett (see p. 158), there is no doubt that fantasy is enjoying a new kind of respect both from young readers and from the adults who manage the book business.

Surely J. K. Rowling deserves a good share of the credit. If there is a more popular writer in the world than J. K. Rowling, we have no idea who it could be. Many people have stories to tell about her influence. Grandparents brag about a grandchild for reading one of the books clear through on the day it came out, and college professors say that Rowling changed the nature of their teaching

In our ASU classes, we've been holding Harry Potter Day right after Halloween, when we can get bargain prices on decorations, food, and costumes. The committee in charge wears costumes, figures out games and crafts, and assigns us all to bring refreshments. This past year a big part of the entertainment was showing some wonderful online parodies.

because, for the first time, they have males enrolling in their classes in children's or YA literature. One of the best stories we heard was from a New Zealand woman who told us that she had been to an all-night-in-the-park read-aloud when one of the books was released and the well-known New Zealand author Margaret Mahy had been one of the readers.

Why is Harry so popular? Even a cursory reading of the series would suggest some answers. Harry is a remarkable character. He is almost impossible to dislike; he's an incredibly apt student of magic at the Hogwarts School of Witchcraft and Wizardy; he's athletic in the game of Quidditch (played in midair by students on broomsticks); he's clearly a fighter; and he has friends who are attractive to readers.

His parents were murdered by the evil Voldemort, and there are enough reminders of Luke Skywalker, Darth Vader, and other aspects of *Star Wars* to fascinate readers for years. Rowling told not only a wonderful story, but as she recently quipped in an interview, she is among the few who managed to make money out of a degree in classics. See Chapter 6 on humor (p. 213) which details the careful attention Rowling paid to creating humorous and memorable names for people and places.

Different Kinds of Fantasies

We used to think of fantasy as a single genre, but now that it has become so popular it is easy to see that there are clearly several different types of fantasy. It stands to reason that this would be true because the human mind has infinite capabilities to imagine many more worlds than we can see and touch. So here in alphabetical order we are giving a sampling of types of fantasy. And even our subcategories are just a sampling because authors are always coming up with new ways to write old stories. One of the most basic techniques is for an author to create a parallel universe, one which exists alongside the regular world. J. K. Rowling was clever in the Harry Potter books to make her alternate universe the main one, with our world of *muggles* being the odd one out. See Focus Box 5.1, "Alternate Universes in Fantasies," on page 150 for books that illustrate alternate universes.

Animal Fantasies   Animal stories aimed at instructing humans are as old as Aesop and as recent as today's book review. Many teenagers have fond memories of such books as E. B. White's *Charlotte's Web,* Jane Langton's *The Fledgling,* Robert C. O'Brien's *Mrs. Frisby and the Rats of NIMH,* Kenneth Grahame's *The Wind in the Willows,* and Richard Adams's *Watership Down.* They may be ready to read Walter Wangerin, Jr.'s, *The Book of the Dun Cow,* a delightfully funny theological thriller retelling the story of Chauntecleer the Rooster. Supposedly the leader for good against evil (the half-snake, half-cock—Cockatrice—and the black serpent—Wyrm), Chauntecleer is beset by doubts. He is aided by the humble dog Mondo Cani, some hilariously pouting turkeys, and assorted other barnyard animals. In *The Unseen* by Zilpha Keatley Snyder, Xandra Hobson feels that she is unloved by her family, but the fun of the story is the way she finds this to be untrue after she rescues a bird from some hunters and it leaves her a feather, which is really a key to another world.

By viewing dragons as animals, we can include Jane Yolen's *Dragon's Blood, Heart's Blood,* and *A Sending of Dragons,* which comprise a series with two extraordinarily likable young people fighting for their lives and for their dragons. Patricia C. Wrede's *Dealing with Dragons* and *Talking to Dragons* are funny adventure stories. Her best work can be found in *Book of Enchantments.* And as Anne McCaffrey has said, she purposely set out to give dragons some long-overdue positive PR. It is interesting that in stories from the Far East, dragons are considered friends, while in traditional stories of European descent, the dragons are feared.

Clare Bell sets her *Ratha's Creature* books twenty-five million years ago. Ratha leads a group of intelligent wild cats who have developed their society and who have learned to herd and keep other animals. Erin Hunter's *Warriors: Into the Wild* portrays four clans of wild cats living in a loose harmony with each other as they share a forest, but when one clan becomes too powerful, the equilibrium is threatened. *Warriors: Fire and Ice* continues the saga. *Fire Bringer* by David Clement-Davies is about intelligent deer who have developed a complex society predicated on their own myths. He later wrote *The Sight,* about an intelligent wolf society. The birth of two pups, Fell, who is black, and Larka, who is white, leads to the acceptance of an ancient myth about foreseeing the future. A 2007 sequel, *Fell,* tells the story of one of the grown-up pups, his betrayal of the family, and then his redemption. For his *A Glory of Unicorns,* Bruce Coville collected twelve stories about his favorite creature, the unicorn, and how it works with and affects people.

In Patricia McKillip's *The Forgotten Beasts of Eld,* the great-granddaughter of a wizard controls enchanted beasts, but she fears men who come into her private world. In *Soul Eater,* Book Three of *The Chronicles of Ancient Darkness* by Michelle Paver, Torak is a gifted boy, who lives 6,000 years ago in

Focus Box 5.1

Alternate Universes in Fantasies

Beautiful Darkness **by Kami Garcia and Margaret Stohl. Little Brown, 2010.** Ethan, Link, and Liv go into the tunnels under Gatlin to save Lena from becoming a Dark Caster. This is a romantic sequel to the 2009 *Beautiful Creatures.*

Betrayed **by Gillian Shields. HarperCollins, 2010.** In this sequel to *Immortal* (Catherine Tegen Books, 2009), the boarding school that sixteen-year-old Evie returns to is named Wyldcliff, an appropriate name for a place where Evie must fight the demons to rescue Sebastian.

Bone Chiller **by Graham McNamee. Random House, 2008.** An evil demon has bitten Danny, so Danny and his friends are hunting down and trying to kill the creature before the venom kills Danny. They corner the demon, but it's not an easy fight.

Daughter of Smoke and Bone **by Lani Taylor. Little, Brown, 2011.** The hero of this romantic thriller is seventeen-year-old Karou, an art student in Prague, who was raised by demons. She makes her living by running errands for Brimstone, her foster parent who is a supernatural chimera. She sets out on a quest to rescue her demon family and to figure out where she belongs, and uncovers so many complications that readers will be eager for a follow-up book.

Destined **by P. C. Cast and Kristin Cast. St. Martin's Griffin, 2011.** *Destined* is a continuation of the highly popular House of Night series of paranormal romances, which includes *Awakened, Burned, Chosen, Dragon's Oath, Hunted,* and *Marked.* P. C. Cast, who writes with her college-age daughter, taught high school English for fifteen years. She has also edited a collection of essays written by teachers and other readers interested in providing a guidebook to the series, *Nyx in the House of Night: Mythology, Folklore and Religion in the PC and Kristin Cast Vampyre Series,* Smart Pop, 2011.

Draw the Dark **by Ilsa J. Bick. Carolrhoda, 2010.** Christian sees a "sideways" place in his mind. He can also see into the minds of other people. He's looking for his missing parents, and uncovers the past and present of the small town where he lives.

Entwined **by Heather Dixon. Green Willow, 2011.** After her mother's death, Princess Azaela and her sisters are forbidden to dance, court, laugh, or even step outside. Finally, Azaela finds a magic space in the castle, thanks to a silver-threaded handkerchief that once belonged to her mother.

Extraordinary **by Nancy Werlin. Dial/Penguin, 2010.** In this urban fairy tale, Faerie Mallory enters the human world in hopes of ensnaring Phoebe in a trap that will save the faerie realm.

Fever Crumb **by Phillip Reeve. Scholastic, 2010.** Reeve wrote *Fever Crumb,* the first of a trilogy, as a prequel to his Hungry City Chronicles. Fever Crumb is a girl orphan raised in the Order of Engineers. She escapes her cloistered life with the help of a theater troupe travelling to London where she thinks she will help on an archaeological dig. Instead she faces all kinds of new challenges. The second book, *A Web of Air* (Scholastic, 2011) finds her in Mayda-at-the-World's-End, a community built on cliffs among frightening mountains. Some of the chapter titles hint at what's ahead: "An Engineer Calls," "Aeroplane," "Wings of the Future," and "Lost Maps of the Sky." Fever's knowledge of engineering is sought by both the evil and the good forces that are envisioning something like a train in the sky.

Northern Europe. He can inhabit the souls of animals, and when one of his best friends, Wolf, is captured by the Soul Eaters, Torak must save him. In *Listening at the Gate* by Betsy James, Kat falls in love with a seal/man, not at all like her father's repressive fellow merchants. The starred review in *School Library Journal* gives James credit for "redrawing the pattern of the classic hero's quest."

In many fantasy books, the animals play only small parts, but they still contribute to the book's success. In Zilpha Keatley Snyder's *The Unseen,* the heart of the story is Xandra Hobson's feeling that she is unloved by her family, but the fun of the story is the way she finds this to be untrue after she rescues a

Foundling (from Monster Blood Tattoo Series, Book No. #1) by D. M. Cornish. Putnam, 2006. In this new and refreshing series, Rossamünd Bookchild ventures out of the orphanage and into the fascinating but dangerous world of Half-Continent. *Lamplighter* followed in 2008 and *The Foundling's Tale Part Three: Factotum* in 2010.

Leviathan by Scott Westerfeld, illustrated by Keith Thompson. Simon & Schuster, 2009, followed by Behemoth, 2010, and by Goliath, 2011. These three beautifully illustrated books are the ultimate example of fantastic technology as World War I is fought in a world divided into Clankers (those who use technology) and Darwinists (those who use DNA to create helpful animals).

Lies: A Gone Novel by Michael Grant. HarperCollins, 2010. All the grownups have disappeared from the FAYZ, leaving the kids to fend for themselves. Two leaders emerge from the kids, Caine's group plans to escape by boat to an island mansion, while Orsay's followers plan to wait until they're fifteen, at which time they think they can join their families wherever they have ended up.

London Calling by Edward Bloor. Knopf, 2006. When an old radio takes Martin back in time to London during World War II, he makes some startling discoveries.

The Lost Conspiracy by Frances Hardinge. HarperCollins/Bowen Press, 2009. Two sisters are the heroines in this fantasy set on a lush, but treacherous, island world. One girl is viewed as being a Lost, i.e., an oracle with special abilities. Her sister is her attendant. Both girls play vital roles in the future of the island.

Magic or Madness by Justine Larbalestier. Penguin/Razorbill, 2005. A girl named Reason grows up in the Australian bush fearing and avoiding her grandmother, but when she is fifteen, her mother goes insane and Reason is sent to live with her frightening grandmother. She escapes through a magic door, only to find herself in New York City.

Reckless by Cornelia Funke. Little Brown, 2010. When his little brother follows Jacob, who has been slipping through his mirror into another realm, all kinds of complications occur in this book for middle schoolers. Funke is the author of the popular *Inkspell* books, which provide a wonderful example of an alternate universe.

Skeleton Man by Joseph Bruchac. HarperCollins, 2001. Young teens may get nightmares from this story based on a Mohawk legend about a man so hungry that he eats himself.

Stork by Wendy Delsol. Candlewick, 2010. When Katla's parents divorce, and she moves with her mother from California to her parents' home town in Minnesota, she is surprised to find that she is not only a member of the Icelandic Stork Society, but that she has been awarded the prestigious second chair of this mysterious society that guides unborn souls to the correct mothers.

Summerland by Michael Chabon. Hyperion/Talk Miramax, 2002. In this original story, a Little League baseball player is recruited by an old-timer from the Negro leagues to play in a game that has the potential to save the world.

Un Lun Dun by China Miéville. Del Rey, 2007. The title is really an allusion to a London that is not quite normal. Twelve-year-olds Zanna and Deeba find themselves in this alternate reality where typewriters "seep," umbrellas are sentient, and milk cartons make endearing pets. It is recommended to readers who liked Norton Juster's *The Phantom Tollbooth* and Neil Gaiman's *Coraline*.

bird from some hunters and it leaves her a feather, which turns out to be a key to another world.

Surely a large part of the pleasure in Philip Pullman's Golden Compass trilogy comes from the animal daemon that each human has, while much of the fun in the Harry Potter books comes from the animals, including Fang, Hedwig, Scabbers, Greyback, Pigwidgeon, and Crookshanks. The animages, Prongs, Padfoot, Moony, and Wormtail, play important parts in the plot, while a good joke is when Hagrid's hippogriff, Buckbeak, is on the Ministry's "Wanted" list and Hagrid thinks he can hide or at least disguise this huge flying creature by changing his name from Buckbeak to Witherwings.

Young Scholars Speak Out

Alaya Swann on Exploring Serious Problems with Parents in Dark Young Adult Literature

I recently attended *Harry Potter and the Deathly Hallows: Part I* with my thirteen-year-old brother. As we exited, he crowed enthusiastically, "It actually *earned* its PG-13 rating." Then he explained, "That part with the scary old lady before she turned into the snake was the creepiest part, and it was awesome!" At the age of thirteen, my brother thought the scariest part was also the coolest part.

The desire to push against boundaries that adults have set is nothing new, but it is new to find authors leading children to think about and explore deeply emotional problems with their parents. For example, Neil Gaiman's *Coraline* leads readers (and later, viewers of the film) to contemplate Coraline's recognition of her mother as "other." This is a key psychological development that is valuable to both a child, who is just beginning to confront the task of growing up, and to an adult, who has vivid memories of that same process.

This kind of dark young adult fantasy has become more common in recent young adult literature. The premise of the first book in Suzanne Collins's *Hunger Games* trilogy is a government-orchestrated fight to the death by specially chosen children. Katniss, the sixteen-year-old protagonist, curtly tells the readers about her father's death in a coal mine explosion and the lingering psychological effects this event had on her: "There was nothing even to bury. I was eleven then. Five years later, I still wake up screaming for him to run." Katniss also describes the trauma she experienced during her mother's deep depression following the death of her husband. Katniss tries to remember how much her mother must have loved her father to give up her home in an affluent district and follow him to this poor coal-mining district. But still "all I can see is the woman who sat by, blank and unreachable, while her children turned to skin and bones. I try to forgive her for my father's sake. But to be honest, I'm not the forgiving type."

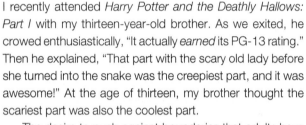

Dark and Gothic Fantasy   It is almost impossible to separate dark literature into fantasy as opposed to science fiction because there are often technology-related contributing factors. An example is Rick Yancey's 2009 horror story, *The Monstrumologist,* which is supposedly the diary of a man, William Henry, who lived to be something like 130 years old, perhaps because of the chemicals he came in contact with when as a boy he worked as an assistant to a self-educated "doctor" in 1888 New England. This doctor, Pellinore Warthrope, hoped to become as famous as Charles Darwin; however, his fame would come not from the study of living creatures, but of horrible creatures from the afterlife that he and Will would collect from graveyards.

If you are listening to these kinds of horror stories as a way of going to sleep and having pleasant dreams, you will probably be motivated to get up and change the CD. This happened to the Nilsens when we were listening to James Dashner's 2010 *The Scorch Trials*. In this sequel to his 2009 *The Maze Runner,* Dashner created a grim and terrifying picture of young people who at first can communicate with each other through mind-think, but then lose this ability when

Katniss's remarks demonstrate how deeply wounding this exposure to parental depression was for her, and how intensely she regards this depression as parental failure. This passage is a far more open confrontation with the effects of parental depression than one might expect in a book for young adults, even in a realistic YA "problem novel." Katniss becomes a caretaker and manages to support her mother and her sister, but her relationship with her mother remains bitter. This psychological scarring provides a backdrop for the dark and horrifying events of the trilogy.

Philip Pullman also deals with strained parent-child relationships and mental illness in his Dark Materials trilogy. In the first book of the series, *The Golden Compass,* Lyra's parents are first absent, then manipulating and immoral. In the second book, *The Subtle Knife,* Will Parry's father is missing and his mother shows signs of paranoid schizophrenia. Early on in the book, a flashback reveals seven-year-old Will's first realization of his mother's mental illness when his mother becomes terrified and paranoid after losing her purse: At first Will thinks that there is a real external danger, but over the next few months he "slowly and unwillingly" comes to understand that "those enemies of his mother's were not in the world out there, but in her mind." He concludes that the enemies are "no less real, no less frightening and dangerous; it just meant he had to protect her even more carefully."

Unlike Katniss's response to her mother's debilitating depression, Will is not angry with his mother for failing her parental duties, and he willingly becomes her caretaker. Will's determination to keep his family together despite his mother's mental illness provides a framework for Will's character development during the rest of the story, and his experiences reflect a real and serious problem that children do encounter.

Pullman's and Collins's candid discussions of these problems reflect a growing desire on the part of authors to face serious real-world problems through fantasy. Just as my brother appreciated the dark moments in the *Harry Potter* film, readers also demonstrate an increasing interest in engaging with young adult fantasy that does not shy away from serious situations. Perhaps fantasy provides a kind of freedom for both authors and readers to dig more deeply into such serious issues and confront the emotional challenges that arise.

Alaya Swann is a Ph.D. student at Arizona State University, where she studies medieval English literature. Her research focuses on female mystics in the late Middle Ages, and she also teaches composition and literature to college students. She has always loved fantasy and young adult literature, and she continues to read it every chance she gets. Her goals include becoming a professor and teaching at the college level, and she hopes to engage as many students as she can in the joys of literature.

they are imprisoned in a large oval-shaped building where the windows are suddenly bricked up and all communication with the outside is cut off. They have access to water but not food, and so all they can do is wait to see what happens.

We knew from reading a preview that the young prisoners were going to be forced to run through one hundred miles of Scorch, with its solar flares, severe storms, and "cranks." The cranks are diseased and deformed people who have been driven mad from earlier contacts with those now in control. We were eager to finish listening to the book, but in the light of day rather than as a soporific.

We probably should not be so surprised to see how fascinated young people are with the afterlife. Since none of us want to die, we naturally want to envision an afterlife. Whether we do it seriously through religion or playfully through jokes and Halloween costumes, or through false bravado by subjecting ourselves to really scary movies and fiction, we are all tiptoeing around the question of "What's next?" Today's authors have provided a wealth of imaginative books for a generation that grew up reading R. L. Stine's Fear Street books and watching *Buffy the Vampire Slayer* on television.

In Michael Grant's *Lies: A Gone Novel*, all the grownups have disappeared from the FAYZ, leaving the kids to fend for themselves. Two leaders emerge. Caine leads a group who plans to escape by boat to an island mansion. Orsay's followers plan to wait until they're fifteen at which time they think they can join their families wherever they are.

Bliss by Lauren Myracle is about the daughter of two hippies, who gave her the name Bliss in the Morning Dew. The story begins when they drop her off at her grandmother's house in Atlanta so they can be free to go north to Canada. Her grandmother enrolls Bliss in an elite prep school, but when Bliss begins to hear the voice of a long dead student, she finds herself in the midst of a plan to release and empower the girl's spirit. Myracle softens some of the chills with humor, but the book is still pretty dark.

Some of the new books are so dark that adults are seriously worried about young people reading them. In her September 14, 2010, blog, Valerie Straus wrote about an interdisciplinary conference being held at Cambridge University on "The Emergent Adult—Adolescent Literature and Culture." The questions being asked by literary scholars, psychologists, and sociologists circled around the differences in teenage and adult minds and whether teenagers are more vulnerable to suggestions. In answer to Straus's question of "Are kids' brains really changed after they read the 'Twilight' saga or 'Harry Potter,' and what does change mean anyway?" conference director Maria Nikolajeva wrote back:

> We have always known that encounters with art and literature affect our senses. We feel joy, sorrow, fear, anxiety, grief. We empathize with the characters. We learn from them about ourselves and about other people. What we know today from neuroscience is that there are spots in the brain that are responsible for these feelings, that it is possible to identify parts of the brain affected by reading or watching a film. The adolescent brain goes through a significant and rapid change, everything that affects it leaves deep imprints. Very dark fiction creates and amplifies a sense of insecurity, which is typical of adolescence; but it can also be a liberation when readers "share" their personal experience with that of fictional characters. So yes, all readers' brains are changed after they have read a book, but teenage brains are especially perceptive and therefore vulnerable. (Downloaded, Sept. 4, 2010)

In a 2008 book, *The Gothic in Children's Literature: Haunting the Borders* (Edited by Anna Jackson, Karen Coats, and Roderick McGillis, Routledge Press), Roderick McGillis has an essay, "The Night Side of Nature: Gothic Spaces, Fearful Times," in which he praises M. T. Anderson's writing ability, but is very critical of Anderson's 1997 book *Thirsty* and the description of Chris (a teenage vampire) cutting himself so as to get the blood he desperately wants. We had not seen reviews of the book when it first came out, which was a few years before the teen vampire craze, but when we looked it up on Amazon.com in August of 2011 we saw that it had been reissued by Candlewick as a paperback in 2008. No review was given from *School Library Journal*, but there was a *Publisher's Weekly* quote saying it was "a cut above" most other books on the subject.

Education Week (April 4, 2007) published a front page story on "Dark Themes in Books Get Students Reading" by Kathleen Kennedy Manzo. The full-page continuation (p. 16) was headlined "Critics Fear that Dark Themes Could Haunt Young Readers." Books pictured as an illustration were Laurie Halse Anderson's *Speak*, Yann Martel's *Life of Pi*, and Jennings Michael Burch's *They Cage the Animals at Night*. Many prominent educators were interviewed about the new trend. Jeffrey D. Wilhelm's quote about a survey he conducted with colleague Michael W. Smith was highlighted: "It was almost completely agreed upon that school reading sucks and that students hate it." In one class, they found that not one of the students actually read the assigned text, Shakespeare's *Twelfth Night*, but they confided thirty different ways that they had fooled the teacher into thinking they had read it.

Time magazine devoted a one-page article in its September 7, 2009, issue to the question of violence in Suzanne Collins's *The Hunger Games*. Lev Grossman described the first book in the trilogy as "a chilling, bloody and thoroughly horrifying book, a killer cocktail of *Logan's Run*, *Lord of the Flies*, *The Running Man*, reality TV and the myth of Theseus and the Minotaur." His conclusion was:

> *The Hunger Games* and *Catching Fire* [*Mockingjay* had not come out yet] expose children to exactly the kind of violence we usually shield them from. But that just goes to show how much adults forget about what it's like to be a child. Kids are physical creatures, and they're not stupid. They know all about violence and power and raw emotions. What's really scary is when adults pretend that such things don't exist." (p. 65)

The same month, *The Costco Connection* devoted its "Arts & Entertainment" page to an article, "Supernatural Success: Paranormal Fiction Gains Popularity with Teens," written by J. Rentilly. Of course, Costco's motivation was to sell more books, but Rentilly had nevertheless interviewed knowledgeable people who made some interesting observations. David Levithan, editorial director at Scholastic, said that he thought the two literary series—Harry Potter and Twilight—were primarily responsible for the sudden surge in paranormal prose aimed at teenagers. He called it a "trickle-up" trend. Adult readers grabbed the books and because of the paranormal elements did not "feel silly or stigmatized for reading kids' books." Megan Tingley, senior vice president and publisher at Little, Brown Books for Young Readers, who acquired and edited the Twilight series, said that the new paranormal books

> . . . put children's fiction on everyone's radar screen, and that, along with the rise of the Internet, set the stage for the YA explosion. Suddenly, everyone was looking for another great book to read and the media was looking for a new, great publishing story, and the Internet provided a way for fans to share their passion for a new author or book at lightning speed. It was like pouring gasoline on a fire. (p. 36)

Humorous and Lighthearted Fantasy   *The Hitchhiker's Guide to the Galaxy* is a genuinely funny spoof. The book began as a BBC radio script, progressed to a television script, and ultimately became a novel. When Arthur Dent's house is due for demolition to make way for a highway, he finds Ford Prefect, a strange friend, anxiously seeking a drink at a nearby pub. Ford seems totally indifferent to Arthur's plight because, as he explains, the world will soon be destroyed to make way for a new galactic freeway. Soon the two men are safe aboard a Vogon Construction Fleet Battleship, and that is the most easily explained of the many improbabilities that follow.

Artemis Fowl in Eoin Colfer's books (Hyperion, beginning in 2001) is described as the "most ingenious criminal mind in history." Actually, Artemus can be compared to the bright, charismatic, and subversive Irish rogues in such adult books as Sean O'Casey's *Juno and the Paycock,* J. P. Donleavy's *The Ginger Man,* and John Synge's *Playboy of the Western World.* Rogues are heroes in Ireland because they were the ones who fought back when the British were taking over. They are high spirited and manage to diffuse real violence with humor or trickery. After the initial *Artemis Fowl* in 2001, Colfer followed up with at least six more books, each beginning with *Artemis Fowl* and then the subtitles: *The Arctic Incident, The Eternity Code, The Opal Deception, The Lost Colony, The Time Paradox,* and *The Atlantis Complex.*

Part of Colfer's humor comes through visual imagery and his descriptions of the Irish "wee" folks that Artemis associates with. They include centaurs, demons, dwarves, elves, fairies, gargoyles, gnomes, goblins, gremlins, imps, krakens, leprechauns, pixies, quaggas, sprites, trolls, and warlocks, all from Irish folklore but with some notable changes. As we might expect the dwarfs are small, compact, and earthy, but Colfer also gives them the ability to unhinge their jaws so they can eat great quantities of food, dirt, or fairy people. Mulch Diggums (*aka* Lance Digger, Mo Digence, and The Grouch) is a kleptomaniac, who often gets apprehended for "digging and entering." Whatever he eats goes through his body and out the bottom end. He loves to unbutton his bum flap and destroy whoever is behind him with a blast of stinky air. With this kind of humor, we shouldn't have been surprised that when Colfer came to speak in Phoenix, the audience was primarily junior high boys.

Gothic fantasy often includes humor to serve as comic relief—sort of an intermission from the horror. One of the few features of humor that all scholars agree on is that there has to be a surprise of some kind. This is a feature that is overdone in horror movies where body parts unexpectedly fall off or unbelievable creatures suddenly emerge from unlikely places, causing audiences to first gasp and then laugh. But Gothic humor can also be very sophisticated as shown by the wordplay in Neil Gaiman's *The Graveyard Book,* which was described by the 2009 Newbery selection committee as "A delicious mix of murder, fantasy, humor, and human longing," in which a child marked for death by an ancient league of assassins escapes into an abandoned graveyard, where he is protected and raised by creatures not of his own ilk. For a fuller discussion of Gaiman's humor, see page 210 in Chapter 6.

Also see the write-up on Terry Pratchett, page 158, who was the first humorous fantasy writer to be chosen for the Margaret A. Edwards award. In his irreverent fantasies, much of his humor comes through the sarcastic comments that characters make to each other when they are communicating the kinds of feelings that most of us have about our real-life situations. His books have been translated into nearly forty languages. It is fortunate that Pratchett relies heavily on sarcasm, rather than on such wordplay as puns and metaphors, because

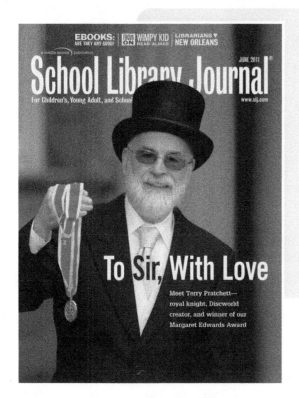

Since its beginning in 1988, School Library Journal *has been the co-sponsor of the Margaret A. Edwards Award, which is announced at the midwinter meetings of the American Library Association. Each June, the Journal features the winner on its cover and includes a three or four page interview on the inside. Here is the cover honoring Terry Pratchett, the 2011 winner. The photo was taken when he was knighted by Queen Elizabeth in 2009.*

sarcasm translates into other languages better than does wordplay, where the key words may not have the same multiple meanings in languages other than English. Also, having characters who are not quite "normal" and placing them in extraordinary situations allows Pratchett more freedom to have his characters make the kinds of surprising comments that bring smiles to his readers.

Nancy Farmer's *The Sea of Trolls* and its sequel, *The Land of the Silver Apples,* have been recommended for some lighthearted moments. So have Sally M. Keehn's *Gnat Stokes and the Foggy Bottom Swamp Queen* and the Bartimaeus Trilogy (*The Amulet of Samarkand, The Golem's Eye,* and *Ptolemy's Gate*) by Jonathan Stroud.

A totally different kind of humor appears in Vivian Vande Velde's *Never Trust a Dead Man.* It is set in medieval times; as the novel starts, seventeen-year-old Selwyn has had a bad week. He loves Anorea, who prefers the richer Farold, and the two boys fight for her favors. Then Farold is found dead, stabbed in the back with Selwyn's knife, and Selwyn is found guilty by public acclaim and sentenced to death. But because their medieval world is full of superstitions about what to do with dead bodies and murderers, the populace decides to entomb Selwyn with Farold's decomposing body until Selwyn dies—or whatever. Selwyn is interred, waiting for the rats or the gas to kill him, when a wander witch, Elswyth, in search of ingredients for a spell, appears. He asks for her help, and in return for his pledge to be her servant for years to come, he escapes along with Farold, brought to life to help find the murderer but accidentally transformed into a bat.

Middle school and junior high readers might also enjoy Stacy Kramer and Valerie Thomas's *Karma Bites* about Fanny Flanders and her granny, whose solution to problems is to bake goodies from her magical box with recipes for

Winner (2011)
Terry Pratchett, A Writer Who Makes Us Smile

Presenting the 2011 Margaret A. Edwards Award to Terry Pratchett was extra poignant because in December of 2008, while Pratchett was still in his fifties, he was diagnosed with a rare form of early-onset Alzheimer's. By the time he was chosen for the award, he had already donated nearly one million dollars to Alzheimer's research and had been featured in a BBC documentary, *Terry Pratchett—Living with Alzheimer's.* He was also knighted by Queen Elizabeth, chosen for the 2008 *Los Angeles Times* Book Prize, and won the 2009 *Boston Globe-Horn Book Award.*

He is a British author, who many of us came to know fairly late in his career when his "serious" book *Nation* was a runner up for the Printz Award and was on our Honor List. But we soon found out that many of our students had been reading his books for years. He is best known to the world-at-large for his Discworld series, which he began in 1983 with *The Color of Magic* (one of the books that the committee honored). The series now has thirty-eight books in it, with five of them being for young adults. All-in-all, Pratchett has written fifty books, with some of them being translated into as many as thirty-seven languages. We have seen sales figures ranging from 35 to 65 million individual purchases.

When Pratchett was interviewed for the cover story in the June 2011 *School Library Journal,* he told Jonathan Hunt that his Alzheimer's is "the kind called posterior cortical atrophy, which in a sense is much, much better than what we call the normal Alzheimer's—although they all end up pretty much the same way." He then said that he had no way to predict how many more books he can write. Depending on his health he intends "to keep going on until I can't go any further, and then regrettably, I will stop."

This wording reminded us of a joke he made on page 11 of *Equal Rites* when Farmer Gordo Smith asks Granny Weatherwax how wizards want to be buried, and she says "Yes." And then when he asks again, "Well, how?" she answers, "Regretfully."

For some time, Pratchett has been unable to type, but he has been working on a voice-activated computer. His health kept him from attending, in person, the January luncheon honoring him at the American Library Association

"Brilliant Banana Bread" and "Make It Better Munches Mix." Polly Shulman's *The Grimm Legacy* is about a library which checks out magical objects instead of books. When the objects begin to lose their powers, Elizabeth and her friends try to figure out what's gone wrong. *Princess Ben: Being a Wholly Truthful Account of Her Various Discoveries and Misadventures, Recounted to the Best of Her Recollection, in Four Parts* by Catherine Gilbert Murdock is the story of fifteen-year-old Princess Benevolence, who is pushed into training to rule after her parents and uncle are attacked and presumed dead. She just happens to discover that there's magic in the castle walls, and with this leg-up, she proves her mettle.

Myth-Based Fantasy   Rick Riordan deserves much of the credit for reviving interest in the Greek and Roman gods. When he came and spoke on a Sunday afternoon in Phoenix during the spring of 2010, the large high school auditorium was completely filled with young teens—as many, or maybe even more, boys than girls—and their parents. He explained that he was an English teacher and was heartbroken when one of his sons hated school. He would climb under the annual meeting, but instead of complaints or expressions of disappointment from those who bought tickets, we heard only expressions of "Best wishes" and hopes that he may be able to continue by coauthoring. Back in 1996, he coauthored a book with his friend Neal Gaiman, *Good Omens: The Nice and Accurate Prophecies of Agnes Nutter, Witch,* that was published as a mass market paperback by Ace and advertised as a descendant of *The Hitchhiker's Guide to the Universe.*

Pratchett gives a wonderful description of an alternate universe when he says his Discworld is a place where things are less as they are, and more like people imagine them to be. Physically, he describes it as "bigger than the biggest, most unpleasantly armed starcruiser in the imagination of a three-ring filmmaker." It is a turtle, ten thousand miles long, which carries "on its meteor-pocked shell four giant elephants who bear on their enormous shoulders the great round wheel of the Discworld" (page 1 of *Equal Rites*). The Edwards Committee chose to honor nine of his books (more than any other recipient). Books honored by the committee and not already mentioned are listed here in alphabetical order with their original publication dates. HarperCollins is the American publisher on all these books.

The Amazing Maurice and His Educated Rodents (2001). Winner of the Carnegie Medal, this is the story of a talking cat helped in his shenanigans by talking rats.

Going Postal (2004). A clever swindler named Moisit Van Lipwig is scheduled for a public hanging, but when he falls through the trapdoor he is surprised to find himself not dead, but instead working for the post office.

Guards! Guards! (1989). The noble dragons have invaded Ankh-Morpork in this book which laid the groundwork for the first Discworld computer game.

A Hat Full of Sky (2004). Tiffany Aching, a witch-in-training, is threatened by a sinister monster and even Granny Weatherwax, the world's greatest witch, can't help her out.

I Shall Wear Midnight (2010). Pratchett said he has a lot of emotional attachment to the book because it may be the final adventure for Tiffany Aching, now sixteen, and *the* witch of the Chalk region.

Small Gods (1994). Pratchett says that "The gods swarm as thick as herring roe," which means that there are also priests galore.

The Wee Free Men (2003). Tiffany Aching saves her little brother from the Queen of Fawiries. *The New York Times* described the book as "Celtic mythology fused with *Buffy the Vampire Slayer*." ●

dining room table and cling to the support pole in the middle so as to keep from having to do his homework.

Riordan started telling him stories from the myths and tying them in with his son's homework as well as his real life. When he ran out of the "real" stories, he started making them up, and thus began his new career of telling stories, not just to his own son, but to millions of other kids. When a boy from the audience asked Riordan if he "believed in" the stories, Riordan said that he "believed in them as wonderful stories," but if he thought of them as really true then he couldn't very well change them and make up new ones.

Riordan's two sons, now in their teens, are still his first audience. If they don't laugh at a joke, he deletes it. Or if they look puzzled about something, he goes back and changes it. Riordan is published by Hyperion, with his first *Percy Jackson and the Olympians* coming out in 2005. It has the subtitle of *The Lightning Thief.* Book Two has the subtitle of *The Sea of Monsters* (2005); Book Three, *The Titan's Curse* (2007); Book Four, *The Battle of the Labyrinth* (2008); and Book Five, *The Last Olympian* (2009). He is now moving on to explore Egyptian mythology with his Kane Chronicles. The first ones to appear are *The Red Pyramid* and *The Throne of Fire.*

In addition to stories clearly based on the myths, there are many intriguing new books where an author tucks in a mythical allusion. For example, readers who adore the three books in Suzanne Collins's The Hunger Games series will probably be interested to know that Collins's ideas for the story came not only from surfing TV and coming across reality TV shows back-to-back with battle stories from Iraq, but also from mythology. Spartacus, who was a slave forced to become a gladiator and fight to the death while the aristocracy watched for entertainment, later became a face for the rebellion, much like Katniss, the hero of *The Hunger Games,* does. A myth even more closely related is that of Theseus. Every year, seven Athenian boys and seven Athenian girls were sent to Crete as a tribute. The Cretans hosted a lavish banquet for these tributes, dressing them and feeding them before sending them into the Labyrinth to face the Minotaur. Theseus offers to take the place of one of the tributes (as Katniss took the place of her sister, Primrose). At the banquet, Princess Ariadne falls in love with Theseus and explains a way for him to survive the Labyrinth. This allows Theseus to escape after he defeats the Minotaur, which is a hybrid creature that is half-man, half-bull—c.f. the genetically engineered *mutts* in *The Hunger Games.*

In Ally Condie's *Matched,* there is a more direct reference to a classical myth. While Cassie and Ky (the two young people perhaps "planned" for each other by The Society) are hiking up a hill as part of their mandated physical training, Ky mentions Sisyphus. Cassie, who has always lived in the controlled Society, which has only one approved list of stories that can be shared, presses Ky to tell her about Sisyhus. Ky explains that it is an old story his father told him. "Sisyphus was crafty and sneaky and always causing trouble for the Society and the Officials." Because of this, the Society decided to give Sisyphus a special punishment that would show people they should not be like him in daring to "think he could be as clever as one of them, when he wasn't an Official, or even a citizen. He was nothing. An Aberration from the Outer Provinces." It is interesting how Ky has adapted the story to the vocabulary of the present-day Society using the words of "An Aberration from the Outer Provinces" which have been applied to him. He goes on to describe the job:

"He had to roll a rock, a huge one, to the top of a mountain."

"That doesn't sound so terrible." There's relief in my voice. If the story ends well for Sisyphus, maybe it can end well for Ky.

"It wasn't as easy as it sounds. As he was about to reach the top, the rock rolled back to the bottom and he had to start again. That happened every time. He never got the rock to the top. He went on pushing forever." (234–235).

Another example comes from *In the Belly of the Bloodhound: Being an Account of a Particularly Peculiar Adventure in the Life of Jacky Faber* by L. A. Meyer (Harcourt, 2006). We classify the Jacky Faber stories as fantasy, but some people might argue that they are just great adventure tales. Anyway, the allusion to a myth comes when a girl has her feelings hurt because she and her coworkers, who have had the job of killing rats with homemade bows and arrows, are referred to as "the Dianas." Jacky sighs and explains the reason. "It was back in the old countries—Greece and Rome and Egypt," where everything started. The people had lots of gods—men gods, boy gods, dwarf gods, and even girl gods. Then she tells the discouraged girl about Athena and Juno, and Ceres, and finally about Diana, who was always shown with a bow and her arrows. She concludes with "It's a compliment, really," and the discouraged girl goes back to her job with a new sense of pride.

In response to all the interest in the myths, teachers might want to have on hand some informative books telling the original stories. George O'Connor has written an Olympian series published by First Second Books. Titles include *Athena: Grey-Eyed Goddess, Hera: The Goddess and her Glory, Zeus: King of the Gods,* and *Hades: Lord of the Dead.* Students might also enjoy Diana Wynne Jones's *The Game,* which is about a dangerous game that allows players to enter the "mythosphere" and ride in and out of folktales and myths. It's a game forbidden by parents but kids play it anyway.

Supernatural Fantasy Fears of death, the unknown, and the supernatural probably go back to prehistoric times, when shadows in a cave and light and dark mystified and frightened humans. While demanding answers, we have settled on myths and legends. Now, amidst all our modern knowledge and sophistication, we hold on to our fascination with the unknowable. We delight in chambers of horrors, tunnels of terror, and haunted houses. We claim to be rational beings, yet we read astrology charts. We mock the superstitions of others yet hold as pets one or two of our own, joking all the time while we toss salt over our shoulder, avoid walking under ladders, and knock on wood. We follow customs without wondering why they came about. Black is assumed to be the appropriate dress for funerals because it is dark, gloomy, and demonstrates solemnity. We may not know that black was worn at a time lost in history because spirits, sometimes malignant or perhaps indignant, were thought to linger near a corpse for a year. Wearing black made it more difficult for these evil spirits to see the living. As long as spirits were around, danger lurked; hence, long mourning periods took place in black dress.

Whether Shakespeare believed in ghosts or witches is anyone's guess. Certainly, his audiences often did, and they apparently delighted in or were frightened by them in plays such as *Macbeth, Hamlet,* and *The Tempest.* Few people will admit to believing in supernatural elements, yet they listen eagerly to urban legends and stories about mysterious happenings. Alvin Schwartz was happily surprised when his books *Scary Stories to Tell in the Dark, More Scary Stories to Tell in the Dark,* and *Scary Stories 3: More Tales to Chill Your Bones* began winning statewide contests as kids' favorite books. At the same time, the books also climbed to the top of the American Library Association's list of banned books. Stephen Gammell's creepy illustrations are probably as much to blame as are the stories themselves. Let's hope that Derek Landy's 2007 *Skulduggery Pleasant* does not meet the same fate even though it too has a skeleton on the cover and is written for young teens.

Supernatural novels have well-established ground rules. Settings are usually in an eerie or haunted house or in a place where a mysterious event occurred

Young Scholars Speak Out

Lisa Maxwell Arter on How I Learned to Relax and Live with "Wabbit Literacy"

I have always loved mythology, and when I was teaching language arts in middle schools, I worked all year long with Greek and Latin roots and affixes to teach both spelling and vocabulary. But the best part came at the end of the year when we submerged ourselves in mythology. We made family trees of the Greek gods (most of which curved back in on themselves) and rearranged the room to journey through the Underworld. My stuffed Fluffy from Harry Potter stood guard on the other side of the River Styx while Charon (dressed in my black graduation robe) led each student past him and toward the three judges. I still get messages from former students (many of whom are now in college or beyond) commenting on the latest Percy Jackson book or telling me about some new connection to one of the myths they have run across.

This has been wonderful, but it spoiled me for supervising student teachers and for teaching in college where I find that most of my students have had only the slightest introduction to mythology. Even though my students live in or near the city of Phoenix, named for the mythological bird which bursts into flames and is reborn from the ashes,

most of them miss the metaphor of how this describes what it felt like to be summertime residents in the "Valley of the Sun" before there was air conditioning or electricity to freeze ice and run fans. They also miss out on the kinds of allusions that make my daily tasks a little more pleasant. When I scrub my home with *Ajax* cleanser, I am reminded of the Greek warrior in the Iliad who really "cleaned up" in battle. When I shave my legs with a *Venus* razor, I am performing an act of ironic vanity because I am trying to look beautiful in a way that ancient Roman women never did. When I download *Hyperion* published books to my Kindle, I do so through *Amazon.com*. When I email my sister, she receives it on her *Juno* account and when I go to my GPS system for navigation directions, I am reminded of how much easier it is than getting out the heavy *Atlas* from the family bookshelves.

When I started teaching young adult literature classes, I worried about the students who were reading Rick Riordan's Percy Jackson stories and thinking that Riordan created such a complex world from scratch. I felt sorry that they were missing out on a lot of the connections,

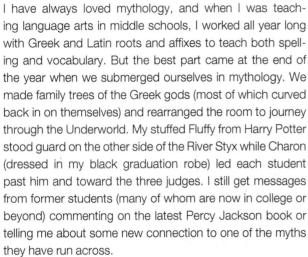

years ago. Some thrillers occur in more mundane places, perhaps a brownstone in New York City or a hotel shut down for the season, but readers know the mundane remains calm only for a short time before frightening events begin and strange people come out to play. Darkness is usually essential, but not always physical darkness. The protagonist is oblivious to evil for a time but ultimately recognizes the pervasive power of the darkness of the soul. Sometimes the wife or husband sells out to evil and entices the spouse to join in a black mass. Rituals or ceremonies are essential. Family curses or pacts with the devil have become commonplaces of the genre. Alfred Hitchcock, that master of suspense, reminds us over and over that the most terrifying things can happen in the most commonplace settings. In *North by Northwest,* on a lovely day in the middle of a South Dakota cornfield, Cary Grant is suddenly attacked by a crop-dusting airplane. In but then I heard from humor scholars about the concept of "Wabbit Literacy" (named after Warner Brothers' Bugs Bunny, aka "that Wascally Wabbit"). They point out that in today's world, most children meet classical figures through television parodies and other pop culture allusions, rather than in the "real" stories. To older generations, this seems absolutely backwards and counterproductive, but young humor scholars argue that it is just part of today's literary "deconstruction" followed by "reconstruction." The pop culture allusions serve as "readiness" and attention getters for the "real" stories. Besides, who is to say which versions are the "real" stories? They all grew out of oral storytelling traditions with various tellers adding their own insights and details, which is what makes them so strong.

I feel comforted by this idea and have vowed to keep leading my students to both "new" and "old" versions of the myths. And as I have been pondering the growing body of new stories that rely on the myths, not always for the whole stories but at least for occasional allusions, I have discovered a new reason for doing this, which is that the Greek and Roman myths include a cast of strong women (e.g., *Pomona* as seen in the name of what started as a farming town in Northern California and *Athena* as seen in the name of Athens, Georgia; *Ceres,* who we honor every morning when we eat our "cereal"; *Psyche,* who still blesses us with her understanding of "psychology"; *Arachne,* who was such a good weaver that the world's spiders are named for her; *Aphrodite,* the Greek goddess of love and beauty, whose power we still invoke when we search for

NEW VERSIONS OF OLD MYTHS

"aphrodisiacs"; and *Diana,* who was the Goddess of the Hunt usually shown carrying a bow and arrows).

We pride ourselves in this "enlightened" age of supposed gender-equality that our girls are stronger and more self-assured than ever before. While there may be some truth in this, I believe it does both genders good to read stories of women who are intelligent, brave, and self-reliant; and who contribute to the world in their own right, not just because they happened to catch the eye of a prince charming who happened to be passing by and whisked them off to "live happily ever after."

• Lisa Maxwell Arter earned her bachelor's and master's degrees in English Education at La Sierra University in Riverside, California. She taught for eight years at Mt. View Junior High in Beaumont, California, where she coordinated and taught literacy intervention courses. She completed her Ph.D. in 2011 and is now teaching English/Language Arts Methods courses at the Polytechnic Campus of Arizona State University.

The Birds, a placid setting alongside the ocean suddenly turns to a scene of terror when sweet little birds begin to tear into human flesh.

In the 1989 edition of this textbook, Robert Westall observed that supernatural books break quite naturally into horror stories and ghost stories. The horror stories make the point that "the human organism is a frail thing of flesh subject to an infinity of abuse, and that it is painful and undignified for the human spirit to have to dwell in it." Such a depressing fact may be well worth saying but not over and over again. Even the books by such ingenious and powerful writers as Poe and Lovecraft, he noted, are not something you would want to read if you are "on the way to build the Taj Mahal, or paint the Sistine Chapel ceiling, or even have a happy love affair."

Knowledgeable people in the publishing world have conjectured that it is the dark elements in the new YA books that have made teen books attractive to adults. Readers can enjoy all the pleasure of good teen fiction, especially the romances, without feeling embarrassed that they are reading "kid lit." See Focus Box 5.2 "The Supernatural: Ghosts, Vampires and Other Undeads," on page 166 for new books that are being enjoyed by teens and adults.

On the other hand, the ghost story is about the undying spirit, not the dying flesh. . . . [Ghosts] add an exciting fifth dimension to the often-boring four dimensions of real life. They make it possible for us to escape into the land of the impossible where, delightfully, anything can happen. They are also a comfort: a reassurance of our own immortality. I would adore to spend my first few years of death as a ghost, drifting round the world painlessly in the company of other friendly ghosts, seeing all the things I never got round to seeing in life because there were other boring earthbound things to be done.

Westall went on to explain that we need ghost stories:

In terms of love and the passing of time, we are all haunted houses, full of rooms we have shut off because of loss, or fear, or regret. To spend all our time wandering through such rooms would lead to madness. But to wander sometimes can be agonizingly sweet and rich. And never to dare to wander through them can make life a dusty boring hell

When Stephenie Meyer published her first book, *Twilight,* in 2005, it immediately jumped to the top of the *New York Times* best-seller list and into the hearts of teenagers. The sequel, *New Moon,* was published in 2006, *Eclipse* in 2007, and *Breaking Dawn* in 2008. By now her stories are so famous that we hardly need to say anything about them. We were amused when we saw a preview for the 2010 *Gulliver's Travels* movie starring Jack Black. It opened with a scene of the hero applying for a job as a journalist. He tells his interviewer that he wants to be a writer. When she asks him what writers he admires, he says something like "Oh, Shakespeare and Krakauer, and that hot mother in Arizona who writes about vampires!"

Other recent vampire stories include Cynthia Leitich Smith's *Tantalize* in which seventeen-year-old Quincie lives with her uncle in Texas, and between the two of them they manage the Italian restaurant that was left to her when her parents died. Quincie decides to rename it Sanguinis and to decorate it with a vampire theme. But when the chef is mauled to death and replaced by a strange, fair-haired man with red eyes and some alarming recipes, readers know something is afoot.

Cal, in Scott Westerfeld's *Peeps,* leaves Texas—the home of shape-shifters—and moves to New York. Upon his arrival, he immediately loses his virginity and then learns that in the Big Apple a new kind of vampirism is an STD (sexually transmitted disease). His kind prefers not to use the v-word, but instead call themselves Peeps, for "Parasite Positive." As the hero of the book, he of course comes over to the good side and becomes one of the Night Watchers, working to understand and defeat the condition. The sequel is *The Last Days,* which has the extra fun of involving rock music as a solution to the problem.

We've heard two theories about why teenagers are especially attracted to vampire and werewolf stories. One is that their bodies actually are undergoing tremendous changes and so they are attracted to stories where young characters change even more than they do. Another is the idea of forbidden love. Especially in Meyer's *Twilight,* girls can revel in all the satisfactions of being an ordinary girl who is suddenly courted and adored and yet does not have "to go all the way." The more-than-perfect Edward loves Bella so much that he exerts utmost control over his "natural" instincts so that he will not accidentally bite Bella and turn her into a vampire or lose control and kill her by sucking out her blood.

The dilemma of most vampire and werewolf stories is whether we can accept someone disturbingly different even when we mostly admire and trust the person. The question that is asked in stories ranging from Frankenstein to Stephen King's work is whether we are willing to go below the surface in judging people? King is a former high school English teacher who frequently includes likable young people among his characters. The fact that he writes about them without condescension is not lost on the audience. "The Langoliers" (from *Four Past Midnight*) is the story of a late-night flight from Los Angeles to Boston. The plane goes through a time rip, and the only passengers who survive are the ten who happened to be sleeping. Fortunately, one of them is a pilot; otherwise, there wouldn't have been much of a story to tell. There is also the blind Dinah, a young girl on her way to Boston for an operation on her eyes. She has such a super-developed sense of hearing that she is mistaken by the mad Craig Toomy, the ultimate yuppie gone awry, as the chief Langolier. The character most closely filling the role of a young adult hero on a romantic quest is Albert Kaussner, a gifted violinist on his way to enroll in a Boston music conservatory. In his own mind, he's not Albert or Al, but Ace Kaussner, "The Arizona Jew" and "The Fastest Hebrew West of the Mississippi." The journey turns out to be much more difficult than anything faced by Ace's mythical heroes of the Old West, and it even requires him to sacrifice his beloved violin. At the end of the trip, he is rewarded with his first love and the feeling of growth and confidence that comes with having passed a difficult test.

Stephen King's first book, *Carrie,* appeared in 1974 and sold well for a then unknown writer. From that point on, King maintained his place as *the* writer of the genre. Carrie is a young outsider, the daughter of religious fanatics, and the

The Supernatural: Ghosts, Vampires, and Other Undeads

Alex Van Helsing: Vampire Rising by Jason Henderson. HarperCollins, 2010. When young Alex is sent to a boarding school, he learns about his great great grandfather, Alex Van Helsing, who was a vampire.

Anya's Ghost by Vera Brosgol. First Second, 2011. In this beautifully done and highly praised graphic novel, Anya is an immigrant from Russia to the United States. She's hell-bent on becoming an American, even refusing to associate with a Russian boy at her school, who she thinks is too "fobby" (fresh off the boat). Then she accidentally falls into an abandoned well, where she meets an American girl ghost. When she is rescued, the ghost follows her up and works as a kind of devious assistant, until Anya learns more about her. People expecting this to be an innocent and playful little comic book will be surprised by the language as well as by the actions of Anya and her high school "friends."

Birth of a Killer: The Saga of Larten Crepsley by Darren Shan. Little Brown, 2010. This is a prequel to Shan's The Cirque du Freek series. After Larten kills the factory foreman responsible for his brother's death, he becomes a vampire to escape the complications of his behavior.

Bloodlines by Richelle Mead. Razorbill, 2011. This is a spin-off from Mead's popular Vampire Academy series. Many of the same characters are in the story but in this one, Sydney, the alchemist, is ordered into hiding in a California high school. A related Vampire Academy gothic novel series is also being released.

Creature of the Night by Kate Thompson. Roaring Brook, 2009. The International interest in the supernatural is revealed in this thriller about a fourteen-year-old Irish boy who moves to the countryside from Dublin, but then gets involved in a murder case.

Elsewhere by Gabrielle Zevin. Farrar, 2005. Liz Hall awakens in a strange bed near a strange companion who has a small red wound at the base of her skull. Both girls are dead and heading for Elsewhere and some unusual experiences.

The Entertainer and the Dybbuk by Sid Fleischman. HarperCollins, Greenwillow, 2007. In this highly original book, readers get a new look at the anti-Semitism of the World War II era. Former American pilot Freddie Birch works as a ventriloquist and is surprised to find himself partnering with a dybbuk—a spirit or ghost.

Everlost by Neal Shusterman. Simon & Schuster, 2006. Nick and Allie are killed in an automobile accident and get acquainted as they head down that mythical tunnel toward "the light." They learn they are Afterlights, who cannot be seen or heard by the living.

It Sucks to Be Me: The All-True Confessions of Mina Hamilton, Teen Vampire, 2009, and *Still Sucks to Be Me: The All-True Confessions of Mina Smith,*

brunt of cruel jokes. She possesses the power of telekinesis, and she uses it to destroy the school, the students, and the town in a fit of justified rage. *Firestarter* is far better, with its portrait of an eight-year-old girl with the power to start fires merely by looking at an object.

Among young adult writers specializing in supernatural themes, Lois Duncan (see her write-up as an Edwards Award winner on p. 253) has been consistently popular. In *Summer of Fear,* Rachel Bryant's family is notified that relatives have died in a car crash, leaving seventeen-year-old Julia behind. The girl, who looks surprisingly mature, arrives and changes the lives of everyone around her. Trickle, the family dog, suspects something is wrong, but Trickle does not live long, and neither does anyone else who gets in Julia's way. Duncan's *Stranger with My Face* and *The Third Eye* were enjoyable but lacked the power of *Summer of Fear.* See Focus Box 5.2 "The Supernatural: Ghosts, Vampires, and Other Undeads," for other examples of supernatural stories written for teens.

Teen Vampire by Kimberly Pauley. Mirrorstone, 2010. In the sequel, Mina has been sent by the Vampire Relocation Agency to the southern states, where she learns how to shape-shift and protect her friend Serena. She has all of the complications of regular school added to the complications of being a vampire.

Kiss Me Deadly: 13 Tales of Paranormal Love edited by Trisha Telep. Running Press Teens, 2010. The stories are collected from authors of books or series and so might be used to introduce readers to the styles of such authors as Maggie Stiefvater, Carrie Ryan, Daniel Waters, and Sharah Rees Brennan.

Liar by Justine Larbalestier. Bloomsbury, 2009. A girl who has a hard time telling the truth is implicated in the murder of a fellow student. The complications of the matter are slowly revealed in this supernatural thriller.

The Lovely Bones by Alice Sebold. Little, Brown, 2002. Fourteen-year-old Susie Salmon is on her way to school when she is raped and murdered in a cornfield. She tells her story from heaven as she watches over her family. A beautifully done film helped the book gain its popularity.

The Old Willis Place: A Ghost Story by Mary Downing Hahn. Clarion, 2004. The events in this spooky and beautifully written story are told through the eyes of two girls, Diana and Lissa, who call the Old Willis Place home. While they keep to themselves and consider making friends "against the rules," their reasons are different.

They Suck, They Bite, They Eat, They Kill: The Psychological Meaning of Supernatural Monsters in Young Adult Fiction by Joni Bodart. Scarecrow Press, 2012. Bodart wrote this for adult librarians and teachers who are trying to get a grasp on this genre. Most readers will be surprised at how many books there are.

The Van Alen Legacy: A Blue Bloods Novel by Melissa de la Cruz. Hyperion, 2009. In this fourth book of the Blue Bloods series, readers learn the history of the New York coven of vampires, which existed in ancient Rome as angels and demons, but have now turned into vampires.

The Wish List by Eoin Colfer. Hyperion/Miramax, 2003. When Meg and her friend Belch try to rob their elderly neighbor, Lowrie McCall, a nearby gas tank explodes and sends Meg through that long tunnel to the afterlife. However, Saint Peter and Beelzebub can't decide who should get Meg and so they send her back to patch things up with Lowrie McCall.

Zombies vs. Unicorns edited by Holly Black and Justine Larbalestier. Simon & Schuster, 2010. These two respected authors of fantasy, went hunting for stories featuring either zombies or unicorns and put them together in a wonderful collection. Each of the editors has a favorite and set out in hope of convincing readers to their way of thinking. The book probably fell short of doing this, but *School Library Journal* praised the twelve stories for going beyond the stereotypes in inspiring readers to "ponder themes of love and loss, moral dilemmas, and the state of modern society."

Support for allowing young adults to read supernatural books comes from Jeanine Basinger, the chair of film studies at Wesleyan University, who was quoted in a *New York Times* article titled "The Chills, The Thrills, The Profits" (Aug. 31, 1999). While her words were aimed at horror films, they apply equally well to books:

It never really goes away, this appetite for horror. . . . We have all of these tragedies on our minds. In modern life it's just one damn thing after another, and we seek to explain it to one another. And if there's some experience that gives closure to it, gives an explanation or at least gives us reassurance that we're not the only ones having the scaries, it reassures us.

Traditional or Mabinogion Fantasy   The *Mabinogion* is a collection of medieval Welsh tales, first published in English in 1838 to 1849 by Lady Charlotte Guest.

The eleven stories deal with Celtic legends, myths, and personalities. There are also four independent tales and four Arthurian romances. Guest was more of a collector than a creative writer. By preserving these old stories, she helped to provide the kind of general knowledge that influenced some of our most popular writers, who, in turn, have influenced other writers. Here in alphabetical order are some of the best-known writers whose works have built what most of us in western cultures think of as "traditional" fantasy.

Lloyd Alexander, who died on May 17, 2007, is best known for his *Chronicles of Prydain*. Alexander grew up in Pennsylvania, but in World War II he was trained in Wales to work as a staff sergeant in intelligence and counterintelligence. His years in Wales provided him with knowledge of the Mabinogion, as well as some interesting settings, both of which he later used in his fantasies. The Prydain chronicles consist of five volumes about Taran, the young Assistant Pig-Keeper, who through *The Book of Three, The Black Cauldron, The Castle of Llyr, Taran Wanderer,* and *The High King* (awarded the Newbery Medal in 1969) saves his country and makes a place in the world for himself.

Peter Dickinson presents readers of *The Ropemaker* with adventures, ideas, and an initiation rite. For twenty generations, the Valley has been safe from barbarians to the north and the evil Empire to the south through powerful magic, but now that the magic grows thin, people from the Valley set out to find help. They learn of the Ropemaker, a powerful magician who has been protecting their Valley, but in the end they discover that a young girl, Tilja, is their protector. In *A Bone from a Dry Sea,* Dickinson uses two narrators, one contemporary, one historic. In his stunning *Eva,* a famous scientist is devoting his life to working with chimpanzees. When the family gets in an automobile accident and his daughter is almost killed, he transplants her brain into a chimpanzee that had been raised by the family.

Alan Garner is known largely for *The Owl Service* (1968), which when it appeared in the United States created something of a sensation among the teachers and librarians who read it. Based on the Mabinogion legends, three young characters find a set of dishes. As the three get to know each other better, they also find that the pattern reflects a story of love and jealousy and hatred, which is one of the Mabinogion's tales of a triangular love that ends disastrously.

Diana Wynne Jones's versatility delights her readers. In *Howl's Moving Castle,* Sophie is changed into an old crone by the Wicked Witch and finds shelter in a strange moving castle owned by a wizard named Howl, who has also been cursed by the Wicked Witch. *Howl's Moving Castle* is a fantastic story, which was later filmed in animation by Hayao Miyazaki. *A Charmed Life,* about young witch Gwendolyn Chant and her brother, Cat, is set in an enchanted England where the government is in charge of magic. In her 2010 *Enchanted Glass,* Aiden and Andrew must join forces to stop chaos from the faerie realm from slipping into their field of care.

Robin McKinley's *Beauty: A Retelling of the Story of Beauty and the Beast* and the more recent *Rose Daughter* are so amusing and so spirited that they led the way for many others to take on the challenge of rewriting old fairy tales. McKinley also created the mythical kingdom of Damar, the setting for her first heroic fantasy, *The Blue Sword*. Harry, a female orphan, is kidnapped by the Hillfolk and slowly convinced that she should take up the legendary blue sword to free the Hillfolk. McKinley won the 1985 Newbery Medal for *The Hero and the Crown*, a prequel to *The Blue Sword*.

Christopher Paolini surprised the world in 2003 with *Eragon*, a quest fantasy, and the first book in the *Inheritance* trilogy. Paolini was a home-schooled boy living in Montana who, when he was fifteen, began writing the story of a middle-ages farm boy who finds a strange blue stone. He takes it home, where it hatches into a dragon. The boy keeps the dragon secret, but then terrible things start happening. In 2002, when Paolini was seventeen, his parents helped him self-publish and sell 10,000 copies of the 500-page book. At this stage, the book came to the attention of Knopf, a major publishing house, which edited and promoted the book worldwide. The 2006 movie was also well received (the video game not so much), as have been *Eldest* and *Brisingr*. With *Inheritance* in 2011, the trilogy changed to a series.

Tamora Pierce's books that are most appreciated by our students are the ones about Beka Cooper, including *Bloodhound: The Legend of Beka Cooper* and *Terrier*, along with *Trickster's Choice* and *Trickster's Queen*. We especially like *Shatterglass*, the concluding volume of her second quartet of the Circle Opens series, because of the way it combines mystery and magic. Pierce explained in an October 1993 article in *School Library Journal* that kids like fantasy because it is a literature of empowerment in a world where they have little to say about how things work. But in fantasy, whether readers are short or fat, unbeautiful or weak, and so on, they find a realm in which those things are negated by strength. But there's always a catch, which is that when they are empowered by winning, their new stature brings new trials and challenges, much like in real life.

J. R. R. Tolkien is the writer against whom all other fantasy writers are measured. *The Hobbit, or There and Back Again* began in 1933 as a series of stories that Tolkien told his children at night about a strange being, Bilbo the Hobbit. *The Lord of the Rings,* his three-part series, is even better known, especially with the release of three movies made from the Ring series revealing his love of adventure and his fascination with language. The Associated Press reported on May 6, 2007, that more than 900,000 copies had been printed of *The Children of Hurin,* a prequel to *The Lord of the Rings* that Tolkien had started in 1918 and eventually abandoned. Long after Tolkien's death in 1973, his son, Christopher, took out the manuscript and edited it for publication.

See Focus Box 5.3, "Books Reflecting Traditional Tales and the Mabinogion," on page 170 for other books that in some way reflect the traditions of the old stories from northern Europe and England. But stand warned that these new stories are written by creative authors, none of whom are interested in simply

Focus Box 5.3

Books Reflecting Traditional Tales and the Mabinogion

A Conspiracy of Kings by Megan Whelan Turner. **HarperCollins, 2010.** In this fourth book of the Queen's Thief series, Saphos studies to be the king of Sounis, but he is kidnapped and sold into slavery. The story focuses on his attempts to escape and accept his rightful place as king.

Crispin: At the Edge of the World by Avi. **Hyperion, 2006.** In this continuation of *Crispin: The Cross of Lead* (Hyperion, 2002), Crispin and Bear are again hunted by men who have decided that Bear is a traitor to their Brotherhood. Troth, a disfigured girl, joins Crispin and Bear in crossing the English channel.

The Demon's Covenant by Sarah Rees Brennan. **S&S, 2010.** This is the second volume of the Demon's Lexicon series. The Obsidian Circle magicians want to recruit Jamie. Mae asks Nick and Alan to protect Jamie.

The Exiled Queen by Cinda Williams Chima. **Hyperion. 2010.** Princess Raisa flees in hopes of avoiding marriage and receiving military training. She meets Han and is attracted to him, but again her hopes of love are thwarted.

Fade by Robert Cormier. **Delacorte, 1988.** Paul Moreaux, a young French Canadian, discovers that he has inherited a family gift/curse that comes to only one person in each generation: the ability to be invisible.

Finnikan of the Rock by Melina Marchetta. **Candlewick, 2010.** The son of the king's guard tries to lead his people home in this extraordinary tale about the emotional price of living in exile.

Fire by Kristin Cashore. **Dial, 2009.** Winner of the 2010 Amelia Elizabeth Walden Award, *Fire* is a sequel to *Graceling* (2008). In the first book, Katsa is "graced" with a gift for fierce fighting, which comes in handy when she must defy her brutal uncle and save the grandfather of the king of a neighboring kingdom. In both books, there is danger, mystery, adventure, and romance.

Green Witch, by Alice Hoffman. **Scholastic, 2010.** In this sequel to the 2003 Green Angel, the city is being rebuilt after the Hoard has almost destroyed it. Green and Troy search for Diamond and for Troy's sister.

Here Lies Author by Phillip Reeve. **Scholastic, 2008.** Reeve turns King Arthur's character upside down in this story. He is a petty tyrant who protects his English neighbors from the Saxon invaders only for a hefty price. The real hero of the story is Myrddin, who is a kind of poet and trickster. He devises and tells the stories of Arthur's greatness that have come down in history. The book is recommended as an insightful exploration of the power of story both in contemporary life and in history.

The Hunter's Moon by O. R. Melling **(Chronicles of Faerie Series). Abrams/Amulet, 2004.** Successfully published in Ireland in 1992 and in Canada in 1993, Melling's story about a teen who must save her unwilling cousin from the Faerie lands is a blend of Irish mythology and geography.

King of Ithaka by Tracy Barrett. **Holt, 2010.** Reviewers praised this as a perfect introduction to the tale of Odysseus. It is told through the eyes of Telemachos, who is accompanied by a centaur and a run-away weaver. He is looking for the father he barely knows and in the process meets terrifying creatures and other dangers on both land and sea.

The Last Conspiracy by Frances Hardinge. **HarperCollins, 2009.** Two sisters, one who is revered as an oracle with extrasensory powers, have vital roles to play in saving their land, which is on a lush, but treacherous, island.

Linger by Maggie Stiefvater. **Scholastic, 2010.** In this sequel to the 2009 Shiver, the werewolf Sam in his human form is trying to help Grace postpone turning into a werewolf after she has been bitten. Grace, Sam, and Cole try to manage their various stages of *werewolfery*.

The Lion Hunter (The Mark of Solomon Series Bk. #1) by Elizabeth Wein. **Viking, 2007.** Set in sixth-century Africa, this story has all the intrigue and imagination of an Arthurian legend but in a very different part of the world. It continues the story of the boy Telemakos, whom readers met in The Sunbird (Viking, 2004).

The Naming by Alison Croggon. Candlewick, 2005.
When sixteen-year-old Maerad meets Cadvan, her life changes because he is a magically gifted Bard who begins teaching her about her own gifts and abilities and the responsibility he sees for her future.

The Navigator by Eoin McNamee. Houghton Mifflin, 2007. Owen, the Navigator, is chosen by the resisters to save the world from their enemies, the Harsh.

Numbers by Rachel Ward. Scholastic, 2010.
Fifteen-year-old Jenn has the ability to see into people's eyes and know when they will die. She keeps her talent secret until a gawky but persistent boy befriends her, and the two together get involved in a terrifying adventure where her talent proves valuable.

Ring of Solomon: A Bartimaeus Novel by Jonathan Stroud. Hyperion, 2010. A crafty Djinni, the servant of the Queen of Sheba's chief guard, inadvertently saves the country from the powerful King Solomon. It's a fantasy with some very funny moments.

The Scorpio Races by Maggie Stiefvater. Scholastic, 2011. When the water horses (carnivorous *capaill uisce*) rise from the sea, the men of the island must prove their strength and bravery through a race to outrun the creatures. Kate decides to be the first girl to enter the race, but the story gets more complicated when her strongest competition comes from Sean, a boy that she is attracted to.

Shadowspell by Jenna Black. St. Martin's, 2010.
In this second book of the Faeriewalker series, the Erlking arrives with his motorcycle gang. He is both handsome and ruthless, threatening Dana and her Faeriewalker powers.

StarCrossed by Elizabeth C. Bunce. Scholastic, 2010.
When Llyvraneth outlaws magic and forces everyone to believe in the king's religion, Digger camouflages himself as a maid in Meri's wealthy home and learns the ulterior motives of the guests.

A Tale Dark and Grimm by Adam Gidwitz. Dutton, 2010. This intriguing story was on several best book lists recommended for middle school readers. It includes eight retellings of the Grimm brothers' fairy tales, but with new characters that provide both amusement and food for thought.

Tender Morsels by Margo Flanagan. Knopf, 2008.
Flanagan rewrites the Grimm Brother's "Snow White and Rose-Red" and in doing so explores both bad and good aspects of human behavior and what a mother will go through to protect her daughters.

13 Treasures by Michelle Harrison. Little Brown, 2010.
Invisible fairies torment and bully Tanya, and then it gets serious when children start disappearing. Tanya turns detective, enters the Fairy Realm, and in the end defies death.

Treasury of Greek Mythology: Classic Stories of Gods, Goddesses, Heroes & Monsters by Donna Jo Napoli, illustrated by Christina Balit. National Geographic, 2011. Napoli uses the same wonderful writing style as she has used in several well-received YA novels, to bring to life 25 of the best known stories. They are beautifully illustrated and the book would make a worthy addition to any classroom where readers want to compare new tellings to traditional ones.

Troll Fell by Katherine Langrish. HarperCollins, 2004. Viking ships and some fantastic creatures add a Scandinavian touch to this adventure about young Peer Ulfsson, who discovers after his father dies that his greedy uncles are going to sell him to the Troll king, who wants to give him as a slave to his newly married son.

The Turning by Gillian Chan. Kids Can/KCP Fiction, 2005. After his mother's death, sixteen-year-old Ben Larsson goes reluctantly with his folklorist father on a sabbatical to England. He learns that he has inherited "old blood, hero's blood" from his Icelandic grandfather and now is needed to combat the evil designs of the Faerie folk.

Wicked Lovely by Melissa Marr. HarperCollins, 2007. Aislinn is a human who can see fairies. When the Summer King decides Aislinn is the Summer Queen he has long lusted for, the Winter Queen sets out to destroy her.

***The Adoration of Jenna Fox* by Mary E. Pearson. Holt, 2008.** In this dystopian novel, seventeen-year-old Jenna wakes from a yearlong coma and slowly realizes that her parents are hiding a terrible secret.

***After* by Francine Prose. HarperCollins, 2003.** After a nearby school shooting, Central High School receives a threat and administrators vow to protect the students. And protect them they do with random locker searches, urine tests, and a whole list of restricted items including wearing anything red (a gang color) and reading J. D. Salinger's *The Catcher in the Rye* because Holden Caulfield is "a highly negative role model."

***Black Hole Sun* by David Macinnis Gill. HarperCollins/ Greenwillow, 2010.** Described as the "year's funniest dystopian thriller," this is the story of a village of unlucky miners who hire a disgraced teenage lawman and his girlfriend to save them from a gang of cannibalistic marauders. The *School Library Journal* reviewer wrote "Think *Seven Samurai* on Mars with wisecracking dialogue worthy of a Bob Hope-Bing Crosby 'road' flick."

***The Carbon Diaries 2015* by Saci Lloyd. Holiday House, 2009.** In this dystopian look at a future only a few years away, Laura and her older sister find their family in dire straits because carbon is now rationed, meaning that travel is limited and so is the use of electricity and gas. Health standards have sunk and food shortages are everywhere.

***The Dirt Eaters* by Dennis Foon (The Longlight Legacy Trilogy Series Book No. #1). Annick, distributed by** Firefly, 2003. In this dystopian story, fifteen-year-old Roan is forced to leave his peace-loving village after it is destroyed and his younger sister is taken to the city. Follow-up books include *Freewalker* and *The Keeper's Shadow*.

***Divergent* by Veronica Roth. HarperCollins, 2011.** Sixteen-year-old Beatrice lives in a Chicago of the future that is divided into factions devoted to such virtues as Amity, Abnegation, Candor, Dauntless, and Erudite. Beatrice parts company with her family as she makes her own choice, but she soon finds out that the highly structured society is not as perfect as she has been lead to believe.

***Dreamquake: Book Two of the Dreamhunter Duet* by Elizabeth Knox. Farrar, 2007.** In a unique blend of fantasy and history, Edwardian heroines Rose and Laura uncover a government plot involving the creation of horrible dreams, which are used for such nefarious purposes as controlling prisoners.

***Epic* by Connor Kostick. Viking, 2007.** In New Earth, everyone plays a fantasy computer game called Epic. An unfair ruling by the Central Allocations Committee leads young adults to challenge the committee and to eliminate Epic.

***Firestorm* by David Klass. Farrar, 2006.** Jack learns he is not an all-American boy but rather a visitor from the future sent to save Earth.

***Glow* (Bk. 1 of Sky Chasers Series) by Amy Kathleen Ryan. St. Martin's/Griffin, 2011.** Fifteen-year-old Waverly and her boyfriend Kieran have always lived on a space ship, but when it is attacked by their sister ship,

repeating the same old stories, and so there are going to be surprising additions. For example, in Jenna Black's *Shadowspell*, the Earlking and his warriors arrive on motorcycles, while in L. G. Bass's Moonshadow Series, the conflict may have similarities to the old European ones, but the surface details are more like a classical Chinese epic combined with a Kung Fu film.

Conventions of Science Fiction

The first science fiction was built around the idea of space travel and the related idea that other planets have intelligent or frightening life forms that may differ drastically from Earth's humans. Contemporary problems are projected

New Horizon, everything changes and Waverly sets out to rethink issues connected to power, religion, morality, and survival.

The Hunger Games by Suzanne Collins. Scholastic, 2008. Although the strong emotions are what most readers remember from Collins's trilogy, it is the technology that makes the games the kind of television spectacular that will distract citizens from thinking about all the unfairness in their country. First are the almost magically hidden television cameras, then the amazing weapons, followed by the specially bred animals, for example, the *trackerjackers* (yellow-jacket wasps that not only inflict poisonous stings, but also hunt out their victims) and the *muttations* (the spirits of killed tributes who come back as horrible dogs to renew their fight against those still alive).

Life as We Knew It by Susan Beth Pfeffer. Harcourt, 2006. A family survives when a meteor hits our moon and causes floods and assorted other catastrophes.

Little Brother by Cory Doctorow. Tor, 2008. Marcus is a computer whiz who develops a secret online replacement for the internet after terrorists have attacked San Francisco. He is organizing rebels against the Department of Homeland Security's clampdown on the city. His friends have been wrongfully incarcerated and tortured for information.

Matched by Ally Condie. Putnam, 2010. In this utopia-turned-dystopia, Cassia is matched to Xander, but for just a flicker on her message board, she is also matched to Ky, who is considered "unmatchable." Xander does not agree that Ky is unmatchable, and this triggers changes for the entire community.

The New Policeman by Kate Thompson. HarperCollins/Greenwillow, 2007. In this lively Irish story, a fifteen-year-old musician sets out to find where all the time has gone in hopes of filling his mother's birthday request of having more time. And while Liddy makes it to the Land of Eternal Youth, he is surprised that it isn't the utopia he expected, but rather is filled with fantasy, folklore, and music.

Rash by Pete Hautman. Simon, 2006. Bo examines a future society that's given up freedom in favor of safety. Sent to a prison, he survives by his own athletic ability and an artificial intelligence program.

Sapphique by Catherine Fisher. Dial, 2010. In this sequel to *Incarceron* (2009), which is about the all-powerful computer named Incarceron, Finn has to prove that he, rather than the computer, is the rightful heir to the throne.

The Secret Under My Skin by Janet McNaughton. HarperCollins, 2005. The year is 2368 when a technocaust has destroyed most of the technology. Scientists are blamed for the disaster and sent to concentration camps, but as the world begins to heal a new class of specialists develops. Blay, who tells the story, starts out as a young orphan scrounging through garbage, but then she becomes an assistant and an observer in her own right.

Wither. The Chemical Garden Trilogy Book One by Lauren DeStefano. S&S, 2011. Genetically perfect humans are born, but the boys die at the age of twenty-five, and the girls at twenty. "Gatherers" go looking for girls, born to parents not genetically altered, who can be sold to the newly perfected, but short-lived families. Two more books are promised in the trilogy.

hundreds or thousands of years into the future, and those new views of overpopulation, pollution, religious bickering, political machinations, and sexual disharmony often give readers a quite different perspective on our world and our problems.

The prime requirement for "good" science fiction (the kind listed in Focus Box 5.4, "Utopias and Dystopias in Science Fiction") has been the idea that the technology in science fiction must fit into natural laws, that is, readers must be able to believe in at least the possibility of the events that occur in a story. In a 1983 *Nightcap* talk show on Arts Cable Television, Isaac Asimov agreed that "The best kind of sci-fi involves science," but then he went on to say that even though he knows that "Time travel is theoretically impossible," he wouldn't want to give it up as a plot gimmick. What he was saying is that "rules" count, but that plot and excitement count even more. The internal consistency and plausibility of a postulated imaginary society creates its own reality.

Science fiction was never as popular on radio as it deserved to be, although *Dimension-X* and *X Minus One* had many fans. Television was a different story. From Rod Serling's *The Twilight Zone* on through the ever-new incarnations of *Star Trek,* viewers seemed to find TV science fiction irresistible. A more recent entry in the field, *The X-Files,* was different enough that it found an audience. N. E. Genge's *The Unofficial X-Files Companion* is a record of the plots and characters along with the serial killers, cults, werewolves, robots, and other strangenesses that have roamed through *X-Files* episodes.

Because of the increasing abilities of filmmakers to create special effects, science fiction is a natural source for films (see Film Box 5.1, "Fantasy, Science Fiction, and Dystopias in the Movies," for some all-time favorites). In March 2007, even the United States Postal Service joined in a *Star Wars* celebration by releasing fifteen Star Wars stamps, which featured an explanation on the back of the sheet:

> For 30 years, the *Star Wars* Saga has thrilled moviegoers with its epic story of good versus evil. Set across a fantastic galaxy of exotic planets and bizarre creatures, the saga tells the mythic tale of the disintegration of the Old Republic, the creation of the Empire, the rise of the evil Darth Vader, and the ultimate victory of the Rebel Alliance. From the wisdom and power of Yoda to the brave deeds of Jedi Knights and improbable heroes, *Star Wars* has inspired generations of fans with its unbridled sense of adventure, advancing the art of filmmaking while leaving an indelible mark on our cultural imagination.

Carl Sagan, the late Cornell University astronomer/author, has said that science fiction is what brought him to science. Kurt Vonnegut, Jr., also applauded science fiction through having his character Eliot Rosewater, in *God Bless You, Mr. Rosewater,* stumble into a convention of science fiction writers and drunkenly announce that he loves them because they are the only ones who:

> . . . know that life is a space voyage, and not a short one either, but one that'll last billions of years. You're the only ones with guts enough to really care about the future, who really notice what machines do to us, what wars do to us, what cities do to us, what big, simple ideas do to us, what tremendous misunderstanding, mistakes, accidents and catastrophes do to us.

Then he goes on to praise them for being "zany enough to agonize over time and distances without limit" and "over mysteries that will never die, over the fact that we are right now determining whether the space voyage for the next billion years or so is going to be Heaven or Hell."

Why does science fiction appeal to both young adults and adults? First and probably most important, it is exciting. Science fiction may have begun with the "rah-rah-we're-off-to-Venus-with-Buck-Rogers" sensational fiction, and although it has gone far beyond that, the thrill of adventure is still there. Science fiction writers do not write down to their audience, and this is recognized and admired. Science fiction allows anyone to read imaginative fiction without feeling the material is kid stuff. Science fiction presents real heroes to readers who find their own world often devoid of anyone worth admiring. These heroes are doing something brave, going to the ultimate frontiers, even pushing these

Fantasy and
Sci-fi Films

MOVIE PREVIEW

Because of filmmakers' abilities with special effects, sci-fi and fantasy films attract huge audiences. See Film Box 5.1, "Fantasy, Science Fiction, and Dystopias in the Movies," on page 176 for information about some of the best sci-fi movies.

frontiers farther back, all important at a time when many young people wonder if any new frontiers exist.

Science fiction has a heritage of fine writers and important books. Some critics maintain that the genre began with Mary Wollstonecraft Shelley's *Frankenstein: Or, The Modern Prometheus* in 1818. Others argue for Swift's *Gulliver's Travels* in 1726 or the much earlier Lucian's *The True History* in the second century AD. No matter, for nearly everyone agrees that the first major and widely read writer was Jules Verne, whose *Journey to the Center of the Earth* in 1864 and *Twenty Thousand Leagues Under the Sea* in 1870 pleased readers on several continents.

The first American science fiction came with Edgar Allan Poe's short story "The Unparalleled Adventures of One Hans Pfaall," which appeared in the June 1835 issue of the *Southern Literary Messenger* and was included in *Tales of the Grotesque and Arabesque* in 1840. Hans Pfaall's balloon trip to the moon in a nineteen-day voyage may be a hoax, but the early trappings of science fiction are there. Dime novels occasionally used science fiction, particularly in the Frank Reade series, as did some books from the Stratemeyer Literary Syndicate, particularly in the Tom Swift and Great Marvel series.

These books were readable and fun, and they were read over and over by many people who had no idea how good most of the stories were. Most critics, however, were snobs about science fiction. Some fans didn't consider the genre respectable, but the fact that science fiction, or whatever it was called in the early days, was not part of mainstream writing may have made it more attractive to readers who were not seeking literary respectability so much as they were looking for books that were entertaining.

Types of Science Fiction

Space travel, with the possibility of having visitors from other planets, is the most obvious type of science fiction, and probably the first to be read by many later fans of more complex books. It is the simpleminded but effective story of

Film Box 5.1

Fantasy, Science Fiction, and Dystopias in the Movies

2001: A Space Odyssey (1968, 141 minutes, G, Writers: Stanley Kubrick and Arthur C. Clarke, Director: Stanley Kubrick) The Computer (HAL) and the human (Bowman) are in a race to reach the monolith placer on the moon, allowing the winner of the race to reach the next stage of evolution.

Avatar (2009, 162 minutes, PG-13, Writer and Director: James Cameron; with Sam Worthington, Zoe Saldana, and Sigourney Weaver) A paraplegic marine uses the body of an avatar to visit the moon Pandoram where he learns of a greedy corporate's attempt to drive off the native humanoid *Na'vi* in order to mine for the precious material that is scattered through the moon's rich woodland.

Blade Runner (1982, 118 min., color, R; Director: Ridley Scott; with Harrison Ford and Rutger Hauer) A former police officer is hired to destroy Androids who have come to Earth illegally. From Philip Dick's Do Androids Dream of Electric Sheep?

Children of Men (2006, 100 min., color, R; Director: Alfonso Cuaron; with Clive Owen and Julianne Moore) By 2027 women can no longer become pregnant. Then a young girl is found pregnant, and Theo devotes his life to saving her. From P. D. James's novel.

Cloverfield (2008, 84 min., color, PG-13; Director Matt Reeves; with Lizzy Caplan, Jessica Lucas, and T. J. Miller) Five young people are attending a going-away party for a friend when a monster the size of a skyscraper attacks New York City. They are the tellers and the photographers of this truly scary story.

Frankenstein (1931, 71 min., black and white; Director: James Whale; with Boris Karloff) Mary Shelley's story of a man-created being and what he did.

Groundhog Day (1993, 102 min., color, PG; Director: Harold Ramis; with Bill Murray) A bored TV weatherman finds he is trapped, repeatedly replaying the same day.

Howl's Moving Castle (1994, 119 min., color, PG; Director: Hayao Miyazaki; with the voices of Jean Simmons and Christian Bale). A young girl falls under a witch's spell and discovers a moving castle. From Diana Wynne Jones's novel.

Ladyhawke (1985, 124 min., color, PG; Director: Richard Donner; with Michelle Pfeiffer and Rutger Hauer). A medieval story about two lovers caught up in an evil spell.

wild adventure, usually with a touch of sociological or environmental concerns. H. G. Wells's *The War of the Worlds* spawned many imitations about this group of aliens invading Earth and that group of aliens attacking another threatened outpost of civilization. Such books combine the best of two worlds—science fiction and horror.

Time and space travel have been themes in science fiction since H. G. Wells's *The Time Machine*, while in many other books authors work with the wonder and danger of space travel. For example, in Larry Niven and Jerry Pournelle's *The Mote in God's Eye*, humans have colonized the galaxy and an alien society sends emissaries to work with the humans. When the aliens accidentally die, the humans must send representatives dashing through space to ward off disaster and war. Space travel is a popular theme in movies. See Film Box 5.1 for some all-time favorites.

Mad scientists or the threat of science gone sour or insane is another popular technique. Philip K. Dick's *Do Androids Dream of Electric Sheep?* (reissued as *Blade Runner* in 1982 when the film adaptation came out) presents a gloomy view of the future. A cop/bounty hunter searches for human-created androids

Men in Black (1997, 98 minutes, PG-13, Writers: Lowell Cunningham and Ed Solomon, Director: Barry Sonnenfeld; with Tommy Lee Jones and Will Smith) Two Men in Black (Agents K and J) are part of a top-secret organization designed to monitor and police alien activity on Earth. Several sequels followed with one scheduled for release in 2012.

Pan's Labyrinth (2007, 112 min., color, R; Director: Guilleremo del Toro; with Ivana Naquero, Sergi Lopez, Maribel Verdu, and Doug Jones) Ofelia meets a tall faun who tells her she must complete three tasks to return to the underworld.

Pleasantville (1998, 123 min., color/black and white, PG-13; Director: Gary Ross; with Reese Witherspoon, Tobey Maguire, and Jeff Daniels) A brother and sister are transported within their TV to a 1950s happy sitcom, Pleasantville.

The Purple Rose of Cairo (1985, 87 min., black and white/color; Director: Woody Allen; with Mia Farrow and Jeff Daniels). A Depression-era waitress finds relief from her misery in films until her favorite actor walks out of his film.

Star Wars (1977, 121 min, color, Writer and Director: George Lucas; with Ewan McGregor, Liam Neeson and Carrie Fisher) This space-age story with such memorable characters as Luke Skywalker, Darth Vader, Obi-Wan Kenobi, Yoda, and Princess Leia won six Oscars. So many successful sequels (called *Episodes*) followed that it became a cultural reference point.

Stranger Than Fiction (2006, 105 min., color, PG-13; Director: Marc Foster; with Will Ferrell, Dustin Hoffman, and Emma Thompson) An IRS auditor hears an audible voice repeating his own thoughts.

Super 8 (2011, 112 minutes, PG-13, Writer & Director J. J. Abrams with Joel Courtney, Kyle Chandler, Elle Fanning, Amanda Michalka) In a kind of tribute to Steven Spielberg's early movie making, a group of small-town high-school friends shoot an amateur movie in 1979 when they witness a train crash, that brings all kinds of high-tech mystery to their town.

The Time Machine (1960, 103 min., color; Director: George Pal; with Rod Taylor and Yvette Mimieux) A scientist creates a time machine that can go forward to see what humanity has done to itself. Although all scientists agree that such a thing is impossible, it is nevertheless a popular theme in many later films.

Young Frankenstein (1974, 105 min., black and white, PG; Director: Mel Brooks; with Gene Wilder, Peter Boyle, Cloris Leachman) A loving parody of Frankenstein with touches of Bride of Frankenstein tossed in.

who have escaped from another planet to come back to a horribly drizzling and bleak Earth.

Harry Turtledove's *Worldwar: In the Balance* is a kind of "what if" science fiction. The author changes history as when Turtledove sets his story in 1942 when the Allies are at war with the Axis powers. An alien force of lizard-like things invades Earth with a technology that far surpasses human knowledge.

Cyberpunk is one of the wildest, rampaging kinds of science fiction today. Gene LaFaille defined *cyberpunk* in the December 1990 issue of the *Wilson Library Bulletin* as:

A subgenre of science fiction that incorporates our concern about the future impact of advanced technologies, especially cybernetics, bionics, genetic engineering, and the designer drug culture, upon the individual, who is competing with the increasing power and control of the multinational corporations that are extending their stranglehold on the world's supply of information. (p. 14)

Cyberpunk is about technology and the power of communication as it is used to manipulate people. William Gibson's 1984 *Neuromancer* was the novel

Margaret A. Edwards Award

Winner (2007)

Lois Lowry, Who Gave Us *The Giver*

Most of Lois Lowry's books are written for children, although young teens love both *Number the Stars* (a Holocaust story that won the 1990 Newbery Medal) and her first book, the 1977 *A Summer to Die*, in which Lowry shares the emotions, although not the actual events, connected to the childhood death of her sister, Helen. The Margaret A. Edwards Award committee honored Lowry for *The Giver,* which won the 1994 Newbery Medal, and is accessible to readers as young as twelve or thirteen, while at the same time being rich enough to stimulate serious thinking on the part of adults and college students.

The Giver is set in a futuristic society which has as its goal to make everything "the same." Babies are born to designated birth mothers and raised in a nursery until at age two they are either "released" (a euphemism for *killed*) or assigned to a "family," which will consist of two parents and a son and a daughter. The society is so controlled that the citizens are conditioned not to see colors and not to question authority or such things as "releases" and the making of lifelong work assignments when children turn twelve. At school, the children learn the values of their culture, but not its history or anything about neighboring societies. The group's memories are entrusted to a single individual, a man designated as The Giver.

The book's protagonist is a twelve-year-old named Jonas, who is startled when at the society's annual end-of-the-year ceremonies he is designated to be the next Giver. He is to start training immediately to become the Receiver of the community's memories. Lowry told Anita Silvey, who interviewed her for the June 2007 *School Library Journal,* that this unusual idea was inspired by visits she made in the early 1990s to her mother and father when they were in their late eighties and living in a nursing home in Staunton, Virginia. Lowry would fly down from Boston and on the trip home always had things to ponder.

Her mother was blind and very frail, but her mind was intact and she shared many experiences with her daughter, even talking about the painful ones including the death of Lois's older sister, Helen. In contrast, Lowry's father was physically healthy but his memory was gone and so as they would look at the scrapbook that Lowry and her brother had put together for him, she would have to tell him over and over again about such things as Helen's death. He would feel sad for a few minutes, but then, in contrast to the deep sadness with which Lowry's mother would relive some of her experiences, he would soon forget and ask again about the girl in the scrapbook.

This unpredictability of memory and what goes on in the human mind is what Lowry set out to explore when she wrote *The Giver.* She says she had no intention of writing a dystopian novel; it just turned out that way. This may be why the first few pages of the book seem so bright and why readers feel the negative aspects all the more strongly when they become privy to the memories that Jonas receives from The Giver. Lowry further explores the mystery of memory in her 2006 *Gossamer,* in which a girl called Littlest is being trained as a dream giver to bring better dreams to a troubled boy. In 2000, she published *Gathering Blue* as a companion volume to *The Giver.* The protagonist is a crippled girl who is skilled at embroidery and is taken from her village to the palace where her job of restoring the ceremonial robes that tell the story of her people is made more difficult by the ruling powers and their philosophy of "management."

When we brought *The Giver* to class after it won the 1994 Newbery Medal, our YA students predicted that it had a great future as a book for common reading. They were correct in this prediction, but they were wrong in their companion prediction, which was that teachers would have no censorship problems with it because the book has "no sex, no violence, and no objectionable language." Within a couple of years, *The Giver* had become a frequently censored book. We suspect that the dystopian vision of a society that bears some resemblance to our own frightens and depresses some adults, but because this is a difficult concept to recognize, much less communicate, they look for specific incidents to protest such as the use of "released" as a *euphemism* for "death" and the mention of the pills that children take as they reach puberty and begin to feel "the stirrings." ●

that brought cyberpunk to readers' attention. *Steampunk* is a little stronger term, which we've seen used in relation to Scott Westerfeld's 2009 *Leviathan,* which gives a new history for World War I when the Clankers, who rely on machinery, are fighting the Darwinians, who develop new species to help them win the war. In *Leviathan Book Two: Behemoth,* the Darwinists create a fierce creature to be used by the British navy. In Suzanne Collins's *The Hunger Games,* the Capitol, while not relying on these terms, uses both Clanker technology as in the advanced photo equipment for televising all the details of the games and even the participants' private lives, and Darwinian techniques through the use of the genetically altered *Mutts* and the *Jabberjays,* who are birds bred to spy on individuals.

In 2002, M. T. Anderson set a high bar for books about bioscience when he wrote *Feed.* It is set in a not-too-distant future when all young people and most adults have Internet feeds implanted into their brains. Every citizen's consciousness is flooded nonstop with consumer ads, instant messaging, and social guidance from an anonymous corporate entity that is more puppet-master than government. Teenagers are especially susceptible to influence from the feed as they rush to buy everything from music to clothes to recreation. But it is different for Violet, whose father has a feed that is an external unit. He can put it on and take it off.

Violet's implant was placed in her brain so late in life that it causes life-threatening health problems. Violet and her father are passive-aggressive resisters of the consumer culture foisted on society by the feed or, actually, by the corporations that control the feed. Her resistance results in behavior unpredictable enough to prevent a profile from being constructed from her history of purchases. In the end it also prevents her from getting the medical help she needs. Anderson's book is not lighthearted. Instead, it is true to its dystopian genre and the author's desire to present a cautionary tale portraying a dark future that grows out of human foibles manifested in the present.

Nancy Farmer's 2002 *The House of the Scorpion* is a grim, futuristic novel, in which the owner of an opium farm near the Mexican border of the United States raises cloned children to provide replacement body parts for himself. He is now 110 years old. Readers meet Matt, a future clone, when he is six years old and follow him through his escape and "rescue" into a work camp that is a modern equivalent of the kinds of orphanages that Charles Dickens wrote about. Farmer's highly honored book was one of the first to seriously develop biotechnology. When Farmer was being honored at one of our Arizona Book Fairs—she grew up in Yuma, Arizona, which is on the Mexican border—she laughingly explained that she was an insomniac and got her idea of a powerful man cloning children to supply him with body parts from listening to talk radio.

Neal Shusterman's 2007 *Unwind* is set in a futuristic society where parents have a chance to return teenagers who aren't turning out to be the young adults their parents had dreamed of. They turn them into the government to be *unwound,* which simply means that their body parts will be harvested for use by other people. Connor's parents have agreed to turn him in. He runs away, but then is betrayed and found. It is an exciting, but creepy story.

When Mary E. Pearson wrote her 2008 *The Adoration of Jenna Fox* about a girl with a bionic arm, she wanted to stay ahead of what might actually be possible. She told interviewer Rebecca Hill, for an article titled "Is the Robot Really Real?" (*VOYA,* June 2011, pp. 150–151), that she had to keep "upping the ante" in relation to bionic body parts because science was moving so fast. Her sci-fi story is even more close to reality today because of all the research and work being done with wounded veterans who have come home from Iraq and Afghanistan determined to live active lives.

Lauren DeStafano's 2011 *Wither, The Chemical Garden Trilogy: Book One* is a story about genetically perfect humans. However, there is one flaw. The boys all die at the age of twenty-five, and the girls at twenty. "Gatherers" go looking for girls born either before the new technology or from parents who have not participated in the program, so that they can be sold to the newly perfected, but short-lived families.

Utopias and dystopias are neither science fiction nor fantasy, but they share characteristics with both. Readers must suspend disbelief and buy into the author's vision, at least for the duration of the story. As with science fiction, utopian and dystopian books are usually set in the future, with technology having played a role in establishing the conditions out of which the story grows. Unlike science fiction, and more like fantasy, however, once the situation is established, authors focus less on technology and more on sociological and psychological or emotional aspects of the story.

The centuries-old fascination with utopias is suggested by the Greek origin of the word, which includes two meanings, "no place" and "good place." Most of us, in idle moments, dream of a perfect land, a perfect society, a place that would solve all our personal problems and, if we are altruistic enough, all of the world's problems, as well. In our nightmares, we also dream of the opposite, the dystopias, which are diseased or bad lands. But few of us do more than dream, which may explain why readers appreciate authors who transfer their dreams to the printed page.

We used to say that dystopian stories are not likely to be popular with teenagers because young people are basically optimistic and have not lived long enough to become disgruntled about the aspects of modern society most likely to be satirized in dystopian novels. However, Lois Lowry's *The Giver* proved us wrong. It is a prototypical dystopian novel, but also one of the all-time most popular books for both school and independent reading. See page 178 on Lois Lowry as winner of the Margaret A. Edwards Award. Also see Focus Box 5.4 for descriptions of other dystopian novels that young people appreciate. In his *Republic* in the fifth century BC, Plato presented his vision of the ideal world, offering suggestions for educating the ruling class. With wise philosopher-kings, so Plato maintained, the people would prosper, intellectual joys would flourish (along with censorship, for Plato would ban poets and dramatists from his perfect society), and the land would be permanently safe. Later utopias were geared less to a ruling class and more to a society that would preserve its peace and create harmony and happiness for the people.

Yearning for the simpler life in which we dream of being part of something greater than ourselves is natural. For some young people, however, the search has led to religious groups less like communes and more like cults. Robert Coover explored the power and madness of a cult in *The Origin of the Brunists*. In that novel, a mining explosion kills ninety-seven people, but one survivor believes that God has saved him to proclaim the approaching end of the world.

Dystopias are more dramatic and exaggerated than their counterparts and for that reason are more successful in attracting young adults. Dystopias warn us of society's drift toward a particularly horrifying or sick world lying just over the horizon. They are sometimes misinterpreted as prophecies alone, but books such as Aldous Huxley's *Brave New World* and George Orwell's *Nineteen Eighty-Four* and *Animal Farm* are part prophecy, part warning. Readers who have engaged with the characters are never again able to regard a discussion of individual freedom in an abstract way.

Significant Science Fiction Writers

Isaac Asimov's response to a question of what he would do if he knew he were going to die the next day is said to have been "Type faster!" And before his death in 1992, he indeed typed fast. He wrote more than five hundred books in so many fields that he comes close to being a truly Renaissance figure. But whatever his contributions to the study of the Bible or Shakespeare, no one can question his contributions to science fiction. The several volumes in his Foundation series established the basis for a multidimensional society that an incredible number of readers have temporarily inhabited and accepted. Asimov's first book of short stories was entitled *I, Robot;* when Twentieth Century-Fox released the film, *I, Robot,* starring Will Smith in 2004, they credited Isaac Asimov's stories.

Ray Bradbury, while arguably less interested in the mechanics of science fiction, may have been the most sensitive of the early writers about humanity's ability to befoul Earth and the rest of the universe. He seemed to have almost no interest in how his characters moved from Earth to Mars, but *The Martian Chronicles* is a wonderful set of semirelated short stories about the problems of being human in a universe that does not treasure our humanity. In a prefatory note to Bantam's 1954 edition, Clifton Fadiman described Bradbury as "a moralist who has caught hold of a simple, obvious, but overwhelmingly important moral idea—that we are in the grip of a psychosis, a technology-mania, the final consequences of which can only be universal murder and quite conceivably the destruction of our planet."

Arthur C. Clarke is regarded as one of the fathers of science fiction. His *Childhood's End* is one of the classics in the field, and his short story *2001: A Space Odyssey* was developed into a full-length film and is perhaps the most widely cited of any work in science fiction. In the introduction to his 1953 *Profiles of the Future,* Clarke wrote:

A critical—the adjective is important—reading of science-fiction is essential training for anyone wishing to look more than ten years ahead. The facts of the future can hardly be imagined *ab initio* by those who are unfamiliar with the fantasies of the past. . . . I do not for a moment suggest that more than one percent of science-fiction readers would be reliable prophets; but I do suggest that almost a hundred percent of reliable prophets will be science-fiction readers—or writers.

We thought of Clarke's statement when, just after the September 11, 2001, terrorist attacks, we heard a commentator say that readers of science fiction did not take nearly as long as did other Americans to realize that an airplane flying into one of the Twin Towers was not an accident.

Robert Heinlein in a *Library Journal* article defined science fiction as speculative fiction based on the real world, with all its "established facts and natural laws." He went on to say that while the result can be extremely fantastic in content, "it is not fantasy: it is legitimate—and often very tightly reasoned—speculation about the possibilities of the real world." Heinlein began his career writing young adult books, and then moved on to adult material and never looked back. Books for the young such as *Farmer in the Sky* and *Pokayne of Mars* are today largely forgotten, but for many young people, they provided a new vision of the future which Heinlein later developed in *The Moon Is a Harsh Mistress* and *Stranger in a Strange Land* (Vol. 78, July 1953, p. 1188).

William Sleator's books are in the genre spawned by H. G. Wells's *The War of the Worlds* in which a group of aliens invade Earth. The genre combines science fiction and horror. In *Interstellar Pig,* sixteen-year-old Barney is intrigued to discover that three different neighbors moved next door. Soon, Barney and the three are playing a board game called Interstellar Pig, and Barney learns fast enough that he stands between the neighbors and the destruction of Earth. *Parasite Pig* is an intelligent sequel. Sleator's *House of Stairs* illustrates how mad psychologists can become to prove their point. Five young people are brought to an experimental house made up almost entirely of stairs madly going everywhere, and the young people learn that adults can be truly cruel. Similar emotions emerge in Sleator's *The Last Universe,* in which a mysterious maze in the garden behind Susan's house terrifies her.

Scott Westerfeld's books that most enchant our students started with *Uglies* in 2005, followed the same year by *Pretties,* then in 2006 by *Specials,* and in 2007 by *Extras*. They are set in a futuristic society where all sixteen-year-olds can have an operation to make them beautiful, but not everyone wants to lose what makes them unique. The job of the *Specials* is to keep the *Uglies* down and the *Pretties* stupid. *Extras* gets its title from the large adoring crowds that in the old days were hired for films.

Concluding Comments

The books we've talked about in this chapter start with life as we know it and attempt to stretch readers' imaginations. All of us need to dream, not to waste our lives but to enrich them. To dream is to recognize humanity's possibilities. In a world hardly characterized by undue optimism, the genres treated here offer us challenges and hope, not the sappy sentimentalism of "everything always works out for the best" (for it often does not) but realistic hope based on our noblest dreams of surviving. If we go down, we do it knowing that we have cared and dreamed and found something for which we are willing to struggle.

Poetry, Drama, Humor, and New Media

The genres in this chapter are primarily social, and for the most part are shared orally, being transferred to paper mainly for safekeeping and preservation. Poetry, drama, and humor all existed before the printing press, and if we want students to enjoy them for their emotional impact, as well as for their intellectual content, we need to do whatever we can to bring them alive through talk and oral presentations. In the section on New Media we are writing briefly about comics, graphic novels, and video games. And with these latter items, many of the stories being told are basic—even primitive—in contrast to the high-tech equipment through which they are being shared.

Poetry for Young Adults

Students love poetry, but they do not always love the same poetry their teachers have learned to love through many years in college and graduate school, meticulously poring over classic poems and ferreting out the literary genius in each one. If Louise Rosenblatt's Reader Response Theory gives clues to the difference, it is that the poetry our young readers love provides an accessible venue for identification while classic poems most often do not. Like any other genre of young adult literature, poetry must speak to our students through topics and issues that are relevant to them using language and rhythm which they find appealing. This does not mean that they will not one day learn to appreciate poems from long ago and far away, but for now their hearts and minds are touched by modern poetry, poetry written to express the emotions they feel on a day-to-day basis. "Tintern Abbey" and "La Belle Dame sans Merci" may very well become beloved favorites one day, but not until our students have developed a love of poetry in general and acquired the literary skills and adult life experience to understand and appreciate them. Contemporary poetry, written for young hearts and minds, can often provide a bridge to classic poems when paired for study, but first young readers need to experience poetry that resonates with them.

Poetry Slams

Reading poetry and "experiencing" poetry aren't necessarily the same thing. Young people today are more accustomed to poetry that is performed, often described as "poetry for the stage," rather than "poetry for the page." Competitions, called *poetry slams,* are held regularly in which young poets perform their own verse with passion and prosody. Merriam Webster defines *prosody* as "the rhythmic and intonational aspect of language," and poetry slams are judged not only on the content of the poems but also on the poet's ability to express the poem's message through rise and fall in tone and volume, variation in speed, and strategic emphasis on certain words and certain syllables. Young people are accustomed to performance poetry which utilizes elements of sound to help convey its meaning, both devices of sound intentionally written into the poetry and manipulation of sound as the poem is performed by the poet.

According to the National Poetry Slam website (http://nps2011.com/about/what-is-poetry-slam/), the poetry slam model was invented in the 1980s by a Chicago construction worker named Marc Smith. Slam is a fast-paced competition where poets have a limited amount of time to impress judges randomly selected from the audience. Performers use all the tricks of storytelling, song writing, theatre, stand-up comedy, and cold hard poetry to wheedle points out of the judges from 0.0 (terrible) to 10.0 (perfect!).

Obviously, poetry slams operate democratically rather than authoritatively, emphasizing that poetry is not an esoteric art form intended only for the enlightened, but is, instead, an art form that makes a statement about life from the poet's perspective that should be accessible to anyone—if the poet is successful. Poetry slams may be conducted under the National Poetry Slam organization and act as qualifying events leading up to the national final competition, but most poetry slams are local events, put on at coffee houses, universities, schools, or libraries, and organized by local aficionados of poetry who work as volunteers. A perusal of Poetry Slam, Inc. revealed no fewer than ninety-five local slam events from Fairbanks, Alaska, to Haiku, Hawaii, to Lauderhill, Florida, to Manchester, New Hampshire. National Poetry Slam set-up rules are usually followed even at local events: three-minute time limit (penalty for going longer), and no costumes or music. Judges are chosen from the audience and given little in the way of guidelines for assigning a numeric score to each poem/poet based on content and performance, usually on a scale of 1–10. Usually, five judges are chosen and for each performance the high and low scores are discarded and an average is computed from the remaining scores. Those in attendance at poetry slams are encouraged to treat the performers in ways which would make Shakespeare's groundlings proud,

The poetry slams we hold in our classes are not nearly as formal as the ones described on national websites. We let our students present either their own poetry or someone else's. Here's what we need:

1. *An uninhibited volunteer to serve as master of ceremonies.*

2. *Numbered participation tickets on which students write their name and the name of their poem. They hand this to the MC, who records their scores and keeps them for the awarding of prizes.*

3. *Minimal room decorations and simple refreshments.*

4. *Two sets of Olympic style judging cards.*

5. *Miscellaneous prizes for the winners.*

clearly expressing their opinions of the poem and its performance loudly and sometimes obnoxiously.

Poetry slams do not demand a specific genre of poem. According to Poetry Slam, Inc. (http://www.poetryslam.com/): "You'll find a diverse range of work within slam, including heartfelt love poetry, searing social commentary, uproarious comic routines, and bittersweet personal confessional pieces. Poets are free to do work in any style on any subject." *Slam poetry* is not synonymous with *hip hop poetry* although hip hop poetry can be performed at a slam. Slam poet organizers prefer the term *spoken word* poetry to indicate the difference between slam poetry and what might be called traditional poetry, meaning poetry that is written intentionally for live performance versus poetry written to be read silently by someone other than the poet.

Many National Poetry Slam poets make school visits and recite poetry that is perfectly appropriate for school. Many of their poem performances can also be found online, especially on YouTube at www.youtube.com. Among the poet/performances we recommend are:

1. Taylor Mali ("Why Falling in Love Is Like Owning a Dog," "Like Totally Whatever")

2. Danny Sherrard ("The Distance," "Bus Boy")

3. Janean Livingston ("Dare to Dream")

4. Anis Mojgani ("Four Stars," "Galumpf")

Hip Hop, Gangsta Rap, and Brave New Voices

Hip hop poetry is a distinct genre popular with young people and is often performed at poetry slams, but hip hop is its own art form with its own origins and purpose. Hip hop originated as a type of music that had very clear and distinctive beats, created by disk jockeys as they mixed sounds from different records and added some of their own words and sound patterns. Hip hop music provided a means of self-expression to inner city youth and has been credited with providing an outlet, through dance, for feelings of frustration and alienation from mainstream society. Hip hop lyrics were socially conscious and illuminated the frustrations of life in the inner city with little hope for improvement due to a status quo designed to keep disenfranchised people in their stations and keep the privileged in control. Hip hop resulted in major dance and cultural events, beginning in the Bronx in New York City in the late 1970s and spreading throughout the world such that multiple countries and locations worldwide have their own versions of hip hop culture with some commonalities. Resulting commodification of hip hop has created its own fashion and recording industry worth $90 billion per year according to an online survey by Harris Interactive, according to GrabStats .com (http://www.grabstats.com/statmain.asp?StatID=1301). With this commodification has come the complaint that hip hop as a mirror of society's ills has become a farce, and that its original purpose—a means for expressing discontent with the social ills of urban life in the United States—has been subverted by commercialization. One example of this is what is known as "gangsta rap," a form of poetry that evolved out of hip hop, which is spoken over music and has a pronounced rhythmic background. Criticism of gangsta rap holds that while it may have begun as an accurate portrayal of street life, it has morphed into a genre that romanticizes gang life, violence, racial hatred, and misogyny.

One of the most influential efforts to evolve from the hip hop movement and poetry slam events has been the Youth Speaks organization and its Brave New Voices program which was televised as *Russell Simmons' Brave New Voices: Def Poetry Jam* on HBO. Youth Speaks, founded in 1996, is intended for young poets, ages thirteen to twenty-four, and according to its website (http://www .bravenewvoices.org/):

> Youth Speaks Inc. is a multi-faceted organization that understands and believes that the power, insight, creativity, and passion of young artists can change the world. In addition to a wide variety of arts education, youth development, and presentation programs that serve thousands each year in the Bay Area, we house a repertory theater company (The Living Word Project) that commissions, produces and tours internationally-recognized new work in new aesthetics, host an annual gathering of young poets and poetry organizations from throughout the world (Brave New Voices), and have built a network of like-minded organizations developed on our model throughout the country. (FAQs, par. 1)

Youth Speaks, founded in the San Francisco Bay Area, has grown into a national program which reportedly serves an annual estimate of 200,000 young people in its events, not including those accessing resources online or on television. Youth Speaks has launched or helped to launch local poetry programs around the country and continues to sponsor events, competitions, and workshops for poets, teachers, and other nonprofit organizations. Youth Speaks can be found on Facebook at http://www.facebook.com/youthspeaks and on Twitter at http://twitter.com/#!/youthspeaks.

The Brave New Voices project began when Youth Speaks held its first national poetry slam, *The Brave New Voices International Youth Poetry Slam Festival,* in 1998. *Def Poetry Jam,* originally launched on Broadway, aired on HBO in 2002 and was produced by Russell Simmons. *Russell Simmons' Def Poetry Jam: Brave New Voices,* including documentary style background exposés on young poets in the Brave New Voices competition, as well as the actual performance, began with the 2008 competition in Washington, DC. These poets are representative of an important youth voice, a voice that may change the world. According to the Brave New Voices website (http://www.bravenewvoices.org/hbo/):

> All over the United States, a new generation of poets is emerging. This new HBO series captures teenagers picking up the pen and taking hold of the microphone with passion, intelligence, creativity, honesty and power. These voices of 21st Century America transcend race, class, gender, orientation, and red state/blue state politics as they show us all what the next generation of leaders looks and sounds like.

We recommend all of the Brave New Voices performances, but some which are especially appropriate for school viewing and discussing, all of which are available on YouTube, include:

1. B Yung ("Change," "Magician")
2. Devin Murphy ("Tourette's," "Jordan")
3. Jasmine Williams ("Miles Apart")
4. Joshua Bennett ("Carbon Copy," "Tamara's Opus")

One of our own favorite hip hop poets, Myrlin Hepworth, shares a poem that is representative of the concern and frustration young people feel about where the world is headed:

Love Is My God
by Myrlin Hepworth

I think of the prayer books my *abuelita* sends me
while my friend explains to me

that he believes the world is ending and that it is hopeless

and I wonder if he's right
maybe it is hopeless . . .

If a third of the world's natural resources have been consumed,
if polar bears are becoming hermaphrodites

if the air in Darfur still smells like rotting corpses
if the air in New Orleans still smells like the air in Darfur

is it hopeless?
if self-esteem could be bought worn or driven with enough money

then what happened to Kurt Cobain
Whitney Houston, Britney Spears, Lindsay Lohan?

Why are so many of our actors and models addicted to cocaine?
I watch my *abuelita* pray to god, she refers to god as "him,"

"give him your heart" she says
and I wonder if god is a man.

Why would god be a man?

I wonder if god is a woman?
why would a god be a woman?

When did god become a gender?

Why do so many followers of God kill each other?
Why do terrorists read the Bible and the Koran?
Why do humanitarians read the Bible and the Koran?

Are we killing ourselves for god?
Taking control of our final moments

like men and women leaping from the World Trade Center
their final prayers swallowed by the jet fuel,

do you call their deaths a leap of faith?
How do suicide bombers encourage more suicides?

What is the point in questioning if it only leads to more questions?
Is this poem a suicide bomber?

What flavor was the Kool Aid in Jonestown that day?
Are we all drinking our own separate versions of the same Kool Aid?

If religion helped to inspire the hearts
of Timothy McVeigh and Osama Bin Laden,

if religion helped to inspire the hearts
of Martin Luther King and Ghandi,
is it hopeless?

If Martin Luther King Blvd is crowded with black and brown men
killing each other?
If the Pakistani India border is crowded with men waiting to kill each
other?

Is it hopeless
if democracy found big business,
if religion found a war,
if hippies found drugs,
if Jesus found a cross,

if Martin Luther King and Ghandi both found bullets
is it hopeless?

Where are we going?

Is it all for nothing? Is nothing the scariest word we know?

Nothing like beyond 7th avenue and Buckeye,
Nothing like beyond the moon,
beyond the stars, beyond the universe,
where nothing exists?

Is religion an answer for the word nothing?

I see my *abuelitas* face
"give your heart to god *mi jito,*"

she says, and I wanna tell her
that I don't know what god is,

and I don't know if I believe in god
but I believe in something,

I believe in the love you poured into my heart as a little *chavalito*
I believe in the tears of widows,

in the frail arms of soldiers holding their dying friends.
I believe in the prayers of muslims

and christians. I believe in a piece of paper,
in an idea, in a dream.

I believe there is not hope on this earth without love
so love has to be my God.

Love has to be my suicide bomber
so let me live my seconds out with conviction

let me die for this belief,
let me die with the words "hope" and "love"

as the only words written on my gravestone.

Multiple Voices, Multiple Narrators, Multiple Cultures, and Multiple Worries

Poems written in multiple voices, as illustrated through Focus Box 6.1, "Poetry: Multiple Voices, Multiple Narrators, and Multiple Cultures," page 191, have a special connection for young people, perhaps because they are looking for their own voices, or perhaps because they are wondering what other people are thinking about a common experience.

Family or personal dysfunction is no longer taboo in young adult literature, and the vast majority of young people have witnessed it through their peers if not experienced it themselves: abuse, drug addiction, alcoholism, violence, and more. Poetry provides a means for young readers to explore these experiences as fictional protagonists attempt to make sense of their lives. In *Dark Sons* (Jump at the Son, 2005), Nikki Grimes narrates in verse the lives of two teenage boys experiencing a father who abandons them and their mothers. Alternating chapters follow Ishmael and his mother, Hagar, from the Holy Bible as they are cast out

MULTI-VOICED
POETRY

As shown in Focus Boxes 6.1 "Poetry: Multiple Voices, Multiple Narrators, and Multiple Cultures" (p. 191), 6.2, "Stories Told through Free-Verse Poetry" (p. 192), and 6.3, "More Poets and Poetry" (p. 198), there are many kinds of poetry being published for young readers, in addition to the many online sources.

by Abraham when his elderly wife, Sarah, miraculously bears him an heir and modern day Brooklyn dweller Sam, whose father leaves his mother for a younger woman. The poetry gracefully exposes the conflict of emotions that both boys feel for fathers whom they love and hate at once.

In her popular free-verse trilogy, *Crank* (2004), *Glass* (2007), and *Fallout* (2010), Ellen Hopkins introduces readers to Kristina, a character based on Hopkins's own daughter. Kristina, a model child, becomes her own antithesis when she goes to visit her divorced father and meets a young man who sets her on the path to methamphetamine addiction. Using innovative verse form, reminiscent of ee cummings, Hopkins continues the story through three books, the last one told by Kristina's children.

Poetry for the Average Man, Woman, or Teen: Poetry 180

While famed poet Billy Collins was United States Poet Laureate from 2001–2003, he strove to bring poetry back into the mainstream and away from the academic elites where he perceived it had come to rest. He devised what he called a "180 degree turn back to poetry" and put it on the Poetry 180 website (http://www.loc.gov/poetry/180/) hosted by the United States Library of Congress. It was his intention that a new poem be read at school each day, and since there are approximately 180 school days in most schools in the United States, he selected 180 poems to go on the website where he welcomes us:

> Welcome to Poetry 180. Poetry can and should be an important part of our daily lives. Poems can inspire and make us think about what it means to be a member of the human race. By just spending a few minutes reading a poem each day, new worlds can be revealed.

Poetry: Multiple Voices, Multiple Narrators, and Multiple Cultures

Bronx Masquerade **by Nikki Grimes. Speak, 2003.** The voices of eighteen high school students tell their stories as if it is "Open Mike Friday" in Ms. Ward's English class.

Cool Salsa: Bilingual Poems on Growing Up Latino in the United States **by Lori Carlson. Holt, 1994.** Carlson brings together a group of beloved writers who portray the nuances of bicultural life. In 2005, she followed with *Red Hot Salsa: Bilingual Poems on Being Young and Latino in the United States*.

Joyful Noise: Poems for Two Voices **by Paul Fleischman. HarperCollins, 1988.** Fleischman was one of the first poets to come up with the idea of doing poetry to be performed sometimes by one person and sometimes by two people. The idea came from his childhood when his father, Sid Fleischman, would direct the family in such performances.

More than Friends: Poems for Him and Her **by Sara Holbrook and Allan Wolf. Boyds Mills, 2008.** These poems come in pairs, one poem from a boy's perspective and one poem from a girl's perspective, both on the same topic, such as "Making the First Move" or "What to do When He [or she] Looks at You."

My Own True Name **by Pat Mora. Arte Publico, 2000.** Mora takes a look at life along the border of Mexico and the United States through the eyes of young and old, sometimes in the same poem.

Night Is Gone, Day Is Still Coming: Stories and Poems by American Indian Teens and Young Adults **by Betsy Franco and Traci L. Gourdine. Candlewick, 2003.** This collection includes poems about adolescent struggles with indignities, injustices, and ignored history and heritage.

19 Varieties of Gazelle: Poems of the Middle East **by Naomi Shihab Nye. Greenwillow, 2005.** Naomi Shihab Nye shares sixty poems exploring the experiences of people young and old and perspectives about being an Arab-American. In *Time You Let Me In: 25 Poets under 25* (Greenwillow, 2010), Nye acts as editor for a collection of poems from young poets attempting to make sense of life. Other well received books by Nye include her 2011 *Transfer*, her 2009 *Honeybee: Poems & Short Prose,* and her 1998 *The Tree is Older than You Are: A Bilingual Gathering of Poems and Stories from Mexico* with paintings by Mexican artists.

Requiem: Poems of the Terezin Ghetto **by Paul B. Janeczko. Candlewick, 2011.** Janeczko is a talented poet that in previous editions of this textbook we have identified as a "national treasure," so we were happy to see this new book that he wrote after researching the Czech town that during World War II was used as a way stop for Jews on their way to the gas chambers. Most of the poems are given the name of a person and the kind of identification number that would have been tattooed on their arm.

You Don't Even Know Me: Stories and Poems about Boys **by Sharon Flake. Hyperion, 2010.** Flake explores life stories of African American teens including fifteen poems about young men who do their best in life but have a hard time succeeding, as well as boys who choose a path of crime.

Woven Stone **by Simon Ortiz. University of Arizona Press, 1992.** Simon writes about growing up in Acoma Pueblo as well as coming into conflict with the world outside the Acoma Nation. In "Bony," Ortiz explains the love his family felt for a dog his father delivered "in a gunny sack," and in "How to Make a Good Chili Stew," he outlines a recipe that is about much more than food."

Poetry 180 is designed to make it easy for students to hear or read a poem on each of the 180 days of the school year. I have selected the poems you will find here with high school students in mind. They are intended to be listened to, and I suggest that all members of the school community be included as readers. A great time for the readings would be following the end of daily announcements over the public address system.

Focus Box 6.2

Stories Told through Free-Verse Poetry

***Fortune's Bones: The Manumission Requiem* by Marilyn Nelson. Front Street, 2004.** Nelson tells the true story of a slave who in the late 1700s was owned by a Connecticut doctor. When he died, the doctor dissected his body and boiled down the bones to use for anatomy studies. Nelson's rich telling of this unique story could be an effective reader's theater production.

***Frida: Viva la Vida!* by Carmen T. Bernier-Grand, Marshall Cavendish, 2007.** Free-verse poems, each paired with one of Frida Kahlo's paintings, do a good job of introducing a new generation to this famous Mexican painter.

***Heartbeat* by Sharon Creech. HarperCollins, 2004.** Middle school readers will enjoy the rhythm of the verses in this story of twelve-year-old Annie who loves to run, not to win a race, but to feel the earth and sky.

***Hoop Kings* by Charles R. Smith, Jr. Candlewick, 2004.** Shaq O'Neal's shoe sole (actual size) is featured as a fold-out in this gorgeous book of sports poems. The pages feature twelve super-heroic basketball players with equally vibrant poems.

***Keeping the Night Watch* by Hope Anita Smith, illus. by E. B. Lewis. Holt, 2008.** Thirteen-year-old C. J. is angry when her absent father returns and tries to regain the family's trust. C. J.'s young siblings are ecstatic, but it takes C. J. much longer to forgive her father for leaving.

***Locomotion* by Jacqueline Woodson. Putnam's, 2003.** Woodson uses a teen voice to create the free verse, the sonnets, and the haiku that tell Lonnie's story as he moves through group and teen homes.

***Make Lemonade* by Virginia Euwer Wolff. Holt, 1993.** This winner of the National Book Award was one of the earliest books in which the author lent dignity to a problem novel by using a spacious free-verse format. In the sequel, *True Believer* (2001), LaVaughn's horizons extend beyond her neighborhood, but she does not lose her determination.

***Out of the Dust* by Karen Hesse. Scholastic, 1996.** In diary-like entries, Billie Jo tells how her dreams get lost in the swirling winds of the 1930s Oklahoma dustbowl. The book won the Newbery Medal.

***Split Image* by Mel Glenn. Morrow/HarperCollins, 2000.** Poems from observers show how Laura Li, a dutiful Asian daughter, has a hard time figuring out how to manage her heritage and her new life. Glenn's other poetic stories include *Foreign Exchange: A Mystery in Poems* (1999), *The Taking of Room 114: A Hostage Drama in Poems* (1997), *Jump Ball: A Basketball Season in Poems* (1997), and *Who Killed Mr. Chippendale?* (1996).

***The Voyage of the Arctic Tern* by Hugh Montgomery. Candlewick, 2002.** Unlike most of the new prose poets who are writing realistic problem stories, Montgomery spins a high-seas adventure story.

***The Watch that Ends the Night: Voices from the Titanic A Novel* by Allan Wolf. Candlewick, 2011.** Wolf retells the Titanic tragedy though the poetic voices of individuals. Readers first meet "John Snow: The Undertaker," who has come for the bodies. They next meet "The Ship Rat," and then "Bruce Ismay, The Businessman" followed by "E. J. Smith, The Captain." The pages are spacious and the stories dramatic. The last thirty pages of this big and beautifully designed book are "The Notes" which give real-life details for each of the characters, as well as miscellaneous information about the ship and its tragic end.

***The Way a Door Closes* by Hope Anita Smith, illustrated by Shane W. Evans. Holt, 2003.** The first twelve poems are about the happiness that C. J. experiences in his family, but the thirteenth, "The Way a Door Closes," lets readers know that the father of the family is leaving. The rest of the book (twenty-two more poems) describe C. J.'s up-and-down emotions.

***Who Will Tell My Brother?* by Marlene Carvell. Hyperion, 2002.** Carvell's sensitive story treats the issue of offensive Indian mascots used by sports teams.

As he clearly states, he wants the poems to be read over the intercom to the entire school by all members of the school community from coaches to kids, explaining that: "teachers should aim at creating a broad spectrum of readers to encourage the notion that poetry belongs to everyone." Billy agrees with our previous nod to prosody, meaning skillful attention to intonation, pronunciation, variation in volume and pace, and emphasis on words and syllables: "And we know that a poem will live or die depending on how it is read," and so he gives four helpful instructions on how to prepare and how to deliver a poem. He also insists that poems be allowed to speak for themselves for the most part and not be analyzed to death, a custom he parodies in the very first of the 180 poems, "Introduction to Poetry," a poem of his own, in which students assault a poem with a rubber hose, attempting to beat the meaning out of it. Collins chose the poems with high school in mind; nevertheless, some of them may not be very interesting to high school students, and so we recommend trying them out on a focus group first to see which poems are most likely to succeed. They are all great poems, but among the ones that have been most successful for us are:

"Introduction to Poetry," Billy Collins

"The Summer I Was Sixteen," Geraldine Connolly

"Wheels," Jim Daniels

"Fat Is Not a Fairy Tale," Jane Yolen

"Football," Louis Jenkins

"The Grammar Lesson," Steve Kowit

"God Says Yes to Me," Kaylin Haught

"The Rider," Naomi Shihab Nye

"How to Change a Frog into a Prince," Anna Denise

Each of the poems in Poetry 180 that resonate with young readers touches upon some aspect of the adolescent experience that is especially poignant. For example, being an adolescent is largely about firsts in life: first love, first death of a loved one, first time you are truly alone, first driver's license, first time you realize you are different, first time you are away from home, and so on. One of our favorite poets, Alberto Rios, a National Book Award Finalist and recipient of the Arizona Humanities Council Arizona Literary Treasure Award, shares this poem about an early trip to the doctor and his first x-ray.

Dark Rubies in a Pirate's Chest
by Alberto Rios

With a flourish and a whoosh sound
The doctor walked into the room

Sticking the photograph up
Against a white light.

I closed my eyes at the suddenness,
At the bright room made even brighter.

The first time I had an x-ray
I opened one eye to look at it,

I had swallowed a white xylophone—
Apparently. I opened my other eye:

Two white xylophones.
I looked harder, and tried not to think

Xylophone too loudly. Maybe
These were not xylophones.

Nobody seemed to want to bang on them,
Which is what I would do,

Not even the doctor who had already
Tapped my knees—he had the thing

You need to play the xylophone, but no.
He didn't make a move to get it. I looked again.

Harder. I saw in there inside myself
Two trellises in the night, white in black,

A mist or a fog enveloping them,
Mystery everywhere, the movie

Starting, dogs howling, Sherlock Holmes
Frowning in the distance, the crime

Ready to happen. The murder.
It's nothing. Everything's fine,

The doctor pronounced, squinting his eyes
The same way I was.

That didn't sound right to me.
But *chest* didn't sound right to me, either,

My chest. It was hard to figure. I had a chest,
Which I knew was the front of me, but

I had a chest of drawers, too, and—
Here's the thing, what I had been hoping for—

I had once seen a picture of a pirate chest
Full of gold coins and dark rubies,

Emeralds and teeth-strings of pearls. Everything
Shiny. This was not that. I wanted *that*.

Mine inside was simply a small space, quiet
Xylophones, a crime scene, perhaps,

A dark, cloudy night. Inside me.
A dark night, black and gray,

Even though I had eaten oranges for lunch.
And some ketchup, some red ketchup, I was sure.

Should I have mentioned that? Because
Everything was certainly not all right.

Poetry has great power. It touches us in ways only figurative language can. Whether it is hip hop, a funny poem heard at a poetry slam, or a poem about the first experience with some aspect of life, poetry has great power to help young people, and all people, to understand and make sense of their lives.

Teaching Young Adult Poetry

Chapters 10 and 11 list detailed activities to use with students as they process their reading of young adult literature. Many of those activities will work just as well or even better with poetry as with prose because it is actually easier to convince students to do a "close" or a "deep" reading of something as small as a poem, rather than of a whole play or a novel. So, how does the classroom teacher facilitate students as they first engage with a poem? How should a poem be introduced to the class for the very first time before the activities?

Step Number 1: Pick a Good Poem   Use a poem that will be meaningful to readers as well as interesting and artful. Boring, irrelevant poems, even if they are in the literature anthology, will make the act of teaching poetry geometrically more difficult than it should be and rob students of their intrinsic motivation to learn about poetry. In addition, boring poems can kill any chance of a lifelong relationship with poetry. Teachers would be missing the point of Poetry 180 if they failed to take heed of Collins's hope that students take each poem and "hold it up to the light," rather than "torture a confession out of it" (from "Introduction to Poetry"). We have all had the experience of torturing poems to death in English class although we may have felt more like we were the ones being tortured in the process. First and foremost, Collins recommends that students have a pleasant experience with the poems, or as he puts it in the second installment of his Poetry 180 project, *180 More* (Random House, 2005), an "immediate injection of pleasure." Lest students come to the conclusion that poetry is punishment, we want to ensure they enjoy it early on, creating a welcome place in their hearts and minds for the reading of, the listening to, and the discussion of poems.

Step Number 2: Provide an Effective Reading of the Poem   A video of the poet on YouTube or Vimeo, for example, can be magical, but the teacher, a student, or even a volunteer will suffice, provided careful attention to prosody is given. Reading a poem cold (i.e., without any preparation) can do a great disservice to the poem. Using a video camcorder to practice is ideal because it enables the reader to experiment with different emphases and speeds and to manipulate tone until the reader feels satisfied that the poem's meaning and feeling is now there for the audience to discover. In class, read/perform the poem at least two times and, if at all possible, provide the students with the written text. But hold off on handing out copies until the second reading so that during the first reading your students will be free to relax and concentrate on the sounds of the words.

Step Number 3: Discuss the Students' Reaction to the Poem as a Group   First, however, give them some time to sit with it and time to write down their thoughts and feelings as they read back over the written text. On their copy, have them mark the words, phrases, or lines that especially got to them, and make a few notes explaining what it made them think or feel. Treat their reactions to the poem with respect. Louise Rosenblatt's Reader Response Theory tells us that when each individual and a text come together, something new is created that never existed before. As we begin discussion of the poem, which would be better termed *response* than *discussion,* we should be careful to honor each student's reaction and to encourage students to make their own meaning of the text, but also consider a group dynamic in the process. Reader Response theorist Robert Probst, in a January 1986 *English Journal* article titled "Three Relationships in the Teaching of Literature," explains the teacher's role in this and what he hopes the result will be if teachers:

> . . . go through the act of making meaning with students, students may see that the process is tentative and probing, that it begins in unarticulated response and is gradually shaped into coherent statements about self and text. (p. 66)

The teacher's role in this, then, is to encourage students to react fearlessly with their hearts and minds to a poem, secure in their knowledge that they will not be held to that first impression and can change their minds and their reactions to the poem as they hear from their classmates. Also, they need to know that we are interested in their personal reaction to the poem and not the regurgitation of a preconceived "correct" reaction arrived at years ago by a university professor who logged it into the teacher's guide part of an anthology. If a class has a number of students who are too timid to speak in front of the whole class, have them work in pairs or small groups, sharing their reactions to the poem, then choosing one thing to share with the whole class. Acknowledging that some repetitions will occur is perfectly okay. See Focus Box 6.3, "More Poets and Poetry," on page 198 for additional examples.

Step Number 4: Discuss the Artist's Craft   As students learn about the elements of poetry, including scansion, figurative language, and so on, they delight in recognizing these elements in a poem. Help them to see that poetic devices do not exist in a vacuum, but rather that they serve the grand purpose of poetry: to evoke emotion and/or stir the imagination. Poets use rhyme and metaphor, for example, to achieve a response, to provoke a reaction from the reader as they, the poets, make a statement about the human experience. That statement is the most important thing, and the technique comes next (but is still important). The better the poet can use metaphor, meter, allusion, and so on, the more effectively the message comes across, and so it is important not to separate the device from its purpose. Teachers are wise not to begin with the poetic term and move backwards to the poetic event but to do the exact opposite. As Alberto Rios, National Book Award Finalist, who kindly let us use his poem "Dark Rubies in a Pirate's Chest," told us back in 2002 when we interviewed him for an article in the January issue of *English Journal:*

> In general, the deductive approach—starting with the names of devices, understanding them as vocabulary, and then moving to an example—has not been effective; instead, starting with the example and then trying to understand the vocabulary within which the event occurs is what helps it to make sense.

So, begin with what the poem does to young readers by asking them how it makes them feel, what it makes them experience in their imaginations, and what it makes them think. After they have exhausted discussion about what the poem does, ask them about the how, the poetic devices that touched their hearts and minds so powerfully. They may not know the terms, but this is where the teacher comes in explaining, for example, that "Frost's unqualified reference to Adam and Eve in 'So Eden sank to grief' (in "Nothing Gold Can Stay") which you said made you wonder if the human race has always been subject to moral decay all the way back to the beginning of time is called a biblical allusion," or that the *ta dump ta dump* rhythm you said makes you feel as if you're riding a horse (in "Horses vs. Hosses," by S. Omar Barker) is called iambic pentameter, which means there are five feet in a line and each foot has one stressed syllable in it. (Shakespeare was very fond of this scheme). At which point the teacher can mark in the meter of the line on a projection of the poem and maybe even throw up a few lines from Sonnet 18 ("Shall I compare thee to a summer's day?"). Students can mark in all the resulting artist's craft discussed on their own copy of the poem, which will help them to make connections to other poems using the same techniques or provide for comparison between poems that use very different techniques.

Anyone who has ever been to a dude ranch and "panned for gold" should get the concept of letting the students mine for gold themselves as they engage with poetry. They see and hear the poem performed to its full potential, react with the full force of their hearts and minds, and pan for gold, so to speak. As the teacher helps them in uncovering the nuggets mixed among the pebbles and grains of sand, they are learning to analyze poetry and discovering how the poet used age-old techniques to convey a message or a feeling.

In reference to Alberto Rios's poem, "Dark Rubies in a Pirate's Chest" here are some of the things that you might lead students to pan for, remembering that they—not you—are doing the search. You are only the trailblazer and the one who provides the map and the tools. You will probably want to start with students' personal reactions and their memories of going to a doctor and being left in an examination room. There needs to be enough discussion that everyone in the class understands the literal event that is being talked about before moving on to visit about what makes this writing *poetic* rather than *prosaic*. One of the characteristics of poetic language is words that suggest sensual imagery in the five different ways that humans are equipped to understand.

- **Sight** as with *photograph, dark, night, white in black, a dark night, grey and black, misty, fog, picture, shiny, cloudy, gray,* etc.
- **Sound** as with *whoosh, sound xylophone, tap, bang, howling, quiet,* etc.
- **Smell** as with *dogs, oranges, lunch, ketchup,* etc.
- **Taste** as with *swallowed, teeth, eaten, oranges, lunch, red ketchup,* etc.
- **Touch** as with *sticking, harder, enveloping, small,* etc.

Another characteristic is the use of rhetorical devices called *schemes*, which deal with the surface structure of the language (rhyme, rhythm, repetition, alliteration, assonance, etc.) and tropes which deal with the deep structure of the

Focus Box 6.3

More Poets and Poetry

Crush: Love Poems by Kwame Alexander. Word of Mouth, **2007.** Naomi Shihab Nye wrote the title poem; other featured poets are Pablo Neruda, Nikki Giovanni, and Sherman Alexie. An intriguing variety of verbal formulas may inspire teens to submit their own poems to a related website.

Every Thing On It by Shel Silverstein. HarperCollins, **2011.** Kids who grew up giggling over Silverstein's collections, are the most likely to appreciate this posthumous collection. The title poem is about all the things you can get "with everything on it." This deserves a place on bookshelves next to his world famous *Where the Sidewalk Ends, A Light in the Attic,* and *Falling Up.*

Good Poems, compiled by Garrison Keillor. Viking, **2002.** After a lighthearted introduction, Keillor presents three hundred poems that he has read on his PBS radio show, *A Prairie Home Companion.* They range from the well-known to the obscure, but they are all accessible.

Heart to Heart: New Poems Inspired by Twentieth-Century American Art, edited by Jan Greenberg. Abrams, **2001.** In this Printz Honor Book, Greenberg commissioned poets to write in response to some of the greatest twentieth-century American paintings. She arranged the paintings and the poems according to the poet's approach.

I Am the Darker Brother: An Anthology of Modern Poems by African Americans, revised edition, edited by Arnold Adoff, illustrated by Benny Andrews. **Simon & Schuster, 1997.** Since its publication in 1968, this has been the premier anthology of black poetry. Twenty-one new poems are included with pieces coming from nine women, including Rita Dove and Maya Angelou.

I, Too, Sing America: Three Centuries of African American Poetry, edited by Catherine Clinton, illustrated by Stephen Alcorn. Houghton Mifflin, **1998.** This attractive, large-sized book is a good resource for classrooms and libraries.

Immersed in Verse: An Informative, Slightly Irreverent and Totally Tremendous Guide to Living the Poet's Life by Allan Wolf, illustrated by Tuesday Mourning. **Sterling/Lark, 2006.** This is both a how-to and a book of encouragement for anyone who's even slightly tempted to write a poem. The illustrations add an upbeat tone.

Love Speaks Its Name: Gay and Lesbian Love Poems, edited by J. D. McClatchy. Knopf, **2001.** The 144 poets featured in this collection include Sappho, Walt Whitman, Frank O'Hara, and Muriel Rukeyser.

Pierced by a Ray of Sun: Poems about the Times We Feel Alone, selected by Ruth Gordon.

---

language so as to include metaphors and similes and the use of words that have more than one meaning.

- **Schemes** include the rhythm of the poem as shown by how smoothly it reads and the repetition of such words as *xylophone* and the phrase *everything's all right.* The lines do not rhyme with each other, but certainly they go well together.

- **Tropes** are what give this poem so much power with its various meanings of the word *chest* and then when the boy sees the ribs in his chest as one *xylophone* and then two *xylophones* and the doctor's little *hammer* as a tool to use on the *xylophones,* which have now changed into a *trellis* or maybe a crime scene, leaving readers to figure out just what the *dark rubies* are in the boy's *treasure chest* and why *Everything was certainly not all right.*

A third aspect of poetic language is that poets have *poetic license.* Poems do not follow the grammar of either a written language or of a spoken language, but

HarperCollins, 1995. These seventy-three poems all explore human loneliness. Also recommended are Gordon's earlier collections including *Time Is the Longest Distance* (1991), *Under All Silences* (1987), and *Peeling the Onion* (1993), all HarperCollins.

Poetry Speaks: Hear Great Poets Read Their Work from Tennyson to Plath, **edited by Elise Paschen and Rebekah Presson Mosby. Source Books, 2001.** A bonus to this book are the three CDs presenting many of the forty-two poets doing interpretive readings.

Reflections on a Gift of Watermelon Pickle, **edited by Stephen Dunning and others. Scott, Foresman, 1967, reissued, 1994.** A landmark book, this collection proved that young readers could enjoy modern poetry without the help (or hindrance) of teachers. Its sequel, *Some Haystacks Don't Even Have Any Needle, and Other Complete Modern Poems* (Lothrop, 1969), is almost as good.

Time You Let Me In: 25 Poets Under 25 **by Naomi Shihab Nye. HarperCollins, 2010.** A highly respected poet has chosen these poems from young poets and written a beautiful introduction to a set of poems that is timeless in its expression of the "hope, humor, intelligence, passions, and complications" that come with being on the cusp of adulthood.

Tour America: A Journey through Poems and Art **by Diane Siebert, illustrated by Stephen T. Johnson. CIP Chronicle, 2006.** Children, teens, and adults can all enjoy this book of poems and paintings that takes readers to twenty-six of the author's favorite places in America—ranging from Alaska and a view of the aurora borealis to Chicago and a view of the El.

Truth and Lies: An Anthology of Poems, **edited by Patrice Vecchione. Holt, 2001.** Vecchione adds illuminating notes to help young readers enjoy the poems that she carefully chose from across centuries and across cultures.

Wáchale! Poetry and Prose About Growing Up Latino in America, **edited by Ilan Stavans. Cricket Books/Carus Publishing, 2001.** A reviewer described the vivid word pictures in this bilingual collection as speaking from the heart and lingering in the mind.

Walt Whitman: Words for America **by Barbara Kerley, illustrated by Brian Selznick. Scholastic, 2004.** Beautiful pictures and a generous format make this a good book for introducing one of America's most famous poets.

Why War Is Never a Good Idea **by Alice Walker, illustrated by Stefano Vitale. HarperCollins, 2007.** Folk art paintings make Walker's poem especially powerful. Skilled teachers can use the book to bring both an artistic and a thought-provoking experience to groups from ages eight or nine on up.

each poem has its own grammar. It's fun to discover how particular poets choose to exert their poetic license. Since this is a free-verse poem, there are no heroic couplets like the kind that Shakespeare used; nevertheless, the phrases are so carefully crafted that they can be blocked like poetry but not prose. The word at the beginning of each line is capitalized, but the ends of the lines do not always have periods. Once students see this in a poem, they will be better able to appreciate the books listed in Focus Box 6.2, "Stories Told through Free-Verse Poetry."

Making Drama a Class Act

We used to say that playwrights did not write plays for teenagers because teenagers were not the ones buying tickets to Broadway plays or flying to London on theater tours. That's still true, but today's teenagers make up a healthy portion of television and movie audiences; therefore, talented writers are now writing serious plays designed for young people either to read or to

Today's students want to make their own dramatic productions whether they are making movies to enter in a film festival or to post online. When kids in our Tempe neighborhood were making a zombie film, we got there in time to hear a cooperative neighbor asking, "You want me to do what!?" She was probably even more alarmed by the afternoon when the boys had gotten what looked like real guns and were acting in front of a green screen so that they could substitute a more exciting backdrop than that of our typical suburban neighborhood.

perform. Be warned, however, that these are not the kinds of nondescript plays that were found in books for high school students a generation ago. They are plays which question fitting in, popularity, sex, drugs, making choices, and taking chances. And now with YouTube and the easy accessibility of cameras and related equipment, many teenagers are much more interested in making their own movies, like the kids did in the successful 2010 *Super 8,* which had Steven Spielberg as one of its producers. The film was based on his own teen years as a neighborhood maker of movies.

Jerome McDonough has been labeled "father of young adult drama" because of the powerful and easy-to-produce plays he creates for the young adult stage. They are fifty to seventy minutes long, have flexible casts so the plays can be adapted to however many actors are available, and have contemporary settings. Hindi Brooks, who has been a writer for television's *Fame* and *Eight Is Enough,* has also written plays specifically for young adults. (Both McDonough's and Brooks's plays are available from I. E. Clark in Schulenberg, Texas.) Samuel French in Hollywood and Dramatists Play Service in New York also offer play scripts written for teenagers. For the first time, when the ALAN Workshop was held in New York City in November 2007, it included a panel of playwrights talking about their scripts. Without encouragement from teachers, few teenagers read drama because it needs to be read aloud with different voices and it is hard to visualize the scenery and the stage directions. One of our graduate students, Alison Babusci, who came to study in Arizona State University's well-known program in Children's Theater, drew up these five suggestions for teachers who are planning to have students read and study such plays as those listed in Focus Box 6.4, "Plays Commonly Read in English Classes."

1. Make students feel like they are "on the inside" of the theatrical world by bringing in photocopies of sets and costume designs. Obtain a stage diagram and teach students stage directions; the more they

Plays Commonly Read in English Classes

Children of a Lesser God by Mark Medoff. Dramatists, **1980.** Especially since the success of the movie, students appreciate this Tony Award-winning play about a deaf young woman and her relationship with a hearing teacher.

Driving Miss Daisy by Alfred Uhry. Dramatists, **1988.** The impressive film serves as a backdrop for reading this play that helps students learn what is involved in a lasting friendship.

The Effect of Gamma Rays on Man-in-the-Moon Marigolds by Paul Zindel. Dramatists, **1970.** This moving story of the damaging forms that parent–child love can take brought Paul Zindel to the attention of the literary world.

Fences by August Wilson. Drama Book Shop and New American Library paperback, **1995.** Wilson's play won the Pulitzer Prize for the way it shows an African American family losing its dreams in the 1950s.

Inherit the Wind by Jerome Lawrence and Robert E. Lee. Dramatists, **1955.** Based on the Scopes trial, this play is especially interesting in relation to current controversies over creationism versus evolution. The lines are easy to read aloud, and there is a good balance between sharp wit and high drama.

Les Misérables by Tim Kelly. Dramatists, **1987.** With eleventh and twelfth graders, the boys like action, the girls like romance, and they all like music. So here's a play that answers everyone's needs.

A Man for All Seasons by Robert Bolt. Baker (also French), **1960.** This play is good for its portrayal of one of the most famous periods of English history and for its exploration of a hero. Interesting comparisons can be drawn to works treating heroes of noble birth, as in *Antigone* and *Hamlet,* and heroes of ordinary birth, as in *Death of a Salesman* and *The Stranger.*

"Master Harold" . . . and the Boys by Athol Fugard. Penguin, **1982.** This powerful one-act play asks students to examine the psychological effects of racism on whites.

The Miracle Worker by William Gibson. Baker (also French), **1951.** Students love the poignancy of the story of Helen Keller and Annie Sullivan, but it is also a good illustration of flashbacks, foreshadowing, symbolism, and dramatic license when compared to such biographies as Nella Braddy's *Annie Sullivan Macy* and Helen Keller's *The Story of My Life.* Gibson's *Monday After the Miracle,* a continuation of the story, is also a good read.

Sorry, Wrong Number by Lucille Fletcher in *Fifteen American One-Act Plays,* edited by Paul Kozelka. Pocket Books, **1971.** Because it is a radio play written to be heard and not seen, it is ideal for reading aloud.

A Storm in Summer by Rod Serling in *Great Television Plays,* Vol. 2, edited by Ned E. Hoopes and Patricia Neale Gordon. Dell, **1975.** Students like the way Serling relates an encounter between a ten-year-old Harlem boy and a bitter, sarcastic, Jewish delicatessen owner in upstate New York.

The Teahouse of the August Moon by John Patrick. Dramatists, **1953.** The way Patrick lightheartedly pokes fun at American customs and values is refreshing.

Visit to a Small Planet by Gore Vidal, in *Visit to a Small Planet and Other Television Plays.* Little, Brown, **1956.** Because this play was written for television, the action is easy to visualize and the stage directions simple enough to discuss as an important aspect of the drama itself.

What I Did Last Summer by A. R. Gurney, Jr. Dramatists, **1983.** As Anna tells fourteen-year-old Charlie in this play about the last summer of World War II, "All choices are important. They tell you who you are."

know about the production of a play they are reading, the more interested they will be.

2. Become "friends" with the cast by having students copy the cast list (dramatis personae) from the beginning of the play and then write their own descriptions of the characters and their relationships.

3. Involve students by leading them to form their own opinions and images.

4. Let students see the play. Before deciding on what play to read, contact theater groups in your area and find out what plays they will be producing over the next year, or choose a play available on video.

5. Instead of always having students read parts aloud, try letting them improvise selected scenes. Also think of ways to combine drama with music, fine arts, dance, or other physical activities. People do not fall asleep when their bodies are active.

Her concluding advice was that teachers have to be excited by drama. Students will quickly identify and adopt the teacher's attitude: If the teacher is bored, students will be bored. Because so many students work after school and are involved in extra heavy academic loads, some high schools are trying alternative ways to get drama included; for example, offering theater programs during the summer or as extracurricular events.

Paul Zindel's career (see his Margaret A. Edwards Award write-up on page 215) as a popular playwright, screenwriter, and author of young adult books is a good illustration of how teen readers appreciate the immediacy and the directness of characters talking with each other as they do in films and plays. See Focus Box 6.5, "Books Recommended for Read-Alouds or Adaptations into Mini-Plays," for books that include this kind of vivid language.

A favorite play for reading aloud is Reginald Rose's three-act television play *Twelve Angry Men*, the story of a jury making a decision on the future of a nineteen-year-old boy charged with murder. Some classes affectionately refer to

Storytelling is an important piece of drama, especially when students can bring in their own cultures. The National Council of Teachers of English website has several articles about bringing in multicultural stories. Two of their books might be particularly helpful to teachers wanting to include Native American literature: Roots and Branches: A Resource of Native American Literature *by Dorothea M. Susagand,* Reading Native American Literature: A Teacher's Guide *by Bruce A. Goebel. See Focus Box 6.5 on page 203 for books that have been recommended as good materials, in general, for storytelling or dramatizing.*

Navajo Story Teller's Doll

***Black Cat Bone: The Life of Blues Legend Robert Johnson* by J. Patrick Lewis, illustrated by Gary Kelley. Creative Editions, 2006.** This story of Robert Johnson, a blues musician, could be used as a wonderful introduction to a music event.

***Carver: A Life in Poems* by Marilyn Nelson (Boyds Mills, 2001).** Nikki Giovanni praised this winner of the 2001 Boston Globe Horn Book Award by writing, "Oh, Marilyn Nelson, what a magnificent job you have done to bring the past so alive it looks like our future." The individual poems make for an easy way of dividing up this biography of George Washington Carver for a class presentation.

***A Gift from Zeus: Sixteen Favorite Myths* by Jeanne Steig, pictures by William Steig. Joanna Cotler Books/HarperCollins, 2001.** William Steig's drawings, as in *Sylvester and the Magic Pebble*, and his Dr. DeSoto books have always been brute art. Now that he is in his nineties, his style is even more succinct and could serve as a model for kids to do their own giant-sized drawings to assist them in storytelling.

***Here in Harlem: Poems in Many Voices* by Walter Dean Myers. Holiday House, 2004.** Myers did for Harlem what Edgar Lee Masters did in his 1915 *Spoon River Anthology*. The rich text and the variety of voices (up to fifty) make it appealing either for choral readings, individual presentations, or a mixture of both.

***The Hitchhiker's Guide to the Galaxy* by Douglas Adams. Ballantine, 1980.** Arthur Dent and Ford Prefect are on a perilous and very funny journey through the galaxy. The stories were originally produced in England as radio shows and so work well as read-alouds.

***Keesha's House* by Helen Frost. Frances Foster Books/FSG, 2003.** These first-person accounts from seven teenagers show that kids who are pushed out of their own homes and are dealing with such "heavy" issues as abandonment, racism, addiction, delinquency, and sexual consequences can still come together and help each other.

***Short Circuits: Thirteen Shocking Stories by Outstanding Writers for Young Adults,* edited by Donald R. Gallo. HarperCollins, 1992.** Several of these suspenseful and ghostly stories can be used for humorous read-alouds. Alvin Schwartz's *Scary Stories to Tell in the Dark, More Scary Stories to Tell in the Dark,* and *Scary Stories 3: More Tales to Chill Your Bones* (HarperCollins, 1981, 1984, and 1992) are also the kind that will make the hair on listeners' arms stand up straight.

***The Song Shoots Out of My Mouth: A Celebration of Music* by Jaime Adoff, illustrated by Martin French. Dutton, 2002.** Jaime Adoff is the son of Virginia Hamilton and Arnold Adoff and as a musician has put together a poetic tribute to all kinds of music.

***Talkin' about Bessie: The Story of Aviator Elizabeth Coleman* by Nikki Grimes, illustrated by E. B. Lewis. Scholastic, 2002.** An unusual biography is presented through twenty-one poetic speeches given at the funeral parlor where people have come to mourn the early death of the first African American woman to become a licensed pilot. See also Grimes's *Stepping Out with Grandma Mac* (Scholastic/Orchard, 2001) in which poems capture and celebrate the experiences shared by a teenaged girl and her grandmother.

***Tough Boy Sonatas* by Curtis L. Crisler, illustrated by Floyd Cooper. Boyds Mills/Wordsong, 2007.** Driving through the industrial town of Gary, Indiana, will not be the same for readers who absorb these thirty-eight fierce and muscular poems about the boys who run in this harsh town and who, like LaRoy, sing "I am not a failing flashlight. I am an Inspired/ Inspiration."

***What My Mother Doesn't Know* by Sonya Sones. Simon & Schuster, 2001.** These free-verse poems can stand on their own, but when read all together they tell the story of fourteen-year-old Sophie's longings as well as her adventures.

***Witness* by Karen Hesse. Scholastic, 2001.** It is 1924 and a small town in Vermont is caught up in intrigue and prejudice. Hesse uses carefully constructed free verse to present a little-known piece of U.S. history through the eyes and voices of eleven different townspeople.

***Your Own Sylvia: A Verse Portrait of Sylvia Plath* by Stephanie Hemphill. Knopf, 2007.** This is a book to promote alongside Sylvia Plath's still-popular *The Bell Jar* (HarperCollins, 1971).

the play as *Twelve Angry People* because girls as well as boys are assigned parts. Teachers have offered the following reasons for the play's success, which can serve as guides when predicting the potential of other scripts.

1. It calls for twelve continual parts, enough to satisfy all students who like to read aloud.
2. It teaches practical lessons of value to students' lives.
3. It may serve as a springboard for research and further discussion on how the judicial system works.
4. It creates a forum for students to prove the psychology of group dynamics and peer behavior.
5. It sparks student excitement from the beginning and sustains it throughout.
6. It can be read in two-and-a-half class sessions.
7. The "business" is minimal and can be easily carried out as students read from scripts.
8. Pertinent questions can be asked when the jury recesses after Acts I and II.
9. Students are attracted to the realism, and they can relate to a motherless slum youth of nineteen.
10. The excellent characterization allows students to discover a kaleidoscope of lifelike personalities.

Play scripts are sold through distributors, most of whom will happily send free catalogues to teachers who request them. A typical script price for a one-act play is under $10.00 with a typical royalty charge of less than $100 for the initial production, less for each subsequent production. Teachers wanting scripts for in-class reading rather than for production should so note at the time of ordering so that no royalty is charged. If the play is to be produced, whether admission is charged or not, the producer should pay the fee when the scripts are ordered. A royalty contract is mailed along with the scripts. Check online for information from these distributors:

Brooklyn Publishers Free Scripts for High Schools and Middle Schools:
http://www.brookpub.com/

Horton's One-Act Play Scripts:
http://www.stagepage.info/oneactplayscripts/_oneact.html

I. E. Clark in Schulenberg, Texas:
http://www.ieclark.com/childmen.html

Dramatists Play Services in New York:
http://www.dramatists.com/

Free One-Act Plays for High Schools:
http://plays.about.com/od/plays/tp/freeplays.htm

Play Scripts Blog for Middle Schools:
http://www.playscripts.com/blog/tag/middle-school-plays/

Play Scripts Inc. for High Schools:
http://www.playscripts.com/high

TheatreFolk: Plays for High School and Middle School:
http://www.theatrefolk.com/

But even better than launching yourself on a solitary tour of such guides as these is to go and visit the theater teacher, who will probably have several catalogues that have arrived in the mail. Borrow them. Read the quick plot summaries and order some plays to read with your classes. Perhaps you can share costs with the theater department, while your students serve as first readers—as scouts—for appealing new scripts. Reading new plays from professionally prepared scripts is one of the simplest ways to follow Alison Babusci's suggestion that we make students feel "on the inside" of the theatrical world. Another way is to let students create their own plays from such books as those listed in Focus Box 6.5.

Humor Matters

Despite what must seem obvious truth to good teachers and librarians—that a sense of humor is essential for the survival of educators and students—some deadly serious people wonder if this (or any other time, presumably) is the time for levity. The answer is, of course, yes. Given their enforced world of school and an ever-demanding society, young people need laughter every bit as much as—maybe even more than—adults.

What do young people find funny? Lance M. Gentile and Merna M. McMillan's article, in the January 1978 *Journal of Reading* titled "Humor and the Reading Program" offers a starting point. Their stages of children's and young adults' interest in humor, somewhat supplemented, are as follows:

1. *Ages ten to eleven:* Literal humor, slapstick (e.g., The Three Stooges), laughing at accidents (banana-peel humor) and misbehavior, sometimes mildly lewd jokes (usually called "dirty jokes"), and grossness.

2. *Ages twelve to thirteen:* Practical jokes, teasing, goofs, sarcasm, more lewd jokes, joke-riddles, sick jokes, elephant jokes, grape jokes, tongue twisters, knock-knock jokes, moron jokes, TV blooper shows, and grossness piled on grossness.

3. *Ages fourteen to fifteen:* More and more lewd jokes (some approaching a mature recognition of the humor inherent in sex); humor aimed at schools, parents, and other adults in authority, as in television's *Malcolm in the Middle;* and grossness piled on even greater grossness. Young adults may still prefer their own humor to their parents' humor, but they are increasingly catching on to adult humor and may prefer it to their own.

4. *Ages sixteen and up:* More subtle humor; satire and parody now acceptable and maybe even preferable, witticisms (rather than last year's

half-witticisms, which they now detest in their young brothers and sisters). Adult humor is increasingly part of their repertoire, partly because they are anxious to appear sophisticated, partly because they are growing up (pp. 343–350).

From Chills to Giggles

Something in the human mind encourages crossovers between fear and amusement, as shown by how often people who have suffered a fright burst out laughing as soon as the danger is over. Humor about death can be traced back at least as far as the early Greeks. English speakers refer to this blend of humor and horror as Gothic because they associate it with the grotesque gargoyles and other frightening figures in tapestries, paintings, sculptures, and stained glass windows, which were created to represent the devil and to frighten people into "proper" beliefs and behavior. Instead, people coped with their fears by turning such icons into objects of amusement.

People still do this at Halloween with spiderwebs, skeletons, black cats, bats, rats, ghosts, coffins, tombstones, monsters, and haunted houses. Halloween developed out of the sacred or "hallowed" evening preceding All Saints Day, which falls on November 1. The holiday is now second only to Christmas in the amount of money expended for costumes, parties, and candy to be given to trick-or-treaters.

The world has had great fun with Mary Shelley's story *Frankenstein: Or, the Modern Prometheus,* but when it was written many people viewed it as a cautionary tale against medical experimentation. Shelley's story followed close on the heels of the development of autopsies and of dissection for purposes of medical study. Such practices made people nervous and fearful. One way of calming such fears was by laughing at them. While Shelley's story was itself rich in Gothic details with a complex plot and fully developed characters, hundreds of parodies and imitations are comic in nature.

Gothic novels underwent a similar kind of transformation from scary to funny when, in the same year that Shelley published *Frankenstein* (1818), Jane Austen published *Northanger Abbey* as a gleeful parody of the earlier novels. Later Gothic stories in the mid and late 1800s included some darkly humorous moments caused by visits from the dead as in Edgar Allan Poe's "The Fall of the House of Usher," Emily Brontë's *Wuthering Heights,* and Charles Dickens's *A Christmas Carol* with its Ghosts of Christmas Past, Christmas Present, and Christmas Future. In *Bleak House,* Dickens creates a character who spontaneously combusts; in *Little Dorrit,* the prison resembles a haunted castle; and in *Great Expectations,* Pip meets the criminal in a graveyard and has a hallucinatory vision of Miss Havisham's hanged body "with but one shoe to the feet."

Bram Stoker's 1897 *Dracula* is not the first story about a vampire, but it is the one that established such Western traditions as a vampire's need for periodically sucking blood, the requirements of a prolonged relationship before a human can be turned into a vampire, vampires sleeping in coffins during the day and arising for action only after dark, the impossibility of killing vampires with ordinary human weapons, and the use of such conventional techniques for repelling vampires as garlic, a silver crucifix, and a wooden stake through the heart.

Bud Abbott and Lou Costello were among the earliest film comedians to take advantage of the possibilities of film for stretching viewers' emotions between the frightening and the ridiculous. Their 1948 *Abbott and Costello Meet Frankenstein* still appears on all-time best comedy lists. In the mid-1960s, *The Munsters* was a popular television show. Also, Charles Addams's ghoulish cartoons, which had been published in the *New Yorker,* were adapted into the pseudoscary *The Addams Family.* Laughs come mostly from the surprise of seeing ordinary family life conducted in a spooky old mansion by scary-looking individuals with such names as Uncle Fester, Morticia, Gomez, Wednesday, and Pugsley.

Other Gothic movies that made people both shiver and laugh include the 1973 *Rocky Horror Picture Show,* a spoof of a Gothic novel, which originally failed at the box office but soon developed a cult following. The 1984 *Ghostbusters* starred Bill Murray and Dan Aykroyd, while the 1986 *Little Shop of Horrors* starred Steve Martin, Rick Moranis, and a plant that eats people. Also in 1986, *The Witches of Eastwick,* based on John Updike's novel, starred Jack Nicholson, Cher, Susan Sarandon, Michelle Pfeiffer, and Veronica Cartwright. This fascination with horror led right into the Batman movies of the 1990s, in which New York City was renamed Gotham City. Its underground tunnels and sewer systems were made to serve as modern substitutes for the secret passageways, hidden entries, and basement crypts of the castles and mansions in Gothic novels.

In 1975, folklore collector Alvin Schwartz was happily surprised when his 1981 *Scary Stories to Tell in the Dark* and its sequels, *More Scary Stories to Tell in the Dark* and *Scary Stories 3: More Tales to Chill Your Bones,* started winning state contests where children voted on their favorite books. Today, Schwartz's books are still on the American Library Association's list of frequently banned books, but kids still love them. They are kids' versions of some of the scary urban legends published in such adult books as Jan Harold Brunvand's *The Vanishing Hitchhiker: American Urban Legends and Their Meanings* and Joseph C. Goulden's *There Are Alligators in Our Sewers and Other American Credos.* A similar, but newer, book that includes such stories as "The Stolen Kidney," "The Scuba Diver in the Forest Fire," and "Aliens in Roswell, New Mexico," is Thomas Craughwell's *Alligators in the Sewer and 222 Other Urban Legends.* In the mid-1980s writer Robert Lawrence Stine, who had written joke books for Scholastic as well as a *How to Be Funny* manual under the pen name of Jovial Bob Stine, created the Goosebumps series for eight-, nine-, and ten-year-olds and the Fear Street series for young teens. Even though interest in Gothic humor has peaked, Stine is still a publishing phenomenon. A few years back, when First Lady Laura Bush was invited to a book promotion event with Mrs. Putin in Russia, she offered to bring an American author with her. She was told that the only author Russian children would know was R. L. Stine, and so Mrs. Bush and Mr. Stine went on a goodwill tour to Russia.

Ethnic-Based Humor

Discussions and news stories about political correctness have made everyone aware of the fact that ethnic-based humor can be used in negative ways. However, the other side of the coin is that such humor can also be used for positive purposes. Among members of their own groups, people use ethnic-based humor as a way of bonding and as a sign of solidarity and group pride. For example, humorous undertones often run through the Spanglish that young Hispanics use and through the exaggerated slang that is part of Black English.

An important point is that positive uses of ethnic humor usually come from within the group itself. This does not mean that all elements of criticism are avoided. Just as individuals sometimes use self-deprecating humor, they also use group-deprecating humor. The difference, when such humor comes from inside versus outside a group, is that the insider is probably chiding the group to change, while the outsider is making fun of, and cementing, old stereotypes.

When ethnic-based joking finds its way into books or films, thoughtful readers or viewers can learn a lot about each other. Henry Spalding has described the way that Jews use self-deprecating humor as "honey-coated barbs" at the people and things Jews love most. He says that he and his relatives verbally attack their loved ones and their religion, but always with a grand sense of affection, "a kiss with salt on the lips, but a kiss nevertheless."

Sherman Alexie's 1998 movie *Smoke Signals,* based on a short story from his book *The Lone Ranger and Tonto Fistfight in Heaven,* has some of this same kind of humor in it. The story is set on the Coeur d'Alene Indian Reservation in northern Idaho, and while it is about such serious problems as alcoholism, alienation, and broken dreams, it does not shy away from wry humor. When we went to see the film in Scottsdale, Arizona, the audience was almost equally divided between whites and Native Americans. Both groups laughed at such parodies as a T-shirt advertising "Fry Bread Power" and at "the miracle of the fry bread" when Victor's mother magically feeds a crowd that is twice as big as she had expected. She simply raises her arms heavenward and solemnly rips each piece of bread in half. Both groups also laughed at the KREZ radio station announcer who sounds like Robin Williams when he shouts, "It's a great day to be indigenous!" Indian viewers seemed more amused by Victor's telling Thomas to shut off the television, "There's only one thing more pathetic than Indians on TV and that's Indians watching Indians on TV."

Indian viewers also laughed uninhibitedly at the two gum-chewing, soda-drinking sisters who sat sideways facing each other in the front seat of their old car as they listened to rock music and drove backward. While white viewers were troubled by such practical questions as, "Is the gear shift broken?" and "Can't they afford to get it fixed?" the Indian viewers appeared to accept the women as genuinely funny versions of contrary clowns. Several tribes rely on contraries for their humor. These are clowns that do the opposite of what is expected. They dress in buffalo robes in the summer and go stark naked in winter snow. In Thomas Berger's 1964 *Little Big Man,* made into a film of the same name, a contrary clown arrives riding backward on a horse with his body painted in motley colors. He says "Goodbye" for "Hello," "I'm glad I did it!" for "I'm sorry," and cleans himself with sand before striding off by walking through the river.

The point is that humor is a powerful literary technique that can be used for a multitude of purposes. Because humor is so intimately tied to the culture of particular groups, it will probably be one of the last things that outsiders catch onto. Nevertheless, it is well worth whatever attention we can give to it, whether working with middle-school readers or older readers. See Focus Box 6.6, "Books to Make Readers Smile," on page 210.

Teaching Literary Humor

Students are sometimes disappointed because an adult recommends a "funny" book. When they read it, they don't feel like laughing all the way through. The fact is that for people to laugh, they have to be surprised, and there is no way that an author can surprise a reader on every page. Instead, authors sprinkle humor throughout their books. The greater the contrast between the rest of the book and the humor, then the bigger the surprise and the more pleasure it will bring to the reader. Our job at school is not just to repeat the same kinds of humor that students get on the Comedy Central channel or through lists of jokes on the Internet but to help students mature in their taste and appreciation. We need to educate students to catch onto a multitude of allusions and to have the patience required for reading and appreciating subtle kinds of humor.

At one of the International Society for Humor Studies meetings, Jacque Hughes, who teaches at Central Oklahoma University in Edmond, presented an example of how drawing relationships between raucous humor and more subtle humor can help students move to new levels of appreciation. She was having a hard time getting her eighteen-year-old freshmen to understand the dark humor in Flannery O'Connor's "A Good Man Is Hard to Find." Then she happened to see *National Lampoon's Vacation* starring Chevy Chase. It was wonderfully funny, and, because most of her students had seen the movie, class members were able to compare the personalities and the incidents. When they realized that the similarities were too extensive—and too funny—to be coincidental, they gained a new appreciation for O'Connor's skill to do only with words what cost the movie producers millions of dollars to do with words and film.

Types and Features of Literary Humor Used by Outstanding YA Authors

Teaching about humor is doubly challenging because there is no such thing as "a sense of humor." One person might have a sense, or an appreciation, of irony, while another might be amused by wordplay, and someone else by being made to feel superior. In other words, there are many different types of humor (gothic, slapstick, parody, insult, sudden-insight, etc.) and for each type there are many

As we point out, there are many different kinds of humor and what is funny to one person may not be funny to someone else. Nevertheless, the books listed in Focus Box 6.6, "Books to Make Readers Smile" (p. 210), are known to have made many readers smile, and some to laugh out loud.

Angus, Thongs, and Full-Frontal Snogging and ***On the
Bright Side, I'm Now the Girlfriend of a Sex God:
Further Confessions of Georgia Nicolson*** **by Louise
Rennison. HarperCollins, 2000 and 2001.** There's
also a third book in the series, but it doesn't have quite
the sparkle of these first two British imports.

Bucking the Sarge **by Christopher Paul Curtis.
Random/Wendy Lamb, 2004.** "The Sarge" is Luther's
mother who is a big-time landlady and a master at
running scams on both her tenants and her business
associates. Luther has to use his own creative abilities
to establish his independence and break free from his
mother's deviousness.

Diary of a Wimpy Kid **by Jeff Kinney. Amulet, 2007.**
Several sequels, including *Roderick Rules,* are already
out. The popularity of these middle school books
was helped by the successful films. When *Roderick
Rules* was released on the same day as George W.
Bush's autobiography, late-night comedians had fun
telling about how it outsold the former president's
book.

Gilda Joyce: Psychic Investigator **by Jennifer Allison.
Dutton, 2005.** Gilda is a cross between *Harriet the Spy*
and the 2007 *Nancy Drew* film, especially in relation to
moving to California and living in a grand old Victorian
mansion that appears to be haunted.

***How Angel Peterson Got His Name: And Other Out-
rageous Tales about Extreme Sports*** **by Gary
Paulsen. Random/Wendy Lamb Books, 2003.**
Paulsen is at his storytelling best in these entertaining
sketches. His *Harris and Me: A Summer Remembered*
(1993) and *Lawn Boy* (2007) are equally funny—and
exaggerated.

I'm Not Joey Pigza **by Jack Gantos. Farrar, Straus and
Giroux, 2007.** In his Joey books, for middle school readers, Gantos walks a fine line between creating humor and
empathy for a hyperactive boy with more than his share
of family troubles. Titles include *Joey Pigza Swallowed the
Key* (1998), *Joey Loses Control* (2000), and *What Would
Joey Do?* (2002).

***Lemony Snicket's Series of Unfortunate Events from
Book the First: The Bad Beginning, or, the Orphans!***
(1999) to ***Book the Thirteenth: The End*** **(2006) by
Daniel Handler (under the pseudonym of Lemony
Snicket). HarperCollins.** Written and illustrated as old-
fashioned melodramas, the series, with its wry humor
and unexpected allusions, began as books for children,
but by and large Handler managed to retain his audience
as they grew older by writing longer and more sophisticated stories. Handler's smart allusions refer to such
pop culture icons as Monty Python and Isadora Duncan
and to such authors as Edgar Allan Poe, T. S. Eliot,

different features (surprising, thoughtful, mean-spirited, exaggerated, etc.). And in
each of our minds these many types and features are jumbled together sort of like
the pieces of shiny material in a kaleidoscope. We each carry around a different
set—different sizes, different colors, and different weights—and for no two people do they fall into exactly the same pattern. The reason we said it was *doubly*
challenging is that the same thing is true for the authors who create the humor,
which means that whenever connections are made so that we end up being amused
together, we should be doubly grateful. Here in alphabetical order we describe some
of the favorite techniques used by outstanding authors of young adult literature.
One point we want to illustrate is how differently they approach their material.

Neil Gaiman's *The Graveyard Book* (HarperCollins, 2008) opens with an
eighteen-month-old newly orphaned boy wandering into a graveyard and needing a name. After many of the "residents" of the graveyard suggest names in
memory of people they knew, Mrs. Owens, who has agreed to care for the boy,

J. D. Salinger, George Orwell, Virginia Euwer Woolf, and Sappho.

Martyn Pig by Kevin Brooks. Scholastic, 2002. The humor is pretty dark, but it's here in the story of a boy and the girl next door (an aspiring actress) who work to cover up the accidental death of Martyn's drunken and mean father.

The Misadventures of Maude March, or, Trouble Rides a Fast Horse by Audrey Couloumbis. Random, 2005. This historical piece resembles a dime novel, partly because the pioneer heroine has grown up reading such stories and therefore uses them as the basis for decision making. She and her sister steal two horses and head out for Independence, Missouri, where "nobody cares about your past."

No More Dead Dogs by Gordon Korman. Hyperion, 2000. Twelve-year-old Wallace is tired of reading books in which the dog always dies. He gets in trouble at school when the drama club decides to put on a play about Old Shep and Wallace takes steps to keep the fictional dog alive.

Slob by Ellen Potter. Philomel, 2009. Owen's story is a lot more serious than most books set in middle school, but it has the same kind of humor. Owen is a fat and smart seventh grader in New York City, who is all tied up in inventing a television set that will work as a recorder of things from the past.

Son of the Mob by Gordon Korman. Hyperion, 2002. Television's *Sopranos* has nothing on this story about seventeen-year-old Vince Luca, whose "family" business keeps interfering with his regular life.

The Secret Diary of Adrian Mole, Aged 13¾ and The Growing Pains of Adrian Mole by Sue Townsend. First published in England in 1982, reissued as HarperTempest, 2003. These very funny books are taken from Adrian's diaries as he recounts his life struggles, in which no one (especially the BBC) fully appreciates the value of his sensitive writings, nor does the beloved Pandora long for Adrian's caresses as much as Adrian longs to caress Pandora.

The Vacation by Polly Horvath. Farrar, 2005. As she did with her 2003 National Book Award winner, *The Canning Season*, Horvath places a parentless young person under the care of some very strange, but not purposefully harmful, relatives. Readers probably find the situations funnier than do the characters.

Uncle Boris in the Yukon and Other Shaggy Dog Stories by Daniel Pinkwater, illustrations by Jill Pinkwater. Simon & Schuster, 2001. In his usual style, Pinkwater starts with a smidgen of autobiography and then adds large helpings of exaggeration.

Zen and the Art of Faking It by Jordan Sonnenblick. Scholastic, 2007. Middle schoolers love the unpretentious style of Sonneblick's writing. Here he tells the realistic story of San Lee, an adopted Chinese kid whose con-artist father is in jail. As San Lee starts a new school he vows to stand out instead of slinking into the background.

says firmly, "He looks like nobody." And Silas, who is a leader in the graveyard, concurs, "Then Nobody it is. Nobody Owens." In everyday use the name is shortened to Bod, sometimes misheard as Boy. Madame Lepescu calls him Niminy. Bod's guardian is Silas, and when he decides that it's time for Bod to learn to read, he brings in two alphabet books, along with *The Cat in the Hat*. He assigns Bod to practice his lessons by finding each letter of the alphabet on a headstone. It's lucky for Bod that Ezekiel Ulmsley's tombstone is still readable.

The Graveyard Book is filled with onomastic play as when the Hounds of Heaven that come from the Ghoul Gate are identified as the Duke of Westminster, the Honorable Archibald Fitzhugh, the Bishop of Bath and Wells, the Emperor of China, and the 33rd President of the United States. Elizabeth Hempstock was killed and buried as a witch and so was given no headstone. Bod sets out to get one for her and when he asks what should go on it, she replies, "My name. It must have my name on it, with a big E, for Elizabeth, like the old queen that died when I was born, and a big Haitch, for Hempstock." Mother Slaughter's tombstone is so weathered and covered with lichen that it now reads only LAUGH. Chapter 7 is entitled "Everyman Jack," an allusion to Charles Dickens, who in his *Tale of Two Cities* has a Jacque One, Jacque Two, and Jacque Three. It is because *Jack* is a term for the common man that we have such modern words as *jack hammer, jack knife, carjack, hijack,* and even *jacket.* In Gaiman's book his Jacks-of-All-Trades are the assassins with the names Jack Frost, Jack Tar, Jack Dandy, Jack be Nimble, and Jack Ketch.

Jack Gantos, who won the 2012 Newbery Award for *Dead End in Norvelt*, makes wonderful use of irony and surprise; plus he's a genius at picking out dramatic details that help him create eccentric characters. He's especially hard on old people, but with empathy. As far as we can remember, *Dead End in Norvelt* is the first laugh-out-loud book to win the Newbery Award. The humor is all the more delightful because it is imbedded in a wonderful piece of historical fiction, set a few years after World War II in the small planned community of Norvelt, which is named after Eleanor Roosevelt because of her support for home ownership. We identified with the story because of the details of the time, which we can still remember. We too had a father who brought home a war surplus "gizmo," which was about as useless as the small airplane that Jack's father purchased and tried to rebuild, a mother who adored Eleanor Roosevelt, a town nurse who doled out strange advice for everything from bloody noses to arthritis treatments, a friend who lived above the mortuary that her family ran, a relative who wrote up community events—including "uncommon" obituaries—for the local newspaper, and a backyard that was home to a struggling victory garden plus a few animals that were supposed to be providing our daily food. Both *The New York Times* and Jon Scieska have recommended *Dead End in Norvelt* as a sure-fire winner for boys. We predict that senior citizens will also love it because of the memories it will trigger and maybe even the inspiration to write their own life stories in such a way that their grandchildren will read them.

Yann Martel's *Life of Pi* (Harvest/Harcourt, 2001) won Britain's Booker Prize, and in the United States spent several months on the *New York Times* bestseller list. It was also chosen for several One-Book programs, including the one we have in Arizona. Although it was published as an adult book, teenagers picked it up and began reading because it is about a boy their same age and they related to several of his dilemmas even though he was a boy who grew up in India. Much of the book's success is based on the way that Martel used the concepts of equivocation, language play, and suspension of disbelief to explain analogies and similarities between fiction and religion. Martel is an expert at using a single word to mean more than a single thing. Because one of the friends of Pi's family was a world-class swimming champion, and because this swimmer's favorite swimming pool was the Piscine Molitor, in Paris, Pi was given the name of Piscine Molitor Patel. Thus, Pi and the Parisian swimming pool had the same name. Pi's friends would mispronounce his name to "Pissing Patel," and ask him, "Are you Pissing?" So this was a third meaning of his name. In desperation, when he went from elementary to high school he had the idea of shortening his name. He stood in front of the class and said, "My name is Piscine Molitor Patel, known to all as Pi Patel." And then he drew the symbol for the mathematical term *pi* and a large circle sliced in two. To further reinforce his new name, he explained that *pi* equals 3.14.

Pi resented the idea of having to choose a single religion; he wanted to be a Hindu, a Muslim, a Jew, and a Christian, all at the same time. In one of the most exciting parts of the book, when Pi discovers that he is sharing a lifeboat with an uncaged lion, he swears in all four religions: "Jesus, Mary, Muhammad, and Vishnu."

Terry Pratchett is a master at sarcasm. In *The Color of Magic* (HarperTorch 2000) Rincewind characterizes Twoflower as "If complete and utter chaos was lightning, he'd be the sort to stand on a hilltop in a thunderstorm wearing wet copper armour and shouting, 'All gods are bastards.'" In *Equal Rites* (HarperTorch 2000) he says that "for animals, the entire universe has been neatly divided into things to (a) mate with, (b) eat, (c) run away from, and (d) rocks." In *Mort* (HarperTorch 2001), he says about the city of Ankh-Morpork, "Perhaps it's the sheer zestful vitality of the place, or maybe it's just that a city with a million inhabitants and no sewers is rather robust for poets, who prefer daffodils—and no wonder." In *Sourcery* (Harpertorch 2001), he wrote that the citizens of Ankh-Morpork had always claimed that the river water was incredibly pure. They reasoned that, "Any water that had passed through so many kidneys had to be very pure indeed." In *Wyrd Sisters* (HarperTorch 2001), Pratchett describes the duke as having a mind that ticked like a clock, "and like a clock, it regularly went cuckoo." In *Guards! Guards!* (HarperTorch 2001), he describes the dwarfs as having beards and wearing up to twelve layers of clothing, and then he adds, "Gender is more or less optional." And in *The Light Fantastic* (Harper 2005), he says that Herrena the Henna-Haired Harridan "would look quite stunning after a good bath, a heavy-duty manicure, and the pick of the leather racks in Woo Hung Ling's Oriental Exotica and Martial Aids on Heroes Street." But this wasn't the case. In fact, "she was currently quite sensibly dressed in light chain mail, soft boots, and a short sword."

J. K. Rowling in her Harry Potter series of seven books (Scholastic 1998–2007) created much of her humor through unexpected alliterations. For example, the house founders at Hogwarts are named Godric Gryffindor, Helga Hufflepuff, Rowena Ravenclaw, and Salazar Slytherin. The names also contain sound symbolism in that Gryffindor alludes to a mythical creature, the Griffin; Ravenclaw is reminiscent of the gargoyles of a Gothic cathedral; Hufflepuff is a fun name for a teacher; and Slytherin is what a snake does. Characters in these novels are given amusing and slightly insulting names like Filius Flitwick, Madeye Moody, Bathilda Bagsot, Dudley Dursley, Nymphadora Tonks, and Stan Shunpike (the driver of the Knightbus). Some of the names are even more insulting, like Grawp, Rufus Scrimgeour (the Minister of Magic), and Kingsley Shacklebolt. The nicknames are even more fun as when Mundungus Fletcher is called *Dung*, Horace Slughorn is called *Slug*, Elphias Doge is called *Dogbreath*, Remus Lupin is called *Moony* (he's a werewolf), Sirius Black is called *Padfoot* after the dog star, James Potter is called *Prongs* because his Patronus is a stag, and Peter Pettigrew is called both Scabbers and Wormtail because he becomes a rat, in both senses of the word. Even the ghosts get funny names like Moaning Myrtle and Nearly Headless Nick. The inventions created by the Weasley twins have such names as Decoy Detonator, Fiendfyre, Nosebleed Nouggats, Puking Pastilles, Skiving Snackboxes, and Weasley's Wildlife Whiz Bangs.

J. K. Rowling uses humorous names not only for amusement, but also to help readers remember the names of her people, places, and things. Characters must cross over to her parallel universe of Hogwarts by boarding the train on Track Nine and Three Quarters at Kings Cross Station. When they get there they will find both Diagon Alley (a play on *diagonally*) and Knockturn Alley (a play on *nocturnally*). And in this parallel world, Rowling reminds readers that they are in a "foreign country," with such spellings as Kreature for "Creature," the Knight Bus for "Night Bus," Elderflower wine for "Elderberry wine," and Butterbeer as a blend of Butterscotch and Rootbeer.

Louis Sachar's *Holes* (FSG, 1998) contains many examples of wordplay. There is ambiguity in the name of Stanley Yelnats because his father and grandfather had the same name, plus it's a palindrome (spelled the same back-to-front as well as front-to-back). Zeroni's name is shortened to Zero, an ironic reference to Zero's brain. The K.B. on the gold cap which Stanley finds stands for Kate Barlow who is also known as the Kissing Bandit. And when the boys discover that the name on the sunken boat that they found was Mary Lou, they assumed that the boat had been named after someone's sexy girlfriend instead of after a fifty-year-old donkey with halitosis. *Holes* also has many exaggerations and contradictions as with the Kissing Bandit who died laughing, the miraculous nature of the lizards, the life-saving nutrition of the onions, a warden who puts rattlesnake venom in her nail polish, and a mountain shaped like the "Thumb of God." Exaggerated characters range from Clyde "Sweet-Feet" Livingston, to the clairvoyant Madame Zeroni, and on to the lovesick Elya Yelnats. When Mr. Pendanski asks Stanley if he knows who is responsible for Stanley's predicament, Stanley remembers hearing about a family curse and innocently responds with "My no-good-dirty-rotten-pig-stealing-great-great-grandfather."

In *Holes* the adults have the power, the money, and the prestige, so the kids must live by their wits. When Stanley arrives at Camp Green Lake (which is not a lake and has very little greenery) he reads a sign declaring that it is "a violation of the Texas Penal Code to bring guns, explosives, weapons, drugs, or alcohol onto the premises." Stanley's response was "Well, duh!"

Holes is a Comedy of Manners not only in the hierarchy established by the adults vs. the children, but also the hierarchy of the children themselves. Zigzag, Magnet, Squid, Armpit, Caveman, Barfbag, and Xray all have strangely appropriate names. Zero and Stanley are the lowest ranking kids in the camp, but they are also the two kids who are able to escape from the camp and end up with something less (but not a lot less) than a million dollars.

Types and Features of Humor with Examples from the Web and from Films

Don Nilsen recently taught a university class in humor, which is where he began to understand and appreciate the idea of how differently individuals respond to different kinds of humor, and how much more excited students were to find and share humor from the Web that they could bring to class and use as part of their explanation of particular humor features. The following text lists and defines important features of humor and gives the websites that his students gathered as examples. If by the time you are reading this the websites have changed, you will probably be able to find other sites that exemplify the same feature. The point is not just to have funny things to show a class, but instead to help students understand some of the complexities of humor and its

Paul Zindel, **And His Legacy**

Paul Zindel's Margaret A. Edwards Honor Books include *The Pigman; The Pigman's Legacy; The Pigman and Me; My Darling, My Hamburger;* and *The Effect of Gamma Rays on Man-in-the-Moon Marigolds: A Drama in Two Acts.* Zindel also wrote many other books and several successful screenplays including the 1972 *Up the Sandbox,* the 1973 *Mame,* and the 1986 *Runaway Train.*

Zindel graduated from Wagner College on Staten Island where, even though he majored in chemistry, he took a concentrated ten-day course in playwriting from Edward Albee. At the time, Albee was well known for his one-act plays *The Zoo Story* and *The Death of Bessie Smith,* and would soon be even better known for *Who's Afraid of Virginia Woolf?* Zindel was entranced. He said he wanted to be Edward Albee. He wanted his career, his popularity, and, most of all, his money!

After graduation, Zindel taught chemistry for ten years at Tottenville High School on Staten Island, while moonlighting by writing plays. In one of his classes, a girl had answered an ad from the back of a comic book that promised for one dollar to send seeds that had been exposed to gamma rays at Oak Ridge Laboratories. She got the seeds and grew them for her science fair exhibit, which she named "The Effect of Gamma Rays on Man-in-the-Moon Marigolds and Celestial Cabbage." Zindel loved her title—once he dropped off the part about cabbage—and his first successful play grew out of his love for this title. It was a story about the relationship between a sensitive girl, her epileptic sister, and their bitter and controlling mother. It opened in 1965 at the Alley Theatre in Houston and went on to win the Pulitzer Prize, a New York Drama Critics Circle Award, and an Obie. When, in 1970, it opened off-Broadway, it played 819 performances. In 1966, a shortened screen version was produced on public television. Harper and Collins editor Charlotte Zolotow saw it and was so impressed at Zindel's skill in creating interesting and believable teenage dialogue that she contacted Zindel and convinced him to try his hand at writing a book for young adults. Her invitation resulted in *The Pigman,* which was published to widespread acclaim in 1968.

At the time of the invitation, Zindel was saving on his rent money by living in and "guarding" empty houses that were up for sale. When he saw a teenaged boy trespass onto the property he went out to scold him, but instead ended up listening to the boy's many adventures. Zindel thought of a girl in one of his classes who was named Lorraine and who was so sensitive that she would cry at any mention of death or sadness. He was struck with the idea of putting two such different people in a book and having them interact with an eccentric, old man whose character Zindel based on an Italian neighbor that he remembered. Zindel later wrote more about this same neighbor in *The Pigman and Me* and *The Pigman's Legacy.*

Both Robert Cormier and M. E. Kerr acknowledged that before they decided to enter the field of young adult literature they read Zindel's *The Pigman* and weighed the fact that a Pulitzer Prize-winning playwright was putting forth his best efforts for teenagers. Joan Bauer has said that the first respect as an author that she received from her teenage daughter was when in 1994 she was asked to be on a panel about creating humor with Zindel. And at the time of his death in 2003, other writers of YA books spoke about his influence on their own careers. Will Hobbs described Zindel as a "chemistry teacher turned alchemist," and went on to say that Paul was "so good I couldn't stand it; I had to try writing young adult novels of my own." Alex Flinn said that Zindel was one of only three YA authors that he remembers reading when he was young. He feels as if he "met John and Lorraine just yesterday." Lauren L. Wohl, the marketing director for Roaring Brook Press, thanked Zindel in the June 2003 *VOYA* for allowing her to finally score with her teenaged son when she mentioned that she was working with Paul Zindel.

"The Pigman Paul Zindel?"

I nodded.

"You're kidding."

"Nope. Really!"

"Cool!" ●

importance in modern communication. Ambitious students can also be encouraged to find examples of these same humor features in written forms.

Double Entendre (Intentional Ambiguity)   When ambiguity is unintentional, it is a bad thing, but when it is intentional, it is a good thing. To distinguish between *bad* or accidental ambiguity and *good* or purposeful double entendre, a listener has to know the author's intent. If the author is writing or saying something meant to be entertaining, double entendre is often a good thing. But if the author is trying to get a good grade on a basic composition assignment, ambiguity is a bad thing. In Stephen Colbert's *The Colbert Report* (pronounced with a French accent), Stephen Colbert is a liberal playing the role of an ultra-conservative, so his use of double entendre allows him to use words with meanings opposite to that of their more common meanings (something that C. S. Lewis also does in his *The Screwtape Letters*): http://www.colbertnation.com/home

Exaggeration   The cello part in Pachelbel's "Cannon in D" consists of eight quarter notes played over and over. They are D, A, B, F#, G, D, G, A. In "Pachelbel Rant," cello player Rob Paravonian explains how much he hated these eight notes until he found the same eight notes in many other types of music: http://www.youtube.com/watch?v=JdxkVQy7QLM. The narrator in "Animal Power Moves" uses exaggerated voice inflection to talk about the ten most amazing offensive and defensive power moves in the animal kingdom: http://www.youtube.com/watch?v=GkYbFr7dcIs

Gallows Humor   The fact that many of these "Animal Power Moves" result in death and destruction makes the moves all the funnier: http://www.youtube.com/watch?v=GkYbFr7dcIs. Gallows humor can also be seen in the film *Pulp Fiction*. When a car hits a bump, the guy in the front seat unintentionally shoots and kills the guy in the back seat, and they end up washing the blood from their clothing on Quentin Tarentino's real front lawn. Another example of gallows humor appears in *Fargo* when the killers are trying to dispose of a dead body by putting the body parts into a tree chipper, and the stuff that comes out of the chipper turns the snow red.

Incongruity and Incongruity Resolution   Most people expect music to be something for the ears, but if a group of monks has taken a vow of silence, then they must find some other way to sing the Hallelujah Chorus in "The Messiah." These monks have a creative, and funny, way of "singing" without using their voices: http://www.youtube.com/watch?v=ZCFCeJTEzNU&feature=related.

Irony (Trick, Twist, or Hoax)   Basic juggling is difficult enough, but what about juggling on a piano keyboard to play "We Wish You a Merry Christmas"? That's even more difficult, but if you watch carefully when you see it being played, you can see that it is a hoax. There are no individual keys on the keyboard, which is simply programmed to play "the next note" every time it is hit. All the juggler has to do is hit the keyboard, which is considerably easier than hitting individual keys. http://www.break.com/usercontent/2006/11/3/amazing-piano-juggler-178127. Another hoax is a video clip of a kid who sounds like President

Bush II talking about global warming. Here is the video clip: http://www.youtube.com/watch?v=BWdiHtv6T6s. But this is a double hoax; it is not the kid's voice. It is the voice of Will Farrell. Here is the original parody: http://www.youtube.com/watch?v=jOjfxEejS2Y&feature=related. To prove that George W. Bush can take a joke, here is a Bush impersonator side-by-side with the real President Bush II: http://www.youtube.com/watch?v=XlzFohgYbnA&feature=related.

Parody   "The Onion" is not the news; it is a parody of the news. In parody, it is possible to observe exaggeration, understatement, and wordplay, often with a dead-pan expression. Here is the website for "The Onion": http://www.theonion.com. Jon Stewart's *The Daily Show* is also a parody. http://www.thedailyshow.com/. "The Onion," *The Daily Show,* and *The Colbert Report* can be considered "fake news shows." Nevertheless, many viewers depend on these "fake" programs for their "real" news. Another example of parody is "Tortoises" from Saint Saëns' "Carnival of the Animals." Here is the website for "Tortoises": http://www.youtube.com/watch?v=AHvqaRaDzQE. Because a tortoise is so slow, this musical representation of the tortoise is also very slow. However, "The Tortoise" is actually a parody of "the Can Can" which came from Jacques Offenbach's opera "Orpheus and the Underworld": http://www.youtube.com/watch?v=bRgWtRXhzUg&feature=related. Many of the poems that are in Lewis Carroll's *Alice in Wonderland* and *Through the Looking Glass* are parodies of the didactic poetry that was popular at the time. Because the style of Edgar Allan Poe's "Bells," "Annabelle Lee," and "The Raven" is so distinctive, the poems have been frequently parodied, something that you might encourage your students to do.

Role Reversal and Props   In *The Colbert Report,* Stephen Colbert, whose website was previously given under "Double Entendre," is also a good example of the skilled use of props to support his claim to be an ultra-conservative, overly patriotic American. He uses the American Eagle, the American flag, and the shield of Captain America to support the role he has created for himself. Props have been used throughout history as a way of saying to the audience, "This is not me speaking; this is my persona." In the Middle Ages and the Renaissance, the king had a fool or jester who was likely to be of small stature or to have a hump back. His props included a cap and bells, motley dress, and a scepter, perhaps with a caricature of his face on one end of it. These comical props gave the fool the power to say outrageous things that only a fool would say. From this custom came today's ventriloquists, people who have one persona as themselves and a different persona through their dummy (who has a very different persona). Other comedians use such props as a cigar, a fright wig, strange glasses, an unusual hat, or other clothes. Or it might be a piano as in the following clip by Igoodesman and Joo: http://cartoonando.blogspot.com/2008/04/1000-posts.html.

Sarcasm and/or Hostility   Sarcasm is probably the favorite genre of high school and college students. A good example of in-your-face sarcasm is Auto-Tune the News: http://www.youtube.com/watch?v=tBb4cjjj1gI. Another good example of sarcasm is a two-minute presentation of all thirteen of Daniel Handler's Lemony Snicket books: http://www.youtube.com/watch?v=ej3hAZ1QnqA.

Stronger sarcasm, with a bit of hostility and superiority thrown in, is the norm on *Tosh.O*'s video clip, as in this one, "Women can do anything men can do": http://www.youtube.com/watch?v=qMwPq-a-8W4. Another perfect example of strong sarcasm is Mel Brooks's "Springtime for Hitler": http://www.youtube.com/watch?v=ZGp0hCxSg98.

Satire   Probably one of the bests satirists of our time is Mel Brooks, as can be seen in *Blazing Saddles* and *The Producers*. The Monty Python group also presents excellent satire, as in *The Life of Brian,* which ends with everybody being crucified and singing "Always Look on the Bright Side of Life": http://www.youtube.com/watch?v=WlBiLNN1NhQ. Again, for good satire, don't forget "The Onion": http://www.theonion.com. and Jon Stewart's *The Daily Show:* http://www.thedailyshow.com/.

Surprise   Suppose it is half-time at a Phoenix Suns game and you look out on the basketball court to see something strange that you can't figure out. Then it gets even stranger, because it is the "Human Slinky." In ways it is human; in other ways, it couldn't be human. It's a surprise, but it's also an example of incongruity and incongruity resolution. Here it is: http://www.youtube.com/watch?v=d0Eln4gneYk. Now suppose you go to a symphony, and the program tells you that one of the pieces is entitled "Typewriter," and that it is written by Leroy Anderson. "Typewriter" is a strange name for a musical composition, but when the orchestra performs the piece the audience can see that it is a perfectly appropriate name. Here it is: http://www.metacafe.com/watch/803796/the_typewriter_song/.

Understatement and Dead-Pan Presentation   Although exaggeration is an excellent way to signal that a piece of writing is intended as a parody, as irony, or as satire, understatement can also be used to signal the same thing, which in itself is ironic. Notice that in "Kleptomaniac," Jack Webb does everything he can to keep from smiling, and even Johnny Carson has to hold back his laughter to keep the skit from falling to pieces: http://www.youtube.com/watch?v=mhLLU0H34ms. In this clip, notice how Demetri Martin uses understatement and a dead-pan expression to parody the presentation of a pedantic university professor: http://www.youtube.com/watch?v=vaGa3kjRS7o.

Wordplay   Of course wordplay is used in all of the previous categories. Nevertheless, wordplay is a primary ingredient in some video clips, where wordplay is the point of the clip. In "Kleptomaniac" by Johnny Carson and Jack Webb, the wordplay is based on words containing the /k/ sound: http://www.youtube.com/watch?v=mhLLU0H34ms. Victor Borge also uses a great deal of wordplay in his presentations: http://www.youtube.com/watch?v=BcV19rylSZc. And in "Yiddish *Dick and Jane,*" the wordplay is bilingual in nature because sprinkled through the English script are such Yiddish expressions as *mensch, schlep, Bubbe, Gornicht, Oy Gevalt, Shpilkes, mishpucka,* and *ibbledick altercocker:* http://www.youtube.com/watch?v=NlO5vUS5KnU.

New Media

The Graphic Novel: Sequential Art Narration

Although the unenlightened may cling to the idea that *graphic novel* is nothing more than a euphemism for *comic book,* the term *graphic novel* actually covers a wide variety of texts, all of which are accompanied in some fashion by illustrations. As graphic novel scholar James B. Carter, assistant professor of English at the University of Texas El Paso, explains:

> regardless of the conscientious scholars and creators who have written on the graphic novel as being a form beyond genre, many students, teachers, and professors continue to refer to sequential art narration (comic strips, comic books, and graphic novels) as a genre rather than, as I think is more accurate, a form or format.[1]

Graphic novel experts and professional librarians Kristin Fletcher-Spear, Merideth Jenson-Benjamin, and Teresa Copeland also go to great lengths to explain that: "'graphic novels' is an imprecise term used to describe a format that uses a combination of words and sequential art to convey a narrative. Graphic novels can be of any genre on any topic."[2] Or, according to Scott McCloud's definition back in 1994 in *Understanding Comics* (which is itself in comic book form): "juxtaposed pictorial and other images in deliberate sequence, intended to convey information and/or to produce an aesthetic response in the viewer."[3] McCloud is, himself, a graphic novelist, comics creator, and theorist on sequential art narration.

The key terms across definitions seem to be words (or narration) and sequential art, or art in sequence to tell a story. Carter, Fletcher-Spear, Jenson-Benjamin, and Copeland all agree that it is much more accurate to think of the graphic novel as a format and not a genre. Actually, any number of genres can be housed in the graphic novel format, from fantasy to nonfiction, the commonality always being sequential narrative art.

Graphic novels, including comic books, have been rising higher and higher on the librarian's shelf of respectability over the past two decades. Art Spiegelman's *Maus I: A Survivor's Tale,* the story of his father's life as a Jew in Nazi Germany prior to and during WWII, won a Pulitzer Prize Special Award in 1992. *Maus,* which was followed by *Maus II: And Here My Troubles Began,* depicts various groups of people as cartoon animals dressed as people: Nazis are cats, Jews are mice, Polish are pigs, and Americans are dogs. The novel follows the factual events of his father's life, taking advantage of the caricature provided by the cartoon animal characterization.

American Born Chinese by Gene Luen Yang (First Second, 2006) won the 2007 Eisner Award for Best Graphic Album: New, which was no surprise, but it also won the 2007 Printz Award, the first graphic novel to do so, and was a finalist for the 2006 National Book Award. *American Born Chinese* is actually three stories that come together in the end: a fantasy/myth, a parody/satire, and a modern problem/realistic story. The book has a powerful social and psychological message about stereotypes, immigration, cultural heritage, and self-image. Yang's

Using Graphic Novels with Children and Teens: A Guide for Teachers and Librarians *is distributed free by Scholastic publishers as a way to help educators learn about the graphic novel. Check the websites of the publishers of graphic novels to see what else is available.*

skillful storytelling and information-dense illustrations allow him to tell a very detailed set of stories in only 240 pages.

Graphic novels are earning a place in formal curriculum, as well. In his seminal work *The Power of Reading: Insights from the Research,* Stephen Krashen, University of Southern California Professor Emeritus, lays out research supporting the idea that K–12 students gain literacy skills faster when allowed to read what they enjoy, including graphic novels, and that English language learners flourish in their literacy development when reading comic books.[4]

The tendency may be to think of graphic novels as long comic books about superheroes, but *American Born Chinese* is evidence that this is not the case. In fact, as per Carter and our other experts, the graphic novel is a format that encompasses fantasy, mystery, adapted classics, superhero, horror, political satire, historical fiction and historical fact, science fiction, love and romance, and more. Graphic novels can be incredibly complex and contain a myriad of information couched in words and pictures. Consider Eric Shanower's 31 issue Age of Bronze series, depicting the Trojan War. The first graphic novels in this series were printed in 1998 and are projected to continue to twice the current number by the seventh volume's conclusion. Research for the writing of this series has been phenomenally broad and deep as the author/artist explains:

> I've gathered many of the different versions of the Trojan War—poems, plays, stories, paintings, opera—and I'm combining them all into one long story, while reconciling all the contradictions. And I'm not leaving anything out. So over the years I've made a lot of trips to libraries, and whenever I go into a bookstore, I always check the mythology and archaeology sections.[5]

Shanower's research into actual artifacts from the Greek Mycenaean age provided him with visual images, not only of ships, weapons and armor, homes, clothes, and hairstyles, but also of social order as depicted by the relationships among figures on frescoes, vases, pots, and cups. Greek ruins provided plenty of information about buildings, as did recovered shipwrecks from that time period. Sculptures also provided information about hairstyles and clothing, and sometimes even the features of a famous person, such as Thetis, Mother of Achilles.[6] Shanower's cartoon depiction of Odysseus shows him wearing armor and helmet, as well as carrying a shield and spear modeled on what is known as the "Warrior Vase," an artifact from the Late Bronze Age.[7] All graphic novelists do not research their topics to this degree, of course, but the level of investigation is indicative of the information that is packed into the cartoon panels. Shanower twice won the highest award given to comics writers/graphic novelists, the Will Eisner Award for his work on Age of Bronze.

The term *manga,* common in graphic novel circles, refers to sequential narrative art that originated in Japan and has become popular internationally. Stylistic commonalities have been appropriated around the world, generating local manga outside Japan. The term *anime* refers to animation of such stories as seen on television and in movies. Japanese manga, like all sequential narrative art, is actually a format, not a genre, and can be about anything from nonfiction to fantasy. Although historians trace the roots of manga through hundreds of years in Japanese history, the most obvious origin of modern manga is the post-WWII *Astro Boy,* a superhero who is actually a robot modeled after a real boy, who fights for justice and peace. Popularity of manga in the United States skyrocketed in the 1990s.

Graphic novels have developed their own canon over the years, and we provide our own top ten here:

Batman: The Dark Knight Returns, Frank Miller

Blankets, Craig Thompson

Bone, Jeff Smith

A Contract with God, Will Eisner

Ghost World, Daniel Clowes

Maus & *Maus II,* Arthur Spiegelman

Sandman, Neil Gaiman

Trickster: Native American Tales: A Graphic Collection edited by Matt Dembicki.

V for Vendetta, Alan Moore

Watchmen, Alan Moore & David Gibbons

One last plus for graphic novels is their diversity; there is surely something to appeal to any and every reader in terms of genre, cultural heritage, and interest.

Video Games as Interactive Literature

Starting with the third edition of this textbook, we began mentioning interactive fiction, something predicted to go way beyond those Choose Your Own Adventure novels that kids had fun with back in the 1970s. But we always sort of begged off from writing about it because the idea wasn't fully developed yet. Even now that full-blown interactive fiction has arrived by way of video games played either on computers or on game platforms such as the Nintendo Game Cube or a Sony PlayStation, many of us hesitate to embrace it. We're frightened away by such names as Warcraft, Gears of War, Counterstrike, and Grand Theft Auto.

In a survey we took of nearly three hundred local high school students, we asked those who played video games to list a favorite and tell why they liked it. Eighty-four of the students responded, with hardly any of them listing the same game, which made us nostalgic for the old days when our grandchildren were all playing Pokémon and we had a chance of joining in their conversations. One of the boys filling out the survey had obviously had experience with negative adult judgments because he appended a note after he wrote that Stalker was fun: "No—you don't stalk people." Another boy said he liked Day of Defeat because he owns *noobs,* which he kindly explained are "beginners, like *newbys.*" Another boy said he didn't like to play the games, but he loved "hunting for them online."

Besides the online card games, which seven students mentioned, there are basically four kinds of video games: first-person shooter games, fantasy role-playing games, real-time strategy games, and simulation games. The shooter games came first because they were the easiest to program. As designers became more skilled and figured out how to let their characters talk, both the number and the variety of games have expanded; in fact, the video-game industry now makes as much or more money than does the film industry. We heard on an NPR broadcast that the 2006 Japanese economy was saved by the marketing of manga, anime, and computer games around the world, especially to the United States.

James Paul Gee makes the point, in *What Video Games Have to Teach Us about Learning and Literacy,* that many adults are looking at the games from the wrong perspective. We think the games must be a waste of time because they are not teaching content as textbooks do. However, Gee says, some of them *do* teach content while at the same time involving players in the kinds of active and critical learning that prepares them for the decision-making and the modes of operation that are an increasingly big part of modern life. He organizes his book around over thirty "Learning Principles," a few of which he discusses in each chapter under such titles as Semiotic Domains, Learning and Identity, Situated Meaning and Learning, and The Social Mind.

A point he makes throughout the book is that video games often provide a greater potential for learning than does much of what happens in school. His principles illustrate *active* learning. As an illustration of what he means by active learning, Gee says that when game players pick up the direction manual that accompanies the games, they find the reading tough going. Younger players just start experimenting and playing the games in different ways, while older players who have grown up with different attitudes read the manuals over and over and fret if they cannot foresee exactly what they should do. Finally, out of frustration, they turn to the game and start playing. Then, when they go back to the manual to check on some detail, they are happily surprised to discover that it is now much easier to read and understand.

We kept Gee's claims about active learning in mind as we read the reasons that students in our survey wrote for liking particular games. Two students said they were learning history from Age of Empires, while several mentioned cognitive processes in relation to particular games.

- Feeding Frenzy: "It takes multitasking."
- Warrior Worlds: "It's fast paced and allows for strategy."
- Ragdog Avalanche: "Because it's challenging."
- Gameball: "Because you have to pay attention."
- Command and Conquer: "Strategic, real-time overview, fun and challenging."
- Monopoly Tycoon: "Because it tests my brain."

When we adults walk by and see kids focusing so intently on their computers, we worry that they are growing up as loners or as antisocial beings, but students countered this idea with comments related to particular games:

- Starcraft: "I love this game because I can verve my friends online and it's strategic."
- Guild Wars: "I can communicate with people around the world and build teamwork, skills, and strategies."
- Infantry: "Because it's a shooting game and you have to use strategy. Your opponents are other people online."
- Runescape: "It's fun. You walk around and talk to other players, get your skills up and do quests."
- Gears of War: "I play with about fifteen of my friends."
- Action: "I love the challenge and puzzles that come."

The simulation games appear to come the closest to what English teachers would define as interactive fiction, and these were also the ones mentioned the most by girls. These four commented on some version of Sims.

- Sims: "It's fun and challenging," "Because you can control people. I get to build houses and the people who live in them, ha ha!" "Building and designing homes and defining what happens."
- Star Wars 2: "It's cool to change your characters and they're funny."
- World of Warcraft: "I like the fiction and the ability to create your own character."
- Axis and Allies: "I like it because you can be either of these two teams."

While twelve students mentioned having fun, only a couple mentioned humor. At the 2007 International Society of Humor Studies conference held at Salve Regina University in Newport, Rhode Island, we heard a panel presentation on the humor (or lack of humor) in video games. The presenters explained that because the figures are so small, it is hard to reproduce the facial expressions which bring

Margaret A. Edwards Award

Winner (2012)

Susan Cooper, Journalist, Author, Playwright

Among the most interesting facts that we learned when we set out to explore Susan Cooper's career is that she was the first woman at Oxford University to edit *Cherwell,* the student newspaper, and that when she graduated with a degree in English she went to work as a reporter for the *Sunday Times,* where Ian Fleming, the creator of James Bond, was her boss.

Cooper was honored by the committee for her Dark Is Rising series, which began in 1965 with *Over Sea, Under Stone,* and then continued with *The Dark Is Rising* in 1973, *Greenwitch* in 1974, *The Grey King* in 1975, and *Silver on the Tree* in 1976. *The Dark Is Rising* was a Newbery Honor book, while *The Grey King* won the Newbery Medal. Between the first and second book in the *Dark Is Rising* series, Cooper wrote the 1970 *Dawn of Fear,* which is almost entirely autobiographical in telling the story of a child in wartime England. She was born in 1935, and so was at an age to remember the experiences, but she explains that for the sake of the book, she turned herself into a boy.

Cooper lived in England—sometimes in the places that she used for the settings in her Dark Is Rising books—until 1963, when she married Nicholas Grant, a scientist at M. I. T. and moved with him to Boston area. She still lives in Massachusetts in a small town a short way from her children and grandchildren. Her *Dark Is Rising* books are in the tradition of J. R. R. Tolkien, Lloyd Alexander, C. S. Lewis, and Alan Garner. Because Cooper's hero, Will Stanton, was only 11-years-old, Cooper may have been the author who introduced many children to the old Celtic mythologies and beliefs including such concepts and terms as *Old Ones, the seventh son of a seventh son, boggarts, runes, golden harps, crystal swords, grails,* and other magical artifacts, along with such ideas that magic comes in varying degrees and that bad weather, restless animals, and darkness foretell a coming evil that can be fought off only by a "special" young person.

In July of 1997, Jim Henson Pictures optioned the film rights to *The Dark Is Rising* because it was a favorite book of company president Brian Henson. However, the project never got off the ground and so in 2005, Henson sold the rights to Walden Media, which spent two years and 45 million dollars making a film, which was less than successful. The new company did not have the same respect for the book and so instead of leaving the story in the 1960s, they made it contemporary and they changed the age of Will from 11 to 14, in hopes of cashing in on the teen market. For the United States, they also changed the title to *The Seeker: The Dark Is Rising*. In reviewing the film, A *New York Post* critic joked that Susan Cooper must be "trembling in fear of being sued for ripping off J. K. Rowling's ideas and publishing them 20 years in advance."

It's too bad that the company did not involve Cooper in writing the script, because like Paul Zindel and Orson Scott Card, who wrote plays as well as teen novels, Cooper has used her skill with producing dialogue to write scripts for Broadway, television, and film. More recent books by Susan Cooper include her 1983 *Seaward,* 1993 *The Boggart,* 1997 *The Boggart and the Monster,* 1998 *King of Shadows,* 2002 *Green Boy,* and 2006 *Victory*. ●

Each year, since 1998 a YALSA committee has chosen to bring attention to ten books that were published for adults, but that are predicted to have special appeal to teen readers. The award is named after Margaret Alexander Edwards (called Alex by her friends) because when she first started looking for books that would appeal to sophisticated teenagers, she had to look at books published for adults because nearly all publishers focused on either adults or children. The idea of the award was at first controversial because people feared that once teen readers moved over into "adult" fiction, they were unlikely to return to teen books and would therefore miss out on a whole stage of reading.

But in the last few years, as genres and designated age levels have blended, and as all kinds of new formats have come into existence, the Alex Award has gained wider acceptance. As we compiled the descriptions of the ten books that were chosen, we noticed that even though they are published as books for a general adult audience, they fit with most of the characteristics of YA literature that were listed in Chapter One. For example, the protagonists are young, their peers are important to them, and several are involved in the kinds of quests appropriate to a bildungsroman.

Big Girl Small by Rachel DeWoskin. FSG, 2011.
Sixteen-year old Judy Lohden is an above-average student with a wonderful singing voice. The fact that she is only three feet, nine inches tall, doesn't keep her from telling a story that made one reviewer on Amazon.com conjecture that she might be "our new John Hughes," and another one to predict that she just might "stuff Holden Caulfield right back into his dusty museum case."

In Zanesville by Jo Ann Beard. Little, Brown, 2011.
A fourteen-year old late bloomer relates the story of her 1970s American girlhood in one of our country's "innumerable Zanesvilles."

The Lover's Dictionary by David Levithan. FSG, 2011.
This is the first book for adults written by Levithan, who is responsible for several popular teen books. His love story, told in the format of dictionary entries, was praised for its poignant vignettes and emotional candor.

The New Kids: Big Dreams and Brave Journeys at a High School for Immigrant Teens by Brooke Hauser. Free Press, 2011. "Some walked across deserts and mountains to get here. Others flew in on planes. One arrived after escaping in a suitcase. And some won't say how they got here," is an example of the writing that made committee members praise this nonfiction book as a "multicultural mosaic" and "a singular work of narrative journalism."

The Night Circus by Erin Morgenstern. Doubleday, 2011. In this "spell-casting" novel of a magical, and somewhat scary, circus, two young magicians (Celia and Marco) are pitted against each other as competitors, but nevertheless they fall in love.

Ready Player One by Ernest Cline. Crown, 2011. Wade Watts is the teenage protagonist who in this "genre busting" science fiction/romance escapes his dull life by going online as Parzival. An "extra" is that the story is rooted in the 1980s, but with reviewers insisting that it is more than a "nostalgic romp."

Robocalypse: A Novel by Daniel H. Wilson. Doubleday, 2011. Archos, is a shy human boy who is one of the first to notice that the dazzling technology of the future is assuming control over the global network and hence over humankind's future.

Salvage the Bones by Jesmyn Ward. Bloomsbury, 2011. In this winner of the National Book Award, which was described as the "best Katrina-drenched" book, fourteen-year-old Esch is pregnant and she and her three brothers are without help from adults as they try to get ready for a hurricane that is building over the Gulf of Mexico.

The Scrapbook of Frankie Pratt: A Novel in Pictures by Caroline Preston. HarperCollins, 2011. In 1920 Frankie Pratt receives a scrapbook and her father's old Corona typewriter plus a package of vintage postcards, letters, magazine clippings, and other memorabilia. Readers are privileged to get a glimpse at Frankie's treasures because her goal is to go off to college and become a writer.

The Talk-Funny Girl by Roland Merullo. Crown, 2011. Seventeen-year-old Marjorie Richards lives in such an isolated family, that they have their own way of speaking, but that is just one of the problems that Marjorie faces in a poverty-stricken rural area of New Hampshire where teenage girls are disappearing.

much of the humor to comics and cartoons. And while some of the best designers are starting to bring in humor, for now the humor is coming mostly from the way players mock the characters and create their own parody stories.

Related to this, authors who grew up playing video games are bringing them into their writing, as with Conor Kostick's 2007 *Epic,* a fantasy story about a society where violence is forbidden and people must solve their differences through the game world of Epic, while simultaneously trying to accumulate wealth and status in both the real world and the fantasy world.

Concluding Comments

Of all the chapters in this book, this is the one that begs for some kind of out-loud sharing. We hope that in class you can have a poetry slam (or jam) and that selected students will perform an excerpt or an improvised scene from a play or do a humorous reader's theater presentation. It would also be a good experience for you to go to a local high school production of a play, or make a few phone calls to the central administration of your local library to locate a teen poetry slam that you could observe. And in relation to the new media of graphic novels and video games remember when, as English teachers, we used to assign students to write a follow-the-direction essay telling us how to make a peanut butter sandwich? Surely, it would be more interesting all the way around if you invited students to write a follow-the-direction essay telling you how to play their favorite video game or a comparison/contrast piece on two graphic novels.

Notes

1. James B. Carter, "Die a Graphic Death: Revisiting the Death of Genre with Graphic Novels, or 'Why Won't You Just Die Already?'" *The ALAN Review* 36.1 (Fall 2008): 15–25.
2. Kristin Fletcher-Spear, Merideth Jenson-Benjamin, and Teresa Copeland, "The Truth about Graphic Novels," *The ALAN Review* 32.2 (Winter 2005): 37–44.
3. Scott McCloud, *Understanding Comics.* New York: HarperCollins, 1994.
4. Stephen Krashen, *The Power of Reading: Insights from the Research.* Englewood, CO: Libraries Unlimited, 1993.
5. Eric Shanower "The Art of the Graphic Novel," *The ALAN Review* 32.2 (Winter 2005): 32–36
6. Shanower, 35.
7. Shanower, 35.

Adventure, Westerns, Sports, and Mysteries

chapter

7

Remembering English teachers who pleaded with us to "read only the best—the classics," many of us feel vaguely worried when we read books simply to enjoy characters and their adventures. Somewhat defensively, we make claims that are hard to substantiate. For example, we claim that reading about adventures makes us more interesting people, sports books teach us the game of life, mysteries are psychologically helpful to our inner well-being, and if our emotions sometimes seem less-than-honorable, they are a substitute for aggression. These claims may have some truth, but they are hard to prove. We will be on safer ground if we simply accept the idea that reading for pleasure is a worthy activity and a goal in and of itself. If we, and our students, gain something more than pleasure, we should be grateful that serendipity is still at work in today's complex world.

Adventure Stories

"Once upon a time" is a magical phrase. The concept opens not only fairy tales but also adventure tales. It suggests actions and excitement. Certainly we care about the people—which is why we prefer nonfiction to fiction—but we may care equally—or more—about the actions to come. The greatest of these is implied violence, things we fear that will happen. The pace and tempo force the action to move faster and faster and to speed us into the tale. Adventure books sell well, for good reason. Anthony Brande, in *American Heritage* 51, noted that the country was mad for adventure:

> The whole country seems bent on getting out there and having adventures, and if you can't do it, you can read about it. Magazines like *Men's Journal* and *Outside* that specialize in the subject are thriving. The staid old National Geographic Society has launched its own magazine, *National Geographic Adventure,* to take advantage of what has reached the state of a craze. (January 2001, p. 43)

The author then added, "A taste for adventure is as old as the human race itself, a function of an evolutionary development that rewards risk takers over the timid and the meek." The best adventure story takes us outside ourselves (see Table 7.1). In an article on the dangers of being in Yosemite National Park, an ecologist and wilderness guide told the London *Independent* (June 30, 1995, p. 18), "There are incredible benefits to our life of modern luxury. But we pay for it by domesticating ourselves. When we set out in a park like Yosemite, we enter a world for which we are not very well trained. You don't practice sitting on top of 3,000-foot-high cliffs. You don't get that at the office."

He's right, of course, and that's why we crave all sorts of excitement by reading about people who live the adventure and the thrills and chills we have denied ourselves by living in our comfortable and safe world. The best adventure tales demand more than a plot and a series of actions. Good writers provide believable characters amid those thrills and chills, at least a likable and imperfect (and probably young) protagonist and a wily and dangerous antagonist (or villain). Because we are primarily interested in action, we're likely to be irritated by long descriptive or meditative passages. Writers must reveal characterization through the plot—what could happen, what might happen, how all incidents tie together. We want surprises and turns of the screw. Heroes become trapped, and the only way to safety is through even greater jeopardy. Adventure tales usually focus either on person-against-person or on person-against-nature, with person-against-self becoming important only as the tale unfolds and the protagonist faces frustration and possible failure.

TABLE 7.1	Suggestions for Evaluating Adventure Stories
A good adventure story has most of the positive qualities generally associated with good fiction. In addition, it usually has:	**A poor adventure story may have the negative qualities generally associated with poor fiction. It is particularly prone to have:**
A likable protagonist with whom young readers identify	A protagonist who is too exaggerated or too stereotyped to be believable
An adventure that readers can imagine happening to themselves	Nothing really exciting about the adventure
Efficient characterization	Only stereotyped characters
An interesting setting that enhances the story without being in the way of the plot	A long drawn-out conclusion after the climax has been reached
Action that draws readers into the plot within the first page or so of the story	

When talking about kids and the natural world, Will Hobbs says, I believe there is a part of the human heart that longs for wild places. We yearn for that connection to nature that helped form our consciousness over the millennia. Our sense of beauty derives from natural forms: our sense of adventure and discovery, in real life and in books, finds ready fulfillment on the grandest stage of them all, the outdoors. I've always felt that our connection to the American earth is the great subject of American literature.

I like to think of my novels as "adventure-plus." In Jason's Gold, *for example, winter survival is embedded in the history of the Klondike gold rush. In* Go Big Or Go Home, *I laced the escapades of two boys with a lot of weird-but-true science and the search for life on Mars.* Take Me to the River *is a suspense story that will acquaint readers with border issues of a different kind than those I wrote about in* Crossing the Wire. *Novels are a great way for kids to learn content because they're affective, and the brain remembers what the heart cares about.*

Much closer to what we view as traditional adventure are the stories written by Gary Paulsen, who leads all other YA writers in adventure tales. See p. 231 for the write-up on him as an Edwards Award winner. Coming in a close second is Will Hobbs, whose interests in hiking, whitewater rafting, archaeology, and natural history are reflected in his books. See his photo and a recent comment he sent us.

Hobbs's stories are more action-packed than Paulsen's and sometimes less introspective, though in *Downriver* the change that Jessie makes in her life is impressive. In both *Far North* and *Jason's Gold,* readers learn what it is like to be really cold. *Jackie's Wild Seattle* is about mountain climbing, while both *Ghost Canoe* and *Down the Yukon* are canoeing adventures. In *Wild Man Island,* fourteen-year-old Andy Galloway has a run-in with a grizzly bear, he hears wolves howling, he sees a dog where none should be, he finds an abandoned cannery, and more frightening—and intriguing—he runs into "a giant of a man overgrown with gray hair." *Wild Man Island* becomes a combination of adventure mixed with Andy's need to justify his father's archeological theories.

Hobbs's *Crossing the Wire* is especially relevant to young people in Arizona, where there are many immigrants from Mexico, both legal and illegal. Adventure is imposed on fifteen-year-old Victor Flores. Victor's father is dead, he is the sole breadwinner of his family, and that means he must illegally cross the border (the "wire") into the United States to find work. He has no green card, no command of English, no trade skills, and no money to pay the "coyotes" to guide him. His struggle to cross the border and to face drug smugglers, gang violence, and starvation makes for a compelling and disturbing novel.

Part of the charm of adventure stories is their variety of settings—both in time and space. Cornelia Funke's *The Thief Lord* is set on the watery "streets" of modern Venice. Two orphans, who are fleeing from cruel relatives, meet a group of other kids and a charismatic young man who calls himself the Thief Lord. She uses puckish humor to make the Thief Lord different from Charles Dickens's Artful Dodger in *Oliver Twist*.

In Kenneth Oppel's *Airborn*, fifteen-year-old Matt Cruse, a cabin boy on the luxury airship *Aurora*, watches a balloon sink slowly. Matt saves the old balloonist, but he dies that night. A year later, Kate, the granddaughter of the balloonist, travels on the *Aurora*, hoping to learn more about her grandfather's last voyage. *Skybreaker* carries on the story with Matt and Kate joining forces with a pirate's daughter and a swashbuckling ship's captain to salvage a ghost airship that disappeared forty years earlier.

Adventurous Girls

In Avi's Newbery Medal-winning *The True Confessions of Charlotte Doyle*, a young girl is forced to overcome circumstances before they overcome her. Charlotte is raised in an upper-class family with a strong father. Even though she is warned not to board the brig *Seahawk*, bound from Liverpool, England, to Providence, Rhode Island, her father has told her to take the ship, and so she goes on board, the only female on a ship commanded by evil and cruel Captain Jaggers. Trapped by the captain, she evades his plan to kill her and watches as the ship tips and plunges in a storm and the captain goes overboard. The crew makes her the ship's new captain—mostly because Charlotte is the daughter of an officer of the ship's company—but also because she has shown courage in facing down the captain and aiding the crew.

While most readers enjoyed Charlotte's adventures, at least one reviewer had qualms. Anne Scott MacLeod wrote in *Horn Book Magazine* (Jan./Feb. 1998), "It's a fine and vicarious adventure story. It is also preposterous" (p. 20). Avi took exception to the exception and in the Summer 1999 *Signal* wrote, "It is a legitimate task . . . of fiction to re-invent the past, if you will, so as to better define the future. . . . Historical fiction—among other things—is about today's possibilities" (p. 21). Perhaps both MacLeod's and Avi's statements illustrate the truth of what critic Henry Seidel Canby said way back in 1929 in the *Saturday Review of Literature*, "Historical fiction, like history, is more likely to register an exact truth about the writer's present than the exact truth of the past" (Dec. 31, p. 491).

Another girl at sea is the heroine of L. A. Meyer's books about Bloody Jacky, who starts her adventures as a ship's boy. The first book begins with Mary Faber's childhood in late eighteenth-century London, where her family has died from the plague. After cutting off her hair, and being a member of Rooster Charlie's gang, she spots a way out of London and her dreary world. She sees a ship, *The Dolphin,* and she tells a member of the crew that she can read (her father taught her). She becomes the ship's cabin boy, and off she sails, facing the wind and all the problems destined to come her way. She receives the inevitable rough treatment from the crew, she has no idea what life at sea is like, and she has no notion of the duties of a ship's boy. Most of all, she puts off the inevitable discovery of her sex almost longer than readers can believe. She has

Margaret A. Edwards Award
Winner (1997)
Gary Paulsen, Adventurer and More

Among Paulsen's two hundred plus-or-minus books, the ones honored by the Margaret A. Edwards Award are *Hatchet, Woodsong, The Winter Room, The Crossing, Canyons,* and *Dancing Carl.* We would add to the list of his very best *Harris and Me, Brian's Winter, Soldier's Heart: Being the Story of the Enlistment and Due Service of the Boy Charley Gaddard in the First Minnesota Volunteers, The River, The Beet Fields,* and *Guts.*

Gary Paulsen is most famous for the survival story that he tells in *Hatchet,* about thirteen-year-old Brian, who is flying to visit his father in the Canadian wilderness. The pilot has a fatal heart attack and the plane goes down. Brian's only survival tool is a hatchet that was a gift from his mother. While that wasn't much, it allowed him to survive.

Hatchet has become a classic adventure and survival story, mostly for boys although lots of girls also love it. Paulsen received a number of letters from readers who liked the book but questioned if Paulsen had taken the easy way out by having Brian rescued at the end of summer. They asked, what if Brian had not been rescued? Could he have survived a winter? Paulsen answered by writing another book, *Brian's Winter,* in which Brian is not rescued and has to face a bleak winter.

If that wasn't enough, Paulsen wrote other books about Brian, the most impressive being the nonfiction *Guts: The True Story behind Hatchet and the Brian Books.* Maybe the inspiration for this book was that a reader questioned Paulsen on the accuracy of *Hatchet* or the likelihood that Brian would survive, given the odds against him. In *Guts,* Paulsen writes about his own adventures that parallel Brian's problems. In successive chapters, Paulsen recalls his own near plane crashes, his tangles with a moose, his run-in with mosquitoes, and his ability to handle a gun—or a bow—when it was necessary. His education learning to eat in the wilderness is announced by the title of Chapter Five, "Eating Eyeballs and Guts or Starving."

Young people love Paulsen and his books. Some of that adulation comes from a simple fact, that Paulsen has lived a rugged life and has done most of the things that appear in his book. He has lived in the Canadian wilderness and in mountains and in canyons. He has sailed around Cape Horn. He has owned a motorcycle. He rides horses. He has played professional poker. He loves dogs and has raced them in the Alaskan Iditarod, and one dog, Cookie, saved his life. He has worked in a beet field, and he has worked for a carnival.

Paulsen is a master writer of adventure books, all essentially rite-of-passage. But he has written other kinds of books as well. *Harris and Me* is an autobiographical story of his early youth when he was dumped off on some relatives because his own folks were drunks. He learns to love his relations, particularly his cousin, Harris, who has a wild scheme for every occasion. Both boys learn the questionable fun of peeing on an electric fence or wrestling three hundred-pound pigs. *The Beet Fields* is as likely to be read and enjoyed by adults as young people. It's the story of Paulsen's sixteenth year, when he goes to work in the beet fields and learns that migrants can go up and down the rows much faster than he, and he will never get rich at weeding beets. It's the story of his working for a carnival and meeting Ruby. It's a gritty autobiography, and as Paulsen says this is "as real as I can write it, and as real as I can remember it happening." His 2010 book, *Woods Runner,* is about a thirteen-year-old boy who, during the Revolutionary War, sets out to rescue his parents who were captured and taken to a New York prison by British soldiers.

Gary Paulsen writes for young adults, and they recognize honesty and goodness in his words. In *The Winter Room,* he tells the reader, "If books could have more, give more, be more, show more, they would still need readers, who bring to them sound and smell and light and all the rest that can't be in books. The book needs you."

The book always needs the reader, and Paulsen provides books that find the reader over and over.

adventures aplenty, all of them well handled by Meyer. A sampling of the dozen or so books includes—*Curse of the Blue Tattoo: Being an Account of the Misadventures of Jacky Faber, Midshipman and Fine Lady; Under the Jolly Roger: Being an Account of the Further Nautical Adventures of Jacky Faber;* and *In the Belly of the Bloodhound, Being an Account of a Particularly Peculiar Adventure in the Life of Jacky Faber.*

In 2002, Nancy Farmer proved in *The House of the Scorpion* that she could write an exciting survival story, but since this was a science fiction dystopian novel, readers had other things to focus on besides the adventure. In her 1997 *A Girl Named Disaster,* however, survival—physical as well as emotional—is the main focus. The realistic story takes place in the early 1980s in Mozambique and Zimbabwe, when there was considerable hostility among white people, the Shona, and the Matebele. Crossing borders was dangerous because of land mines. The protagonist is an eleven-year-old orphan, Nhamo, who, with the help and encouragement of her grandmother, runs away from her village to escape being married to a villainous old man who already has three wives. She is traveling by boat but she misses the place where two rivers come together just before emptying into the huge Lake Cabora Bassa. Nhamo is forced to live on a small island for almost a year, finding her own food and dealing with baboons and also a leopard. Finally, with the kind of strength that would have made her grandmother proud, Nhamo builds herself a new boat and sets out to find the river she had missed before.

We should probably mention here that as we looked for new adventure books, we were surprised to see how many authors have slipped bits of fantasy or magical realism into the kinds of stories that even five or six years ago would have been straight adventure stories. What this means is that many of the books recommended in Chapter 5 as "fantasy" will also have many of the characteristics described in this chapter as "adventure."

Ship Ahoy! The Excitement of Pirate Stories

Johnny Depp has starred in four pirate films—*Pirates of the Caribbean: The Curse of the Black Pearl* (2003); *Pirates of the Caribbean: Dead Man's Chest* (2000); *Pirates of the Caribbean: At World's End* (2007), and *Pirates of the Caribbean: On Stranger Tides* (2011)—that have made multimillions of dollars along with millions of happy fans. Pirates are big business in film. They are equally entertaining to read about in books, as long as their cruelty and their bloodshed is confined to the printed page.

YA writers have not ignored the attraction pirates hold for young people, although now that real pirates are wreaking havoc in the South Pacific the books may be losing some of their charm. Tanith Lee's *Piratica: Being a Daring Tale of a Singular Girl's Adventure upon the High Seas* and its *Piratica II: Return to Parrot Island* are playful fantasies. In Celia Rees's *Pirates,* Nancy Kington runs off from an arranged marriage to an evil man to join a pirate crew, and when pirates begin raiding Savage Island in Lenore Hart's *The Treasure of Savage Island,* fifteen-year-old Molly warns the settlers, saves her father, and finds a long-lost treasure.

In William Gilkerson's *Pirate's Passage,* when Captain Johnson of the good ship *Merry Adventure* washes up in Nova Scotia, a boy and his mother welcome him, but while the captain's extensive knowledge of pirates and pirates' ways excites the boy, it also makes him suspicious. In Iain Lawrence's *The Wreckers,* a young man who longs for the sea but is denied it by his businessman father becomes involved in the dangerous business of looting wrecked ships. His adventures continue in *The Smugglers* and *The Buccaneers.* Lawrence's *The Convicts* begins with Tom, a fourteen-year-old boy charged with murder and sentenced to the Lachesis, a prison ship for boys. In the sequel, *The Cannibals,* the boys' lives are even more brutal as they plot to escape from a convict ship taking them to Australia.

Geraldine McCaughrean's *The Pirate's Son,* set in the 1800s and packed with derring-do, opens with the death of Nathan Gull's father. Nathan must leave school since he has no money. Luckily for him, Tamo White, son of a pirate, decides to leave school, too, and take Nathan with him. The first half of McCaughrean's *The Kite Rider* is even more exotic and action-packed. The setting is thirteenth-century China, after the Mongols have conquered it, and hatred and distrust between Chinese and Mongols permeate the land. When twelve-year-old Haoyou's father takes his son to see his ship, the boy is thrilled until the first mate takes offense when the father insults the Khan's wife. The mate kicks Haoyou off the ship and, worse yet, attaches the father to a kite hoisted over the ship to determine whether the winds augur a profitable voyage for the ship and the crew. Horrifying as this is, Haoyou is unprepared when his father catches the wind and is lifted high aloft, only to be as suddenly plummeted to his death. It is now up to Haoyou to carry on the duties of the family and the honor of his father. He manages admirably, and a bonus for readers is that they get to meet Mipeng, a girl cousin, who is clever, funny, and wise in ways that save Haoyou from himself.

Nonfiction Adventures

Nonfiction adventures in which people set out to challenge nature (see Focus Box 7.1, "Adventures of Real People Challenging Nature," page 234) have an extra level of excitement because readers know that human lives are at stake. While young people seldom have what it takes to embark on such purposeful adventures, they can nevertheless read about them. They can also imagine what they would do if they happen to be forced into such an adventure, as were the young people whose story is told in *Alive* (see the discussion in Chapter 9, page 292).

Climbing mountains is one of the ways that people face off against nature because, as Reinhold Messner reminds us in his 1979 *Everest: Expedition to the Ultimate,* "In all true adventure, the path between the summit and the grave is a narrow one indeed." Nowhere is that clearer than in Jon Krakauer's *Into Thin Air: A Personal Account of the Mount Everest Disaster.* In the spring of 1996, fourteen groups of climbers were making their way up Mount Everest. Krakauer reached the summit on May 10, as did five teammates, but five others died, and nineteen others were stranded for a time when a freak storm hit and left them to survive temperatures of 100 degrees below zero. Ultimately, Everest took twelve lives that spring. Krakauer describes the work that went into planning and setting up the camps, the difficulties of the climb, the heroism shown by many of

Focus Box 7.1

Adventures of Real People Challenging Nature

Amelia Lost: the Life and Disappearance of Amelia Earhart by Candace Fleming. Random House, 2011. Younger teens will enjoy the account of a woman celebrity who loved a challenge.

Breaking Trail by Arlene Blum. Scribner, 2005. Blum organized and helped lead climbs on Mount McKinley, Annapurna, Everest, and more.

Endurance: Shackleton's Incredible Voyage by Alfred Lansing. McGraw-Hill, 1959. When his ship was crushed by ice in 1915, Sir Ernest Shackleton and his twenty-seven-member crew camped for five months on Antarctic ice floes and drifted at sea.

Ghosts of Everest: The Search for Mallory and Irvine by Jochen Hemmleb, Larry A. Johnson, and Eric Simonson. The Mountaineers, 1999. The authors set out to find the bodies of two climbers—George Mallory and Andrew Irvine—who died on Everest on June 4, 1924.

Hippie Chick by Joseph Monninger. Front Street, 2008. Lolly didn't set out to challenge nature, she just happened to be in a sailing accident. Manatees actually help in her survival.

The Long Exile: A Tale of Inuit Betrayal and Survival in the High Arctic by Melanie McGrath. Knopf, 2007. When Inuit hunters on the Ungava Peninsula in the east Arctic found game increasingly harder to find, the Canadian government decided to move 1,200 of them to Ellesmere Island where there were no permanent residents. This forced relocation to a place the Inuits had no understanding of and led to disaster.

Mountains of the Mind by Robert Macfarlane. Pantheon, 2003. Macfarlane writes about the history of the relationship between humanity and mountains from when mountains were seen as eyesores or obstacles to now, when they are regarded with awe.

No Shortcuts to the Top by Ed Viesturs. Broadway, 2006. Viesturs set out to climb the summits of the world's fourteen highest mountains without using bottled oxygen. He accomplished his quest in 2005.

Off the Map: Tales of Endurance and Exploration by Fergus Fleming. Atlantic Monthly Press, 2005. Fleming's book includes forty-five biographical essays covering the history of geographical discovery.

Savage Summit: The True Stories of the First Five Women Who Climbed K2, the World's Most Feared Mountain by Jennifer Jordan. Morrow, 2005. All five who climbed K2 died, three on the descent, two while climbing other mountains.

Scott of the Antarctic by David Crane. Knopf, 2006. Scott's background—middle-class upbringing amid genteel poverty, and the navy he joined which, in peacetime, recruited upper-class officers—made life difficult for him during the expedition to the Antarctic.

the climbers—and some incidents that exhibited cowardice or selfishness—but he cannot explain fully why anyone should take such risks.

Krakauer had agreed to take part as a climber and writer for *Outside* magazine, but when he delivered his article—on time—he learned about the bitterness of many of the friends and relatives of those who died. He wrote *Into Thin Air*, which was published by Villard in 1997, in an attempt to get the story straight and to explain what role he had in saving a few climbers and in being unable to save others. It is also one more effort to explain why it is that anyone would climb a mountain, specifically Everest.

People who don't climb mountains—the great majority of humankind, that is to say—tend to assume that the sport is a reckless, Dionysian pursuit of ever-escalating thrills. But the notion that climbers are merely adrenaline junkies chasing a righteous fix is a fallacy, at least in the case of Everest. What I was doing up there had almost nothing to do with bungee jumping or skydiving or riding a motorcycle at 120 miles per hour. Above the comforts of Base Camp, the expedition in fact became an almost Calvinistic undertaking. The ratio of misery to pleasure was greater by an order of magnitude than any other mountain I'd been on. I quickly came to understand that climbing Everest was primarily about enduring pain. And in subjecting ourselves to week after week of toil, tedium, and suffering, it struck me that most of us were probably seeking, above all, something like a state of grace.

Krakauer's story has taken on extra weight over the last few years. First because, with his background of climbing in Pakistan and Afghanistan, he took it upon himself to investigate the death of Pat Tillman, the football player who gave up his million dollar contract with the Arizona Cardinals to become an Army Ranger and fight in both Iraq and Afghanistan. When Tillman was killed in Afghanistan, the Army first tried to use his "heroic" death for purposes of recruitment, but then stories began to leak out that he was killed in what used to be called *friendly fire,* that is, he was shot by an American soldier.

Krakauer launched a full scale investigation and wrote a book released by Doubleday in October of 2009. *Where Men Win Glory: The Odyssey of Pat Tillman* became an immediate best seller. Although it was not written for teen readers (the Army language in it is way beyond what Harry Mazer and Walter Dean Myers have been challenged for in their books about the military) many young adults are reading it, at least here in Arizona where Tillman played on ASU's football team and where the Pat Tillman Foundation is located. They consider Tillman a hero and his adventures to be grand and tragic, but not in the same way that the U.S. Military public relations officers tried to portray the story.

The second reason that Krakauer is in the news is that, because of his mountain climbing experience, he was in a position to check some of the supposedly factual accounts in Greg Mortenson's runaway best seller, *Three Cups of Tea,* which is about Mortenson's mountain climbing in northern Pakistan near the Afghan border, getting separated from his climbing party, and at last being rescued by villagers in the high mountains of Pakistan. In gratitude for their rescue, Mortenson launched a charitable campaign to gather money and build schools in Pakistan and Afghanistan. But in the spring of 2011, Krakauer charged Mortenson with fraud about some of the incidents in his book, especially those relating to his climbing and being rescued by the villagers. In *Three Cups of Tea,* he also wrote about being held for a time by the Taliban, but Krakauer recognized some of the people in the photo and said that in fact they were local leaders who were honoring Mortenson. Krakauer took his suspicions to the producers of CBS's *60 Minutes,* which launched an investigation and, on April 15, 2011, devoted a large part of their Sunday evening television show to the matter. This caused cancellations of speaking engagements and also changes in plans by universities which had already assigned incoming freshman to read *Three Cups of Tea* in preparation for discussing it in various classes.

The whole incident shows how eager readers are to experience vicarious adventures. At the same time, however, we really want to believe them, especially if we are reading them in a book that is labeled "true." We are much more willing to suspend our disbelief at the movies because we know that trick

photography and special effects are there to help us forget that losing is more common than winning.

Westerns

The appeal of the American West is as old as the first explorer who saw it and marveled. Dime novelists of the 1870s and 1880s glorified the wildness and vitality of miners, cowboys, mountain men, soldiers, and outlaws. From the beginning, *westerns* were written for mass appeal, so they are easily accessible to teen readers.

If anything else were needed to make the West the heartland of adventure, movies provided rootin'-tootin'-shootin' cowboys and rustlers, good guys and bad guys—always easy to spot by who wore white hats versus who wore black. Films may not have been needed, at least not at first, because Owen Wister's *The Virginian,* written in 1902, had already established the central characters of too many westerns. There is the quiet and noble hero, the schoolmarm heroine, the hero's weak friend, the villain, and rustlers, along with such basic plot devices as cattle drives, the inevitable showdown between hero and villain, violence aplenty, revenge, and more revenge.

Many readers were not looking for realism from these books. Instead, it was romanticism as exemplified by the highly popular novels of Zane Grey,

This portrait of Will Rogers hangs on the wall of the Student Union at the University of Central Oklahoma as a constant reminder to contemporary students of the past that is celebrated in many of the westerns mentioned in this chapter.

especially his 1910 *The Heritage of the Desert* and his 1912 *Riders of the Purple Sage.* But an amazing number of fine writers lived and breathed the real West and wrote accurate and nonromanticized novels—for example, A. B. Guthrie with *The Way West* (1949) and Charles L. McNichols with *Crazy Weather* (1944). The prototype of the western came with Jack Schaefer's *Shane* (1949), which was consistently praised by critics and teachers. Frank Waters, one of the best writers of his time, wrote a loving and lyrical novel of a young man caught between two cultures in *The Man Who Killed the Deer* (1942).

Conventions of the western were so well established by this time that writers knew what was expected. The setting is obviously the West, preferably some time between 1880 and 1895, the high point of cowboy life. Suspense and excitement pervades the novel, as it rarely did for real cowboys back then—rustlers, lynchings, bank robberies, jailbreaks, crooked lawyers, ladies of the evening, the cavalry riding to the rescue, and on and on. Violence was more likely portrayed than implied. The hero (a marshal, ex-gunman, drifter, wagonmaster) will be moral, though that may have come after a reformation, which he will rarely be willing to talk about save to the heroine and only then in a particularly trying or tender moment. Morality will ultimately triumph as the hero plays a successful Hamlet and puts the world aright.

Fortunately, some western writers have been able to ignore or work around these conventions. Louis L'Amour's books continue to sell well, though he has been dead for a number of years. Teachers who have introduced his books to their classes have been happily surprised at how many teens become real fans. L'Amour knows the West as a historian, so the West he writes about is accurate. *Down the Long Hills* is one of his best. In it, a seven-year-old goes searching for his horse, which has wandered away. He returns to find his entire wagon train massacred. He and his sister head west, facing starvation, blizzards, and wild animals. It's a remarkable survival tale.

Three writers have focused on gunfighters and violence in small towns. E. L. Doctorow's *Welcome to Hard Times* shows how dismal a dying western town can be when an outlaw sets out to destroy it over and over. Charles O. Locke's *The Hell Bent Kid* is about a man who kills a man in self-defense and then must flee for his life. The best known of the three is Glendon Swarthout's *The Shootist,* about a gunfighter dying of cancer who in his last shootout rids the town of some rough gunfighters. It may be more famous for being the last film made by John Wayne, but its renown is well deserved either as book or film.

Two great books are about a West that is dead. Robert Flynn's *North to Yesterday* is the story of a group of misfits who gather to ride old cattle drive trails long after they have dried up. Edward Abbey's *The Brave Cowboy* is a portrait of a cowboy who has outlived the wide open plains. He hates barbed wire fences and anything that encloses anything or anyone. He breaks into jail to free a friend, but when the friend indicates he is willing to serve his term, the cowboy breaks himself out and a long manhunt begins.

Westerns are so often serious that it is pleasant to read two books that are genuinely funny—deliberately so. David Wagoner's *The Road to Many a Wonder* is simply one of the funniest books in English. Ike Bender, age twenty, leaves home to find gold and is soon followed by his soon-to-be bride. Their struggles to get to Colorado and find the pot at the end of their rainbow are believable, generally, and utterly delightful. Bruce Clements's *I Tell a Lie Every So Often* is about a fourteen-year-old boy who begins his tale with this long and complex paragraph, which is a reasonably accurate description of the book that follows:

> I tell a lie every so often, and almost always nothing happens, but last spring I told a lie that carried me five hundred miles and made a lot of things happen. Somebody got shot because of it, and I had a visit with a beautiful naked girl who stood up in front of me early in the morning and talked in a foreign tongue, and I saw a ball game with a hundred men on one side and a hundred men and one girl on the other side, and a boat sank, somewhat, under me, and my brother Clayton started acting strangely and sleeping with a loaded rifle, and there were some more things, too.

Kathryn Lasky's *Beyond the Divide* is a YA novel of the western movement. Another good western written from the perspective of a young person is Marian Calabro's *The Perilous Journey of the Donner Party*. Calabro tells her meticulously researched story of a group of unfortunate western settlers stranded in an early California snowstorm. Her heroine is twelve-year-old Virginia Reed, the young survivor who throughout the months of the ordeal hid her rag doll inside her clothes.

A new YA novel, Marcus Sedgwick's 2009 *Revolver,* has all the thrills and chills of a western, although the frontier of its setting is way north of our usual western. It begins in 1910 outside of Giron, a small community located at 68 Latitude North in the Arctic wilderness where the protagonist, fourteen-year-old Sig, lives with his older sister, Anna; his stepmother, Nadya; and his father, Einar. They are part of a rag-tag group who were lured to the Arctic by dreams of gold.

The second chapter is a flashback to 1899, when the family first came to Nome, Alaska, which is two latitudes south of Giron. The young children attracted attention because their father was the only adventurer who came with a wife and two children. They were saved from starvation when the most important man in Nome gave Einar the job of assaying the gold that the prospectors would bring in. The man figured that Einar would be honest because he had a family and, therefore, had more to lose than did any of the other men.

As it turns out, Einar was far from honest, and several years later, readers see the children, now teenagers, finding their father frozen to death out on the ice-covered lake that is between their house and the town. They get his frozen body onto his dogsled and get him home and into the house. Anna and Nadya go to the village for help, leaving Sig at home with the frozen and deformed corpse of his father laid out on the dining table. A huge, menacing stranger appears at the door and addresses Sig as "Son." With this, Sig is drawn into a desperate and complicated game that for almost a decade had been going on between the now-dead Einar and this evil man, who informs Sig that as his father's son, it is up to him to fulfill his father's obligations.

The denouement of the story is a postscript coming from the New York City Warwick Hotel in 1967, when readers are let in on the circumstances that encouraged Sigfried Anderrson, now an old man, to pick up a pen, a small black notebook, and tell his story as if it were "about someone else, some other family."

Sports and the Game of Life

Because we lack the space to say everything that adults working with young people need to know about sports books, we recommend that interested readers find Chris Crowe's *More Than a Game: Sports Literature for Young Adults*. Several of the most popular and most talented YA writers tell sports stories. For example, see the Edwards Award pages on Chris Crutcher and on Robert Lipsyte (pages 240 and 241). As shown by the listing in Focus Box 7.2, "An Armful of YA Sports Fiction," most sports books, whether fiction or nonfiction, include information about the training that is needed; the expected rewards, tangible or not; and the inevitable disappointments that make the rewards even sweeter. Early sports books in the 1800s and 1900s focused on the character-changing possibilities of sports along with an inning-by-inning or quarter-by-quarter account. The minute-by-minute account was almost never successful. But the excitement and the euphoria that sometimes comes to players has remained. Occasional nonfiction writers have focused almost exclusively on a player's character flaws, an iconoclastic approach that seems to have had its day.

The excitement of sports is what readers want, just as winning is the only acceptable verdict for fans. In the 1950s and early 1960s such writers as H. D. Francis and John Carson wrote good novels filled with heroes reeking of sweat. Their heroes often examined the price of fame and the temptation to

It is understandable that, in this library, the "Teen Sports Fiction" is one of the biggest signs because it points the way to the section that teen boys—and some girls—are always looking for. See Focus Boxes 7.2, "An Armful of YA Sports Fiction," (on p. 242) and 7.3, "Sports Nonfiction—Real Life Dreams" (on p. 244) to see why these books are popular.

Margaret A. Edwards Award

Winner (2000)
Chris Crutcher, And His
Sports-Plus Novels

The six books that Crutcher was honored for were *Staying Fat for Sarah Byrnes, Athletic Shorts: Six Short Stories, Chinese Handcuffs, The Crazy Horse Electric Game, Stotan,* and *Running Loose.* We want to add *Ironman, Whale Talk,* and *The Sledding Hill.*

When *Running Loose* was published in 1983, reviewers recognized that an accomplished first novelist had arrived on the YA scene, and it did not take long before teachers found Crutcher and began recommending him to their students. Critics began to call his books "honest" and "intense" and to argue over whether *Running Loose* or later books were his best. *Running Loose* is at least partly autobiographical. Few YA novels have parents so decent and so understanding as does Louie Banks. He also has a warm and believable girlfriend in Becky Sanders, but on the down side he has a vindictive football coach willing to do anything to win games, and that includes taking the opposition's star player out through dirty play. Louie protests the foul, but the coach ignores him, and the coach is supported by the principal. Louie is no longer on the team, and then he faces a far greater problem when Becky is killed in a car crash. Later, at the funeral, Louie is almost comatose until he hears the minister saying a litany of funeral clichés about God's moving in "strange and mysterious ways." Louie yells, "He doesn't move in strange and mysterious ways. He doesn't move at all! He sits up there on His fat butt and lets guys like you earn a living making excuses for all the rotten things that happen." No applause follows.

That scene is almost topped by a brief interlude when Louie learns that the principal plans to erect a plaque in Becky's memory and set it in concrete. Later, as Louie leaves school, he sees the plaque and reads all the stuff on it about Becky's work on cheerleading and student council and Honor Society and more. It's too much for Louie, partly because the principal had signed his name at the bottom of the plaque. He was the one school official that both Louie and Becky disliked and so at night Louie takes a sledgehammer to the school. He hammers the plaque loose from the concrete, puts it in the back of his pickup, and dumps it in the river where Becky died.

One of our college students who picked up *Running Loose* expected to write a negative review because she had always hated sports books. She ended up admitting she was wrong because, instead of being about sports, this was a book "about so many things—love, death, loyalty, anger, compassion, and courage. It's about being responsible. It was not about my boyfriend. It was about me." She concluded with, "Crutcher asks the right questions that young people need somehow to find answers to. That's what I learned from reading *Running Loose.*"

Stotan carries on with Crutcher's tests of endurance, loyalty, and challenge. In it, four young men begin the Stotan, a test of physical and emotional strength to develop their swimming team. Each swimmer is also faced with a significant personal problem. In *Staying Fat for Sarah Byrnes,* Sarah has been horribly burned and pretends to be catatonic to escape her evil father. In *Ironman,* Bo writes letters to radio talk-show host Larry King at the same time he is constantly angry with his father and his English teacher (an ex-football coach). In *Whale Talk,* a young male—black, white, and Japanese—refuses to be in organized sports but joins a swimming team and talks other outsiders into joining him.

In the third edition of this text (1989), Chris Crutcher wrote, "I think it is incredibly disrespectful and potentially damaging to foster the myths of our society—myths of the unconditional sanctity of the family, myths of the innate good of any particular institutional spirituality, myths of unexamined patriotism, and on and on. In other words, we owe the same thing to young adult readers as we do to adult readers: that is the honest depiction of our observations—the truth as we see it."

In *Deadline,* eighteen-year-old Ben Wolfe is diagnosed with an incurable kind of leukemia. Because he's of legal age, he doesn't have to let his parents know and so he sets out on his own to pack a lifetime of experience into his senior year at his small Idaho high school. When he contemplates playing on the football team and courting Dallas Suzuki—the girl of his dreams—he has to keep reminding himself that some insects live only one day. ●

Margaret A. Edwards Award

Winner (2001)
Robert Lipsyte, A Contender

All the Way

Robert Lipsyte's honored books include *The Contender, The Brave, The Chief,* and *One Fat Summer.* If the award were given today, we would vote that *Raiders Night* also be on the list. Lipsyte is a professional sports writer and television and radio commentator who, in 1967, was inspired to write *The Contender* when he was in a gymnasium and one of the grand old boxing coaches put a finger to his lips so they could both listen to the way a boy was running up the stairs. As they listened, the coach shared his judgment that this newcomer was going to be "a contender." He could tell from the energy that the boy put into running up the stairs.

The Contender made Lipsyte a name in YA literature because the story of a would-be fighter wandering into a gym in hopes of becoming a contender is a fresh allegory that fit the role filled by many young men in real life. For earlier editions of this text, Lipsyte wrote that he thinks boys don't read as much as we'd like them to partly because current books do not deal with the real problems and fears of boys. And then as educators we tend to treat boys as a group—which is where males are at their absolute worst. He suggests that boys "have to be led into reading secretly and one at a time." *The Contender, The Brave,* and *The Chief* are about individuals who suffer from being in a group. They find hope as soon as someone recognizes them as individuals. His 2010 *Center Field* is a strong book about a strong baseball player, who loses control and has major conflicts with his over-controlling coach.

Lipsyte's *Raiders Night* is about being an individual and speaking out when it is needed. The book may seem like yet another football story until a terrifying and crucial event. Matt Rydek is co-captain of the Nearmont High School Raiders football team. He and the other players are treated royally by fans who love them unconditionally. Matt, however, has two problems. First is his pushy father, who does not know or understand his son, and second is his co-captain, Ramp, who is mean and more sadistic than anyone suspects. In the locker room, Ramp singles out a new player named Chris for humiliation because he has made Ramp look bad.

Ramp marches around during a team initiation waving a small white plastic bat, and when Chris will not humble himself, Ramp pulls down Chris's shorts and sodomizes him with the white plastic bat. Vomit rises in Matt's throat, but even though he has always disliked and distrusted Ramp, he does nothing except feel guilty.

When the coaches and others learn of Ramp's actions on Raider Pride Night, Matt's first impulse is to keep his mouth shut and pretend that nothing happened. Matt's father tells Matt to keep "it in the locker room." At the book's end, when Matt stands up for Chris and himself, his father calls him an "ungrateful little sonuabitch," and says, "Everything I did was for you, busting my back so you could have everything you ever needed, best equipment, baseball and football camps, money in your account, you know how much safe steroids cost. I'm not going to let you throw it away." Matt says, "It's my call."

Of all the ugly episodes in *Raiders Night,* none is more nauseatingly unctuous than Pastor Jim's homily at the Welcome Home Rally. Long after the sodomy scene, Pastor Jim "asked God to give the Raiders the strength to get back up when they were knocked down, to forgive cheap shots, and to win clean." He added, "You know, if Jesus came back, he'd be a Raider, hitting hard and hitting clean."

When Lipsyte was asked if he was surprised that *Raiders Night* was a subject of censorship, he said that *censorship* is too strong of a word for what he has been experiencing. It has been more insidious, as when he is invited to a school by a librarian or an English teacher and then is uninvited by a coach, an athletic director, or a principal. He does not think it is because of the language or the sex or the mention of steroids. Instead, it is because the book takes a negative look at jock culture, which is something those guys are really invested in.

Is *Raiders Night* working? Yes it is. It must be to attract the attention of the greatest advocates of American sportsmanship, these holy three—coaches, athletic directors, and principals. ●

***Ball Don't Lie* by Matt de la Peña. Delacorte, 2005.** A seventeen-year-old white boy, Sticky, lives mostly on the street and, because of his basketball skill, is pretty much accepted by black peers. However, his situation is far more precarious than is that of Maniac McGee in Spinelli's book for younger readers. Still, readers come away feeling optimistic.

***Becoming Joe DiMaggio* by Maria Testa. Candlewick, 2002.** While their father is in prison during World War II, an Italian American family struggles to move on, with DiMaggio and radio always in the background.

***The Boxer* by Kathleen Karr. Farrar, Straus and Giroux, 2002.** In New York City of the 1880s, John Aloysius Xavier Woods works in a sweatshop, but daily he goes by a saloon soliciting would-be bare-fisted boxers. Because boxing is illegal in New York, he's tossed in jail. When he comes out, he's now Johnny "The Chopper" Woods.

***Checkered Flag Cheater* by Will Weaver. FSG, 2010.** Weaver's Motor Novels series has excitement, girls, and lots of racing details. This is the third book in the series.

***Dairy Queen* by Catherine Gilbert Murdock. Houghton Mifflin, 2006.** D. J. Schwenk takes on her father's dairy work when he is injured, but her heart is set on training Brian, the rival school's quarterback, and even going out for her own school's football team. Her story is continued in *The Off Season* (2007), where life becomes more challenging.

***Fighting Ruben Wolfe* by Markus Zusak. Scholastic, 2001.** This story of two brothers joining an illegal fight circuit to earn money for their family received positive votes from all fifteen members of the Best Books for Young Adults committee of ALA.

***Gym Candy* by Carl Deuker. Houghton Mifflin, 2007.** It's ironic that the name of the gym where running back Mick Johnson works out is named Popeye's because this is where he figures out that popping supplements isn't enough. But when he moves to injecting himself with steroids, he gets more than he bargained for. Readers who like *Gym Candy* will probably also enjoy Deuker's 2003 *High Heat* about a baseball pitcher, and his 2010 *Payback Time,* in which a new football player discovers a mystery that someone doesn't want uncovered.

***In a Heartbeat* by Loretta Ellsworth. Walker, 2010.** Eagan is a competitive ice skater. When he dies in an unexpected accident, his heart is given to Amelia, who is surprised to find herself taking on Eagan's personality.

***Leverage* by Joshua C. Cohen. Dutton, 2011.** This story of a friendship between a football player and a gymnast tackles some disturbing aspects of sports programs.

***Love, Football, and Other Contact Sports* by Alden R. Carter. Holiday, 2006.** This collection of short stories developed around Argyle West High School's football team is realistic, ironic, and sometimes funny.

***Missing in Action* by Dean Hughes. Atheneum, 2010.** Jay, who loves baseball, and his mom move back to Delta, Utah, to stay with his grandparents when his father, who is a soldier in WWII, is reported missing in action. Jay is part Navajo and suddenly feels shy about trying to make friends and play baseball, but then he makes friends with an older Japanese boy who is in a Utah Japanese Internment Camp.

***A Passing Season* by Richard Blessing. Little, Brown, 1982.** In one of the best YA novels ever, Craig Warren has potential greatness but his play is erratic.

***Planet Middle School* by Nikki Grimes, Bloomsbury, 2011.** Middle school girls are the most likely fans of this story about Joylin Johnson, an athletic girl facing the joys and challenges of middle school. It is told in Grimes's beautiful free-verse poetry.

***Slam* by Nick Hornby. Putnam, 2007.** Fifteen-year-old Sam is a skateboarding whiz who hits a bump when his girlfriend gets pregnant. Luckily, Sam has Tony Hawk, the world's greatest skater, to talk to him from the giant poster on Sam's wall.

***Under the Baseball Moon* by John Ritter. Philomel, 2006.** Andy Ramon's love life consists of Glory Martinez. He loves music, and Glory loves playing softball. The arrangement works for both of them; Andy plays his trumpet and that inspires Glory's hitting and pitching.

***Wrestling Sturbridge* by Rich Wallace. Knopf, 1996.** Ben and Al are best friends. The only problem is that they are the two best 135-pound wrestlers in the state, and they attend the same high school.

believe—always doomed—that fame would last. Writers as powerful as John Updike killed that dream much as F. Scott Fitzgerald had killed other dreams about the permanence of the glories to be found in society or business. The sentimental fiction of the 1950s and 1960s was never real, but it had a charm that we have lost, and with it some readers of more innocent sports books.

Two particularly impressive books about baseball that mature high school students can appreciate are about love and friendship and fatherhood. They are Mark Harris's *Bang the Drum Slowly* and Donald Hall's *Fathers Playing Catch with Sons*. Harris's story of a second- or third-string catcher dying of leukemia is touching, just as it is good baseball. Hall, a major poet, offers a warm and almost sentimental account of his love for sports, particularly baseball. The first two sentences of his introduction tie together the two worlds he loves and needs: writing and baseball: "Half of my poet-friends think I am insane to waste my time writing about sports and to loiter in the company of professional athletes. The other half would murder to take my place." Later, he distinguishes between baseball and football to the detriment of the latter: "Baseball is fathers and sons. Football is brothers beating each other up in the backyard, violent and superficial."

Angry Sports Books

Anger is part of sports—anger at oneself, anger at teammates, anger at coaches, anger at the opposing team. The following three books are angry in quite a different way. They are angry with the system; with unfeeling parents who care only that their son or daughter is a star, never just a member of a team; with people who take the fun out of sports and replace it with a machine; with people who pretend that sports will build character; and with people who lead young people to embrace the violence that is at the heart of sport.

James Bennett's *The Squared Circle* focuses on Sonny Youngblood, a high school star basketball player now entering Southern Illinois University as the hope of the athletic department. Whether Sonny even likes the sport is a question that Sonny avoids asking, mostly out of fear for the consequences of the answer. His father long ago walked out on the family. Sonny did not like his high school coach and now he finds that he is the only non–African American player on the squad and he hates the fraternity he is ready to join. If all that isn't bad enough, he has a cousin, who is an art professor at the university, and she wants Sonny to work out for himself what he wants to do with his life. Sonny is slow to act, but when he does, he solves several problems all at once. This is a powerful book.

Chris Lynch's *Inexcusable* is also powerful. It is about a high school jock, Keir Sarafian, who rapes his girlfriend, something readers find out on page 1. Keir has fully bought into the world of football. He knows that violence is very much a part of his world, but he also "knows" that he is a good boy. In his own mind, he adds what others would say—that Keir is "rock solid, the kind of guy you want behind you, a straight shooter, loyal, polite, funny, good manners, he was brought up the right way, that boy was." Keir has also crippled an opposing player and now has the nickname Killer. Keir likes being liked, though his sisters do not like him. His only fan is his father, who is oblivious to what Keir has become. When he and his friends tear down a statue, they know it's a prank. When they get drunk, as Keir regularly does, he and his friends pass it off as boyish fun,

Focus Box 7.3

Sports Nonfiction— Real-Life Dreams

Babe Didrikson Zaharias: The Making of a Champion by **Russell Freedman. Clarion, 1999.** Freedman's biographies are a pleasure to read because of the care he takes with the research and the writing as well as with the design of the book.

Between Boardslides and Burnout: My Notes from the Road by **Tony Hawk. HarperCollins, 2002.** Full-color photographs add to this realistic journal of a skateboarding champion.

Big League Dreams: Baseball Hall of Fame's First African-Canadian, Fergie Jenkins by **Richard Brignall, Lorimer, 2010.** Readers will identify with Jenkins and how hard he had to work to become the first African-Canadian to play big league baseball.

The Boys of October: How the 1975 Boston Red Sox Embodied Baseball's Ideals—and Restored our Spirits by **Doug Hornig. Contemporary Books, 2003.** Hornig prepared a hymn to the glories of his favorite team.

Crazy' 08: How a Cast of Cranks, Rogues, Boneheads, and Magnates Created the Greatest Year in Baseball History by **Cait Murphy. Smithsonian Books, 2007.** Fans of the Chicago Cubs have a strange rallying cry: "Remember 1908!" the last time the Cubs won the World Series. A marvelous and wacky book about a marvelous and wacky time.

The Greatest: Muhammad Ali by **Walter Dean Myers. Scholastic, 2001.** Myers brings his skill as a writer to this biography, along with his knowledge of what Muhammad Ali meant to African Americans. In 2011, he also did a picture book biography covering Ali's childhood up to the time of his lighting the torch in the 1996 Olympics.

Indian Summer: The Forgotten Story of Louis Francis Sockalexis, the First Native American in Major League Baseball by **Brian McDonald. Rodale, 2003.** Sockalexis was recruited by the Cleveland Spiders in 1897 and drank himself out of baseball by 1910. This is a sad story.

Let Me Play: The Story of Title IX: The Law That Changed the Future of Girls in America by **Karen Blumenthal. S&S/Atheneum, 2005.** A law that started as almost an accident has made a profound difference in the lives of America's young women. Blumenthal's take on the matter is shown both through facts and human interest stories.

Race across Alaska: First Woman to Win the Iditarod Tells Her Story by **Libby Riddles and Tim Jones. Stackpole Books, 1998.** Readers who know Gary Paulsen's *Woodsong* (Bradbury, 1990) will enjoy this different perspective on the race.

The Story of Negro League Baseball by **William Brashler. Ticknor & Fields, 1994.** Brashler takes up the history of Negro baseball and its important players (e.g., Bob Gibson and Smokey Joe Williams).

Winning Ways: A Photohistory of American Women in Sports by **Sue Macy. Holt, 1996.** Both in this book and in her *A Whole New Ball Game* (Holt, 1993), Macy presents wonderful photos and intriguing details to show that women have a sports heritage.

just as he refuses to listen to Gigi when she says *no* because he knows that people just don't say *no* to a football star.

Since 1967, when Robert Lipsyte wrote *The Contender,* he has had dual careers—one as a professional sports writer and commentator, and the other as an author of powerful young adult books, mostly about sports. His angriest book, *Raiders Night,* was published in 2007. It is the story of a football team and what one team member does to another team member and then what fear and shame can do to the entire team. For more about *Raiders Night* and Lipsyte's other sports books, see the write-up regarding his Margaret A. Edwards Award.

Because sports is a subject where high school readers admire adult athletes and look forward to joining their ranks, both YA and adult books are included in Focus Box 7.3, "Sports Nonfiction—Real-Life Dreams." What also is worth remembering, periodically, is that sports are enjoyable, a way of relaxing with friends, a way of becoming part of the majority, and a chance to exchange ideas about what the coaches, or players, should have done last Sunday, or Saturday. And as shown by the books in the Focus Box, sports no longer belong exclusively to boys and men. Title IX, a law that came into being almost accidentally, has made a profound difference in the lives of America's young women. It's a good thing that this change is starting to be reflected in the literature.

Mysteries

Why are mysteries so enduringly popular? Basically they are unrealistic and, as mystery writers cheerfully admit, usually have almost nothing to do with real-life detection by police or private agents. They demand that we suspend most of our disbelief, and we gladly do so. Mysteries are mere games, but we love games. Some of us claim that we want to beat the detective to the murderer, but we rarely do, and when we succeed, we feel cheated.

The popularity of mystery movies and the number of hotels, ships, and individuals who sponsor parties in which a mock murder takes place, with the partygoers playing detectives, shows the entertainment value of mayhem, murder, and suspense. Because of the high entertainment value of mysteries and their sometimes easy reading level, many mysteries published for a general audience find their way into the hands of young adults.

Daniel's detection of the guilty Elders in "The Story of Susanna" in the *Apocrypha* may be the world's first detective story. Critics generally agree, however, that the modern mystery begins with Edgar Allan Poe's "The Murders in the Rue Morgue," although "The Purloined Letter" is more satisfying today. Poe's detective, C. Auguste Dupin, is unquestionably the first criminal investigator.

Writer and critic Hillary Waugh has said that the skeletons on which mysteries hang are "nothing more nor less than a series of ironclad rules" (*The Basics of Writing and Selling Mysteries and Suspense* 10, 1991: 6–8). The rules are essential to present the puzzle properly and to ensure fair play. He lists them as follows:

Rule One: All clues discovered by the detective must be made available to the reader.

Rule Two: The murderer must be introduced early.

Rule Three: The crime must be significant.

Rule Four: There must be detection.

Rule Five: The number of suspects must be known, and the murderer must be among them.

Rule Six: The reader, as part of the game of fair play, has the right to expect that nothing will be included in the book that does not relate to or in some way bear on the puzzle.

Types of Mysteries

The characteristics of the traditional murder mystery are well known and relatively fixed, although devotees are always interested in variations on the theme of murder. A mystery short story may settle for theft, but a novel, of course, demands murder. Accompanying crimes such as blackmail or embezzlement may add to the delights of murder, but they never replace murder. The ultimate crime normally takes place a few chapters into the book, after readers have been introduced to the major and minor characters, including the victim and those who might long for his death. The detective appears, clues are scattered, the investigation proceeds, the detective solves the case, the guilty are punished, the innocent are restored to their rightful place, and the world becomes right again.

Shannon Ocork, on pages 10 to 12 of the same journal in which Waugh published his "rules," classified mysteries into these six types:

1. *The amateur detective:* At least in the older stories, the amateur detective was male (e.g., C. Auguste Dupin or Sherlock Holmes and, later, Rex Stout's Nero Wolfe). These detectives are altruistic and usually optimistic. They are bright and see what others do not. Sometimes called traditional, golden-age, or classic mysteries, these flourished from the 1920s through the 1940s.

2. *The cozy mystery:* These stories are close to the amateur detective stories. They are usually set in a small English village, although New England is increasingly popular. Agatha Christie, who began writing in the 1920s, is the most obvious writer of cozies. She scattered her best books throughout her life. Her 1939 *And Then There Were None* is her best book without a detective. Others include her 1950 *A Murder Is Announced,* a Miss Marple book, and her 1968 *By the Pricking of My Thumbs,* in which the usually tiresome Tommy and Tuppence Beresford stumble into a believable mystery.

3. *The puzzle:* These stories are exercises in ingenuity as we are led into an intricate murder, with the detective daring us to figure out the end of the story. Ellery Queen's early mysteries had a "Challenge to the Reader" about three or four chapters from the end, when the writer announced that we had all the clues Queen had and should be able to solve the mystery. Luckily, we rarely succeeded.

4. *The private detective:* These hard-boiled mysteries differ from other mysteries in significant ways. Private detectives lack altruistic motives. They enter cases for pay rather than for love of the chase or intellectual fondness for the puzzle. Working out of a cheerless office and around even less cheerful people, they are tired and cynical about the courts, the police, class distinctions, and life in general. Many are former police officers who left the force under a cloud. They have seen too much of the seamy world to feel hope for anything or anyone, and they know that detective work is hard and mostly routine and dull. With patience, any bright person could do what they do. Not only does violence come with the territory, it is the territory. Moreover, we are surprised, even disappointed, if the violence is not there.

5. *The police procedural:* Police procedurals are often the most believable mysteries because the central characters are officers doing their mundane

jobs and tracking down murderers with scientific methods and machines available only to the police. The books of Ed McBain are probably the most popular police procedurals today.

6. *The thriller:* These are usually spy thrillers. They may have bits of mystery tucked into them, but as in Ian Fleming's James Bond series, the mystery involves not so much who did it as how our hero can escape his latest impossible situation with even more than his usual derring-do.

Some Popular Mystery Writers Accessible to Teens

Nevada Barr created Park Ranger Anna Pigeon out of her own experiences as a park ranger. Since 2000, Anna Pigeon has been a ranger and amateur sleuth in various national parks including the Natchez Trace Parkway in *Deep South;* the Dry Tortugas in *Flashback;* and in 2005 the Rocky Mountain National Park in *Hard Truth.* Barr's books combine love of the environment and lore of the place mixed with first class suspense.

Sue Grafton has been among the hottest mystery writers since 1982 when *"A" Is for Alibi* appeared. Her alphabetical series (e.g., *"M" Is for Malice* and *"T" Is for Trespass*) shows Kinsey Millhone working as an insurance investigator in California. She follows the advice of one of the best writing teachers in history, the Roman poet and critic Horace, who urged writers to begin in *media res,* that is, in the middle of the story.

Tony Hillerman holds an honored place in the community of mystery writers. His books breathe of the desert and sand and lonely and quiet places and are inevitably about Hopi or Navajo Indians in the Four-Corners area of the Southwest. When we were editors of *English Journal* and solicited answers to "Who is your favorite writer of detective stories?" Hillerman won by a margin of ten to one. *The Blessing Way* in 1970 was his first book, where readers were privileged to meet Officer Joe Leaphorn.

Ed McBain's police procedurals have delighted fans since 1956, and his later books, like *The Frumious Bandersnatch* and *Fiddlers,* seem to be getting better and better. Part of his charm lies in McBain's knowledge of his imaginary city, Isola, presumably New York City, and anyone and everyone who might want to live there as part of the 87th precinct.

Kathy Reichs, in her day job, is a forensic anthropologist who works professionally out of North Carolina and Montreal. Her detective is Temperance (Tempe) Brennan, also a forensic anthropologist, in books like *Fatal Voyage, Monday Mourning: A Novel, Cross Bones,* and *Break No Bones.*

Sherlock Holmes and His Descendants

Arthur Conan Doyle wrote two kinds of book: popular books of his times, like *The White Company,* which he considered literary and made him proud, and potboilers like the Sherlock Holmes adventures and mysteries, which gave him little pleasure though much money and whose popularity annoyed him. So he took the easy way out; he killed Holmes at the Reichenbach Falls in Switzerland, but the public outcry at Holmes's apparent death made Doyle rethink the matter.

Doyle had written four collections of Sherlock Holmes stories—*The Adventures of Sherlock Holmes* (1892), *The Memoirs of Sherlock Holmes* (1894), *The Return of Sherlock Holmes* (1905), and *The Case Book of Sherlock Holmes* (1927)—and one excellent novel about Holmes, *The Hound of the Baskervilles* (1902). That was all from Doyle.

But it was not the end of Sherlock Holmes. His admirers in England and America founded an organization called the Baker Street Irregulars devoted to Holmes's memory and to writing scholarly (mostly pseudoscholarly) articles mixed with the occasional imitation Holmes story published in the *Baker Street Journal*. Over the years, the articles and the stories (some of them now parodies and pastiches) multiplied. Many of the best were published under the editorship of Ellery Queen as *The Misadventures of Sherlock Holmes* (Little, Brown, 1944) and more recently under the editorship of Peter Ridgway Watt as *The Alternative Sherlock Holmes* (Ashgate, 2003).

Three recent Sherlock Holmes books deserve mention for their variety, if nothing else. Cheng Xiaoqing's *Sherlock in Shanghai: Stories of Crime and Detection* is set in 1920s and 1930s Shanghai and features a Chinese Holmes imitator named Huo. The second one is Steve Hockensmith's *Holmes on the Range* (St. Martin's, 2006), which is set in the Old West of the 1880s with two brothers working as ranch hands. The third one is Mark Haddon's *The Curious Incident of the Dog in the Night-Time,* in which Christopher John Francis Boone—fifteen, autistic, and a Sherlock Holmes devotee—sets out to solve the murder of a poodle in a rich, warm, and often funny novel.

The most successful writer who has taken on Holmes is Laurie R. King, who wrote *The Beekeeper's Apprentice* (1994). King's protagonist is Mary Russell, a brilliant fifteen-year-old who stumbles onto Sherlock Holmes, now a beekeeper in Sussex. The two soon become a team and ultimately solve the kidnapping case of an American senator's daughter. Several more books are in the Mary Russell series.

Middle-grade readers might get introduced to the whole genre through Tracy Mack and Michael Citrin's *Sherlock Holmes and the Baker Street Irregulars.* The "Irregulars" are a gang of street urchins who help the great detective. When the authors spoke at the 2006 ALAN workshop in Nashville, they left even some of the grown-ups eager to start solving the "Three Gruesome Deaths" that were promised in the first book. Another book that might get students interested in Sherlock Holmes is Peter Abrahams's *Down the Rabbit Hole: An Echo Falls Mystery,* whose protagonist, Ingrid Levin-Hill, is also a devoted fan of Sherlock Holmes. In a delicious and suspenseful book, Ingrid sets out to find the murderer of a strange old woman associated with a theater group.

Judging by how long we had to stand in line to buy tickets for the December 2011 film, *Sherlock Holmes: A Game of Shadows* (Directed by Guy Ritchey and starring Robert Downey, Jr., Jude Law and Jared Harris) there is little chance that Holmes will soon disappear from public awareness.

Mysteries Written for Young Adults

While many teenagers have fond memories of such detectives as Encyclopedia Brown and Nancy Drew, and young teens happily read the Sammy Keyes books by Wendelin Van Draanen, most teenagers are looking for something a bit more complex. However, YA authors shy away from doing whole books focused on murder and mayhem, which means that most YA mysteries are concerned with more than the crime. They are also shorter than mysteries for adults, and instead of having professional detectives, the protagonists are likely to be bright and energetic young people, not yet cynical about the world. The violence is more likely to be underplayed, possibly at the edge of the story. The victim is often connected to the protagonist—a family member, a friend, an admired adult, a boyfriend or girlfriend—and the protagonist is virtually forced to enter the game and examine the puzzle.

Robert Cormier's *The Rag and Bone Shop* illustrates most of these characteristics. Seven-year-old Alicia is found murdered only a few hundred yards from her home, and the police have no physical evidence and no suspects. Twelve-year-old Jason, a neighbor and friend, was the last person to see her. To satisfy community pressure, the police arrest him and then bring in an out-of-town interrogator who has a reputation for getting confessions out of suspects. The interrogator, named Trent, works more quickly than did the psychiatrist/interrogator in Cormier's earlier mystery *I Am the Cheese*. In *The Rag and Bone Shop*, there is some evidence that Jason has antisocial attitudes, but mostly he is just shy. It is because he can't stand up to the neighborhood bullies that he spent so much time with the younger Alicia.

The interrogator is particularly motivated because he is hoping that solving this high-profile case will bring him a political appointment. His behavior is all

Now that many restrictions about "appropriateness" have been lifted, teen mysteries are read by almost as many adults as teens. See Focus Box 7.4, "Edgar Award Winners as Year's Best YA Mystery Since 2000," to learn more about them.

Focus Box 7.4

Edgar Award Winners as Year's Best YA Mystery Since 2000

NOTE: The books won the prize in the year following publication.

Acceleration by Graham McNamee. Philomel, 2003.
Seventeen-year-old Duncan has a job at the Toronto subway lost-and-found, where he sifts through piles of junk and finds a strange, leather-bound diary of a would-be serial killer. Since the police don't seem to be interested, he has to take matters into his own hands, so with his two best friends he tries to track down and trap the murderer before he can strike.

The Boy in the Burning House by Tim Wynne-Jones. FSG, 2001. Ruth Rose, a teenage girl, overhears the creepy confessions of her smiling but vicious stepfather. He is the Pastor of the Church of the Blessed Transfiguration in a remote farming community. The confession is about the murder of Jim Hawkins's father, Hub. Later, Jim discovers that his father and Ruth's father had been involved in a fire that caused the death of a teenage boy thirty years before.

Buried by Robin M. MacCready. Penguin, 2006.
Claudine's mother is an alcoholic who runs a small art business during the summer months, when she claims to be sobering up. But in the autumn, she always falls off the wagon, and sometimes disappears, leaving Claudine to clean up all of the bottles and stains on the rug. Claudine tells her therapy group that her mother has checked herself into rehab, and after a while Claudine begins to believe her own lie. In the end, Claudine has to deal with years of angry denial and enabling, but her successes allow readers to be encouraged and uplifted.

Counterfeit Son by Elaine Marie Alphin. Harcourt, 2000. Pop kidnapped children, but when he was killed, resisting arrest, Cameron, one of the children that Pop had abducted, tried to pass himself off as Neil Lacey as a way of distancing himself from what Pop had done to him and the other boys. As Neil Lacey, Cameron was a rich kid who sailed his own boat, but when Cougar, one of Pop's old accomplices in crime, gets out of prison, he tracks down Cameron and presents him with an ultimatum: share the wealth or be exposed.

In Darkness, Death by Dorothy Hoobler and Thomas Hoobler. Philomel, 2004. Judge Ooka investigates the murder of Samurai Lord Inabu, who was killed while sleeping in his palace in Edo. A paper origami butterfly is a clue that is left at the scene of this bloody crime. This is the third book of the Samurai Mysteries.

the more repulsive when he keeps pursuing the "confession," even after readers suspect that he knows Jason is innocent. But, thankfully, readers—and Jason—get a reprieve in the very last sentence.

For a good sampling of what is considered to be "the best" in young adult mysteries, look at Focus Box 7.4, "Edgar Award Winners as Year's Best YA Mystery Since 2000," to see the winners of the Edgar Award, which is given each year for the best young adult mystery.

One of the most intriguing books on our 2008 Honor List was Judy Blundell's *What I Saw and How I Lied.* Although the fine print in the front of the book recommends cataloguing it as *coming of age, secrets, Florida,* and *20th-century history,* we think it qualifies as an intriguing mystery. It is set in 1947 just after World War II, when Evie's stepfather, Joe, comes home to reunite with Evie and her mother, along with Joe's mother.

While Joe was fighting the Germans in Europe, the three women had been fighting each other as they lived together in a house in Queens that belongs to Joe's mother. The story starts after the family has been back together long enough for Joe to buy and open a couple of appliance stores. Evie and her mother are happily

Interrogation of Gabriel James by Charlie Price, FSG, 2010. Gabriel James, a Montana teenager who has been the eyewitness to two killings, is being interrogated by police about the murders. Gabriel gradually comes to realize the link between one of his classmate's disturbing home life and the outbreak of local crimes. During the interrogation, Gabriel also becomes increasingly confused about his own culpability in the crimes.

Last Shot by John Feinstein. Knopf, 2005. Stevie Thomas and Susan Carol Anderson win a fourteen-and-under writing contest about basketball. Part of their prize is that they receive press credentials to the Final Four games in New Orleans, where they overhear Michigan State University's star player, Chip Grabber, being blackmailed. When they later talk with Chip, they discover that if Chip doesn't throw the game, Chip's dad, the MSU coach, would be fired, and all of the team wins for the season would be taken away. Chip and his friends work together to try to stop the blackmailer.

Paper Towns by John Green. Penguin, 2008. Quentin is reunited with Margo, a childhood friend he has loved for years. After a night of breaking into Sea World and exploring closed tourist shops, Margo disappears and Quentin and his friends set out to find her, following obscure clues they think she left for them.

Rat Life: A Mystery by Tedd Arnold. Penguin, 2007. In this gritty teen mystery set in 1972, Todd learns of a dead body that has been recovered in the Chemanga River. Todd struggles with the pressures of his creative writing assignments, his responsibilities at his parents' motel, and his grandmother's failing health, plus his job at a local drive-in theatre working for an under aged Vietnam vet by the name of Rat.

Reality Check by Peter Abrahams. HarperCollins, 2009. Cody is the quarterback of a pretty good high school team, and the college scouts are checking him out. He's doing well in his classes, and is dating Clea, the hottest girl in school. But then things start to go South when Clea is sent to a prep school in the East, and Cody tears his ACL, leaving him on the bench for the rest of the season, and maybe the rest of his football career. His grades plummet and he drops out of school, and then he hears that Clea has gone missing. . . .

The Wessex Papers, Vol. 1–3 by Daniel Parker. Avon, 2002. *The Wessex Papers* is a trilogy resolving a long and involved mystery. The first book, *Trust Falls* introduces the reader to an old-money rebel named Sunday Winthrop, a middle-class rebel named Fred Wright, and the complex social world of snobbish Wessex Academy. In *Fallout,* the second volume, Sunday and Fred reveal their feelings for each other. And in the final volume, Sunday and Fred reveal the blackmailers to the school, making everybody's life much more pleasant.

dreaming about moving out of Joe's family home and into a house of their own, but mostly fifteen-year-old Evie is thinking about the opening of school and how soon she can start smoking and wearing lipstick. Just before the school year starts, Joe suddenly decides that he will take Evie and her mother on a family trip to Florida.

The book opens with a scene that fits into the story much later, but is reprinted on page one because it is crucial that readers understand both the mother in the story and the relationship between Evie and her mother. Evie is the narrator and begins with the following: "The match snapped, then sizzled, and I woke up fast. I heard my mother inhale as she took a long pull on a cigarette. Her lips stuck on the filter, so I knew she was still wearing lipstick. She'd been up all night." As the air around Evie is filled with cigarette smoke and My Sin perfume (her mother's "smell"), Evie pretends to be asleep, while Evie's mother pretends not to know that Evie is awake.

Money—how people get it and what they do with it—is a big part of the story, and so is the post-war prejudice that many people felt against Jews, but the part that is probably going to resonate the most forcefully with girl readers is Evie's developing sexuality and the niggling feeling of competition that she had with her mother, while also feeling a fierce loyalty that goes back to the time before Joe entered the picture. All of this comes out when tragedy strikes the day before the family is scheduled to return from Florida to New York.

What I Saw in the title has two meanings. It includes what Evie literally saw, but more importantly it alludes to what she figures out because of knowing her parents so well and from her keen observations of what is happening all around her. The Florida visit is complicated by the unexpected appearance of Peter, a young soldier who had served under Sergeant Joe in Germany. It turns out that Joe had suddenly decided on the trip to Florida as a way of avoiding contact with Peter. But Peter is not to be thwarted and so he steals a car and follows the family to Florida.

Another clue to the meaning of the story is that the second part of the title is not *Why I Lied,* but *How I Lied.* Evie's court testimony is way too sophisticated to have been plotted out either by her parents or their lawyer, and certainly not by a fifteen-year-old girl. However, it is a testament to Blundell's writing that the court accepts Evie's testimony as the truth. It is also a testament to Blundell's writing that readers accept it for what it is: a concoction so sophisticated that both we as teachers, along with our students, will have a hard time explaining just which parts are "true" and which parts are "lies." We'll also have to put on some heavy-duty thinking caps as we discuss the motivation and the likely results of Evie's decision to punish herself and her family.

Other YA books that have been popular include Patricia Windsor's *The Christmas Killer,* which is set in a Connecticut town terrorized by a killer, and Joan Lowery Nixon's *Whisper from the Dead* which is about a young girl who discovers a body floating in a pool, a typical ploy for Nixon, who is eager to grab her readers' attention. Kevin Brooks's *The Road of the Dead* features fourteen-year-old Ruben who knows absolutely that his sister has been murdered, so Ruben and his brother, Cole, travel to Dartmoor to bring her body home and to find her killer. Joaquin Dorfman's *Playing It Cool* focuses on Sebastian, who solves problems for his friends. When he agrees to track down a friend's birth father, he also agrees to switch identities with his friend, and that is when the trouble begins. For many teens, Lois Duncan's *Killing Mr. Griffin* is still their favorite. See the write-up on her as a winner of the Margaret A. Edwards Award on page 253.

A new mystery that is getting a lot of attention is Craig Silvey's *Jasper Jones,* which is much more than a *who-dunnit.* The title character is an outcast in a small Australian town who discovers the corpse of one of the town's prominent young women hanging from a tree near his "home" in the glade. He sneaks to the house of the only friend he thinks he can trust and knocks on the window of fourteen-year-old Charlie Bucktin. The two boys set out to solve the murder. They can't just go to the police because they know that Jasper Jones will be blamed. Reviewers praised the book but cautioned that because of the language it probably will be more appropriate for older teens.

Jenny Hubbard's *Paper Covers Rock* goes beyond just uncovering "the truth." It is set in a boarding school in the 1980s. One of the boys at the school drowns and 16-year-old Alex worries about his part in the tragedy. He is not certain about what happened; nevertheless he does not tell what he knows even though his silence destroys a young teacher's career. A survival story for

Margaret A. Edwards Award

Winner (1992)

Lois Duncan, **A True Storyteller**

The Margaret A. Edwards committee honored Duncan for her autobiographical *Chapters: My Growth as a Writer* and for her mystery/suspense books, *I Know What You Did Last Summer; Killing Mr. Griffin; Ransom; Summer of Fear;* and *The Twisted Window.*

Of all the Edwards Award winners, Duncan probably became a professional at the youngest age. She began submitting stories to magazines when she was ten. She sold her first short story when she was thirteen to *Calling All Girls,* and her first young adult novel, *Debutante Hill,* when she was twenty. At age twenty-seven, she found herself a single mother needing to support three young children. As she told Roger Sutton in a June 1992 *School Library Journal* interview, she grew up fast while learning to write not only the page-turners that kids love her for, but also children's books and articles for women's magazines including *Ladies Home Journal, McCall's, Redbook,* and *Reader's Digest.* She did not want to be the kind of author who wrote the same story over and over again and so as soon as she finished with one book, she refreshed her palate with a different kind of writing and then went back to telling a new YA story.

Killing Mr. Griffin is one of her best-known books. She said it was inspired by her oldest daughter's first real boyfriend. While he was "the most charming young man you could ever meet," he was also a budding psychopath—"the kind of guy who would swerve in the road to run over a dog." She began wondering what a boy like this could do, how he could influence other teenagers, if he put his mind to it. Out of this wondering came a book that since 1978 has been read by hundreds of thousands of teenagers in spite of the fact that it regularly makes its way onto lists of censored books.

I Know What You Did Last Summer is also well known, partly because it was made into a major film. For an earlier edition of this textbook, Duncan confessed that one of the most exciting evenings of her life was going to the theater to see "her" story, but her excitement soon turned into such disappointment that she forgot to eat her popcorn. The film was so different from the book that at first she thought she was in the wrong theater, but then she recognized some of her teenage characters, just not the adults or the setting. She had no boat in her story, but most of the movie takes place on a fishing boat owned by an insane man who chases the teenagers with a large meat hook. A boy, new to the story, gets shoved into a vat of boiling water, and when her heroine opens the trunk of a car she finds a corpse with crabs coming out of its mouth. But this is nothing compared to when she has to hide in a bin of ice surrounded by the cut-off heads of her friends.

Duncan said that she has always taken pride in being professional about the business side of her career and she understands that changes sometimes have to be made between a print edition and a film edition. "But the soul of a story should not be destroyed in the process. For a book that has been a mainstay in middle school literature classes for over 23 years, to be transformed into a slasher film without the knowledge and consent of the author goes past what is acceptable."

Fortunately, Duncan has had much better experiences with recent movies. Her agent began selling some of her older stories to Hollywood. Six aired as television dramas, but the most successful *Hotel for Dogs* went to the big screen. The producers even let Duncan come and be in one scene. She was amazed at how many trained dogs they had and at how each dog had a twin, so they could take turns in their acting roles. She shared these details at the 2010 ALAN Conference in Florida. Another interesting detail that she shared is that ten of her YA suspense novels are being re-released and she has been asked to "update" them. She didn't realize how many of her plots were based on troubles caused by characters not being able to communicate. So now her biggest challenge is figuring out credible ways for her totally modern kids to somehow lose their cell phones. ●

older readers is Andrew Smith's 2008 *Ghost Medicine.* Set in the mountains of California, it is about seventeen-year-old Troy Stotts who carries the huge responsibility of saving his family's ranch after his mother unexpectedly dies. His job is made that much harder by the sheriff's son, who hates Troy for embarrassing him in front of a girl.

Carl Hiassen's *Scat* is a new addition to his ecology-based stories for middle school readers. As with his earlier books it is set in Florida and it is the kids who do much of the detective work when a biology teacher disappears during a field trip. Another book for younger readers is Siobhan Dowd's *The London Eye Mystery,* in which two siblings—one who is good at reading emotions and one who is good at deduction—join together to find their cousin who has disappeared.

A New Kind of Mystery for Teens

Because of the ever-growing popularity of fantasy with teens, we probably should not have been surprised to read a new book that is a combination mystery and fantasy novel. It is Franny Billingsley's 2011 *Chime,* which is a National Book Award finalist and one of our 2011 Honor List books. It is about two twin sisters, Briony and Rose Larkin, who live in the far north of England in the early 1900s. A major theme in the book is what sometimes happens when new technology comes face-to-face with old beliefs and superstitions.

An engineer from London comes to the village of Swampsea, bringing with him his "bad boy" son, Eldric. Actually, Eldric is more playful than "bad" and more a man than a "boy." The engineer's job is to figure out how to drain the large swamp which practically surrounds the parsonage where the Larkin family lives. Eldric's job is to live at the parsonage and to receive tutoring, in hopes of getting re-admitted to college. Clergyman Larkin, who according to Briony, "irons his voice" before speaking has the job of supervising Eldric's tutoring.

We Nilsens first tried listening to *Chime* on a CD, but then found that the chapters, the paragraphs, and even some of the sentences were so "full" that we needed to read the book in its print version so we could circle back to lines and paragraphs that were especially intriguing. Early in the book, Billingsley has her protagonist, Briony, reminisce about the day her stepmother died and how she stood outside the sickroom door, wondering if she should enter:

> Why did I hesitate? I was afraid of awakening her, I suppose, which I'd call ironic if I were a poet, but I'm not, and anyway, I hate poetry. A poem doesn't come out and tell you what it has to say. It circles back on itself, eating its own tail and making you guess what it means.

We aren't poets either, but still we would say Briony is making an ironic statement because she is the narrator of the story, and it has been a long time since we read a more poetic book or one that circled back on itself forcing us to get involved in figuring out what is happening and in transferring the images from Billingsley's mind to our own minds.

Briony and Rose's mother died early, and the girls were raised by a stepmother, who recently died from arsenic poisoning. Briony and Rose are "porcelain" twins, meaning they are beautiful to look at but oh-so-fragile. Rose has something akin to Asperger's or Autism, while Briony, thanks to her stepmother's manipulative "teachings," is convinced that she is a witch. Briony is left-handed, a "witchy" characteristic that she tries to hide. Also, Briony has "no birthday," another mark of being a witch. This apparently happened because while Rose was born ten minutes before midnight, Briony was born exactly at midnight and apparently the midwife did not know which date to record and so she left the space blank.

Rose has never been outside of Swampsea and other than communicating with her stepmother and trying to appease Rose, her companions have been the Old Ones—the spirits, both good and bad, that she envisions as inhabiting the bog. The residents of Swampsea are generally unhealthy, perhaps from tuberculosis, but Briony thinks they get the Swamp Cough when the Old Ones are displeased, which surely they must be now that engineers are coming to town figuring out how to build a railroad and how to drain the swamp. Briony is convinced that she is responsible both for Rose's condition and that it is her fault that the Old Ones gave Rose her condition and have now given her the Swamp Cough. Rose goes to the swamp to talk to them and even to make blood (she cuts herself) and salt sacrifices. She is also convinced that she was responsible for her mother's death. It is a backwards kind of mystery, in which the person on trial (which is where the book opens) is convinced she is guilty, while it is the jury's duty to convince her otherwise. Thanks to Eldric—the "bad boy-man" Rose is not hung as a witch.

We were surprised to read on the back of the book that Billingsley graduated from Tufts University and the Boston University School of Law because she sounds for-all-the-world like a native of northern England or Scotland. But then we went to her website and learned that she grew up in a family with five children and every night her father would sing songs to the children once they were in bed. Each child could choose two songs, and Franny often chose the old Scottish ballads that her father loved to sing. She spent fifth grade going to school in Denmark, "a fairytale place" where she immersed herself in the stories of Hans Christian Anderson. She wrote:

> My memories of that year come to me now as though through a magical lens: the statue of the little Mermaid rising from the gray waves of the Copenhagen harbor; myself at Christmas, wearing a crown of lighted candles; the Snow Queen's palace, present everywhere in the dark afternoons, the drifts of snow, the moonshot ice.

It isn't so much Billingsley's memories, but the spirit and the magical wording which makes her book so unusual. It could as easily be considered a book of historical fiction or a book about relationships between humans and nonhumans, but we chose to put it in this chapter as a mystery to illustrate the point that young adult authors are continually taking chances and coming up with new combinations of old genres.

Another book that we might include as combinations of mystery and fantasy is *The Monstrumologist* by Rick Yancey. This horror story is supposedly the diary of William Henry, who lived to be something like 130 years old, because of what he came in contact with when as a boy he worked as an assistant to a self-educated "doctor" in 1888 New England. The doctor hoped to become as famous as Charles Darwin; however, his fame would come not from the study of living creatures, but of horrible creatures from the afterlife that he and Will collected from graveyards. The book has some similarities to Marcus Sedgwick's *White Crow,* which is a chilling mystery about a girl who goes on a seaside vacation with her father to an English village. She makes friends with a local girl and then finds herself pulled into the 18th century where a local rector communicates with corpses.

Concluding Comments

This chapter has been about literature that is sometimes treated as "nonessential," mostly because it tugs at emotional more than intellectual parts of our brains. In today's high-tech world, however, it may be that this is the very kind of reading that serves to remind us of our humanity and our need to reach out and understand the emotions of others.

Historical Fiction: Of People and Places

The United States has always viewed history in its own way. More than a century ago, Ralph Waldo Emerson described the great American tradition as "trampling on tradition," and Abraham Lincoln said that Americans had a "perfect rage for the new." But by the beginning of the twentieth century, Americans were feeling more confident and began to look back. U.S. history became a standard part of the school curriculum, thousands of towns erected statues of Abraham Lincoln and Ulysses S. Grant, and historical pageants flourished, including in the South, where Confederates began to look back with pride on their role in the Civil War.

We are focusing on fiction in this chapter and saving nonfiction for Chapter 9, but we confess that we haven't been perfect in making this distinction. The two genres are so closely associated in people's minds that authors of fiction sometimes feel it necessary to include some kind of a clue in their titles, as with the full title of *The Boy in the Striped Pajamas: A Fable* by John Boyne and with the title of *When My Name Was Keoko: A Novel of Korea in World War II* by Linda Sue Park. And in the case of *Annexed*, a 2010 book by Sharon Dogar, it would be hard to explain this fictional book without tying it into the nonfiction *The Diary of Anne Frank*. Dogar wrote her book to tell the story from the point of view of Peter van Pels, the boy whose family hid Anne's family in their attic annex. Some critics are worried about having a fictional book stand alongside a nonfiction account, but teachers should probably view the "matching" books as a way to explore some of the differences between fiction and nonfiction and also as a good way to teach about point of view.

We will first address historical fiction in general and then, in the second part of the chapter, discuss fiction that in some way relates to war. And occasionally we will include materials written for both adults and young adults because the reporting of history for a general audience is often done in a manner accessible to young readers.

Historical Fiction about a Variety of People and Places

Reading historical novels satisfies our curiosity about other times, places, and people; even more importantly, it provides adventure, suspense, and mystery. As with any literary form, there are standards for judging historical novels. They should be historically accurate and steeped in time and place. We should recognize totems and taboos, food, clothing, vocations, leisure activities, customs, smells, religions, literature, and all that goes into making one time and one place unique. Enthusiasts forgive no anachronism, no matter how slight. Historical novels should give a sense of history's continuity, a feeling for the flow of history from one time into another. Historical novels should tell a lively story with a sense of impending danger, mystery, suspense, or romance. See Focus Box 8.1, "Historical Fiction Set in the United States," for examples of such books. And most importantly, authors need to avoid simplifying the issues and stereotyping "the bad" vs. "the good." The characters need to be so fully developed that they will "come alive" so that readers will realize they have things in common. And of course they also need to have excitement and romance, or they won't have readers. Because of the excitement, some of the novels in this chapter could just as easily have been placed in Chapter 7 on Adventures, which, in fact, is what we did when we decided to place the westerns in that chapter instead of in this one.

Historical novels allow us—and at their best, they force us—to make connections and to realize that despair is as old and as new as hope, and that loyalty and treachery, love and hatred, compassion and cruelty were, and are, inherent in humanity, whether it be in ancient Greece, Elizabethan England, or post–World War I Germany. As with most writers, historical novelists may want to teach

Although most of the books in Focus Boxes 8.1, "Historical Fiction Set in the United States" (p. 259), and 8.2, "Historical Fiction Set in the World-at-Large" (p. 260), take place much earlier than the 1960s, psychologists are finding that young readers have a hard time imagining time periods older than the oldest people they know, which is probably their grandparents.

U.S. HISTORICAL FICTION

**Historical Fiction Set
in the United States**

***Bread and Roses, Too* by Katherine Paterson. Clarion, 2006.** As she did in her 1992 *Lyddie*, Paterson writes about the awful labor conditions that existed in the New England mills at the turn of the last century when prejudices and ethnic rivalries added a new layer of danger to already tense labor protests.

***Copper Sun* by Sharon Draper. S&S/Atheneum, 2006.** The worst aspects of slavery and the best sides of friendship are illustrated through this story of a fifteen-year-old girl taken to a Carolina plantation from her African home.

***Counting on Grace* by Elizabeth Winthrop. Random, 2006.** Winthrop's story was inspired by a Lewis Hines 1910 photo of a French Canadian girl, who was one of the "mill rats," working long hours in terrible conditions.

***Crooked River* by Shelley Pearsall. Knopf, 2005.** This story for young teens, set in 1812 Ohio, is about the friendship that develops between thirteen-year-old Rebecca Carver and Amik, an Indian man accused of murder and chained in the loft of the Carvers' cabin.

***The Evolution of Calpurnia Tate* by Jacqueline Kelly. Holt, 2009.** In this book for middle school readers, Charles Darwin's *Origin of Species*—with a little help from Calpurnia's grandfather—helps a young girl get through a long, hot Texas summer in the late 1890s.

***The Horse Thief: A Novel* by Robert Newton Peck. HarperCollins, 2002.** It is 1938 in Chickalooke, Florida, and seventeen-year-old Tullis Yoder has a job taking care of the horses in a rodeo. When the owner falls on hard times and decides to sell the horses to a slaughterhouse, Tullis and various "helpers" steal the horses and lead them to life.

***How It Happened in Peach Hill* by Marthe Jocelyn. Random, 2007.** During the Roaring Twenties, fifteen-year-old Annie travels through upstate New York with her mother who advertises herself as a spiritual adviser and fortune-teller. In a short-lived scheme, Annie pretends to be severely retarded so she can tell her mother what she overhears.

***Lizzie Bright and the Buckminster Boy* by Gary D. Schmidt. Clarion, 2004.** Schmidt was on summer vacation in Maine when he heard the haunting story of how at the turn of the century an African American community was "cleared off" from a Maine island so that a nearby community could develop its tourist industry.

***No Promises in the Wind* by Irene Hunt. Follett, 1970.** During the Great Depression, fifteen-year-old Josh leaves home with his brother and a friend to find shelter and food.

***Sacrifice* by Kathleen Benner Duble. Simon & Schuster, 2005.** In 1692 Massachusetts, Abigail and her sister are accused and imprisoned for being witches. Their mother comes up with a terrible plan to free them.

***Three Rivers Rising: A Novel of the Johnstown Flood* by Jane Richards. Knopf/Borzoi, 2010.** This free-verse novel recreates the disastrous Eastern Pennsylvania Flood of 1889, and in the process reveals some of the complications of class differences when a coal-miner's son and the daughter of a wealthy family work together.

***Uncommon Faith* by Trudy Krisher. Holiday House, 2003.** Cataclysmic events nearly always have repercussions long after the event itself, and Krisher's book illustrates this in relation to a Millbrook, Massachusetts livery fire that killed six people and injured many others in the summer of 1837.

***The Unresolved* by T. K. Welsh. Dutton, 2006.** On June 15, 1904, more than a thousand people from the German section of New York City die in a terrible fire that occurs during an afternoon pleasure cruise on the *General Slocum* steamship. Welsh gives the story a supernatural slant through the part played by the ghost of fifteen-year-old Mallory Meer, whose Jewish boyfriend (a survivor) is accused of starting the fire.

***Where the Great Hawk Flies* by Liza Ketchum. Clarion, 2005.** Two boys in 1782 are enemies and later friends—one white and one half-Indian.

particular lessons. Christopher Collier, for example, makes no pretense about why he and his brother write about the American Revolution in their historical novels. He wrote in the August 1982 *School Library Journal* that:

> The books I write with my brother are written with a didactic purpose to teach about ideals and values that have been important in shaping the course of American

***The Book of Mordred* by Vivian Vande Velde. Houghton Mifflin, 2005.** After the fall of Camelot, a young widow seeks help from young Sir Mordred. Velde portrays a lost time when King Arthur and Mordred disagree on what is right for Camelot.

***Broken Song* by Kathryn Lasky. Viking, 2005.** Reuven, a Jewish boy in Russia at the turn of the last century, made his first appearance in Lasky's 1981 *The Night Journey,* but now he's back for this well-researched account of anti-Semitism in Russia and what it took for him to save his sister and himself.

***The Canterbury Papers* by Judith Koll Healey. Morrow, 2004.** Queen Eleanor of Aquitaine asks Princess Alais of France to bring back a packet of letters hidden in Canterbury Cathedral. Alais learns that she is not the only one interested in the letters.

***Dante's Daughter* by Kimberley Burton Heuston. Front Street, 2003.** This fictional memoir is a good illustration of how an author can make a story more interesting to young readers by having it told through the eyes of a young person, in this case, Dante's only daughter, Antonia Alighieri, who eventually entered a convent.

***The Edge on the Sword* by Rebecca Tingle. Putnam, 2001.** Set in late ninth-century England, this is the imagined story of the teen years of Ethelflaed of Mercia, an extraordinarily accomplished woman noted in the Anglo-Saxon Chronicle.

***Guantanamo Boy* by Anna Perera. Albert Whitman, 2011.** Just after 9/11, a British boy who is visiting in Pakistan is arrested and detained at Guantanamo Bay.

***Incantation* by Alice Hoffman. Little, Brown, 2006.** Hoffman uses the background of the Spanish Inquisition to tell a powerful story of friendship, faith, jealousy, resilience, and love. The protagonist is sixteen-year-old Estrella, whose family pretends to be Catholic but secretly keeps their Jewish faith.

***Life: An Exploded Diagram* by Mal Peet. Candlewick, 2011.** This look at two British kids (star-crossed lovers) during the Cuban Missile Crisis and Englands class war was praised for its ambition and sophistication.

***A Single Shard* by Linda Sue Park. Clarion, 2001.** This winner of the Newbery Medal is set in twelfth-century Korea and is a good illustration of the archetypal journey. A young orphan apprentices himself to a master craftsman of celadon pottery and must take a sample of his master's work to the royal palace.

***Thursday's Child* by Sonya Hartnett. Candlewick, 2002.** This novel makes clear that life in the Australian Depression was no better than that during the American Depression.

history. This is in no way intended to denigrate the importance of the dramatic and literary elements of historical novels. Nothing will be taught, and certainly nothing learned, if no one reads the books. (p. 32)

Collier later wrote in the *ALAN Review* that "there is no better way to teach history than to embrace potential readers and fling them into a living past." Novelist Patricia Lee Gauch observed in the Fall 1993 *ALAN Review* that:

> Surely the appeal of historical story has something to do with the ironies of history. Because we know the ending, the twists of fate, the upside downness of history, and the unpredictability, it is particularly poignant. Not only is there craziness . . . but add to the games of history the obvious capriciousness that a long look at historical events reveals. (p. 13)

We used to make World War II our dividing line between *contemporary* and *historical* fiction, but as we have gotten older and our students have gotten younger, we changed and made our dividing line the Vietnam War. We may have been influenced by reading what Cathi MacRae wrote in the September 1991 *Wilson Library Bulletin* where she told about the research of Harvard psychologist Diana Paolitto on how children develop their concepts of time. Paolitto was astonished to find that her teenage subjects were unable to conceive of a past unless they knew someone who had lived at that time. "In other words," she reported, "the furthest back most young adults can extend credibility is the lifetime of the oldest people they know, probably grandparents." She said that this probably means that teenagers can hardly relate intimately to any time prior to the twentieth century. She was writing this twenty years ago, and so today she might have said prior to the 1950s. Then she concluded with asking, "Is there research to indicate at what age people begin to believe in history? Could it be when individuals have lived long enough to have a history of their own?" (p. 102).

Certainly in our classes we have found that students believe the first sentence in the Prologue to L. P. Hartley's *The Go-Between*, where he wrote, "The past is a foreign country: they do things differently there." This is a good comparison because there are so many different kinds of historical fiction—mysteries, comedies, adventures, realistic problem stories, and several other genres—that no single characterization can be used to define them. The only thing all the books have in common is that they are set in the past. Once our students stop expecting all historical novels to be like grand, movie spectaculars, such as *Gone with the Wind* or *The Ten Commandments*, then they can sit back and think of many books they have read and loved that were "historical."

Historical novels can take readers any place they want to go—or fear to go—and in any period of time they would like. In the last few years, a virtual industry of books about Shakespeare and his time have appeared. Gary Blackwood's *The Shakespeare Stealer* and its sequels, *The Shakespeare Scribe* and *Shakespeare's Spy*, introduced readers to fourteen-year-old Widge, who knows a form of shorthand, becomes a member of Shakespeare's company, falls in love with Shakespeare's daughter, and attempts to finish a play begun by Shakespeare. Lisa Fiedler's *Dating Hamlet: Ophelia's Story* revealed a new view of Ophelia, a woman who loves and stands by Hamlet and is willing to act mad to move Hamlet's plan forward. Fiedler's *Romeo's Ex: Rosaline's Story* moved Romeo and Juliet to the sidelines and focused on the fair Rosaline and her many suitors. Carolyn Meyer's *Loving Will Shakespeare* gives insights into Anne Hathaway's fear of being unloved and her recognition that Will Shakespeare at eighteen is handsome and intelligent. Philip Gooden sets *Alms for Oblivion: A Shakespearean Murder Mystery* in Shakespeare's company where a young member finds another member murdered and other bodies soon appear.

There are unlimited time periods and places in which writers might set their stories. For example, Donna Jo Napoli's *Daughter of Venice* is set in late sixteenth-century Venice with all its sinister intrigues. A trip to King Arthur's time can easily be had through Sarah L. Thomson's *The Dragon's Son*, with its newly created legends about Arthur. An equally easy trip can be made to the Crusades in *The Book of the Lion*, by the prolific and reliable Michael Cadnum, with his portrait of the adventures and horrors experienced in the Holy Land by a seventeen-year-old knight crusader's squire. Kathryn Lasky's

Beyond the Burning Time is a fine novel focusing on the terrors of the Salem witch trials. We suggest offering it to students along with Stephanie Hemphill's 2010 *Wicked Girls: A Novel of the Salem Witch Trials,* which is told in free verse. Hemphill illustrates how "group-think" can have dreadful consequences, whether in the seventeenth or the twenty-first centuries.

Jennifer L. Holm's *Turtle in Paradise,* a 2010 Newbery Honor Book, is a wonderful example of the concept of *roman à clef,* a literary term taken from French where *roman* means "novel" and *clef* means "key." The idea is that the historical details are the key to the story. This is the same *roman* that we see in *romance* (which comes from the *Romance* languages originating in Rome) and, less obviously because it has been affected by German, in *bildungsroman,* to refer to a novel about the "building" of the protagonist's character.

In connection to Holm's story, which is set in Florida during the Great Depression of the 1930s, her protagonist is named Turtle, because she "has a hard shell." When Turtle is introducing herself to the readers, she explains that "Mama has soft blue eyes and all she sees are kittens and roses. My eyes are gray as soot, and I see things for what they are." The gang of middle school boys she makes friends with includes one boy called Beans because he's always near his friend Pork Chop, (i.e., they are Pork and Beans). The boys call themselves The Diaper Gang because they earn their spending money by giving exhausted mothers an afternoon break by taking their babies for rides in their wagon. Holm demonstrates how in the 1930s the movies, the radio, and the funny papers provided the entertainment necessary for people to escape from their worries over the bad economic times. The children make such remarks as "The Diaper Gang Knows . . . ," which comes from their listening to *The Shadow* on the radio. They also talk about their favorite heroes from the funny papers: *Terry and the Pirates, Krazy Kat, Flash Gordon,* and especially *Little Orphan Annie.* And when Turtle gets depressed she sings Shirley Temple's "On the good ship lollipop," song, but her real fantasy is getting into the movies and beating out Shirley for an Academy Award. She even knows what intonation she will use when she says, "Sorry, Shirley. Maybe next year."

Zora and Me by Victoria Bond and T. R. Simon is another 2010 example of a *roman à clef* story appealing to junior high readers, and maybe to older readers who have already met Zora Neal Hurston through her writing. It too is set in a small Florida town, except earlier because Hurston was born in 1891 and in the story she seems to be about ten. It is told through the eyes of Carrie and Teddy (Carrie is the narrator), two friends of the most amazing storyteller they have ever met. The book opens with a mystery. A young man's body is found lying by the railroad tracks. His death upsets the town, but Zora jumps in with an imaginative explanation that she's willing to share, even with the sheriff. The next big problem that her creative mind goes to work on is the existence of a murderous, shape-shifting gator-man who is half-man and half-gator. The book, which was especially fun to listen to on CD, is being praised for its liveliness and its humor and for the careful research into Hurston's life and her work, which is reflected only indirectly in the story.

A piece of historical fiction that sets an entirely different tone and is for older readers is Chris Crowe's *Mississippi Trial 1955,* about the killing of Emmett Till, a black teenager from the North who had the foolish, or bad, manners to joke with a white Southern woman. Crowe also wrote a nonfictional account of the event, *Getting Away with Murder: The True Story of the Emmett Till Case.* We taught both books together and, for a change of pace, included Marilyn Nelson's 2005 *A Wreath for Emmett Till,* in which Nelson used an arcane poetic form to prepare "a crown of sonnets" to honor Till.

Five Recent and Important Historical Novels

M. T. Anderson's *The Astonishing Life of Octavian Nothing, Traitor to the Nation* and its sequel, which has the subtitle of *Volume II: The Kingdom on the Waves,* are novels set in 1760s and 1770s New England. In the first book, Octavian, the narrator; his mother, the lovely Cassiopeia brought from Africa; and Mr. Gitney, a member of the Novanglian College of Lucidity, live in a luxurious house of scholars intent on observing Octavian and giving him the best possible education in hopes of settling the old question of whether nature or nurture is the primary influence on what children grow to be. Members of the College divine secrets of the universe by writing poetry, drawing, and performing sundry experiments that are heartless and pointless. Their absurdity may remind readers of *Gulliver's Travels* and the Grand Academy of Lagoda with all its madness.

Octavian is taught Greek, Latin, mathematics, botany, and music—he plays the violin superbly. His food is weighed before he eats, and his excrement is caught on a gold platter and also weighed. Gitney assures Octavian his education equals that of the princes of Europe. The boy has no idea who or what he is, but Gitney's black valet assures Octavian that he is as African as the valet. Asked why he is treated as he is, Mr. Gitney replies, "We wish to divine whether you are a separate and distinct species." Unsure what that means, Octavian asks, "You wish to prove that I am the equal of any other?" Gitney corrects the boy, "We wish to prove nothing. We simply aim at discovering the truth."

Later, when the College desperately needs money, it comes from a consortium anxious to prove that Africans are inferior to white people. At that point, Octavian's education changes and the novel opens up into a sweeping story that takes in the Revolutionary War.

Volume II opens with little that suggests safety. A boat that seems to promise safety offers no help until Dr. Trefusis, in a scholarly gesture, addresses the boatman as "Gentle Charon" and adds, "I have obols on my tongue." The boatman is no scholar and, not understanding the allusion, threatens violence. Octavian immediately translates, "My master offers you money," and Octavian and Trefusis are on their way to Boston.

But Boston is a disappointment. Octavian seeks work without success, but finally a skill that Octavian learned at the Novanglian College of Lucidity serves them. He gets a job with his violin playing in the orchestra that performs for the British troops. However, that is about the only good luck that Octavian has. He is generally treated as an outsider by both blacks and whites, and it matters not, when the British run out of money and so sell the black soldiers who had sworn loyalty to England back into slavery.

M. T. Anderson is a master storyteller. His impressive accomplishments include the description of the horrors of wars and contagions, his portrait of the insanity of the Novanglian College of Lucidity, his picture of the Revolutionary War that is a terrible contrast to what we learned in our history classes, and his

Allison and Chelsea are creative writing majors. They enrolled in our YA literature class because that's the genre they most enjoy reading and so that's what they want to write. Here they are wondering if they could ever be as clever as was Markus Zusak in The Book Thief.

creation of Octavian Nothing as a believable human that readers care about. Anderson's plot, full of convolutions, horrors, and, surprisingly enough, humor, will keep readers interested and alert through two very long books.

Markus Zusak's *The Book Thief* is, in some ways, an even more complicated novel than *Octavian Nothing*. It is set during World War II and, on the first page, Zusak introduces his narrator, Death, who immediately says,

> ***HERE IS A SMALL FACT***
>
> You are going to die.
>
> I am in all truthfulness attempting to be cheerful about this whole topic, though most people find themselves hindered in believing me, no matter my protestations. Please trust me. I most definitely can be cheerful. I can be amiable. Agreeable. Affable. And that's only the A's.

That is Death talking, which two pages later explains:

> It's just a small story really, about, among other things:
> - A girl
> - Some words
> - An Accordionist
> - Some fanatical Germans
> - A Jewish fist fighter
> - And quite a lot of thievery.

That's the cast, along with much of the action of the book. The girl is Liesel. She will lose her brother to Death in the next few pages. The accordionist is Hans Hubermann who, with his wife Rosa, will adopt Liesel. The fanatical Germans are Nazis who cause trouble, particularly when they burn books or oppress Jews. The Jewish fist fighter is Max Vandenburg who comes to stay with the Hubermanns and becomes one of Liesel's best friends. The thievery concerns Liesel, who finds a book in the graveyard when she goes to watch her young brother being buried. It is *The Gravedigger's Handbook,* which she treasures. At night with her foster father's help, she learns to read that book. Later, Liesel will steal other books.

It is a long and rich story that Zusak tells. Readers will care about many people in the story. They will be horrified by some events, but the one person they will not forget is Liesel.

Laurie Halse Anderson's *Fever 1793,* which tells how fourteen-year-old Mattie's life changes, is a wonderful example of good writing. Church bells ring out, announcing the yellow fever that strikes down hundreds of people in Philadelphia, including one of Mattie's friends. Mattie's family struggles to keep their coffeehouse open, but when Mattie's mother becomes ill, Mattie tries to escape. Laurie Halse Anderson's novel, pairs well with Jim Murphy's *An American Plague: The True and Terrifying Story of the Yellow Fever Epidemic of 1793.*

Anderson's 2008 *Chains* opens with a sad but joyous event for Isabel and Ruth, who are young sisters owned as slaves by the unusual Miss Finch of Tew, Rhode Island. Miss Finch passes away in May 1776. She had promised Isabel and Ruth their freedom upon her death. She had also taught Isabel to read and write. But Miss Finch's brother, Robert, shares none of his sister's mindset and, as the inheritor of her property, sells the sisters to the Lockton family in New York. Thirteen-year-old Isabel had promised her late mother she would always take care of her younger sister Ruth, who, in the vernacular of the day, is *simple* and suffers from epilepsy, a disease badly misunderstood in the eighteenth century. Ruth is the constant target of abuse because she lacks the guile to hide her thoughts and feelings and to present the happy, obedient façade that slave owners expect. In the Lockton family, the two girls experience physical and psychological mistreatment beyond anything they could have imagined in Miss Finch's household. Isabel realizes that they must somehow gain the freedom they were promised or suffer horrible consequences, including separation or even death.

Anderson has once again proven that she can create characters so appealing that readers take their plights to heart and hurt along with them at every tragedy, just as she did in *Fever 1793.* The book was a nominee for the National Book Award and is a fulfillment of Anderson's stated commitment to tell the stories of the human race that need to be told and haven't been.

See page 402 for a write-up on Anderson as winner of the 2009 Margaret A. Edwards Award. Also see Focus Box 8.2, "Historical Fiction Set in the World-at-Large," on page 260 as an illustration of how much variety there can be in historical fiction.

Other Consistently Good Writers of YA Historical Fiction

Tracy Chevalier is a writer of books for adults, but many teenagers consider her one of their own. Her *Girl with a Pearl Earring* is about sixteen-year-old Griet, who must help to support her family. She is hired by the Johannes Vermeer family and immediately disliked by the wife and daughter. Vermeer is constantly in debt, mostly because he paints so slowly and produces few canvases. Griet grows closer to the painter as she mixes and prepares paints, and Vermeer uses Griet as a model for his most famous painting. *Girl with a Pearl Earring* was filmed in 2003 and is almost as good as the book.

In *The Lady and the Unicorn*, the impecunious Nicholas des Innocents convinces a nobleman to commission six tapestries of unicorns—with Nicholas's designs—to be placed in the nobleman's mansion. Nicholas goes to Brussels to visit a master weaver. In all these travels, the successfully virile Nicholas meets and seduces women, all of whom become part of his designs in the tapestries. As Wendy Smith concluded in her review of Chevalier's book in the December 21, 2003, *New York Times Book Review*, Nicholas is "still no saint, but through him, Chevalier reminds us that art has the power to illuminate the understanding of those who make it as well as those who view it."

Bruce Clements in *The Treasure of Plunderell Manor* has written a very funny book that is at once an historical novel and a spoof of historical and Gothic novels. It begins with Laurel heading for Plunderell Manor to become the maid of Alice, heir to the manor. Laurel meets Lord and Lady Stayne who ask Laurel to spy on Alice. Later, sanctimonious Lady Stayne asks Alice if she is well. Then she turns to Laurel, who is Catholic, and says,

> And you? We must concern ourselves with your soul, too. Catholics go to hell, from the Pope on down. Just because you are simple and ignorant and weak, God will not forgive you for being a child of Rome. You may do as you wish, of course, but my advice is that you join the Anglican Church immediately.

Here the adventures begin. The Staynes drop Laurel and Alice at a deserted monastery, assuming the girls will soon die of cold or starvation. Alice is incapable of doing anything remotely helpful, but Laurel saves the day. In fact, she's forced to save several days during the rest of the book.

Christopher and James Lincoln Collier are two brothers who specialize in historical fiction. Their best-known book, *My Brother Sam Is Dead,* comes from the time of the Revolutionary War and was a Newbery Honor book. *The Bloody Country* and *The Winter Hero* continue the story. Another trilogy, *War Comes to Willy Freeman, Jump Ship to Freedom,* and *Who Is Carrie?*, focuses on African Americans and their role in early American history. Throughout the 1990s, the two produced the Drama of American History series for Benchmark Books.

Karen Cushman has chosen to write about girls embarking on journeys to discover themselves. Her 2010 *Alchemy and Meggy Swann* is a sixteenth-century adventure in which crippled Meggy Swann goes to London to find her estranged father who is trying to turn base metals into gold. She discovers herself to be friendlier, zestier, feistier, and more resourceful than she had thought possible. Cushman's first two books are also set in medieval times. *Catherine Called Birdy,* a Newbery Award book, is the diary of a fourteen-year-old daughter of a knight whose feisty and witty observations bring the thirteenth century to life in ways that few historians could. In *The Midwife's Apprentice,* Cushman looks at the same period, but at a different part of the social scale. She writes about an orphan who manages to get herself apprenticed to a midwife. Her 2003 *Rodzina* has a similar plot, except that it is set in the American West in 1881. Rodzina is a large, ungainly

Polish American girl who is sent west on an orphan train. As the train moves along, she sees the younger and more attractive children adopted. The two invitations she receives are disastrous and she runs away and returns to the train, finally making herself so useful that she becomes an assistant to the woman she calls "Miss Doctor." California's gold rush is the setting for *The Ballad of Lucy Whipple.* Lucy, whose original name was California Morning Whipple, finds herself dragged "like a barrel of lard" from Massachusetts to Lucky Diggings, California. The gold she finds is in pie-baking. *The Loud Silence of Francine Green* is a recent work by Cushman. Set in 1949 in Los Angeles during an early anticommunist hysteria mixed with worries about the atomic bomb, thirteen-year-old Francine is an average girl until she meets Sophie, a thorough-going nonconformist. Francine learns about freedom and life, and she begins to question everything from her parents' indifference to Sister Basil's punishment of Sophie for the "sin of intellectual curiosity."

Jennifer Donnelly was immediately recognized as a major writer when *A Northern Light* was published in 2003. It is based in part on the sensational murder of Grace Brown, whose body was found in Big Moose Lake in the Adirondack Mountains. While not the center of Donnelly's novel, the murder is always there, lurking in the background. It's better known to most adults as the basis for Theodore Dreiser's *An American Tragedy.*

Donnelly's novel is about sixteen-year-old Mattie, who lives a life of near poverty in 1906. Her mother is dead, and her father has hardened and is almost unreachable. Mattie, her sister Beth, and Weaver, a young African American boy who is Mattie's closest friend, love to play with language. Each day, one of them selects a word, like *inquisition,* and the three duel back and forth, supplying synonyms until they are bored. When Mattie's friend has twins and Mattie helps, Mattie learns an important distinction between reality and literature. Of all the books she had read, "not one of them tells the truth about babies. Dickens doesn't. Oliver's mother just dies in childbirth and that's that. Brontë doesn't. Catherine Earnshaw just had her daughter and that was that. There's no blood, no sweat, no pain, no fear, no stink. Writers are damned liars. Every single one of them."

Mattie takes a job as a waiter at a resort on Big Moose Lake. She meets Grace Brown, a resort guest, who leaves a packet of letters with Mattie. Before she goes boating with her boyfriend, Grace asks Mattie to burn these letters if she doesn't return. Grace does not return, and hence we get the story.

Donnelly's 2010 *Revolution* is a YA book not because it is a quick and easy read, but because it is two stories in one—both about mature teenage girls who lived two hundred years apart—one in contemporary Brooklyn Heights and one in Paris during the French Revolution. For insights into it, see Melissa Williamson's Young Scholars Speak Out on page 268, "How Being a Music-Loving Goth Chick Helped Me Read Jennifer Donnelly's *Revolution.*"

Leon Garfield set a standard for historical writing that few can match. His is the world of Fielding and Smollett—lusty, squalid, ugly, bustling, and swollen, full of life and adventure and the possibility that being born an orphan may lead you ultimately to fame and fortune. His stories play with reality versus illusion, daylight versus dreams, flesh versus fantasy. His ability to sketch out minor characters in a line or two is impressive. Of a man in *The Sound of Coaches,* he wrote, "He was one of those gentlemen who [e]ffect great gallantry

Young Scholars Speak Out

Melissa Williamson on How Being a Music-Loving Goth Chick Helped Me Read Jennifer Donnelly's *Revolution*

In 1999, it was odd going from being invisible to having people stare at me as I walked down the hallway. I was a quiet high school junior who dyed my blonde hair with blue streaks. My favorite shirt was one that I bought in 1996, advertising my favorite grunge band. Then April 21st rolled around and suddenly people were staring at me.

No one had noticed the grunge clothes or the blue hair, but now people reacted to what happened the day before—the shots from Columbine that were heard 'round the world! Faces were plastered on the news: the deceased, the wounded, and of course, the killers. Marilyn Manson was to blame! I couldn't believe it. The white faced guy who sang "The Beautiful People"? Well, whatever. Good song, though. The killers were apparently part of a clique called "The Trench Coat Mafia."

But I didn't own a trench coat. Why were they staring at me?

Because I was the "goth chick."

I hadn't realized this either. I liked *Bush* and *Nirvana*—grunge bands. I remember *The Cure* from my childhood. I first heard "Lovesong" when I was a kid; it was my first *goth* song. But I didn't think I was a goth chick. I was just quiet and shy: just me.

Columbine, though, changed my life. After the Columbine shootings, the security guard followed me around because I had a tiny chain wallet. (If only he could've seen what that chain wallet turned into years later. I probably could've killed someone with the beast of a chain wallet I carried through four years of college.)

Again, I was just being me. I certainly didn't realize I was a goth chick until the end of that year in my AP American History class. My teacher allowed us to choose a partner and research any contemporary issue. During one of the presentation days, two boys talked to the class about "goth culture." I vaguely remember what they said because my own thoughts were racing through my head: *This is me. Maybe I am a goth chick. I like that. It makes me cool. It makes me different. Hey, I like being different.*

At the end of the presentation, my teacher leaned forward and said, "I hope you weren't offended by any of that." He was an intimidating man, and I hated giving presentations because he grilled you and pushed you to the limits at times. But on that day, I found out that he was also sensitive to our issues and our personalities. After nearly twelve years, I remembered his words verbatim. My AP American History teacher realized what I was and who I was.

On that day, I was proud to call myself a "goth chick."

Now, more than a decade later, I was surprised that I was still a "goth chick," who, like the main character in Jennifer Donnelly's prize-winning novel, *Revolution* (Random House, 2010), is a lover of music. I was being called on to "educate" my professors and fellow students about the musical references in this book, which provided readers with a crash course not only in the French Revolution, but also in connections between both popular and classical music.

Donnelly's *Revolution* is about Andi Alpers, a troubled young woman about to be expelled from a top private

to all the fair sex except their wives." Of the protagonist we are told, "although jealousy was ordinarily foreign to Sam's nature, they did, on occasion, talk the same language." The funniest of Garfield's books are *The Strange Affair of Adelaide Harris* and its sequel, *The Night of the Comet*. In *Adelaide*, Bostock and Harris, two nasty pupils in Dr. Bunnion's Academy, become so entranced with stories of Spartan babies abandoned on mountaintops, there to be suckled by wolves, that they borrow Harris's baby sister to determine for themselves school in New York City. Her little brother was killed when he was caught in a cross-fire at a neighborhood crime scene. Her mother had gone mad, and her father had been out of the picture for a long time. Andi relied on her iPod, her guitar, and an antidepressant to keep her sane. But she had a senior thesis to write. Her father, who was a Nobel Prize-winning DNA pioneer, decided to come back into Andi's life. He arranged for his former wife to go into a mental hospital and, over the Christmas break, he took Andi with him to Paris, where he had serious work to do investigating whether a small heart found preserved in a bottle in the royal palace was that of the young dauphin, Louis-Charles. While her father worked, Andi wrote her thesis and read from an old diary found in a locked guitar case about a girl named Alexandrine (Alex) Paradis who entertained the dauphin during the French Revolution. Andi's plan for the thesis was to trace the influence of a fictional French musician from the eighteenth century named Amade Malherbeau. He was a stand-in for all the classical musicians that Andi hoped to prove had an influence on today's musical groups. The topic turned out to be a musical DNA search going from the fictional Malherbeau to the modern band *Radiohead*.

When Andi was trying to explain to her father the basis for Malherbeau's influence, she mentioned Jimi Hendrix's "Purple Haze," and told him about *tri-tones,* which are an augmented fourth, also known as the *Diabolus in Musica,* or "The Devil in Music." This sound was included in the opening bars of "Purple Haze," one of the most popular *psychedelic rock* songs of the 1960s. The sound occurred when a pianist played an interval of an augmented fourth (a *C* and an *F-sharp*). If it was played over and over again, listeners would think they were watching a horror movie.

At first Andi's father seemed interested in her scientific-sounding descriptions, but then lost interest when she explained that in the 1700s, when musicians first developed the idea, the priests forbade it. They were the ones who named it after the devil, and held it up as a symbol of rebellion and sacrilege, at which point Andi's father lost interest because he had seen more rebellion coming from his daughter than he cared to contemplate.

One of the most influential bands for Andi was early *heavy metal* band *Led Zeppelin*. *Led Zeppelin* also became a favorite of Malherbeau's when Andi woke up in his time period, during a serious drug trip. He asked her "about the man Led, surname Zeppelin, and what sort of instrument he used to make the sounds on 'Immigrant Song'."

Later, Andi walked in the words of Alex's diary and ended up shot. Malherbeau found her and she told him to keep playing guitar and making music. That day, he wrote his famous Concerto in A Minor, "The Fireworks Concerto." When she presented her topic at school, she demonstrated the likeness between Malherbeau's Concerto in A Minor and "Stairway to Heaven."

Andi believed that if Malherbeau didn't write music, the modern rock band *Radiohead* wouldn't exist either. Andi used *Radiohead*'s song "Idioteque" to reference the Tristan Chord, a chord made up of four notes that can be heard at the beginning of German composer Richard Wagner's *Tristan and Isolde*. Malherbeau listened to various songs on her iPod and asked Andi to explain them to him. "Is this truly the music of the future? [. . .] the future is a very strange place," he asked Andi. She answered, "It's got nothing on the past." True that.

> • Before studying for a doctorate in English Education at Arizona State University, Melissa Williamson taught high school English in Northern Virginia. Her work revolves around exploring new ways to rock out with students in the classroom.

the truth of the old tales. Therein begins a wild comedy of errors and an even wilder series of coincidences, near duels, and wild threats.

Carolyn Meyer's *White Lilacs* examines prejudice, injustice, and bravery that were part of Rose Lee Jefferson's life in the 1920s when she lived in Freedomtown, Texas. Meyer's *Mozart's Shadow: His Sister's Story,* tells how Nannert Mozart was a musical *wunderkind,* like her brother, Wolfgang

Amadeus Mozart, but it was Wolfgang's talents that were showcased in the courts of Europe. *Duchessina: A Novel of Catherine de' Medici* tells about sixteenth-century Catherine de' Medici's youth and early marriage and ends with her coronation as queen of France. Her 2011 *Cleopatra Confesses* gives a glimpse into the life of Cleopatra from the age of ten until her death by suicide.

Meyer has explained that when she wrote nonfiction books, she frequently found herself coming up against blank walls where she could find no more information. Because she wanted the stories to continue, she began asking, "What if?" and so began her career as a writer of fiction. In addition to *White Lilacs,* her most highly acclaimed books are probably *Mary, Bloody Mary,* about the youth of the woman who became one of England's most unpopular rulers; and *Where the Broken Heart Still Beats: The Story of Cynthia Ann Parker,* about a woman who was captured by Comanche Indians at age nine and unsuccessfully "rescued" by white settlers years later. In *Patience, Princess Catherine,* a young princess goes to England to become queen, only to have her young husband die. In *Marie, Dancing,* Meyer writes a fictional portrait of the ballet dancer who was the model for Degas's statue, "The Little Dancer."

Scott O'Dell's *The King's Fifth* is probably his most convincing work, with its picture of sixteenth-century Spaniards and the moral strains put on anyone involved in the search for gold and fame. It is convincing, often disturbing, and, like most of O'Dell's historical novels, generally worth pursuing. Students coming to high school with a good reading background probably already know O'Dell from his *Island of the Blue Dolphins* and *Sing Down the Moon,* both of which present original and positive portrayals of young Native American women suffering at the hands of white settlers in the middle to late 1800s. He was a pioneer in featuring strong young women in these two books, and within the last couple of decades several good writers have followed his lead.

Ann Rinaldi's well-received books include *A Break with Charity: A Story about the Salem Witch Trials* and *Cast Two Shadows: The American Revolution in the South.* She tackled a particularly ambitious subject in *Wolf by the Ears,* a fictional story of Sally Hemmings's family. Sally was a mulatto slave in Thomas Jefferson's household, and it is now believed that Jefferson fathered several of her children. The book's title comes from Jefferson's statement about slavery: "as it is, we have the wolf by the ears and we can neither hold him, nor safely let him go. Justice is in one scale, and self-preservation the other." Several of Rinaldi's numerous books deal with some aspect of the Revolutionary or the Civil War. *An Unlikely Friendship: A Novel of Mary Todd Lincoln and Elizabeth Keckley* tells how after Abraham Lincoln is assassinated, Mary Todd Lincoln asks to have her best friend, former slave, and dressmaker Elizabeth Keckley brought to her. In *Or Give Me Death: A Novel of Patrick Henry's Family,* Patty and Anne, the daughters of Patrick Henry and his mentally ill wife, tell their moving story.

Rosemary Sutcliff has been acclaimed as the finest writer of British historical fiction in the world. She began publishing in 1954 with *The Eagle of the Ninth,* and continued for forty years. It is said that she was still writing on the morning of her

Winner (1990)

Richard Peck, And the Magic of the Journey

Richard Peck's honored books include *Are You in the House Alone?*, *Father Figure*, *The Ghost Belonged to Me*, *Ghosts I Have Been*, *Secrets of the Shopping Mall*, and *Remembering the Good Times*. Since winning the Margaret A. Edwards Award, Peck has written several other wonderful books, including *A Long Way from Chicago* (Dial, 1999) and its follow-up, *A Year Down Yonder* (Dial, 2000), which won the Newbery Medal. These last two books are set during the Depression. Joey and Mary Alice Doudel are young teens who live in Chicago, but for the past few years have traveled by train to spend time during summer vacations with their Grandmother Doudel who lives in a rural area of downstate Illinois. At the height of the Depression in 1937, Joey and Mary Alice's parents are having terrible financial problems, and so, in *A Year Down Yonder,* Joey goes to work in a government-sponsored Civilian Conservation Corps (CCC) camp while Mary Alice is sent by herself (except for her pet cat) to spend a year or more with Grandma Doudel. Even though her coat is ragged and she has come as a kind of charity case, the local kids view her as the rich girl from Chicago, so life isn't easy, but thanks to Grandma Doudel, neither is it boring.

Several years ago when Peck came to Tempe, he spoke to one of our classes at ASU and explained that authors like to write journey stories, not just because the archetypal journey is inherently pleasing, but because such plots provide room for interesting developments as protagonists are removed from their old associates and patterns of life and are challenged by meeting new people and new situations. The two books about Joey and Mary Alice are perfect examples of this. He followed these two books with *Fair Weather* (Dial, 2001), which is a reversal on the idea of city kids going to farm country. In this one, a farm family receives a surprising invitation from a rich relative to come to Chicago and attend the 1893 Chicago Columbian Exposition.

In our ASU visit with Peck, he also shared an interesting insight based on a bell curve. He showed how his readers come from the high middle of the curve where lots of kids fit in, but the plots of his stories come from the flat ends of the curve. The most exciting stories are about young people who are "different," people who are doing unusual and out-of-the-ordinary things. When he can, he writes about these "different" characters from the perspective of someone from the middle. For example, in *Don't Look and It Won't Hurt* (Holt, 1999), the story is about a pregnant teenager who is sent away to live in a home for unwed mothers, but it is told through the voice of her sister. In his 2007 *On the Wings of Heroes* (Dial, 2007), which is set in the 1940s during WWII, the story is about a soldier going to war, but it is told through the eyes of Davy Bowman, the soldier's younger brother, who is left at home to collect tin cans for shell casings and milkweed for stuffing life jackets.

Peck told Linda Castellitto in a 2003 interview for BookSense.com that he couldn't imagine writing for young people without having spent several years teaching them. Spending time with junior high readers convinced him that they wouldn't be interested in reading the kind of living autobiography that many first novelists offer the public. He had to go looking for something else, and in a large part that something else has been humor. He told Castellitto that his real goal has been to write a book that would make a teacher "break down and weep with laughter." Of course he wants young readers to laugh too, but he thinks this is a greater challenge because kids aren't used to laughing, except at each other, which is something he has tried to change, especially in his ghost stories and in the ones about Grandma Doudel.

For an example of how Peck combines what he knows about writing with what he knows about teaching, see pages 380–382 for his list of ten questions—accompanied by Ulterior Motives—to ask students about a book they have read. You might also want to find his 2004 *Past Perfect, Present Tense: New and Collected Stories.* It includes eleven previously published stories and two new ones, along with information and inspiration to help aspiring authors. ●

death in 1994. We need to find ways for librarians and teachers to get her books, many of which are being redesigned and republished, to the right young readers—those who care about history and a rattling good story, and who are not put off by a period of time they know little about. Her 1980 *Frontier Wolf* is about a young commander of a group of scouts in northern England who must retreat from the forces of native tribes. *The Shining Company* may be harder to sell than her earlier books about the Normans and the Saxons (e.g., *The Shield Ring* and *Dawn Wind*) because it is set in a more obscure time, seventh-century Britain. Sutcliff cared about people who make history, whether knaves or villains or, in this case, naïve men who trusted their king and themselves beyond common sense.

Mildred D. Taylor used her own family history for the material in her prize-winning series. *The Land* won the 2002 Coretta Scott King Award. It was written as a prequel to the earlier books *Song of the Trees; Roll of Thunder, Hear My Cry; Let the Circle Be Unbroken;* and *The Road to Memphis.* Together, the series chronicles the generations of the Logan family, African American landowners near Vicksburg, Mississippi. *The Land* opens in post–Civil War Georgia when Paul-Edward Logan is about to leave his childhood behind. He is the son of a white plantation owner and a former slave of African American and Native American descent, and he is confused by his station in society. He has always been treated much like his white brothers, but now that he is approaching manhood, his father begins to treat him differently. The father thinks he might save the boy's life by teaching him that his welfare will always be subject to the whims and desires of white men. In 1999, Chris Crowe wrote, *Presenting Mildred D. Taylor.* Reviewers praised it as "a fine, readable introduction to Taylor's life and work," which answers those who criticize Taylor's books for their painful representation of racism. Crowe shows how she maintains a balance between realism and hope. Family photos might also interest students.

Frances Temple's *The Ramsay Scallop* is a wonderful book about medieval Europe. In it, Frances Temple describes the apprehension that thirteen-year-old Eleanor of Ramsay feels as she awaits marriage to twenty-two-year-old Lord Thomas of Thornham. Thomas is no happier about his upcoming marriage because he has become cynical about life and religion after fighting in the Crusades. Father Gregory sends them off on a pilgrimage to the cathedral in Santiago, Spain, and asks that they remain chaste during the trip. Temple's portraits of the people and the time, the friendships they form, and the deceit and pain they meet are brilliant. Temple has written several more contemporary books about young refugees as in *Grab Hands and Run* and *A Taste of Salt.*

Historical Fiction about War

By dividing this chapter basically into two parts, we do not want to imply that war is as important as all the rest of life put together. In fact, one of the things that we criticize history textbooks for is their emphasis on war and the way that they leave out what was happening to the rest of the people while the men were fighting. Struggling to survive in war is not an adventure we would choose, but so many people have been forced into horrible circumstances that books about war—histories, diaries, letters, interviews, fiction—are among the most powerful books young people can read.

Young adults may be conscious of the nearness of war, although they likely know little of the realities of war and even less about the details of past wars. Reading literature about war, fiction or not, acquaints young people with the ambiguous nature of war: on one hand, it illustrates humanity's evil and horror, while on the other hand, it reveals humanity's decency and heroism.

The Current War in the Middle East

When looking for books that young people will want to read, it makes sense to look for books written about a war that young people know, and that is written from their perspective. An almost perfect example of such a book is Dana Reinhardt's 2010 *The Things a Brother Knows,* which was discussed in Chapter 1 as an example of a book in which a young adult makes a worthy accomplishment.

Reinhardt is skilled at observing powerful details that communicate the dynamics of this American Jewish family, plus the book is a good illustration of such basic archetypes as The Seeker, The Friend, The Caregiver, The Warrior, The Sage, The Lover, and The Brother. She goes a step further than most writers by illustrating how in real life people slip out of one role and into another.

While Levi and Boaz start out as literal brothers, only at the end of the book do they become archetypal Brothers, with a capital *B.* This is after Levi and readers of the book learn some terrible details about Boaz's role as a Warrior, and finally as a Brother, not only to Marine Staff Sergeant Jack Gradfore, who Boaz was coming to visit at Walter Reed Hospital, but also to a young Afghan man named Wadhar Amar and three of his Brothers: Jassin Hassad, Tareq Majid, and Bashit Amar. Boaz leaves their names, accompanied by a bloody shirt, at the Vietnam Memorial.

Because it takes a while for authors to come to terms with particular wars, there are relatively few novels relating to the Afghan war. One written by an elementary school teacher, who was in the National Guard and quite unexpectedly found himself shipped off to Afghanistan, is *Words in the Dust* by Trent Reedy. Katherine Paterson wrote the introduction and Scholastic published it in 2011, targeted to middle school and junior high girls. The protagonist, who is also the narrator, is a young teen named Aulaikha. She has a cleft lip and, after many complications, undergoes surgery in a U.S. military hospital to repair her lip. Because the Nilsens lived for two years in pre-war Afghanistan, we loved the authenticity, the descriptions of unique Afghan customs and buildings, and the use of many Afghan words and phrases. The most believable part was the way that Reedy described all the complications of making the arrangements. The process was not at all like having a Fairy Godmother, in the guise of the U.S. military, touch Aulaikha with a magic wand and heal her deformity.

Another book that is not directly related to the current war, but that would never have been written if not for the arduous history of Afghanistan, is Khaled Hosseini's 2007 *The Kite Runner,* which is appreciated by older high school and college students, especially since the film was released. Some young adults are going on to read the 2009 sequel, *A Thousand Splendid Suns.*

The Kite Runner had its beginnings in the time period when the Nilsens lived in Afghanistan just before the Soviet take-over. Even though it is officially fiction, we found many connections to the life we saw and what we watched for in the news after we came home in 1969.

See the Margaret A. Edwards write-up on Walter Dean Myers on page 275 to read about the successful fiction he has written regarding young people in recent wars, including his 2008 *Sunrise over Fallujah,* the story of a boy named Robin (also called Birdy) who, after September 11, joins the Army and finds himself in more danger than he had ever dreamed of.

The Vietnam War

Two YA novels about Vietnam stand out. Valerie Hobbs's *Sonny's War* is about a garage mechanic who ignores his younger sister's advice to flee to Canada and ignore the draft; he is subsequently sent to Vietnam. What makes this novel different is the author's attention to the antiwar movement as it is preached by a local history teacher.

The other outstanding YA novel is Walter Dean Myers's *Fallen Angels.* Harlem is hard on Richie Perry, so he flees Harlem and joins the army. To his surprise, Richie finds himself dreaming of Harlem and wanting to get back to a world he thought he wanted to forget.

Most of the books about Vietnam are nonfiction and so they are treated in Chapter 9. Counting fiction and nonfiction, there are enough different books about the Vietnam war that, when a class works on this subject, students can choose which book(s) they want to read, and chances are they can check them out from libraries. There are also good films that can provide common experiences for the whole class. Besides such famous films as those directed by Oliver Stone (*Platoon* in 1986 and *Born on the Fourth of July* in 1989), HBO produced a film version of *Dear America: Letters Home from Vietnam* by Bernard Edelman that works well in class. So does the 1999 *Regret to Inform,* a seventy-two-minute film directed by Barbara Sonneborn. In 1968 her husband was killed in Vietnam. In 1992 she went to Vietnam to document what other war widows—American and Vietnamese—suffered.

World War II

Several novels about World War II are especially worth reading. One of the most recently published is *Between Shades of Gray* by Ruta Sepetys, a 2011 Honor List book. It is dedicated "In memory of Jonas Sepetys," who must be Rita Sepetys's father, because in the author's note she is identified as "the daughter of a Lithuanian refugee." Told through the voice of a sixteen-year-old Lina, the book is the story of what one family endured when they were taken as part of Josef Stalin's plan to "intellectually cleanse" the nations of Lithuania, Latvia, and Estonia, so that he could make them part of the USSR (which they were between 1941 and 1990). On the back of the book, Laurie Halse Anderson, Richard Peck, and Susan Campbell Bartoletti give glowing recommendations, which we totally agreed with after listening to the book on a CD, read by Emily Klein. The title documents Lina's growing awareness over their long trip by train and truck to a Soviet work camp in Siberia where their first duty was to dig a big hole, that looks suspiciously like a grave for their own little group of people who were rounded up by the NKVD (the Soviet

Winner (1994)

Walter Dean Myers, National Ambassador
for Young People's Literature

Hoops, Motown and Didi, Amiri and Odette: A Love Story, Fallen Angels, and *Scorpions* were the books the Margaret A. Edwards committee honored when they chose Walter Dean Myers for the award. But since 1994 Myers has written so many other wonderful books that he could win the prize all over again. His name dominates the list of Coretta Scott King Awards, and in 2012 he was named National Ambassador for Young People's Literature by the Library of Congress.

We chose to feature Myers in this chapter that includes fiction about war because of his 1989 *Fallen Angels,* which was an unusually powerful book about a young soldier in Vietnam. Richie Perry, the main character, desperately wishes to turn off the war for a while. He fantasizes that it's a movie and he can step out for popcorn.

Now a generation later, readers get to meet Richie Perry's nephew, a boy named Robin, but called Birdy. He is the protagonist in Myers; 2008 book, *Sunrise Over Fallujah.* Birdy was primed to go to college when the Twin Towers were destroyed and so he changed his mind about college and enlisted. And now he is in Iraq and readers are identifying with another young soldier frightened by "an enemy we can't identify and friends we're not sure about."

Myers has frequently told audiences of booklovers how, when he was in something like third or fourth grade, he discovered from reading and from looking at the pictures in books that he was "different." He seldom found a black face in a book, and if it was there, it was a picture of someone he could not identify with. For an earlier edition of this textbook, he wrote that he "began to accept the values, or rather the lack of values, assigned to people of *my* race." Then he went on, "I was simply looking for those human values that the school ascribed to white Americans but neglected to give to black Americans." He tried to become an intellectual and do all the things that black kids did not do, so of course he planned to go to college. When his parents told him they did not have the necessary money, he was devastated and dropped out of high school. He joined a gang and then the army, both of which gave him "macho identities," which were acceptable to him simply because he did not see alternatives. After the army he had a few menial jobs, and then started writing again. He wrote about things he knew: Harlem, basketball, gangs, and the army. He vowed to put in his books the values that he did not find when he was a child.

His best known book is probably his 2000 *Monster,* which was a finalist for the American Book Award and winner of the 2000 Printz Award. The protagonist is a sixteen-year-old boy charged with being an accomplice in the murder of a Harlem drugstore owner. What makes the book so unusual is that the boy (Steve Harmon) is a budding screenwriter and so finds it easier to talk about his alleged crime as if it were being played out in a movie rather than in real life. Steve goes over and over his actions as he puts them into the script he is writing. The underlying question that he tries to push away from his mind is whether he is the monster that the prosecuting attorney describes.

Myers got the idea for the book and the way the boy uses third person from interviewing inmates in New York and New Jersey prisons. In a February 4, 2000, interview for www.teenreads.com, Myers said he was struck by how frequently the young men denied being responsible for their actions. They used all kinds of verbal tricks to maintain their belief that they were really good people just caught up in bad circumstances.

But not to leave you with the idea that Myers writes only serious, hard core realism, we are recommending his 2007 *What They Found: Love on 145th Street,* which is a delightful collection of short stories all set in one neighborhood. When we put it on our Honor List we described it as "delicious and funny and sad." The first story is about a funeral like none you've ever attended, while the last story circles back around to show a young soldier who spoke at the funeral now under fire in Afghanistan, where he is being comforted by a fellow soldier, a female. ●

secret police) from a middle-class neighborhood in Kaunas, Lithuania. Because the book shows a side of the war different from Hitler's persecution of the Jews, it will probably find its way into classrooms to be read alongside books about Anne Frank. The story begins on June 13, 1941, with Lina's statement:

THEY TOOK ME IN MY NIGHTGOWN.

Thinking back, the signs were there—family photos burned in the fireplace, Mother sewing her best silver and jewelry into the lining of her coat late at night, and Papa not returning from work. My younger brother, Jonas, was asking question. I asked questions, too, but perhaps I refused to acknowledge the signs. Only later did I realize that Mother and Father intended we escape. We did not escape.

We were taken.

The title comes from Lina's growing awareness and ability to accept the behavior of the other people who were taken to the work camp with her and her mother and brother. It also alludes to Lina's work as an artist, which plays a part in the plot and in helping readers identify with Lina as "special."

William Wharton's *A Midnight Clear* is about six high-IQ American soldiers in an intelligence and reconnaissance platoon sent to determine whether there are German troops near a French chateau. The six play bridge, chess, and word games, and begin to believe they have nothing to do with the war. Then the Germans show up, and instead of warfare, everyone engages in a snowball fight. They sing Christmas carols and set up a Christmas tree and wonderful peace reigns. Then war starts again and the killing resumes, and what had been warm is now cold and bloody.

English novelist Robert Westall writes about young people who refuse to stay outside the war in *The Machine Gunners* and the sequel, *Fathom Five*. The first novel begins in an English coastal town during 1940 and 1941. Rumors of a German invasion are rife, and Chas McGill wants to help win the war. Chas and his friends locate a downed German plane, find the machine gun in working order, and hide it. When a school is hit by a German plane somewhat later, Chas steals sandbags to create a fortress, a safe place to display the machine gun. The rear gunner of the downed plane stumbles into their fortress and becomes the boys' prisoner. All this childish innocence dies when adults discover the fortress, the German is shot, and the young people are rounded up by their parents. *Fathom Five* is a rousing spy story set later in the war and the story of Chas's lost love and lost innocence. Westall had an amazing ability to portray the ambivalence of young people and the alienation they feel, mixed with love and duty. See Focus Box 8.3, "Fiction about War's Effects on Young People" for other examples.

Harry Mazer's *The Last Mission* is set near the end of World War II. Jack Raab uses his older brother's identification to lie his way into the Air Force to destroy Hitler and to save democracy, all by himself. That dream lasts only a short time before Jack learns that the Air Force involves more training and boredom than fighting. When Jack does go to war, his first twenty-four bombing raids go well, but on the last mission, his plane is hit, all his buddies die, and he is captured. When he returns home, the principal at his old high school asks him to talk.

Focus Box 8.3

Fiction about War's Effects on Young People

Annexed by Sharon Dogar. Houghton Harcourt, 2010. Dogar tells the same story that Anne Frank told in her diary, except that she imagines it through the eyes of Peter, the 15-year-old boy whose family was sheltering the Frank family.

Badd by Tim Tharp. Ember, 2012. Tim Tharp's 2008 *The Spectacular Now* was a National Book Award finalist. In Tharp's new book he demonstrates some of the same kind of honesty, but the story is sadder. It's told from teenager Ceejay's viewpoint when she is left trying to reconnect with her brother when he arrives home from the Iraq war earlier than expected. He seems fine physically, but something is definitely missing, including his old connection with his sister. Tharp was inspired to write the book when he met veterans with PTSD (Post-Traumatic Stress Syndrome) at the college where he teaches.

The Boy in the Striped Pajamas: A Fable by John Boyne. Random/David Fickling Books, 2006. Nine-year-old Bruno, the only child in an affluent German family, is shocked when his family moves to a place in Poland where, from his new bedroom window, he can see a high wire fence and hundreds of people wearing striped pajamas.

Dancing on the Bridge of Avignon by Ida Vos. Houghton Mifflin, 1995. In Nazi-occupied Holland, Rosa finds solace in her violin while being Jewish becomes more and more dangerous. Read also *Anna Is Still Here* (Houghton Mifflin, 1993) and *Hide and Seek* (Houghton Mifflin, 1991).

Dogtag Summer by Elizabeth Partridge. Bloomsbury, 2011. This book for middle school readers is about a 7th grader who knows that she was adopted from Vietnam when she was six-years-old. But when she and her friend, Stargazer, find a mysterious box in her garage a whole lot of questions follow and Stacy begins to wonder if she really belongs in the United States.

Or Give Me Death: A Novel of Patrick Henry's Family by Ann Rinaldi. Harcourt, 2003. Patty and Anne, the daughters of Patrick Henry and his mentally ill wife, tell their moving story in this book that found a place on *VOYA's* Top Shelf Fiction for Middle School Readers.

Hiroshima: A Novella by Laurence Yep. Scholastic, 1995. Though the story is centered around Hiroshima residents, Yep also tells the story of the bomb itself.

Lord of the Nutcracker by Iain Lawrence. Delacorte, 2001. It is 1914 and a ten-year-old London boy is sent, for safety, to live with his aunt in the country. He lives the war, first its patriotism and then its horror, through tin soldiers that his toymaker father sends to him.

The Loud Silence of Francine Green by Karen Cushman. Clarion, 2006. It is August of 1949 and Francine is an eighth grader at All Saints School for Girls in Los Angeles. It is the Cold War and she gets in trouble for challenging her teachers' description of "the Godless" communists.

Purple Heart by Patricia McCormick. HarperCollins, 2009. McCormick's book is about a combat soldier who arrives home haunted by the death of an Iraqi civilian. She told a *USA Today* reporter, that books like hers open the door for kids to have conversations about what it's like to be the one at home waiting for a letter or an e-mail, or for that dreaded knock on the door from two officers, who have come with sad news.

Slap Your Sides by M. E. Kerr. HarperCollins, 2002. Jubal Shoemaker is a Quaker who, in the midst of the patriotism of World War II, has mixed feelings about his brother's being a conscientious objector. See also Kerr's *Linger* (HarperCollins, 1993) about patriotism during the Persian Gulf War.

Soldier Boys by Dean Hughes. Atheneum, 2001. Parallel stories tell about two young soldiers, American Spencer Morgan and German Dieter Hedrick, who enter their country's service full of idealism, only to learn how hellish war is.

Someone Named Eve by Joan M. Wolf. Clarion, 2007. Wolf tells a fictionalized story of a young Jewish girl from the Czechoslovakian village of Lidice who was one of the ten children chosen from the doomed village to be taken to a Lebensborn center for "Germanization."

Under the Blood-Red Sun by Graham Salisbury. Delacorte, 1994. The bombing of Pearl Harbor on December 7, 1941, changes the life of a young Japanese American as he searches for his father and grandfather.

When My Name Was Keoko: A Novel of Korea in World War II by Linda Sue Park. Clarion, 2002. A brother and a sister use the loss of their Korean names as the focus of their memories of the 1940s when Japan occupied Korea.

"I'm glad we won," he said. "We couldn't let Hitler keep going. We had to stop him. But most of all, I'm glad it's over." Had he said enough? There was a silence . . . a waiting silence. There was something more he had to say.

"I don't like war. I thought I'd like it before. But war is stupid. War is one stupid thing after another. I saw my best friend killed. His name was Chuckie O'Brien. My whole crew was killed." Now he was talking, it was coming out, all the things he'd thought about for so long. "A lot of people were killed. Millions of people. Ordinary people. Not only by Hitler. Not only on our side. War isn't like the movies. It's not fun and songs. It's not about heroes. It's about awful, sad things, like my friend Chuckie that I'm never going to see again." His voice faltered.

"I hope war never happens again," he said after a moment. "That's all I've got to say."

He sat down. He hardly heard the applause. The floor of the radio room was still slippery with Chuckie's blood . . . Dave was still fumbling with his chute . . . the plane was still falling through the sky.

Many years after writing *The Last Mission,* Mazer wrote a trilogy about World War II. In *A Boy at War: A Novel of Pearl Harbor,* Adam Pelko signs up for high school classes while his father is on duty on the Battleship Arizona in Pearl Harbor, Hawaii. Adam is tired of being a military brat, but at least he finds a good friend in Davi Mori. Davi explains to Adam that he, Davi, was born in Hawaii and is *nisei* while his parents were born in Japan and are *issei.* Out fishing one day, Adam sees the bombing of Pearl Harbor and the sinking of the *Arizona.*

In *A Boy No More,* Adam and his mother live in Bakersfield. Davi writes from Hawaii that his father is being held by authorities and, later, that his father has been taken to the United States. Adam finds that the Mori family is at Manzanar, an internment camp in the California desert, and he visits them. Davi tells Adam that he always thinks about his father, "the way they treated him like a traitor. For nothing. They put him in prison for nothing. He never says anything, but it hurts him."

In the third book, *Heroes Don't Run,* Adam goes back to his grandfather in upper New York State and then joins the marines. In the meantime, Davi joins the army. When Adam's unit fights in Okinawa, Adam's life becomes violent, explosive, and at times bloody.

Aidan Chambers's *Postcards from No Man's Land* (winner of the 2002 Printz Award) has reminded young people of the ugliness of World War II, and particularly the long-term effects war can have on us. Chambers tells his story in alternating chapters set in 1944 and 1995. In the latter year, seventeen-year-old Jacob Todd travels to Holland to visit his grandfather's grave on the fifty-first anniversary of the Battle of Arnheim and to see Geertrui Wesseling, the last person to see his grandfather alive. Jacob has no presumption that this trip will be at all interesting, but a Dutch saying he hears early on in Amsterdam—"Nothing in Amsterdam is what it appears to be"—should have alerted him to all he would find out about his grandfather, the war, and Jacob himself.

James Forman's finest work, too little known, is *Ceremony of Innocence.* Hans and Sophie Scholl, brother and sister in Nazi Germany, print and distribute literature attacking Hitler. Arrested by the Gestapo, they are urged by friends to escape. A lawyer, who Hans suspects is a Nazi, encourages them to plead insanity. They refuse, endure the mock trial, are found guilty, and are taken away to be executed. Hans is the last to die by the guillotine.

> Hans heard the sound of rollers, and at last there burst from his throat a cry, uttered in a great voice, a voice that combined anger, reproof, and an overwhelming conviction for which he was willing to die.
>
> "Long live freedom!"
>
> Then the greased blade fell. His teeth met through his tongue, and it was over.

Literature of the Holocaust

Not many years ago, anyone wishing to read about the Holocaust would read Anne Frank's *The Diary of a Young Girl*. Today, an outpouring of films and books about the Holocaust means that no one can pretend not to know about the happenings and the evils that went with it. Most of the material about the Holocaust is nonfiction and so will be treated in Chapter 9.

Younger students continue to read and love Johanna Reiss's *The Upstairs Room* and its sequel, *The Journey Back*. The first book is a true story of the author and her sister, two young Jewish girls in Holland, kept safely in hiding by a gentile family for over two years during the Nazi occupation. The girls detest having to stay inside all the time, but when they learn from an underground newspaper what is happening to Jews across Europe, they realize the precariousness of their situation. The second book is about their trip back to their hiding place after the war.

Some recent YA novels have focused on the obvious fact that the same kind of bigotry that was at least a partial cause of the war endures. In Lois Ruby's *Skin Deep*, Dan comes from a fatherless home. When multiethnic quotas keep him off the swimming team and from getting a job at the University of Colorado, he turns to the local skinheads for support, adopting their dress code but never quite accepting their racism. Han Nolan's *If I Should Die Before I Wake* portrays a young girl, a neo-Nazi initiate, who is in a coma from a motorcycle accident. In her dreams in the hospital, she becomes a young Jewish girl whose family lives in a ghetto and then Auschwitz.

The Wave by Morton Rhue (pen name of Todd Strasser) has proved incredibly popular with many young people. In a high school history class, students wonder why the non-Nazi Germans let the Holocaust happen. The teacher responds by introducing students to a new movement, *The Wave*, which captures the imaginations and the hearts of students apparently longing for indoctrination and belief in certainties.

The best of these books is Fran Arrick's *Chernowitz!* Bob Cherno, fifteen, looked back on his fights with Emmett Sundback, a bigot who ridiculed Bob's Jewishness. When Bob's school shows a film about the concentration camps, some students who have ridiculed Bob leave in tears because they understand the horrors of the Nazis' treatment of Jews and other minorities. To Arrick's credit, Sundback does not change and remains the creep that he was.

Internment of Japanese Americans in World War II

The most shameful American action during World War II began in January 1942 when President Roosevelt ordered the forced evacuation of anyone of Japanese ancestry on the West Coast into detention camps scattered in desolate places.

More than 120,000 people were moved from their homes into the meager and arid camps. As disgraceful as was the government's decision to do this, equally disgraceful was the fact that the families' neighbors were eager to buy out Japanese farmers or merchants on their way to internment camps for a few cents on the dollar.

Jeanne Wakatsuki Houston and her husband James D. Houston's *Farewell to Manzanar* describes the first author's life in a camp ringed by barbed wire and guard towers and with open latrines. The three-year ordeal destroyed the family's unity and left them with a burdening sense of personal inadequacy that took years to remove.

John Armor and Peter Wright discovered many photographs taken by Ansel Adams for his ironically titled 1944 book *Born Free and Equal*. They added a text to go with the photographs and titled their book *Manzanar*. With a commentary by John Hersey, *Manzanar* is a record of a people who had a right to be bitter but who were instead generally making conditions at the camp work for them.

In February 1983, a Congressional committee concluded deliberations and agreed that the internment of Japanese Americans was a "grave injustice." The commission noted that the relocation was motivated by "racial prejudice, war hysteria, and failure of political leadership," not by any military considerations. Five years later, the House passed and sent on to President Reagan legislation giving apologies and $20,000 tax-free payments to Japanese American survivors of World War II internment camps. Even so, it was 1990 before the first checks were issued.

Two novels about the internment are outstanding. Cynthia Kadohata's *Weedflower* opens just before the bombing of Pearl Harbor. Sumiko's family grows flowers in California, and after the bombing they are sent to the bleak, dusty, and very hot internment camp in Poston, Arizona. Sumiko and Frank, a Mohave boy, become friends. Boredom sets in for many internees, as it did for Sumiko, but she was strong enough to make her way through depression and out into the sunlight.

Each chapter in Julie Otsuka's *When the Emperor Was Divine* is narrated by a member of the family who was sent to an internment camp called Topaz in the Utah desert in 1942. They spent three years and five months at Topaz. And when they left and returned to what their home was, neighbors and former friends cut them almost as deeply as Topaz did.

One other novel about internment camps is often forgotten, which is a shame because it was written at a time when befriending or being fair to the Japanese was not in fashion. Florence Crannell Means had written many books about minorities, but *The Moved-Outers* (1945) may be her best work. It is about how Sue Ohara's life changed after December 7, 1941, and Pearl Harbor. Her father was taken into custody by the F.B.I. and Sue, her brother Kim, and her mother were taken to a Relocation Camp and then to a camp in Arizona. Conditions could not be worse, but the family survived. Means's novel has its problems. It is dated—few YA books survive more than fifty years—and at times it seems condescending, but it was one of the few contemporary books, YA or adult, that took a moral stand against the treatment of Japanese Americans.

Earlier Wars

Of course, there are books about young people written in relation to World War I and to the Civil War and even back to the Revolutionary War, but most of them are considered children's literature, or they are grouped in with general historical fiction. Remember that the focus on writing books for a teenage audience is a relatively recent idea. However, Michael Morpurgo's *Private Peaceful,* which was a 2004 Honor List book, is set during World War I. It is the story of a young, naïve British soldier who goes willingly into the Army, but then is disillusioned and frightened. He ends up being shot by his superiors for cowardice. Only because we had read Morpurgo's book did we know what to make of an August 20, 2006, Associated Press story which reported that the British Government was preparing to pardon 306 World War I soldiers who were executed for desertion or cowardice after summary trials, similar to the one in Morpurgo's *Private Peaceful.* British Defense Secretary Des Browne announced, "The circumstances [of World War I] were terrible, and I believe it is better to acknowledge that injustices were clearly done in some cases, even if we cannot say which, and to acknowledge that all these men were victims of war." A retired teacher who founded a pressure group, Shot at Dawn, said the government had relented after three lawsuits were filed by families. Records show that the wartime trials were speedy, some lasting no more than twenty minutes. In one case, a soldier was tried and executed on the same day.

Morpurgo is also the author of *War Horse,* which was copyrighted in 1982, but published here in the United States as a Scholastic hardback in 2007 and as a paperback in 2010. *War Horse,* a high budget and highly praised film about World War I was directed by Stephen Spielberg and released on Christmas Day in 2011. Movie-goers who had already read Morpurgo's *Private Peaceful,* will be more likely to notice the immediate, on-the-field execution of two young soldiers who had left the battlefield and hidden the War Horse, along with his partner horse, inside the covering of a Dutch windmill.

Technologies in Imagined Historical Fiction

What impressed us the most when we saw the *War Horse* film, was the re-creation of First-World-War technologies, including the importance of barbed wire and wire cutters as well as the swords and bayonets and the pitched battles. The giant wheels with their great wooden clogs on the gun carriers—which were pulled by horses and pushed by men—reminded us of the *walkers* that Keith Thompson drew for Scott Westerfeld's Leviathan series (*Leviathan, Behemoth,* and *Goliath*). When Westerfeld was on a book tour for *Goliath,* he spoke at the Changing Hands Bookstore in Tempe, Arizona (October 3, 2011) and was quick to give credit to his illustrator, Keith Thompson, and to the research that Thompson had done in old records and sketches of proposed inventions. His three books are a retelling of World War I, as it might have been fought in an alternate world where one side relied on technology (these were the Clankers) while the other side relied on help from nature (these were the Darwinists). The Darwinists were the most interesting because they even managed to have animals join forces to build a dirigible which, in a simplified explanation, would float with the help of bodily gasses. They had learned to manipulate DNA to make animals even more sophisticated than those that Suzanne Collins created for her *Hunger Games* trilogy.

A point that Michael Cart made in his December 15, 2011 "Carte Blanche" column in *Booklist* magazine is that in today's YA fiction there is a "bending and blending" among such genres as romance, historical fiction, science fiction, fantasy, and mystery. Brian Selznick's *The Invention of Hugo Cabret* is a perfect illustration of this new kind of historical fiction. Surely there could never have been a boy like the one in the book (and the *Hugo* film) keeping the great clocks in the Paris train station running, nor was there such an advanced robot as "The Automaton" that the boy was trying to repair in hopes of getting a message from his deceased father. However, there was a real George Mélios (1870–1940), a great filmmaker who was pushed out of the new industry and ended up using his genius to make and repair mechanized toys for children.

These books differ from other fantasies in that they allude to real people and real events not back in medieval times, but in the not too distant past. They are mostly set in the early 1900s, when industrialization was changing the world. It may be that as a culture we are nostalgic for a time which in retrospect seems, not necessarily easier, but at least easier to understand. We got this idea from a visit to the Music Instrument Museum in Phoenix, Arizona, where one of the most popular exhibits is on "Mechanical Music Makers" including a Nickelodeon, an Apollonia, a Barrel Organ, an Organillo, a Violano Virtuoso, and a couple of Player Pianos. When we looked at the intricate punching on the long roll of heavy-duty paper designed to be fed into a huge player piano, we realized that this was a prelude to the first computer cards that people worked with back in the 1970s.

Geraldine McCaughrean's *The White Darkness* (HarperCollins 2007) is another Honor List book that is historical, but at the same time filled with mystery and fantasy connected to technology—or maybe to just insanity—related to the early 1900s. It is the story of a contemporary fourteen-year-old British girl named Sym, who is fascinated with the story of Capt. Lawrence (Titus) Oates who was with the 1911 Scott Expedition in Antarctica. As she explains, even though he's been dead for 90 years, "In ninety years I'll be dead too and then the age difference won't matter."

When the Scott Expedition was stranded in Antarctica, without food or any likelihood of rescue, and it became obvious that Titus could no longer pull his share of the work, he told his companions on March 16, 1912, his 32nd birthday, that he was "just going outside and may be gone some time." Titus Oates's courage and dedication in sacrificing himself for the good of his company, was honored by the entire British nation, which is why Sym agrees to go with her Uncle Victor on a trip to Antarctica to explore his belief that around the North and South Poles there are holes through which they could go to find the planets that exist inside of our own planet. Uncle Victor turns out to be quite mad and the trip is a disaster, but the book is nevertheless fascinating as well as haunting and Sym, along with one other member of the exploration group, does manage to survive.

Concluding Comments

While historical fiction has more variety than nonfiction—for example, it can take place as long ago as Jean M. Auel's prehistorical *The Clan of the Cave Bear* or as recently as the Iraq War, as with Walter Dean Myers's *Sunrise over Fallujah*—many of today's readers prefer memoirs and nonfiction accounts, much like the material seen on the History Channel. Another recent trend is for authors to look past the movers and shakers involved in big dramatic events and to focus instead on ordinary people and show how their lives have been affected by natural disasters and by developments and changes in society. These are trends that will be illustrated in Chapter 9, which will focus on nonfiction accounts of many of the same historical periods treated in this chapter.

Nonfiction
Information, Literary Nonfiction, Biographies, and Self-Help Books

chapter

9

While fiction usually gets the lion's share of attention when it comes to reviewing and recommending books for teenagers, in libraries and schools nonfiction gets the lion's share of the budget. After leaving school, many adults go for years without reading a novel or even a short story, but virtually everyone reads nonfiction whether in newspapers, magazines, on the Internet, or on a cereal box.

In an *English Journal* issue devoted to nonfiction, Paul Hirth wrote the introductory piece, "The Truth about Nonfiction." He said that while English teachers usually feel more inspired or more challenged when they focus on aesthetics, he thinks it can be just as satisfying to help students revel in the "joy of facts" and the "poetry of prose." Teachers scoff, he says, because they think students "are already versed in reading for the literal." But he knows that students need help in reading for irony, in recognizing the subtleties of an argument, and in applying facts and details to the development and interpretation of thought. "Too often," Hirth says, teachers "begin with the assumption that students can't or won't read anything with a text more demanding than a billboard, yet they seem to devour the Internet with ease." He concluded that "just as the study of fiction, drama, and poetry help students explore their thoughts and feelings, nonfiction can offer a reality check—a second opinion, if you will," with which students, and their teachers, can measure their individual responses (*English Journal*, March 2002, pp. 20–22).

Margaret A. Edwards Award

Winner (2010)

Jim Murphy, A Book Lover
Ever Since Sixth Grade

Jim Murphy has a wonderful smile and he's had lots of opportunities to use it since he won the Edwards Award. He told Anita Silvey, who interviewed him for the June 2010 cover story in *School Library Journal,* that his first reaction to hearing the good news was to check and see who else had won it. First, it made him happy to see what good company he was in, but then he started worrying because he felt obligated to live up to the honor.

He doesn't need to worry because his work habits are so ingrained that he couldn't write a sloppy or a bad book even if he wanted to. Plus, he's had a lifetime of searching out the little details that make his stories more than what he calls his "father's history," the kind that is full of numbers, and dates, and facts. Instead, he writes what he calls *experience* books. One of the experience stories that he told Silvey about becoming a book lover was that his father—who was an accountant—had a hobby of refinishing furniture. Jim begged his father to let him refinish a little cherrywood bookcase. It took him weeks of hard work, and when he finally moved it into his bedroom he proudly brought people in to see it. But they began asking why it was empty. "Where are the books?" Jim ran around the house picking up books and bringing them back to his bookshelf. Then people began asking him about the books, and so he started reading, and hasn't stopped since.

The other experience story he told Silvey was about how he started working in publishing at age twenty-three. During high school, teachers gave him encouragement to write and publish in the school's literary magazine. And one summer after he had taken a job working at his father's accounting firm, both parents agreed that he needed to find a different career from that of his father. So when he went to Rutgers University, he majored in English, and he also took lots of history classes. At graduation time, he wrote letters to every publisher in New York asking if he could come in and visit with them about a job. He had lots of good visits, but since he had never taken a class in typing, which is still a pretty important skill for someone in the beginning ranks of a publishing firm, he didn't get a job. However, his uncle, who was a shop steward for a construction company, gave him a job as an iron worker in New York City.

Jim was working up on the twenty-second floor of the Grace Building when he got the telephone call he had been waiting for. There were no such things as cell phones, just his fellow workers shouting from floor to floor: "Get Murphy!" "Hey Murphy, you have a phone call!" The caller was Jim Giblin from Clarion, who was amused at how long it took for Jim to get down to the telephone and at all the construction noises he heard in the background. In spite of Murphy's poor typing skills, Giblin hired him as the company's assistant secretary. And because the company was fairly small—as publishing houses go—Jim had lots of different experiences and gradually worked his way up to becoming an editor, a job he held until he was thirty.

Then he decided—even though he had only $500 in the bank—to step back from editing to do his own writing. His very first book was *Weird & Wacky Inventions,* published in 1978. This was followed by one on the history of tractors, which his accountant father suggested might be "a big hit in Russia!" One of the reasons that Murphy wanted to write his own books is that he was always coming up with what he thought were "good ideas." He would offer them to the authors he was working with and they would look at him strangely. The problem was that they did not envision the original, but daunting ways that he went about doing his research. For example, when he decided to write *Blizzard: The Storm That Changed America,* which is about the 1888 snowstorm in New York City, he learned that the public library had 1,500 first-hand accounts from people who had lived through the storm. He knew that out of all these individual stories he could find enough information to write the book, which reviewers later described as not only humorous, jaw-dropping, and thought-provoking, but also *chilling.* His other books that were cited by the Edwards Award committee are *An American Plague: The True and Terrifying Story of the Yellow Fever Epidemic of 1793, A Young Patriot: The American Revolution as Experienced by One Boy, The Great Fire,* and *The Long Road to Gettysburg.* ●

Information Books

When the American Library Association made history by awarding its coveted 1988 Newbery Medal to Russell Freedman's *Lincoln: A Photobiography,* Milton Meltzer, who long championed the cause of nonfiction, applauded by saying, "It was a terrific thing to do, but it took fifty years to do it." People expressed a similar kind of enthusiasm in 2010 when, for the first time, a nonfiction author—Jim Murphy—was chosen to receive the Margaret A. Edwards Award for a lifetime contribution to young adults. See his write-up on page 284.

When Meltzer made his comment, he was talking to Betty Carter and Richard F. Abrahamson, the authors of *Nonfiction for Young Adults: From Delight to Wisdom.* In their book, Carter and Abrahamson cited twenty-two research studies. Here are some of their findings:

- An interest in reading nonfiction emerges at about the fourth grade and grows during adolescence.
- Interest in reading nonfiction crosses ability levels; one study showed that nonfiction made up 34 percent of the leisure reading of academically able teenagers and 54 percent of the control group's leisure reading.
- Nonfiction makes up a much larger proportion of boys' reading than of girls' reading.
- One study categorized the seven most popular types of nonfiction as cartoon and comic books, weird-but-true stories, rock stars, ghosts, magic, stories about famous people, and explorations of the unknown.
- Remedial readers prefer informative nonfiction and read "primarily to learn new things."
- Students choose nonfiction for a variety of reasons often unrelated to school curricular matters.
- When students gave reasons for reading particular books, it became clear that the purpose of the reading is guided more by the student than

As school budgets shrink, more responsibility falls on libraries to support the arts. The "Art" statue that teenagers sit around on the front steps of the Boston Public Library in Copley Square at least shows young adults that someone values art. See Focus Box 9.1, "Books to Support the Curriculum," on page 286.

Focus Box 9.1

Books to Support the Curriculum

***The Absolutely True Tale of Disaster in Salem* written and illustrated by Rosalyn Schanzer. National Geographic, 2011.** Reviewers praised Schanzer's telling both for its dramatic style and for the black and white ink prints with red accents.

***Artist to Artist: 23 Major Illustrators Talk to Children about Their Art* by Eric Carle. Philomel, 2007.** Let's hope that the word *children* in the title will not turn teen readers away from this collection of some of the best known picture book art explained and commented on by the artists themselves. The featured work was mostly chosen from the Eric Carle Museum.

***Cave Paintings to Picasso: The Inside Scoop on 50 Art Masterpieces* by Henry Sayre. Chronicle, 2004.** The paintings range from cave drawings dated 22,000 BC to Rene Magritte's *The Son of Man,* painted in 1964. Each one is explained and set in its own time period as well as charted on an overall timeline.

***First People: An Illustrated History of American Indians* by David C. King. DK, 2008.** Starting with the ice age, King moves to the present in this beautiful photographic history of Native Americans. Boundaries, differences, and key events are all included.

***Flesh & Blood So Cheap: The Triangle Fire and Its Legacy* by Albert Marrin. Knopf/Borzoi, 2011.** Marrin's book is more than a history of the devastating 1911 fire in New York. He shows how the tragedy is a part of the early history of America's movement to guarantee rights to its workers and draws parallels between these workers of a century ago and the workers in today's sweat shops in developing countries. A second highly recommended history book by Marrin is his 2009 *Years of Dust: The Story of the Dust Bowl* published by Dutton.

***Frozen Secrets: Antarctica Revealed* by Sally M. Walker. Carolrhoda, 2010.** Walker went to Antarctica to make sure what she was writing was true.

The book includes photos and illustrations. She found the area as fascinating as she had imagined from her research.

***Harlem Stomp! A Cultural History of the Harlem Renaissance* by Laban Carrick Hill. Little, Brown/Megan Tingley Books, 2004.** It is refreshing to find a history book that focuses not on conflicts and wars but on creativity in literature, drama, and the arts. Photos and reproductions add to the satisfying result.

***King George: What Was His Problem? Everything Your Schoolbooks Didn't Tell You About the American Revolution* by Steve Sheinkin, illus. by Tim Robinson. Roaring Brook, 2008.** History teachers will probably appreciate Sheinkin's lively writing style as much as, or maybe more than, do young readers.

***Skywalkers: Mohawk Ironworkers Build the City* by David Weitzman. Flash Point, 2010.** Weitzman explains how things came together so that Native Americans from the Mohawk Nation were instrumental builders of some of today's famous skyscrapers. Readers will also learn about the development of America's iron and steel businesses.

***The Teen Guide to Global Action: How to Connect with Others (Near and Far) to Create Social Change* by Barbara A. Lewis. Free Spirit, 2008.** A variety of concrete suggestions are made to show teens how they can get involved in local and international groups focusing on seven major concerns.

***Tracking Trash: Flotsam, Jetsam, and the Science of Ocean Motion* by Loree Griffin Burns. Houghton Mifflin, 2007.** Burns shows how currents, weather, climate, and the environment are interrelated. Read this book if you want to find out about ghost nets, nurdles, and the differences between flotsam, jetsam, plankton, ice floes, and other debris.

by the type of book. One boy read books on subjects he already knew about because it made him feel smart; others preferred how-to books so that they could interact with the author while learning to draw, care for a pet, program a computer, make a paper airplane, and so on; and still others preferred *The Guinness Book of World Records.* Even here purposes differed. Some read the book to discover amazing facts, but others read it to imagine themselves undergoing strange experiences.

Focus Box 9.2

Information about Bodies and Minds

Chew on This: Everything You Don't Want to Know about Fast Food by Eric Schlosser and Charles Wilson. Houghton Mifflin, 2006. Schlosser and Wilson give colorful stories, photographs, anecdotes, and other eye-opening information to explain such slogans as "Supersize me!" and "Have it your way!"

Danger! by Laura Buller et al. DK, 2001. One of the tween reviewers for *VOYA* said, "This book had so many dangerous places, animals and things, I was scared to put it down!" It's actually a refreshing change from most books about taking care of yourself.

Eating Disorders Information for Teens, edited by Sandra Augustyn Lawton. Teen Health, Omnigraphics, 2005. Chapters alternate between narrative overviews covering causes, symptoms, preventions, and treatments of different problems. Quick tips, FAQ, and "Remember!" boxes give direct advice.

For Teens Only: Quotes, Notes, and Advice You Can Use by Carol Weston. HarperTrophy, 2003. Each page starts with an intriguing quote from people as different as Homer Simpson and Edna St. Vincent Millay. Weston expounds on the quotes and concludes with a boldfaced moral, almost like those at the ends of fables.

Inside Out: Portrait of an Eating Disorder, written and illustrated by Nadia Shivack. S&S/Atheneum, 2007. Shivack named her eating disorder Ed, and over the years she kept track of Ed on whatever scraps of paper she could find. These are worked into the book, along with hindsight comments, websites, and lists of resources.

Is It a Choice? Answers to 300 of the Most Frequently Asked Questions about Gays and Lesbians, 3rd edition, by Eric Marcus. HarperCollins, 2005.

Questions range from what to call same-sex parents to how people know if they are gay. Dating, telling parents, socializing, and political activism are all treated.

It's Okay to Say No: Choosing Sexual Abstinence by Eleanor Ayer. Rosen, 1997. Both physical and emotional health are touted as benefits of abstinence. While the message fits in with many religious teachings, the author does not focus on religion but instead on self-respect and preparing for a healthy marriage.

101 Questions about Sex and Sexuality: With Answers for the Curious, Cautious, and Confused by Faith Hickman Brynie. 21st Century Books, 2003. While emphasizing that abstinence is the only sure way to avoid STDs and pregnancies, Brynie also provides contraceptive information. The questions were collected from middle school and high school students.

Stay Strong: Simple Life Lessons for Teens by Terrie Williams with an introduction by Queen Latifah. Scholastic, 2001. Chapters include "Life Isn't Fair and Nothing You Do Matters," "How I Talk Is My Business," and "It's the 'In-Crowd' That Matters."

The Way We Work: Getting to Know the Amazing Human Body by David Macaulay with Richard Walker. Houghton, 2008. Macaulay's large colored-pencil illustrations add humor and clarity to his guided tour of what he calls "the most remarkable piece of engineering" and what other people call the human body.

What the World Eats by Faith D'Aluisio, photos by Peter Menzel. Tricycle, 2008. This young adult version of *Hungry Planet* shows the food choices of families in twenty-one countries. Color photos and thought-provoking facts make this a savory book.

Students are sometimes seeking the kinds of information that can supplement what they are learning in school, as in Clive Grifford's 2009 *10 Explorers Who Changed the World,* which would be good support for a history class. See Focus Box 9.1, "Books to Support the Curriculum." If they want something closer to their own lives they might select Lisa Cohn and Debbie Glasser's 2009 *The Step-Tween Survival Guide: How to Deal with Life in a Stepfamily.* See Focus Box 9.2, "Information about Bodies and Minds." Or if students just

The Book of Potentially Catastrophic Science by **Sean Connolly. Workman, 2010.** At least the experiments are described in chronological order so maybe kids who are trying them out will slowly work up to the most complicated.

Bootleg: Murder, Moonshine, and the Lawless Years of Prohibition by **Karen Blumenthal. Roaring Brooks, 2011.** Blumenthal skillfully traces America's relationship with alcohol and the unexpected consequences of the 18th amendment which was devised to curtail drinking, but ended up encouraging crime.

The Captivating, Creative, Unusual History of Comic Books by **Jennifer M. Besel. Capstone Press, 2010.** In keeping with its subject, this book is colorfully illustrated. It not only goes from the beginning of the genre but dares to make predictions about the future.

Gangs by **Richard Swift. Groundwork Guide, 2011.** Swift explores the growth of gangs in major cities around the world, which he says have grown out of "a witch's brew of violence, guns, drugs, racism, and poverty." He hopes that by analyzing and revealing the contributing factors and the results, he can awaken both young people and adults to the dangers.

The Good, the Bad, and the Barbie: A Doll's History and Her Impact on Us by **Tanya Lee Stone. Viking, 2010.** Lee sent emails to thousands of people asking for their experiences with the Barbie Doll. She welded the responses into a remarkably readable and entertaining book that reveals fascinating relationships between marketing, popular culture, and social history.

Ideas That Changed the World by **Julie Ferris et al. DK, 2010.** In its usual style of beautifully illustrated books, this one will inspire as well as inform.

Killer Lipstick: And Other Spy Gadgets. 24/7: Science Behind the Scenes by **Don Rauf. Franklin Watts, 2009.** Good photos of spy equipment and real life examples make this a fascinating look into a business that many teenagers fantasize about joining.

Lucy Long Ago: Uncovering the Mystery of Where We Came From by **Catherine Thimmesh. Houghton, 2009.** In 1974, anthropologists discovered the skeletal fragments of a 3.2 million-years-old primate who walked on two feet and had an incredible brain. The remains were affectionately named Lucy and scientists are still trying to figure out what she says about human existence.

Mysterious Bones: The Story of Kennewick Man by **Katherine Kirkpatrick, illustrated by Emma Stevenson. Holiday House, 2011.** This well received book is suggested as a companion book to Patricia Lauber's *Who Came First?: New Clues to Prehistoric Americans* (National Geographic, 2003). It tells about the discovery of a 9000-year-old Paleoindian skeletal remains and the uproar that took place as Native American tribal groups went to work under the Native American Graves Protection and Reparation Act (NAGPRA) to be sure that the remains were treated lawfully and with respect. Scientists eventually received a moderate "go-ahead," which is just now being acted on.

No Choirboy: Murder, Violence, and Teenagers on Death Row by **Susan Kuklin. Holt, 2008.** The stories of four young men convicted of violent crimes are presented alongside the stories of people affected by their actions. Kuklin's well-researched narrative puts a human face on what is normally read only as a newspaper headline.

The North Pole Was Here: Puzzles and Perils at the Top of the World by **Andrew C. Revkin. New York Times, 2006.** Revkin is a *New York Times* reporter who accompanied modern day scientists to the top of the world. His book tells not only the contemporary story, but also those of previous explorers as it introduces readers to what climatologists and oceanographers do.

want to relax with an amusing book, they might choose Ruth Freeman Swain's 2008 *Underwear: What We Wear Under There*, illustrated by John O'Brien. For more books whose authors have worked hard to find unusual topics, look at Focus Box 9.3, "Intriguing Facts."

Narrative or Storytelling in Nonfiction

When Thomas Keneally's 1982 *Schindler's List* won a Pulitzer Prize in fiction, there was considerable controversy over whether the book was eligible because it was supposedly a journalistic account of a true event. E. L. Doctorow spoke to the same issue when he said in his acceptance speech for the National Book Critics Circle Award for *Ragtime,* "There is no more fiction or nonfiction, only narrative."

Three hundred English teachers who responded to a survey asking for ten adolescent novels and ten adult novels worthy of recommendation to teenagers gave further evidence that in people's minds fiction and nonfiction are blending together. Twelve of the top twenty recommended "novels" were actually such nonfiction books as Piers Paul Read's *Alive,* James Herriot's *All Creatures Great and Small,* Robin Graham's *Dove,* Alvin Toffler's *Future Shock,* and Dee Brown's *Bury My Heart at Wounded Knee.*

The blending of fiction and nonfiction has occurred from both directions. On one side are the nonfiction writers who use the techniques of fiction, including suspense, careful plotting and characterization, and literary devices, such as symbolism and metaphor. On the other side are the writers of fiction who do considerable research so that they won't be so likely to make mistakes in their fiction. For example, in a preface to *Izzy, Willy-Nilly,* Cynthia Voigt acknowledges help from medical personnel who taught her about the many physical and mental aspects of amputation. And in *A Single Shard,* it is obvious that Linda Sue Park has done extensive research on celadon pottery.

Good novels are fiction in the sense that fictional names are used and the authors combine bits and pieces of many individual stories. Nevertheless, in another sense, these stories are more real and actually present a more honest portrayal than some pieces labeled nonfiction that are true accounts of bizarre or strange happenings.

Literature—fiction and nonfiction—is more than a simple recounting or replaying of the life that surrounds the writer. It is a distillation. For example, Alex Haley's nonfictional *Roots* became real to millions of television viewers as well as to millions of readers, yet the book has to contain many fictional elements. The imagination of Haley's readers was captured by the fact that on September 29, 1967, he "stood on the dock in Annapolis where his great-great-great-great-great-grandfather was taken ashore on September 29, 1767," and sold as a slave to a Virginia plantation owner.

From this point, Haley set out to trace backward the six generations that connected him to a sixteen-year-old "prince" newly arrived from Africa. What the public might not stop to consider is that in the generation in which Haley started his story with the young couple, Omoro and Binta Kinte, and the birth of their first son, Kunta, there were 256 parents giving birth to 128 children, each one of whom is also a great-great-great-great-great-grandfather or grandmother to Alex Haley. The point is that even though Haley was writing nonfiction, he had an almost unlimited range of possibilities from which to choose. With the instincts of a storyteller, he selected powerful incidents and telling details. Someone with the instincts of an accountant or a clerk might have told a more complete, but less interesting, family history.

Young Scholars Speak Out

Mary Powell on Bringing Nonfiction and Music Together

With today's emphasis on high stakes testing and standardized curriculum, the arts have, unfortunately, been forgotten in many urban schools. As a high school English teacher in a Latino, low income, inner city school, I can relate to these pressures. After reading Connie Zitlow and Lois T. Stover's article in the spring 2011 *ALAN Review,* "Portrait of the Artist as a Young Adult: Who Is the Real Me?" I was inspired to integrate music into my ninth-grade language arts classroom. In their article, Zitlow and Stover describe the power that young adult authors have when they incorporate the arts into their books. Students are able to incorporate the therapeutic properties of dance, music, and drawing into their lives. Zitlow and Stover wrote that this was particularly true in relation to young adult novels because the books include characters of the students' same age, plus they are undergoing similar conflicts that everyday teens face. After reading this article, I wondered, what would happen if I asked my students to explore music through young adult, nonfiction books?

When I asked if they would be interested in doing something with music for their last project in the spring of 2011, they were enthused. I proposed that we would read about musical instruments and then create brochures to teach their classmates about an instrument of their choice.

I checked out a suitcase full of books on music from our public library, and wheeled them into class. Texts varied from books about music in Latin America, Asia, and Africa, to texts about the history of a variety of instruments including the banjo, keyboard, and guitar. I asked students to come up, peruse these books, and select a few pages that they wanted to read and incorporate into their brochures. This naturally became an exercise on how to limit a research topic, and on writing concisely, as I reminded my students, "This is a pamphlet to educate your peers, not an essay, so remember to limit your topic and be brief." It was also a fun, artistic activity as students decorated their brochures with symbols, pictures, and illustrations. Some students incorporated technology by creating them on the computer.

On the day the brochures were due, students volunteered to share their pamphlets with the class. One boy explained that he had selected the flute because he has played it for two years, and he wanted to find out more about it. When he explained that flutes can be made from gold, silver, and platinum, he was asked whether flutes sound differently based on what they are made from. A few students chose the guitar or piano because they had relatives who had played them, and they thought they "looked fun." Some expressed an interest in taking lessons, which showed that the project created interest beyond those who already had a strong musical connection.

During a presentation on the violin, the student presenter mentioned that it was once "the instrument of peasants." Although he could not explain the rationale behind this label, a girl in the class raised her hand and explained,

New Journalism, Literary Nonfiction, and Nonfiction Novels

Roots is part of the genre sometimes labeled *new journalism* or *literary nonfiction.* Truman Capote created the term *nonfiction novel* for *In Cold Blood,* his account of an especially brutal murder and the subsequent trial. Other terms

MUSIC IN
NONFICTION

Jazz **by Walter Dean Myers (Holiday House, 2006)** came with bold illustrations by Christopher Myers and melodious captions that explained the history behind be-bop, Louie Armstrong, and various jazz instruments. It also included a glossary of jazz terms, a timeline on jazz music, and an audio CD.

Musical Instruments of the World by M. J. Knight (Smart Apple Media, 2006) is a series with a book on brass and woodwinds, another on keyboards, and another on stringed instruments. Students especially liked the pictures from around the world.

Punk Rock Etiquette: The Ultimate How-to Guide for DIY, Punk, Indie, and Underground Bands **by Travis Nichols (Flash Point/Roaring Brook, 2008)** is a book for students beyond my freshmen in musical talent. Nonetheless, they still enjoyed the humor and the non-condescending attitude in telling teens what they need to know to start their own band.

"Wood was in higher supply so they were easier to make. And because servants would play violins for royalty, the upper classes considered it a peasant's instrument." I was happy to see the students involved and discussing music that came from different cultures and different times in history—even from today's digital world when synthesizers bring in noises from telephones and computers.

Having a whole array of books all different, but still related, inspired them to create their own variations on a theme. And when I went to search out the books, I was amazed at how new and how attractive they were. Here are some of the books that my students gravitated to, although it probably isn't necessary to use the very same books.

Raggin' Jazzin' Rockin': A History of American Musical Instrument Makers **by Susan VanHecke (Boyds Mills, 2011)** presents the history of the cymbal, piano, and guitar, and explains the role played by such musicians as John Phillips Sousa, the Beatles, and Larry Hammond, who instituted electricity into sound.

Two other books that Mary later found and plans to bring in the next time she does a project with music are Jennifer Armstrong's 2004 *What a Song Can Do: 12 Riffs on the Power of Music.* Armstrong edited the book and among the contributors are Joseph Bruchac, Ron Koertge, and David Levithan. The other one is Arnold Adoff's 2011 *Roots and Blues: A Celebration.* It is illustrated by R. Gregory Christie and was chosen as a 2011 "Best Book"

Mary Powell has taught high school English for eleven years. She was a 2011 Frederick Douglass Scholar at West Chester University in Pennsylvania, where she taught a young adult literature course to preservice English teachers. Mary has published articles on her classroom in the *English Journal* and in *Teaching & Learning: The Journal of Natural & Reflective Practice.* She is earning her Ph.D. in English education from Arizona State University and is writing her dissertation on the impact of a writing community on teachers' identities as educators and as writers.

that are used include *creative nonfiction, literary journalism, journalistic fiction,* and *advocacy journalism.* Although its roots were growing right along with journalism in general, it did not begin to flower until the 1960s. Part of the reason for its development is the increased educational level of the American public. Newspaper readers and television viewers, including young adults, are not satisfied with simplistic explanations. They want enough background information that they can feel confident in coming to their own conclusions.

Affluence, combined with modern technology, helps make the new journalism possible. Compare similar incidents that happened 126 years apart. In 1846, a group of travelers who came to be known as the Donner party were trapped in the high Sierras by an early snow. They had to stay there all winter without food, except for the flesh of their dead companions. After they were rescued, word of their ordeal gradually trickled "back east," so that for years afterwards sensationalized accounts were made up by writers who had no chance to come to the scene or interview the survivors.

Compare that with 1972. A planeload of Uruguayan travelers crashed in the Andes Mountains, and the survivors, who waited 2½ months for rescue, ate the flesh of those who died. The news, once discovered, was immediately flashed around the world. Author Piers Paul Read flew to Uruguay, where he stayed for several months interviewing survivors, government officials in charge of the search, and family and friends of both the deceased and the survivors. More than a year later, Lippincott published *Alive: The Story of the Andes Survivors*, which was on the *New York Times* best-seller list for seven months, and is a popular class-read in many high schools.

The fact that the survivors were in their early twenties undoubtedly helped teenagers to identify with the story, but so did the literary techniques that Read used. He focused on certain individuals, presenting miniature character sketches of some and fully developed portraits of others. The setting was crucial to the story, and he described it vividly. He was also careful to write so that the natural suspense of the situation came through. His tone was consistent throughout the book. He admired the survivors but did not shy away from showing the negative aspects of human nature when it was sorely tried. In a preface he said that the only liberty he allowed himself was the creation of dialogue between the characters, although, whenever possible, he relied on diaries and remembered comments and quarrels as well as his acquaintance with the survivors' speaking styles.

Literary nonfiction combines factual information with emotional appeal. Such books might be classified as biography, history, drama, essay, or personal experience, but regardless of classification, such books serve as a bridge between childhood and adult reading because of the straightforward, noncondescending style that is characteristic of good journalism.

Nonfiction best sellers often outsell fiction best sellers, and television producers have learned the appeal of "reality" shows. They also know they can add millions of viewers if they advertise a program as "a documentary" rather than "a drama."

Evaluation of Nonfiction

Evaluating nonfiction for young readers is more complicated than evaluating fiction because

1. People select informational books primarily on the basis of the subject matter, and because there is such a variety in subjects, people's choices vary tremendously, resulting in a lack of consensus on what is "the best."

2. Informative books on such topics as computers and car repair become dated more quickly than fiction books. Students preparing to take the SAT tests, wanting advice on handling money, or planning for a career need the most recent information. The constant turnover of informative books leaves us with few touchstone examples.

3. The transitory nature of informative nonfiction books discourages teachers and critics from giving them serious consideration as instructional materials. Although well-written personal experience narratives have long life spans, people who have made up their minds that they are not interested in nonfiction find it easy to ignore all nonfiction.

4. Reviewers and prize givers, many of whom come from English teaching backgrounds, may not feel competent to judge the technical or other specialized information presented in many informative books.

We suggest that the evaluation situation can be improved by readers looking at the intended audience and the content of the book. (What is it about? What information does it present?) Then look at the appropriateness and success with which each of the following is established.

Setting/Scope. Informative books may be historical, restricted to regional interests, or have a limited scope. In evaluating these, ask whether the author set realistic goals and whether the reading level of the intended audience matches the amount of space and backup graphics.

Theme. Informational books also have themes or purposes that are closely tied to the author's point of view. Is it meant to persuade someone to a particular belief or to inspire thoughtfulness, respect, or even curiosity? Some authors shout out their themes; others are more subtle. As you evaluate the theme, check for consistency throughout the book.

Tone. The manner in which an author achieves a desired goal sets the tone of a book. Is it hard-sell, strident, one-sided, humorous, loving, sympathetic, adulatory, scholarly, pedantic, energetic, or leisurely? Authors of informative books for children used to take a leisurely approach in hopes of enticing children into becoming interested in their subject, but today's young readers are just as busy as are their parents and often go to nonfiction books for quick information. A boy or girl who wants to repair a bicycle does not want to read the history of the Wright brothers and their bicycle shop before getting to the part on slipped gears.

Style. The best informative books also have style. As author Jane Langton said when she was asked to serve as a judge, the good books "exude some kind of passion or love or caring . . . and they have the potential for leaving a mark on the readers, changing them in some way." A problem in examining an author's style is that each book must be judged according to the purpose the author had in mind. From book-to-book, purposes are so different that it is like the old problem of comparing apples and oranges. Some books are successful simply because they are different—more like a mango than either an apple or an orange.

Contemporary Influences on the Publishing of Informational Books

Before the 1960s, the work published for young readers was mainly fiction (novels or short stories), poetry, or textbook material to be used in school. Few publishers thought that young readers would be interested in factual books unless they were forced to study them as part of their schoolwork. Then the Soviet Union launched *Sputnik,* and Americans were sincerely frightened that Russia was scientifically and technologically ahead. In 1961, Congress passed the National Defense Education Act, which gave millions of dollars to school libraries for the purchase of science and math books (later expanded to include

The older teens get, the more varied are their interests. Seventeen-year-old Assiris liked reading Walter Dean Myers's Time to Love: Stories from the Old Testament *because of the illustrations and the fact that they weren't interrupted by "all those Bible numbers." Seventeen-year-old Luke chose to read Lisa Smedman's* From Boneshakers to Choppers: The Rip-Roaring History of Motorcycles *because everyone in his family owns a motorcycle and he wanted to learn some things the others didn't know. See the Focus Boxes in this chapter for several equally disparate choices.*

all books). Publishers competed to create information books that would both qualify for purchase under the Act and attract young readers.

The rise in nonfiction's popularity has paralleled the information explosion and the rise in the power and influence of the mass media. Today there is simply more information to be shared between reader and writer. Television, radio, movies, newspapers, magazines, and now the Internet all communicate the same kinds of information as do books. But because whatever is produced by the mass media must be of interest to a *mass* audience, writers for newspapers and television are not as free to look for unusual topics or to present them from unusual viewpoints as are the writers of books. Teenagers are especially interested in books that present the extremes of life's experiences, which is why our college students get nostalgic smiles on their faces when we mention *The Guinness Book of World Records*. Whatever is the biggest, the best, or the most unusual is of interest, as shown in Focus Box 9.3, "Intriguing Facts," page 288. Authors also search for an angle that will tie the subject to teenagers. A good example is the *Junior Chronicle of the 20th Century* produced by Dorling Kindersley. Each of the oversized pages is illustrated with photographs from the year that is being shown. The editors were careful to find at least one youth-oriented photo for each double-page spread.

Books to Support and Extend the School Curriculum

Informational books purchased by school libraries are usually referred to as "books to support the curriculum," but a more accurate description would probably be "books to extend the curriculum" because these books seldom help students who are doing poorly in class. Instead they provide challenges for successful students to go further than their classmates. We do not have room in this textbook to print more than a sampling of the kinds of nonfiction that teenagers read. Some of it serves as models for research. It can go beyond the obvious facts to present information that is too complicated, too detailed, too obscure, or too controversial to be included in textbooks. For example, a legitimate complaint often voiced about history books is that they focus on war and violence and leave out life as it was lived by most people. Another complaint is that they leave out the experiences of women and minorities. For example, school history textbooks do not mention contraception, but nothing has changed women's lives more than the birth control pill. Well-written and well-illustrated trade books serve as a counterbalance to these omissions.

New books that help students prepare, or at least think about, careers range from something as focused as Peter Larson and Kristin Donnan's *Bones Rock! Everything You Need to Know to Be a Paleontologist* to something as general as Gloria Skurzynski's *Sweat and Blood: A History of U.S. Labor Unions*. Donna M. Jackson's *ER Vets: Life in an Animal Emergency Room* may disillusion animal lovers who have romantic fantasies of saving beautiful pets for grateful people, while *Steven Caney's Ultimate Building Book* may inspire future architects and builders. When selecting such books, librarians and teachers should remember that because young readers lack the kind of background knowledge that most adults have, it is especially important that informative books be well organized and indexed in such a way that readers can look up facts without reading the whole book. Unclear references or confusing directions are especially troublesome in how-to books, which range from books as practical and up-to-date as Ron Miller's *Digital Art: Painting with Pixels* to something as ambitious as Arlene Hirschfelder's *Kick Butts! A Kid's Action Guide to a Tobacco-Free America*.

How-to books are seldom best sellers, simply because they are so specialized that they appeal to fairly limited audiences. The challenge for the educator is to let students know about their availability. Once students find their way into the library to check out a book that helps them accomplish a particular goal, they are likely to return for other books.

With sports books, obviously the first thing a reader looks for is the particular sport; consequently, authors choose titles that practically shout to potential readers. But one thing to watch for in a how-to sports book is whether costs are mentioned. It is almost cruel for an author to write a glowing account of a child star in tennis, gymnastics, skating, swimming, or dancing and leave young readers with the impression that all it takes is hard work. Those readers whose parents do not have time or money for transportation, lessons, entry fees, equipment, and clothes should be let in on the secret that there's more to how you play the game than meets the eye. A similar warning needs to be given about books telling kids how to establish their own businesses or how to get into show business. Such wish-fulfilling books about unusual successes are likely to set the stage for disappointment among the thousands of more typical kids who find themselves working in fast-food restaurants or as grocery store courtesy clerks for minimum wages. There's a need for more books about these less glamorous jobs as well as for the kind of commonsense guidance found in Neale S. Godfrey's *Godfrey's Ultimate Kid's Money Book*.

For academically inclined high school students, it is important to bring books about college to their attention early on because the actual application process takes eighteen months, and its success or failure may depend on what classes a student took as a freshman. High school libraries should have recent editions of such books as *The Fiske Guide to Colleges* and the Princeton Review's guide to *Visiting College Campuses* as well as various practice books designed to help students do well on admissions examinations.

Biographical Books

Today's biographies for young adults are likely to provide a balance of both strengths and weaknesses. They demonstrate how the subject and the reader share similar emotions. Both have fears and insecurities, and both succumb to temptations and vanities. After reading a good biography, the reader feels a kinship with the subject, not so much in spite of as because of the character's human frailties.

To say that a biography is written *objectively* does not mean that it is written without feeling. For biographies to ring true, the author must become immersed in the subject's life so that he or she can write with passion and commitment. This implies a point of view, not one imposed by an author who set out to prove a preconceived idea but a unifying force that guided the person's life and was discovered by the author through his or her research. It used to be that, especially with biographies written for children, authors praised their subjects and made them seem almost too good to be true. But then people began to point out that the end result of such adulation was counterproductive because children knew they could never be that perfect and so they just gave up trying.

Today we are more likely to read debunking than fawning biographies because authors are tempted to capitalize on the attention that goes with knocking a hero or an institution off from a pedestal. Some people call such books anti-hero, but while they may be "anti-hero" in the popular sense of the word, they differ from true examples of the literary meaning because the subject of a debunking biography is not written about with sympathy. The best authors try to balance out their reporting as did Elizabeth Partridge when she wrote *John Lennon: All I Want Is the Truth,* which won a BCCB Blue Ribbon Nonfiction Book Award. She wrote about Lennon's razor-sharp wit and his activism for peace and for female rights. She showed him to be a complicated and contradictory figure who would chant peace, but hit women and fight men. He was extremely strong and independent, but he needed someone to contain him—his Aunt Mimi, Paul McCartney, and finally Yoko Ono.

Claudette Colvin: Twice Toward Justice won a 2009 National Book Award for its author, Philip Hoose. It was a touching moment at the November 18 National Book Awards ceremony when Hoose was declared the winner in the young readers division and he and his guest, a not-so-young Claudette Colvin, walked slowly toward the podium. He assured her that she didn't need to hurry because this was her "moment."

On March 2, 1955, Claudette, "a bespectacled, studious looking" fifteen-year-old school girl, was forced off a city bus in Montgomery, Alabama; arrested; and charged with violating segregation laws, disturbing the peace, and "assaulting" a police officer. Others who had been arrested on similar charges had pleaded guilty, but Claudette felt she had done nothing wrong—she certainly had not "assaulted" a police officer—and so she refused to plead guilty.

Black leaders rallied around Claudette, raising money, writing letters, and meeting with legal officials. When she was found guilty on all charges, "The verdict was like a bombshell." It contributed to the outrage and the sense of togetherness among the Blacks in Montgomery, and this is when the leaders decided to ask Rosa Parks, a dressmaker and seamstress who was a leader in the Montgomery National Association for the Advancement of Colored People (NAACP), to repeat Claudette's action. They thought that an older, more respected community member would be a better representative for their cause than the young Claudette, so Hoose was telling the truth about the awards ceremony being Claudette's "moment." His prize-winning book has given Claudette her rightful place in history.

It is because of the actions of so many young people in the American Civil Rights Movement of the 1950s and 1960s that authors have written many young adult books about the movement. See Focus Box 9.4, "Young People and Civil Rights" on page 298. Also see Focus Box 9.6, "Starred Biographies of Atypical Heroes." One of the books in the biographies will be Deborah Heiligman's beautifully written and researched story of *Charles and Emma Darwin: The Darwins'*

***Birmingham Sunday* by Larry Dane Brimmer. Boyds Mills, 2010.** This is a good book to go with Christopher Paul Curtis's fictional *The Watsons Go to Birmingham, 1963.* Brimmer tells the story, with photos and other documentation, of the children who died in the church bombing on September 16, 1963.

***Black and White Airmen: Their True History* by John Fleischman. Houghton Mifflin, 2007.** John Leahr was black and Herb Heilbrun was white in a time when racism was rampant. They grew up together and went into the WWII Air Force, successfully flying fifty missions as partners. Their story is only one of many about black and white airmen fighting together after Pearl Harbor.

***Cause: Reconstruction America 1863–1877* by Tonya Bolden. Alfred Knopf, 2005.** Archival photos, excellent graphics, and political cartoons help Bolden achieve a sense of storytelling as she writes about the Civil Rights Act of 1866, the plight of Native Americans and freed slaves, and the women's suffrage movement during a time of national expansion.

***Denied, Detained, Deported: Stories from the Dark Side of American* Immigration by Ann Bausum, National Geographic, 2009.** This 130-year history of U. S. immigration policy will help to put into perspective the current debates about "border control."

***Fort Mose: And the Story of the Man Who Built the First Free Black Settlement in Colonial America* by Glennette Tilley Turner. Abrams, 2010.** This is a bit of American history that has been ignored so it's a step in the right direction for Turner to have done her careful research and equally careful writing.

***Freedom Riders: John Lewis and Jim Zwerg on the Front Lines of the Civil Rights Movement* by Ann Bausum. National Geographic, 2006.** Bausum tells the story of the 1960s civil rights movement through the eyes of two young men—one white and one black—who joined in the freedom rides of the 1960s. Bausum's book was honored as the most distinguished piece of youth literature written in 2006 by a Wisconsin resident.

***Heart and Soul: The Story of America and African Americans* written and illustrated by Kadir Nelson. HarperCollins, 2011.** Nelson's dramatic paintings illustrate the stories that are related by an unnamed narrator. They are about his relatives and the roles they played in crucial American events that range from fighting alongside George Washington to marching with Rev. Martin Luther King, Jr. Another Kadir Nelson book that has proved popular, especially in its audio version narrated by Dion Graham, is *We Are the Ship: The Story of Negro League Baseball.*

***Little Rock Girl 1957: How a Photograph Changed the Fight for Integration* by Shelley Tougas. Compass Point Books, 2011.** Tougas tells the story of the now famous photo of two high school girls—one white and one black—whose picture was taken on the day that the fifteen-year-old Elizabeth Eckford arrived all by herself to enroll in Central High School in Little Rock, Arkansas. The dramatic photo taken by newspaper reporter Will Counts was flashed across the country. Many years later, Counts returned and took a picture of the same two women reconciling in front of their old high school.

***Marching for Freedom: Walk Together, Children, and Don't You Grow Weary* by Elizabeth Partridge. Viking, 2009.** Partridge's book focus on the 1963 voting rights protests in Selma, Alabama. It is described as having an eloquent text, accompanied by haunting images.

***New Boy* by Julian Houston. Houghton, 2005.** It is the 1950s and fifteen-year-old Rob Garrett comes from the South to be the first African American to attend a prestigious Connecticut boarding school. He learns that prejudice wears different faces, especially when he visits a cousin in Harlem and meets Malcolm X and his followers.

***The Power of One: Daisy Bates and the Little Rock Nine* by Judith Fradin and Dennis Brindell Fradin. Clarion, 2004.** Daisy Bates and her husband, L. C. Bates, published the *Arkansas State Press,* which in the 1950s presented news from the local black community not only for Little Rock, but for the world. She was the mentor and constant supporter of the nine African American students who in 1957 integrated Central High School in Little Rock.

***We Shall Overcome: The History of the Civil Rights Movement As It Happened* by Herb Boyd, Ossie Davis and Ruby Dee. Sourcebooks MediaFusion, 2004.** Boyd uses a clear, journalistic style to tell his living history which begins with the murder of Emmett Till in 1955 and ends with the assassination of Dr. Martin Luther King, Jr., in 1968. Each chapter is dedicated to a specific person or event.

Focus Box 9.5

Nonfiction Books about War and Its Effects on Young People

Anne Frank: Her Life in Words and Pictures from the Archives of the Anne Frank House by Menno Metselaar, Ruud Van der Rol, translated by Arnold J. Pomerans. Flashpoint, 2009. This non-fiction account, with its many photographs, including family photos, makes a good addition to all of the other Anne Frank books now available.

Bearing Witness: Stories of the Holocaust by Hazel Rochman and Darlene Z. McCampbell. Orchard, 1995. This marvelous collection of material will shock readers just as other selections will give them pictures of real heroes.

The Beautiful Days of My Youth: My Six Months in Auschwitz and Plaszow by Ana Novac. Holt, 1997. As Nazis kill and cremate concentration camp victims, Novac keeps a diary of the horrors.

The Diary of Anne Frank hardly needs an introduction but the 1995 definitive edition of *Anne's Frank's Diary* adds some details and makes her appear more human. Also of interest is Miep Gies's *Anne Frank Remembered* (S&S, 1987), which is the autobiography of the woman who helped hide the Frank family.

Ghosts of War by Ryan Smithson. HarperCollins, 2009. Smithson is one of the youngest veterans to come home from Iraq and Afghanistan and to get his memoir published. He was in high school on 9/11 and enlisted in the Army when he was only 17 and was sent to Iraq when he was 19.

Hidden Child by Isaac Millman. Farrar/Frances FosterBooks, 2005. For middle school students, this seventy-three-page biography tells the story of a Jewish boy whose Parisian mother bribed officials to take him out of the deportation line and to a hospital. Six years later, when he is fifteen, he is adopted by an American Jewish family.

Hiding to Survive: Stories of Jewish Children Rescued from the Holocaust by Maxine B. Rosenberg. Clarion, 1994. Fourteen Americans, now in their fifties and sixties, remember what they can of being hidden.

I Never Saw Another Butterfly: Children's Drawings and Poems from Terezin Concentration Camp, 1942–1944 by Hana Volavkova. Schoken, 1978. This oversized book contains reproductions of art work done by imprisoned children. It is often used in middle school to introduce a unit on the Holocaust.

Never to Forget: The Jews of the Holocaust by Milton Meltzer. Harper, 1988. Meltzer did his usual fine job of collecting and reporting in this book. Ten years later he wrote the story of how Gentiles saved Jews in the Holocaust.

The Tragic History of the Japanese-American Internment Camps: From Many Cultures, One History by Deborah Kent. Enslow, 2008. A general overview is given, plus many personal accounts.

Truce: The Day the Soldiers Stopped Fighting by Jim Murphy. Scholastic, 2009. Murphy not only gives authentic details about how five months into World War I, soldiers all along the front began emerging on Christmas Day for an impromptu cease-fire. He also recounts the events leading up to the war and includes old photos from the era. Ambitious students might enjoy making a comparison with Scott Westerfeld's imagined account of World War I in the Leviathan series.

War Is . . . : Soldiers, Survivors, and Storytellers Talk about War edited by Patty Campbell and Marc Aronson. Candlewick Press, 2008. The two editors/collectors have opposing views about the inevitability of war, but they both believe that young people need to hear—or in this case, read—honest statements from people with first-hand experience.

The War to End All Wars: World War I by Russell Freedman. Clarion, 2010. World War I, which either directly or indirectly cost the lives of 20 million people, was so terrible that the world vowed it would be the last world war. As we now know, the cautionary prediction did not come true. Freedman's book is part of a renewed interest in the period.

When Elephants Fight: The Lives of Children in Conflict in Afghanistan, Bosnia, Sri Lanka, Sudan, and Uganda by Eric Walters and Adrian Bradbury. Orca, 2008. One child from each country is featured as the centerpiece for the history and conditions surrounding the wars going on in their countries.

Zlata's Diary: A Child's Life in Sarajevo by Zlata Filipovic. Penguin, 1994. A fifth-grade girl kept a diary of the horrors, the friendships, and the love and the blood that she saw during the Serbian-Croatian war.

Amelia Earhart: This Broad Ocean **by Sarah Stewart Taylor and James Sturm. Hyperion, 2010.** Here's a graphic novel that is as inventive and lively as its heroine.

American Slave, American Hero: York of the Lewis and Clark Expedition **by Laurence Pringle. Boyds Mill, 2006.** Beautiful paintings add to the story of the man who went on the Lewis and Clark Expedition because he was "owned" by William Clark. His documented contributions went way beyond what was expected.

Becoming Billie Holiday **by Carol Boston, illustrated by Floyd Cooper. Boyds Mills/2008.** Boston uses lines from Holiday's songs as the titles of her narrative poems that tell a powerful story of how a poor and neglected girl from the streets lifts herself into a position of respect and fame. Cooper's illustrations are a good match for Boston's poetry.

Black Elk's Vision: A Lakota Story **by S. D. Nelson. Abrams, 2010.** Nelson's beautiful illustrations, combined with archival photographs and solid research, makes for a book that will introduce readers to the complex history of Native Americans.

Cleopatra Rules: The Amazing Life of the Original Teen Queen **by Vicky Alvear Shecter. Boyds Mills, 2010.** Shecter's lively writing style and the seductive cover will draw readers to the book and might even make them decide that history can be fun.

The Duel: The Parallel Lives of Alexander Hamilton & Aaron Burr **by Judith St. George. Viking, 2009.** St. George tells a fascinating story of two prominent political leaders through alternating chapters that lead up to the July morning in 1804 when they face each other in a duel.

Frederick Douglass: A Noble Life **by David Adler. Holiday House, 2010.** This commanding biography uses black and white photos and reproductions of documents to tell the story of the first slave to become an eloquent spokesperson for his people.

I Heard God Talking to Me: William Edmondson and His Stone Carvings **by Elizabeth Spires. Farrar, 2009.** Spires uses free-verse poems in this biography of an African American stone sculptor who explored the mysteries of life with his "rock-solid-faith."

The Lincolns: A Scrapbook Look at Abraham and Mary **by Candace Fleming. Random, 2008.** Primary sources and archival photos help Fleming present side-by-side portraits of the famous first couple.

The Notorious Benedict Arnold: A True Story of Adventure, Heroism and Treachery **by Steve Sheinkin. Roaring Brook, 2010.** There is much more to Benedict Arnold than his name as a traitor. In the Continental Army, he was a general known for his long-time courage and loyalty.

Onward: A Photobiography of African-American Polar Explorer Matthew Henson **by Dolores Johnson. National Geographic, 2005.** Henson was hired to go on Robert E. Peary's trip to the North Pole as Peary's manservant, but he became much more than that as the group faced terrifying conditions. He was posthumously awarded the National Geographic Society's Hubbard Medal.

Rachel Carson **by Ellen Levine. Viking, 2007.** Part of the Up Close series, this book introduces Carson as someone readers would like to know. It also shows why she deserves so much credit for being a pioneer in the environmental movement.

10 Explorers Who Changed the World **by Clive Gifford, illustrated by David Cousens. Kingfisher/Macmillan, 2008.** Done in the style of a colorful graphic novel, the book starts with the first explorers and goes through the 1990s. A "Life Links" part shows how they and their accomplishment are connected to each other.

The Trouble Begins at 8: A Life of Mark Twain in the Wild, Wild West **by Sid Fleischman. HarperCollins, 2008.** Samuel Clemens's mischievous childhood and rambunctious youth fits well with Sid Fleischman's playful writing style. The nineteenth-century photographs and reproductions reveal how Samuel Clemens, by the age of thirty, had become America's resident wit under the name of Mark Twain.

The Voice That Challenged a Nation: Marian Anderson and the Struggle for Equal Rights **by Russell Freedman. Clarion, 2004.** In his usual style, Freedman creates a beautifully designed and well-told biography of the talented singer who became a star in the political as well as the entertainment world.

Leap of Faith. It was a finalist for the National Book Award, the Printz Award, and the *L. A. Times* Book Prize. It stood out from the dozens of books about Darwin that were published that year in honor of his 200th birthday because it focused on both Charles and Emma. Heiligman thought she was the perfect person to write such a book because she majored in religious studies in college and shortly after graduation met and married a science writer. He told her about how Charles Darwin and his wife, Emma, loved each other, but that the religious Emma was worried that Charles "would go to hell and they wouldn't be together for eternity." Heiligman put this conversation in her closing acknowledgments and added, "If bells had chimed . . . or fireworks had exploded in the sky. . . . I would not have been surprised [because] I knew right then I had a book to write."

Although, in their deep structure, biographical books share the same purpose of letting readers learn about individuals who for some reason are of special interest, in their surface structures or their forms they differ as described in the following text.

Autobiographies have an immediate and obvious appeal to readers. "Who," we ask ourselves, "would know more about this person than the person? Who could better tell us this person's story?" The truth may be that almost anyone else could do a better job. Most of us want to look good to others. This means that we might leave out a significant piece of our lives that still embarrasses us or humiliates us or leaves us feeling unsure of ourselves and our motives. This is not to say that autobiographies are automatically untrustworthy, only that they may not tell the whole story or that certain parts may be left out, possibly for good reason, possibly not.

While celebrity autobiographies and biographies are the ones that get in the news and are likely to be requested from libraries, some of them present problems for educators. By the time a biography or autobiography of some new celebrity has gone through a rigorous selection procedure, the subject may no longer be of interest. Also, many of the books present questionable or outright immoral concepts. For example, Wilt Chamberlain's *A View from Above* has a chapter, "On Sex and Love: What Rules the World," which makes clear that he believes he is lucky because he has had sexual relations with nearly 20,000 women. That may impress Chamberlain, but it is likely to bother most adults.

With questionable books, it's usually better that teenagers have a chance to read the whole book rather than just get the smatterings of sexual or violent titillation that appear in the media. One thing we can feel confident in suggesting is that when it comes to selecting books about which you are unsure, check out your initial reaction with others. Talk to colleagues, parents, and students, especially students, because unless someone starts young people along such a line of thinking, they may never understand that reading about someone's life does not necessarily mean emulating everything about that person. As librarian Mary Mueller observed in a *School Library Journal* article:

> Our past and present are full of personages who lived outside traditional rules. They often used poor judgment or acted in a less-than-exemplary fashion. . . . How can we expect our students to really see the personality of Harry Truman without letting them see the tenacity, salty language, and temper that so characterized him? (Nov. 1991, pp. 55–56)

Several authors have told us that young readers seem to be put off by the terms nonfiction *and* biographies, *and so whenever feasible they prefer to identify themselves as authors of* historical adventures.

The decision whether to consider a book a personal experience or an autobiography is often up to the reader. For example, Maya Angelou's *I Know Why the Caged Bird Sings* and its three sequels are usually considered either autobiographies moving chronologically through Angelou's life, or as personal experience stories.

Collective biographies have become increasingly popular because authors can write about individuals whose lives may not have been chronicled fully enough to provide information for an entire book. Collective biographies are also an efficient way to get information about previously ignored individuals into a library. Authors usually bring together the stories of people who have something in common. For example, Russell Freedman's *Indian Chiefs,* the biographies of six western Indian chiefs during the 1800s, is a stronger condemnation of white treatment of Native Americans than it would have been had he told only one of their stories. *Gold Rush Women* by Claire Rudolf Murphy and Jane G. Haigh takes a look at twenty-three women who were among the adventurers flocking to Alaska in the 1890s when gold was discovered. *The Smithsonian Book of the First Ladies: Their Lives, Times, and Issues,* edited by Edith P. Mayo, tells the equally interesting and unique stories of women at the opposite end of the social scale.

Memoirs differ from biographies because there is no obligation for a writer to tell about his or her whole life. They can choose just the part that hangs together or that tells a good story. A memoir can be a quite ordinary story of growing up in ways that make young readers feel privileged to get acquainted with a new friend. For example, the first paragraph in Mark Salzman's *Lost in Place: Growing Up Absurd in Suburbia* is witty and certainly likely to grab the attention of most readers:

When I was thirteen years old I saw my first kung fu movie, and before it ended I decided that the life of a wandering Zen monk was the life for me. I announced my willingness to leave East Ridge Junior High School immediately and give up all material things, but my parents did not share my enthusiasm. They made it clear that I was not to become a wandering Zen monk until I had finished high school. In the meantime I could practice kung fu and meditate down in the basement. So I immersed myself in the study of Chinese boxing and philosophy with the kind of dedication that is possible only when you don't yet have to make a living, when you are too young to drive and when you don't have a girlfriend.

The best memoir that we have read in the last few years is Jack Gantos's *Hole in My Life,* which was a runner-up for the 2002 Printz Award. As shown by the smoothness and the power of the writing, Gantos has written this story probably dozens of times, if not on paper, at least in his head. It is an account of the fifteen months he spent in a federal prison between high school and college. He had helped to sail a boatload of hashish from the Virgin Islands to New York City, where he used a shopping cart to make the deliveries that his employers, Ken and Hamilton, had set up. As Jack explains one morning after the ritual head-count at the prison,

> I was in. Counted in. After breakfast I was counted. Before dinner I was counted. After dinner. Before lights out. Then while I slept. And even then I turned that phrase over and over in my mind: "Count me in." Those were three words I'd take back if I could. They were my words to Ken and Hamilton. "Count me in." Now I was counted in my cell every day, and I was counted on to be there morning, noon, and night.

The first time Jack wrote this story, he squeezed it in between the lines of a prison library copy of Dostoevsky's *The Brothers Karamozov* (journals were not allowed). When he was released, the prison guard who searched his suitcase took out the book for return to the library. Although he never saw it again, it is likely that his memories are more vivid because he wrote them down. When he received an early release from prison because of good behavior and because he had gotten himself accepted at a junior college, he began writing "brutal stories about prison, about New York street life, about the men I knew who had hard lives and hard hearts." Then one day he grew "tired of all the blood and guts and hard lives and hard hearts and began to write more stories" about his childhood. Middle school readers know him best for *Joey Pigza Swallowed the Key* and *Joey Pigza Loses Control* (a 2001 Newbery Honor Book).

In recommending this book to readers, adults need to realize that it is written for mature high school students, not the kids who read the Joey Pigza books. When Gantos came and spoke to our students at Arizona State, he said that the book was as much a cautionary tale for adults as for kids. He wants adults to get the message that we should not give up on kids who are in trouble. With the right help, and a lot of luck, they may survive and go on to become the kind of adult who can make the world a better place.

The success of personal experience books depends largely on the quality of the writing because there isn't a plot for readers to get excited about, and honest accounts lack the kinds of literary exaggeration that make for intriguing villains and heroes. One aspect of personal experience books that makes them attractive to young readers is that they are by people looking back on experiences they had when they were young. For example, Robin Graham, author of *Dove,* was only sixteen when he set sail on his own boat to go around the world. Steven Callahan, author of *Adrift: Seventy-Six Days Lost at Sea,* was twenty-nine when he set sail. In the personal experience books about adult protagonists that teenagers enjoy, the adults are likely to be unencumbered by family responsibilities. For example, mature young readers enjoy such travel books as Peter Matthiessen's *African Silences,* Charles Kuralt's *A Life on the Road,* and Bruce Chatwin's *What Am I Doing Here?*

Teenagers' Emotional and Physical Health

When young adult specialist Patty Campbell spoke at an American Library Association annual meeting, she pointed out that teenagers are so wrapped up in what the psychologists have labeled the "adolescent identity crisis" that they have neither the time for, nor the interest in, sitting down and reading about the world in general. What they are looking for are books that help them decide on who they are and where they fit into the scheme of things. Informative books they judge to be helpful include sex education books, some physical and mental health books, selected how-to books, and memoirs or fictional accounts of experiences teenagers can imagine themselves or their acquaintances having. For many teens, the only other "information" books they consult are read under duress—only because teachers assign reports and research papers.

Marie Hardenbrook, former librarian at McClintock High School in Tempe, Arizona, told us that teenagers especially appreciate books that give advice on managing one's life and being successful right now. Her "Inspirational" display and booklist was consistently popular. She included such sports-related books as Richard E. Peck's *Something for Joey,* William Blinn's *Brian's Song,* and Shannon Miller's *Winning Every Day: Gold Medal Advice for a Happy, Healthy Life.* The runaway best loaners, however, were Jack Canfield's Chicken Soup books, including two volumes of *Chicken Soup for the Teenage Soul: 101 Stories of Life, Love, and Learning;* and others in the series with such subtitles as *The Pet Lover's Soul: Stories about Pets as Teachers, Healers, Heroes, and Friends;* and *The Woman's Soul: 101 Stories to Open the Hearts and Rekindle the Spirits of Women.* Teens also look for books that will offer answers to such specific questions as:

Can I get AIDS from French kissing?

Do I have diabetes?

Why do I feel like crying all the time?

What's the difference between just trying a drug and becoming addicted?

The best books offering answers to such questions have good indexing, clear writing, suggestions for further reading, and, where appropriate, information about Web pages, telephone numbers, and support groups. The *Need to Know Library,* put out by Rosen publishers, is a dependable series of self-help books. Each book is sixty-four pages and includes a glossary, index, photos, and suggestions for further reading. With self-help books, girls make up the majority of

While nearly all self-help and advice books contain information about physical health and safe sex, what most kids are really interested in are the emotional aspects.

readers; hence, authors and publishers work hard to create such books as Erika V. Shearin Karres's *Mean Chicks, Cliques, and Dirty Tricks: A Real Girl's Guide to Getting Through the Day with Smarts and Style* and *Girlsource: A Book by and for Young Women about Relationships, Rights, Futures, Bodies, Minds, and Souls*. And even a more neutral sounding title such as Florence Cadier and Melissa Daly's *My Parents Are Getting Divorced: How to Keep It Together When Your Parents Are Splitting Up* will probably attract more girl than boy readers.

The exploration of sexual matters in books for young readers is an especially sensitive area for the following reasons:

- Young adults are physically mature, but they probably have had little intellectual and emotional preparation for making sex-related decisions.

- Parents are anxious to protect their children from making sex-related decisions that might prove harmful.

- Old restraints and patterns of behavior and attitudes are being questioned, so that there is no clear-cut model to follow.

- Sex is such an important part of American culture and the mass media that young people are forced to think about and take stands on such controversial issues as homosexuality, premarital sex, violence in relation to sex, and the role of sex in love and family relationships.

- Talking about sexual attitudes and beliefs with their teenage children may make parents uncomfortable, especially if the father and the mother have different views. This means that many young people must get their information outside of the home.

While some books focus specifically on a problem such as AIDS or pregnancy, it is more common for books to cover emotional as well as physical aspects of sexual activity. No single book can satisfy all readers, and this is true of those dealing with sex education. An entire collection must be evaluated and books provided for a wide range of interests, attitudes, beliefs, and lifestyles. Those who criticize libraries for including books that present teenage sexual activity as the norm have a justified complaint if the library does not also have sex education books that present, or even promote, abstinence as a normal route for young people.

Materials dealing with sex are judged quite differently from those on less controversial topics. For example, in most subject areas, books are given plus marks if they succeed in getting the reader emotionally involved, but with books about sex, some adults feel that it is better for young readers to be presented with straightforward "plumbing manuals"—the less emotional involvement the better. Other adults argue that it is the emotional part that young people need to learn. Coming to agreement is not at all easy because adults have such varying attitudes and experiences.

College students in our YA lit class each brought in a sex-education book to share in small groups. Each group was to choose the most "interesting" example—for better or for worse—to share with the class. Everyone giggled when the teacher brought out a "sexometer" and said the groups needed to decide on a number for the sexiness of their book. It was a good exercise to demonstrate how differently individuals viewed the books. The groups had a hard time agreeing on something as basic as defining "sexiness," much less on how to incorporate the idea into their evaluation of particular books. This is not an exercise suggested for high school students. Even the college students felt awkward about it and did not want their faces shown in a photograph setting the "sexometer" for their group presentation.

The issue today which is deservedly getting lots of attention from educators and parents relates to the prevention of bullying, especially in relation to GLBT (Gay, Lesbian, Bisexual, Transgendered) issues. *Acting Out! Combating Homophobia through Teacher Activism,* edited by Mollie V. Blackburn, Caroline T. Clark, Lauren M. Kenney, and Jill M. Smith (Teachers College Press, 2010), has just been chosen as the 2011 winner of the Richard Meade Award given by the Conference on English Education (a unit of the National Council of Teachers of English) for outstanding research in English Education. The authors first began giving serious thoughts to the matter in 2004 when the State of Ohio was involved in a "brewing battle over same-sex marriage." Later, they acknowledged that their book probably had its informal beginning six years earlier when they were horrified at the October 1998 murder of Matthew Shepherd, a university student who was tortured and left to die on a prairie near Laramie, Wyoming. Witnesses testified that he was killed because of his sexual orientation. A combination of these events led a group of English teachers to form a study group to see what they could do about what they viewed as a very real problem. In the foreword to their book, they ask the question:

> How many times in classes, social groups, or relationships—in the daily living of our lives—do we blunder, insult, objectify, marginalize, remain silent, silence others, or assume too much or too little?

For many people, Shepherd's death, followed by several teen suicides connected to bullying related to sexual orientation, was the beginning of a new kind of consciousness-raising about the evils of a prejudice that in many ways has been practiced and protected not only by individuals, but also by social, religious, educational, and government agencies. While many of us view such actions as mean-spirited, other well-meaning people think they are protecting the overall good. In their view, homosexuality should be made to look abhorrent so that people will not choose to make it part of their own lifestyles.

One of the things that made us give some serious thought to this is what M. E. Kerr told us about her speaking visits to middle schools. She said that school principals wait for her in the parking lot so they can tell her not to mention her books that refer to lesbianism because they want to "protect the children." Kerr's view of such behavior is that what is being protected is the prejudice, not the children, who in today's culture already know that gay people exist.

Both mass media and professional journals have been paying considerable attention to the matter. For example, the July 25, 2011, *Newsweek* devoted four pages to an article, "Why Gay Marriage Is Good for Straight America." And in a July 25, 2011, three-page feature movie review and chronology of the Harry Potter films, *Time* magazine gave prime space to the October 19, 2007, quote from J. K. Rowling, who at a Carnegie Hall book-tour event announced that Dumbledore was gay. When the audience burst into clapping and cheering, Rowling quipped, "If I had known this would have made you this happy, I would have told you years ago."

The June 2011 issue of *VOYA* carried an article by Haydee Camacho, "Where GLBT Literature Is Going and Why It Matters" (pp. 138–139). Camacho began with, "When the first teen novel featuring gay characters, *I'll Get There. It Better Be Worth the Trip* by John Donovan was published in 1969, the Stonewall Riots starting the gay rights movement had not yet taken place." Then Camacho pointed out that Donovan's book, which has been out of print for years, was reissued by Flux Books in September 2010.

To get information for her article, Camacho queried members of the American Library Association's GLBT Round Table, the Rainbow Project, and the Stonewall Book Award Committee. Lynn Evarts, a librarian in central Wisconsin and chair of the ALA Rainbow Project Committee, told Camacho that she appreciates the fact that GLBT literature is at a transition point where GLBT characters are in the book, but their sexual identity is not the main point of the book. Other librarians said they were glad to see that publishers are now seeking out well-written stories about GLBT characters. As more talented authors are considering the matter, the quality of the books is going up. John Green and David Levithan's upbeat *Will Grayson, Will Grayson* (Dutton, 2010) was the first gay-themed book to make it to the *New York Times* Best Sellers list.

Evarts is also encouraged that more students are reading the literature and passing it on because in her community there are people who believe "we don't have gay people here." She thinks it is good for students to read about gay characters because it might make them think, "That sounds like someone I know or could know." Evarts also likes the Rainbow Project book list because it supports librarians who can say, "This book is on an ALA list. It's okay to put it on my library bookshelf and I can defend it."

However, librarians and teachers will still feel more comfortable if they read books—even books on notable lists—before offering them to students so that they will be able to talk about them either with student readers or with their parents. It would be good to know, for example, that the 2010 Stonewall Book Award winner, Nick Burd's *The Vast Fields of Ordinary* (Dial, 2009), was criticized because the kids in it were "bad" (i.e., they were not good role models for teens). Librarian Lisa Johnston from Sweet Briar College in Lynchburg, Virginia, who chaired the committee, responded with, "No, these are real kids." What the committee wants to see is a variety so that different readers can find different characters to identify with. Dale McNeill, librarian in Queens, New York, added that "It's important that there are urban gay kids, promiscuous kids, some who don't care about school and others who do. You want a classroom of kids to see themselves."

He then went on to point out that the gay experience now appears in movies and on television shows, such as *GLEE*. However, these shows cannot tell viewers what the characters are feeling. Because television is a social medium with other people hearing and seeing it, viewers miss "that delicious privateness of a book," which "can be yours alone." Victor Schill, a Texas librarian and an ALA Rainbow Project member, said that GLBT literature is part of the bigger movement to diversify literature for all readers.

> It is like any young adult materials for tweens and teens. It is like Latino or African American or Asian American children reading books without those characters. You have to see the diversity of the society we live in. There are different groups of people and ways of loving people. It is all part of our experience in something mysterious.

A couple of useful articles for teachers have also appeared in *The ALAN Review*. "Creating a Space for YAL with LGBT Content in Our Personal Reading" by Katherine Mason (Summer 2008, pp. 55–61) was a report on a survey that Mason conducted with twenty-one preservice English teachers from Kennesaw State University and fifty-one middle and high school teachers in suburban school districts near Atlanta, Georgia. Before she embarked on her study, she looked at findings from a 2005 study of 1,700 young respondents by the Gay, Lesbian & Straight Education Network (GLSEN):

- 64.3 percent reported feeling unsafe at school because of their sexual orientation.
- 40.7 percent felt unsafe because of how they expressed their gender.
- Only 16.5 percent said that faculty and staff intervened when they heard such homophobic terms as *faggot* and *dyke,* or heard something described as "That's so gay!"
- 18 percent said they had heard teachers themselves use that type of language.

In Mason's own study, she found a high correlation between teachers' resistance to bringing LGBT books into their classrooms and having ever read one. Many teachers said something to the effect that they don't bring books about heterosexual activities into their classes, so why should they bring in books about homosexual activities. Others said that a student's sexual orientation was not the teacher's business, while nearly half of the teachers said they were worried about the reaction of parents and administrators if they should bring such books into their class. Mason ended her article with a plea that teachers should at least read some of the books before walling them off from their students.

The other article from *The ALAN Review* was Emily S. Meixner's, "Would You Want to Read That? Using Book Passes to Open Up Secondary Classrooms to LGBTQ Young Adult Literature" (*The ALAN Review*, Summer 2009, pp. 92–98). She has devised what she calls "Book Passes" as a way of introducing her students to new books and helping them to develop skills in making quick decisions on what books they want to read. She begins her procedure by collecting a large set of appealing YA books, some of which include GLBT incidents or characters, either in a major or a minor way. She seats her class in pairs in a large circle that fills the whole room. Then she gives each pair a Book Pass Chart, printed on a half-sheet of paper. There are five lines (one for each book the pairs will look at) divided into four columns identified as Title, Author, Topic, Rating ("Yes, I want to read it," or "No, I don't want to read it.").

Each pair of students is given a book and instructed to do the following:

1. Look at the front cover.
2. Flip the book over to read the synopsis or excerpt or quotes provided on the back.
3. Quickly skim the inside cover of the jacket.
4. Begin reading the first couple of pages.
5. Fill out the form, including your rating of the book.

While the students, working in pairs, are following the directions, she circles the room, listens to comments, and answers questions. Then, after about five minutes, she signals that it is time for each pair of students to pass their book to the couple on their left. After each group has looked at as many books as time permits, she calls a halt and leads the class in a discussion of the process and the ratings given to the books.

Besides teaching students how to make sound decisions for their own reading when they are browsing in a bookstore or at a library, Meixner recommends this activity for setting a tone of openmindedness, acceptance, and inclusivity. It also puts the books in the hands of those students who need and want them and gives all the students an introduction to books they may not have heard about. And without preaching, she models a way to talk about the books without using the kinds of insulting terms students might be accustomed to hearing. Books that could be included in this activity, along with several other good YA books, include the following:

Almost Perfect by Brian Katcher (Delacorte, 2009) is the story of Logan, a senior in a small town high school who falls in love with Sage, a "different" but new girl in town. Eventually Sage tells Logan that she was born a male and is in the process of becoming a female. Logan is horrified that maybe he is gay because he fell in love with a male. The story has a somewhat happy ending, but not until after tragic events ensue.

Annie on My Mind by Nancy Garden (Farrar, 1981) is a beautifully written love story about two older high school girls. It is probably the most famous young adult book related to the issue of gayness. (See page 311 where Nancy Garden tells about her censorship troubles with the book.)

Deliver Us from Evie by M. E. Kerr (Harper, 1994) is a realistic story of two girls almost ready to graduate from high school, Evie Burman and Patsy Duff. The title comes from the way a boy, who wants to date Evie, sits behind her at church and when the "Lord's Prayer" is recited, changes the *Deliver-us-from-evil* line, and then acts as if he has made a good joke.

Freak Show by James St. James (Dutton, 2007) is about Billy, who calls himself a "Gender Obscurist," even though other people at the Eisenhower Academy are more direct. Reviewers used such adjectives as *fast-paced, snarky,* and *playfully naughty* for this story about a "queen" who turns things upside down by running for Homecoming Queen.

I Am J by Cris Beam (Little, Brown, 2011) is about a child who was named Jennifer, but from early on preferred to wear pants and shirts, to play with rough and tough boys, and to be called J instead of Jennifer. As a teen, J decides to explore testosterone treatments and to enroll in a special school for transgendered youth.

Luna by Julie Anne Peters (Little, Brown, 2004) is the story of Regan, which is intricately tied to the story of her transgendered brother. The reviewer for *School Library Journal* described the book as a "sensitive and poignant portrayal of a young man's determination to live his true identity."

Margaret A. Edwards Award

Winner (2003)
Nancy Garden, Stretching
Our Minds on Sexuality

Garden was honored for her 1982 *Annie on My Mind,* but other well-written books include her 1984 *Prisoner of Vampires,* 1991 *Lark in the Morning,* 1996 *Good Moon Rising,* and 1999 *The Year They Burned the Books. Endgame,* a powerful story about the rippling effects of school bullying, was published in 2006. The book starts with fifteen-year-old Gray Wilson waiting in juvenile detention for his trial as a murderer. The heart of the story is what leads up to the day that Gray, who has been bullied in increasingly mean ways at two different high schools, takes a gun to school and starts shooting.

Nancy Garden has two worlds: one the world of her books, the other the world of censorship and defending her books. In *Annie on My Mind, Lark in the Morning,* and *Good Moon Rising,* Garden has dealt honestly with what it is like to be a gay young adult in our world. The protagonists speedily learn that prejudice is a given and ignorance is rampant. Garden has confessed that she finds it hard to avoid using her characters as "mouthpieces" for her own views. It would be all too easy to stand them up on soapboxes and have them shout, "Hey, we're decent people, most of us; like every other group, we're not all good or all bad—and it's wrong that we're often treated unfairly, or harassed, or beaten up."

Unquestionably, Garden's best-known book is *Annie on My Mind.* Earlier books concerned with same-sex love ended unhappily, presumably proving that was the way such loves should expect to end. In the beginning, Garden's *Annie* appears on its way to a similar ending, but Liza and Annie eventually handle their problems and accept their love for each other. It's a problem novel marvelously well-handled and touching.

Lark in the Morning may be a better book than *Annie.* The protagonist is gay but her sexuality is not the central concern of the book. Rather, two runaways that Gillian discovered hiding near her summer home take up her attention and make her lesbianism less important in the book.

Garden told Christine A. Jenkins, who interviewed her for the June 2003 *School Library Journal,* that she was at a writers' conference when someone asked her if she'd had any troubles with *Annie on My Mind.* She responded that she had not. Two days later a phone call notified her that *Annie* had been burned in Olathe, Kansas.

The event soon made her a controversial young adult author. YA novels don't come to trial very often, and even less often are authors asked to participate. But her visit to the scene was not altogether unpleasant. Garden said,

> When I was in Kansas, people would come up to me even before the case was filed saying that they were embarrassed that this had happened where they lived. There were a lot of people who didn't believe in the First Amendment, and a lot of people who were pretty homophobic. But there were a lot of very good people also, and that was a very good thing to learn.

The trial also gave her strong opinions about censorship, some of which she put into *The Year They Burned the Books.* "It's important to remember that censorship is a two-way street," she says. "If you can ban a book you don't like, I can ban one you do like! If everyone could remove books they disagree with, I'm not sure there'd be a lot of books in the library any more." At the trial, Garden braced herself for hostile questions, but after her lawyer finished asking her questions, the other side chose not to cross-examine, which she assumes means that they didn't think she would help their case.

Much of the language in District Court Judge G. T. Bebber's November 29, 1995, opinion in the case, *Stevana Case et al. v. United School District No. 233* comes from the Supreme Court's language in *Pico v. Board of Education, Island Trees (NY) Union Free School District.* The lawyer representing the Olathe students said, "I think it's a clear message to schools and school libraries that they can't remove books simply because they disagree with the views expressed in a book. That's what the rule of the *Pico* case is. This decision very strongly reaffirms that principle." ●

Night Kites by M. E. Kerr (HarperCollins, 1986) might have been the first YA novel about the effects of AIDS. In it, a beloved older brother, who unknown to his family is gay, comes home to die from AIDS.

Parrotfish by Ellen Wittlinger (S&S, 2007) takes place between Thanksgiving and Christmas, when Grady McNair, formerly known as Angela, comes out as transgendered and falls in love with "the hottest" girl in school. In 1999, Wittlinger also treated GLBT issues in *Hard Love* (S&S).

Punkzilla by Adam Rapp (Candlewick, 2009) is about fourteen-year-old Jamie, who is running away from a military school where he was enrolled by his father, who thought that such a strict environment would keep Jamie from becoming gay, like his older brother. Jamie is called Punkzilla because of his love for music. The story is written through the letters that Jamie writes (but does not mail) as he tries to make his way to see his brother, who is dying.

Sister Mischief by Laura Goode. Candlewick, 2011. Three girls found an all-girl hip-hop group, along with a hip-hop gay-straight alliance. Marcy is DJ *SheStorm,* Tess is *The Contessa,* while Rowie is *MC Rohini.* It is an unusual story partly because it is set in a conservative Minnesota town.

Will Grayson, Will Grayson by John Green and David Levithan (Dutton, 2010) is about two boys named Will Grayson. A student recently told us about reading this funny book where two boys had the same name. We were pleased that he thought of this first, rather than the fact that some of the characters were gay.

The Stonewall Children's and Young Adult Book Award for 2012 was given to Bil Wright's *Putting Makeup on the Fat Boy* (Simon & Schuster). The four Honor Books were Lili Wilkinson's *Pink* (HarperTeen), Brian Farrey's *With or Without You* (Simon Pulse), Ilike Merey's *a + e 4ever* (Lethe Press), and Paul Yee's *Money Boy* (Groundwood Books).

Well-planned and well-written books can present information about different viewpoints, and teachers and librarians are performing a worthwhile service if they bring such books to the attention of young people. Of course, our students can find much of their information about sex online, but especially in relation to sex education, this may not be ideal. In a summer school class, which had an unusually large number of parents in it, someone remarked that maybe there was no longer a need for sex education books because kids could get all the information they wanted from the Internet. There was an immediate uproar from the parents in the class who were united in saying there was a greater need than ever for well-thought-out and well-designed books, because they did not want their children entering into sex-related online conversations.

When helping young adults make reading decisions in this area, we need to consider the reader's purpose. If the reader wants basic information, nonfiction is far superior because it can present a wider range of information in a clear, unambiguous way. But if the reader desires to understand the emotional and physical aspects of a particular relationship, an honest piece of fiction usually does a better job.

Schools and libraries need to seek community help in exchanging ideas and developing policies. Family values must be respected, but honest, accurate information must also be available for those who seek it. Charting a course along this delicate line is more than any one individual should be expected to do, which is why people need to communicate with each other. Professionals working with books are also obligated to find and study the latest, most authentic information and to bring that information to those who are helping to shape policies and practices. The general public may get away with objecting to or endorsing ideas and books that they have never explored or read. Not so for the professional charged with leading a group to consensus or compromise. The more you know about the materials, and the more you understand about individual and group differences, the better able you will be to participate in book selection, discussion, and, sometimes, defense.

Outstanding Authors of Nonfiction for Young Adults

We will close this chapter on nonfiction by presenting a sampling of the talented and hard-working authors who are devoting their professional careers to writing books for young adults. Here are descriptions of some of them, but please do not pass over an interesting new book simply because the author's name is not listed here, as new authors are always joining the field. Also, realize that the books mentioned in each write-up are only a sampling that focuses on the authors' most recent books. Check their websites to see what else they have written.

Marc Aronson states on his website: "I try to write each book with the same care I would put into a novel, but with the same respect for truth as a judge in a court of law." Aronson is both an editor and an author of nonfiction books, so of course he has an interest in how nonfiction is promoted to young people. He worries about the fact that schools choose "safe and familiar" textbooks and that bookstores seem to consider nonfiction for kids to be "owned" by the schools so they do little to promote it. Even parents and grandparents shy away from buying nonfiction books as gifts. In mid-July of 2007, he sent an email to *School Library Journal* in which he said,

> I suspect that the very size of the problem is the beginning of the solution. That is, the general ignorance of and aversion to nonfiction is so widespread that it is ripe to be toppled. What I felt from the crowd today—and I've seen in other similar gatherings is . . . a craving that is all the stronger because people didn't even realize they had it—they simply did not know that nonfiction could come to them in exciting and new ways.

Aronson is working to create a revolution of rising expectations in which people will "know that nonfiction can offer more, so they demand more." They will recognize "what is wrong with the mix of textbooks that have no narrative power and reading lists dominated by fiction." A crucial element in Aronson's "revolution" is simply getting more people to read books that are written with passion and a deeply felt interest in the subject. Aronson chooses to write about topics that are complex. He presents different sides of the stories that haven't been told before as in his *The Real Revolution: The Global Story of American Independence* and in his *Race: A History Beyond Black and White*. His biographies focus on a range of people as different as Bobby Kennedy, John Winthrop, and Oliver Cromwell. His *Sir Walter Raleigh and the Quest for El Dorado* won a Boston Globe/Horn Book Award and was praised for exploring a contradictory and complex Elizabethan figure. His *Art Attack: A Short Cultural History of the Avant-Garde* did an excellent job of tying together art, music, and literature with available Internet resources. Other recent books on intriguing facts include *Sugar Changed the World: A Story of Magic, Spice, Slavery, Freedom, and Science; If Stones Could Speak: Unlocking the Secrets of Stonehenge*, and *Trapped: How the World Rescued 33 Miners from 2,000 Feet below the Chilean Desert*. http://www.mararonson.com

Susan Campbell Bartoletti's books do a good job of illustrating how authors can take a subject of general interest and make it more interesting to young readers by putting the focus on someone of their own age, as she did in her Newbery Honor Book, *Hitler Youth: Growing Up in Hitler's Shadow*. Her 1997 *Growing Up in Coal Country* won several prizes, and so did her *Black Potatoes: The Story of the Great Irish Famine, 1845 to 1850*. Her 2011 *They Called Themselves the KKK: The Birth of an American Terrorist Group* puts a new slant on the Ku Klux Klan by tying it into today's fear of terrorism. The Klan is a subject that is glossed over in many history books, as shown by an incident at a local Arizona high school. Three boys, who were good friends, all had names

When Joseph Bruchac came to Arizona State University for an event celebrating the release of his Code Talker: A Novel about the Navajo Marines of World War Two, *many young Navajos came to get a glimpse into this exciting part of their tribal history. Here a girl takes a picture of three of the code talkers who helped Bruchac write his book: Samuel Holiday, Joe Kellwood, and George Willie.*

that started with *K* and so they declared themselves "The Three K's" (one even put it on his car's license plates). They were totally surprised to learn that they were sending an unintended message. http://www.scbartoletti.com

Joseph Bruchac, who traces part of his ancestral heritage to the Abenaki tribe in the Adirondacks, is a prolific writer of books about Native Americans, several of which are appropriate for young teens. In the spring of 2011, he came to Arizona and visited with groups of Native Americans, both on the Navajo reservation and in urban areas, to celebrate publication of his book *Code Talker: A Novel about the Navajo Marines of World War Two.* See the photo taken when he visited Arizona State University, along with three of the Navajo Code Talkers he worked with in writing his book. They were part of the elite group of communicators who relied on an adapted form of their Navajo language to communicate through the only code that was not broken by the Japanese. Bruchac's 2007 *Squanto's Journey* tells the story of Thanksgiving from an Indian perspective. His 2008 *Sacajawea* uses the alternating voices of Sacajawea and William Clark to tell the story of the Lewis and Clark expedition. Other recent books are *March toward the Thunder, Whisper in the Dark* (both 2009), and *Bearwalker* (2010). His *Jim Thorpe: Original All-American* was especially appreciated by young athletes, who learned that the real Pop Warner was the coach at the Carlisle Indian School in 1911 when Carlisle beat Harvard by a score of 18 to 15. http://www.josephbruchac.com

Russell Freedman wrote his first book, *Teenagers Who Made History*, in 1961, and it wasn't until 1988, nearly thirty years later, that he won the Newbery Medal for *Lincoln: A Photobiography*. Since then he has been honored with the Laura Ingalls Wilder Award, given every five years to honor a lifetime contribution. Among his most recent books are *Who Was First? Discovering the Americas; The Voice That Challenged a Nation: Marian Anderson and the Struggle for Equal Rights;* and *Children of the Great Depression.* His *Confucius: The Golden Rule; Martha Graham: A Dancer's Life;* and *Babe Didrikson Zaharias: The Making of a Champion* contain between 175 and 200 pages and, as such, are longer than his earlier books. A turning point in Freeman's career came when he attended an exhibition of historical photographs and found himself "communicating" with the young faces that stared out at him from the old photos. He searched out these and other pictures for a book, *Immigrant Kids.* Since then he has made a specialty of finding evocative photographs to use not as decoration but as an integral part of his books. He won the Orbis Pictus Award and the Boston Globe Honor Book Award for his 1990 *Franklin Delano Roosevelt.* His 1991 *The Wright Brothers* was a Newbery Honor Book and so was his 1993 *Eleanor Roosevelt: A Life of Discovery.* In his 1994 *Kids at Work: Lewis Hine and the Crusade against Child Labor,* he wrote directly about the power of photography to document social conditions under which U.S. children labored. In his 2006 *The Adventures of Marco Polo* he helped to answer the question of whether Marco Polo was the world's greatest explorer, or the world's greatest liar. His 2010 *Children of the Great Depression* is especially timely in the way it explains the complexities of the stock market crash and its effect on children. http://www.ric.edu/astal/authors/russellfreedman.html

James Cross Giblin was in elementary school during World War II, and the image of Hitler was all around him—in movie newsreels, on recruiting posters, and on the covers of weekly news magazines. In nearly every picture, Hitler was shown as a raving monster, foaming at the mouth and barking out commands. Even as a boy, Giblin found these portrayals hard to accept, especially when they made Hitler seem funny rather than frightening. He had read enough about his brutal actions—even before the world knew about the Holocaust—to know that Hitler was not "funny." However, the images and the questions stayed with Giblin his whole life, so that when people asked why he wanted to write about such a "monster," he would answer, "I don't believe any human being is born a monster. So how and why did Hitler become one? That's what intrigues me— and that's what I want to try to find out."

This little story illustrates Giblin's belief that the best nonfiction books are written about topics that have been in the authors' minds and hearts for a long time. Giblin is fascinated with telling two sides of a story, which he did admirably in his 2005 *Good Brother, Bad Brother: The Story of Edwin Booth and John Wilkes Booth*. The two brothers were in ways similar, but one of them ended up assassinating President Lincoln. Giblin created vivid images of the brothers and the effects of the assassination on the nation in general and on the Booth family in particular. His *Secrets of the Sphinx* shows readers a world before written history as Giblin explores clues and various theories about the pyramids, Atlantis, and the Rosetta Stone, which is a large stone slab covered with writing in three different languages. It is what enabled linguists to decipher one of the world's first writing systems. He has written biographies of several presidents, as well as one of Paul Revere and Senator Joe McCarthy. His *The Truth about Unicorns* serves as an excellent model for research as it traces the history of beliefs, superstitions, stories, and art about this mythical creature. His *Charles A. Lindbergh, A Human Hero*

In nonfiction about historical events and in biographies, students and their teachers expect documentation by way of letters, photos, newspaper accounts, interviews, and websites where they can go for further information. This kind of real-life documentation strengthens the books in Focus Boxes 9.4, "Young People and Civil Rights" (p. 298), 9.5, "Nonfiction Books about War and Its Effects on Young People" (p. 299), and 9.6, "Starred Biographies of Atypical Heroes" (p. 300).

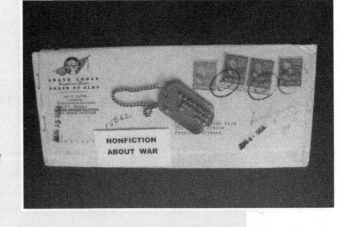

NONFICTION ABOUT WAR

was chosen for several "Best Book" lists based on Giblin's meticulous research and the skillful way that he balanced information about "an all-too-human hero." His 2008 *Did Fleming Rescue Churchill? A Research Puzzle* (with Eric Brooks) is a clever children's book in which a boy named Jason is assigned to write a research paper about Alexander Fleming, the inventor of penicillin. Jason learns on the Internet that Fleming had once rescued Winston Churchill from drowning. But now Jason (and the reader) must use historical clues to determine whether or not this is a true tale. http://www.orrt.org/giblin/bibliography.html

Albert Marrin earned a Ph.D. in history from Columbia University in 1968 and shortly thereafter began publishing history-related books. In his 2006 *Saving the Buffalo,* readers learn that Native Americans had more than a hundred uses for the buffalo and never killed more than they needed. In the same year, he wrote a fascinating book, *Oh, Rats! The Story of Rats and People,* which is an anecdotal history of the love–hate relationship between rats and humans. In some cultures rats are venerated; other cultures try to exterminate them. Marrin's *The Great Adventure: Theodore Roosevelt and the Rise of Modern America* tells about Teddy Roosevelt, who published around eighteen million words and won a Nobel Prize. Roosevelt was also known to have been an uninhibited dancer, a big game hunter, and an environmental-conservation activist. The book also tells about the Brownsville Incident and other times that he acted badly.

In 1985, Marrin's *1812: The War Nobody Won* was given a Boston Globe/Horn Book Honor Award for nonfiction. Marrin has written well-received biographies on historical figures ranging from Abraham Lincoln to Adolf Hitler and from Sir Francis Drake to General Robert E. Lee. His *Dr. Jenner and the Speckled Monster: The Search for the Smallpox Vaccine* is a timely book because of fears about vials of frozen virus preserved in laboratories around the world. His *Secrets from the Rocks: Dinosaur Hunting with Roy Chapman Andrews* is the story of a pioneering paleontologist who led five expeditions into China between 1922 and 1930. Less-thoughtful writers would have been satisfied to focus on the excitement and danger of traveling into the Gobi Desert of Mongolia, but Marrin goes further and shows how the expeditions would have been different under today's sensibilities. For example, women were excluded from the expeditions, and Andrews had no compunctions about shooting rare animals or loading up treasures and bringing them out of the host countries he visited. A *School Library Journal* reviewer praised Marrin's *The Spanish-American War* for delineating "how American jingoists, expansionists, 'big navy' advocates, yellow journalists, and filibusterers maneuvered the nations into taking part in what politicians called 'A splendid little war!'" http://www.fun-books.com/books/albert_marrin.htm

Laurence Pringle is a respected and prolific writer of science-related books for young readers. For an earlier edition of this text, he discussed the challenge of being "fair" when writing about decision making that involves both social and scientific knowledge and attitudes. Because idealistic young readers may be especially vulnerable to one-sided arguments, he says that writers have a responsibility to present all sides of an issue and to show the gray as well as the black and white. He quickly adds, however, that being fair is not the same as being objective: "anyone who is well informed on an issue is not neutral," but that does not mean that he or she cannot work "to help kids understand the issues so they can make their own decisions." Among his well-received books are *Imagine a Dragon, Alligators and Crocodiles! Strange and Wonderful, Bats! Strange and Wonderful* and *Cicadas! Strange and Wonderful*. One of his earliest "Strange and Wonderful" books (2007) is about the seventeen species of penguins, which range in size from the blue penguin at sixteen inches tall to the emperor penguin which is close to four feet tall. Some are named for how they look (the black-footed penguin) or from where they originated, as with the Galapagos penguin.

Other Pringle books include *Billions of Years, Amazing Changes: The Story of Evolution and Oil Spills: Damage, Recovery and Prevention*. http://www.laurencepringle.com/

Catherine Reef is the modern counterpart of the frontier housewife who always saved a little dough from a batch of bread to serve as starter yeast for the next batch. On her website, Reef tells how her interest in African American history led her to write *This Our Dark Country: The American Settlers of Liberia*, and then to go on and write *William Grant Still: African-American Composer* and *African Americans in the Military*. In 2000, she wrote *Paul Laurence Dunbar: Portrait of a Poet* and then six years later she wrote *e. e. cummings: A Poet's Life*. One of the anecdotes that teens could probably relate to about Cummings is that he had such bad acne that, when he rode on a streetcar, he would always hide his face behind a newspaper. Her other successful books include *Alone in the World: Orphans and Orphanages in America; Childhood in America: An Eyewitness History; Sigmund Freud: Pioneer of the Mind;* and *George Gershwin: American Composer*. Her most recent books include *Ernest Hemingway: A Writer's Life, African Americans in the Military,* and *Jane Austen: A Life Revealed*. http://www.catherinereef.com/

Concluding Comments

As we conclude this chapter on nonfiction, we will simply repeat the statement that we made at the beginning of this chapter: In the real world, nonfiction gets a greater share of people's money and attention than does fiction. Because there is so much of it, adults working with young readers have an even greater responsibility to help to winnow the wheat from the chaff and to bring to students' attention the books that they are likely to want and need. We also have an obligation that Mary E. Mueller pointed out in an "Up for Discussion" piece in the November 1991 *School Library Journal*. She said that with shrinking budgets, we all know that we need to buy new computer books, but we hesitate to spend money on new historical and informative books and on new biographies. But with changing attitudes and outlooks—which, we add, is even more true for self-help books—these sections of a library need just as much loving care and attention, including weeding, replacing, and promotion, as do any other sections of the library.

Her statement is even truer today than it was then, and teachers, along with librarians, need to give it some serious thought.

Evaluating, Promoting, and Using Young Adult Books

chapter

10

In this chapter we are writing about the various responsibilities common to the work of librarians, English teachers, reading teachers, social studies teachers, parents, and counselors or youth workers. (See Chapter 11 for more specific information for English teachers.) These areas were chosen to give focus and organization to the information, but there is considerable overlap. For example, all of us who work with young readers and books need to get in the habit of both writing and reading book reviews to increase our knowledge and skill as well as to help us have the knowledge necessary to suggest the right book for the right student, or to at least point someone in the right direction.

When two people are talking about a book they both enjoyed, there is no way to divide the conversation into such discrete categories as literary analysis, personal feelings, sociological implications, and evaluation of potential popularity. Librarians find themselves discussing books as if they were classroom teachers. Teachers can adopt some of the promotional techniques that librarians use, and librarians can use some book discussion tactics that teachers use. In short, this chapter's organization may make it appear that librarians work with young readers and books quite differently from the way that teachers and counselors work with them, but in reality nearly all adults who work with young readers and books have much the same goals and share many of the same approaches.

To begin this chapter, we asked for advice from Diane P. Tuccillo, whose work we watched for nearly twenty-five years when she was Young Adult Coordinator for the nearby City of Mesa Library. Here she gives her "top

Diane Tuccillo's Top Ten Pieces of Advice for Librarians with Teenage Patrons

1. Start or improve a library teen advisory group and/or teen volunteer group. Both school and public libraries can have vibrant, engaging, empowering advisory groups with the right adult leadership, advocacy, and commitment. Not only will library teen advisory groups bring more teens to the library, they allow teens to promote library events and teen literature to their peers, and they help create lifelong readers, library users, and library supporters.

2. Help teens form book discussion groups at their library. Allow them to select the books, with objective guidance, and to conduct the actual discussions. Give them book discussion guides from publishers or encourage them to find guides online.

3. Use the library as a way to encourage theatrical or artistic connections to literature. Start a puppet or theater troupe of teens who enjoy acting. Have them write scripts based on classic children's books, or use prewritten scripts to which they add their own creative touches for performances. Let teens create bulletin boards or do window painting to encourage interest in books and reading.

4. Bring teens to YA literature events or other appropriate conferences or forums. For example, state library associations might offer opportunities for teens to present at their conferences. At the American Library Association conferences, the Young Adult Library Services Association holds the Best Fiction Teen Feedback Session where teens are invited to come and give their reactions to newly published YA books. Also, college level YA literature instructors sometimes welcome panels of local teens to discuss current trends in teen reading. Keep your eyes and ears open for opportunities to give teens a voice about their literature!

ten" pieces of advice to librarians who want to succeed with teenage patrons. After her statement, we will fill in with a few other observations and comments about the important role of librarians, followed by advice on writing about YA books and using young adult literature with English language learners. We will conclude this chapter with short sections tying YA books in with reading teachers, social studies teachers, parents, and others, such as counselors and volunteers in youth groups, who work to help young people talk and think about human relations and values.

Young Adult Literature and Librarians

Most public libraries have young adult sections, even if they can no longer afford a librarian totally devoted to YA books. The thinking behind setting up special rooms for young adults is that teenagers enter a children's section

5. Allow teens to conduct fundraisers based on reading. A read-a-thon might support your library; a local agency that serves teens, like the Boys and Girls Club; Books for a Better World; or some other worthy cause. Ask your teens about what group they would like to raise funds for by getting pledges for time spent reading.

6. Take teen opinions to heart. Invite teens to join focus groups or strategic planning groups to improve your library. If a new teen space is being created, ask for teen input on its design and on the materials collection. Get teen representation on the adult library board and/or the Friend of the Library board.

7. Teach teens to be peer reader advisors. Show them how to write book reviews. Post the reviews on the library Web page. Allow teens to make bookmarks announcing their recommendations and to put them in the books, have them create booklists, and teach them to perform booktalks.

8. Get teens to help design and maintain your school library or public library teen Web page. Listen to their opinions about both layout and content. Teach them to make book videos or partner with your school district's recording studio to create book review shows. Have teens contribute links, reviews, booklists, blogs, and book videos or recorded shows to the page.

9. Find ways to connect teens with real live authors. Bring authors to the library and have teens introduce and host the events. Film teens interviewing authors. Invite local authors to come to the library to teach teens the ropes about writing and publishing.

10. Get your Friends of the Library or school PTO to fund teen advisory group or teen volunteer T-shirts. Have a teen design the T-shirt with a catchy name or phrase or have a contest for several artists. T-shirts attract attention, give teens a sense of camaraderie and purpose, and can be a great promotional item for reading and the library! They are also a reward, one of many possible ways you can (and should!) thank and praise your actively involved teens.

Diane Tuccillo is currently Teen Service Librarian at the Poudre River Public Library District in Fort Collins, Colorado. Her writing regularly appears in professional journals. She has been the president of ALAN (Assembly on Literature for Adolescents of NCTE), and has been a member of the Printz, Morris, and Walden book award committees. She is a long-standing member of the VOYA (Voice of Youth Advocates) editorial advisory board and is the author of Library Teen Advisory Groups (Scarecrow, 2005) and Teen-Centered Library Service: Putting Youth Participation into Practice (Libraries Unlimited, 2010).

reluctantly, and their size, voices, and active natures intimidate the children who are there. Also, one of the purposes of young adult services is to provide a transition from the children's collection to the resources of the total library, and a librarian watching over children would not be free to walk with a teen to a different part of the library. Furthermore, it's hard for the same person who runs programs for preschoolers and reads dozens of new children's books each year to switch gears to the interests and the technologies that teenagers prefer. The biggest challenge that YA librarians have is probably connected to questions of selection and censorship. It takes considerable knowledge and experience to pave the way for a library to offer "serious" high-quality literature rather than to rely only on "safe," noncontroversial literature.

Certainly these worries are valid, and we all need to do what we can to persuade decision makers that young adult librarians serve an important role. But if the choice is between having a library open only four days a week and having separate librarians for children and teenagers, most library boards vote to keep the library open. This dictates more flexibility and more challenge for the librarian who serves both age groups. Parents who have both teenagers and young children vouch for the differences between the two, yet they manage somehow. Many librarians have to do the same. We hope this textbook helps.

Matching Books with Readers

Commercial programs and CD-ROMs allow students to search for books using key words. Many YA authors have their own websites and blogs, and clever booksellers do, on an international level, the same kind of promotional work that teachers and librarians have been doing locally for years. Electronic aids are wonderful, but nothing can substitute for a large and varied reading background and the ability to draw relationships between what students tell or ask and what the librarian remembers about particular books. Experience sharpens this skill, and those librarians who make a consistent effort to read a few new books every month rapidly increase their repertoire of books.

With all their other responsibilities, few librarians have as much opportunity as they would like to guide individual reading on a one-to-one basis. The next best thing is to give presentations or booktalks to groups. A booktalk is a short introduction to a book, which usually includes one or two paragraphs read from the book. Booktalks are comparable to movie previews or teasers in presenting the characters and a hint of the plot, but they should never reveal the ending. Booktalks are tiny slices of pie so delicious that they will tempt the reader to want more. The simplest kind of booktalk may last only sixty seconds. In giving it, the booktalker must let listeners know what to expect. For example, it would be unfair to present only the funniest moments in a serious book—a reader might check it out expecting a comedy. If a book is a love story, some

Even though it's fun to supplement booktalks with media clips, hands-on booktalks are also memorable. Here, Jim Blasingame brought in his old shovel that is worn flat across the front, which means it picks up more dirt than does a new shovel that has a pointed scoop. He used it to explain why the experienced boys in Louis Sachar's Holes *were not at all appreciative when, on his first day, Stanley offered to use one of the old shovels.*

clue should be given, but care needs to be taken because emotional scenes read out loud and out of context are likely to sound silly. The cover of a book often reveals its tone, which is one of the reasons for holding up a book while it is being discussed or for showing PowerPoint slides or color overheads if a presentation is being given to a large audience.

Diane Tuccillo suggested training students to give booktalks. The hardest thing for our students to learn is to be concise; especially if they haven't prepared and are therefore "winging it," they go on-and-on, not realizing that it takes time and concentration to select the "heart" of a story. But what our students are much better at than we are is managing technology so that they can supplement regular booktalks with brief movie clips, something from an author's website, or even something relevant from YouTube.

Most young readers do not want to hear a ten- or fifteen-minute talk on one book unless it is dramatic and used as a change of pace along with shorter booktalks. Even with short booktalks, people's minds begin to wander after they've listened for ten or fifteen minutes. The ideal approach is for the teacher or librarian to give booktalks frequently but in short chunks. However, this may not be practical if a librarian from a public library is making a special effort to leave the library and come to a classroom as a way of getting acquainted and encouraging students to sign up for library cards and begin to use the public library.

School librarians have an advantage in that they can arrive in class with a cart full of books ready to be checked out. A half-hour or so can be devoted to the booktalks, with the rest of the time saved for questions and answers,

In one of her classes, Alleen Nilsen brought in biscuits she had baked with the silhouette of the mockingjay on them. She sprinkled cinnamon and sugar through a waxed paper cutout before baking them. The little biscuits illustrate how cleverly the people in Suzanne Collins's Hunger Games trilogy began to show their allegiance to Katniss. If they were in danger of being discovered, they just popped their mockinjay wafers into their mouths and started chewing.

browsing, signup, and checkout. In cases like this, it's good to have a printed bibliography or bookmark to leave with students for later use in the library.

This kind of group presentation has the advantage of introducing students to the librarian. Students who feel acquainted are more likely to initiate a one-to-one relationship, which is a valuable part of reading guidance. Group presentations also give students more freedom in choosing books that appeal to them. When a student asks a librarian to recommend a good book, the librarian has time to tell the student about only two or three titles, and the student probably feels obligated to take one of these books regardless of whether it sounds appealing. But when the librarian presents ten to fifteen different titles, students can choose from a much larger offering. This also enables students to learn about and to select books that might cause them embarrassment if they were recommended on a personal basis. For example, if a girl is suspected of having lesbian leanings, it may not help the situation for the librarian to hand her Nancy Garden's *Annie on My Mind*. But if this book were included among several books introduced to the class and the student chose it herself, it might fill a real need. And when librarians talk about a book, showing they have read it, the door is opened for students to initiate conversations either about a specific book or books in general.

Another advantage to group presentations is that they are efficient. For example, if a social studies class is beginning a unit on World War II in which everyone in the class is required to read a novel having something to do with the war and also write a small research paper, it makes sense for the librarian to give the basic information in one group presentation. Being efficient in the beginning enables the librarian to spend time with individual students who have specific questions rather than making an almost identical presentation to thirty individuals.

Displays

When we took a survey for the last issue of this textbook, one-third of the students said that browsing in a library was one of the ways they gathered reading ideas. This hints at the importance of making displays that will at the very least let browsers see the covers of books and know that someone thought these books were good enough to deserve special attention. Displays can be fairly simple, perhaps nothing more than a sign that says, "Like to Watch Dr. Phil?—You'll Love These" (personal experiences and social issues books, although not identified in just that way), or "Kleenex Books" (books about sadness, death, and loss). Preparing displays can bring the same kind of personal satisfaction that comes from decorating a room or setting out a bouquet of flowers. People with negative feelings toward making displays and bulletin boards have probably had experiences in which the results did not adequately compensate for the amount of time and effort expended. Following are some general principles that will help to increase the returns on a display while cutting down on the work:

1. Go window shopping in the best stores—the ones that appeal to the young adults that you are wooing. When you see a display that you like, adapt its features to your own purposes.

2. Promote more than one book and have multiple copies available. Enthusiasm wanes if people have to put their names on a list and wait.

As a backup, have color photocopies of the book jackets so that, as the books are checked out, you can keep your display from looking skimpy by replacing books with the photocopies mounted on foam board.

3. Tie displays into current happenings. Connect the books to popular movies, the school play, a neighborhood controversy, or various holiday celebrations.

4. Use displays to get people into the library. Offer free bibliographies and announce their availability through local media.

5. Put displays in high-traffic areas where everyone, not just those who already use the young adult collection, will see them.

6. Get some height and variety into the display by using interchangeable parts such as leaning boards with hooks to hold books, or boxes covered with drapes. To focus attention on the books, plain backgrounds are better than figured ones.

7. Take advantage of modern technology. Buy stick-on letters, use your computer and your desktop publishing skills to prepare attractive bibliographies and signs, and for big events splurge on a banner at a copy store.

The changing location of portable displays is in itself an attention getter. A portable display can be as small as a two-foot sandwich board set in the middle of a table or as large as a pup tent surrounded by books about camping, hiking, backpacking, ecology, and nature foods. If space is a problem, small bulletin boards can be hung from the ceiling or stood against pillars or walls. Involve students by displaying their art work or snapshots of their pets under such headings

Making signs or banners that can be stored flat (or hung) and then brought out for use with various sets of books is efficient. It's also a good idea to solicit help from young artists as with this MANGA display.

as "The Comforts and Delights of Owning a Dog," or ". . . of Being Owned by a Cat." And don't overlook the possibility of putting up posters such as those offered by the American Library Association or tying commercial posters in with books; remember the part that the poster message "Don't disturb the universe" played in Cormier's *The Chocolate War*.

Programs

Stores have special sales and events to get people into the marketplace, where they will be tempted to buy something. In the same way, ambitious librarians sponsor video-game nights and put on special programs both to do something special for regular library users and to bring nonusers into the library. Besides the suggestions from Diane Tuccillo, we have only a couple of ideas to add. One is that coordinating with schools and other community agencies will help you publicize your special event, which goes a long ways toward communicating to people that your library is an open and inviting place. Also, it's better to have a casual setting planned for a relatively small group, with extra chairs available, in case more people come than you expect. Bustling around at the last minute to set up extra chairs gives an aura of success that is more desirable than having row-on-row of empty chairs. And as Diane Tuccillo mentioned, such events are wonderful places to involve young people in the preparation. If you go the extra mile and teach them to write thank-you notes, you will be making a true contribution to the world.

Program possibilities include outdoor music concerts featuring local teenage bands, a film festival showing videos or films created by teens, poetry readings in a coffeehouse setting, or workshops in computer programming, photography, creative writing, bicycle repair, and so forth. Guest speakers are often invited to discuss subjects that schools tend to shy away from, such as self-defense and rape prevention, drug and birth control information, and introductions to various hotlines and other agencies that help young adults.

View programs as opportunities to encourage library visitors to become regular book users. Route traffic past the young adult section, pass out miniature bibliographies on bookmarks, and arrange scheduling so that attendees have time to spend a few minutes in the library before or afterwards.

When an author is invited to speak, the host librarian needs to begin publicity several weeks in advance to be sure that people are reading the author's books. English and reading teachers should be notified so that they can devote some class time to the author's work. When Ann Brashares, author of *The Sisterhood of the Traveling Pants,* came to Arizona to speak at Changing Hands Book Store, four girls (Britney, Paula, Audrey, and Ashley), who were sharing a pair of $4.00 jeans purchased at Goodwill, were interviewed for a pre-publicity news story in the local newspaper. At the presentation and book signing, they each gave a one-minute introduction of their favorite author.

Many authors' websites tell how they can be contacted for school or library visits. Google the Children's Book Council and look under "Author and Illustrator Sites" for information on how to contact particular authors. See Focus Box 10.1 "Good Internet Resources for Teachers and Librarians," for several other helpful websites.

Focus Box 10.1

Trailee Awards for a New Kind of Book Talk

One of the newest awards announced at the ALA 2012 Mid-winter Meeting were the Trailee Awards, which were given for the best on-line book trailers in six different categories.

1. Publisher/Author Created for Elementary Readers, which went to Katie Davis for her *Little Chicken's Big Day.*

2. Publisher/Author Created for Secondary Readers, which went to Quirk Books for *Miss Peregrine's Home for Peculiar Children* by Ransom Riggs.

3. Student Created for Elementary Readers, which went to the members of the Bookie Woogie Book Blog for *Where the Mountain Meets the Moon* by Grace Lin.

4. Student Created for Secondary Readers, which went to Daniel Neal, a student at Flower Mound High School in Flower Mound, Texas under the direction of Librarian Sherry Thompson, for *Tenderness* by Robert Cormier.

5. Adult created for Pre-K–12 Readers, which went to Amy Oelkers, an MLS student at St. Catherine's University in St. Paul, Minnesota for *Incarceron* by Catherine Fisher.

6. Educator/Librarian Created for Pre-K–12 Readers, which went to Analine Johnson, Library Media Specialist at Rodolfo C. Centeno Elementary in Laredo, TX for *The Cabinet of Wonders* by Marie Rutkoski.

This was the second year of the competition, which was sponsored by School Library Journal. More than 80 entries were submitted. From those the five judges selected 24 finalists (four in each category) and invited the public to vote. Over 3,000 votes were received. The idea behind the new competition is that short videos are a wonderful way to introduce readers to books, and even more important, when students make the videos they develop a deep and long lasting connection to the book. To find samples, you can search the general term of "book trailers for kids" or go to these specific sites.

Book Trailers for All
www.Booktrailersforall.com

Kidlit Book Trailers-Kids Books . . . in Action!
www.Kidlitbooktrailers.ning.com

43 Book Trailers Sites to Inspire, Instruct, and Share
www.darcypattison.com/marketing/book-trailers

Booktalks/Book Trailers – Deborah Fanslow's School Library Portfolio
www.redfrn.weebly.com/booktalksbook-trailers.html

Evaluating and Writing about Books

At the same time that we want to give young people choices, we want to do all that we can to make available the kinds of choices that will encourage them to read and help them make good use of the time they invest in it. It is ironic that, in a time when there are more books to choose from, most schools and libraries have less money to spend. Also, book prices have increased more than budgets, so that if a purchasing mistake is made, especially with a series or a set of books, a proportionately larger bite is taken out of school, library, and personal budgets. One of the ways for us to help see that our money is wisely spent is to help in decision processes by serving as book reviewers and as contributors to professional journals. Here is a summary of the kinds of writing you will do over your career listed in ascending order of difficulty and challenge:

Keeping a record of your own reading, probably by typing paragraph-length descriptions complete with publishing information (author, publisher, original year of publication), the genre of the book, and whatever information you anticipate wanting in the future. If the book might be controversial, jot down any prizes it has won or where you could find a review.

Making annotations, like the little descriptions that are in the focus boxes throughout this textbook, is a good habit to get into. Thanks to computers, teachers or librarians can easily reorganize their annotated lists to fit such different purposes as giving them to a teacher planning a unit on the Holocaust or making a flier to go with a display of love stories for Valentine's Day. Try to be more creative than starting each annotation with, "This book. . . ."

Writing reviews for locally or nationally published newsletters, magazines, or journals. Thanks to amazon.com, both you and your students can send in reviews and get them posted for others to read. Also, thanks to several online services, you can also read different reviews of the same book and develop your own ideas of what makes a helpful review. One of the main things that people reading reviews want is for some sensible person to tell them whether or not this particular book is worth an investment of money, trouble, and time. Teachers and librarians also want to be alerted to potential censorship problems and if there is a tie-in with an upcoming movie or some other event. Probably fewer than two dozen people in the United States are full-time reviewers of juvenile books. Most reviews of children's books (which is where YA lit is categorized in the publishing world) are written by teachers and librarians who evaluate books both as part of their assigned workloads and as a professionally related hobby.

Writing pedagogical articles, which are related to teaching and intended for fellow educators. Such articles are often about how you have been successful at using a particular book with a class or in finding three or four books that worked well together. These kinds of articles appear in such journals as those listed in Appendix C.

Writing scholarly articles is a way of engaging in literary criticism and in making original observations about some aspect of books in our field. Some Ph.D. dissertations are pedagogical in nature, while others are looking at the literature itself, rather than at how it is used. Look in Appendix C, "Some Outstanding Articles and Books about Young Adult Literature." Because young adult literature is a relatively new development, there is ample opportunity for original research and observation, whether from the viewpoint of a literary scholar, a teacher, a librarian, or a counselor or youth worker. The field as a whole will grow strong as a result of serious and competent criticism and analysis.

The field of juvenile reviewing is sometimes criticized for being too laudatory because the reviews are written by book lovers who are anxious to "sell" literature. One reason is that the publishers of well-established authors are the ones who can afford to send out review copies. Also, those editors of journals who have room for only a limited number of reviews devote their space to the books they think are the best, so of course the reviews are usually positive.

The fact that juvenile books are reviewed mostly by librarians and teachers working on a part-time basis slows down the reviewing process, especially if the reviewers take time to incorporate the opinions of young readers. With adult books, reviews often come out before or simultaneously with the publication of the book, but with juvenile titles it is not uncommon to see reviews appearing a full year or more after the book was released. Once young adult books are launched, however, they are likely to stay afloat much longer than adult best sellers because teachers work the best books into classroom units, librarians promote them, and paperback book clubs keep selling them for years. And most importantly, children continue to grow older and to advance in their reading skill and taste, so that every year a whole new set of students is ready to read *A Separate Peace, The Catcher in the Rye,* and *The Outsiders.*

Evaluation Criteria

People generally evaluate books based on literary quality, reader interest, potential popularity, or what the book is teaching (i.e., its social and political philosophy). Evaluators should make clear their primary emphasis lest readers misunderstand them. For example, although a critic may review a book positively because of its literary quality, a reader may interpret the positive review as a prediction of popularity. The book is purchased and put on the shelf, where it is ignored by teenagers. Consequently, the purchaser feels cheated and loses confidence in the reviewing source. In an attempt to resolve that kind of conflict, when Mary K. Chelton and Dorothy M. Broderick founded *VOYA* (*Voice of Youth Advocates*), they devised the evaluation code shown in Table 10.1. Each review is preceded by a Q number, indicating quality, and a P number, indicating popularity. They suggest that a fringe benefit to using such a clearly outlined code is that it helps librarians analyze their buying patterns. Those who lean heavily toward either quality or popularity see their biases and are able to strike a more appropriate balance.

A quite different set of criteria from either popularity or literary quality is that of social or political values. Most reviewers—whether or not they realize it—are influenced by their personal feelings toward how a book treats social issues. Of course, none of us—neither authors nor reviewers—are free from personal biases. Note how all of our "Young Scholars" who have written the "Speaking Out" pages are making statements reflecting their own viewpoints.

TABLE 10.1   VOYA Evaluation Code

Quality	Popularity
5Q: Hard to imagine it being better written	5P: Every young adult was dying to read it yesterday
4Q: Better than most, marred only by occasional lapses	4P: Broad general young adult interest
3Q: Readable without serious defects	3P: Will appeal without pushing
2Q: A little better editing or work by the author would have made it 3Q	2P: For the young adult reader with a special interest in the subject
1Q: Hard to understand how it got published	1P: No young adult will read unless forced to for assignments

That's fine. The fun and excitement of working in a creative field is that we aren't expected to act like robots, but at the same time book reviewers need to be clear in their minds, and communicate to their readers what criteria they are using. Censors, for example, who might be offended about a philosophy or a lifestyle in a particular book will often avoid talking about their real discomfort and instead will focus on such matters as language and style.

Young Adult Books and English Language Learners

Much of the material for teaching English to speakers of other languages has been designed either for young children or for adults. This means that middle school and high school teachers are eager for materials that they can use with teenagers. Young adult literature would seem to be an obvious choice because many YA books are shorter and less complex than books traditionally read by high school students. We agree that YA books are fine for those students whose English skills are fairly advanced, but we have found that students who have barely worked their way out of "sheltered" or specialized classes into regular English classes need extra help.

We came to this conclusion because, over the years, several of our graduate students have had internships or part-time jobs teaching English language learners either in regular schools or in weekend and after-school classes offered by service or religious organizations. They have come and borrowed boxes of YA books to take to their students for individualized reading. After a few weeks or months, when they come to return the books and visit with us, we of course ask how things went. Sadly, none of these teachers reported having grand successes.

The major problem has been that while our offices are filled with hundreds of books, most of them were sent to us by publishers as ARCs (advanced reading copies) and so we had only single copies to loan our teachers. This means that students were left to choose and read the books all on their own. They could not share and talk with other students about their particular book, nor did the teachers have time to devise helpful techniques to go along with so many different books. A second problem—certainly not one that we had anticipated—was that some of the students thought the books were "too much fun to read." They worried that they were not learning "enough" and would therefore fall behind ELL students in other classes who were spending their time doing more formal exercises.

Current educational policies in our state are to move English language learners as quickly as possible from specialized classes into regular English classes. This means that virtually all classroom English teachers are also teachers of English as a second language. Because of this experience we developed the following set of guiding principles that we now share with our future English teachers.

Expect and prepare for success: Remember that on a daily basis your job is to teach, not to test, students, and so your goal should be to figure out multiple ways to help students succeed. Choose pieces that are fairly short and easy to read. Look for white space on the pages, as with poems and novels in verse. It is better to work with a short story or an excerpted chapter that everyone can understand than with a big, long book that overwhelms students. It is fine to share condensations with the students, or even to find graphic novels that will present the same stories that students will later read. This kind of prereading is designed to give students the overall idea of the book and get them ready to read the author's original words because that's where they will get the spirit, the voice, and the beauty of the author's language.

Do whatever you can to relieve feelings of anxiety and fear: We talked with a teacher of American Literature at a university in Chile, who told us that he never teaches an American novel that has not been made into a film. He shows the film first so as to remove the students' fear of misunderstanding the plot. When students are reading authentic material that has not been simplified for a textbook version, they have to make what we call "intelligent guesses," and if they understand the direction of the story these "guesses" are more likely to lead them in the right direction. A teacher of American literature who works in Bologna, Italy, told us that she goes looking for film versions of whatever book she has assigned that can be watched in three different formats: first dubbed into Italian, then the English version but with Italian subtitles, and finally just in English. After these three viewings, her students are ready to read the book and concentrate on the language, the subtleties, and what is different about the book and the film.

Help students meet the characters before reading about them: In an *English Journal* article, "Words, Words, Words: Reading Shakespeare with English Language Learners" (September 2009, pp. 44–49), Christina Porter told about teaching thirty-page excerpts of Shakespeare plays. To help students get ready, she introduces the characters by drawing stick figures on the board and then drawing lines between them as she explains how they relate to each other. She also passes out "pantomime" cards with simple directions so that small groups come up and act out something that happens in the story without using any words. Later when students are reading, they look forward to recognizing the words that go along with the pantomime they just saw.

Get off to a good start by letting students read with their ears as well as their eyes: Start off by having students follow along in their copy of a book as you read the first few pages, or arrange for them to listen to a tape recording of the first chapter, and later of parts that are especially well-recorded. We have heard people say that children should never be asked to read a poem out loud to fellow students if they have not already heard it read by a fluent speaker. The idea is that the language of poetry is "different" from the language of prose and so children will feel more comfortable if they have heard it at least once. With English language learners, the rhythm and the flow of most written English will be different from what they are accustomed to, and so it is helpful if they can hear enough of the piece that it will resonate in their minds as they read the rest of it themselves.

Bring in children's literature, but only when you have a special reason: Teenagers are likely to feel insulted if they think the teacher is offering them easy-to-read books made for first or second graders because that's all she thinks they are capable of reading. However, if the teacher has a genuinely interesting reason for bringing in a children's book then it might be fine. For example, we just ran across a news story about Dr. Seuss's *Green Eggs and Ham* (which Seuss wrote using only fifty words) being the fourth highest selling book in America—and maybe in the world. We have our doubts about this statistic, but we do know that when Dr. Seuss was given an honorary doctorate at a university the audience spontaneously stood up and in unison recited the whole book for him. Bringing in such a news clipping, along with the book, might be a perfectly fine way to liven up a day's lesson, especially if you can find suitable images on the Web so that the class can read the book all together. Also, see page 371 in Chapter 11 for other suggestions of ways to use picture books in high school classrooms.

Include opportunities for lots of small group consulting and talking: Even if everyone in the class is reading the same book, try to devise opportunities for students to consult with each other in small groups so they can practice talking about what's happening in the story. Students from different cultures will have different experiences to bring to the table and it is quite likely that they will know different words so they can help each other in developing their vocabularies in natural and comfortable ways. To keep small groups on task, it's good for them to have an obligation to present something to the other students. This could be as challenging as writing an original script for a three- to five-minute play related to what they are reading, or it could be an oral reading of a few pages of a graphic novel with different students taking the part of particular characters.

While we were disappointed in our experience of simply loaning out individual YA books to English language learners, we have been thrilled with the success of a more structured service learning program in which our college students could earn three upper division credit hours for participating in a reading class at a local high school. As far as I can remember, all of the college students were native speakers of English, but we would have been happy to include non-native speakers if any had applied. They would probably have been inspirational to the high school students, who consisted of about half native speakers and half non-native speakers of English. They were all high school freshmen with low reading skills. The high school paid one of our graduate students a small stipend (less than $1,000) to serve as a group leader for four or five of our undergraduate students. They travelled to the local high school two days a week to work for one hour throughout an academic semester. Our university sponsored the program for several years at two different high schools, but in 2010 it was cancelled because the high schools could no longer afford the stipend, nor could we find anyone to pay for the sets (five copies each) of popular young adult books that our students took with them to read.

With today's economic challenges, probably few of you will be able to set up such a program, but we are nevertheless explaining how it worked in hopes that you can adapt some of the principles to your own situations. All of us involved thought it was worthwhile because, in every case, the students in the classes where our college students were helping made significantly higher gains in their reading scores than did the students in the same schools who were in classes without the extra help. In other high schools, it might be feasible that seniors who have finished their graduation requirements could be recruited into this kind of a service-learning project, especially if they are interested in becoming linguistics majors or in teaching English in a foreign country. As part of a teen outreach program, libraries might also sponsor this kind of partner or small-group reading club.

In our program, the college students had to have either taken, or be currently enrolled in, a young adult literature or a children's literature class. They met at the university for four hours of training before going to the high schools. On their first day, each student went to class with multiple copies of a YA book that they had chosen because they personally liked the book, not to mention that it was fairly easy to read. As part of their individual introduction to the high school students, they gave a short booktalk on the YA novel they held in their hands. After the booktalks, the high school students were asked to write down a first and second choice of which book they wanted to read. Our graduate student supervisor immediately sorted the requests so that the students could go right to work with their leader and the other four students in their group. See Table 10.2 for do's and don'ts of booktalks.

The high school students probably made their choices based on the personalities of the college students, as much as on the YA books they each offered. Nevertheless, the system worked well because the students were working in small groups and were excited to have been given some choice about the matter. Three weeks were allotted to the reading of a book, and on the final day each group made some kind of a presentation about their book to the rest of the class. Time was saved at the end of this "Performance Day" for the college students to again give booktalks and for the students to write down their first and second choices so that at the next class meeting everyone started over in a new group with a new leader and a new book. This meant that, during the semester, students read and worked closely with at least four different books, plus they had a chance to get acquainted with four different college students and to work closely with the native and non-native speakers in each group.

Common sense, as well as professional advice, tells us that the best way for students to build their vocabularies is to read lots of books. We agree, but we have also found that English language learners need some extra help and so we have devised some fairly simple ways to build vocabulary lessons based on student reading. If we had taught this to our students who borrowed the boxes of books to take to their English language learners, their students probably would not have come back worried that they were "just having fun" reading YA books, rather than learning what they needed to know.

The best vocabulary lessons need to come directly from students' reading. Serious English language learners know that they must learn the meanings of thousands of new words, and part of this knowledge has to be deciding which of a word's many meanings is the one intended. We often tell students to "use the context" to figure out a meaning of a word. But actually, what the context mainly does is disqualify meanings that are inappropriate. Students usually need to have some idea of the many possible meanings of a word before they can settle on the author's intended meaning.

TABLE 10.2	Do's and Don'ts for Booktalking

Do	Don't
1. Prepare well. Either memorize your talks or practice them so much that you can easily maintain eye contact.	1. Don't introduce books that you haven't read or books that you wouldn't personally recommend to a good friend as interesting.
2. Organize your books so that you can show them as you talk. To keep from getting confused, you might clip a note card with your talk on it to the back of each book.	2. Don't "gush" over a book. If it's a good book and you have done an adequate job of selecting what to tell, it will sell itself.
3. When presenting excerpts, make sure they are representative of the tone and style of the book.	3. Don't tell the whole story. When listeners beg for the ending, hand them the book. Your purpose is to get them to read.
4. Even though you might sometimes like to focus on one or two themes, be sure, over the months you meet with any group, that you present a wide variety of books. Include informative books that young readers would probably like to know about but might be too embarrassed to ask for.	4. Don't categorize books as to who should read them, for example, "This is a book you girls will like"; or show by the books you have brought to a particular school that you expect only Asian Americans to read about Asian Americans and only Native Americans to read about Native Americans, and so forth.
5. Experiment with different formats, for example, a short movie, some poetry, or one longer presentation, along with your regular booktalks.	5. Don't give literary criticisms. You have already evaluated the books for your own purposes, and if you do not think they are good, do not present them.
6. Keep a record of which books you have introduced to which groups. This can be part of your evaluation when you compare before and after circulation figures on the titles you have talked about. Also, good record keeping helps you not repeat yourself with a group.	
7. Be assertive in letting teachers know what you will and will not do. Perhaps distribute a printed policy statement explaining such things as how much lead time you need, the fact that the teacher is to remain with the group, and how willing you are to make the necessary preparation to do booktalks on requested themes or topics.	

Helping students learn these many meanings takes some preplanning on the part of teachers, as well as help from many other speakers. This is why we recommend that for English language learners, either small groups or whole classes of students read the same book so that students can share information with each other, and the teacher can mentally prepare by looking ahead and giving some thought to the various meanings of the words and phrases that students might need help with.

One of the Newbery Medal winners that we are recommending for this purpose is the 2007 winner, *The Higher Power of Lucky* by Susan Patron. It is 134 pages long and is spaciously printed, with small drawings by Matt Phelan appearing every few pages. However, teachers need to be warned that it is the most controversial of all the Newbery winners. Protests began as soon as the award was announced because the word *scrotum* appears on page 1. We suspect that it was not just this word that brought out the censors and the protestors, but the whole edginess of the story.

Ten-year-old Lucky Trimble is the protagonist. She lives in a fairly isolated trailer park in the desert community of Hard Pan, California, which is a long way from the movie image of life in California portrayed through most Hollywood movies. Lucky has one of the few "paying" jobs in town, which is to sweep off the patio and pick up all the trash at the Hard Pan Found Object Wind Chime Museum and Visitor Center. The reason there is always trash on the patio is that practically every day a group of twelve-step addicts gather and as soon as they are through talking they come out on the patio to relax. The Gamblers Anonymous leave smashed beer cans and candy wrappers, and of course the recovering alcoholics hate to see or smell beer cans, just as the smokers hate to see the cigarette butts left by the overeaters, who in turn hate to see the candy wrappers left by the gamblers.

Chapter 1 is entitled "Eavesdropping." Readers meet Lucky "crouched in a wedge of shade behind the dumpster." She is listening to Short Sammy, an alcoholic, tell his story of how he reached rock-bottom, and was inspired to seek his "higher power." Lucky loves to hear his story, first because it really is dramatic, and second because each time he tells it he adds little details that make it longer and longer. The climax of Short Sammy's story is that while listening to Johnny Cash and drinking homemade rum, he fell asleep in the front seat of his parked '62 Cadillac. He woke up suddenly and fell out of his car when "he saw a rattlesnake on the passenger seat biting his dog, Roy, on the scrotum."

Here are the words that we highlighted, just from page 1, as probably needing some explanation for English language learners—and maybe for other readers, too. As part of teaching these words and phrases, it makes sense to talk about them in additional contexts—so that students understand they are learning the words for more than just this one story. Our approach would be first to read page 1 aloud while students follow along in their own books and then to return and share such information as the following with students. Many teachers have students keep a word journal where they write down such words and, if feasible, draw a little picture to help them remember.

> *Eavesdropping:* First, see if students know what *eaves* are. Talk about the concept and see if they can tell you a word in their own language or whether houses where they come from have *eaves*. Then demonstrate how if someone stands under the eaves of a house and leans close to a window, she might be able to hear what is being said. The eaves have the effect of holding the sound in so that it is easier to hear. Then look at the picture of Lucky. Do we see any *eaves* on the building? No. This means that it is a metaphor. She is listening through a tiny hole in the wall, but it is still called *eavesdropping*. Talk about other ways of *eavesdropping* (e.g., holding a glass up to a wall, listening through keyholes, or even "planting" hidden microphones in rooms).

> *Crouched:* The picture in the book does a good job of demonstrating this action, but you might want to have students *crouch* by their desks for a minute so they will have the extra help of "muscle memory" in planting the word in their minds. You might also talk about how animals *crouch* before attacking and also see if students can give some other examples of why people might *crouch* down (e.g., to hide from someone, to look under a table, to get through a small opening, etc.).

> *Wedge of shade:* Talk about both of the nouns in this phrase. Draw a picture of a *wedge of pie* or hold up a rubber or wooden *wedge,* if you have one in your room to prop the door open. Ask someone to explain why the last

person on an elevator might have to *wedge his way in* or ask someone to go out into the hall and then *wedge his way* back into the room. Help students to generalize that it is a long triangular shape. Then, if you are brave, you might talk about boys giving each other *wedgies,* which is the kind of slang term that kids really want to learn. *Shade* is a very old word in English and in many other languages, so your students might have examples they can contribute from their own languages. When it is hot, English speakers like to stand in the *shade,* and sometimes airline attendants will ask passengers to pull down the window *shades* so as to help cool the plane. Cognate words include *shadow, shadow-boxing, shady dealings,* and *shadowing someone* as when a detective follows a suspected criminal. In old plays and stories, ghosts were sometimes called *shades.*

Dumpster: While the word *dump* is very old, *dumpster* is a fairly new word to name large metal containers which hold trash. Being *down in the dumps* is a metaphor meaning that you are feeling "low" or "trashy." *Dump trucks* are made so that the bed lifts up and whatever is in them can be *dumped* onto the ground behind them or, if it's trash, into an official *city dump.*

Hard Pan's Found Object Wind Chime Museum and Visitor Center: We could not find a real California town named *Hard Pan,* so Susan Patron must have made up the name of the town and then of its only "community center" to reflect the town's "hard times." It is almost a ghost town now, but was originally settled by men who came to California hoping to pan for gold. This would have been hard, indeed, because *panning for gold* requires flowing streams, which are not to be found in this desert. So instead, the men had to dig for gold, hence the old mine that later plays a part in the story. Or maybe *Hard Pan* refers to the dry, hard soil which metaphorically resembles a flat frying pan with the town sitting in the middle, like a fried egg. People who live in desert areas often pick up interesting rocks or other "*found objects,*" which they would want to share with the community or with people stopping by on their way to someplace more interesting. It is also common for people in dry, windy areas to make wind chimes from interesting pieces of wood or from stones that they find. For the story, the important point is that the town is so small that it does not have any churches, schools, or other community places.

Rock-bottom stories: When digging a hole, whether it's digging for water near a ranch house, or digging for gold out in a desert, once the digger gets through all the soil and hits "rock-bottom," there is hardly anything that can be done, at least in the days when this phrase became part of the language. Today, powerful explosives can be used, but still the meaning that the people in the self-help groups are thinking about is that they have gone as far down as they can go, and so it's time to change their lives and go in a new direction.

Higher power: The idea of finding something more important and more powerful to lean on and to borrow strength from is the whole idea of the book. Many religions talk about their higher power being God or Jesus, but this phrase is meant to include more than just Christian religions, and is what ten-year-old Lucky Trimble is looking for in her own life, which has been hard, indeed. We suspect that the idea that a little girl has to work so hard to find a "higher power" is more likely the cause of adult discomfort than is the one-time use of the word *scrotum*.

Scrotum: When you explain that this is the formal term for the male genitalia, be sure to let students know that it is not commonly used and that it would be a social mistake for them to use the word in public. You might go online and find some of the news stories about the controversy. Again, this is the kind of edgy information that won't be in formal ESL textbooks, but is really what students want and need to learn.

A bonus to working with *The Higher Power of Lucky* is that it is also an excellent way to teach students about the concept of intertextuality (i.e., an author referring to other well-known books or characters to help put over an original idea). Patron does this with P. D. Eastman's 1960 *Are You My Mother?*, which five-year-old Miles, who lives with his grandmother, carries around and constantly asks Lucky to read for him. The other book is Peter Sis's 2003 *The Tree of Life*, which is a beautifully illustrated biography of Charles Darwin. Lucky carries it with her because she envisions herself as the same kind of careful observer and note taker as was Charles Darwin. And after her teacher reads the book to them, Lucky names her dog *HMS Beagle*, after the ship that carried Darwin around the world. As part of a class reading of *The Higher Power of Lucky*, you might read these two children's books to your class and help students conjecture on why and how each of the books plays a role in *The Higher Power of Lucky*. This kind of prethinking about why something might be in a book helps readers anticipate the plot of a book.

To summarize our advice on using YA books with English language learners, we are saying that reading authentic young adult literature, especially when there is someone to help and guide the reader, is a wonderful experience for these students. It is good practice for their reading skills, while at the same time it introduces them to cultural attitudes and values and gives them a good chance to socially interact with other students. And if the students feel successful, they are more likely to continue reading for pleasure and listening to recorded stories when they are out of the classroom.

We sent a note to Elle Wolterbeek, our doctoral student who directed several sections of these classes, to ask which of the YA books were most successful. She graduated in 2010 and is now teaching college students near Boston, but she clearly remembered the popular books because she had to go out and keep buying additional copies. The all-time favorites were Orson Scott Card's *Ender's Game*, which she paired with a graphic novel, and Rebecca Stead's *When You Reach Me*. Others that were especially enjoyed were Louis Sachar's *Holes*, Caroline B. Cooney's *Driver's Ed*, Paul Zindel's *The Pigman*, and Wendelin Van Draanen's *Flipped*. The students also liked Jerry Spinelli's *Star Girl*, which had something extra going for it because its western setting made Arizona readers feel right at home. Elle was surprised about the popularity of Stead's *When You Reach Me*, which includes time travel and allusions to Madeleine L'Engle's *A Wrinkle in Time*, which she thought the non-native speakers would not relate to. The fact that they loved the complicated story reminded her that non-native speakers want to stretch their minds just as much as do native speakers. See Focus Box 10.2, "Recommended Books for Reading with English Language Learners."

Alexander and the Terrible, Horrible, No Good, Very Bad Day **by Judith Viorst, illustrated by Ray Cruz. Simon, 1972.** Although this is a picture book, ELL students would probably enjoy knowing that, in 2009, *Newsweek* magazine carried a blurb that told how reporter Seth Cotler Walls had found the title of Viorst's book used in fifty different news stories about politicians and other celebrities, including Attorney General Alberto Gonzales, Senator Ted Stevens, Treasury Secretary Tim Geithner, and cabinet nominee Tom Daschle, who were having their own bad days. After reading the story, students might have fun writing about their own bad days.

The Giver **by Lois Lowry. Houghton Mifflin, 1993.** One reason we are recommending this "classic" for English language learners is that most native English speakers in high school classes will have already read it and might, therefore, be willing to serve as group leaders or reading partners for their fellow students, who are struggling to learn English.

The Giving Tree **by Shel Silverstein. HarperCollins, 1964.** The words are simple in this classic story, but there's something about the story that touches people deeply. Many years ago, we had a returned veteran from the Vietnam War, who was paralyzed from the waist down, in one of our classes. The women in the class were arguing that the book was sexist because the tree, which happily gives up everything to the greedy little boy/man, is referred to as *she*. This discussion was cut short when the soldier raised his hand and told the class that in Vietnam when he was in the hospital and learned that he would never walk again, he planned to commit suicide. Then a nurse came in and laid the book on his bed. As he lay there reading and re-reading it, he changed his mind. We were all so touched by his story that we decided to ignore the choice of pronouns.

Holes **by Louis Sachar. Farrar, 1998.** As adults, we forget how much fun children have when they are learning their first language—remember all those second-grade riddles! Fortunately, Louis Sachar is here to provide some of that same kind of fun for kids learning their second language as when he named his characters—Zero, Armpit, Magnet, Squid, X-Ray, and Barf Bag, or when *Stanley Yelnats'* name turns out to be a palindrome and the recreation room at Camp Green Lake is called the W-R-E-C-K room.

A Light in the Attic: Poems and Drawings **by Shel Silverstein. HarperCollins, 1981.** We are not suggesting that students be given this whole book to read all at once, but that the poems be scattered throughout a school year to bring light and life to a class. The drawings are as important as the words.

Out of the Dust **by Karen Hesse. Scholastic, 1997.** This powerful story about a family's misfortune is set during the Great Depression in the 1930s and is told in easy-to-read free-verse. Fourteen-year-old Billie Jo is the protagonist whose mother and unborn baby brother are killed in a fire that Billie Jo feels partly responsible for.

The Voice That Challenged a Nation: Marian Anderson and the Struggle for Equal Rights **by Russell Freedman. Clarion, 2004.** Freedman's nonfiction books are smoothly written and illustrated with high-quality photographs. Marian Anderson (1897–1993), a talented contralto, African American singer, won a competition to sing with the New York Philharmonic Orchestra, but was largely denied operatic roles because of discrimination against African Americans. In 1939, she was scheduled for a concert at Washington's Constitution Hall, but then at the last minute was denied the opportunity, and so she sang an outdoor concert from the steps of the Lincoln Memorial for thousands of people of all races who were happy to stand up while listening to her beautiful voice. A companion book for other students in the class to read would be Freedman's *Lincoln: A Photobiography* (Clarion, 1987).

Young Adult Books and Reading Teachers

Including a section on reading in this text is in some sense superfluous because this whole book is devoted to teaching and promoting reading, but the interests and responsibilities of teachers of reading differ in some ways from those of English teachers or of librarians. One difference is that, except for remedial programs, teaching reading as an academic discipline in the high schools is a fairly recent development. The assumption used to be that normal students had received enough formal instruction in reading by the time they completed elementary school. They were then turned over to English teachers who taught mostly literature, grammar, and composition. Certainly English teachers worked with reading skills, but they were not the primary focus. Today, more and more states are passing laws setting minimal reading standards for high school graduation, and this has meant that reading has become almost a regular part of the high school curriculum. In some schools, all ninth graders now take a reading class; in other schools, such a class is reserved for those who test one or two years below grade level. Depending on how long it takes them to pass the test, students may take basic reading classes for several semesters.

In the teaching profession, the reluctant reader is nearly always stereotyped as a boy from the wrong side of town, someone S. E. Hinton would describe as an outsider, a greaser. Actually, reluctant readers come in both male and female varieties and from all social and IQ levels. Many of them have fairly good reading skills; they simply don't like to read. Others are poor readers partly because they get so little practice. What these students have in common is that they have been disappointed in their past reading. The rewards of reading—what they received either emotionally or intellectually—have not come up to their expectations, which were based on how hard they worked to read the material. They have therefore come away feeling cheated. The reading profession has recognized this problem and has attempted to solve it by lowering the price the student has to pay (i.e., by devising reading materials that demand less effort from the student). These are the controlled vocabulary books commonly known as *high-low books,* meaning high interest, low vocabulary. They are only moderately successful because the authors are rarely creative artists; they are educators who have many priorities that come before telling a good story. An alternative approach is making the rewards greater rather than reducing the effort. This is where the best young adult literature comes into the picture. It has a good chance of succeeding with reluctant readers because:

1. It is written specifically to be interesting to teenagers. It is geared to their age level and their interests.

2. It is usually shorter and more simply written than adult material, yet it has no stigma attached to it. It isn't written down to anyone, nor does it look like a reading textbook.

3. There is so much of it that individual readers have a good chance of finding books that appeal to them.

4. As would be expected, because the best young adult books are the creations of talented, contemporary authors, the stories are more dramatic, better written, and easier to get involved in than the controlled vocabulary books.

5. The language used in good adolescent literature is more like the language that students are accustomed to hearing. In this day of mass-media communication, a student who does not read widely may still have a fairly high degree of literary and language sophistication gained from watching television and movies.

Taking all this into account, some types of adolescent literature will still be enjoyed more than others by reluctant readers. In general, reluctant readers want their stories told faster and in less space. If it's information they are looking for, they want it to be right there. If they are reading a book for thrills and chills, they want it to be really scary. If they're reading for humor, they want it to be really funny. And if they're not sure about committing themselves for a large chunk of time, they want books in which they can get a feeling of accomplishment from reading short sections, paragraphs, or even sentences, as with various kinds of trivia books.

The Young Adult Library Services Association (YALSA) puts together an annual list of "Quick Picks," based on the selection criteria of short sentences, short paragraphs, simplicity of plot, uncomplicated dialogue, a sense of timeliness, maturity of format, and appeal of content. Fiction must include "believability of character and plot as well as realistic dialogue." This list, along with another YALSA list, "Popular Paperbacks for Young Adults," can prove helpful for reading teachers. The lists are available on the American Library Association's (ALA) website, http://www.ala.org/yalsa. The ALA also publishes a yearly book, *ALA's Guide to Great Reading*, which includes all of their "Best Book" lists ready for photocopying. Reading teachers should also pay extra attention to the section on Free Reading on pages 342–343 and take a look at Stephen Krashen's article, "Free Reading: Is It the Only Way to Make Kids More Literate?" in the September 2006 *School Library Journal*.

At our university we have a strong physical education program in which teachers are being trained under the PLAY (Promoting Lifelong Activity for Youth) philosophy. In the new PE classes, children no longer play elimination games in which the least skilled are the first to sit down. Nor does the PE teacher put children on display to be laughed at if they cannot climb a rope or do a push-up. And rather than having children wait apprehensively to see if they will be the last one picked for a team, children are allowed to select their own activities from such sports as skating, jumping rope, juggling, playing with Frisbees and hula hoops, and so on. Older students play badminton or tennis, jog or run, and work out on the kinds of equipment now found in adult fitness clubs. The idea is that if students enjoy and understand the value of what they are doing, they are more likely to continue it when no teacher is applying pressure.

Physical education teachers are absolutely certain that when today's kids grow up they will need to exercise their bodies and control their diets and so they are trying to teach wellness and food management, along with the pleasures of physical activity. We literacy teachers do not have such a specific view of our students' future needs, but we know that it is getting harder, rather than easier, to manage literacy needs. Modern media encourages divided attention as people multitask by talking on the telephone while handling their email and by listening to television newscasts while reading on-screen crawlers about different events. Also, today's world is filled with purposeful obfuscation in that many political, commercial, and philosophical messages are written more for legal protection or for persuasion than for clarification. And because of the complexity of such things as today's computer manuals, prescription drug warnings, and income tax forms, the reading material we need for managing our daily lives is more complicated than what our grandparents needed.

The major lesson we can learn from the PE teachers is the importance of student choice. The idea is unsettling because presiding over a gym or a room filled with students all engaged in the same activity gives teachers a satisfying sense of control. But whether students are doing the same calisthenics, chanting the same phonics lessons, or reading the same book, the activity is probably not something they will look forward to doing in their adult lives because humans, like cats, do not want to be herded.

When students are allowed to be the teacher's partner in choosing reading materials, they gain a sense of ownership and pleasure, plus they get practice in one of the most important literacy skills they will need in their adult lives. Because each day we are presented with so much to read, all of us are forced to perform triage: Category One—*Ignore*; Category Two—*Skim*; and Category Three—*Read*. Children seem less troubled by this than are most of us, but the problem is that many pieces find their way into students' *Read* category only because of pressure from us. Once students graduate, there will be no pressure from teachers and so it is important that we think ahead.

Instead of always assigning students to answer textbook or teacher-prepared questions, we need to give them practice in talking about their reading with small groups of fellow students. This will lay a foundation for future literary talk with friends about something they found on the Internet, a movie they just saw, a TV series, or a book they have read. We also need to model and encourage students to show respect for different literary genres and tastes. We need to extend the old saying about not judging a book by its cover to something like "Don't judge a story by the medium of its telling."

Of course, we want to offer books to readers that portray their own cultures and their own lifestyles, but we also need to provide readers with access to books beyond our own expectations. One of our best lessons in the diversity of reading tastes came from an Arizona woman who, as a volunteer, drove the Reading-Is-Fundamental bookmobile through northern Arizona. One morning when she was parked high on a desert mesa on the Hopi Indian Reservation, she saw an elderly man leaning against a cedar tree. She assumed he had come with a grandchild, but a couple of hours later when he was still standing there she invited him to come in and pick a book for himself. He stayed quite a while and at last chose Robert Louis Stevenson's *Treasure Island*. He must have sensed her surprise because he offered an explanation: "I started it at boarding school, but I didn't get to finish it."

Probably not one of us would have "matched" this book to this particular reader, but the incident shows that there are many kinds of diversity and that if we want to succeed in turning people into lifelong readers, we need to provide many choices and then to respect those choices that students make.

Four Ways of Teaching While Offering Students Choices: Free Reading, Studying Archetypes, Working with Illustrations, and Analyzing Names

Teri Lesesne in her 2006 book for teachers in middle grade schools, *Naked Reading: Uncovering What Tweens Need to Become Lifelong Readers,* is well aware of the wide disparity between the literacy practices of young people and how much they want to have something to say about what they read. A good idea that she has for helping teachers cope with the new reading strategies is what she calls *Template Activities,* teaching techniques that can be used with a variety of books. Middle school teachers would do well to find her book and see which of her Template Activities might work for them. Here we will describe three Template Activities that have worked for us with older students.

Free Reading

In Ken Donelson's thirteen years of teaching high school English, free reading is the activity that won more students over to the satisfaction (and maybe even the joy) of reading than anything else he tried. He remembers it as the hardest work he did, but also the most satisfying. In today's world of high-stakes tests and accountability, some schools are tempted to label the activity—whether it's a whole semester's course or a couple of days each week—*guided* or *individualized reading.* However, such titles go against the basic philosophy of the course, which in the mid-1930s grew out of Lou LaBrant's English teaching at Ohio State University's Lab School. The great benefit of *free reading* is that students have freedom of choice in what they read, which might include books that are too new to have been included in the curriculum. For example, when on February 7, of 2012 we went to Hamilton High School in Chandler, Arizona to help celebrate Charles Dickens's 200th birthday, the book that students wanted to talk about was John Green's 2012 *The Fault In Our Stars.* Green had come to a local bookstore on a book tour (an activity supposedly invented by Charles Dickens), plus the February 6, 2012 *Time* magazine had devoted a full page to a review written by Lev Grossman, "The Topic of Cancer. A Young-adult novel that triumphs with humor and pathos."

One of the chief reasons for providing students time to read in class is to prevent the dropoff in reading that usually occurs when students begin high school and their social and work schedules leave little time for reading. A classroom library is provided, containing multiple copies of popular young adult and adult titles from which students make their own selections. It is wise for teachers to send a note of explanation to parents indicating that the choice of books is up to the student and his or her parents.

When students finish a book, they hold a conference with the teacher, who preferably has also read the book. The purpose is not to test the student as much as it is to encourage thinking about the book and the author's intentions and to give teachers an opportunity to suggest other books that the student might enjoy. Teachers need to show that they respect the reading of popular young adult books by being familiar with many of them and by being genuinely interested in what students have to say about them. The class is doomed to failure if teachers view it as a kind of focused study hall in which their job is to do little more than keep control and keep kids reading. It's also doomed to failure if students view it as a "cake" class; for this reason, successful teachers are fairly stringent as they devise various systems for giving credit. Students keep records of the number of books (or number of pages) read, they assist the teacher in judging the difficulty of the material, they mark their improvement over the semester (perhaps shown by a test score or by the number of pages the student reads in a class period), and they receive grades on their preparation for the individual conferences.

Various studies summarized by Dick Abrahamson and Eleanor Tyson in "What Every English Teacher Should Know about Free Reading" have shown:

1. Free reading is enjoyed by both students and teachers.
2. Over a semester, students pick a variety of books, ranging from easy to difficult and from recent to classic.
3. Reading skills improve, with some of this improvement undoubtedly related to attitude change.
4. Students taught through free reading are more likely to read as adults and to foster reading activities with their children.
5. Individual conferences help literature come alive for students.
6. The conferences also help to break down barriers between students and teachers.
7. Good teachers employ the concept of reading ladders; for example, helping a girl move from a frivolous romance to a Laurie Halse Anderson book and on to *Gone with the Wind* and *Jane Eyre* (*The ALAN Review,* Fall, 1986, pp. 54–58, 69).

With so many benefits, why isn't the course taught more often? Part of the reason is an image problem. Many people suspect that if students are having a good time they can't also be learning. Another problem is that the teacher's role is practically invisible. Being able to listen to students while working ever so subtly to suggest books that will raise levels of reading takes a knowledge of hundreds of books plus tact and considerable talent in communication. Yet this teaching occurs in private sessions between two people. One of our favorite graduate students is a high school reading teacher who teaches an individualized reading class along with some of the more traditional remedial reading classes. She laughs in frustration about her principal's visits to her individualized reading class. After popping his head into her room on several different occasions and seeing the kids reading and her talking with a student at her desk, he sent her a note requesting that she let him know "when you are going to be teaching," so that he could come and observe.

She's still trying to educate him about the type of class she's teaching. It is not for the dysfunctional or disabled reader. It is for the average or above-average student who simply needs a chance to read and discuss books. In effect, it is one last try on the part of the school to instill in young people the habit of reading for pleasure. An alternative discussed in Chapter 11 is the organization of literature circles.

Archetypes in Literature and Pop Culture

Another Template Activity is to work with archetypes as they are reflected in literature and in pop culture. A benefit of supervising student teachers is that we get to see successful classroom activities, and one that excited us was on archetypes taught by Cynthia Kiefer and her student teacher, Jessica Zellner, at Saguaro High School in Scottsdale. On our third visit, we walked in and found every bulletin board, practically every chalkboard, and every inch of the wall covered with one-page "posters." Cynthia said it was the only assignment she had ever given where every student in every class followed through and brought in their work to be explained to the other students and pinned or taped up for everyone to see. Each poster had a downloaded picture of a celebrity or a character from a film, a television show, or an advertising campaign, plus the identification of an archetype and a couple of paragraphs written by the student explaining why this character fit into the particular archetype. The most surprising part was that we saw very few duplicates of the specific characters, but many repeats of particular archetypes being illustrated.

Studying archetypes is a perfect way to bring some consistency and commonality to discussions and considerations of the variety of literacy experiences illustrated through the Media Watch in Chapter 3 and in the comments from students taking our survey. Working with archetypes helps people understand the circular way in which literature and popular culture work together to create the collective unconscious, that is, those images related to the deepest, most permanent aspects of people's lives including death, fear, love, ambition, the biological family, and the unknown.

Carl Jung, Joseph Campbell, and Northrop Frye have all written on how these images find their way into people's minds and underlie the way we communicate with each other. People not privy to such cultural images could not understand the thirty-second commercials we watch on television, the cartoons that tell a whole story in one picture, the cover lines that attract us to magazine stories, and so forth. The small "bubbles" from which comic strip characters speak allow for only a few words, while the small screens on cell phones used for Instant Messaging encourage the creation of even more succinct messages. This push toward efficient communication promotes a reliance on archetypal images

We had students help us make these mini-posters illustrating various archetypes. We keep the set in a filing cabinet and then pull it out on the day we introduce the concept of archetypes. Each poster, along with a big sheet of butcher paper for their own notes, goes to a small group of students who within fifteen or twenty minutes can think of a surprisingly large number of examples to "teach" the rest of us about their assigned archetype.

in which just three or four words or the mention of a name is enough to trigger full-blown images in the minds of readers or listeners.

Beth Ricks, one of our Ph.D. graduates who now teaches at the University of Louisiana–Monroe, wrote to tell us about her frustrations in trying to get the high school students she was teaching to approach literature through a critical lens or perspective. They would lose interest long before she could teach them the backgrounds for Marxism or feminist theory, or even Reader-Response,

> But when I used archetype theory as a way to introduce mythology and Homer's *Odyssey,* they were actively involved. And I realized it's because they already have the foundation with archetypes because the archetypes are part of the subconscious and myth is part of who we are. They easily picked up the concept of looking at texts through an archetypal lens. So far, we have applied archetypes to film, music, the newspaper, magazines, and of course, the *Odyssey.* We watched *Shrek* in class, and they saw it through new eyes. . . . With my senior class, we watched an Adam Sandler movie and they wrote essays in which they traced the Innocent's Journey. They loved this exercise and from it realized that many of the books they had previously read included an Innocent embarking on a journey.

In closing, she said the best part was that her students had fun and that for the first time they understood they could criticize literary texts without being negative. And long after the class studied archetypes, students were still identifying and arguing about the archetypal roles of particular characters. In a spillover to real life, one of her students reported on how she tried to calm her parents by explaining the nature of the archetypal Seeker when they were upset about their popular new minister's resigning and going to "find himself" in a different town. They weren't impressed until she explained the concept of a Shadow Seeker as someone who has the archetypal characteristics to such an extent that they go beyond reason—for example, the interfering mother-in-law is a Shadow Caregiver just as the control freak or micromanager is a Shadow Leader or Shadow Ruler.

The following are brief descriptions of archetypes that we have found easy for students to understand and to "discover" in both the popular culture and in the literature we are reading. We took most of these from Carol S. Pearson's *Awakening the Heroes Within: Twelve Archetypes to Help Us Find Ourselves and Transform Our World* (HarperOne, 1991), but over the years we've changed the descriptions and added a couple of new ones, including the Junex versus the Senex.

The Innocent Embarking on a Journey is the most archetypal of all stories. It begins with a young person setting out either willingly or through some kind of coercion on a journey or a quest and meeting frightening and terrible challenges. After proving his or her worth, the young person receives help from divine or unexpected sources, so that readers rejoice in the success of the young protagonist as when David slays Goliath, when Cinderella is united with the noble prince, and when Dorothy and Toto find their way back to Kansas. In every culture, legends, myths, and folk and fairy tales follow the pattern of the adventure/accomplishment romance. They are called romances because they contain exaggeration. The bad parts are like nightmares, while the good parts are like pleasant daydreams. Such romances came to be associated with love because the traditional reward for a successful hero on such a quest was the winning of a beautiful maiden.

The biblical story of Joseph is a prototypical example of a worthy young hero being forced to go on a journey and, after great trials and tribulations, proving his worth both with the Pharaoh and with his brothers when they come to beg for food. A distinguishing feature of such romances is the happy ending achieved only after the hero's worth is proven through a crisis or an ordeal. Usually as part of the ordeal the hero must make a sacrifice, be wounded, or leave some part of his or her body, even if it is only sweat or tears. The real loss is that of innocence, but it is usually symbolized by a physical loss, as in Norse mythology when Odin gave one of his eyes to pay for knowledge. J. R. R. Tolkien used a similar theme in *The Lord of the Rings* when Frodo, who has already suffered many wounds, finds that he cannot throw back the ring and so must let Gollum take his finger along with the ring.

Among the world's great stories of journeys are Homer's *Iliad* and *The Odyssey,* John Bunyan's *The Pilgrim's Progress,* Jonathan Swift's *Gulliver's Travels,* and the biblical story of Adam and Eve being banished from the Garden of Eden. Modern children's journey stories include William Steig's *Sylvester and the Magic Pebble,* Ezra Jack Keats's *The Snowy Day,* and Maurice Sendak's *Where the Wild Things Are.* See Focus Box 4.1, "Literal Journeys/Figurative Quests" (p. 105), for examples of YA stories that follow this archetypal pattern.

The Archetypal Seeker has much in common with the real lives of young adults because they know that sooner or later they must leave their parents' homes and make a life for themselves. In the Bible, Joseph was forced to go on his journey; in contrast, Moses, who led the Jews in their Exodus from Egypt, comes closer to being a Seeker because he chose to go forth and find a better life. The Pharaoh, who wanted the Jews to stay and work for him, represents the part of the human psyche that resists change and wants to preserve the status quo.

An important part of being a Seeker is knowing when to stop. Shadow Seekers—those for whom the grass is always greener on the other side—abound in modern culture as with marriage partners and the owners of cars and houses, who continuously "trade up." The boy in Willa Cather's short story "Paul's Case" is a Shadow Seeker who wants to live in the fantasy world of the theater and in the glamorous world that he imagines for the wealthy. Paul commits suicide rather than face the dreary life he foresees for himself after his father repays the money he stole to finance his trip to New York.

The Junex versus the Senex archetype simply represents another way of talking about the conflict that exists between young and old. From an adult viewpoint, this is the idea of the *Dennis the Menace* cartoons and *The Little Rascals* movie gang. From a child's viewpoint, this is perhaps what is behind referring to someone as a Scrooge, with implications of stinginess; to someone as an old Witch or a Grinch, with implications of mean-spiritedness; or to someone as a dirty old man, with implications of sexual exploitation. This archetype is often referred to as the generation gap, but in fact it does not have to cross a whole generation. With teenagers, only a few years can make a difference in one's attitudes and loyalties, as when high school seniors "lord" it over freshmen, or when older siblings make life miserable for younger brothers and sisters. Because of where they are on their life journeys, teenagers find this archetype important.

In an interesting switch, a reversal is sometimes shown in which young protagonists skip a generation and identify with people of their grandparents' ages. This may relate to the fact that teenagers and elderly people are both living on the edges. They are not really in control of their lives, and so as "outsiders" they may join with each other to present a united front against the mainstream adults in the middle. Examples include Jimmy and his grandmother in Walter Dean Myers's *Somewhere in the Darkness*, Miracle McCloy and her grandfather in Han Nolan's *Dancing on the Edge*, and Tree and his grandfather in Joan Bauer's *Stand Tall*.

The Orphan has always been a well-loved character, probably because deep in our subconscious all readers fear being the lost child. Harry Potter is the latest orphan to tug at our heartstrings, but before Harry, we had the orphans in Charles Dickens's *Little Dorrit* and *Oliver Twist*, the children in C. S. Lewis's *The Lion, the Witch, and the Wardrobe*, and the endearing young redhead in Lucy Maud Montgomery's *Anne of Green Gables*. To play the literary role of orphan, young protagonists can have lost both of their parents, as in Robert Cormier's *I Am the Cheese*, or only one parent, as in Mark Twain's *Huckleberry Finn*. A child might be a temporary orphan, as was the boy in the *Home Alone* film, or the protagonist might still have one or both parents, but the parents are unable to play their role, as with the mother in Cynthia Voigt's *Homecoming* series. A higher percentage of orphans appear in children's literature than in real life because many authors figure out some way to get rid of the parents so that the children can be free to make decisions and get credit for their own actions.

The Caregiver comes from the world's bank of great stories where we have such characters as The Good Samaritan, Robin Hood, Snow White, Jiminy Cricket, Mary Poppins, Wendy from Peter Pan, and Charlotte from E. B. White's *Charlotte's Web*. Even preschoolers know about Horton, the wonderfully patient elephant from Dr. Seuss's *Horton Hatches the Egg*, and about the mother duck who majestically leads her ducklings through Boston traffic in Robert McCloskey's *Make Way for Ducklings*. One of the most touching contemporary stories about a caregiver is Katherine Paterson's *The Great Gilly Hopkins*. Galadriel, shortened to Gilly, is in foster care because, as one of our students described the situation, her "flower-child parents went to seed in the garden of motherhood." While searching for her birth mother, Gilly fails to appreciate her larger-than-life foster mother until it is too late.

The Wicked Stepmother is a universally understood archetype of the Shadow Caregiver (i.e., someone who takes the characteristics of the archetype to the extreme and therefore fails). Bruno Bettelheim, along with other critics, has suggested that the Wicked Stepmother is not really a stepmother, but instead is the dark side of everyone's mother—the scapegoat for the resentments that build up as part of the Junex–Senex conflict. The character is portrayed as a Wicked Stepmother instead of a wicked stepfather because on a daily basis the mother enforces discipline and teaches children a sense of responsibility as well as the skills of daily living.

The Sage offers spiritual and intellectual care as opposed to the physical care that is thought of as being part of the Caregiver role. The Giver in Lois Lowry's book of that name is an archetypal Sage. By holding the community's memories, he shields the members from responsibilities. In his wisdom, he questions this role and leads Jonas, who has been chosen to be his successor, to also question it. In more traditional literature, Merlin is a Sage, and it could make an interesting study to compare how authors ranging from C. S. Lewis to T. H. White and from Mary Stewart to Walt Disney's scriptwriters have portrayed this legendary Sage. Jeff's father at the beginning of Cynthia Voigt's *A Solitary Blue* is portrayed as a Shadow Sage. In response to his wife's leaving the family, Jeff's father places himself in "an ivory tower," but finally, as the book progresses, he is able to come down and relate to his son. Some of our students have argued that Darth Vader from *Star Wars* is a Shadow Sage because he is obsessed with perfection and being right, but at the same time is cynical and wants to obtain wisdom not so he can help others, but so he can feel superior and criticize them.

A true Sage is wise enough to realize that people cannot search for just one truth, but instead must understand a multiplicity of truths. This is the point made in Hisako Matsubara's *Cranes at Dusk*, set in post-World War II Japan. When a Shinto priest allows his daughter to attend Christian services he is putting into practice his belief that "No religion is enough to answer all the questions."

The Friend in literature ranges from Robin Hood and his Merry Men to Harry Potter, Ron, and Hermione. Friendship is the theme of some of the most popular children's books—for example, Arnold Lobel's *Frog and Toad Are Friends,* Lois Lowry's Anastasia books, Barbara Parks's Junie B. Jones books, and Beverly Cleary's Ramona books. Middle school girls have loved the friendships shown in books by Judy Blume, Ellen Conford, and Paula Danziger. Friendship was also at the root of the success of The Babysitters' Club and the Sweet Valley High series. (See Focus Box 4.2, "Love and Friendship," p. 109, for books that explore friendships among contemporary teens.) Since the story of David and Jonathan in the Old Testament, there have been strong stories about friendships between boys, as in John Knowles's *A Separate Peace.* The runaway success of Ann Brashares's 2001 *Sisterhood of the Traveling Pants* shows that friendships among girls can also be satisfying.

The Lover is such a popular protagonist that for general readers lovers have co-opted the whole genre of romance. From a literary standpoint, the first romances were stories told in the Roman (or Latin) manner; that is, those told by speakers of Latin, Italian, Spanish, and French. These stories were often about bold adventurers slaying dragons, rescuing princesses from ogres, and defeating the wicked enemies of a righteous king. Love came into the stories because a successful knight was often rewarded by being given the hand of a beloved maiden. The world's lovers are as different as Adam and Eve, Beauty and the Beast, Jane Eyre and Rochester, Catherine and Heathcliff, and even Tarzan and Jane. Shadow Lovers, those whose love is out of control or damaging, might include Samson and Delilah, J. Gatsby and Daisy, Humber Humbert and Lolita, and perhaps even the gangsters Bonnie and Clyde.

Being rewarded with the love of a respected character is a common theme in YA books. Stories of star-crossed lovers, the most famous of which is Shakespeare's *Romeo and Juliet,* are intrinsically interesting because of the possibility for greater suspense and tension. Such protagonists come close to being Shadow Lovers if their actions bring about tragic results. The possibility for tragedy and conflict used to be at the heart of YA books about love between characters of the same sex, but in fairly recent years YA authors have begun to portray lesbian and gay characters filling the role of Lovers rather than Shadow Lovers.

The Warrior, the Hero, the Villain or Destroyer are archetypes of strong characters; people who will stand up and fight. Those who become Heroes or Superheroes choose to fight on the side of good, as with Superman, Spiderman, Wonder Woman, and Batman and Robin. If Warriors make the wrong choice and go in the other direction, they become Villains or Destroyers. Female Villains are called such names as Jezebels or Witches, while male Villains might be referred to as Hitlers or Devils. A fairly new eponym for a Destroyer Warrior is a Rambo, taken from the name of the lead character in David Morrell's *First Blood*, made famous in the Rambo movies starring Sylvester Stallone. Another reason the name caught on is that society was becoming aware of a new kind of Destroyer—young, hostile males who were not thieves or criminals in the old sense of the word, but instead were toughs and bullies. Thirty years after Morrell created his Rambo character, society is even more puzzled by these kinds of Destroyers and the ripple effects of their actions in schools and communities. (See Focus Box 4.4, "Buddies and Bullies," page 127.)

The Ruler is more likely to be called a Leader in the United States because of the country's history as a haven for common people and its rejection of the idea of royalty and inherited power. The good Ruler is like Aslan in C. S. Lewis's *The Lion, the Witch, and the Wardrobe* or like Simba in Walt Disney's *The Lion King*. Alison Lurie in her 1991 *Don't Tell the Grownups* observed that the great appeal of the Winnie the Pooh books to young children is that the child Christopher Robin gets to play the role of the beneficent dictator in charge of the whole "Hundred Akre Woods."

Great Rulers make mistakes, but when this happens, they are mature enough to recognize their folly and to learn from it. A recognition of this fact has brought changes in the biographies written for young people. It used to be that authors put in only the positive aspects of Leaders' lives, but today they include both the good and the bad, in the hopes that young people will be even more inspired to see that "imperfect" people, which all of us are, can still make great contributions.

The Fool and the Trickster are archetypes that appear in American jokes about "The Little Moron," in some of the Muslim stories about Mullah Nasruddin (sometimes he's wise and other times he's foolish), in Jewish tales about the Fools of Chelm, and in European and American folktales about Foolish Jack. Readers and listeners enjoy the humor that comes from the surprise, incongruity, spontaneity, and violations of social norms that are part and parcel of stories about fools or clowns. Children have an extra reason for enjoying stories about Fools—because of their powerlessness and lack of experience, they are often left feeling foolish and so are glad when they find characters even more foolish than they are, as when in the Amelia Bedelia stories the housemaid constantly misinterprets the meanings of words. For adults, literary Fools include such characters as Sheridan's Mrs. Malaprop, who always mixes up her words, and Thurber's Walter Mitty, whose mind keeps wandering away from real life and into fantasy daydreams.

Tricksters are only pretending to be Fools so that they can get away with something, as when Tom Sawyer tricks the neighborhood boys into whitewashing the fence. Ulysses was a Trickster when he managed to escape with most of his men from the cave of the Cyclops. The Joker in the Batman movies is a Trickster. In YA books, portrayals of Fools and Tricksters are fairly subtle and usually have the serious purpose of teaching young people not to be Fools or to be tricked, a point discussed in more detail in relation to realistic problem novels in Chapter 4.

The Magician appears in stories of fantasy where authors create a make-believe world with no explanation of how the magic works. Internal consistency is all that is required. Ursula Le Guin's books about Earthsea are especially good at illustrating the role of the Magician. Ogion is the Magician/Sage, but readers are most interested in the young people who are training to become Magicians, as when the boy Sparrowhawk is destined to become the archmage named Ged, the girl Goha is destined to become the wise woman Tenar, and in the last book, an abused Orphan is destined to become the next archmage under the name of Tehanu. Honest Magicians use their powers for good, while Shadow Magicians use their powers for evil or destructive purposes. Some stories about Magicians and Creators are cautionary tales that warn against humans trying to take the power of the gods for themselves, as illustrated by the host of troubles released when Dr. Frankenstein created his monster.

The Creator does not wave a wand or pronounce magical words to make happy endings possible; instead, he or she transforms reality by changing the way characters perceive matters, often with long-term effects on the real world. The Wizard in Frank Baum's *The Wonderful Wizard of Oz* was this kind of a magician when he convinced Dorothy's companions that he was giving them what they obviously already had: courage for the lion, brains for the scarecrow, and a heart for the tin woodman. In old folktales, the role of the magical Creator was filled by dwarves, elves, fairy godmothers, fortune-tellers, shamans, witches, healers, and priests and priestesses. In modern life, psychiatrists, therapists, religious leaders, politicians, teachers, friends, and parents are more likely to play these roles. Shadow Creators are the con artists who exploit people's emotional needs for selfish purposes. Both kinds of Creators are commonly included in YA books where authors explore some fairly subtle differences between Creators who play a positive role and those who play a negative role by killing others' dreams— usually through being overly controlling or overly negative, as were parents and coaches in Robert Lipsyte's *Raiders Night,* already discussed in Chapter 7.

Working with Illustrations in Young Adult Books

When Scott Westerfeld spoke at Changing Hands Bookstore in Tempe, Arizona on October 3, 2011, celebrating the release of *Behemoth,* the third book in his *Leviathan* series, he started with an ode to the power of illustrations. He told how when his Uglies series was translated into Japanese, the publishers choose to have it illustrated, sort of manga style, something he had never dreamed of. When he was sent a digital copy, he sat for hours happily "reading" his books, even though he does not know a word of Japanese.

It was so much fun that he put a few of the illustrations on his website, and was amazed at how many readers sent in notes asking why they couldn't have illustrations in the copies of *their* books. This is when he decided that for his next book he would work closely with an illustrator, which he did in his Leviathan series. In his speech, he gave full credit to the illustrator Keith Thompson. The fully illustrated books are officially listed as being "by Scott Westerfeld and Keith Thompson." Although the two men did not sit side-by-side working on the books, the Internet made it possible for them to send ideas and drawings back-and-forth. And it was often Thompson whose historical research into old drawings and proposals, influenced what Westerfeld wrote, especially in relation to the *walkers* that in Westerfeld's alternate telling of World War I took the place of heavy-duty wagons and wheeled carts for carrying cannons.

Westerfeld was surprised to find out that a century ago most fiction books for adults were illustrated. Earlier, we had heard that it was the paper shortage connected to World War II that "killed" the idea of the frontispiece artwork in novels, but Westerfeld reported that the art work in many books went far beyond just a single front page. He was amused to discover, for example, that the image we all have in our minds of Sherlock Holmes in his hunting cap, with the brim and the flaps tied on top of his head, was totally the invention of the illustrator. Nowhere in the books does Holmes go out riding in a forest, although he sometimes carried a riding crop, which he would in extreme cases put to good use. Since then we've seen an online picture of a "NO SMOKING" sign in the Baker Street train station in London which as an ironic attention-getter is printed in front of multiple images of Sherlock Holmes's silhouette with his pipe and his hunting cap.

Activities that group leaders might use to encourage readers to look at and appreciate the resurgence of artwork in YA books include guiding students to examine the format and design of well-done graphic novels so that they will think of them as more than just pictures in a row. For example, students might work on small segments of Vera Brosgol's *Anya's Ghost* to count the number of panels on each page, noting the differences in size, shape, and placement and what these differences convey to readers. Other questions students might work with include whether someone is speaking, or if there is one big "comic-book" kind of word provided by the artist, who with graphic novels plays the role of the narrator. A bulletin board of such "comic-book" words as *KRAK, THUD, HEEELP! RRRING, YIPE! SLAM,* and so forth could be used to show how such words were forerunners to text speech. You could also talk about what it means if a drawing "bleeds" off the page as on the cover of *Anya's Ghost* or on page 91 where the ghost is telling her story. What does it say about tone when a page is mostly grey, mostly white, or mostly black? Why does p. 60 have a dotted line around it? How is it different? How many different facial expressions does Brosgol achieve mainly through the positioning of the pupils in Anya's eyes? An alternative to a traditional book report could be the making of a story board for turning a short story or part of a regular book into a graphic novel or a book illustrated in the style of Westerfeld's Leviathan books or Brian Selznick's *The Invention of Hugo Cabret*. Another idea for a bulletin board is to encourage students to make enlarged drawings of figures they particularly appreciate.

Several recent novels, all highly acclaimed, feature young people whose lives—at least their emotional lives—are saved by their love for sketching and drawing. Gary D. Schmidt's *Okay for Now* was a finalist for the National Book Award and is on our 2011 Honor List. The book is set in the late 1960s when eighth-grader, Doug Swieteck has to move with his family from Long Island to a small town in upstate New York. His father lost his job, but arranges, with the help of an old drinking buddy, to get a similar job at a paper mill. Doug's father and his older brother are as despicable as his mother is lovable in spite of how she is constantly berated by her husband. This means that it is mostly up to strangers in the new town to nurture and encourage Doug, i.e., to make things "Okay, for now." At the beginning of the book, Doug is attracted to a drawing of an arctic tern done by John James Audubon and on display under a glass-covered table in the town library. While Doug's fingers itch to try drawing the bird (paper, pencils, and even an eraser, are provided near the exhibit), he resists because he knows only "chumps draw." His personal growth is shown by the way he gradually changes his mind thanks to the encouragement of an assistant librarian and of the friends he makes when he works as a Saturday morning delivery boy for a small grocery.

Ruta Sepetys's *Between Shades of Gray* is the story of a young Lithuanian girl, Lina, who drew pictures as a way of keeping her spirits and her hopes alive of somehow contacting her missing father, when she and her mother and younger brother were taken to Siberia in 1941 as part of Stalin's plan to conquer the Baltic countries and make them part of the USSR. Lina also wrote short, coded notes along with her sketches. The idea behind the novel is that we have the story because Lina had buried her pictures and her notes in hopes that someone would find them and learn about her life. According to the novel, they were found in 1995 in an area in Lithuania, which was being cleared for construction. A note in the bottle said that Lina had buried the package in 1954 after she had returned from her twelve years of imprisonment in Siberia and discovered, along with all the other returning refugees, that it was still not safe to talk about their experiences.

Laura Lee Gulledge's *Page by Paige* is a graphic novel in which a sixteen-year-old girl, named Paige, is uprooted by a move from Virginia to Brooklyn. She vows to draw a few pages each week, and sticks to telling her own story over an eight-month period. The book was praised by its *School Library Journal* reviewer for its cleverness, the excellent use of panel size and placement, and the "brilliant" way that Gulledge manages to express emotions both through her art and through such spot-on descriptors as "agents of whimsy," "fluent in Paige," "clickage," and "a redhead island."

Allan Say's 2011 *Drawing from Memory* is a beautifully illustrated retelling of Say's lifelong love of comics and of the different reactions he got from adults when he began drawing as a child. He is the Japanese-American author and illustrator of books that some teens might remember reading in elementary school: *Kamishibi Man* (2005), *Grandfather's Journey* (2008), and *Tea with Milk* (2009).

Daniel Handler, who many students already know and love because he is the man who wrote the Lemony Snicket books, cleverly illustrated by Brett Helquist, has written *Why We Broke Up*, a realistic problem novel illustrated by Maira Kalman. The plot has some similarities to Jay Asher's *Thirteen Reasons Why*, but it isn't nearly as somber. The girl in this story is actually doing the "dumping" of her boyfriend and instead of leaving him a box of tapes explaining her suicide (as in Asher's book) she leaves him a box of mementos from their courtship. These are mostly just everyday items, but they are made special because of the way the girl tells how they fit into their story and because of Kahman's paintings, which are printed in full-color on heavy-weight art paper. Our hope is that *Why We Broke Up* might inspire similar partnerships between teen writers and artists who might be encouraged to take a new look around them and find items worthy of such careful attention.

Names and Naming in Young Adult Literature

Looking at names and naming in YA books is a fourth Template Activity for working with different books under an overall umbrella topic. Paying extra attention to the way that authors choose names for their characters can be a revealing activity. One reason is that, with rare exceptions, all other words that we speak or write already have generally agreed-upon meanings. However parents are free to make up original names for their newborn infants, a practice that is becoming increasingly popular, while authors of fiction are forced to make up new names, or at least new combinations of names, lest they get accused of pointing fingers at real people.

Teenagers have an extra reason for being interested in names because their main interest at the stage of life they are in is to develop their own identities, separate from their parents. And one of the ways they express this interest is to experiment with changing their names, as when, in *The Great Gatsby*, F. Scott Fitzgerald introduces his title character with:

> James Gatz—that was really, or at least legally, his name. He had changed it at the age of seventeen and at the specific moment that witnessed the beginning of his career—when he saw Dan Cody's yacht drop anchor over the most insidious flat on Lake Superior. It was James Gatz who had been loafing along the beach that afternoon in a torn green jersey and a pair of canvas pants, but it was already Jay Gatsby who borrowed a rowboat, pulled out to the *Tuolumne* and informed Cody that a wind might catch him and break him up in half an hour.
>
> I suppose he'd had the name ready for a long time, even then.

One of the most successful writing topics for college freshman, and we imagine it would also work for older high school students, is for them to tell the story of their names. We usually learn that about half of the class members go by a name that has in some way been adapted or changed from what their parents wrote on their birth certificates. Before having students launch into thinking and writing about their own names, we work with name changes in fiction and among celebrities. For example, we talk about how Ursula K. Le Guin in the Earthsea books gives her main characters two names. Readers first get to know them by their *use-names,* but then later their *true-names* are revealed.

Robert Cormier was a master at using name changes as a significant part of his plots. In *I Am the Cheese,* the whole plot revolves around the Farmer family being taken into the U.S. Government Witness Protection program and having to get new names. In his *After the First Death,* there is a fascinating scene in which the terrorist Artkin and his trainee Miro call a waitress by the wrong name and then argue with her that there's no way she can know this isn't her name. Cormier uses the scene to demonstrate the difference between the young terrorist, who is totally comfortable with his assigned name, and the waitress who is made to feel frightened and insecure by whatever "game" these two "foreigners" are playing on her.

Margaret A. Edwards Award

Winner (1993)

M. E. Kerr, A Genius with Names

Kerr's Edwards Honor Books include *Dinky Hocker Shoots Smack!; Gentlehands; ME ME ME ME ME: Not a Novel;* and *Night Kites.* Other highly acclaimed books include *Little Little; If I Love You, Am I Trapped Forever?;* and *Deliver Us from Evie.*

One of Kerr's first jobs when, in 1972, she wrote *Dinky Hocker Shoots Smack!* was to choose a pen name to use with her YA books since she was already known as a writer of mysteries and of love stories about lesbians. Her real name is Marijane Meaker, and so for her pen name she chose M. E. Kerr, a play on her surname. The next thing she had to do was to argue with her publishers, who wanted a softer title than *Dinky Hocker Shoots Smack!*

The story is about a do-gooder mother who is oblivious to the needs of her own overweight daughter, who is ironically called Dinky. The title comes from what Dinky paints on the walls and the sidewalk for people to see when her mother exits a meeting where she is being honored for her work with drug addicts. In a lighter, naming incident, Dinky names the stray cat she finds cowering under a car Nader, in honor of Ralph Nader, who, as a critic of the American automobile industry, also spent considerable time under cars.

In *I'll Love You When You're More Like Me,* Wally has a crush on a girl who has created for herself the fancy sounding stage name of Sabra St. Amour—she used to be plain old Maggie Duggy. When Wally meets her at the beach and she asks him for a cigarette, he tells her she has to be a little crazy to let the cigarette companies manipulate her with such names as Merit and Vantage. She responds that she came to the beach for a swim and some sun, not for a lecture, but Wally goes right on asking her if True, More, and Now mean that she will get more out of life by living for the moment because she won't live long if she is being True to her filthy habit. While this isn't enough to convince Sabra to quit smoking, she becomes interested in Wally as a "thinker."

Kerr's *Gentlehands* is the story of a post-WWII hunt for one of the cruelest of the Nazi SS guards at Auschwitz. He taunted Jewish prisoners from Rome by playing Puccini's opera *Tosca* and singing "O dolci mani," which translates to "gentle hands." The plot centers around whether Buddy's mysterious German grandfather is this man. He has named his keeshond dog Mignon, a name that he says comes from an opera, but a more gruesome interpretation could be that it comes from filet mignon, as a reminder of how Gentlehands used to turn selected prisoners over to his dogs.

Deliver Us from Evie is the story of a lesbian relationship between Evie Burrman and Patsy Duff, two high school seniors who live in the fairly prosperous farming community of Duffton. A boy from a neighboring farm, Cord Whittle, would like to court Evie and when she turns him down he gets even with her in church during the recitation of "The Lord's Prayer." He stands near her and says in an extra loud voice, "Deliver us from Evie," and then laughs and nudges Evie as if he has made a good joke.

Kerr named the protagonist of her YA mysteries John Fell so she could have such titles as *Fell, Fell Back,* and *Fell Down,* and then make such additional puns as "fell apart," "fell to pieces," and "fell in love." *Little Little* is about a girl who is a dwarf and her relationship with Sidney Applebaum, a dwarf with a humpback who grew up in the Twin Oaks Orphans home run by Miss Lake. The boys, all deformed in some way, called their home Mistakes Cottage, and chose for themselves such names as Wheels, Cloud, Pill, and Worm. Miss Lake objects, but she does not understand that the boys have taken "naming rights" for themselves so as to take away the pain that might come from outsiders calling them names. In keeping with their attitude, they refer to "regular" people as Sara Lee, an acronym for "Similar And Regular And Like Everyone Else." ●

Louis Sachar, Polly Horvath, Gary Paulsen, and of course, J. K. Rowling, use names to bring smiles to readers. A good example is the title story in Paulsen's collection, *How Angel Peterson Got His Name*. Also, see the Edwards Award write-up on M. E. Kerr and how she uses names both for amusement and for more serious purposes. While Robert Cormier uses his carefully chosen names mostly to set a somber tone, Francesca Lia Block uses names to establish a playful kind of magical realism as illustrated by some of the names in her Weetzie Bat books. Besides Weetzie, she has characters named My Secret Agent Lover Man, Dirk, Duck, Cherokee, and Witch Baby. Their pets include Slinkster Dog, Go-Go Girl, Pee Wee, Wee Wee, and Tiki Pee. Names that establish time periods are especially useful for historical fiction. For example, Karen Cushman uses the same kinds of linguistic processes to create historical names that fit into particular time periods, as with her medieval books, *Catherine, Called Birdy, The Midwife's Apprentice,* and *Alchemy and Meggy Swann,* and her California gold rush story, *The Ballad of Lucy Whipple*. The names are very different but created through the same four processes that historical linguists describe as being responsible for 90 percent of the surnames created in England and Europe during medieval times, which is when people began living in towns and cities so that they needed more than a single name. Most surnames, many of which also became first names, were either:

1. Based on place names,

2. Descriptions of personal characteristics,

3. Descriptions of a person's occupation, or

4. Patronyms, based on the personal name of a father or another admired person.

Besides using character or place names to establish time periods, authors use them to establish locations. Nancy Farmer's *A Girl Named Disaster* is set in present-day Mozambique and Zimbabwe, where the custom is to devise names for children that "send a message" to other members of the family. Yann Martel

We were amused in our 2010 summer travels to discover that it wasn't just thousands and thousands of newly born baby girls who were being named after Stephenie Meyer's Bella. Apparently the owner of this newly painted beauty shop is also a fan of the Twilight books.

***The Absolutely True Diary of a Part-Time Indian* by Sherman Alexie. Little, Brown, 2007.** Alexie's first book written specifically for teenagers won the 2007 National Book Award in the category of young people's literature. Alexie writes about the mysterious Turtle Lake which he and his friend Rowdy dare each other to dive into. He explains that Indians love mysteries and that some people say that Turtle Lake, which no one has ever been able to find the bottom of, got its name because of being home to a giant snapping turtle that ate Indians. Then he shows the universality of such exaggerations by going on to call it "A Jurassic turtle," "A Steven Spielberg turtle," and "A King Kong versus the Giant Reservation Turtle turtle."

***Colibri* by Ann Cameron. Farrar/Frances Foster Books, 2003.** A twelve-year-old Guatemalan girl, whose original name meant "Hummingbird Star," learns that at age four she was kidnapped by "Uncle" Baltasar, a man who calls her Rosa and uses her as his assistant while he pretends to be blind.

***Jip: His Story* by Katherine Paterson. Lodestar, 1996.** When the story starts, the year is 1855 and Jip West is probably eleven or twelve years old. No one knows for sure because he was abandoned on West Hill Road when he was a toddler. Townspeople named him Jip thinking that he must have fallen from a Gypsy wagon, but actually he was purposely left behind by his slave mother who was being taken back to the South and did not want her boy to be a slave.

***The Joy Luck Club* by Amy Tan. Random House, 1989.** Waverly was named for the California street where her immigrant family lived. She is an adult before she learns that her mother named her oldest brother, Winston, because she "liked the meaning of those two words wins ton," and her second brother, Vincent, because it "sounds like win cent, the sound of making money."

***The Lone Ranger and Tonto Fist Fight in Heaven* by Sherman Alexie. Grove Press, 2005.** Alexie's book is set on the Coeur d'Alene Indian Reservation in northern Idaho and much of the humor comes from the way he mixes Indian and white naming practices as when he writes, "I was always falling down; my Indian name was Junior Falls Down. Sometimes it was Bloody Nose or Steal-His-Lunch. Once, it was Cries-Like-a-White-Boy, even though none of us had seen a white boy cry."

***The Meaning of Consuelo: A Novel* by Judith Ortiz Cofer. Farrar, Straus and Giroux, 2003.** Consuelo, whose Spanish name means "consolation" or "joy," is the older sister in a middle class Puerto Rican family. She is the "good one," while her younger sister, Mili,

---

and Orson Scott Card use names to establish their fantasy settings, while Daniel Handler filled his Lemony Snicket books with jokes related to the names of famous American literary and pop culture figures. While children missed many of these allusions, their parents were amused, which made the books favorites for families to listen to while on car trips. See Focus Box 10.3 "Names and Naming in Multicultural Books" on for examples of how authors use names to quickly identify ethnicities. Also see Cynthia Nicholson's essay in Chapter 3 on page 88 in which she writes about the importance of respecting the names of African Americans.

Critics have complained that J. K. Rowling's character names are not as "authentic" as are the character names in J. R. R. Tolkien's books. This is true, but Rowling had different goals. Besides using names to create a parallel world and to amuse readers, she created descriptive names that not only helped with characterization, but also with memory. Jim Dale, who recorded the Harry Potter books for Scholastic, explained that for just one book, he had to create 125 different voices. It is amazing that readers (both old and young) were able to remember this many different characters, not only while reading a single book, but also while waiting a couple of years for the next book to appear.

whose name is short for "miracle" or "wonder," drifts into increasingly bizarre behavior and then suicide. Consuelo must decide whether to stay and "console" her family or move to New York and make her own life. *Call Me María: A Novel in Letters, Poems, and Prose* by Judith Ortiz Cofer (Orchard, 2004) is written for younger teens.

My Name Is Not Angelica by Scott O'Dell. Houghton Mifflin, 1990. O'Dell dedicated this historical novel "To Rosa Parks, who would not sit in the back of the bus." Raisha and her two young friends, Dondo and Kanje, are put on a slave ship and taken from Africa to St. Thomas. The boys' names are changed to Abraham and Apollo, and Raisha's to Angelica. When revolts and violence occur on the island, the boys commit suicide rather than return to slavery, but pregnant Raisha is determined to live and save her baby, but not ever to think of herself as Angelica.

My Name Is Not Easy by Debby Dahl Edwardson. Marshall Cavendish, 2011. The author has lived in Barrow, Alaska, the northernmost community in North America most of her adult life. Her well-received book is about an Iñupiaq (Eskimo) boy sent from his home near the Arctic Circle to attend a Catholic-sponsored school. The story is told through five narrators, one of whom is "Luke." He explains on the first page, "When I go off to Sacred Heart School, they're going to call me Luke because my Iñupiaq name is too hard. Nobody has to tell me. I already know . . . My name is hard like ocean ice grinding at the shore or wind rounding the tundra or sun so bright on the snow it burns your eyes."

Naming Maya by Uma Krishnaswami. Farrar, Straus and Giroux, 2004. Maya grew up in New Jersey, but now she finds herself back in India with her mother, who is intent on selling the family home after her parents' death. Maya's parents are divorced and Maya falsely thinks their problems started with a disagreement over her name.

Weedflower by Cynthia Kadohota. Atheneum, 2006. Sumiko is a young Japanese/American girl living in California during the years leading up to World War II. Sumiko's family is sent to the Poston Internment Camp, located on a Mohave Indian reservation near Parker, Arizona. The camp was run by Native Americans and Sumiko develops a shy friendship with an Indian boy named Frank. Names and their symbolic meanings are at the heart of several incidents in this well-written piece of historical fiction.

When My Name Was Keoko: A Novel of Korea in World War II by Linda Sue Park. Clarion, 2002. Between 1940 and 1945, South Korea was occupied by Japan and the people were forced to adopt Japanese names and study the Japanese language. Chapters alternate between Keoko and her brother, who is trying to get used to his new name of Sun-hee.

A different names-related topic that students might enjoy talking about is how Stephenie Meyers's Twilight books are changing real-life naming patterns. An article in the *Omaha World Herald* written by Cleveland Evans, one of the former presidents of the American Name Society, was headlined "Vampires, Teen Moms Impacting Top Names." It appeared on May 17, 2011, just after the Social Security Administration released its list of the top baby names for 2010. Here are some of the facts:

- Jacob and Isabella were again the winners with 22,731 Isabellas and 21,875 Jacobs. It is unusual that, for the second year in a row, the #1 name for girls accounted for more babies than the #1 name for boys. There are so many more available girls' names than boys' names that the boys' lists are not as varied.

- Isabella and Bella began their boom in 2009 and increased again in 2010.

- Alice, Edward's sister, also saw her name rise 40 percent in 2010.

- Esme (the name of Edward's mother) was in the top 1,000 in 2010 for the first time ever.

YA Books and Parents

"Tell me a story."

"Read just one more!"

"Can we go to the library today?"

Such requests are among the pleasant memories that parents have of their young children. These memories become even more cherished when parents look at these same children, now teenagers rushing off to part-time jobs or after-school sports or spending so much time with friends or online that they no longer seem to have time to do required school assignments, much less read a book for pleasure. When parents ask us what they can do to encourage their teenage children to read, we find it easier to tell them what not to do because we've observed at least three clear-cut roads to failure.

1. Don't nag. There's simply no way to force young adults to read, much less to enjoy it.

2. If you choose to read the books your teenagers are reading, don't do it as a censor or with the intent of checking up on your child or your child's school.

3. Don't suggest books to your teenager with the only purpose being to teach moral lessons.

Lest we appear unduly pessimistic, we hasten to add that we have also seen some genuinely rewarding reading partnerships between teenagers and their parents. These successful partnerships have resembled the kind of reading-based friendships that adults have with each other. Mutual respect is involved, and the partners take turns making suggestions of what will be good to read. Conversations about characters, plots, authors, and subject matter come up naturally, with no one asking teacher-type questions and no one feeling pressured to talk about what he or she has just read.

Teenagers enjoy being in a helping role (i.e., being experts whose opinions are valued). Some of the best partnerships we've seen have been between our older college students and their teenage children who have volunteered to read and share their opinions on the books their parents are reading in class. A key to enticing young people to read is simply to have lots of books and magazines available. But they need to be available for genuine browsing and reading by everyone in the family, not purchased and planted in a manner that will appear phony to the teenager. A teenager who has never seen his or her parents read for pleasure will surely be suspicious when parents suddenly become avid readers on the day after parent-teacher conferences.

Perhaps a more important benefit than modeling behavior is that when parents read some of the best new books (the Honor List is a good starting place), they gain an understanding of what is involved in being a teenager today. Parents who have read some of the realistic problem novels have things to discuss with their children regardless of whether their children have read the same books. Even when children are not interested in heart-to-heart discussions, parents are more understanding if they've read about the kinds of turmoil that teenagers face in struggling to become emotionally independent. In our own classes, and we understand the same is true for others teaching young adult literature, we are getting an increasing number of adult students who are there simply because they enjoy reading and talking about the young adult fiction that was not being written when they were teenagers. Those who are parents of teenagers consider it serendipitous if their teenagers also get interested and begin reading the same books.

A more structured approach is for parents to work with youth groups and church groups or to volunteer as a friend of either the public library or the school library. These kinds of activities provide parents with extra opportunities to involve young people in sharing reading experiences. In such situations, it is often a benefit to have other young people involved and for parents to trade off, so that they aren't always the leader for the particular group in which their child is a member.

YA Books and Teachers of Human Relations, Counselors, and Youth Group Leaders

Workers with church and civic youth groups, teachers of classes in human relations, and professional counselors working with young adults have all found that reading and discussing short stories or books can be useful. When we talk about using books to help students understand their own and other people's feelings and behavior, we sometimes use the term *bibliotherapy*. It is a word that goes in and out of fashion, at least in reference to the informal kind of work that most teachers and librarians do with young adults. Its technical meaning is the use of books by professionally trained psychologists and psychiatrists in working with people who are mentally ill. Because of this association with illness, many "book" people reject the term. They reason that if a young adult is mentally ill and in need of some kind of therapy, the therapy should come from someone trained in that field rather than from someone trained in the book business or in teaching and guiding normal and healthy young adults.

Most people agree, however, that normal and healthy young adults can benefit psychologically from reading and talking about the problems of fictional characters. All teenagers have problems of one type or another, and simply finding out that other people have them too provides some comfort. We are reassured to know that our fears and doubts have been experienced by others. David A. Williams, a communications professor at the University of Arizona, said in a *Tempe Daily News* interview that he would die happy if he could "prove that a positive correlation exists between the rise in anxiety in the country and the decline of pleasure reading." Research done during the 1950s and 1960s showed that anxiety is directly related to a poor concept of oneself. "It seems to me," he said, "that the human being's major concern in life is to determine what it means to be a human being." The paradox is that before people can see themselves, they have to get outside of themselves and look at the whole spectrum of human experience to see where they fit in. "When we are feeling anxious it is usually because we have a narrow perspective that sees only what it wants to see." Someone who is anxiety-ridden, paranoiac, or resentful selects experiences from life to validate those feelings. For people like this, reading can put things back into perspective. "When we read about others who have suffered similar anxieties, we don't feel so cut off and, although the world doesn't change, we change the way we look at it" (Dec. 15, 1977).

As books put things back into perspective, they open up avenues of communication that successful discussion leaders tap into. It is important, however, for adults to be careful in guiding students to read and talk about personal problems. No one should be forced to participate in such a discussion, and a special effort should not be made to relate stories to the exact problem that a group member is having. In fact, it would probably be best to avoid matching up particular problems with particular students. When someone is in the midst of a crisis, chances are that he or she does not want to read and talk about someone else in a similar predicament. As a general rule, one would probably get the most from such a discussion before or after—rather than during—a time of actual crisis.

Such discussions are usually held in clubs, church groups, classes on preparation for marriage and human relations, and counseling and support group meetings at crisis centers and various institutions to which young people are sent. Because membership in these groups changes from meeting to meeting and there are no pressures for participants to do outside reading as "homework," a leader will probably be disappointed or frustrated if the discussion is planned around the expectation that everyone will have read the book. A more realistic plan is for the leader to use a short story or to give a summary of the book and a ten- to twenty-minute prepared reading of the part that best delineates the problem or the topic for discussion. Using fairly well-known books, including ones that have been made into movies, increases the chances of participation. Using popular books also makes it easier for students whose appetites have been whetted to find the book and read it on their own.

In an adult group of professionals, the same purpose would be accomplished by reading a case study that would then be discussed. But case studies are written for trained adults who know how to fill in the missing details and how to interpret the symptoms. Teenagers are not psychologists, and they are not social workers or philosophers. Literature may be as close as they will ever come to discussing the kinds of problems dealt with in these fields. What follows the oral presentation can be extremely varied, depending on the nature of the group, the

TABLE 10.3 The Powers and Limitations of Young Adult Literature

What literature can do:

1. It can provide a common experience or a way in which a teenager and an adult can focus their attention on the same subject.
2. It can serve as a discussion topic and a way to relieve embarrassment by enabling people to talk in the third person about problems with which they are concerned.
3. It can give young readers confidence that, should they meet particular problems, they will be able to solve them.
4. It can increase a young person's understanding of the world and the many ways that individuals find their places in it.
5. It can comfort and reassure young adult readers by showing them that they are not the only ones who have fears and doubts.
6. It can give adults as well as teenagers insights into adolescent psychology and values.

What literature cannot do:

1. It cannot cure someone's emotional illness.
2. It cannot guarantee that readers will behave in socially approved ways.
3. It cannot directly solve readers' problems.

leader's personality, and the purpose or the goal of the discussion. The literature provides the group—both teenagers and adults—with a common experience that can serve as the focus for discussion. Pressures and tensions are relieved because everyone is talking in the third person about the characters in the book, although in reality many of the comments will be about first-person problems.

Reading and discussing books can in no way cure mental illness, but reading widely about all kinds of problems and all kinds of solutions helps keep young people involved in thinking about moral issues. Table 10.3 shows what young adult literature can and cannot do. When it is used as a tool to teach about human relations and values, the positives outweigh the negatives.

Young Adult Books in the Social Studies Classroom

Turning facts into believable stories that touch readers' emotions is the biggest contribution of fiction to the social studies class. It is important for readers to realize, however, that many different books need to be read because each book presents a limited perspective. Stereotypes exist in people's minds for two reasons. One is that the same attitudes are repeated over and over, so that they become a predominant image. Another is that an individual may have had only one exposure to a particular race, group, or country. For example, readers of Chaim Potok's *The Chosen* don't learn everything about Hasidic Jews, but they know a lot more than they did before they read the book, and their interest may have been piqued, so that they will continue to watch for information and to read other books.

Nearly everyone agrees that by reading widely and sharing their findings, social studies class members can lead each other to go beyond stereotypes. For this to happen on more than an ad hoc or serendipitous basis, however, the teacher needs to identify clear-cut goals and then seek help from professional sources and other teachers and librarians in drawing up a selective list of books to be offered to students.

Social studies teachers have always recognized the importance of biographies and of the kind of historical books featured in Chapter 8, but they may not be as aware of the many books, both fiction and nonfiction, that are available to help them teach students about contemporary social issues. See Chapter 9 for nonfiction books treating topics of interest to teenagers, such as ecology, as well as issues related to sex and health care including questions about transplants, surrogate parenting, euthanasia, animal rights, cloning, stem cell research, and experiments on humans. Books on government ask questions about individual rights as opposed to the welfare of the group. Such questions range from whether the state has a right to require motorcycle helmets and seatbelts to whether it should legislate drugs and sexual preference.

Social studies teachers also miss a powerful resource if they fail to bring in the kind of fiction discussed in Focus Box 10.4, "Teenagers outside the Continental United States." Movies, television, and photographs allow people to see other places, but literature has the added dimension of allowing the reader to share the thoughts of another person. As today's jet age and the Internet shrink the distances between countries and cultures, it is more important than ever that

Between Shades of Gray **by Ruta Sepetys. Philomel, 2011.** This is an unrelentingly sad novel based on the author's family background and her research. The narrator is fifteen-year-old Lina who tells the story about one family's struggle to survive when, just before World War II, Lithuanians were deported to Siberia.

Chanda's Secrets **by Allan Stratton. Annick, distributed by Firefly, 2004.** Sixteen-year-old Chanda lives in sub-Saharan Africa, and is faced with arranging for the burial of her baby brother and eventually for her mother, both of whom succumb to AIDS. The book is now a major film.

City of the Beasts **by Isabel Allende, translated from Spanish by Margeret Sayers Peden. HarperCollins, 2003.** Allende's first novel for young readers is part magical realism and part contemporary politics. A fifteen-year-old boy accompanies his journalist grandmother on an expedition into an Amazon jungle in search of a legendary beast that is perhaps human.

Facing the Lion: Growing up Maasai on the African Savanna **by Joseph Lemasolai Lekuton and Herman J. Viola. National Geographic, 2003.** The author tells his own story of growing up in a nomadic subgroup within the Maasai people in Kenya. By law, each family designates a child to attend school, and he was the one chosen from his family. He went from the mission school to an elite high school and then to college in the United States.

Ostrich Boys **by Keith Gray. Random, 2010.** When Ross dies, his British friends take his ashes to Ross, Scotland, to give him a grand send-off. During the journey the group loses a train ticket, gets involved with girls and bungee jumping, and ends up learning about themselves and the intimate meanings of friendship.

Red Glass **by Laura Resau. Delacorte, 2007.** A shy sixteen-year-old Arizona girl develops new strengths when she and her Bosnian great-aunt Dika get involved in helping a Guatemalan immigrant and his six-year-old son go back across the U.S. border that they had crossed illegally.

Running with the Reservoir Pups, **and *Bring Me the Head of Oliver Plunkett,* and *Seagulls Have Landed* by Colin Bateman. Delacorte, 2005 and 2006.** Bateman is a popular Irish writer for adults, but decided to do an *Eddie and the Gang with No Name* trilogy for tweeners. The books are a welcome contrast to many of the more serious problem novels set in foreign countries.

The Sweet, Terrible, Glorious Year I Truly, Completely Lost It **by Lisa Shanahan. Delacorte, 2007.** Gemma Stone is Australian, but that does not explain why her older sister turns into bridezilla and why, in her fourteenth year, Gemma learns that "Love is doves *and* dog poo."

Tall Story **by Candy Gourlay. Random, 2011.** Bernardo is eight feet tall and lives in a Philippine village, where the people think he is a giant who can protect them from earthquakes. Immigration restrictions keep him separated from his mother, a nurse in England, but finally he gets to join her. It is a serious but heartwarming story, especially for Bernardo and his "little" sister.

What the Moon Saw **by Laura Resau. Delacorte, 2006.** Fourteen-year-old Clara Luna is invited to spend the summer with her father's parents, people she has never met, in a remote Mexican village. Readers get to share her experience as she learns about a lifestyle foreign to the one she has in the United States.

people realize that members of the human race, regardless of where or how they live, have more similarities than differences.

Concluding Comments

This chapter has shown that using and promoting books with young readers is a shared opportunity and responsibility. It belongs not only to librarians and English and reading teachers but also to everyone who works closely with young people and wants to understand them better. It can serve as a medium through which to open communication with young adults about their concerns.

Young Adult Literature in the English Class

Our goal in this chapter is to show how young adult literature can be a welcome addition to most English classes in high schools. Although we recognize that classes, students, teachers, and parents vary considerably, the methods we are discussing have worked for large numbers of teachers and their students.

Principles of Teaching English

We believe in five principles about English teachers and the teaching of literature:

1. *English teachers must never forget that literature should be both entertaining and challenging:* Teachers must alert students to literature they will find challenging and satisfying. Is this easy to do? No, not always, but it might convince students that teachers care about reading and kids.

2. *English teachers must know a wide range of literature:* Teachers should know classics of English and American literature, of course; they should also know American popular literature, young adult literature, and something about Asian and European literature (e.g., Asian folktales, Norwegian drama, French short stories, or Russian novels). They should know women writers and ethnic writers, especially, but not exclusively, from the United States, and what they do not know about literature, they should learn by reading in the way that Gary Paulsen advises: "Read like a wolf eats."

3. *English teachers ought to know enough about dramatic techniques and oral interpretation to be comfortable reading aloud to students:* We need teachers eager and able to read material to students that just might interest, intrigue, amuse, or excite them. Outside of speech or drama, no classes require so much oral performance from teachers as English classes. Reading poetry, drama, and short stories aloud is half the fun of teaching. Obviously, the availability of poetry or fiction on tapes or CDs means other voices can be heard, but that does not mean the teacher's voice should be silent. Ian McKellen's reading of Shakespeare exceeds the grasp of us mortals, but McKellen is not there to explain why he read a passage from *Richard III* or *Macbeth* or *Othello* as he did.

4. *English teachers must remember the distance in education and sophistication between them and their students:* No matter what the rapport, it is almost equally easy for teachers to overestimate as to underestimate their students. Choosing material for an entire class is never easy. Some materials—say, a *New Yorker* short story, a T. S. Eliot poem, or a Harold Pinter play—assume a sophistication that high school students often do not have. Selecting literature for fifteen, thirty-five, or forty-five students is almost inevitably an exercise in frustration and failure, but it is no excuse for not trying to meet all students' needs with that one fabulous, never-to-be-forgotten classroom novel, poem, short story, or play.

5. *Finally, English teachers should teach and use only literature they enjoy:* Teachers should not fake enthusiasm or interest. If a teacher doesn't like Robert Frost's poetry or Stephen Crane's *The Red Badge of Courage,* the teacher has no business using Frost or Crane. There are too many stories, plays, and poems out there about which teachers are presumably enthusiastic. Obviously, this point follows our second point, that teachers are incurable, wide readers.

None of this implies that teachers cannot change their minds about literature or writers; it is sometimes great fun and profitable to work with literature about which you feel ambivalent. Nor should students be discouraged from reading and talking about works for which the teacher has no great enthusiasm.

Our five principles for teaching literature extend to works in the curriculum guide as well as the literary canon of great books. Curriculum guides are developed by human beings with strengths and weaknesses, and they can be changed. Little is to be gained from a bored teacher presenting Poe's poetry to an equally bored class. It is better to assume that in the four years of high school these students will have one English teacher who likes Poe. And if it doesn't happen? There are worse disasters. What if no teacher wants to teach Shakespeare? We cannot imagine an English department so devoid of taste or ability, but if one exists, it is surely preferable that students leave school ignorant of Shakespeare than bored by him.

Literature that a teacher thinks is worth teaching, however defined, ought to encourage honest teaching and honest responses from kids. As Louise Rosenblatt has pointed out in her *Literature as Exploration,* 4th ed., from the Modern Language Association, "No one else can read a literary work for us. The benefits of literature can emerge only from creative activity" on the part of each reader. Readers respond to the little black marks on the page, or to the sound of the words in their ears and "make something of them." The verbal symbols enable readers to combine their "past experiences with what the words point to in life and literature" (pp. 278–279).

Allowing young people time to respond to literature slows down the teacher and the lesson because time is required for thinking and for building, especially for students accustomed to memorizing and spitting back whatever the teacher has said. Students have to be convinced that responding honestly to literature is worth the trouble and hard work.

Using Young Adult Literature in English Classes

One of the reasons we endorse young adult literature for English classes is that students can believe a teacher who asks for their honest response to a book that features a contemporary young person facing a problem that students are likely to face. Young adult literature is often recommended as a bridge to appreciating literary techniques, but its role in developing the trust needed for a response-centered approach to literature may be even more important.

Young adult books work well in class for all the reasons that we mentioned in the previous chapter for using YA books with English language learners. But thanks to the tremendous growth in the field, teachers can find YA books at all levels of sophistication and challenge, plus the covers are attractive and made to appeal to teenagers. As a bonus, young adult authors are often willing to visit with students either in person or electronically.

Back in the February 1972 issue of the *English Journal,* Robert C. Small, Jr., offered an uncomfortable reason that some teachers resist bringing contemporary and YA literature into their classrooms. He said that teachers who want to establish themselves as the literary expert and translator of books to lowly students will be uncomfortable with YA literature because when young people read adolescent

PROFESSIONAL READING

Fortunately, most English teachers love to read because there are always new—and old—books to help you with whatever challenges you are meeting in your class. See Focus Box 11.1, "Professional Books to Help Teachers with YA Lit," for some suggestions of recently published books.

Focus Box 11.1

Professional Books to Help Teachers with YA Lit

NOTE: Teachers should also check out the Twayne Young Adult Author Series, edited by Patty Campbell between 1985 and 1999, as well as the Scarecrow Studies in Young Adult Literature, edited by Patty Campbell from 1998 to the present.

American Indian Themes in Young Adult Literature by Paulette F. Molin. Scarecrow, 2005. This is an important book because there has been so much misunderstanding in this area, specifically the mistaken idea that all Native American tribes think the same way.

Exploding the Myths: The Truth about Teenagers and Reading by Marc Aronson and Bruce Brooks. Scarecrow, 2001. Few people have the writing and editing experience that these authors have, plus the skill in communicating.

Fang-Tastic Fiction: Twenty-First Century Paranormal Reads by Patricia O'Brien Matthews. American Library Association, 2011. Meant as a guide to librarians trying to answer their borrowers' questions, this well-organized book is especially helpful in describing all the series. The books are listed chronologically with a paragraph explaining the major events and what happens to the protagonists. It is also good for identifying such subgenres as urban romance, chick lit, mystery, historical settings, Web resources, and for listing male vs. female protagonists.

Fresh Takes on Teaching Literary Elements: How to Teach What Really Matters about Character, Setting, Point of View, and Theme by Michael W. Smith and Jeffrey D. Wilhelm. NCTE, 2010. Here are good ideas, clearly stated and illustrated.

The Heart Has Its Reasons: Young Adult Literature with Gay/Lesbian/Queer Content, 1969–2004 by Michael Cart and Christine A. Jenkins. Scarecrow Press, 2006. This is a fascinating look at how books for young people reflect cultural beliefs.

Immigration Narratives in Young Adult Literature: Crossing Borders by Joanne Brown, Scarecrow Press, 2010. Chapters in this timely book include "The Golden Door," "The Beckoning Shores," and "The Journey."

Library Collections for Teens: Manga and Graphic Novels by Kristin Fletcher-Spear and Merideth Jenson-Benjamin. VOYA Press, 2011. Besides telling about what librarians probably need (or want) for their libraries, the authors provide sections on such topics as the management of manga (including how libraries in Japan handle it), series overviews, subgenres of manga, and ideas for programming with graphic novels.

Literacy for the New Millennium, edited by Barbara J. Guzzetti. Praeger Perspectives, 2007. The third volume in this set of four focuses on adolescents and includes chapters written by leading scholars. Topics include blogging, literacy tutors, gender issues, digital literacy, and the "best books" for teenagers.

Mixed Heritage in Young Adult Literature by Nancy Thalia Reynolds. Scarecrow Press, 2009. Reynolds looks at an increasingly important topic as she explores the many new YA books that touch on young people of mixed races. She also looks at old books, including *Jane Eyre,* and provides lots of examples to support her interesting observations and advice.

Names and Naming in Young Adult Literature by Alleen Pace Nilsen and Don L. F. Nilsen, Scarecrow Press, 2007. The ideas touched on in this chapter are more fully explored with specific examples coming from the works of some 25 well-known authors.

Not Your Mother's Vampire: Vampires in Young Adult Fiction by Deborah Overstreet. Scarecrow Press, 2006. It's too bad that Stephenie Meyer's *Twilight* and Ellen Schreiber's Vampire Kisses series did not make it into Overstreet's book, but still for those of us wondering why vampires are so "hot," there's lots to bite into.

Once Upon a Time in a Different World: Issues and Ideas in African American Children's Literature

---

books they are the experts, and they may need to serve as translators to adults who wish to understand the adolescent books (p. 222). We hope this is no longer true. See Focus Box 11.1, "Professional Books to Help Teachers with YA Lit."

For many English teachers who use young adult literature in their classes, one exciting development is that students are more than merely willing to talk about by Neal A. Lester. Routledge, 2007. Both children's and YA books are discussed. Specific examples include interesting discussions of such issues as the treatment of hair and the absence of the n-word in books published for young readers.

Radical Change: Books for Youth in a Digital Age by Eliza T. Dresang. H. W. Wilson, 1999. Dresang made so many new and interesting observations about changes coming to the field of YA literature that, in a previous edition of this text, we used her book as the organizing focus for a chapter on pop culture.

Readicide: How Schools Are Killing Reading and What You Can Do about It by Kelly Gallagher. Stenhouse, 2009. Our students brought this book to our attention because they were so impressed at how Gallagher defines *readicide* as "the systematic killing of the love of reading, often exacerbated by the inane, mind-numbing practices found in schools."

Reading Ladders: Leading Students from Where They Are to Where We'd Like Them to Be by Teri Lesense. Heinemann, 2010. Lesense is one of the most well-read and talented professors of young adult literature. Besides teaching at Sam Houston State University, she is the Executive Secretary of ALAN (Assembly on Literature for Adolescents of NCTE). *Reading Ladders* is a continuation of ideas first offered in her 2006 *Naked Reading: Uncovering What Tweens Need to Become Lifelong Readers* (Stenhouse, 2006).

The Rights of the Reader by Daniel Pennac, translated by Sarah Adams. Candlewick, 2008. Illustrator Quentin Blake provides quirky and playful sketches to illustrate Pennac's experiences as a child, a parent, and an inner-city teacher in Paris.

Teaching and Learning about Multicultural Literature: Students Reading Outside Their Culture in a Middle School Classroom by Janice Hartwick Dressel. International Reading Association, 2003. Dressel worked with a teacher of 123 eighth graders, mostly from the dominant culture. They were reading a variety of multicultural literature and Dressel studied their

responses, which focused as much on differences in power as on differences in color.

Thematic Guide to Young Adult Literature by Alice Trupe. Greenwood, 2006. Descriptions of both contemporary and historical titles are included under thirty-two categories or issues.

Transparent: Love, Family, and Living the T with Transgender Teenagers by Cris Beam. Dial Books, 2009. This is not a guidebook for parents or educators, but it is highly praised by adult readers for its narrative power and the way a "secure and sagacious" novelist writes about the range of problems he found when hanging out with transgendered, inner-city youth, many of them homeless.

Using Critical Perspectives to Teach Young Adult Literature by Anna O. Soter, Mark Faust, and Theresa Rogers. Christopher-Gordon, 2008. Several leading scholars have contributed essays that can serve as a motivation to further research and experimentation.

Using Picture Storybooks to Teach Literary Devices: Recommended Books for Children and Young Adults by Susan Hall. Oryx Press/Greenwood, 2002. Most high school students enjoy the change of pace that comes with looking at picture books from their childhood. The literary devices being taught include black humor, hyperbole, internal rhyme, parallel story, and serendipity.

What's the Big Idea? Question-Driven Units to Motivate Reading, Writing, and Thinking by Jim Burke. Heinemann, 2010. Burke, a successful high school teacher, has the ambition and the skill to communicate his ideas in clear and non-condescending language.

What Was It Like? Teaching History and Culture Through Young Adult Literature by Linda J. Rice. Teachers College Press, 2006. Part of TCCU's Language and Literature Series, Rice's book is filled with good ideas for activities and books connected to specific periods of history. English and social studies teachers can get some good ideas.

the novels; they are excited and anxious to talk. That's also true for teachers who have used YA books and adult books together. Patricia Lee Gauch wrote in a *Top of the News* article titled "Good Stuff in Adolescent Literature," Winter 1984,

> Some of the best discussions in my classroom experience have been based on adolescent fiction. We have ranged from the use of animal imagery to the development

of plot to the question of the alienated hero in American fiction. And I have found one of the best ways to use the "good stuff" of adolescent fiction is to yoke it with adult fare. *Roll of Thunder, Hear My Cry* with *I Know Why the Caged Bird Sings; Gentlehands* with *Night; The Chocolate War* with *The Oxbow Incident.* This isn't "babying kids into reading decent prose." It's yoking "good stuff" with "good stuff" to take advantage of the length and teen-centered subject of the younger books. (p. 129)

For an imaginative teacher, young adult books have many uses. An individual title can be studied by the whole class, although that is comparatively rare. It can be paired with adult books, classics or not, as recommended in some of the books in Appendix C, and they work beautifully in free reading and thematic units. Their possibilities extend as far as the teachers' imaginations because they provide what other good novels do plus an almost guaranteed adolescent interest.

Richard Jackson, when he was editor-in-chief at Bradbury Press, predicted that young adult literature will endure because even though society changes from one generation to another, its rites of passage remain and the impulse to record and reconsider those rites strikes all of us.

Teaching Short Stories

Short story author Tim Wynne-Jones, who has been described as "the master of the glimpse," wrote for the sixth edition of this textbook,

> A good short isn't a lot of things. It isn't long, it isn't preachy, and it certainly isn't a novel wannabe. It isn't a sketch, it's a miniature. Not the whole season, just the big game. Not the whole sunset, just one straggler on the beach. It does not presume to grandeur. It is happy to invoke a gasp of surprise, a belly laugh, a single tear.

While warning teachers not to overanalyze short stories, we suggest reading them aloud in class to introduce a topic for discussion or writing, illustrate a point, fill out a thematic unit, provide material for reader's theater and dramatization, and give students enough experience in literary discussion that they can learn the meanings of literary terms from actual experience rather than from memorizing definitions. While there is a place for learning about such concepts as verisimilitude, point of view, synecdoche, and unreliable narrators, it is not from a list to be memorized. Instead, such learning should come naturally from the teachers' discussions as students ponder and talk about a story they have just read. See Focus Box 11.2, "Old and New Recommended Collections of Short Stories."

For all of these reasons, short stories work well in classrooms where students can read fifteen short stories in the time it takes to read one or two novels. Through reading the larger number of short stories, they can meet a greater variety of viewpoints and representatives of different ethnic groups and cultures. And because the best of modern American authors have written short stories, students can experience high-quality writing in pieces that are short enough for comfortable reading.

**Old and New Recommended Collections
of Short Stories**

Am I Blue? Coming Out from the Silence, **edited by Marion Dane Bauer. HarperCollins, 1994.** Several popular writers contributed stories centered on coming to terms with homosexuality.

American Short Story Masterpieces, **edited by Raymond Carver and Tom Jenks. Dell, 1987.** Included are Flannery O'Connor's "A Good Man Is Hard to Find," Bernard Malamud's "The Magic Barrel," and Joyce Carol Oates's "Where Are You Going, Where Have You Been?"

The American Short Story, **Volumes 1 and 2, edited by Calvin Skaggs. Dell, 1977 and 1980.** Among the well-loved stories in these two collections are Faulkner's "Barn Burning," Thurber's "The Greatest Man in the World," Twain's "The Man Who Corrupted Hadleyburg," and Richard Wright's "Almos' a Man."

Athletic Shorts: Six Short Stories **by Chris Crutcher. Greenwillow, 1991.** The athletes in these stories may attract readers to Crutcher's sports novels because several of the protagonists are the same.

Baseball in April and Other Stories **by Gary Soto. Harcourt Brace Jovanovich, 1990.** These eleven fairly simple stories are about everyday events in the lives of Mexican American kids living in the Fresno, California, neighborhood where Soto grew up.

Best Shorts: Favorite Short Stories for Sharing, **edited by Avi. Houghton Mifflin, 2006.** Avi chose such great read-alouds as Isaac Bashevis Singer's "Zlateh the Goat," Frank Stockton's "The Lady or the Tiger?," Robert D. San Souci's "The Caller," Lloyd Alexander's "The Town Cats," and Megan Whalen Turner's "The Baby in the Night Deposit Box."

Girl Goddess No. 9 **by Francesca Lia Block. HarperCollins, 1996.** From reading this collection of nine short stories, readers come away feeling acquainted with some young Los Angeles residents who are a lot more interesting than "the girl next door."

Gothic, **edited by Deborah Noyes. Candlewick, 2004.** Ten original dark tales are written by M. T. Anderson, Vivian Vande Velde, Garth Nix, Celia Rees, and six other masters.

Half-Human, **compiled and edited by Bruce Coville. Scholastic, 2001.** Each of these ten stories is appropriately illustrated with a surrealistic photograph. Coville's

own story ends the collection. Earlier Coville collections include *Odder Than Ever,* 1999, and *Oddly Enough,* 1994, both from Harcourt.

In Short: How to Teach the Young Adult Short Story **by Suzanne I. Barchers. Heinemann, 2005.** These fifteen short stories are by writers like Avi, Neal Shusterman, Gloria Skurzynski, and Vivian Vande Velde. Teaching helps on theme, literary forms, and discussion topics are appended.

Leaving Home: 15 Distinguished Authors Explore Personal Journeys, **selected by Hazel Rochman and Darlene Z. McCampbell. HarperCollins, 1997.** Allan Sherman, Tim O'Brien, David St. John, Norma Fox Mazer, Gary Soto, and Toni Morrison are among the authors represented.

One Hot Second, **edited by Cathy Young. Knopf, 2002.** Stories by Norma Fox Mazer, Ellen Wittlinger, Nancy Garden, Jacqueline Woodson, and others explore the nature of desire.

Point of Departure: 19 Stories of Youth and Discovery, **edited by Robert S. Gold. Dell, 1967 (New printing, Laurel Leaf, 2005).** These stories, all featuring young protagonists, come from the pens (actually the typewriters) of a Who's Who of great American authors.

Sixteen: Short Stories by Outstanding Writers for Young Adults, **edited by Donald R. Gallo. Delacorte, 1984.** Gallo was the first person to reach a mass audience through inviting YA authors to contribute short stories. Since this first book, he has gone on to publish *Visions, Connections, Short Circuits, Join In: Multiethnic Short Stories, Within Reach, Ultimate Sports, No Easy Answers,* and *Time Capsule.* More recent collections include *On the Fringe* and *What Are You Afraid Of? Stories about Phobias.*

21 Proms, **edited by David Levithan and Daniel Ehrenhaft. Scholastic, 2007.** Here is the perfect centerpiece for a spring book display, but you'll need lots of copies. Several talented writers contributed unique takes on this traditional American rite of passage.

Working Days: Short Stories about Teenagers at Work, **edited by Anne Mazer. Persea, 1997.** Mazer's collection helps to counterbalance the way authors, except for Joan Bauer, have mostly ignored the importance of jobs in the lives of teenagers.

There is no single way of getting at any literary work, and several approaches may need to be tried. Students probably come to class already knowing how to listen, the importance of taking assiduous notes on what the teacher says, and to play all this back at test time, but that doesn't have much to do with the reading. In many ways, a careful reading of a work by student A will produce a different work from an equally careful reading by student B or student C because readers base their feelings on past experiences and present morality to yield a different story with each reader, and sometimes a greatly different story. Guiding students—not every time they read a short story, but once in a while—through these steps may be helpful:

1. Read the first sentence carefully (and the first paragraph). What do they tell you about the setting, characters, or tension?
2. Predict from the first paragraph what's likely to follow.
3. Speed-read the story to get some sense of what it's about and who the characters are (probably the only part that can be done outside of class).
4. Isolate the problems in reading the story (e.g., dialect, structure, conflicting characters).
5. Reread the story, doing parts or all of it aloud.

What can we safely say to our classes about virtually all short stories? We can tell students that all fiction is based on conflict, and we might begin by exploring different kinds of conflict. We can say, with some confidence, that

1. The title of the story usually is significant.
2. First-person narrators are similar to readers in being fallible mortals likely to make mistakes in judging people or letting their emotions get in the way.
3. In most short stories, the first words are important because this is the author's opportunity to grab the audience. We might do well to read and re-read aloud the first few lines to see what they tell us.

The questions English teachers pose for students should be carefully thought out and played with. Beginning teachers need to develop and practice the questions before class, while more experienced teachers can rely on mental notes of what makes a discussion worthwhile rather than mere chitchat to take up fifty-five minutes of class. One scheme devised long ago by Edward J. Gordon and Dwight Burton is to start with simple recall questions, which can be reassuring to students in setting up the details of the story. As serendipity, these questions and answers also help the students who did not do the reading to have at least a glimmer of what is going on. Then moving from concrete to abstract questions, you can ask questions that require students to:

- Prove or disprove a generalization made by someone else.
- Derive their own generalizations.
- Generalize about the relation of the total work to human experience.
- Carry generalizations derived from the work into their own lives.

We are certainly not suggesting that teachers come into class and fire off these questions as if they are a spelling test, but that they keep them in the back of their minds as a general guide. Observers of good literary discussions have found that students circle back around to all these levels and that, while students seldom pose questions, they frequently make observations that stimulate other students to comment and add their own opinions.

Probably the most important part of a discussion—and unfortunately the most often ignored—is the summing up. In too many classes, the bell rings in the midst of a discussion and students rush away without gathering their thoughts. Such "fly-away" endings cause students to lose respect for class discussions. If they think the teacher is just filling in time until the bell rings, they won't put forth their best efforts. Successful teachers keep an eye on the clock and save at least a couple of minutes to draw attention to those points that the class basically agrees on, to praise insightful comments that help the rest of the class see something they might have missed, and to lead students to see connections between the present discussion and previous ones.

Within the last two decades, publishers have produced several attractive collections of short stories written by young adult authors (see Focus Box 11.2, "Old and New Recommended Collections of Short Stories" on page 369). Because of all the reasons we've already given for liking young adult literature, we often recommend short stories by YA authors, but we also like to mix in stories about young people written for general adult audiences. Our favorite general anthology is Robert S. Gold's *Point of Departure,* which recently came out in a new printing. Such stories as John Bell Clayton's "The White Circle," Bernard Malamud's "A Summer's Reading," William Saroyan's "Seventeen," Carson McCullers's "Sucker," John Updike's "A&P" and "Tomorrow and Tomorrow and So Forth" can go a long way toward helping young readers increase their literary sophistication while still focusing on teen interests. With sophisticated classes, teachers might lead students to detect the subtle differences in tone between a story written *for* young adults and stories written *about* young adults. The ones that are *about,* but not *for,* teenagers are likely to be more nostalgic, plus the authors might be showing the lack of sophistication or maturity of the young adult as when the boy in Updike's "A&P" quits his job so suddenly. In the stories for YA readers, the protagonists may make mistakes, but they still end up looking "in control" and on their way to bigger and better things.

The genres for short stories include realistic fiction, science fiction, fantasy, humor, animal stories, folklore, and myth. Students who are hung up on a particular kind of book can usually be enticed to try at least a short story in another genre. And within the same genre, students can be encouraged to select more challenging books. Stories by the best YA authors can also serve as introductions to authors, whose longer novels they might also enjoy.

Using Children's Picture Books with High School Students

Some of our best lessons have come from using children's picture books in advanced classes. When author Jack Gantos spoke in one of our classes on December 5, 2011, he showed slides from classic picture books and said that he uses the books as demonstrations with his fiction writing students: *Curious George* to illustrate the importance of focusing on a single character, *Corduroy* to demonstrate the importance of pathos, and *The Lorax* to demonstrate the importance of a worthy topic. He also said that with almost any good picture book, the ending is two-pronged. One is the physical ending—the tying together of the plot—but the more important ending is the psychological climax—the one that leaves readers with an emotional memory.

We have found that picture books provide a welcome break from more tedious work, while for some students they also bring smiles of nostalgia. Besides serving as models for student writing, they can be introductions to new units and new concepts. And by watching for mass media messages which rely for their meanings on allusions to children's literature, teachers and students can get valuable insights into cultural values.

Advertisers, broadcasters, cartoonists, journalists, politicians, bloggers, and whoever else wishes to communicate with large numbers of people regularly allude to children's literature because, in our increasingly diverse culture, memories of childhood books are one of the few things we have in common. Nursery rhymes and folktales are a rich resource because they present a full array of personalities from which to choose characters—*Chicken Little* to represent alarmists, *Pinocchio* to stand in for liars, the *Big Bad Wolf* to warn of danger, *Humpty Dumpty* to point out how easy it is to fall from grace, and *The Frog Prince* to give hope to discouraged women of all ages.

We've always encouraged students to watch for these allusions and to bring them in as news. Over the last couple of years as Americans have suffered from economic downturns and widespread feelings of insecurity, we have seen the nature of the allusions change. In the old jokes about Humpty Dumpty, onlookers looked sympathetic and tried to help, but in the latest cartoon we saw bystanders rushing away shouting "Salmonella!" Housing market woes were illustrated by a puzzled-looking Winnie the Pooh saying, "Oh, Bother!" when he sees that

Children's picture books not only bring nostalgic smiles, but can also serve as the basis for student writing and for some sophisticated cultural and literary observations.

the "100 Aker Realty" company has posted a "Foreclosure" sign on Mr. Sanders' tree-trunk. A different cartoon showed a "Foreclosure" sign placed on the abandoned shoe where the Little Old Woman used to live with her many children. A similar drawing showed two agents standing in front of the big shoe with one of them saying, "It looked kinda dumpy but appraised at a million-two." These were in sharp contrast to the cheerful advertisements we used to see where Hawaiian Punch was being shown as just the thing for a mother with many children. The other big contrast we noticed was with allusions to Dorothy and the Wizard of Oz. In a new cartoon, the Wicked Witch says, "Forget the slippers, I want the Tin Man's Oil!" while in another one Dorothy and her friends have sold the Tin Woodman to a recycling center in exchange for bus fare to get back to Kansas.

In a grammar class, we have taught a sophisticated linguistics lesson by bringing in a stack of Peggy Parish's Amelia Bedelia books about the lovable housemaid who is always in trouble because she misunderstands what people say. For example, when she is told to "put out the lights," she hangs the light bulbs outside; when she's told to "dress the chicken" she puts baby clothes on it; and when she is told to "dust the furniture" she sprinkles bath powder all over the couch. The Amelia Bedelia books, with such titles as *Amelia Bedelia Goes Camping, Merry Christmas, Amelia Bedelia,* and *Amelia Bedelia and the Baby,* were originally published in the 1980s, but were so popular that most libraries still have copies; plus they are now available in various collections offered on Amazon.com. Our lesson works even better if we can also find a couple of the wordplay picture books by Fred Gwynne, which include *A Little Pigeon Toad, The King Who Rained, The Sixteen-Hand Horse,* and *A Chocolate Moose for Dinner,* which were also published mostly in the 1980s. We use the books to help students develop an understanding about how the English language has many, many words that sound alike. Some of them are accidental puns (these are most likely to be spelled differently) while others sound the same and also have the same spelling of the important morphemes (the tiniest part of words that communicate a meaning). In these cases the words are metaphorically related, and so students should try to figure out their common meaning. The point of the lesson is to provide students with skills to help them look for underlying semantic relationships between common words.

We break the class into groups of three or four—or even just partners if we have enough books to go around. Each group reads their book and finds one example of a pun, in which the protagonist has confused two words that sound the same but are not semantically related, and one example of a metaphor, in which the words really do relate to each other in some way, but not exactly as the protagonist thinks. Most high school and college students—at least those who are native speakers—can easily find examples of each type of misunderstanding. For example, the *stamp* we put on letters really does relate to the kind of *stamping* that Amelia Bedelia does with her feet when she is told to "stamp the letters." Stamps descend from the old custom of sealing envelopes shut by stamping or pressing down on the piece of wax that was used to seal important letters. In contrast, *the king who rained* vs. *the king who reigned* is an accidental pun, because the two words just happen to sound alike.

English is one of the richest languages in the world partly because we have borrowed so many words from other languages. If we had to have unique sound patterns for each separate word, our minds (and our speech organs) could not manage. The fact that the words with unrelated meanings have, for the most part, preserved their different spellings helps us in writing and reading to recognize their differences. Students will understand this point much better after each group has reported, and you have talked about, the underlying difference in the two examples they find in their book. Authors Gwynne and Parish include examples of both accidental puns and related metaphors in their wordplay, but you will see that Gwynne tends more toward the accidental puns, while Parish tends more toward words that sound alike because deep in their history they have a meaning relationship.

Here is a listing of some of the other books with related activities that we have either used with our students or that high school teachers have told us about. The fun thing about using children's books is that new ones are always being published and creative teachers are constantly coming up with new ideas of how to use them.

Art & Max by David Wiesner. Clarion, 2010. Art and Max are two Gila monsters, who live in a southwest desert. Art is an artist, who prefers to be called *Arthur*. Max is a younger, more exuberant Gila monster who, when he is invited to paint Arthur, starts by literally throwing paint on him. The book is wonderful fun for examining different styles of art, but it is also an illustration of the literary concept of deconstruction, followed by reconstruction, a process that changes Art (or Arthur) both on the inside and the outside.

Brave Potatoes by Toby Speed. Putnam's Sons, 2000. When the prize-winning potatoes at the county fair leave the exhibition barn for a ride on the midway, they know that Chef Hackemup is watching through binoculars from his restaurant. After being kidnapped, the brave potatoes show their courage and defeat the evil chef. The story, told in verse, is funny and simple, but a good starter for a writing activity in which each student is given a real potato. Students can brainstorm descriptive words that appeal to the senses based on their potatoes and work up to writing a story with a potato main character.

Click, Clack, Moo: Cows that Type by Doreen Cronin. Simon & Schuster, 2000. When the cows get a hold of an old typewriter, Farmer Brown soon finds himself deep into labor negotiations. The cows would like electric blankets, for example, and until they get them there will be no milk. The chickens soon join the cows, and in an attempt to end the uprising, Farmer Brown exchanges the electric blankets for the typewriter. Acting as a neutral party, the ducks deliver the blankets and remove the typewriter. What happens next shows the power of the pen. It's a good starter for writing from different points of view and exercising the aspect of voice in writing.

Fibblestax by Devin Scillian, illustrated by Kathryn Darnell. Sleeping Bear Press, 2000. Students may start thinking about where and how language, as well as individual words, originated after this story is read aloud. Carr is a crude red-faced man who has the authority to give names to things in their village, but a youngster named Fibblestax doesn't like Carr's creations and thinks he can do better. What Carr has named *gloobywickus*, Fibblestax renames *cream*, and what was known as *gunnywunks* in Carr's vocabulary Fibblestax renames *flowers*. Ultimately a naming contest must be held to determine who will be the final, official word creator in the village, the sour Carr or the optimistic Fibblestax. The book is a fun and thought-provoking opening to activities in word etymology, including advanced activities like using the *Oxford English Dictionary*.

If You Give a Mouse a Cookie by Laura Joffe Numeroff, illustrated by Felicia Bond. Geringer, 1985. Arizona English teacher Leslie Standerfer reports that of all the picture books she has used in her teaching, this is the one that gets the best response. She uses it to teach cause-and-effect and to emphasize that as writers we need to make sure we aren't assuming causation and basing our argument on a faulty assumption. This playfully exaggerated story of how one thing leads to another was such a hit that at the end of the year one of her students presented her with the miniature gift version including the stuffed animal mouse.

It's a Book by Lane Smith. Roaring Book Press, 2010. This perfect read-aloud explores the difference between books and computers. There are only two characters: a monkey with a book, and a donkey with a computer. Students enjoy the question-and-answer format and the surprise ending. A good lesson can come from talking about how else the same information might be communicated—either humorously or seriously—and then asking students to follow up with a writing assignment.

The Lorax by Theodore Seuss Geisel. Random House, 1971. A special day deserves a special oral reading, and Earth Day is just the time to open class with *The Lorax*. While you might choose something like Rachel Carson's *Silent Spring* to establish the history of environmentalism and the tradition of Earth Day, Dr. Seuss's tale of reckless overharvesting of resources will get to the spirit much more quickly, plus it's not a bad way to introduce heavier eco-writing like Edward Abbey's *The Monkey Wrench Gang*.

The Mysteries of Harris Burdick by Chris Van Allsburg. Houghton Mifflin, 1984. When Harris Burdick drops off pictures with titles and captions based on a book of short stories he has written, the publisher is intrigued, especially when Burdick never returns with the stories. The slightly spooky pictures never fail to inspire students of all ages to think of their own stories to explain the pictures.

Scary Stories to Tell in the Dark collected from folklore and retold by Alvin Schwartz, drawings by Stephen Gammell. Scholastic, 1989. Long past Halloween, this can be a good place to find a few inspirational examples to use in encouraging students to write their own stories about being scared or to introduce the topic of folklore and how such stories grew, especially in frontier America where people were always meeting new and strange things. You might compare these to the urban legends of today, as well as to the themes in futuristic science fiction stories which develop around new technologies that more or less frighten us.

The Secret Knowledge of Grown-ups by David Wisniewski. HarperCollins, 1998. Grown-ups are full of mandates: eat your vegetables, don't jump on the bed, drink your milk, and so on. They can give a reason, too: vegetables are good for you, the bed will break, and you need to grow tall and have strong bones. The secret knowledge of the real reasons, however, are now released in the formerly classified file, "The Secret Knowledge of Grown-ups." The vegetable mandate, for example, is actually due to millions of years of evolution starting in the era when giant vegetables ruled the Earth and ate human beings. In order to stay at the top of the food chain we must continue to eat our former predators. This book is a good lesson starter for a writing activity in which students explain the real (and humorous) reasons for a common adult-to-child mandate.

Terrible Things by Eve Bunting, illustrated by Stephen Gammell. Harper & Row, 1980. The concept of allegory could not be more clearly illustrated than through a reading of Eve Bunting's story of the species-by-species devastation in the forest. The subtitle even reads "An Allegory of the Holocaust." Reading this out loud takes about five minutes but it sets a mood that is perfect for introducing heavier literature, such as *The Diary of Anne Frank*. Remembering a definition of the literary term *allegory* will be easy when students have applied it as easily as this picture book facilitates.

The True Story of the Three Little Pigs by Jon Scieszka, illustrated by Lane Smith. Penguin Putnam, 1989. The media and the dominant ideology conspired to tell the story of the three little pigs with a very anti-wolf bias, but in Jon Scieszka's more objective handling of the story, the wolf finally gets to share his side of the story. This is good for kicking off a discussion of parody, voice, or, perhaps on a more advanced level, point of view through an unreliable narrator. This is an obviously different spin on a well-known story that might interest advanced students in reading John Gardner's *Grendel,* the monster's spin on the story of Beowulf. You might also want to read Scieszka and Smith's *The Stinky Cheese Man and Other Fairly Stupid Tales* (Viking, 1992) as inspiration for the writing of parodies.

Teaching Novels

Assigning one novel to be read by an entire class became a popular practice with teachers, partly because it seems reassuring to know what's on the agenda for the next few days or, in some classes, the next few weeks. After struggling with grammar and composition, in which class members' abilities are obviously at great distances from each other, it should be a treat for teachers and the students all to join in reading the same book, some in class and some at home. For students with reading difficulties, teachers might suggest that they try checking out an audiotape of the novel from a library. A surprisingly large number of books have been recorded. Students can read along with the tape or CD or just listen to it. Some are condensations, while others are full readings, but either way the listening experience will be better than students resorting to *Cliff's Notes*.

Although many teachers assume that having specific novels read by the entire class has always been a standard part of the English curriculum, the practice is not universally accepted. One of the problems in using novels is the expense of acquiring a full class set of novels of your choice (e.g., Bernard Malamud's *The Assistant,* Robin McKinley's *The Hero and the Crown,* or Mary Shelley's *Frankenstein: Or, the Modern Prometheus*). Another problem is the length of time it takes for students to read the novel (rarely less than a week and more likely two or more). Adults have been known to stop reading when boredom sets in, but no such benediction comes to kids when they're reading a book for a class. More than eighty years ago, Howard Francis Seely wondered about our attraction to novels and asked in the November 1929 *English Journal* just why it is deemed imperative that a whole class read the same novel at the same time. He realizes that the practice is supposed to permit class discussions, which "more often than not turn out to be the answer of factual questions chiefly of a trifling nature." The most frequent and probably the most futile argument he gets from colleagues is "If Johnny hasn't read *The Talisman* in the ninth grade with his group, what will happen to him when he comes to *The Spy* in the tenth?" He went on to say, "That question is generally hurled at me with an air of utter, crushing finality. I can only faintly ask, 'Well, just what would?' With that I'm given up as hopeless."

A few years later, a teacher from England published an article, "The Reading Habit" in *Tomorrow* (July 1934), pointing out that

> Once the novelty has worn off a book, the child's interest in it can very easily flag. . . . Even the best novel rarely occupies us more than a few evenings. It is curious that teachers . . . should so often expect the restless mind of the child to possess a greater staying power in this respect than they possess themselves.

English teachers who wish to use novels for common reading should choose books they believe will appeal to young people. Never choose something solely because it is a "classic" or has won an award. Generally, there is merit in books that win awards, but winners are chosen by human beings, not gods, and human beings make mistakes. Anyone who has been part of a judging committee knows that books are removed from final consideration for reasons having nothing to do with literary merit or adolescent appeal. Compromise is inevitable and this is as true of awards for adults as for young people; Pulitzer and Nobel winners have frequently been controversial and debated for years.

Some teachers do not have to worry about selection because choices are established by school or district curricula. Among the most widely used titles are Orson Scott Card's *Ender's Game,* Robert Cormier's *The Chocolate War,* Charles Dickens's *Great Expectations,* Harper Lee's *To Kill a Mockingbird,* and Mark Twain's *Adventures of Huckleberry Finn.* Not a bad selection, and all are popular with teachers and most students.

But what are teachers to do if none of these seems right for the class they now face? What if other novels, like one of the following, would have been their first choice: Chinua Achebe's *Things Fall Apart,* William Faulkner's *As I Lay Dying,* Lois Lowry's *The Giver,* Herman Melville's *Billy Budd,* Walter Dean Myers's *Fallen Angels,* Mildred Taylor's *Roll of Thunder, Hear My Cry,* or Kurt Vonnegut, Jr.'s, *Slaughterhouse-Five?* All seven of these novels have been widely used in American schools for one grade or another.

Young Scholars Speak Out

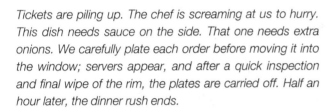 **on What's Cooking in Your YA Literature Class?**

Tickets are piling up. The chef is screaming at us to hurry. This dish needs sauce on the side. That one needs extra onions. We carefully plate each order before moving it into the window; servers appear, and after a quick inspection and final wipe of the rim, the plates are carried off. Half an hour later, the dinner rush ends.

* * *

Thirty-five high school freshmen come bounding into a classroom after lunch. Every one of them is at a slightly different academic level and brings a different life story. My task is to make them all better readers and writers. After fifty-five minutes, the bell rings, and they scamper off to their next period.

Teaching and cooking may seem like completely different professions, but they have more in common than one might think. In fact, my time studying at Scottsdale Culinary Institute and cooking at Gregory's World Bistro profoundly shaped the way that I now teach English. In particular, culinary experience taught me to pay attention to ingredients, timing, presentation, and workspace—elements that are also relevant in the young adult literature classroom.

Ingredients: Let us begin with a lesson in cheese. Is it better to pile on the gloppy kind or buy a slightly more expensive, but much more flavorful variety—like *La Tur, Parmigiano-Reggiano*, or Irish Cheddar—and use less of it? Chefs would reach toward flavor; teachers should, too. With YA literature, our books are our ingredients, so they must pack a punch (no gloppy selections, please). Fortunately, high-quality YA literature is available. Students can read from the Honor List or choose books recommended by someone they trust. Putting powerful books in students' hands will make them hungry for more.

Course topics can add flavor, too. When Alleen Nilsen and I co-taught a college course, students signed up for panels, researched their topics, and shared results with the class. Since students claimed topics well in advance, they had time to *spice up* their subjects and let their ideas

marinate. Their topics included vampires, Harry Potter, censorship, gender issues, and sex-education books. Students ate these up!

Just as a chef might adjust a menu after a trip to a farmers' market, teachers need to be on the lookout for fresh ideas and ripe opportunities. For example, we were lucky to have Arizona State University professor and creative writer Jewell Parker Rhodes visit our class, which inspired many students to read her excellent children's book, *Ninth Ward*. Another chance guest speaker, an ASU graduate student from Afghanistan, sparked a discussion of YA literature about his country. The ingredients for a superb lesson might be right there in your community, so shop locally when possible.

Timing: In addition to high-quality ingredients, the art of timing is vital to cooking and teaching. *Firing sheets* in catering count back from the moment of food service (e.g., 7:00 service, 6:45 buffet line set, 6:30 butter pulled from refrigerator, etc.). Without a firing sheet, it would be impossible to have all buffet items ready simultaneously. Similarly, backwards planning can help teachers manage the steps toward an outcome. For example, if the culminating activity for reading Elie Wiesel's *Night* is a creative response, what must come before that? Students could brainstorm types of creative responses and think about their own talents. To build background knowledge even before reading the text, students could examine primary documents on the Anti-Defamation League's "Echoes and Reflections" site. What must happen before that? Teachers can answer important pedagogical questions if they plan backwards.

Prix fixe menus, or set courses, also require special timing. Usually a theme binds *prix fixe* courses together; however, each dish provides a different experience. Our lessons are like this, too, as teachers strive to create varied activities within a unit. *Prix fixe* menus can begin with an *amusé*, a flavorful first dish of a bite or two to excite the palate. Similarly, in classrooms, our anticipatory sets pique students' interest at the beginning of a lesson, a unit, or even a semester. One of my favorite *amusés* at the start of a semester is a "Find someone who . . ." hunt with each task related to an upcoming course topic. In a YA literature course, this activity might read: "Find someone who has read an e-book, . . . has experienced censorship first-hand, . . . remembers reading a classic in high school," and so on. In planning your menu, be sure to leave plenty of time between courses for proper digestion.

Along with careful planning, timing also involves responding to one's environment in real time. In particular, cooks must monitor their work, peeking in the oven from time to time, using thermometers for more exact reads, and checking sauces using tasting spoons. In the classroom, periodic checks for understanding—both formal and informal—are also essential. Are students getting it? Check. Whether we are cooking or teaching, we stop and check progress often; then we adjust, and even re-adjust, until the results satisfy.

Presentation: In culinary school I loved studying *plating*, which is the art of placing items attractively on a plate. The plate of food should ultimately look interesting and have a variety of colors and textures. Fried parsnip strips can add height. Sauces in squeeze bottles can form dots or lines around the plate, and any pool of sauce should rest beneath a protein rather than masking grill marks. Like chefs, teachers often take great care in the way that they present materials. For panels in Alleen's class, she will make nametags for presenters and arrange chairs into a panel at the front of the room, which she believes helps students feel respected. For a poetry slam, she will decorate the room with a banner, set up a prize table, provide scorecards and robes to judges, and prepare numbered name cards for participants to hand to the emcee. Teachers know that attractive activities can help build student interest.

Presentation need not be additional work placed on the teacher, however. Students could store all of their work for a YA novel unit in an attractive, personalized "foldable" (see one of the many books on foldables for examples). As a culminating unit activity, students could present a YA book to the class using technology, perhaps with an "illuminated text" for the book (see the online example for "Cat in the Rain") or through a student-made film. I have seen secondary students go to great lengths to create beautiful presentations to impress their peers.

Workspace: One last component that teachers and cooks value is workspace. In fact, *mise en place*, or placement, is a concept that cooks live by. Before starting a recipe, cooks gather all the necessary ingredients. Before food service, cooks carefully arrange everything on the line: plates for the hot line are stacked in a warm place, sauté pans are within reach, oil is in a squeeze bottle, and so on. Without the concept of *mise en place*, the kitchen would be absolute pandemonium during the dinner rush! The classroom is very similar: it must be organized for maximum efficiency because classes are short. If a teacher has a lending library, for example, is it set up so that students can check out YA novels efficiently? What if students need book recommendations on a day when the teacher is absent? Also, is there a forum set up so that students can recommend great YA books to each other all year long? Students appreciate a carefully arranged classroom.

Chefs often say to "use the right tool for the job." In other words, while a chef knife is good for nearly any job, it would be awkward for the fanning of strawberries (fanning is delicate work, so a paring knife would work better). Adjust the environment to fit students' tasks, and do not be afraid to switch tools. For example, our students engaged more wholeheartedly in a discussion when we moved the desks into a circle. When they could see their classmates, all of a sudden everyone had something to say about the place of YA literature in the canon. Sometimes small changes can make a big difference.

The classroom environment also needs a positive tone; efficiency alone is not enough. To achieve a positive tone on the first night of class, Alleen has students tell about a book that they remember from their childhood; this exercise does not take any preparation on the teacher's part, and it allows students who have loved the same book to bond. It also fosters a community of readers. Writing and then sharing excerpts from reading autobiographies can also contribute to this community spirit. Usually two or three pages long, the reading autobiographies explain students' reading trajectories in terms of the levels of literary appreciation outlined in Chapter 1. In these papers, students might also comment on their reading preferences, challenges, and memories. Sharing these papers—or excerpts from them—is great fun. Bon appétit!

● *Wendy R. Williams is a doctoral student in English Education at Arizona State University. She has taught secondary English for nine years—both before and after studying at Arizona's highly acclaimed culinary school. While her academic study and research for her dissertation now keep her busy, she cannot resist hosting the occasional dinner party.*

Moving clockwise from the top are photos of some of the class activities that Wendy talked about in her "What's Cooking?" essay. Sarah is shown with her burka folded back as she serves nan (Afghan bread) and nuts and raisins on the evening that our Afghan graduate student came to tell us about his perceptions of such books as Khaled Hosseini's The Kite Runner *and Greg Mortenson and David Oliver's* Three Cups of Tea. *Next is the bag of materials the panel was given at the first of the semester as encouragement to start planning, next are some of the materials we prepared for our poetry slam, and finally there is a copy of Aron's "foldable," in which he kept his reading notes on Laurie Halse Anderson's* Speak.

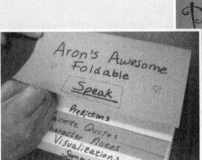

What can a teacher do in that situation? That depends on the school or the district. How rigid is the curriculum guide? Some may be more flexible than teachers expect. How rigid are the department chair or the curriculum coordinator? Certainly it's worth finding out, or even volunteering to serve on a curriculum committee.

Author and former teacher Richard Peck (see his Margaret A. Edwards Award write-up in Chapter 8) devised the following ten questions which were first published in the *ALAN Review* in the spring of 1978 when Donelson and Nilsen were editing that journal. This list of questions proved to be one of the most important and useful pieces that we published. Peck explained that his goal was to help teachers move students past their I-liked-it or I-didn't-like-it reactions. Each question is followed by his UM (Ulterior Motive):

1. *What would this story be like if the main character were of the opposite sex?*

UM: To approach the thinking of the author, who must decide what kind of protagonist or narrator will best embody or express the viewpoint. Could the protagonist of *The Member of the Wedding* be a boy instead of a girl? Could Jerry

Renault in *The Chocolate War* be a female victim of a female gang? Certainly, though each book would seem different in many superficial ways. Such a question might even temporarily defuse the sexual polarization rampant in junior high.

2. *Why is this story set where it is (not what is the setting)?*

UM: To point out the setting as an author's device to draw the reader into the action by means of recognizable trappings. The isolated setting of *Lord of the Flies* is a clear, if negative, example. But why is a soap opera almost always placed in an upper-middle-class, suburban setting? Why do so few YA novels occur in historic or exotic settings?

3. *If you were to film this story, what characters would you eliminate if you couldn't use them all?*

UM: To contrast the human richness of a novel with the necessary simplification of a TV show. Confronted with the need to eliminate some of the characters who add texture, some readers may rise up in defense of their favorites.

4. *Would you film this story in black and white or in color?*

UM: To consider tone. The initial reaction in this florid age is to opt for color in everything. But some young readers may remember that the most chilling *Dracula* films are in black and white, perhaps in part because dark shadows are always darkest and black blood is more menacing than red.

5. *How is the main character different from you?*

UM: To relent for once in our attempts to get the young readers to identify on their own limited terms. Protagonists regularly embody traits for the reader to aspire to. In YA books, they typically have powers, insights, and surmountable drawbacks that readers will often respond to without processing the facts.

6. *Why or why not would this story make a good TV series?*

UM: To contrast the shaping of a book's sequential chapters in the larger shape of the plot to the episodes of a TV series that repeat narrowly but do not rise from their formula to a central conclusion.

7. *What's one thing in this story that's happened to you?*

UM: To elicit an anecdotal response that draws the reader into the book. YA novels typically deal with the shock of recognition in their depicting of highly realistic school, social, and personal situations. Science fiction and fantasy use very human situations to balance their more fabulous elements and to make room for the earthbound reader.

8. *Reread the first paragraph of Chapter 1. What's in it that makes you read on?*

UM: To begin a book where the author must, in assessing the need for immediate involvement in an age not known for its patient attention span. An even more wistful motive is to suggest that young people include in their own writing immediately attractive devices for gaining the attention of the reader, if only the poor teacher.

9. *If you had to design a new cover for this book, what would it look like?*

UM: To consider the often deceptive packaging of the book in this visual era, particularly the paperback cover, and to encourage a more skeptical eye among those who were being bombarded by packaging and commercial claims long before they could read.

10. *What does the title tell you about the book? Does it tell the truth?*
UM: To remind readers that the title may well be the most important words the author writes and to encourage their defenses against titles that titillate and oversell.

Teaching with Thematic Units

The idea behind thematic units is to bring focus to a class and to keep students from feeling so "scattered" in their classwork. Potential themes can be as short as a single word (Friends), or as long as a complete sentence, as with this anonymous quotation: "It is by chance that we met, by choice that we became friends." Themes can come from a famous quotation (e.g., "The course of true love never did run smooth" from William Shakespeare's *Midsummer Night's Dream*), a popular song, an advertising jingle, or any well-known event in history, such as the War in Vietnam or The Holocaust. Themes can also be a topic, as with "Orphans: Children on Their Own," or a subgenre of literature such as "Hanging Out with Vampires and Werewolves." There is simply no limit to the possibilities for themes.

Ideally, a thematic unit will bind together a number of apparently dissimilar elements, including literature, language, media, and popular culture. First, however, we need to distinguish the thematic unit from two other kinds of units. The project unit has a clear end product, with all the steps that lead up to that end. For example, the production of a class play ends when the play is put on, a class-published slang dictionary ends when the booklet is put together and handed out, and reading and talking about a single novel ends with the last discussion and the test. A subject-centered unit consists of a body of information the teacher feels is important for the class (e.g., a unit on the history of English synonyms or the rise of drama in Shakespeare's time). These units have no clear-cut ending, barring a test, but they do have generally clear limits of what is to be included.

The thematic unit is different in that it binds together many elements of English while centering on an idea or motif that runs through a body of literature. For example, a question most of us have asked ourselves is, "Why do some people want to manipulate others?" This question is also asked in Aldous Huxley's *Brave New World*, George Orwell's *1984*, Shakespeare's *Othello* and *King Lear*, F. Scott Fitzgerald's *The Great Gatsby*, Henrik Ibsen's *An Enemy of the People*, Robert Cormier's *Fade*, Sonya Hartnett's *Surrender*, M. E. Kerr's *If I Love You, Am I Trapped Forever?* and Sophocles's *Antigone*. Is this a theme deserving the four or five weeks' time that the usual thematic unit takes? Here are four criteria against which to stack such a question:

1. The theme needs to appeal to kids. If it is too easy, too hard, or too boring, the teacher will lose the students' interest and attention.
2. The theme needs to be worth doing—in other words, intellectually and emotionally respectable for these particular kids at this particular time of their development and at this particular time of the year.

3. There must be lots of easily located literature on the theme.

4. The theme needs to appeal to the teacher; if the teacher is not excited about it, the kids won't be either.

Assuming that the theme meets these four requirements, the teacher must search for literature on the theme that will challenge the students and that they will enjoy, composition topics (written and spoken) worth using and related to the theme, websites and maybe films (short and feature-length) related to the theme and worth viewing, and spelling and vocabulary lists related to the theme. That means the teacher must determine the following:

1. A list of sensible objectives (or learning outcomes or standards if you prefer) for this specific unit (not English classwork in general) that both kids and their parents can understand.

2. A work of some length (usually a short novel or a play) to open the unit and make clear to students what the unit is aiming at. Such a work is not essential, but it's customary and usually helpful.

3. A body of short works (poetry and short stories and essays) to be used throughout the unit because they are related to the theme.

4. A series of composition assignments (usually two or three written assignments and two or three oral assignments) on the theme.

5. A list of vocabulary words related to the unit topic, perhaps twenty to thirty or so, to be talked about and tested five at a time.

6. A list of spelling words related to the unit topic, perhaps twenty to thirty or so, to be talked about and tested about five at a time.

7. A way of beginning the unit that grabs students' attention and interest while focusing on the theme. Obviously, teachers can (and do) begin thematic units with "Hey, kids, how would you like to talk about _____?" or "Hey, kids, we're going to turn to something entirely different now, a unit on _____," but surely there's a slightly more fascinating way. A short film or the teacher reading aloud a short story (or a recent news clipping) might work.

8. A way of wrapping up the unit that ties all the strands together. Tests, the all-American way to wrap anything up, are always possible. Some classes find panel discussions useful, some might profit from a student evaluation of the unit and the literature read, and others might benefit from some creative art project or a dramatization.

9. The problems that the unit—and students—may encounter and how the teacher works through them. Perhaps it's time to incorporate peer editing into the class, and if this unit is as good a time as any other to introduce kids to peer evaluation and editing, the teacher needs to plan on preparing class members to work in small groups. Perhaps the short book chosen to get the unit started (e.g., Monica Hughes's *Hunter in the Dark*) has some vocabulary problems, or Nathaniel Hawthorne's short story "Young Goodman Brown" presents problems getting the kids to understand colonial life and religion. These and similar issues need to be worked through and solutions found.

Thematic units can range from complex and sophisticated topics for college-bound kids to simple topics that are appropriate for junior high. For example, a thematic unit on "Our Ability to Endure," which centers on the theme of survival and power, is a topic of immediate interest to eighth and ninth graders. It could open with words from William Faulkner's much-anthologized Nobel Prize speech and move to one of these as common reading and the remainder as supplementary reading: Avi's *The True Confessions of Charlotte Doyle,* Alice Childress's *Rainbow Jordan,* Robert Cormier's *After the First Death,* James Forman's *Ceremony of Innocence,* Anne Frank's *The Diary of a Young Girl,* Harry Mazer's *The Last Mission,* or Robb White's *Deathwatch.*

A more intellectually and emotionally complex thematic unit on "Redemption" might begin with reading and discussing Katherine Mansfield's "The Garden Party" or Nadine Gordimer's "A Company of Laughing Faces." This might be followed by the class reading Bernard Malamud's *The Assistant,* and sometime during the unit each student might be asked to read at least one supplementary work. Here there's room for a range in difficulty with advanced students doing Dante's *The Divine Comedy* or Dostoevsky's *Crime and Punishment.* Less challenging books include Hal Borland's *When the Legends Die,* F. Scott Fitzgerald's *The Great Gatsby,* Ursula K. Le Guin's *A Wizard of Earthsea,* Fran Arrick's *Tunnel Vision,* Judy Blume's *Tiger Eyes,* Margaret Mahy's *Memory,* and Paul Zindel's *The Pigman.*

Teachers wanting ideas for themes of interest to young people might skim through titles of some of the recent short story collections, many of which are thematically organized; for example, Belinda Hollyer's *You're the Best: 14 Stories about Friendship,* M. Jerry Weiss and Helen Weiss's *Dreams and Visions,* Walter Dean Myers's *What They Found: Love on 145th Street,* and Michael Cart's *Tomorrowland: Stories about the Future.* See Focus Box 11.2, "Old and New Recommended Collections of Short Stories," for ideas.

Of course, you want to have more than a collection of short stories from which to plan a unit, but it is comforting to have something to start with and to show students the possibilities for different interpretations. One of the benefits of thematic units should be that they are flexible enough to inspire different thinking by different students.

However, choosing books to fit the theme needs to be done thoughtfully, with consideration for the interests, needs, and skill levels of the individual students. Ideally, you will have enough books that students will be allowed some choice in what they read. Within thematic units teachers may find it helpful to use the literature circle approach as described below with each circle of students reading a different book and then bringing their experience back to the rest of the class.

Literature Circles

In the last chapter, we talked about using literature circles with English language learners. Each group had a college student serving as a coordinator and helper. But the kind of literature circles we are talking about here are directed by the students themselves. Obvious advantages are that students feel more responsible for the conversation and many more students get to speak than when one teacher leads thirty students in a discussion. Another advantage is that each group can be reading a book, at least partially of its own choosing. Some teachers collect sets of books that are thematically related or that are written by the same author. For example, Jacqueline Woodson (see the Margaret A. Edwards Award description about her on page 386) has written enough books that each of five or six groups in a class could be reading a different Woodson book. In a college class, students could do all of the reading outside of class and spend only an hour in a discussion, with perhaps an extra half-period for group sharing. In high schools, the experience is usually spaced out over two weeks so that the students have time for reading both in and outside of class. If the students have some choice of which book they will read, they are more likely to appreciate their reading experience. Also, when the program succeeds, students often choose to read on their own one or two of the books that their classmates have enjoyed.

The biggest resistance to this approach comes from teachers who feel that if a book is so simple that kids can read and discuss it on their own, there is no use in wasting class time on it. We hear less of this attitude than we used to because today's teachers worry that if they do not lead students to enjoy reading books in school, these students will go through life getting both their enjoyment and their enlightenment from whatever their acquaintances happen to say, or from whatever snippets they happen to find on the Internet or hear through other mass media.

The fact that the teacher cannot be involved in all the groups at once puts greater responsibility on the students. This can be good in that students know that the success of the discussion depends on them, but it can also be a problem in that students are tempted to talk about other things. To encourage involvement, it is a good idea to make a list of jobs that students either volunteer for or receive by assignment on a rotating basis. Here are some of the jobs other teachers have devised. You might choose from the following list or devise additional jobs of your own. While you will probably always want someone to fill the first three categories, be flexible with the others and make sure that over the course of a semester students are assigned to different responsibilities.

1. *The Discussion Leader* helps the members decide how far the participants should read before their next meeting, keeps the group on task, and makes sure all students have a chance to participate. These leaders are encouraged to start with the seeds provided by other students and are cautioned against asking simple fact questions or questions that can be answered with a *yes* or *no*.

2. *The Recorder* takes notes and is responsible for summarizing the group's observations either for the group itself or in a report to the whole class.

3. *Initiators* (probably two or three) make seed cards on which they write questions or ideas for the group to begin discussion. They give these seeds to the discussion leader and stand ready to explain what they meant or what kinds of ideas they hope to elicit.

4. *Character Guides* come ready to describe the personality and the physical characteristics of the main characters and to lead the group in figuring out how and why these characters change.

Margaret A. Edwards Award

Winner (2006)
Jacqueline Woodson, **Writing Against the Fear**

Woodson's honored books include *I Hadn't Meant to Tell You This; Lena; From the Notebooks of Melanin Sun; If You Come Softly;* and *Miracle's Boys.* Among her other writings are several well-received children's books.

Woodson has described her goal as "writing against the fear," by which she means putting on paper the kinds of things that she knows young people worry about but seldom hear honestly discussed. When she was in high school, her favorite authors were James Baldwin, Toni Morrison, and Alice Walker. She wrote her first book at age seven (a book of poetry about butterflies) and carried it around in the back pocket of her jeans to show to whomever she could nab. In college she majored in English and minored in British literature, but all the time, she told Deborah Taylor, who interviewed her for the June 2006 issue of *School Library Journal,* she felt like it was a background for something bigger—something that she is just now beginning to understand.

> *I wrote because I loved writing and the power of writing. I wrote because there were people in my head saying stuff and I wanted to listen and understand. Call it madness. Call it a gift. Call it whatever society needs to call it to understand it. I watched the world and the world was big and amazing and attainable when I wrote.*

One of the reasons that kids pick up Woodson's books is that they are thin. She jokes that she is so talkative that when she sits down to write she has used up all her words. In a more serious vein, she explains that she feels such urgency about the subjects she's treating that she has to strip away the descriptions and just get to the point. Her writing is spare, almost like free-verse poetry. Her succinctness—plus the fact that she treats subjects that other authors have shied away from—keeps kids reading. She includes both black and white characters as she writes about racism and homophobia, first love of an interracial couple, sexual abuse by a parent, and kids being on their own. Bad things happen in her books, but there are also some very good people who step in to help. In *I Hadn't Meant to Tell You This,* black Marie and white Lena become friends. They both live in homes without a mother. Marie's father is a black college professor and, although he resists, Marie makes her affluent home a weekly refuge to the impoverished Lena and her little sister, Dion, who take their Saturday baths at Marie's. What Lena doesn't mean to tell Marie is that her father is sexually abusing her. In the sequel, *Lena,* which Woodson wrote after getting numerous letters from readers who wanted to know what happens, thirteen-year-old Lena takes her eight-year-old sister, Dion, and runs away. They cut their hair and pretend to be boys, unless they happen to be picked up by a woman. Lena's idea is that if they make it to the small town in Kentucky where she thinks their deceased mother grew up, surely some of her people will take them in. They don't go to authorities because they fear they will be separated. As they hitchhike, they make up lie after lie, asking people to drop them off at the hospital in the next big town where they say their mother just had a new baby and has sent for them. They claim they are hitchhiking because they lost their bus money. Only after they are given a ride, two good meals, and an overnight stay by a kindly woman who has cared for foster children and is concerned enough to question their unlikely story does Lena's fear melt enough for her to come to her senses and realize that her dream of finding "family" is pretty unlikely. After all, she and Dion had never heard from any Kentucky relatives, nor did anyone send a card or acknowledge her mother's death. This realization makes Lena ready to accept help from the woman, who gets in touch with Marie's father. As with most of Woodson's books, while all the problems are not solved, they are at least recognized and readers go away with a little more knowledge about what the world needs to do. ●

5. *A Word Detective* watches for unusual words or ordinary words used in different senses. This person jots down the words and the page numbers and comes ready to lead the other students in seeing why these words are special.

6. *A Plot Guide* starts each day's discussion by summarizing events that have happened in the course of the day's reading. He or she invites other group members to speculate on the importance of the events and helps group members become comfortable with such words as *exposition, rising action, climax,* and *denouement.*

7. *Future Authors* select three or four passages that they wish they had written. They come ready to read the passages and to explain what they like about them. Are there interesting allusions or metaphors? Are they particularly surprising in how much information they present in so few words? Do they have underlying humor or foreshadowing?

8. *A Drama Director* suggests how the group might present their book to their classmates through a reader's theater presentation, a television talk show, or a short skit.

9. *A Graphic Designer* figures out and brings the needed supplies for the group to make some kind of a chart or poster that will help explain the idea of their book.

As with everything else suggested in this book, literature circles do not come with a guarantee and there is no exact recipe to follow. You will want to devise your own approach after considering our suggestions as well as those to be found in such books as *Literature Circles: Voice and Choice in the Student-Centered Classroom* by Harvey Daniels and *Literature Circles and Response,* edited by Bonnie Campbell Hill, Nancy J. Johnson, and Katherine L. Schlick.

Using Young Adult Literature in Creative Writing

In an "Up for Discussion" article in the March 1996 *School Library Journal,* contemporary author and creative writing teacher Jack Gantos told how, on the first day of class when he asks his college students about a book they've recently enjoyed, they try to impress him by citing *War and Peace, Crime and Punishment, Wuthering Heights,* and *The Sound and the Fury.* Gantos appreciates and teaches these books in his literature classes, but because not one of his creative writing students "was with Tolstoy when Napoleon retreated from Moscow, or spent part of their youth in a Siberian prison with Dostoyevsky, or wandered the imaginary moors with Emily Brontë while stuck in a parsonage, or sorted mail with Faulkner in Mississippi," he marches his students to the library where he takes them through the stacks and hands them young adult books to read "not for comprehension or analysis, but for inspiration." He wants them to "revel in the juicy details of life" that will help them value their own experiences "with family and friends, in their own communities, observing or participating in the human dramas of the moment" (p. 128).

Language is a social phenomenon, and just as we learned to speak through imitation and trial and error, we learn to write in much the same way. Young adult literature can provide creative teens with inspiration and models to follow because:

- The problems in the books are likely to be ones that readers or their friends have experienced or thought about.
- A variety of ethnic backgrounds and settings enlarges the chance of students finding stories with which they can identify.
- Characters' conversations can serve as models for the writing of dialogue because the speech patterns come close to the everyday, spoken language of teenagers and to the I-wish-I-had-said-that kind of rejoinder.
- Even in historical fiction or in fantasy or science fiction, the protagonists are young, which means that their intellectual and emotional development is similar to that of teenage readers.
- Most YA authors write in a succinct and straightforward style so that readers can "get" the story and still have some intellectual energy to expend in looking at the author's techniques.
- The intriguing details that professional writers include in their stories are the same kinds of details that clever and witty teenagers observe and relate to each other when they are telling about something they have experienced.

While teenagers seldom write scholarly papers, many of them enjoy writing scripts, poems, and short stories, or putting their observations online in blogs or even creating their own zines. See Focus Boxes 11.3, "Encouragement for Student Writers," and 11.4, "Publication Opportunities for Young Writers."

Some teachers of creative writing have found that it works well to use a collection of YA short stories for the text because, for one thing, it's a lot easier to pick out figurative language from contemporary short stories than from Elizabethan drama or early American literature. A collection that has worked well for us is Don Gallo's *Sixteen: Short Stories by Outstanding Writers for Young Adults*. Gallo grouped the stories under the categories of friendships, turmoils, loves, decisions, and families, but for creative writing purposes, we regrouped them into types starting with what we judged to be the easiest for students to imitate, then moved on up to the hardest. We started with wish-fulfilling stories so that students could have fun thinking, talking, and then writing about their daydreams and fantasies. We next looked at stories filled with incongruity and surprise, followed by those showing contrasting points of view. The most sophisticated category of the stories, which we left until last, were the realistic explorations of human emotions.

How much work young writers do depends on their motivation as well as on the setting. Students in a semester- or yearlong class probably have more time to put into their writing than those in a six-week unit or in an after-school writing club sponsored by a library or other community organization. Those in extracurricular writing groups, however, may be more motivated and may be together over several years rather than just for a few months.

Focus Box 11.3

Encouragement for Student Writers

A Maze Me: Poems for Girls by Naomi Shihab Nye, illustrated by Terre Mahere. HarperCollins/Greenwillow, 2005. Nye not only shares her wonderfully fresh poetry, but also advises future poets. One of her sensible suggestions is, "If you write three lines down in a notebook every day . . . you will find out what you notice." She started doing this when she was twelve and hasn't stopped yet.

Blood on the Forehead: What I Know about Writing by M. E. Kerr. HarperCollins, 1998. The title comes from the framed quotation that Kerr keeps above her desk, "Writing is easy: All you do is sit staring at a blank sheet of paper until the drops of blood form on your forehead."

Getting the Knack: 20 Poetry Writing Exercises by Stephen Dunning and William Stafford. National Council of Teachers of English, 1992. The book does exactly what it sets out to do, which is to give young writers specific details about different ways to write poems.

Immersed in Verse: An Informative, Slightly Irreverent & Totally Tremendous Guide to Living the Poet's Life by Allan Wolf, illustrated by Tuesday Mourning. Sterling/Lark, 2006. This is both a how-to book and a book of encouragement for anyone who's even slightly tempted to write a poem. The illustrations add an upbeat tone.

A Kick in the Head: An Everyday Guide to Poetic Forms by Paul B. Janeczko, illustrated by Chris Raschka. Candlewick, 2005. In this follow-up to their 2001 *A Poke in the I*, these two creative men make the study of poetic forms so much fun that we predict kids will want to see if they can follow the "rules" while still being as original as are the sample poems in the book.

The Making of a Writer by Joan Lowery Nixon. Delacorte, 2002. This popular author of mysteries for young readers aimed her memoir at fans in junior high and middle school. All the way through she shares advice and tidbits, ending up with her "top ten" tips.

Poems from Homeroom: A Writer's Place to Start by Kathi Appelt. Henry Holt, 2002. Appelt is a successful writer for children and middle school students and uses her same fresh style in this encouraging book.

Poetry Matters: Writing a Poem from the Inside Out by Ralph Fletcher. HarperCollins, 2002. Fletcher describes poems as "emotional X-rays," and then sets out to equip readers with what they need to create the X-rays of their feelings and observations. Interviews with poets are inspiring as well as instructive.

Seeing the Blue Between: Advice and Inspiration for Young Poets, compiled by Paul B. Janeczko. Candlewick, 2002. Janeczko collected advice and models from thirty-two successful poets and put it all together with the same care that he has used in such previous books as *How to Write Poetry* (Scholastic, 1999), *The Place My Words Are Looking For* (Bradbury, 1990), and *Poetspeak: In Their Work, About Their Work* (Bradbury, 1983).

Technically, It's Not My Fault: Concrete Poems written and illustrated by John Grandits. Clarion, 2004. The title comes from a science experiment gone awry. Middle school students will be the ones most likely to be amused, but high school students might want to see how their own skills stack up with those of Grandits.

A Teen's Guide to Getting Published: Publishing for Profit, Recognition, and Academic Success, 2nd edition, by Jessica Dunn and Danielle Dunn. Prufrock Press, 2006. Although we aren't as enthused as some people are about encouraging teens to become published authors, we at least need to provide ambitious teens with the kind of information that is in this book.

Whatcha Mean What's a Zine? The Art of Making Zines and Mini-Comics by Mark Todd and Esther Pearl Watson. Graphia Books/Houghton Mifflin, 2006. Creative and/or artistic kids can get both inspiration and instruction from this book that is designed to look like a homemade zine. It is the book the authors wish they had run across when they started drawing and telling their own stories long before they knew there was a name for what they were making.

Writing Magic: Creating Stories That Fly by Gail Carson Levine. HarperCollins, 2006. Levine's chapter titles give the tone of her must-read for potential authors: "Liftoff," "Heart and Guts," "Plowing Through," "Digging Deeper," and "Writing Forever."

Publication Opportunities for Young Writers

Amazon.com

http://www.amazon.com: Amazon is one of the original places on the Web where teens can submit book reviews. The Listmania! Lists allows users to create personalized book lists and suggestions on any topic.

Bookbrowse.com

http://www.bookbrowse.com: Teens can write and submit reviews about their favorite books at this site edited and owned by Davina Morgan-Witts.

BookDivas

http://www.bookdivas.com: A collaboration between *Seventeen* magazine and Electric Artists, BookDivas encourages girls to read, review, and discuss books or whatever strikes their fancy.

Book Raps

http://www.oz-teachernet.edu.au/projects/br: At this site, teens can discuss books that are nominated by teachers and librarians. "Book Raps" are scheduled on a monthly calendar and anyone can participate. Book Raps is part of the Oz-Teacher Net of Australia and is maintained by Margaret Lloyd, Jennifer Masters, and Shaun Nykvist.

Favorite Teenage Angst Books

http://www.grouchy.com/angst/: At this appealing site, teens can discuss books related to classic coming-of-age issues, such as relationships, drugs and alcohol, self-esteem, and family problems. The website author, Cathy Young, recently edited an anthology of stories called *One Hot Second: Stories of Desire*.

Guys Read

http://www.penguinputnam.com/static/packages/us/yreaders/guysread: Guys Read is an initiative to improve literacy in boys, created by Jon Scieszka. This site features booklists and tips to help improve literacy among boys. Guys are invited to start their own chapters and communicate about what they are reading.

Merlyn's Pen

http://www.merlynspen.org: Established long before the days of Internet printing, Merlyn's Pen publishes a yearly collection as well as more frequent issues featuring teenage writing.

Read! Literacy and Education for Life

http://www.weread.org/teens/Index.asp: Teens can read and submit stories and book reviews at this site. WE READ is an acronym for "World Enterprise for Reading, Education, and Academic Development" and is in the process of obtaining its nonprofit status.

Reading Rants!

http://www.readingrants.org: Maintained by Jennifer Hubert, middle school librarian at the Little Red School House and Elisabeth Irwin High School in Greenwich Village, Manhattan, Reading Rants! focuses on books geared toward girls.

TeenInk Magazine

http://TeenInk.com/Books/: A monthly print magazine and website written by teens for teens. The website accepts original poetry, fiction, and book reviews from teens.

TeensPoint.org

http://www.teenspoint.org/reviews/index.asp: At this library site, teens have opportunities to read and write reviews of books, music, movies, and websites. It is maintained by the Central Rappahannock Regional Library in Fredericksburg, Virginia.

WordSmiths

http://teenlink.nypl.org/wordsmiths-current.cfm: Sponsored by the New York Public Library, WordSmiths is a site where teens can publish their own creative writing.

While an obvious goal may be the writing of a short story, less ambitious tasks can provide practice as well as feelings of success along the way. For example, students can work in small groups to improvise dialogue for a scene that might have occurred in one of the stories, or they can rework a story into a one-act play or a reader's theater production.

Students love to write scenes for movies or television, and now that there are so many teen-centered television shows, they might practice turning a short story into a TV script. Keeping a response journal helps students focus on a story. Prompts to help readers think of themselves as authors include:

1. The part of this story that comes the closest to something I might write is . . .

2. If I had written this story I would have . . .

3. If I were to write a sequel . . .

4. This author is especially skilled at (choose one) developing characters, writing conversations, describing settings, or creating interesting plots as shown by . . .

In anticipation of creating their own story titles, help students examine the titles in a collection. Which are the most intriguing? The most memorable? For example, in Gallo's *Sixteen* collection, what are the extra meanings in Brancato's "Fourth of July" and Lipsyte's "Future Tense"? Which titles help establish setting by hinting at time and place? Which establish a light tone? How about a dark or serious tone? What is the effect of an author asking a question? Does Cormier's "In the Heat" remind readers of the oxymoronic "In the heat of the night," while Major's "Three People and Two Seats" reminds them of the cliché "two's company, three's a crowd"? The point in relation to students' own writing is to illustrate how much thought authors put into creating titles that honestly convey the sense of their stories while arousing readers' interest.

Other Strategies for Inspiring Reading and Thinking

Reader-response journals empower students to find personal meaning in their reading. Rather than summarizing to prove they did the assignment, or guessing what the book was supposed to mean according to the teacher or study guide, readers become accustomed to making their own meaning out of their reading by making personal connections to it. They write in their journals at regular intervals according to the teacher's requirement, such as at the end of every chapter or after every important event. Teachers then read what students have written and write small responses in the margins. Linda R. Berger, in an article "Reader Response Journals: You Make the Meaning . . . and How" (*JAAL*, 39.5, pp. 380–385), told how she worked with her students to come up with four questions that would help them think of things to respond to in their journals:

What do you notice?

What do you question?

What do you feel?

What do you relate to?

In her classes, the reader-response journals have proven to be excellent springboards for discussion and writing. Students who might normally find it difficult to talk in large or small discussions feel more confident if they can pull out their reader-response journal and share something they had made a note of. The journals also work well as a prewriting activity.

Socratic circles center on interaction in dialogue, but not debate, among a group of students. For help in this process see Matt Copeland's *Socratic Circles: Fostering Critical and Creative Thinking in Middle and High School* (Stenhouse, 2005). He starts with a short passage of text that his students have read critically, then he forms two concentric circles of students. The inside circle of students focuses on exploring the meaning of the text, while students in the outside circle observe their conversation. When the conversation is finished, they report on what they observed and give feedback on the quality of the dialogue as well as the group dynamics. Then the students exchange places and repeat the process. In literature circles, students are working with broader issues, but here they are working with only a passage—probably a couple of pages, which they read and annotate. Obviously, the teacher has to choose a passage that is central to the theme of the book and one that is full enough to provoke lots of discussion.

Silent discussion involves choosing five or six provocative quotations from a book that students are all reading or have just finished reading, and writing a different quote in the center of one of five or six large pieces of butcher paper (three to four feet long) placed on tables spread out around the classroom. Students work in five or six groups with a chosen leader. The groups start at different tables and each student is equipped with a colored marker and a black or blue pen. As the activity begins, each group reads the quotation at their table and discusses it so that everyone understands where it came from in the story and what it means. Then each person (the big piece of butcher paper and the table make it possible for students to write at the same time) uses his or her colored marker to write a response to the quotation. They can agree or disagree with it, give an explanation, connect it to real life or to another story, or write whatever it makes them think of. After about five minutes, the teacher signals and each group rotates to the next table and repeats the process until every group has been to every table. Then the second round starts with students reading other students' comments and using their blue or black pens to respond to at least one of the comments already written. When time is up, the teacher calls a stop and each group (under the direction of their designated group leader) is responsible for taking the poster from the table they are at, taping it up for all to see, and presenting to the rest of the class the one or two observations and the related responses that they found particularly insightful or original. If feasible, the colorful posters can stay up for a few days so that students can ponder comments they did not have time to study carefully.

Banned book on trial can be used with any book, but is especially meaningful with a book that actually was banned in some part of the country or at some time. Students can break into small groups, some forming a jury, some as attorneys for the prosecution and some as attorneys for the defense, and conduct a mock trial as if a particular book were on trial and might be banned. Both sides must present passages from the book that support their contention that the book be banned or not banned. The judge, who may be the teacher, but doesn't have to be, has the role of instructing the jury (and the rest of the class) as to the Supreme Court findings on censorship of school and library books. The jury should have a discussion outside the hearing of the attorneys before announcing their finding and then explain the reasoning they followed to arrive at their decision. Look in Chapter 12 to find basic Supreme Court precedents which the jury, the judge, the plaintiff, and the defendant can consult.

A Character or author day can give students the chance to dress up and perform before either their classmates or before a larger audience in the school cafeteria or auditorium. First, the students choose an author they like and after reading a couple of the author's books and doing some research, they make a display with foam board, cardboard, or whatever items they can gather. This differs from making posters, in that their display needs to be self-supporting so it can sit on a table or a desk with its creator standing nearby. After figuring

On the day we all came to class dressed as a character, it took us a while to figure out that Remington had come as Artemis Fowl, the boy with the "most ingenious criminal mind in history."

out a short speech, the student comes dressed either as the author or as one of the characters in the book. If it's just one class doing the presentations, the teacher might want the students to take turns so that everyone gets to hear everyone else's presentation. But an alternative for larger groups is to have the room arranged as for a science fair with students standing by their displays and informally giving their short presentation and answering questions for whoever stops by. For example a student dressed as Gary Paulsen in jeans, hunting boots, suspenders, flannel shirt, and cap, might begin, "Hello. I'm Gary Paulsen, and I'm from Thief River Falls, Minnesota, where I was lucky I stayed out of as much trouble as I did. If you read my book, *How Angel Peterson Got His Name,* you will find out how I almost drowned going over a waterfall in a barrel. Let me tell you about some of my other books and how they relate to my life. . . ."

In another example, a student dressed up as Ponyboy Curtis from *The Outsiders* in tight jeans, T-shirt, and slicked back hair, might open with, "Hello, I'm Ponyboy Curtis. My parents were killed in a car accident, and now my twenty-year-old brother Darry takes care of me and my other brother, Sodapop. S. E. Hinton wrote about my family and our group, the Greasers, for a class assignment when she was in high school in Tulsa, Oklahoma, and that's where the story takes place. It's a great story, really tough, and 'tough' means good in Greaser talk."

The following rubric (or one you devise with your students) might help students decide what to include and also let them know how they will be graded:

- Facts about author's life
- Character traits of the protagonist and other important characters
- Plot premises from the author's major books
- What a reader will learn about life from these books (what does the author's message say to readers?)

Writing letters to authors is an activity that many teachers encourage. All of the authors we know say they love to get letters from students who have been so touched by their book that they wanted to write a sincere letter and so took it upon themselves to do so; however, these same authors hate to receive what they call *assignment letters,* especially if the letters have not been edited by the teacher, and the students ask questions that they could have easily answered themselves from the authors' websites. They also hate it when students beg for an answer because their teacher promised a better grade if they got an answer. Anyone expecting an answer should at least provide a self-addressed and stamped envelope. If you still want to do this, take your students through all the stages of prewriting, drafting, editing, and publishing (i.e., perfecting them). Then put all the letters from one school in one package, so that the author knows that these were all part of one project and can be answered through one letter. Make the letters relatively short (one page), do not ask for autographed copies of books, and do not ask for help with a report about the author and book (especially not for a report that is due in a couple of days). Look on the author's website and see if it might be more feasible to send one class message to an author via email. And explain to students that authors can only write so many words in a day and if all their readers ask them to write letters then they won't have time to write their books.

Another way to use letters is to have students write letters from one character in a book to another, using elements of the plot to demonstrate their understanding or engagement with the book. For example, the first paragraph of a letter to Matteo, the teen protagonist in Nancy Farmer's futuristic *The House of the Scorpion*, from Tam Lin, the bodyguard with a sordid past but a loyal heart, might read:

Dear Matt,
If you are reading this, then I am dead and you have escaped from El Patrón. Your life is in danger, but at least you now have a fighting chance. Wherever you go and whatever you do in life, I want you to remember that clones are just as human as any other person, and that one life is just as sacred as any other life. You have a right to have your own life and El Patrón can no more own your life than he can own the stars and the moon.

Another example is for students to write a letter to an important character's parents based on events from the book. For example:

Dear Mrs. Pigza:
As Joey's teacher, I am very concerned about his apparent lack of self-control. He has manifested behaviors that suggest he might need some accommodation or help from special resources. Joey is dangerous to himself and others, which he seems to find mildly amusing. Some examples of his behavior include running with open scissors, sticking his finger in the pencil sharpener (both of these stunts resulted in injury to someone), swallowing his house key, and ruining a class field trip (from which he will ineligible until further notice).
Mrs. Pigza, it is imperative that I visit with you and Mr. Pigza here after school one afternoon as soon as is convenient for you.

Students can read their letters out loud in class, and they can answer each other's letters (the letter to which they most want to respond) if class time permits.

Concluding Comments

One of the main points we are trying to make in this chapter is that we hope both teachers and students can enjoy themselves at the same time that they read and learn. We have suggested several activities that should help you accomplish this goal. But our best advice is that you work with other teachers, sharing your ideas and seeing what they do. Seeing a model of a project or hearing about a successful activity from a colleague is more efficient than reading our wordy descriptions. We will therefore close this chapter with a simple listing of additional activities that we have seen or heard about, and encourage you to watch and listen for such activities as you visit with your colleagues to see if they might be something you could use in class. Teachers, as well as students, need to relieve that cloud of boredom that threatens to hang over all of us. One of the reasons that so many researchers get positive results in their studies is simply that the participants have succeeded because they got a shot of adrenalin from directing their students in trying something new. So here is a "Lucky Seven" list of activities you might consider having your students undertake.

1. Make a movie poster based on speculation about their book being made into a movie. Include the proposed title, a color graphic, a meaningful quotation, a rating, and credits for the actors and director.

2. Make a board game similar to Monopoly based on a book; for example, Gordon Korman's *Son of the Mob* could inspire a game putting Vince Luca on the road to a normal life.

3. Write a letter trying to get the characters accepted as participants on a television show such as *Judge Joe* or *Judge Judy* as a way of solving a dispute they are having.

4. Write an alternative ending by having students brainstorm, in groups or individually, to think of possible endings to a novel. Encourage students to pick one and flesh it out as a complete ending.

5. Read scary stories in a darkened room (lit only with battery-powered camp lanterns), with blankets spread on the floor and recordings of night sounds to set the mood. Alvin Schwartz's *Scary Stories to Tell in the Dark* are short and easy; older students can search for scary stories in Stephen King or R. L. Stine books.

6. Write a personal ad for a character (e.g., "Michigan orphan seeks reunion with father who was last seen carrying a trombone and playing in a jazz band. Inquiries can be made at Hooverville. Ask for Bud, not Buddy." Based on Christopher Paul Curtis's *Bud, not Buddy*).

7. Write an obituary or a eulogy for a character who dies in a novel, such as Mr. Pignati in Paul Zindel's *The Pigman*, Violet in M. T. Anderson's *Feed*, or Emmet Till in *Mississippi Trial, 1955*.

Censorship: Of Worrying and Wondering

We live in censorial times. Not only are books being censored, but so are songs, movies, advertisements, student writings, student presentations, and even individuals. In the spring of 2011, for example, President and Michelle Obama were heavily criticized by Fox News and Sarah Palin for inviting the Chicago-based rapper known as Common to be one of the presenters at a White House afternoon of poetry. The Obamas changed their plans to address the criticism and asked Common to come to a less formal evening performance, rather than the original afternoon event. On the day of the event, White House spokesman Jay Carney said that while the president opposes some of Common's lyrics, he appreciates Common as a socially conscious hip-hop artist or rapper, "who in fact, has done a lot of good things."

According to *The Official Blog of the Peter Heck Radio Show,* May 12, 2011 (downloaded 5/23/2011), the controversy began after the Web-based *Daily Caller* announced the invitation and printed some of the rapper's lyrics, which included heavy criticism of former president George W. Bush and "A Song for Assata," with the line "Your power and pride is beautiful. May God bless your soul." Assata Shakur, formerly known as Joanne Chesimard, was convicted in 1973 for the slaying of a state trooper, Werner Foerster, on the New Jersey Turnpike.

This connection drew New Jersey policemen into the controversy. David Jones, president of the State Troopers Fraternal Association union, said that the White House invitation to a rapper who seemed to celebrate Shakur was disturbing. He declared that, "The young people who read this stuff, hear this stuff, are getting a very dangerous and deadly message." A coincidence that added fuel to the fire was that the poetry event at the White House was held the same week that lawmen from across the country were making their annual trek to Washington, DC to honor fallen comrades at the National Law Enforcement Memorial.

We started the chapter with this example because it illustrates several of the reasons that today's educators are increasingly worried about problems with censorship.

- The Internet allows anyone with a complaint to communicate to large numbers of like-minded people, many of whom will be willing to join in a protest and to forward information soliciting support from their own sets of friends.

- The Internet also makes it easy for complainants to find background information that they can use to build a case as when they go back in someone's history to see what they previously wrote or said.

- While the value of protecting "young people" was alluded to by the union president from New Jersey, the early participation of Sarah Palin and Fox News also shows how the idea of protecting young people from "evil influences" is being used for political purposes.

See the photo below for a reproduction of headlines that were in the news during the spring of 2011. One of the reasons that we currently find ourselves living

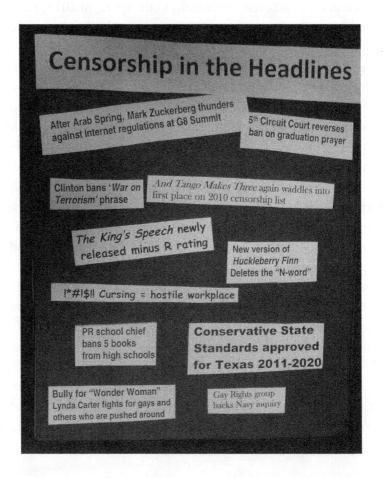

in censorial times is that expectations and standards have changed tremendously for the mass media. Parents who grew up watching *The Dick Van Dyke Show,* where even a photo of a double bed was not allowed, have a hard time finding any television that does not include allusions to, or portrayals of, various kinds of sex and/ or violence. The breakdown of restrictions on television started with pay-for-view and late-night cable TV; to compete, however, the major networks also had to loosen restrictions, and so parents who have fond memories of kid-friendly TV now search out recordings of *The Andy Griffith Show* and *Leave It to Beaver* to share with their children.

In print media, *Playboy* magazine, which sometimes gets the credit for changing America's acceptance of sexual content, now has to rely on marketing its insignia in foreign countries for its profits because its "genteel" photos cannot compete with what is available online or in pornographic films sold for private viewing. One of the reasons that some parents react negatively to teachers or librarians providing *graphic novels* is that they associate the term— maybe just subconsciously—with the old definition of *graphic* as a shortened form of *pornographic,* rather than with the idea of graphic novels being filled with *graphs* or drawings, as in comic books.

In addition, some critics have suggested that parents who know they have little to say about the films their children see, the television they watch, the magazines they read, the songs they listen to, the online sources they look at, and the text messages they receive and send feel encouraged by the idea that they can at least take control over what books their children read in schools. They have the feeling suggested by the line from the old revival song that advised our grandparents to "brighten the corner where you are!"

Other critics subscribe to the idea that hard times encourage censorship. They point to the last seventy years and the major censorship battles that raged over *The Grapes of Wrath* during the Cold War, *The Catcher in the Rye* when Senator Joseph McCarthy was on his rampage, *To Kill a Mockingbird* when we were challenged by segregation and integration, *Go Ask Alice* and *Born on the Fourth of July* during the Vietnam War, and the Harry Potter books during the Iraq War and amid fears of terrorism.

Thirteen Assumptions and Observations about Censorship and Censors

Given the censorship attacks of the last thirty-plus years, we can safely make the following assumptions about censorship.

1. Any work is potentially censorable by someone, someplace, sometime, for some reason. Nothing is permanently safe from censorship.

2. The newer the work, and the more popular it is, the more likely it is to come under attack.

3. Censorship is capricious and arbitrary. Two teachers bearing much the same reputation, credentials, and years of experience and using the same work will not necessarily be equally free from attack (or equally likely to be attacked).

4. Censorship spreads a ripple of fear. The closer the censorship, the greater likelihood of its effect on other teachers.

5. Censorship does not come only from people outside the school. Administrators, other teachers or librarians, or members of the school board may initiate an incident.

6. Censorship is, for too many educators, like cancer or a highway accident. It happens only to other people. Most incidents happen to people who were sure "it couldn't happen to me." It did and it will.

7. Schools without clearly established, school board-approved policies and procedures for handling censorship are accidents waiting to happen. Every school should develop a policy and a procedure that helps both educators and objectors when an incident arises.

8. If one book is removed from a classroom or library, no book is safe any longer. If a censor succeeds in getting one book out, every other person in the community who objects to another book should, in courtesy, be granted the same privilege.

9. Educators and parents should, ideally, coexist to help each other for the good of the young, but the clash of parents with some educators appears to be sadly inevitable. Some people would prefer to see young adults *educated,* which means allowing them to think and wonder about ideas and to consider the consequences of those ideas. Others would prefer to see young people *indoctrinated* into certain community or family values, beliefs, or traditions and to eschew anything controversial. With so little in common between these two philosophies of schooling, disagreement is not only natural but certain.

10. Censors, who try desperately to keep young people pure and innocent, often expose young people to the very things they are protesting. Several years ago in the Phoenix area, a group violently objected to a scholarly dictionary that contained some "offensive" words. As part of making their case to the public, they compiled a list of their "best" examples, which they duplicated and distributed widely, including to students at the school where the dictionary was in use.

11. Censors often have a simplistic belief that there is an easily established and absolute relationship between books and deeds. A bad book, however defined, produces bad actions. What one reads, one immediately imitates.

12. Censors alternately love and hate English teachers and librarians. Censors would appear to hate what educators use, but censors would also appear to approve of great literature, particularly the classics. However, most censors are essentially nonreaders and they know little about

literature except that it must be uplifting, noble, and fine. They assume that classics have no objectionable words, actions, or ideas. So much for *Crime and Punishment, Oedipus Rex, Hamlet, Madame Bovary, Anna Karenina,* and most other classics.

13. Finally, censors use language carelessly or sloppily. Sometimes they cannot possibly mean what they say. The administrator who said, "We don't wish to have any controversial books in the bookstore or the library," must not have understood what the word *controversial* meant. Three adjectives often pop up in the censor's description of objectionable words: *filthy, obscene,* and *vulgar,* along with such intensifiers as *unbelievably, unquestionably,* and *hopelessly.* Such oxymoronic expressions as *pure garbage, pure evil,* and *unquestionable filth* also appear.

Some Important Concepts

Because librarians and teachers are working with limited funds and limited time, they naturally have to make decisions about what books they will purchase and offer to the public. This brings up what is usually referred to as *selection vs. censorship.* When we insist to a protester that "*We select,* but *you censor,*" parents suspect that we are playing word games. A classic distinction between the two ideas was drawn by Lester Asheim when he wrote "Not Censorship but Selection" in the *Wilson Library Bulletin* 28 (September 1953, p. 67). He stated that "Selection begins with a presumption in favor of liberty of thought; censorship with a presumption in favor of thought control." The selector takes a positive approach to a book and seeks out its values in the book as a whole. The censor approaches the matter from the opposite direction, looking specifically for "vulnerable characteristics wherever they can be found." While selection seeks to "promote the rights of the reader to read," censorship seeks to protect the readers from the "fancied effects" of what they are reading. "The selector has faith in the intelligence of the reader, the censor has faith only in his own." This is a point also made by Laurie Halse Anderson, the 2009 winner of the Margaret A. Edwards Award. See her write-up on page 402.

Censorship, in its broadest sense, refers to all of the concepts being described in this chapter. What they have in common is the goal of suppressing intellectual freedom. But in its narrower sense, *censorship* refers to a book being removed from a school library or classroom, or to part of someone's work being changed or removed. A paragraph or just a few words might be taken out of a speech, a book, a song, a performance, or an article. When Maurice Sendak's 1970 *In the Night Kitchen* was given a Caldecott Honor Award, it instantly became controversial because Sendak included frontal nudity when he pictured a little boy in his dream sliding out of his pajamas and down from his bedroom into the night kitchen where three bakers—all resembling Oliver Hardy—are busy mixing the batter for the morning cake. Some school librarians, who did not want to deal with the controversy, took black felt-tip pens and painted little swimming trunks on the boy. Others just refused to stock the book. As a result, as late as the year 2000, the book was in twenty-fifth place on the American Library Association

Margaret A. Edwards Award

Winner (2009)

Laurie Halse Anderson, A Storyteller and Champion for Free Speech

On the inside of her right wrist, Laurie Halse Anderson has a small, black tattoo. It reads *Hwæt,* the first word in *Beowulf,* the Old English story which was told orally for centuries before it was written down. *Hwæt* was the symbolic way for storytellers to let people know they were launching into a story, but rather than translating it to something like, "Once upon a time . . . ," more fitting translations might be "What's Up!" "Harken!" or "Hear this!" Anderson smilingly explains that she chose to have the word tattooed on her wrist as a reminder of all the work she put in as a linguistics major, but really it is because she likes having a constant reminder that she is a storyteller.

When ALA awarded Anderson the Margaret A. Edwards honor, the committee praised her ability to stretch across time periods and genres, as shown by her 2003 *Catalyst,* a contemporary story about a smart girl who is the daughter of a minister (something true of Anderson) whose life is suddenly turned upside down; her 1999 *Speak,* about a girl traumatized by being raped at a party; and her 2002 *Fever 1793,* which she prefers to call a *historical thriller* rather than *historical fiction.* For more information about Anderson and the amazing number of well-received books she has written, go to her beautifully prepared website http://madwomanintheforest.com.

Since she writes so eloquently in defense of the work of storytellers, we asked her if, as part of this page, we could reprint the statement that she allowed us to use in the eighth edition. She wrote it as an add-on to her 1999 *Speak,* which, as soon as it was published, received numerous challenges from people who did not like to think about the emotional pain that teenagers sometimes suffer. Despite—or maybe because of—its popularity, *Speak* continues to be a challenged book and came in as #60 on the "Top 100 Banned/Challenged Books: 2000–2009" distributed by the American Library Association. Here is what she wrote:

These are scary days in which to raise teenagers. I know. I have four of them. Part of the problem is that we have a generation that has been exposed to unprecedented amounts of sexual behavior in the media and on the Internet. They see it. They talk about it. Their hormones react, and a lot of kids wind up in painful situations.

Literature is the safe and traditional vehicle through which we learn about the world and pass on values from one generation to the next. Books save lives. Contemporary young adult literature surprises some people, because it is an accurate reflection of the way today's teenagers talk, think, and behave. But these books must be honest in order to connect to the teen reader. America's teens are desperate for responsible, trustworthy adults to create situations in which they can discuss the issues that are of the highest concern for them. Reading and discussing books is one of the most effective ways to get teens to think through and learn about the challenges of adolescence.

Most of the censorship I see is fear driven. I respect that the world is a very scary place. It is a terrifying place in which to raise children, and in particular, teenagers. It is human nature to nurture and protect children as they grow into adulthood. But censoring books that deal with difficult adolescent issues does not protect anybody. Quite the opposite. It leaves kids in darkness and makes them vulnerable.

Censorship is the child of fear and the father of ignorance. Our children cannot afford to have the truth of the world withheld from them. They need us to be brave enough to give them great books so they can learn how to grow up into the men and women we want them to be. ●

list of banned books between 1990 and 2000. Once people start looking at a particular piece through the lens of censorship, they often come up with additional reasons that a piece should be censored. For example, the harshest critics of *In the Night Kitchen* ascribed "hidden" or subconscious sexuality to the story because of the phallic shape of the milk bottle as well as the creamy, white milk being stirred into the dough.

Other examples of censorship include the way that some popular songs are re-recorded with the objectionable words being softened or garbled so that the recordings can be sold in big-box, family type stores. Another example is the recent release of an edition of Mark Twain's *Huckleberry Finn* minus the N-word.

Making a complaint is the first, and sometimes the last, action that occurs in a censorship case. This simply means that an interested individual (or perhaps a representative of a group) approaches a librarian, a bookstore owner, or a teacher and asks that a particular book not be offered to young people for reading. Sometimes in school situations, parents will explain that they do not want their child to be required to read a chosen book and so they are asking that a substitute book be made available to their own child. For a teacher who is well prepared with book rationales and who has a strong background knowledge of YA books, this could be a fairly simple matter, even though it takes strength of character for a teacher not to have negative feelings toward the child whose parents have come in wanting to upset a beautifully prepared lesson plan or thematic unit. Teachers need to have empathy for parents who come in because it often takes real courage for parents to come to school and talk to a teacher. However, we would advise giving a little more "negative face" to the complainant if he or she is not a parent of one of your students, but is instead a representative from a group that has decided to launch multiple attacks on a particular book by starting in lots of different schools.

Filing a formal complaint goes a step further. This is when a parent—or other interested individual—has not been satisfied with a visit to the teacher or librarian and so fills out the school's complaint form asking for a public hearing about having the book removed from the school. Complaint forms should be easily accessible and freely distributed. Most such forms ask for a signature documenting that the complainant has read the whole book and has visited with the teacher or librarian. A complaint form should never be used as a stalling technique, and because it asks for two fairly onerous tasks (a visit to the teacher or librarian, and complete reading of the book) everything else about it—the typeface, the kind of paper, the tone of the writing, the procedures that are described—should communicate respect and encouragement.

Holding a public hearing is the next step in the process as described on the complaint form. Such meetings should be announced and open to the public. The people making the complaint are usually given first place on the program, with opponents being given second place. To avoid mass shouting matches, who gets to speak is usually well controlled and decided on ahead of time. We have been to some meetings where speakers had to apply online for a speaking position, or be at the meeting to sign up at least forty-five minutes before the opening. We have also been to meetings where the audience had to sit quietly watching the entire school board meeting because the hearing was written in as the last item on the agenda. Most times there is a time limit for each speaker, but in one district a scheduled complainant could keep talking as long as he or she was on the subject of the book. As soon as the statement wandered off into politics or personal anecdotes, for example, the recorder would ring a bell and the speaker had to yield the floor to the next speaker.

Sadly, the few public hearings that we have attended have been uncomfortable not only for whoever was managing the meeting, but also for those in the audience, especially the ones who came with prepared statements. In one case, the school board had quite clearly already made its decision. This offended the majority of the audience who had come expecting to be heard. At another hearing, the complainant had said he was bringing a whole church congregation, but then he showed up all by himself. The librarian defending the book had arranged for several prominent townspeople to speak for the value of keeping the book in the library. When these speakers were welcomed almost as lifelong friends of various members of the school board, the man obviously felt betrayed. As he left the room following the announcement from the board that, in its secret ballot, it had voted unanimously to allow the book to stay in the high school library, it was clear that the man was unlikely to ever be a friend to the local school system or a supporter of his son's leisure-time reading.

Banning a book is the end result that most complainants are looking for. They want the book totally removed from the classrooms or the library. It is no longer fashionable to gather a crowd to a celebration bonfire, although in the spring of 2011 a minister from Florida did exactly that when he burned a copy of the *Koran*. He clearly admitted that he was looking for publicity, as are most people who want to ban a book, especially if they are using their censorship efforts as a way of soliciting political compatriots. "Banned in Boston" used to be almost a badge of honor for films or stage plays that had been forbidden by police officers in charge of protecting the public from obscenity. The U.S. Postal Service also has the right to refuse what it considers obscene mail. When someone sues in court and wins a legal decision against a book, the banning applies only to the area under the jurisdiction of the court, which is why the most far reaching decisions are the ones coming from the United States Supreme Court. When the American Library Association celebrates Banned Book Week (the last week in September), they are actually celebrating "banned and challenged" books, because many more books are challenged than are banned. And although teachers and librarians are asked to report challenges to particular books (this is how the ALA derives its annual lists) the suspicion is that for every report ALA receives three or four challenges go unreported. So many librarians have been stung by negative news stories and photos that they hesitate to attract unnecessary attention to challenges that have been quietly and respectfully settled.

Taking your case to court is the ultimate step in a complaint. As you will see from reading the final section of this chapter, the circumstances of court cases vary widely and final outcomes are unpredictable. Going to court is costly, and unless a case has a chance of setting a precedent, many attorneys discourage their clients from suing. Teachers probably do not need much convincing to go through a district-designed procedure rather than a court case because they have been trained not to antagonize their superiors and not to challenge community values. But if a teacher is being sued, for all practical purposes he or she has no choice but to get a lawyer.

Most censorship episodes are solved outside of legal hearings and court decisions. When teachers or librarians come under attack, unofficial rumor-mongering charges are lodged against them because someone objects and labels the offending work *obscene, filthy,* or *pornographic.* The case is heard in the court of public opinion, sometimes before the school board, with few legal niceties prevailing. The censors (and too often the school board) almost never operate under any definition of obscenity that a court would recognize, but their interpretations of the issues are operationally effective for their purposes. The book may not always be judged as a whole book (although individual parts may be juicily analyzed), and the entire procedure may be arbitrary and capricious. The decision, once announced, rapidly disposes of the offending book and frequently the teacher or librarian to boot, a variation of old-fashioned Western justice at work. To keep this from happening to you, see Focus Box 12.1, "Books to Help Adults Deal with Censorship Problems."

What and Why Do the Censors Censor?

Although a few textbooks, as well as dictionaries and informative nonfiction, have been attacked in recent years, the overwhelming majority of the books that get censored are novels, probably because these are the books that speak directly to people's deepest feelings. Also, it is more common for a novel than an information book to reach huge audiences. Censors usually do not

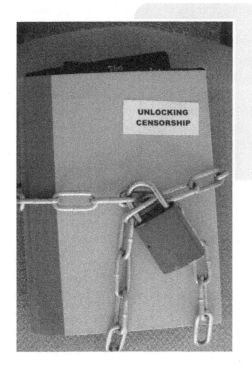

The more you know about censorship, the better prepared you will be to ameliorate the damaging effects that nearly always come to a school or a library when censors arrive. The books in Focus Box 12.1, "Books to Help Adults Deal with Censorship Problems," can be a big help.

Censored Books: Critical Viewpoints, **edited by Nicholas J. Karolides, Lee Burress, and John M. Kean. Scarecrow, 1993.** Among the fifty-six rationales for both YA and adult books are ones for *Annie on My Mind, Brave New World, The Chocolate War, The Crucible, Forever, If Beale Street Could Talk, The Outsiders,* and *Then Again, Maybe I Won't.*

Censored Books II: Critical Viewpoints, 1985–2000, **edited by Nicholas Karolides. Scarecrow, 2002.** Defenses are written for sixty-four popular books including *The Bluest Eyes, Bridge to Terabithia, A Day No Pigs Would Die, Fade, Fallen Angels, The Giver, I Am the Cheese, Killing Mr. Griffin, The Last Mission,* and *Tiger Eyes.*

Censoring Culture: Contemporary Threats to Free Expression, **edited by Robert Atkins and Svetlana Mintcheva. New Press, 2006.** The essays here make a persuasive case that censorship affects everyone.

First Freedoms: A Documentary History of the First Amendment Rights in America **by Charles C. Haynes, Sam Chaltain, and Susan M. Glisson. Oxford University Press, 2006.** One of the truths emerging from *First Freedoms* is that, while the concept of "free speech" sounds like a clearly defined privilege, it is not as easy to figure out as we might expect.

The Fourth R: Conflicts over Religion in America's Public Schools **by Joan DelFattore. Yale University Press, 2004.** DelFattore is the same author who in 1999 wrote the influential *What Johnny Shouldn't Read.*

Freedom for the Thought That We Hate: A Biography of the First Amendment **by Anthony Lewis. Basic Books, 2008.** It wasn't until 1919 that the Supreme Court recognized freedom of speech, and even since then the idea has had a vexed history. Lewis, a long-time columnist and one-time Supreme Court reporter for the *New York Times,* has written a spritely and interesting history of the past 200 years of arguments over the First Amendment.

The Language Police: How Pressure Groups Restrict What Students Learn **by Diane Ravitch. Knopf, 2003.** New York University professor Diane Ravitch's book is a detailed commentary and analysis of a new kind of censorship, in which textbook publishers, school boards, and bias and sensitivity committees go through texts to weed out anything that might somehow or somewhere offend or disturb. She says that if we want to stop censorship, we must recognize that this new kind of censorship "represents a systemic breakdown of our ability to educate the next generation and to transmit to them a full and open range of ideas about important issues in the world."

The Nine: Inside the Secret World of the Supreme Court **by Jeffrey Toobin. Doubleday, 2007.** Reading this book will help put the Supreme Court's work with censorship in perspective with the other kinds of decisions it makes.

Rationales for Teaching Young Adult Literature, **edited by Louann Reid with Jamie Hayes Neufeld. Heinemann, 1999.** Reid's rationales for over twenty books include a short introduction to the book (several of which could work as booktalks), the intended audience, the relationship of the book to the school program, the impact of the material on readers, potential problems and ways to address them, references, alternative and related works, other pieces cited, and a brief note about the author. A concluding chapter, "Afterword: Listening to the Readers," makes the whole effort of teaching seem worthwhile. An updated edition was published in 2009.

What Johnny Shouldn't Read: Textbook Censorship in America **by Joan DelFattore. Yale University Press, 1992.** DelFattore's bottom line of "Don't let Uncle Sam or the local school board raise your child" may have contributed to the rise of home schooling in America.

NOTE: Also see the June 2011 issue of ***VOYA (Voice of Youth Advocates)* magazine,** which has censorship and intellectual freedom as its focus topic.

bother with obscure books. In the fifth century BCE, in Book II of *The Republic,* Plato argued that banishing poets and dramatists was essential for the moral good of the young. His reasoning was that writers often told lies about the gods or made the gods appear responsible for the evils and misfortunes of mortals. Plato's argument that fiction could be emotionally disturbing to the young is still heard today, although not as forcefully as it was in the early 1800s when *The New England Quarterly Magazine 1* (April–May–June 1802) carried an article entitled "Novel Reading: A Cause of Female Depravity." After lamenting women's immodesty and lack of chastity, the author went on to assign the blame by writing:

> Those who first made *novel-reading* an indispensable branch in forming the minds of young women have a great deal to answer for. Without this poison instilled as it were, into the blood, females in ordinary life, would never have been so much the slave of vice.

Notice how this old attitude of needing to protect the young is reflected in the following list of the twenty-five books that the American Library Association reports as having been the most often challenged between 2000 and 2009. For the complete list of one hundred, as well as lists from previous decades, go to the American Library Association's website. Also, notice how many of the books are read mostly by females. American society has always allowed (or even encouraged) more freedom in the reading choices of boys than of girls.

American Library Association's List of Twenty-five Most Challenged Books 2000 to 2009

1. *Harry Potter* (series) by J. K. Rowling
2. *Alice* (series) by Phyllis Reynolds Naylor
3. *The Chocolate War* by Robert Cormier
4. *And Tango Makes Three* by Justin Richardson and Peter Parnell
5. *Of Mice and Men* by John Steinbeck
6. *I Know Why the Caged Bird Sings* by Maya Angelou
7. *Scary Stories* (series) by Alvin Schwartz
8. *His Dark Materials* (series) by Philip Pullman
9. *ttyl; ttfn; l8r g8r* (series) by Lauren Myracle
10. *The Perks of Being a Wallflower* by Stephen Chbosky
11. *Fallen Angels* by Walter Dean Myers
12. *It's Perfectly Normal* by Robie Harris
13. *Captain Underpants* (series) by Dav Pilkey
14. *The Adventures of Huckleberry Finn* by Mark Twain
15. *The Bluest Eye* by Toni Morrison
16. *Forever* by Judy Blume
17. *The Color Purple* by Alice Walker
18. *Go Ask Alice* by Anonymous
19. *Catcher in the Rye* by J. D. Salinger
20. *King and King* by Linda de Haan
21. *To Kill A Mockingbird* by Harper Lee
22. *Gossip Girl* (series) by Cecily von Ziegesar

23. *The Giver* by Lois Lowry
24. *In the Night Kitchen* by Maurice Sendak
25. *Killing Mr. Griffin* by Lois Duncan

It is almost impossible to give specific reasons for *why* particular books are so often censored because sometimes even the censors do not know why they have strongly negative feelings toward one book but strongly positive feelings toward another. In any case, here is a list of "Seven Deadly Sins" likely to bring the wrath of censors down on the heads of authors. We are not providing this list as advice for authors to avoid these ideas or concepts when they write a book. If anything, we are saying that it is the bravery to deal with unsettled issues that makes young adult literature a valuable part of the intellectual life of today's teenagers.

1. Judging by the books that gather complaints, censors are often racists, although they try to hide their feelings behind comments about "questionable" or "unrecognized" authors and "incorrect" language.

2. Many censors are homophobic, which they also try to hide behind comments about "appropriate" role models and the need to preserve the "innocence" of young readers.

3. The "rewriting" of history (i.e., presenting events from the viewpoint of the "little people" in big events) is problematic. Such books offend those people who prefer to think that America is a divinely blessed country and that none of our "founding fathers" ever strayed from being honest and noble.

4. People's attitudes and expectations about sexual matters are so individualized that authors have a good chance of offending parents no matter what viewpoint they take. Many parents do not want school books to encourage their children to think about sex because they hope to postpone sexual thoughts until the children are old enough to make wise decisions.

5. Some censors hate books about immigrant experiences because they think they are "too sad," "too harsh" or "too critical" of American policies. They drag kids into political questions that should be left to adults.

6. Fantasy frightens parents, both because of the "big" possibilities of new worlds, but also because of the "little" coincidences. For example, in the Harry Potter books the proscription against calling Lord Voldemort by his real name may be too close for comfort to Christians who follow the commandment "Thou shalt not use the name of the Lord, thy God in vain!" One of our students came to class and reported that her uncle had just died and she had been assigned to write the obituary. The only phrase that the older relatives specifically requested was that he "was a life-long member of the . . . Church." She blushed when she said it made her feel like she was being asked to distinguish between the "pure" Harry Potter and "the Half-blood Prince."

7. No one enjoys having ideas they hold dear (including their own body images and characteristics) written about in a negative light or made fun of. Comedy author Max Shulman once told us that he tries to "come close, but not too close" to his readers. If he makes fun of someone in a way that makes a reader say, "Aha, I know someone like that!" the reader is happy. But if he is so on-the-spot with his description that the reader thinks, "Oh, no! That's me!" the reader is unhappy. Although he was talking about humor, the same process works for serious fiction and is probably at the root of many more censorship cases than we recognize.

Three Kinds of Censors

Censors generally fall into three kinds of pressure groups: (1) those from the right: the conservatives; (2) those from the left: the liberals; and (3) those who are not so easily identified because they are an amorphous band of educators, publishers, editors, and distributors who we might assume would be opposed to censorship. Look at the sampling of retyped headlines from fairly recent news stories in the earlier photo and, at the risk of overgeneralizing, see if you can guess where the kind of censorship being alluded to originated. As we write about the three types of implied censorship, we will point to the most obvious "sponsor," but as with many cases taken from real life rather than written as a "textbook case," some of the cases are more complex than can be communicated in just a headline. The first two groups operate from different guiding principles, but it is sometimes easy for educators to be confused about whether an attack stems from the right or the left because the coercive methods, the censorial rhetoric, and the messianic fervor seem so similar. The third group is less easily recognized because it does not get in the news as much. Its censorship is often unrecognized because it is unorganized and functions through a personal, ad hoc, case-by-case approach. Nevertheless, censors from this group are more likely than not to feel sympathetic to conservative cases for censorship.

Group One: Censors from "The Right"

The headline regarding *And Tango Makes Three* by Justin Richardson and Peter Parnell (Simon & Schuster, 2005), which received the most challenges of any book in 2010, provides a prime example of the censoring efforts of right-wing conservative groups. This book is the true story of two male penguins in New York's Central Park Zoo who fall in love and take turns sitting on an abandoned egg until it hatches. People protesting the book say that it is putting a stamp of approval on homosexuality and alternate lifestyles. They are especially incensed that the book is for young children.

When the Puerto Rican school chief banned five popular books from high schools, his explanations sounded very similar to those given by U.S. conservative critics. The fact that English professor Alan Gribben has rewritten Mark Twain's *Huckleberry Finn* and throughout the book replaced the N-word with the word *slave* (published by New South Books, 2011) relates to the fact that, over the past several decades, the teaching of this book has been heavily protested, mostly from The Right. However, Professor Gribben says that he is actually coming from The Left because he loves the book and is simply trying to find a way that it can be taught in high schools. At the time that Gribben embarked on his project, *Huckleberry Finn* ranked fourteenth for challenges between 2000 and 2009, and most of these challenges have come from conservative groups. These groups, which continue to *worry* (in the sense of alarm and *harass*) educators, have folksy or clever names such as SOS (Save Our Schools), PARENTS (People of America Responding to Educational Needs of Today's Society), CURE (Citizens United for Responsible Education), and LOVE (Let Our Values Emerge). With few exceptions, the groups seem united in wishing to protect young people from insidious forces that threaten the schools. They want to remove any vestiges of sex education and secular humanism from classes or libraries, to put God back into public schools, and to restore traditional values to education. Few openly announce that they favor censorship of books or teaching materials.

The big news in the story of Mark Zuckerberg, Facebook CEO, was that he wore a suit, instead of his usual sandals and jeans, when he went to battle against censorship of social networking at the G8 Summit being held on May 25, 2011, at the Elysée Palace in France. World leaders were putting their heads together to see if they could better understand the role of social networking in encouraging various uprisings throughout the Middle East in the spring of 2011. The incident also shows the important role being played by young people in a world that is increasingly "flat."

Group Two: Censors from "The Left"

The headlines probably inspired by censors from The Left include the happy headline "Bully for 'Wonder Woman' Lynda Carter," who is fighting against the kind of disrespect often shown to gays. The headline about a gay rights group backing a navy inquiry of an anti-gay film made by the captain of a ship to entertain his sailors has similar reasoning behind it. When complaints about the navy incident first surfaced in the early spring of 2011, one of the late night comedians made his own joke by saying he thought the captain should be punished for "impersonating a comedian." He was implying that rather than being humorous, the amateurly made film was simply hostile to gay people.

Attempts to keep cursing out of the workplace doesn't sound like a kind of censorship coming from The Left, but certainly The Left has been concerned about promoting the idea that people should not have to work in a hostile environment. The headline about the Fifth U.S. Circuit Court reversing a ban on praying at a San Antonio high school 2011 graduation ceremony is coming from both The Right and The Left. An agnostic family (from The Left) had gotten the ban put in place on the grounds that, because of church and state separation, invocations were unconstitutional at public events. The Medina Valley Independent School District filed an emergency appeal, which was granted.

In a June 2, 2002, article in the *New York Times*, N. R. Kleinfield wrote about a new kind of censorship coming from The Left. It was entitled, "The Elderly

Man and the Sea? Test Sanitizes Literary Texts." He told how Jeanne Heifetz was skimming through familiar quotations on the New York State Regents Examination in English and discovered that words were missing. She checked and found several quotations that were cut or rewritten. For example, a quotation from a speech by the United Nations Secretary General was given thus:

> Polls show strong American support for the organization at the grass-roots level.

However, the original quotation was this:

> Polls show strong American support for the organization at the grass-roots level regardless of what is said and done on Capitol Hill.

Surely a major change in meaning took place between quotation one and quotation two. Another alteration in the speech by the United Nations Secretary General occurred when he praised "the fine California wine and seafood." This was altered so that he was praising only "the fine California seafood." When questioned, the director of the testing program explained that they were following her department's "sensitivity" guidelines.

Group Three: Censors from Unexpected Sources

People in this third group mostly come from within the schools: teachers, librarians, or school officials who either censor materials themselves or support others who do. They work behind the scenes, perhaps because they fear being noticed and like to stay anonymous. Or they may regard themselves as highly moral and opposed to whatever they label immoral in literature, and so they feel they are doing their jobs to step in and "make things right." They may think that by striking preemptively, they are avoiding censorship problems.

Many members of the Texas State Board of Education, who every ten years review and revise what will be allowed to be taught in Texas public schools, probably do not think of themselves as censors, but rather as leaders. However, the rest of the country waits with bated breath for the results because they fear that as Texas goes, so goes the nation. Textbook publishers have argued that this is an urban myth, but nevertheless because Texas, with its restrictive lists of approved textbooks, is such a huge part of the school market, U.S. educators are fearful.

For the 2001 edition of this textbook, M. E. Kerr provided a good example of how this third group of censors works. In the early 1990s, prior to the publication of her critically acclaimed *Deliver Us from Evie,* she came out publicly as a lesbian. At about the same time, publishers, as part of a marketing technique to take advantage of the large number of libraries in middle schools, began labeling YA literature as "age ten-and-up" or "Junior High-up." This meant that Kerr was often invited to speak to children in sixth, seventh, and eighth grades. In these situations, it was common for teachers to let her know they did not want to talk about her gay novels. One principal met her in the parking lot and said, "We like your books a lot, Ms. Kerr, but these children are too young for

Night Kites, Deliver Us from Evie or *Hello, I Lied.*" Her response to this kind of censorship is:

Of course kids know about gays: any kid who watches TV does. There are gay characters in sitcoms now, on soaps, on talk shows and featured in movies and made-for TV dramas. Gay performers are on MTV, and there are gay rock stars, singers, and composers. The failure to mention us to children, and to discuss books about us, puts us in a special category. Kids know we're there, but they sense that somehow we're reprehensible. Educators are not protecting the child with this blackout, they are protecting the prejudice.

Another example of behind-the-scenes censors comes from the first year that Alleen Nilsen was teaching in a library science program. Her job started in August, and in September she boldly put up a big window display of banned books. A senior professor called her in and confided that whenever she hears about a banned book she tucks the information away in her mind "and never mentions it to anyone."

This was in 1975, and it was Alleen's first clue that she was going to need to work hard in her new job. Her second clue came a few months later when she was teaching an evening, in-service class to librarians. One of the books the class wanted to read and talk about was Judy Blume's *Are You There, God? It's Me, Margaret* (first published in 1970). One librarian proudly raised her hand and explained that before she let any girls check out the book, she asked them whether or not they had started menstruating. Another one explained that she never let boys check out the book because the girls told her they didn't want boys reading it. Alleen was disappointed that not one of the students in the class recognized their fellow librarians' actions as a kind of censorship that at the least needed to be recognized and talked about.

What to Do before the Censor Arrives

The following are steps you can take to ensure you are prepared for a censorship challenge.

1. Be up-to-date about what books are coming under attack, especially in your own neighborhood. This means keeping up with local news and with what recent court decisions have said about books, as well as reading the *Newsletter on Intellectual Freedom, School Library Journal, English Journal,* and *Voice of Youth Advocates.* Also seek out and subscribe to the websites and news blogs related to these journals. Of course, this is a lot of work, but it is better than facing a censor while totally ignorant of the world of censorship.

2. As mentioned earlier, any teacher who assigns long works (other than text-books) for common reading needs to have given considerable thought to the reason that this particular book is being taught. Even if the book is a district requirement, teachers should go through the process of writing their own rationales in the style of informal essays, not as answers to test

questions. A good rationale tells why the teacher is using this book at this time, what specific goals the teacher has, how the book will meet these goals, and what problems of style, tone, theme, or subject matter exist. Answering such questions makes teachers take a fresh look at a book and think more carefully about the possibilities and problems inherent in teaching it. See Focus Box 12.1, "Books to Help Adults Deal with Censorship Problems," for professional books to help you write rationales. A good idea is to prepare a folder for each book you will be teaching. This folder should contain your rationale, photocopied reviews from respected sources, and ideally samples of work from previous students showing how the book has helped you meet the goals you had in mind when you first chose the book.

3. Most important, make sure that your institution—whether you are a volunteer librarian for one small charter school or one of 450 Language Arts teachers in a big city school district—has developed procedures for handling censorship, should it occur. The National Council of Teachers of English monographs (available online), *The Students' Right to Read* and *The Students Right to Know,* will be helpful, as will the American Library Association's *Intellectual Freedom Manual,* revised for its eighth edition in 2010. Whether adopted from any of these sources or created afresh, the procedure should include a form to be completed by anyone who objects to any teaching material or library book and a clearly defined way in which the matter will be handled after completion of the form. (Will it go to a committee? How many are on the committee? Are people outside the school on the committee? How many teachers? How many administrators?) The procedural rules must apply to everyone (no exceptions should be allowed whether the complainant is the local drunk or the State Superintendent of Schools). Most importantly, the procedures must be approved by the school board. If the board does not approve the document it has no legal standing. If the school board is not periodically reminded of the procedures—say, every couple of years—it may forget its obligation. Given the fact that many school boards change membership slightly each year and may change their entire composition within five or six years, teachers and librarians should take it upon themselves to remind the board. Otherwise, an entirely new board may wonder why it should support something it neither created nor particularly approves of. In the same way that it is important for the school board to have reminders about the policy, it is probably better if you enlist help from fellow educators and administrators to draft the form so that when a complainant arrives at the door of anyone in your school, you will be consistent in the way you politely ask the complainant to fill out the form and then schedule a follow-up meeting. Too many teachers have been negatively impacted when a principal knocks on a classroom door bringing in a parent who is smiling happily because the principal has already assured her that, of course, you will remove the offending book.

4. Woo the public to gain support for intellectual and academic freedom. Invite parents to become "Friends of the Library" or include them in interesting extracurricular activities. Parent-and-kid reading clubs are time consuming, but worthwhile. We have known a couple of divorced dads who felt belonging to this kind of a club was a wonderful way to stay connected to their child. All

communities have readers and former teachers interested in students' freedom to read. Finding them ahead of time is part of the teachers' and librarian's jobs. Waiting until censorship strikes is probably going to be too late.

5. Don't forget to talk about intellectual freedom and censorship with your own students. See Focus Box 12.2, "Censorship and Free Speech in Books for Young Readers." You can also watch for short stories and for real stories from the news that will make for interesting class discussions. Since young people are so often actors in censorship stories, they are interested in such news events. But a word of caution might be in order. We had a case against *Huckleberry Finn* here in Tempe that went all the way up to the Ninth Circuit Court. It was heartbreaking to see the effect that all the publicity had on the child whose mother brought the case.

6. College students in young adult literature classes might benefit from role playing a public hearing. After you have chosen a book from those listed on pages 405–406 or one that has aroused contradictory feelings in your class (the Twilight books have done this in our classes) then let small groups of students sign up for whatever role they want to play. For example, (1) prepare a complaint form for your imagined employer, (2) draw up the procedures to be followed, (3) be the complainant or a supporter of the complainant, (4) play the role of the defendant or a supporter of the defendant, (5) play a member of the school board or be the person conducting the meeting. Other people in the class can choose the role they want to play from nametags like those shown in the photo below. Everyone else in the class can write a supportive letter either for or against the book that is being questioned. The letter should be written to whoever

To get some variety while role-playing, either for a formal hearing or at an informal discussion at a school board, we found that it helps to have participants choose to play a particular role, even if it leads to stereotyping. Here are the name tags we used in one of our classes, but there are many different ways to assign roles. You might get ideas for your role by reading one or more of the books listed in Focus Box 12.2, "Censorship and Free Speech in Books for Young Readers," on page 416.

is going to make the final decision in the case, most likely the president of the school board. Of course, such a staged event will lack the adrenalin and many of the facts that go along with such real-life events, but having participated in this exercise might make participants feel more comfortable should they find themselves as part of a genuine hearing.

What to Do after the Censor Arrives

If you do face a censorship challenge, you can try some of the following steps.

1. **Refuse to panic,** which is easier said than done because censors always have the advantage of being able to determine the time and place for the attack. No matter how well prepared the teacher or the librarian, only the censor can say when.

2. **Do not be too surprised or appalled** if you discover that not all your fellow teachers or librarians will rush in with immediate support. Also, no matter how surprised you are by the complaint, be sure to treat the complainant with dignity and dispatch. As soon as the panicky *fight or flight* feeling has passed, settle down and listen . . . , listen . . . , listen. Sometimes this is all that is needed to open communication links. But realize that even if the complainant comes to see why the offending work was assigned, he or she may still ask that you find a substitute book. We advise complying with this kind of a request, but not just giving up on the matter. The following example shows the wrong approach. The father of a couple of girls in our neighborhood went to their teacher and asked that they not have to read *Catcher in the Rye,* because he remembered reading all the "dirty" pages when he was in high school. He told Alleen that the teacher responded to his request by sending his daughters to the library for the next two weeks where they could read *War and Peace.* The next time Alleen saw the girls she asked them, "How'd it go?" They said that the first day they glanced at the book and found it so "uninteresting" that they put their copies back on the shelf and "played on the computer" for the next nine days. Then on the last day they skimmed through the Cliff's Notes version of *War and Peace,* just in case the teacher asked them about it—which she never did.

 At least this was a better outcome than if their father and the teacher had gotten into a lockdown battle over whether the class as a whole should have been reading *Catcher in the Rye,* but it is nonetheless too bad that the girls totally missed out on talking about a good book with fellow readers. Obviously the father shouldn't have waited until the very day the class was to start on *Catcher in the Rye* to go and make his request, and years ago, when he was in high school, he should have read the whole book instead of just the pages other students had identified as "dirty." It is also easy to criticize the teacher's actions, but the fact that she was teaching four different classes each day with something like 120 students makes her action—or lack of action—at least understandable.

Censorship and Free Speech in Books for Young Readers

The Book Thief by Markus Zusak. © 2005 in Australia, first U.S. Printing Knopf, 2007. Death is the unusual narrator of this amazing story from World War II, which earned prizes and accolades from virtually all YA review sources. It is all about words and what they do for—and against—people. The insights into Nazi propaganda are closely related to the topic of this chapter.

Fahrenheit 451 by Ray Bradbury. Ballantine, 1953. Although Bradbury's classic story of book burning was published as an adult novel, it is now read by more teenagers than adults. When Alleen Nilsen and Ken Donelson were editing *The English Journal* in the 1980s, a high school teacher wrote in to say that his students had paperback "school editions" and when he took a turn reading aloud, they asked him why he "was putting in all those swear words"? They had no swear words in their books. He immediately stopped reading and turned the day's lesson into one on *irony*. Here they were reading a book against censorship . . . which had been censored. Professional groups have since spoken out against such practices and said that, at the least, *expurgated* versions must be so identified on the covers and in sales material. Some authors are so offended by the practice that they do not trust publishers to pull excerpts from their books to be included in either fiction or nonfiction anthologies.

The Harry Potter Series by J. K. Rowling. Scholastic, 1997–2007. Several incidents in the Harry Potter books bring attention to censorship and free speech issues. Why does everyone, except Harry, refer to Lord Voldemort as "He Who Must Not Be Named" or "You Know Who"? Why are there so many secrets? And who are they to be kept secrets from? Is Rita Skeeter an ethical reporter when she literally "bugs" people's conversations? Just what is Filch's *Secrecy Sensor,* and why does he have it? One of Hermione's quotes that was printed on the American Library Association's 2005 Banned Books Week Poster comes from *Harry Potter and the Order of the Phoenix* when Hermione tells Harry that if the new headmistress "could have done one thing to make absolutely sure that every single person in this school will read your interview, it was banning it."

The Higher Power of Lucky by Susan Patron. Atheneum, 2006. As soon as Patron's book was announced as the winner of the 2007 Newbery Medal, it landed in big-time censorship problems because the word *scrotum* appears on page 1. Even though *Higher Power* is a children's book, it is strong enough to hold the attention of teens, perhaps as a read-aloud, where it can serve as the foundation for a discussion on censorship. Was it really the word *scrotum* that got the book into so much trouble, or was it that parents were uncomfortable having their children learn about Alcoholics Anonymous and a whole lot of people whose lives had hit "rock-bottom"?

The Hunger Games trilogy by Suzanne Collins. Scholastic, 2008. Author Suzanne Collins says she got her idea for *The Hunger Games* while channel-surfing at a point where the lines between a reality show competition and coverage of the Iraq War "began to blur in this very unsettling way." The popular trilogy is set in a post-apocalyptic world called Panem, where North America once stood. The books' connection to this chapter is

3. **Call for help**—it is only as far away as your computer. Look on the Internet for the National Coalition Against Censorship or email with specific questions, ncac.org. Visit the websites of the American Library Association and the National Council of Teachers of English. Look first at their home pages because you are likely to find several smaller websites that can provide specific kinds of help. For example, NCTE has a specific anticensorship page, plus information about SLATE (Support for the Learning and Teaching of English) and a list of teachers who are willing to serve as consultants. It also has a Standing Committee on Censorship and "Guideline on the Students' Right to Read," which can be downloaded at no cost.

When you go into the American Library Association website, be sure to see the pages on Banned Books Week, which ALA sponsors along how skillfully and cold-heartedly the Capitol (the main province where all decisions are made) created the spectacle of the Hunger Games in which "chosen" children fight to the death. The Capitol uses the televised spectacle to manipulate and control the emotions of the people who live in the outer provinces, which exist as specialized plantations to provide luxuries for the Capitol.

***Lemony Snicket: The Unauthorized Autobiography.* HarperCollins, 2002.** As part of the madcap adventures in these books for middle school readers, three pages are devoted to a letter from Vice Principal Nero thanking Mr. and Mrs. Spats for sending him the article from *The Daily Punctilio,* which explained "the danger of allowing young people to read certain books." He fired Mrs. K., thus saving the children from reading such books as *Ramona Quimby, Age 8; Matilda;* and *Ivan Lachrymose: Lake Explorer.*

***Madapple* by Christina Meldrum. Knopf, 2008.** Although Meldrum's sophisticated book is a combination murder mystery and contemporary *bildungsroman,* it has all the trappings of an ancient fantasy. While there are many reasons for reading the book—or listening to the well-done recording—the part that relates to censorship is how the mother chooses to raise her daughter, Aslang, in total isolation and ignorance of today's world. The mother was only fifteen when she came to the United States from Denmark not knowing that she was pregnant. At first, the young mother is with her sister, but then they quarrel and the mother takes her two-year-old to the backwoods of Maine where she raises her to know all kinds of ancient languages and religions, but only the minimum required by the home schooling official about today's world. When Aslang is seventeen, her mother dies and the girl finds herself in a very foreign world.

***Matched* by Ally Condie. Dutton Books, 2010.** Condie's book owes a lot to *The Giver,* but hers is written more for a teen audience and it is basically a love story. It opens with Cassia, who is about to turn eighteen, and is getting ready for the traditional "matching" (engagement) ceremony. She lives in a futuristic world where everyone trusts the "Society" to make all the decisions. She eagerly watches her cell phone to see who she will be matched with. For just a few seconds there is a picture of Xander, the new "dangerous" boy who has come to town, but then it is immediately replaced by the picture of Ky Markham, the neighbor boy from the best of families, who she always expected to be with. The interesting part related to freedom and censorship is the way that modern technology is "pasted on" to an old culture. The picture of Xander that Cassia saw was not just an accidental glitch. It is part of an experiment so the Society can learn more about how people "naturally" develop love attachments.

***The Sledding Hill* by Chris Crutcher. HarperCollins/ Greenwillow, 2005.** Crutcher puts himself and a pretend novel entitled *Warren Peece* in this postmodern attack on censors. Rather than sounding angry and resentful, Crutcher turns the story into a playful fantasy about fourteen-year-old Eddie Proffit, whose best friend was killed in an accident but nevertheless decides to hang around and watch out for Eddie.

***The Year They Burned the Books* by Nancy Garden. Farrar, Straus and Giroux, 1999.** Jamie is editor of the school newspaper and a supporter of sex education in schools. Her editorial touches some raw nerves and the fight is on.

with help from the American Booksellers Association, American Booksellers Foundation for Free Expression, American Society of Journalists and Authors, Association of American Publishers, and the National Association of College Stores. It is also endorsed by the Center for the Book in the Library of Congress. If you wish to get further information, you can contact ALA's *Office for Intellectual Freedom* at 1-800-545-2433 ext. 4220.

4. **If you are heading into a formal hearing,** look to see if the author has a website and a "contact me" button. Many authors, and/or their publishers, are willing to step in and lend a hand to a teacher who is well prepared and brave enough to defend a book in a school hearing or a court case.

A Historical Sampling of Censorship Attitudes and Events in the United States

In response to suggestions from earlier users of this textbook, we are condensing the historical part of this chapter. However, further information on these events can be found in the sources listed at the end of this chapter or through an Internet search engine.

1872: Reformer Anthony Comstock founded the Society for the Suppression of Vice in New York. The next year he went to Washington, DC to urge passage of a federal statute against obscenity, abortion, and contraceptive devices. He got himself appointed as a Special Agent of the Postmaster General, and by 1914 had caused the arraignment of 3,697 people for allegedly sending "obscene" material through the mail. Through the 2,740 convictions that he brought about, he raised $237,123.30 in fines, which helped somewhat to pay for the prison sentences totaling over 565 years. When Comstock visited boys in jail and asked what had led them into the world of crime, they told him exactly what he wanted to hear (as they knew full well), that dime novels and drinking and shooting pool were sources of all their present misery.

1877: In the March issue of the *American Library Journal* (p. 278), William Kite, librarian at the Friend Free Library in Germantown, Pennsylvania, worried about the influence of novels. He wrote about a young woman of fine education who for several years had been an inmate of a mental institution all because she "gratified a vitiated taste for novel-reading till her reason was overthrown." He said he could provide many more examples and then asked, "Have we the moral right to expose the young to such cancer?"

1896: While Mark Twain was coming under widespread attack for his less-than-genteel characters, Stephen Crane's *The Red Badge of Courage* was being heavily criticized for its profanity. The December issue of *Library Journal* (p. 144) told how at the annual meeting of the American Library Association, the book was deemed unfit to go "into the hands of a boy." Gen. McClurg, of Chicago, and Col. Nourse, of Massachusetts, were quoted as saying the book was "not true to the life of a soldier," and that "no such profanity" was common.

1897: Under the title "Objectionable Reading for Children," James Buckham wrote in *The Teachers Institute* (November, p. 89), "Let teachers strictly forbid the bringing of any literature, which is merely for entertainment, into the schoolroom. . . . Many a wild escapade has been hatched from a blood-and-thunder story-book under a boy's desk-lid. Many a feverish thought and impulse has come to the romantic school girl from the pages of a light novel which she conceals beneath her textbook."

1913: The first U.S. court decision announcing a definition of, and a test for, obscenity used an 1868 English case, *The Queen v. Hicklin,* as its precedent. The judge in this case had devised a definition which existed in British law for nearly a century and in American law until the 1930s. In this 1913 *United States v. Kennerly* case, Judge Learned Hand ruled against a defendant because his publication clearly fell under the limits of the Hicklin test, but he added a comment about "mid-Victorian morals" as conveyed by the words *obscene, lewd,* or *lascivious,* and questioned whether "in the end men will regard that as obscene which is honestly relevant to the adequate expression of innocent ideas, and whether they will not believe that truth and beauty are too precious to society at large to be mutilated in the interest of those most like to pervert them to base uses."

1933: Judge John M. Woolsey of the Federal District Court for Southern New York did much to overturn the Hicklin test when he found that James Joyce's *Ulysses* was "sincere and honest" and "not dirt for dirt's sake." He ruled that in matters determining what is obscene, the work *must* be judged as a whole, not on the basis of its parts. The next year, Judge Learned Hand of the Federal Circuit Court of Appeals upheld Woolsey's reasoning, and the phrase about a work being "judged as a whole" became an important part of many cases that have followed.

1957: In *Butler v. Michigan,* Butler challenged a Michigan statute that tested *obscenity* in terms of its effect on young people. Butler argued that it was wrong to restrict adult reading to that fit only for children. Justice Felix Frankfurter agreed and declared the law unconstitutional. He wrote that to quarantine the general reading public against books fit for children was "to burn the house to roast the pig."

1957: In *Roth v. United States,* the U.S. Supreme Court announced that obscenity "utterly without redeeming social importance" was not protected by the First Amendment. This was the beginning of several years of arguments questioning the meaning of "redeeming social values," "the average person," and "prurient," as defined by Webster as "arousing an immoderate or unwholesome interest or desire."

1964: In *Jacobellis v. Ohio, contemporary community* was defined as "national rather than local," but a strong minority dissent argued that the very meaning of *community* "meant local."

1968: In *Memoirs v. Attorney General of Massachusetts,* three things were declared necessary for *prurience:* (1) The dominant theme appeals to prurient interest in sex, (2) the material is offensive to community standards, and (3) there is no redeeming social value.

1968: The *Ginsberg v. New York* decision introduced the concept of "variable obscenity" and stated that "the well-being of its children is of course a subject within the State's constitutional power to regulate." It also stated that while studies have not proven that obscenity is "a basic factor in impairing the ethical and moral development of . . . youth," neither have they disproved that a "causal link exists."

1969: The U.S. Supreme Court ruled in *Tinker v. the Des Moines (Iowa) School District (393 U.S. 503)* that neither teachers nor students lose their First Amendment rights "at the schoolhouse gate."

Fortunately, in schools and communities, it is not just English teachers and librarians who are interested in censorship issues. Here our colleague at ASU, Regents Professor Elly Van Gelderen, poses with some of her anti-censorship T-shirts, distributed by the National Coalition against Censorship. She regularly wears them when she teaches her linguistics classes.

1971: In *Presidents Council, District 25 v. Community School Board No. 25,* a New York City School Board voted 5–3 to remove all copies of Piri Thomas's *Down These Mean Streets* from junior high libraries because of its offensive nature and language. When parents sued, the U.S. Court of Appeals Second Circuit held for the school board, but explained that their decision was not based on the dubious literary or educational merit of the book, but on the fact that the state had given the right of selecting school materials to local school boards and so the state had no right to arbitrarily interfere.

1978: The *Presidents Council* decision was cited for several years as the definitive decision, but because it was not a Supreme Court decision it served as precedent only for judges so inclined. In *Right to Read Defense Committee of Chelsea (Massachusetts) v. School Committee of the City of Chelsea* in the U.S. District Court for Massachusetts, a different ruling prevailed when the chairman of the school board decided to remove a paperback anthology, *Male and Female under Eighteen,* which contained a student-written poem with "street language." The final ruling was that because the high school librarian had purchased *Male and Female* for the high school library, it had a kind of "tenure." The judge wrote:

If this work may be removed by a committee hostile to its language and themes, then the precedent is set for removal of any other work. The prospect of successive school committees "sanitizing" the school library of views divergent from its own is alarming whether they do it book by book or one page at a time. What is at stake here is the right to read and be exposed to controversial thoughts and language—a valuable right subject to First Amendment protections.

1979: Three members of the Island Trees (New York) School Board attended a 1975 fall conference sponsored by the conservative Parents of New York—United (PONY-U) where they were given lists of books deemed "objectionable," including the following which they later found in their district libraries: Bernard Malamud's *The Fixer,* Kurt Vonnegut's *Slaughterhouse-Five,* Desmond Morris's *The Naked Ape,* Piri Thomas's *Down These Mean Streets,* a collection of short stories by Negro writers, Oliver LaFarge's *Laughing Boy,* Richard Wright's *Black Boy,* Alice Childress's *A Hero Ain't Nothin' but a Sandwich,* Eldridge Cleaver's *Soul on Ice,* and the anonymous *Go Ask Alice.* In February of 1976, the board gave "unofficial direction" that the books be removed from the libraries and delivered to the board for their reading. They issued a press release attempting to justify their actions, calling the books "anti-American, anti-Christian, anti-Semitic, and just plain filthy." They appointed a review committee, but then went against the committee's recommendations. The conflict was taken to the U.S. District Court in 1979 by Stephen Pico, a student, who along with others brought suit against the school board claiming that their rights under the First Amendment had been denied. The District Court did not agree that students' rights had been taken away, but then the case went on to the U.S. Court of Appeals for the Second Circuit, and finally, through an indirect route, to the Supreme Court. This was the first time that a school-related case had been heard at this level. The Court was careful to communicate that it was not making a judgment about the literature, but about the way that the school board overstepped its boundaries. They judged the school board's actions to have been "narrowly partisan" and "political."

> If petitioners *intended* by their removal decision to deny respondents access to ideas with which petitioners disagree, and if, this intent was the decisive factor in petitioners' decision, then petitioners have exercised their discretion in violation of the Constitution.

1984: While librarians appreciated being supported by the Supreme Court, teachers were not so sure that their rights were equally supported. In *Mozert v. Hawkins County (Tennessee) Public Schools,* parents asked for the removal of three books in the Holt, Rinehart and Winston reading series from the sixth-, seventh-, and eighth-grade programs because they thought the books were teaching secular humanism, Satanism, feminism, evolution, telepathy, internationalism, and other anti-religious beliefs. The parents formed Citizens Organized for Better Schools and ultimately sued the school board. However, U.S. District Judge Thomas Hull dismissed the lawsuit, but on appeal before the Sixth Circuit of the Court of Appeals, a panel of three judges remanded the case back to Judge Hull. Judge Hull ruled in favor of

Quotes I Most Want on a T-Shirt, a Button, or a Bumper Sticker—Chosen by YA Lit Students at Arizona State University

1. "You don't have to burn books to destroy a culture, just get people to stop reading them."
   —**Ray Bradbury**

2. "Everything I know, I learned from reading banned books."
   —**Unknown Source**

3. "If we don't believe in freedom of expression for people we despise, we don't believe in it at all."
   —**Noam Chomsky**

4. "They that can give up essential liberty to obtain a little temporary safety deserve neither liberty nor safety."
   —**Benjamin Franklin**

5. "Censorship, like charity, should begin at home, but unlike charity, it should end there."
   —**Claire Boothe Luce**

6. "I have met thousands of children now, and not even one time has a child come up to me and said, 'Ms. Rowling, I'm so glad I've read those books because now I want to be a witch.'"
   —**J. K. Rowling**

7. "It takes a village to raise a child, but it takes only one complaint to raze a curriculum."
   —**Louanne Reid**

8. "Books and ideas are the most effective weapons against intolerance and ignorance."
   —**Lyndon Johnson**

9. "A censor is a man who knows more than he thinks you ought to."
   —**Granville Hicks**

10. "All the secrets of the world are contained in books. Read at your own risk."
    —**Lemony Snicket**

the complainants, but the U.S. Sixth Circuit Court of Appeals overturned Hull's decision, and the U.S. Supreme Court refused to hear an appeal.

1986: On July 7, 1986, the U.S. Supreme Court announced its decision in *Bethel School District v. Fraser*, upholding school officials in Spanaway, Washington, who had suspended a student for using sexual metaphors in describing the political potency of a candidate for student government.

1988: In *Hazelwood v. Kuhlmeier*, the U.S. Supreme Court ruled that when a school newspaper bears a school's imprimatur and is organized as a teaching tool, as in a journalism class, then the school has a legitimate pedagogical concern in regulating the paper's content. Independent student newspapers, established either by policy or practice as forums for student expression, have a higher level of First Amendment protection.

2003: In *Counts v. Cedarville* in Arkansas, a hearing was held on the Harry Potter series after a parent filed a request. At the hearing, the decision was made to keep the books in the library with no restrictions. However, the school board told the librarian to put them on a restricted shelf. When parents objected that this was a way of denying access, they went to court and the judge agreed.

2007: A Supreme Court decision *(Morse v. Frederick)* began with student Joseph Frederick and his friends unfurling a fourteen-foot-long banner emblazoned with "Bong Hits 4 Jesus" when the students were released from school to celebrate the Olympic torch being carried through Juneau on its way to the 2002 Winter Games in Salt Lake City. Principal Deborah Morse demanded that Frederick take down the banner. He refused, and she ordered him to her office and gave him a ten-day suspension. The resulting lawsuit took five years to make its way through the Supreme Court, with the result being that school officials may reasonably punish speech that "promotes illegal drug use." The Court refrained from going further to say that schools could punish students for speaking out on political or social issues.

2011: The annual young adult book festival in Humble, Texas, was cancelled in the spring of 2011 because Ellen Hopkins, the popular author of the Crank series, which includes *Crank, Glass,* and *Fallout,* was "disinvited" to participate after some parents complained about the subject matter of her hard-hitting series. Rather than just sulking away, she contacted another of the planned speakers, Pete Hautman, who had also experienced being "disinvited" to a speaking engagement because a few parents read his books—or more likely read about protests against his books online—and raised objections. Hautman withdrew his acceptance, and the other authors (Matt de la Peña, Melissa de la Cruz, Brian Meehl, and Tera Lynn Childs) also withdrew in a show of support. Cancellation of the event brought lots of publicity and letters of support for the authors. Among those lending support were the National Coalition against Censorship, the Society of Children's Book Writers and Illustrators, and the National Council of Teachers of English. Local school librarian Camille Powell was quoted in *Time* magazine as explaining, "When middle school parents challenge books, it's often a last gasp to stay involved. Elementary schools are fairly responsive to parental input. However, the junior high transition years are frustrating and difficult for parents as their control over their child and the school gradually erodes."

2011: In June the Supreme Court, by a 7–2 vote, upheld a Federal Appeals Court decision to throw out a California law banning the sale or rental of violent video games to minors. Justice Antonin Scalia wrote that "No doubt a state possesses legitimate power to protect children from harm, but that does not include a free-floating power to restrict the ideas to which children may be exposed." He then went on to cite the kind of violence found in the old "children's stories" about Hansel and Gretel, Cinderella, and Snow White.

2012 and Beyond: At the risk of looking foolish a few years from now, we will go out on a limb and close this chapter with six predictions of what we think will be happening over the next few years in relation to teenagers and questions about censorship, freedom of speech, and ownership of intellectual property.

1. As with the cancelled book festival in Texas and with the rearranged appearance of the rapper Common (both in the spring of 2011), censors are probably going to look toward efficiency and simply label all the books or songs of a particular author or performer as "unacceptable." One reason is that few censors enjoy reading and so it is unlikely that they will discover on their own a book they would want to censor. Instead, they will hear about a book that "needs censoring" from friends or members of a group they belong to. Even with present guidelines on complaint forms, it is hard to get censors to read the entire book that they want to censor. They are not lazy people, but they honestly believe that books can be dangerous to one's mind and so rather than running the risk of "contaminating" themselves by reading multiple books by a "questionable" author, they will want to simplify the matter by just censoring the author as a person, rather than censoring his or her books one-by-one.

2. As state budgets are slashed, the power of teacher and government employee unions is being threatened. This gives rise to worries about teachers and librarians being more likely to cave in to the requests of potential censors because they fear that, without the support of their unions, they may jeopardize their employment if they attract attention to themselves.

3. Lawsuits will continue to increase, but they will focus more on student expressions, as with the case of the Alaskan boy displaying what he called a "meaningless" banner "just to get on TV." We predict more problems of this kind because public schools and colleges are scrambling to "outlaw," or at least discourage, speech that can be interpreted as bullying, hostile, or threatening. Considering the creativity of thousands upon thousands of high school students and of the disparate thinking of thousands of educations, there will, of course, be unanticipated consequences that will need to be thought through.

4. Dress codes will continue to be a bone of contention. Are the T-shirt messages we are recommending on page 420 going to be allowed? What about gang colors (i.e., should the "innocent" student who just happens to wear a certain color combination be treated the same as gang members who have planned to "send a message" by dressing in their colors on a particular day)? What about rings, pins, and sticker messages? There will undoubtedly be problems as educators try to apply overarching "guidelines" to millions of individual cases.

5. Many more cases are going to involve the Internet and what role schools will play. A survey of freshmen at our college showed that what they most want from their technology classes is guidance in building a moral code, or a code of responsibility, as they work online. Some of their biggest questions relate to the ownership of intellectual property and to the complications of engaging in social networking and the sending or receiving of sex-related messages or photos.

6. Questions about free speech and the control of information will remain a hot topic in YA literature, but it will be treated in more creative ways. In the eighth edition of this textbook, we recommended several books where the plot centered around the traditional banning of a book and the fallout on various individuals. Of course, we still have some good books like that, but now we are seeing ideas about censorship and mind control coming into many more books, not as the main focus, but as important contributing

factors. We also see questions about mind control being explored in fantasy, where authors have more freedom to inspire original thinking about the matter, as seen in several of the books in Focus Box 12.2, "Censorship and Free Speech in Books for Young Readers," on page 416.

Concluding Comments

We believe that the school—classroom or library—must be a center of intellectual ferment in the community. This implies not that schools should be radical, but that they should be one place where freedom to think and inquire is discussed, and their consequences thought through. We believe librarians and English teachers must protect these freedoms, not merely in the abstract but in the practical, day-by-day world of the school and library.

A Starter Bibliography on Censorship

Some General Books on Censorship

Bald, Margaret and Ken Wachsberger. *Banned Books: Literature Suppressed on Religious Grounds*. Facts on File, 2006.

Blanshard, Paul. *The Right to Read: The Battle against Censorship*. Beacon, 1955.

Foerstel, Herbert N. *Banned in the U.S.A.: A Reference Guide to Book Censorship in Schools and Public Libraries*. Greenwood, 2002.

Green, Jonathon. *The Encyclopedia of Censorship*. Facts on File, 2005.

Heins, Marjorie. *Sex, Sin, and Blasphemy: A Guide to America's Censorship Wars*. Norton, 1993.

Hentoff, Nat. *Free Speech for Me—But Not for Thee: How the American Left and Right Relentlessly Censor Each Other*. Harper, 1992.

Hentoff, Nat. *The War on the Bill of Rights: And the Gathering Resistance*. Seven Stories, 2003.

Huff, Mickey and Project Censored, Eds. *Censored 2012: Sourcebook for the Media Revolution*. Seven Stories Press, 2011.

Hull, Mary. *Censorship in America: A Reference Handbook*. ABC-CLIO, 1999.

Jones, Derek. *Censorship: A World Encyclopedia*. London: Fitzroy Dearborn Publishers, 2001 (4 Volumes).

Karolides, Nicholas J. *Banned Books: Literature Suppressed on Political Grounds*. Facts on File, 2006.

Karolides, Nicholas J. *Censored Books II: Critical Viewpoints 1985-2000*. Scarecrow Press, 2002.

Karolides, Nicholas J., Margaret Bald, and Dawn B. Sova, eds. *120 Banned Books: Censorship Histories of World Literature*. Checkmark, 2005.

Levine, Judith. *Harmful to Minors: The Perils of Protecting Children from Sex*. University of Minnesota, 2002.

Mill, John Stuart. *On Liberty*. 1859. With John Milton's *Areopagitica*, two of the basic sources in facing censorship.

Milton, John. *Areopagitica*. 1644. The title comes from the Areopagus hills near the Acropolis in Athens where the Upper Council met.

Nakaya, Andrea, ed. *Censorship* (in the Opposing Viewpoints series). Greenhaven, 2005.

Oboler, Eli M., ed. *Censorship and Education*. Wilson, 1981.

Peck, Robert S. *Libraries, the First Amendment and Cyberspace: What You Need to Know*. American Library Association, 2000.

Shinder, Jason, ed. *The Poem That Changed America: "How" Fifty Years Later*. Farrar, Straus and Giroux, 2006.

Sova, Daw B. *Banned Books: Literature Suppressed on Sexual Grounds*; *Banned Books: Literature Suppressed on Social Grounds*; *Banned Plays: Censorship Histories of 125 Stage Dramas*. Facts on File, 2006, and 2004.

The History of Censorship

Boyer, Paul S. *Purity in Print: The Vice-Society Movement and Book Censorship in America*. Scribner, 1978.

Comstock, Anthony. *Frauds Exposed, or How the People Are Deceived and Robbed, and Youth Corrupted*. J. Howard Brown, 1880.

Comstock, Anthony. *Morals versus Art*. Ogilvie, 1888.

Eldridge, Larry D. *A Distant Heritage: The Growth of Free Speech in Early America*. New York University Press, 1993.

Haight, Anne Lyon and Chandler B. Grannis. *Banned Books 387 B. C. to 1978 A. D.* R. R. Bowker, 1978.

Hunt, Pamela. *In Cold Fear: The Catcher in the Rye Censorship Controversies and Postwar American Character*. Ohio State University Press, 2000.

Ingelhart, Louise Edward. *Press and Speech Freedom in the World: from Antiquity until 1998*. Greenwood, 1998.

Knuth, Rebecca. *Libricide: The Regime-Sponsored Destruction of Books and Libraries in the Twentieth Century*. Praeger, 2003.

Neier, Aryeh. *Taking Liberties: Four Decades in the Struggle for Rights*. Public Affairs, 2003.

Perrin, Noel. *Dr. Bowdler's Legacy: A History of Expurgated Books in England and America*. Atheneum, 1959. Brilliant, as is anything by Perrin.

Plato. *The Republic*, especially Book 2.

Stone, Geoffrey R. *Perilous Times: Free Speech in Wartime, from the Sedition Act of 1798 to the War on Terrorism*. Norton, 2004.

Taylor, Jon Tinnon. *Early Opposition to the English Novel: The Popular Reaction from 1760 to 1830*. King's Crown, 1943.

Zeisler, William, ed. *Censorship: 500 Years of Conflict*. Oxford University Press, 1984.

Censorship and the Courts

Abrams, Floyd. *Speaking Freely: Trials of the First Amendment*. Viking, 2005.

Books on Trial: A Survey of Recent Cases; A Report from the Clearinghouse School Book-Banning Litigation, rev. ed.

Bosmajian, Haig A., ed. *The First Amendment in the Classroom*, 5 Volumes. Neal-Schuman.
  Vol. 1. *The Freedom to Read*, 1987.
  Vol. 2. *Freedom of Religion*, 1987.
  Vol. 3. *Freedom of Expression*, 1988.
  Vol. 4. *Academic Freedom*, 1989.
  Vol. 5. *The Freedom to Publish*, 1989.

De Grazia, Edward. *Censorship Landmarks*. Bowker, 1969.

Lewis, Anthony. *Freedom for the Thought You Hate: A Biography of the First Amendment*. Basic Books, 2008.

Lewis, Felice Flanery. *Literature, Obscenity and Law*. Southern Illinois University Press, 1976.

Moffett, James. *Storm in the Mountains: A Case Study of Censorship, Conflict, and Consciousness*. Southern Illinois University Press, 1988.

Rembar, Charles. *The End of Obscenity: The Trials of Lady Chatterley, Tropic of Cancer, and Fanny Hill*. Random House, 1968.

Censorship and Libraries

Bielefield, Arlene. *Library Patrons and the Law*. Neal-Schuman, 1995.

Carrier, Esther Jane. *Fiction in Public Libraries: 1900–1956*. Libraries Unlimited, 1985.

Curry, Ann. *The Limits of Tolerance: Censorship and Intellectual Freedom in Public Libraries*. Scarecrow, 1997.

Geller, Evelyn. *Forbidden Books in American Public Libraries, 1876–1939: A Study in Cultural Change*. Greenwood, 1984.

Jones, Barbara M. *Libraries, Access, and Intellectual Freedom Developing Policies for Public and Academic Libraries*. ALA, 1999.

Knuth, Rebecca. *Libricide: The Regime-Sponsored Destruction of Books and Libraries in the Twentieth Century*. Praeger, 2003.

Kravitz, Nancy. *Censorship and the School Library Media Center*. Libraries Unlimited, 2002.

Peck, Robert S. *Libraries, the First Amendment, and Cyberspace: What You Need to Know*. ALA, 2000.

Robbins, Louise S. *Censorship and the American Library: The American Library Association's Response to Threats to Intellectual Freedom, 1939–1969*. Greenwood, 1996.

Robbins, Louise S. *The Dismissal of Miss Ruth Brown: Civil Rights, Censorship, and the American Library*. University of Oklahoma Press, 2000.

Wiegand, Wayne A., ed. "The Library Bill of Rights," the entire Summer 1996 Issue of *Library Trends*.

Censorship and Schools

Adams, Helen R., foreword by Dianne McCaffee. *Ensuring Intellectual Freedom and Access to Information in the School Media Program*. Hopkins Libraries Unlimited, 2008.

Association for Library Service to Children. *Intellectual Freedom for Children: The Censor Is Coming*. American Library Association, 2000.

Brinkley, Ellen Henson. *Caught Off Guard: Teachers Rethinking Censorship and Controversy*. Allyn and Bacon, 1999.

Brown, Jean E., ed. *Preserving Intellectual Freedom: Fighting Censorship in Our Schools*. NCTE, 1994.

Burress, Lee. *Battle of the Books: Literary Censorship in the Public Schools, 1950–1985*. Scarecrow, 1989.

Davis, James E., ed. *Dealing with Censorship*. NCTE, 1979.

Edwards, June. *Opposing Censorship in the Public Schools: Religion, Morality, and Literature*. Erlbaum, 1998.

Homstad, Wayne. *Anatomy of a Book Controversy*. Phi Delta Kappa Educational Foundation, 1995.

Jenkins, Edward B. *Censors in the Classroom: The Mind Benders*. Southern Illinois University Press, 1979.

Moffett, James. *Storm in the Mountains: A Case Study of Censorship, Conflict, and Consciousness*. Southern Illinois University Press, 1988.

O'Neil, Robert M. *Classrooms in the Crossfire: The Rights and Interests of Studenns, Parents, Teachers, Administrators, Librarians, and the Community*. Indiana University Press, 1981.

Pipkin, Gloria. *At the Schoolhouse Gate: Lessons in Intellectual Freedom*. Heinemann, 2002.

Reichman, Henry. *Censorship and Selection: Issues and Answers for Schools*. American Library Association, 2001.

Scales, Pat. *Teaching Banned Books: 12 Guides for Young Readers*. ALA, 2001.

Scales, Pat. *Protecting Intellectual Freedom in Your School Library: Scenarios from the Front Lines*. American Library Association, 2009.

Simmons, John S., ed. *Censorship: A Threat to Reading, Learning, and Thinking*. IRA, 1994.

Steinle, Pamela Hunt. *In Cold Fear: The Catcher in the Rye Censorship Controversies and Postwar American Character*. Ohio State University Press, 2000.

Glossary of Literary Terms Illustrated by YA Literature

Allegory: An extended metaphor or comparison in which characters, events, or objects are equated with meaning outside of the story. Allegorical stories can be enjoyed on a surface level as well as on a second or deeper level. For example, William Golding's *Lord of the Flies* is on the surface an adventure story, while on the allegorical level it is a warning against lawlessness and how easy it is for people to be corrupted by power.

Allusion: A figure of speech that refers to something likely to be familiar to readers because of their knowledge of history, literature, or popular culture. Allusions are efficient communication because good readers can turn a single reference into an extended idea. For example, Robert Cormier's title *I Am the Cheese* might remind a reader of the old nursery song and game, "The Farmer in the Dell." This alludes to the family's newly given surname of *Farmer* and to the closing lines of the song: "The cheese stands alone" and "The rat takes the cheese."

Antagonist: The character (or sometimes event) that opposes the protagonist.

Archetypes: Images, patterns, or symbols that are part of the collective unconscious. Archetypal images are stronger and more durable than stereotypes. The Innocent setting out on a journey is an especially common archetype in YA literature, and so are generational conflicts in which young people struggle to gain their independence from adults.

Backdrop setting: A context of time and place that is like a stage setting in that it does not play an essential or unique part in the plot. The most common backdrop setting is that of a high school because school is the everyday business of teenagers. The fact that there are only so many ways to describe stairways, restrooms, lockers, cafeterias, classrooms, and parking lots gave a sameness to books for this age group, which may have contributed to the new popularity of fantasy.

Benign humor: Harmless or playful humor that is nonthreatening. Examples include most of the humor in Daniel Handler's *Lemony Snicket* novels and the wordplay in Lewis Carroll's *Alice in Wonderland* and *Through the Looking Glass.*

Bildungsroman: Literally a story (a romance) about the building or growing of someone's character. In some ways, most young adult literature fits into this category because it has something to do with a child moving toward adulthood, even though in very small steps. "Classic" YA examples include Judy Blume's *Are You There, God? It's Me, Margaret,* Robert Cormier's *The Chocolate War,* and S. E. Hinton's *The Outsiders.*

Characterization: Whatever an author does to help readers know and identify with the characters in a story. Common techniques include providing physical descriptions, letting readers know what the characters say and what others say to and about them, showing the characters in action, showing how others relate to them, and revealing what they are thinking. See also **dynamic** and **static characters.**

Deconstruction: The idea that literature is constructed from words, which only approximately represent thoughts or actions. Once we realize this about a piece of literature, then we are able to undo the construct, that is, to examine and pull out different possible meanings. Deconstructing a piece of literature is taking it apart in different ways. Writers can also deconstruct events before they put them in their novels; for example, Virginia Euwer Wolff's *Bat 6* and Karen Hesse's *Witnesses* are told and retold by various characters who each have a unique point of view.

Dénouement: Literally, the untying of the knots at the end of a story. The purpose of the dénouement is to let the reader down after the excitement of the climax. Orson Scott Card softens the ending of *The Lost Boys: A Novel* by alluding to an afterlife when he writes that on the Christmas Eve when Stevie was abducted and murdered, they lost one other thing: their nicknames. No one made a conscious decision, it was just that they were part of a set, and it didn't seem right to use only some of them. "But someday they would use all those names when *Doorman* [Stevie] met them on the other side."

Dialect: Using characters' individual speech patterns to set them apart from mainstream speakers. A dialect might be illustrated through wording as when Hal Borland wrote in *When the Legends Die,* "The Ute people have lived many generations, many grandmothers, in that land," or it might be through "different" grammar and pronunciation as when such African American writers as Ntozake Shange, Maya Angelou, Virginia Hamilton, Toni Morrison, and Walter Dean Myers use black dialect for a variety of purposes, including the communication of pride in ethnic heritage. For the most part, difficulties in spelling and reading make authors rely sparingly on dialect.

Didacticism: Preachiness, as when an obvious moral or a lesson is tacked onto a story. Actually, most people who write for young readers want to teach lessons or impart some kind of wisdom or understanding. When something is described as didactic, it is being criticized for having a lesson so obvious that it detracts from the story.

Doppelgangers: Two characters who have so much in common that they blend together in readers' minds. Examples include Robert Louis Stevenson's *Dr. Jekyll and Mr. Hyde* and Lewis Carroll's *Tweedledum and Tweedledee*. In recent YA lit, the best example is the two leading characters in John Green and David Levithan's *Will Grayson, Will Grayson*.

Dynamic character: One who undergoes some change during the story. A dynamic character usually plays a major role in a story because an author needs considerable space in which to show how the character changes.

Escape literature: That which requires a minimum of intellectual energy so that readers can relax and enjoy the story with little or no intention of gaining insights or learning new information.

Euphemism: The use of circumlocution or an indirect kind of speech, usually to avoid giving offense. The word is cognate with *euphonious,* meaning "pleasing to the ear." Modern writers usually prefer direct speech, but Margaret Craven's title *I Heard the Owl Call My Name* is more intriguing than a bald statement such as "I knew I was going to die," while Hemingway's title *For Whom the Bell Tolls* is both more euphemistic and euphonious than "the one who has died."

Farce: On stage, a violent and physically shocking form of dramatic comedy. But at the same time it is dramatic and exaggerated, it does not offend because the violence is highly stylized and the actors are so skilled that they never really hurt each other. In literature, Eoin Colfer's *Artemis Fowl* books are a kind of farce because of the exaggerated characteristics of Colfer's Little People including Centaurs, Demons, Dwarves, Elves, Fairies, Gargoyles, Gnomes, Goblins, Gremlins, Imps, Krakens, Leprechauns, Pixies, Sprites, Trolls, and Warlocks.

Figurative language: Intentional use of language in such a way that additional meanings are given to what would be expected in standard usage. Metaphors, symbolism, and allusions are figures of speech based on semantics or meaning. Other figurative speech is based on such phonological aspects as alliteration (the repetition of consonants), assonance (the repetition of vowels), rhyme (the repeating of sounds), and rhythm and cadence (the patterning of sounds).

Foreshadowing: The dropping of hints to prepare readers for what is ahead. The purpose is not to give away the ending but to increase excitement and suspense and to keep readers from feeling manipulated. For example, readers would feel cheated if the problems in a realistic novel are suddenly solved by a group of aliens when there had been no foreshadowing that the story was science fiction.

Formula literature: That which is almost entirely predictable because it consists of variations on a limited number of plots and themes. To some extent, this description fits most literature; the difference is a matter of degree. Many of the situation comedies, crime shows, and adventure shows on television are formula pieces, as are many of the mysteries, romances, and even horror stories that young people—and adults—enjoy reading.

Gothic: A stark genre that uses the color symbolism of red (for blood) and black (for night) with much of the action taking place in haunted houses, underground caverns, or dark forests. The old castle that is home to the Hogwarts school in the Harry Potter books is a perfect Gothic setting, and in one of the Twilight movies, Bella has to travel to Europe to get a truly gothic setting.

In medias res: Latin for "in the midst of things." This device of bringing the reader directly into the middle of a story is usually followed by flashbacks to fill in the missing details.

Integral setting: The time and place that an author has created so that it will play an important part in the story. In protagonist-against-nature stories, historical fiction pieces, and regional stories, the settings are often integrated into the plots.

Intertextuality: A term created by Julia Kristeva, who pointed out that writers build their new texts on all that they have absorbed and transformed from their life's reading. When readers compare the similarities among the styles or the topics of various writers, they are doing intertextual analysis. Sharon Creech did intertextual writing in *Love That Dog* when she had her young protagonist become so enchanted with the poetry written by Walter Dean Myers that he began writing poetry himself.

Literature with a Capital L: That which has a degree of excellence not found in the mass of material that is printed every day. Such literature rewards study not only because of its content but also because of its style, universality, permanence, and the congeniality of the ideas expressed.

Magical realism: A kind of magic that happens without genies or good fairies to grant the protagonist's wishes. The magic is all the more startling because of the way it creeps up on the reader as part of what is being read as a realistic story. Francesca Lia Block is usually praised for the way she brings magical elements into her stories. However, some critics suggested it was too jarring when, in *Missing Angel Juan,* Witch Baby found herself in a diner filled with the kinds of humanoids usually reserved for science fiction.

Metaphor: Figurative language in which basically dissimilar things are likened to each other. A metaphor can consist of only a word or a phrase (a *head* of lettuce or the *outskirts* of a city), or it can be a series of interwoven ideas running through an entire book, as when Walter Dean Myers in *Fallen Angels* compares the Vietnam War to various aspects of movies or television.

Mode: A broad term describing the way authors treat their material as comedy, romance, irony, satire, and tragedy. Together these modes make up the story of everyone's life, and in literature as in life, they are interrelated, flowing one into the other.

Narrative hook: A device that authors use to entice readers into a story; for example, a catchy title as in Douglas Adams's *The Hitchhiker's Guide to the Galaxy,* a question as in Richard Peck's *Are You in the House Alone?,* or an intriguing first few sentences as in Paul Zindel's *The Pigman,* when John says, "Now Lorraine can blame all the other things on me, but she was the one who picked out the Pigman's phone number. If you ask me, I think he would have died anyway. Maybe we speeded things up a little, but you really can't say we murdered him. . . . Not murdered him."

Open endings: Those conclusions that leave readers not knowing what happens to the characters. Alice Childress in *A Hero Ain't Nothin' but a Sandwich* did not want to predict either that Benjie would become a confirmed drug addict or that he would go straight because she wanted readers to think about the fact that boys in his situation turn both ways. Books with open endings are good for group discussions because they inspire involved readers to consider the options.

Personification: The giving of human characteristics to something that is not human. For example, Maya Angelou in *All God's Children Need Traveling Shoes* writes, "July and August of 1962 stretched out like fat men yawning after a sumptuous dinner. They had every right to gloat, for they had eaten me up. Gobbled me down. Consumed my spirit, not in a wild rush, but slowly, with the obscene patience of certain victors."

Plot: The skeleton on which the other aspects of a story hang. Plots are made from the challenges, conflicts, and problems faced by the main characters. The most exciting plots are the ones in which the action is continually rising, building suspense, and finally leading to some sort of a climax. Episodic plots are accounts of a series of events as with such memoirs as James Herriot's *All Creatures Great and Small* and Anita Lobel's *No Pretty Pictures.*

Point of view: The vantage point and the distance from which the author decides to tell the story. The point of view that gives the author the most freedom is the one called omniscient or "all knowing," in which authors can plant themselves anywhere in the story, including inside characters' minds. With first-person point of view, the author speaks through the voice of a particular character. While this has the advantage of sounding authentic and personal, only one character's thoughts and observations can be given. Some authors get around this limitation by writing different chapters through the voices of different characters. Third-person point of view is more objective and is used for nonfiction as well as for many fictional stories. In YA books, the third-person narrator is often a character in the story who is writing about another "more interesting" or "more extreme" character.

Protagonists: The main characters in stories, the ones with which readers identify. Novels for young readers usually include only one or two protagonists because the stories are shorter and less complex than something like Leo Tolstoy's *War and Peace.* Protagonist-against-another is the kind of plot in which two people are in conflict with each other, as are Louise and Caroline in Katherine Paterson's *Jacob Have I Loved* and Rambo and the sheriff in David Morrell's *First Blood.* Protagonist-against-nature stories are often accounts of true adventures, such as Piers Paul Read's *Alive: The Story of the Andes Survivors*, Thor Heyerdahl's *The "RA" Expeditions,* and Steve Callahan's *Adrift: Seventy-Six Days Lost at Sea.* Protagonist-against-self is a common plot in young adult literature because so many stories recount rites of passage in which the protagonist comes to a new understanding or level of maturity. In Paula Fox's *One-Eyed Cat,* the conflict takes place inside the mind and heart of eleven-year-old Ned, who has to come to terms with the fact that when he tried out his new gun, he partially blinded his neighbor's cat. Protagonist-against-society stories often feature members of minority groups whose personal struggles relate to tensions between their ethnic groups and the larger society. Examples include Chaim Potok's *My Name Is Asher Lev* and *The Chosen,* Gary Soto's *Baseball in April* and *Jesse,* Louise Erdrich's *Love Medicine,* and Marie Lee's *Finding My Voice.*

Setting: The context of time and place. Setting is more important in some genres than in others. Fantasies are usually set in the far past or in some place where people have never been, while most science fiction stories are set in the future or in outer space. See also **Backdrop** and **Integral settings.**

Static character: One whose personality and actions stay basically the same throughout the story. Because in young adult literature the focus is on the young protagonist, most adult characters (parents, teachers, friends, etc.) are portrayed as static.

Stereotype: Literally, a printing process through which an image is created over and over again. When reviewers say that an author's characters are stereotypes, they are probably making a negative criticism. However, at least some characters must be stereotyped because stories would fall under their own weight if authors had to start from scratch in developing each character. For the sake of efficiency, many background characters are stereotypes. To solve the problem of always having the same people stereotyped, contemporary authors are making an effort to feature as main characters many of those who have previously been ignored or relegated to stereotypes.

Stock characters: Stereotyped characters that authors can use in the way that shoppers pluck items from the well-stocked shelves of grocery stores. While a laughingstock is an object of ridicule, other stock characters include villains, tramps, bad boys, and little princesses.

Style: The way a story is written in contrast to what it is about. No two authors have exactly the same style because with writing, just as with appearance, behavior, and personal belongings, style consists of the unique blending of all the choices each individual makes. From situation to situation, these choices may differ, but they are enough alike that the styles of particular authors, such as Kurt Vonnegut, Jr., Richard Brautigan, and E. L. Doctorow, are recognizable from book to book. Style is also influenced by the nature of the story being told. For example, Ursula K. Le Guin used a different style when she wrote the realistic *Very Far Away From Anywhere Else* from the one she used when she wrote her fantasy *A Wizard of Earthsea.* Nevertheless, in both books she relied on the particular writing techniques that she likes and is skilled at using. J. D. Salinger's *The Catcher in the Rye* has had such an influence on the style of writing about young protagonists that every year promotional materials or reviews compare two or three new books to *Catcher.*

Symbol: An item that is itself but also stands for something else. An example is the title of Linda Sue Parks's *A Single Shard,* in which the one piece of the master's pottery that Tree-Ear manages to deliver to the emperor symbolizes the great challenge that the boy faced on his journey.

Theme: A central idea that ties a story together and answers such questions as what the story means and what there is to think about when it is all over. Some authors are explicit in developing a theme, even expressing part of it in the title, as did Maya Angelou with *All God's Children Need Traveling Shoes* and Virginia Euwer Wolff with *Make Lemonade.* Books may have more than one theme, but usually the secondary themes are less important to the story.

Tone: The author's attitude toward the subject and the readers. Biblical language may lend weight and dignity to a book, as with James Herriot's title *All Creatures Great and Small* or Claude Brown's *Manchild in the Promised Land.* Exaggeration or hyperbole may communicate a flip tone, as in Ellen Conford's title *If This Is Love, I'll Take Spaghetti* and Ron Koertge's *Where the Kissing Never Stops.*

Book Selection Guides

The following sources are designed to aid professionals in the selection and evaluation of books and other materials for young adults. We attempted to include sources with widely varying emphases, but, in addition to these sources—most of which appear at regular intervals—many specialized lists are prepared by committees and individuals in response to current and/or local needs. Readers are advised to check on the availability of such lists with librarians and teachers. Also, publications for adults such as *The New York Times Book Review, The Los Angeles Times,* and *Smithsonian* magazine, give attention to books for children and teenagers, especially in the weeks prior to Christmas when people are looking for gift ideas.

We checked these websites in August of 2011, but if you are unsuccessful with our addresses you can probably find the publications by using a good search engine. We were happy to see how much information each publication provides online. Some require an online subscription to read the full journal, but many provide a surprising amount of information simply for the looking.

The ALAN Review: National Council of Teachers of English, 1111 West Kenyon Road, Urbana, IL 61801-1096, http://www.alan-ya.org/the-alan-review/

Since 1973, this publication, which is devoted entirely to adolescent literature, has appeared three times a year. Subscribers do not need to be members of the National Council of Teachers of English, which is the sponsoring organization. Current editors are Steven Bickmore and Jacqueline Bach from Louisiana State University and Melanie Hundley from Vanderbilt. Each issue contains approximately fifty "Clip and File" reviews written by ALAN members who are mostly secondary school teachers or librarians. Also included are feature articles, news announcements, occasional reviews of professional books, and descriptions of relevant Ph.D. dissertations.

Booklist: American Library Association, 50 East Huron Street, Chicago, IL 60611, http://www.ala.org/template.cfm?Section=booklist

Reviews, which constitute a recommendation for library purchase, are written by professional staff members, who also attach a YA designation to selected adult titles. The "Books for Youth" section is divided into works for older, middle, and young readers. Exceptional books are given starred reviews and sometimes special features are provided on related books. The end-of-the-year "Editors' Choice" issue is especially useful, as are the lists of "Best Books" compiled by various committees affiliated with the American Library Association. Check the website for several lists related to young adults.

Books for the Teenage: New York Public Library, 455 Fifth Avenue, New York, NY 10016, http://www.randomhouse.com/highschool/awards_sub.pperl?top=202&cat=205

The over one thousand recommendations in this booklet come from the young adult librarians in the eighty branches of the New York Public Library. Annotations are minimal, and grouping is by subject with titles and authors indexed. Young adults are invited to enter an art contest for each year's cover.

Books for You: National Council of Teachers of English, 1111 West Kenyon Road, Urbana, IL 61801-1096, http://www.ncte.org/search?q=books+for+you

Committees of English teachers put these books together every few years. They are written for direct use by students and contain concise annotations for between two hundred and one thousand recommended books organized under such categories as "Growing Up," "Issues of Our Time," and "Sports." There is one for senior high students, one for junior high, and one that is high interest/low reading level.

Bulletin of the Center for Children's Books: Johns Hopkins University Press, 2715 North Charles Street, Baltimore, MD 21218-4363, http://bccb.lis.illinois.edu/

This is the journal founded by Zena Sutherland and originally published by the University of Chicago Press. When Chicago's Graduate Library School closed, the *Bulletin* moved to the University of Illinois in Urbana-Champaign but is officially published by Johns Hopkins University Press for the Graduate School of Library and Information Science at the University of Illinois. In each issue staff members review approximately sixty new books, with approximately twenty being identified as appropriate for grades nine through twelve. Reviews are coded with *R* standing for "recommended," *Ad* for "additional title if topic is needed," *M* for "marginal," and *NR* for "not recommended." The website reprints starred reviews and each month features a theme-based list of a dozen recommended titles.

Children's Literature in Education: Springer, 233 Spring Street, New York, NY 10013, http://www.springer.com/education+%26+language/linguistics/journal/10583

In this British/American cooperative effort, the editors show a preference for substantive analysis rather than pedagogical advice or quick once-overs.

A good proportion of the articles are about YA authors and their works. The table of contents is printed online and access is given to selected articles.

English Journal: National Council of Teachers of English, 1111 West Kenyon Road, Urbana, IL 61801-1096, http://www.ncte.org/journals/ej

This is the largest journal published by NCTE with its audience being mainly high school English teachers. It appears six times a year and frequently has articles about young adult literature, plus a regular column on young adult books. For more than a decade it has published our annual Honor List.

Horn Book Magazine: Horn Book, Inc., 11 Beacon Street, Suite 1000, Boston, MA 02108, http://www.hbook.com/magazine/

Since 1924, the *Horn Book Magazine* has been devoted to the critical analysis of children's literature. Many of the articles are written by noted authors, while the book reviews are staff written. Since Roger Sutton, a former YA librarian, became editor, more attention has been given to young adult literature. Big names in YA literature who are either regular contributors or reviewers include Betty Carter, Tim Wynne-Jones, and Patty Campbell. *Horn Book* cosponsors the Boston Globe Horn Book Awards and also prints a yearly "Fanfare" list of best books.

Journal of Adolescent and Adult Literacy (JAAL): International Reading Association, 800 Barksdale Road, Box 8139, Newark, DE 19711-8139, http://www.reading.org/General/Publications/Journals/JAAL.aspx

The audience for this journal is high school reading teachers. Although most of the articles are reports on research in the teaching of reading, some articles focus on reading interests and literature. James Blasingame edits a regular review column on young adult literature.

Kirkus Reviews: Kirkus Service, Inc., 200 Park Avenue South, New York, NY 10003, http://www.kirkusreviews.com/

Kirkus reviews are approximately two hundred words long and are relied on throughout the publishing industry. The big advantage is timeliness and completeness made possible by twice-a-month issues.

Publishers Weekly: 245 West 17th Street, New York, NY 10011, http://www.publishersweekly.com/pw/home/index.html

While the focus is on the general world of adult book publishing, much of the information is relevant to anyone working with books; for example, what will company mergers mean to readers, what are the current best sellers, and who are the prize winners? Staff members write the reviews, which include some for children ages twelve and up.

School Library Journal: (subscriptions) P.O. Box 5670, Harlan, IA 51995-1170, http://www.schoollibraryjournal.com/

SLJ is the most comprehensive of the review media. In monthly installments, it used to try to review all books published for young people, but as the numbers have increased it has begun to group books that are published in series or sets. Still, it publishes more than 4,000 reviews per year with about one-third of them being for readers twelve and older. Advertisements and feature articles provide good information along with the reviews, which are written by a panel of four hundred librarians. A starred review, inclusion on the December "Best Books" list, or both, signifies an exceptional book. Editorial correspondence should go to 160 Varick St., 11th Floor, New York, NY 10013.

Teacher Librarian: The Journal for School Library Professionals: Scarecrow Press, 4501 Forbes Blvd., Suite 200, Lanham, MD 20706, http://www .teacherlibrarian.com/

For over thirty years, *TL* has published both feature articles and regular columns about issues, concerns, and materials for K–12 school librarians. It has started a new Wiki for online reviewing: www.seedwiki.com/wiki/ lmc_reviews.

Voices from the Middle: National Council of Teachers of English, 1111 West Kenyon Road, Urbana, IL 61801-1096, http://www.ncte.org/journals/vm

Sponsored by the National Council of Teachers of English for educators in middle and junior high schools, this journal regularly includes information about YA lit appropriate for tweeners.

Voice of Youth Advocates (VOYA): Scarecrow Press, 4501 Forbes Blvd., Suite 200, Lanham, MD 20706, http://www.voya.com/

Published every other month, this is a journal prepared mainly for librarians who work with teenagers. It was founded in 1978 by Mary K. Chelton and Dorothy Broderick. VOYA consistently has good articles on current trends in literature and youth services in libraries. The editors and contributors do an especially good job with fantasy and science fiction.

Some Outstanding Articles and Books about Young Adult Literature

Articles

Using Young Adult Literature in Libraries and Classrooms

Abrahamson, Richard, and Eleanor Tyson. "What Every English Teacher Should Know about Free Reading." *ALAN Review* 14 (Fall 1986): 54–58, 69.

Adams, Lauren. "Disorderly Fiction." *Horn Book Magazine* 78 (September/October 2002): 521–528.

Alexander, Lloyd. "Seeing with the Third Eye." *English Journal* 63 (May 1974): 35–40.

Anderson, Laurie Halse. "Loving the Young Adult Reader Even When You Want to Strangle Him (or Her)!" *ALAN Review* 32 (Winter 2005): 53–58.

Barker, Clive. "Fearful Symmetry: The Art of Fantasy." *ALAN Review* 32 (Winter 2005): 26–31.

Bickmore, Steven T. "It Is Inexcusable to Deny *Inexcusable* a Place in the Classroom." *ALAN Review* 35:2 (Winter, 2008): 75–83.

Bott, C. J. "Bully Books: More than Damage Control." *VOYA* 31:2 (June, 2008): 118–121.

Bushman, John. "Young Adult Literature in the Classroom—Or Is It?" *English Journal* 86 (March 1997): 35–40.

Bushman, John, and Shelley McNerny. "Moral Choices: Building a Bridge between YA Literature and Life." *ALAN Review* 32 (Fall 2004): 61–67.

Campbell, Patricia. "Prizes and Paradoxes." *Horn Book Magazine* 79 (July/August 2003): 501–505.

Carico, Kathleen M. "Professional Journal Articles and the Novels They Illuminate: A Resource for YA Courses." *ALAN Review* 29 (Fall 2002): 62–66.

Carroll, Pamela Sissi. "Today's Teens, Their Problems, and Their Literature: Revisiting G. Robert Carlsen's *Books and the Teenage Reader* Thirty Years Later." *English Journal* 86 (March 1997): 25–34.

Carter, Linda Purdy. "Addressing the Needs of Reluctant Readers through Sports Literature." *Clearing House* 71 (May/June 1998): 309–311.

Franzak, Judith, and Elizabeth Noll. "Monstrous Acts: Problematizing Violence in Young Adult Literature." *Journal of Adolescent and Adult Literacy* 49 (May 2006): 662–672.

George, Marshall A. "Furthering the Cause: The Study and Teaching of Young Adult Literature." *English Education* 37 (October 2004): 80–84.

Gibbons, Laurel, Jennifer S. Dail, and B. Joyce Stallworth. "Young Adult Literature in the English Curriculum Today: Classroom Teachers Speak Out." *ALAN Review* 33 (Summer 2006): 53–61.

Giles, Gail. "Wanted: Male Models: There's a Good Reason Why Boys Don't Read." *School Library Journal* 54:12 (December 2008): 48–49.

Goodson, F. Todd. "A Pinch of Tobacco and a Drop of Urine: Using YA Literature to Examine Local Culture." *ALAN Review* 32 (Fall 2004): 50–58.

Hale, Lisa A., and Chris Crowe. "'I Hate Reading If I Don't Have To': Results from a Longitudinal Study of High School Students' Reading Interests." *ALAN Review* 28 (Spring/Summer 2001): 49–58.

Harmon, Janis M., and Monica C. Gonzales. "Are These Parents for Real? Students' Views of Parents in Realistic and Historical Fiction." *ALAN Review* 30 (Winter 2003): 57–62.

Hautman, Pete. "How to Win a National Book Award: A Primer." *ALAN Review* 32 (Summer 2005): 24–28.

Hipple, Ted, Lisa Scherff, Jennifer Claiborne, and Amy Cirici Sullins. "Teaching the Mock Printz Novels." *English Journal* 93 (January 2004): 69–74.

Hopper, Rosemary. "The Good, the Bad, and the Ugly: Teachers' Perceptions of Quality in Fiction for Adolescent Readers." *English in Education* 40 (Summer 2006): 55–70.

Lesesne, Teri S. "Audio Talk: Lessons in Listening: Reflecting on the Listening Experience." *VOYA* 34:1 (April 2001): 44–46.

Mason, Katherine. "From Preservice Teacher to Trusted Adult: Sexual Orientation and Gender Variance in an Online YAL Book Club." *ALAN Review* 38:1 (Fall, 2010): 7–15.

Melone, Christine. "Chickalicious: Want to Woo Reluctant Female Readers? Chick Lit May Be the Ticket." *School Library Journal* 56:6 (June, 2010): 32–35.

Pace, Barbara G. "Resistance and Response: Deconstructing Community Standards in a Literature Class." *Journal of Adolescent and Adult Literacy* 46 (February 2003): 408–412.

Peck, Richard. "In the Beginning." *Horn Book Magazine* 82 (September/October 2006): 505–508.

Phelps, Stephen. "Critical Literacy: Using Nonfiction to Learn about Islam." *JAAL* 54:3 (November, 2010): 190–198.

Proukou, Katherine Kim. "Young Adult Literature: Rite of Passage or Rite of Its Own." *ALAN Review* 32 (Summer 2005): 62–68.

Ritter, John H. "Are YA Novelists Morally Obligated to Offer Their Readers Hope?" *ALAN Review* 30 (Spring 2003): 8–13.

Santoli, Susan P., and Mary Elaine Wagner. "Promoting Young Adult Literature: The Other 'Real' Literature." *American Secondary Education* 33 (Fall 2004): 65–75.

Seely, Debra. "You Can't Change History, Can You?" *ALAN Review* 31 (Summer 2004): 20–24.

Sprague, Marsha M., and Lori Risher. "Using Fantasy Literature to Explore Gender Issues." *ALAN Review* 29 (Winter 2002): 39–42.

Stotsky, Sandra. "Is the Holocaust the Chief Contribution of the Jewish People to World Civilization and History? A Survey of Leading Literature Anthologies and Reading Instructional Textbooks." *English Journal* 85 (February 1996): 52–59.

Sullivan, Ed. "Going All the Way: First-Time Sexual Experiences of Teens in Fiction." *Voice of Youth Advocates* 26 (February 2004): 461–463.

Thomas, Melissa. "Teaching Fantasy: Overcoming the Stigma of Fluff." *English Journal* 92 (May 2003): 60–66.

Uhler, Linda. "Every Reader His (or Her) Book: Books for a Diverse Teen Audience." *VOYA* 33:3 (August 2010): 212–218.

Vetter, Amy M. "Cause I'm a G: Identity Work of a Lesbian Teen in Language Arts." *JAAL* 54:2 (October 2010): 98–108.

Whelan, Debra Lau. "A Dirty Little Secret: Self-censorship Is Rampant and Lethal." *School Library Journal* 55:2 (February 2009): 26–30.

Yokoto, Junko. "Asian and Asian American Literature for Adolescents: What's Important for Librarians and Teachers to Know." *VOYA* 33:3 (August 2010): 214–215.

Zitlow, Connie S., and Lois T. Stover. "Portrait of the Artist as a Young Adult: Who Is the Real Me? *ALAN Review* 38:2 (Winter 2011): 32–42.

Commentary and Criticism on Young Adult Literature

Abrahamson, Richard F. "Collected Wisdom: The Best Articles Ever Written on Young Adult Literature and Teen Reading." *English Journal* 86 (March 1997): 50–54.

Alexander, Lloyd. "Fools, Heroes, and Jackasses." *School Library Journal* 42 (March 1996): 114–116.

Angel, Ann. "The Voices of Cultural Assimilation in Current Young Adult Novels." *ALAN Review* 30 (Winter 2003): 52–55.

Aronson, Marc. "The Betrayal of Teenagers: How Book Awards Fail America's Most Important Readers." *School Library Journal* 42 (March 1996): 23–25.

Aronson, Marc. "The Myths of Teenage Readers." *Publishing Research Quarterly* 16 (Fall 2000): 4–9.

Breen, Karen, Ellen Fader, Kathleen Odean, and Zena Sutherland. "One Hundred Books That Shaped the Century." *School Library Journal* 46 (January 2000): 50–58.

Brooks, Wanda. "Reading Representations of Themselves: Urban Youth Use Culture and African American Textual Features to Develop Literary Understanding." *Reading Research Quarterly* 41:3 (Summer 2006): 372–392.

Carlsen, G. Robert. "For Everything There Is a Season." *Top of the News* 21 (January 1965): 103–110. Stages in reading growth.

Carlsen, G. Robert. "Literature Is." *English Journal* 63 (February 1974): 23–27.

Cart, Michael. "Of Risk and Revelation: The Current State of Young Adult Literature." *Journal of Youth Services in Libraries* 8 (Winter 1995): 151–164.

Carter, Betty. "Master of Disaster: Paolo Bacigalupi." *School Library Journal* 57:5 (May, 2011): 34–37.

Crowe, Chris. "The Problems with YA Literature." *English Journal* 90 (January 2001): 146–150.

Daniels, Cindy Lou. "Literary Theory and Young Adult Literature: The Open Frontier in Critical Studies." *ALAN Review* 33 (Winter 2006): 78–82.

Early, Margaret J. "Stages of Growth in Literature Appreciation." *English Journal* 49 (March 1960): 161–167. A major article.

Fitzgerald, Frances. "The Influence of Anxiety: What's the Problem with Young Adult Novels?" *Harpers* 307 (September 2004): 62–63, 66–70.

Gale, David. "The Business of Books." *School Library Journal* 42 (July 1996): 18–21. How publishers take a YA manuscript and turn it into a book.

Glasgow, Jacqueline N. "Reconciling Memories of Internment Camp Experiences During WWII in Children's and Young Adult Literature." *ALAN Review* 29 (Fall 2002): 41–45.

Hinton, S. E. "Teen-Agers Are for Real." *New York Times Book Review*, August 27, 1967, pp. 28–29. Brief and excellent.

Hipple, Ted, and Amy B. Maupin. "What's Good about the Best?" *English Journal* 90 (January 2001): 40–42.

Hipps, G. Melvin. "Adolescent Literature: Once More to the Defense." *Virginia English Bulletin* 23 (Spring 1973): 44–50. Forty-plus years old and still one of the best rationales for adolescent literature.

Holindale, Peter. "The Adolescent Literature of Ideas." *Children's Literature in Education* 26 (March 1995): 83–95.

Hunt, Caroline. "Young Adult Literature Evades the Theorists." *Children's Literature Association Quarterly* 21 (Spring 1996): 4–11.

Knickerbocker, Joan L., and James Rycik. "Growing into Literature: Adolescents' Literary Interpretation and Appreciation." *JAAL* 46 (November 2002): 196–208.

Koss, Malanie D. "Young Adult Novels with Multiple Narrative Perspectives: The Changing Nature of YA Literature." *ALAN Review* 36 (Summer 2009): 73–80.

McLeod, Anne Scott. "Writing Backward: Modern Novels in Historical Fiction." *Horn Book Magazine* 74 (January/February 1998): 26–33.

Meltzer, Milton. "Where Do All the Prizes Go? The Case for Nonfiction." *Horn Book Magazine* 52 (February 1976): 17–23.

Merla, Patrick. "'What Is Real?' Asked the Rabbit One Day." *Saturday Review* 55 (November 4, 1972): 43–49. The rise of YA realism and adult fantasy.

Mertz, Maia Pank, and David A. England. "The Legitimacy of American Adolescent Fiction." *School Library Journal* 30 (October 1983): 119–123.

Myracle, Lauren. "Molding the Minds of the Young: The History of Bibliotherapy as Applied to Children and Adolescents." *ALAN Review* 22 (Winter 1995): 36–40.

Nilsen, Alleen Pace. "The House That Alice Built: An Interview with the Author Who Brought You *Go Ask Alice*." *School Library Journal* 26:2 (October 1979): 109–112.

Nilsen, Don L. F., and Alleen Pace Nilsen. "Naming Tropes and Schemes in J. K. Rowling's Harry Potter Books." *English Journal* 98:6 (July 2009): 60–68.

Paterson, Katherine. "Are You There, God?" *Harvard Divinity Bulletin* 33 (Spring 2005): 50–58.

Peck, Richard. "Huck Finns of Both Sexes: Protagonists and Peer Leaders in Young Adult Books." *Horn Book Magazine* 69 (September/October 1993): 554–558.

Perkins, Mitali. "Straight Talk on Race: Challenging the Stereotypes in Kids' Books." *School Library Journal* 56:04 (April 2009): 28–34.

Pierce, Tamora. "Fantasy: Why Kids Read It, Why Kids Need It." *School Library Journal* 39 (October 1993): 10–14.

Probst, Robert. "Reader Response Theory and the Problem of Meaning." *Publishing Research Quarterly* 8 (Spring 1992): 64–73.

Reeve, Philip. "The Worst Is Yet to Come: Dystopias Are Grim, Humorless, and Hopeless—and

Incredibly Appealing to Today's Teens." *School Library Journal* 57:8 (August 2011): 34–36.

Roxburgh, Stephen. "The Art of the Young Adult Novel." *ALAN Review* 32 (Winter 2005): 4–10.

Salvner, Gary M. "Lessons and Lives: Why Young Adult Literature Matters." *ALAN Review* 28 (Spring/Summer 2001): 9–13.

Smith, Scot. "The Death of Genre: Why the Best YA Fiction Often Defies Classification. *ALAN Review* 35:1 (Fall 2007): 43–50.

Wilson, David E. "The Open Library: YA Books for Gay Teens." *English Journal* 73 (November 1984): 60–63.

History of Young Adult Literature

Carlsen, G. Robert. "Teaching Literature for the Adolescent: A Historical Perspective." *English Journal* 73 (November 1984): 28–30.

Edwards, Margaret A. "The Rise of Teen-Age Reading." *Saturday Review of Literature* 37 (November 13, 1954): 88–89, 95.

Geller, Evelyn. "Tom Sawyer, Tom Bailey, and the Bad-Boy Genre." *Wilson Library Bulletin* 52 (November 1976): 245–250.

Green, Samuel S. "Sensational Fiction in Public Libraries." *Library Journal* 4 (September/October 1879): 345–355. Extraordinarily intelligent comments about young adults and their books. The entire issue is worth reading, particularly papers by T. W. Higginson (pp. 357–359), William Atkinson (pp. 359–362), and Mellen Chamberlain (pp. 362–366).

Hentoff, Nat. "Fiction for Teen-Agers." *Wilson Library Bulletin* 43 (November 1968): 261–264. On the shortcomings of YA fiction.

Kelly, R. Gordon. "American Children's Literature: An Historiographical Review." *American Literary Realism, 1870–1910* 5 (Spring 1973): 89–107.

McCue, Andy. "From Frank Merriwell to Henry Wiggen: A Modest History of Baseball Fiction." *SABR* (Society for American Baseball Research) *Review* 5 (1990): 54–71.

McEntegart, Pete, et al. "The Top 100 Sports Books of All Time." *Sports Illustrated* 97 (December 16, 2002): 126–248.

Messenger, Christian K. "Sport in the Dime Novel." *Journal of American Culture* 3 (Fall 1978): 494–505.

Phelps, William Lyon. "The Virtue of the Second-Rate." *English Journal* 16 (January 1927): 10–14. A marvelous article.

Poe, Elizabeth Ann, Barbara G. Samuels, and Betty Carter. "Twenty-Five Years of Research in Young Adult Literature: Past Perspectives and Future Directives." *Journal of Youth Services in Libraries* 28 (November 1981): 25–28.

Popkin, Zelda F. "The Finer Things in Life." *Harpers* 164 (April 1932): 606–611. Contrasts between what young adults like to read and what parents and other adults want kids to read.

Radnor, Rebecca. "You're Being Paged Loudly in the Kitchen: Teen-Age Literature of the Forties and Fifties." *Journal of Popular Culture* 11 (Spring 1978): 289–299.

Repplier, Agnes. "Little Pharisees in Fiction." *Scribner's Magazine* 20 (December 1896): 718–724. The didactic and joyless goody-goody school of YA fiction in the last half of the nineteenth century.

Scroggins, Margaret C. "Do Young People Want Books?" *Wilson Library Bulletin for Librarians* 11 (September 1936): 17–20, 24.

Small, Dora V. "Extensive Reading in Junior High School: A Survey of Teacher Preparation." *English Journal* 19 (June 1930): 449–462.

Thurber, Samuel. "Voluntary Reading in the Classical High School: From the Pupil's Point of View." *School Review* 13 (February 1905): 168–179. Thurber was a leader of English Education long before NCTE, and his many articles are worth any teacher's time.

Books

Books about Literary Genres

Aldiss, Brian, and David Wingrove. *Trillion Year Spree: The History of Science Fiction*. Atheneum, 1986.

Attebery, Brian. *The Fantasy Tradition in American Literature: From Irving to Le Guin*. Indiana University Press, 1980.

Barnhouse, Rebecca. *Recasting the Past: The Middle Ages in Young Adult Literature*. Heinemann, 2000.

Barron, Neil. *Anatomy of Wonder: A Critical Guide to Science Fiction*, 5th ed. Libraries Unlimited, 2004.

Brown, Joanne. *Immigration Narratives in Young Adult Literature: Crossing Borders*. Scarecrow, 2011.

Brown, Joanne, and Nancy St. Clair. *The Distant Mirror: Reflections on Young Adult Historical Fiction.* Scarecrow, 2006.

Burgess, Michael, and Jill H. Vassilakos, Eds. *Murder in Retrospect: A Selective Guide to Historical Mystery Fiction.* Libraries Unlimited, 2005.

Carnog, Martha, and Timothy Perper, Eds. *Graphic Novels Beyond the Basics: Insights and Issues for Libraries.* Libraries Unlimited, 2009.

Cart, Michael, and Christine A. Jenkins. *Young Adult Literature with Gay/Lesbian/Queer Content 1969–2004.* Scarecrow, 2006.

Carter, James Bucky, Ed. *Building Literacy Connections with Graphic Novels: Page by Page, Panel by Panel.* National Council of Teachers of English, 2007.

Costanzo, William K. *Great Films and How to Teach Them.* NCTE, 2004.

Drew, Bernard A. *100 Most Popular Thriller and Suspense Writers: Biographical Sketches and Bibliographies.* Libraries Unlimited, 2009.

Fletcher-Spear, Kristin, and Meribeth Jenson-Benjamin. *Library Collections for Teens: Manga and Graphic Novels.* VOYA Press, 2011.

Fox, Dana L., and Kathy G. Short, Eds. *Stories Matter: The Complexity of Cultural Authenticity in Children's Literature.* NCTE, 2003.

Gannon, Michael B. *Blood, Bedlam, Bullets, and Bad Guys: A Reader's Guide to Adventure/Suspense Fiction.* Libraries Unlimited, 2004.

Gates, Pamela S., Susan B. Steffel, and Francis J. Molson, Eds. *Fantasy Literature for Children and Young Adults.* Scarecrow, 2003.

Goldsmith, Francisca. *The Readers' Advisory Guide to Graphic Novels.* ALA Editions, 2009.

Herald, Diana Tixier. *Fluent in Fantasy: A Guide to Reading Interests.* Libraries Unlimited, 2000.

Herald, Diana Tixier. *Strictly Science Fiction.* Libraries Unlimited, 2002.

Hintz, Carrie, and Elaine Ostry, Eds. *Utopian and Dystopian Writing for Children and Young Adults.* Routledge, 2003.

Jarrell, Jill S., and Tara C. Cannon. *Cooler Than Fictions: A Planning Guide for Teen Nonfiction Booktalks.* McFarland, 2010.

Johannessen, Larry R. *Illumination Rounds: Teaching the Literature of the Vietnam War.* NCTE, 1992.

Johnson, Sarah L. *Historical Fiction: A Guide to the Genre.* Libraries Unlimited, 2005.

Jones, Diana Wynne. *The Tough Guide to Fantasyland,* rev. ed. Penguin, 2006.

Marcus, Leonard, Ed. *The Wind in the Word: Conversations with Writers of Fantasy.* Candlewick, 2006.

Martinez, Sara E., Ed. *Latino Literature: A Guide to Reading Interests.* Libraries Unlimited/ABC-CLIO, 2009.

Matthews, Patricia O'Brien. *Fang-Tastic Fiction: Twenty-First Century Paranormal Reads.* ALA, 2011.

Polanka, Sue, Ed. *No Shelf Required: E-Books in Libraries.* American Library Association, 2010.

Reid, Suzanne Elizabeth. *Presenting Young Adult Science Fiction.* Twayne, 1998.

Sandoz, Joli, and Joby Winans, Eds. *Whatever It Takes: Women on Women's Sports.* Farrar, 1999.

Stableford, Brian. *The A to Z of Science Fiction Literature.* Scarecrow, 2005.

Stableford, Brian. *Historical Dictionary of Fantasy Literature.* Scarecrow, 2005.

Sullivan, C. W. III, Ed. *Young Adult Science Fiction.* Greenwood, 1999.

Taylor, Desmond. *The Juvenile Novel of World War II: An Annotated Bibliography.* Greenwood, 1994.

Wee, Patricia Hachter, and Robert James Wee. *World War II in Literature for Youth: A Guide and Reference Book.* Scarecrow, 2004.

Wiseman, Rosalind. *Owning Up Curriculum: Empowering Adolescents to Confront Social Cruelty, Bullying, and Injustice.* Research Press, 2009.

Commentary and Criticism on Young Adult Literature

Aronson, Marc. *Beyond the Pale: New Essays for a New Era.* Scarecrow, 2003.

Barron, Neal, Ed. *Fantasy and Horror: A Critical and Historical Guide to Literature, Illustration, Film, TV, Radio and the Internet.* Scarecrow, 1999.

Bilz, Rachelle Lasky. *Life Is Tough: Guys, Growing Up, and Young Adult Literature.* Scarecrow, 2004.

Broderick, Dorothy. *Images of the Black in Children's Fiction.* Bowker, 1973.

Cameron, Eleanor. *The Green and Burning Tree: On the Writing and Enjoyment of Children's Books.* Dutton, 1993.

Cart, Michael, and Christine A. Jenkins. *The Heart Has Its Reasons: Young Adult Literature with Gay/Lesbian/Queer Context, 1969–2004.* Scarecrow, 2006.

Carter, Betty, and Richard Abrahamson. *Nonfiction for Young Adults: From Delight to Wisdom.* Oryx, 1990.

Chambers, Aidan. *Introducing Books to Children*, 2nd ed. Horn Book, 1983.

Dean, Deborah. *Genre Theory: Teaching Writing, and Being*. National Council of Teachers of English, 2008.

Hazard, Paul. *Books, Children and Men*. Trans. Marguerite Mitchell. Horn Book, 1944.

Hogan, Walter. *Humor in Young Adult Literature: A Time for Laughs*. Scarecrow, 2005.

Horning, Kathleen. *From Cover to Cover: Evaluating and Reviewing Children's Books*. Harper, 1997.

Howard, Elizabeth F. *America as Story: Historical Fiction for the Secondary Schools*. ALA, 1988.

Hunt, Peter. *An Introduction to Children's Literature*. Oxford University Press, 1994.

Hunter, Mollie. *The Pied Piper Syndrome and Other Essays*. Harper, 1992.

Kelly, Patricia P., and Robert C. Small, Eds. *Two Decades of the ALAN Review*. NCTE, 1999.

Lynn, Ruth Nadelman. *Fantasy Literature for Children and Young Adults*. Bowker, 1989.

MacCann, Donnarae. *White Supremacy in Children's Literature: Characteristics of African-Americans, 1830–1900*. Garland, 1998.

McCallum, Robyn. *Ideologies of Identities in Adolescent Fiction: The Dialogic Construction of Subjectivity*. Garland, 1999.

Moore, John Noell. *Interpreting Young Adult Literature: Literary Theory in the Secondary Classroom*. Boynton/Cook, 1997.

Nikolajeva, Maria. *From Mythic to Linear: Time in Children's Literature*. Scarecrow, 2000.

Nikolajeva, Maria. *The Rhetoric of Character in Children's Literature*. Scarecrow, 2002.

Rochman, Hazel. *Against Borders: Promoting Books for a Multiracial World*. ALA, 1993.

Silvey, Anita. *500 Great Books for Teens*. Houghton Mifflin, 2006.

Sloan, Glenda. *The Child as Critic*. Teachers College Press, 1975. Northrop Frye's theories applied to YA literature.

Soter, Anna. *Young Adult Literature and New Literary Theory*. Teachers College Press, 1999.

Spencer, Pam. *What Do Young Adults Read Next? A Reader's Guide to Fiction for Young Adults*, 2 Vols. Gale Research, 1997.

Stringer, Sharon. *Conflict and Connection: The Psychology of Young Adult Literature*. Heinmann, 1997.

Sullivan, C. W. *Science Fiction for Young Readers*. Greenwood, 1993.

Sullivan, Edward T. *The Holocaust in Literature for Youth: A Guide and Resource Book*. Scarecrow, 1999.

Townsend, John Rowe. *Written for Children: An Outline of English-Language Children's Literature*, 3rd ed. Lippincott, 1988. Townsend's finest work.

Yolen, Jane. *Touch Magic: Fantasy, Faerie, and Folklore in the Literature of Childhood*. Philomel, 1981.

Zipes, Jack, Ed. *The Oxford Encyclopedia of Children's Literature*, 4 Vols. Oxford University Press, 2006.

Zitlow, Connie. *Lost Masterworks of Young Adult Literature*. Scarecrow, 2002.

Using Young Adult Literature in Libraries and Classrooms

Applebee, Arthur N. *Literature in the Secondary School: Studies in Curriculum and Instruction in the United States*. NCTE, 1993.

Appleman, Deborah. *Adolescent Literacy and the Teaching of Reading: Lessons for Teachers of Literature*. NCTE, 2011.

Appleman, Deborah. *Critical Encounters in High School English: Teaching Literary Theory to Adolescents*. Teachers College Press, 2000.

Bartel, Julie, and Pam Spencere Holley. *Annotated Book Lists for Every Teen Reader: The Best from the Experts at YALSA-BK*. Neal-Schuman, 2010.

Beach, Richard. *A Teacher's Introduction to Reader-Response Theories*. NCTE, 1993.

Blasingame, James. *Books That Don't Bore 'em: Young Adult Books That Speak to This Generation*. Scholastic, 2007.

Bodart, Joni. *Radical Reads 2: Working with the Newest Edgy Titles for Teens*. Scarecrow, 2009.

Books for the Teen Age. New York Public Library, published annually.

Brown, Jean A., and Elaine C. Stephens. *Teaching Young Adult Literature: Sharing the Connection*. Wadsworth, 1995.

Buckley, Eileen Murphy. *360 Degrees of Text: Using Poetry to Teach Close Reading and Powerful Writing*. NCTE, 2011.

Burton, Dwight. *Literature Study in the High Schools*, 3rd ed. Holt, 1970. For many teachers and librarians this was THE book that introduced them to young adult literature.

Carlsen, G. Robert. *Books and the Teen-Age Reader*, 2nd ed. Harper, 1980.

Carr, Jo, Ed. *Beyond Fact: Nonfiction for Children and Young People*. ALA, 1982.

Cawelti, John G. *Adventure, Mystery, and Romance: Formula Stories as Art and Popular Culture.* University of Chicago Press, 1976.

Chambers, Aidan. *Introducing Books to Children.* Heinemann, 1973.

Cole, Pam B. *Young Adult Literature in the 21st Century.* McGraw Hill, 2008.

Dunning, A. Stephen. "A Definition of the Role of the Junior Novel Based on Analyses of Thirty Selected Novels." Ph.D. dissertation, Florida State University, 1959.

Edwards, Margaret A. *The Fair Garden and the Swarm of Beasts: The Library and the Young Adult,* rev. ed. Hawthorn, 1974. The problems, but mostly the joys, of working in a library with young people.

Eiss, Harry, Ed. *Literature for Young People on War and Peace: An Annotated Bibliography.* Greenwood, 1989.

Elliott, Joan B., Ed. *Young Adult Literature in the Classroom: Reading It, Teaching It, Loving It.* IRA, 2002.

Fader, Daniel N., and Elton B. McNeil. *Hooked on Books: Program and Proof.* Berkeley, 1968.

Farrell, Edmund, and James R. Squire, Eds. *Transactions with Literature: A Fifty-Year Perspective.* NCTE, 1990.

Gillespie, John T., and Catherine Barr. *Best Books for Middle School and Junior High Readers, Grades 6–9.* Libraries Unlimited, 2004.

Gilmore, Barry. *Speaking Volumes: How to Get Students Discussing Books—And Much More.* Heinemann, 2006.

Goebel, Bruce A. *Reading Native American Literature: A Teacher's Guide.* NCTE, 2004.

Groenke, Susan L., and Lisa Scherff, Foreword by Alan Sitomer. *Teaching YA Lit through Differentiated Instruction.* NCTE, 2010.

Heller, Frieda M., and Lou LaBrant. *The Librarian and the Teacher of English.* ALA, 1938.

Hertz, Sarah, and Donald Gallo. *From Hamlet to Hinton: Building Bridges between Young Adult Literature and the Classics,* 2nd ed. Greenwood, 2005.

Isaac, Megan Lynn. *Heirs to Shakespeare: Reinventing the Bard in Young Adult Literature.* Heinemann, 2000.

Kajder, Sara. *Adolescents and Digital Literacies: Learning Alongside our Students.* NCTE, 2010.

Kaywell, Joan F., Ed. *Adolescent Literature as a Complement to the Classics.* Christopher-Gordon, 1993.

Latrobe, Kathy H., and Judy Drury. *Critical Approaches to Young Adult Literature.* Neal-Schuman Publishers, 2009.

Lesesne, Teri. *Making the Match: The Right Book for the Right Reader at the Right Time, Grades 4–12.* Stenhouse, 2003.

Martin, Hilias J., Jr., and James R. Murdock. *Serving Lesbian, Gay, Bisexual, Transgender and Questioning Teens.* Neal-Shuman, 2007.

McCann, Thomas M. *Reflective Teaching, Reflective Learning: How to Develop Critically Engaged Reading, Writing, and Speaking.* Heinemann, 2005.

Milner, Joseph O., and Carol A. Pope. *Engaging American Novels: Lessons from the Classroom.* NCTE, 2011.

Monseau, Virginia, and Gary M. Salvner, Eds. *Reading Their World: The Young Adult Novel in the Classroom.* Boynton/Cook, 1992.

Moore, John Noell. *Interpreting Young Adult Literature: Literary Theory in the Secondary Classroom.* Boynton/Cook, 1997.

Peck, David. *Novels of Initiation: A Guidebook for Teaching Literature to Adolescents.* Teachers College Press, 1989.

Petitt, Dorothy. "A Study of the Qualities of Literary Excellence which Characterize Selected Fiction for Younger Adolescents." Ph.D. dissertation, University of Minnesota, 1961.

Probst, Robert. *Adolescent Literature: Response and Analysis.* Merrill, 1984.

Purves, Alan C., and Richard Beach. *Literature and the Reader.* NCTE, 1972.

Purves, Alan C., Theresa Rogers, and Anna O. Soter. *How Porcupines Make Love II: Teaching a Response-Centered Curriculum.* Longman, 1990.

Rochman, Hazel. *Tales of Love and Terror: Booktalking the Classics, Old and New.* ALA, 1987.

Rosenberg, Betty. *Genreflecting: A Guide to Reading Interests in Genre Fiction,* 2nd ed. Libraries Unlimited, 1987.

Rosenblatt, Louise. *Literature as Exploration,* 4th ed. MLA, 1983.

Rosenblatt, Louise. *The Reader, the Text, and the Poem: The Transactional Theory of the Literary Work.* Southern Illinois University Press, 1978.

Scholes, Robert. *Textual Power: Literary Theory and the Teaching of English.* Yale University Press, 1985.

Smith, Michael W., and Jeffrey D. Wilhelm, Foreword by Deborah Appleman. *Fresh Takes on Teaching Literary Elements.* NCTE, 2010.

Trupe, Alice. *Thematic Guide to Young Adult Literature.* Greenwood, 2006.

Welch, Rollie James. *A Core Collection for Young Adults: Teens @ the Library,* 2nd ed. Neal-Schuman, 2011.

Authors of Young Adult Literature

Note: Anyone who wishes to teach about a particular author should go online and search to see if there is a book written about the individual. Heinemann, Scarecrow, Twayne, Greenwood, the National Council of Teachers of English, and the Modern Language Association are among the publishers who produce books about individual authors. The books listed here include information about more than one author.

Bodart, Joni Richards. *100 World-Class Thin Books, or What to Read When Your Book Report Is Due Tomorrow*. Libraries Unlimited, 1993.

Chevalier, Tracy. *Twentieth-Century Children's Writers*, 3rd ed. St. James Press, 1989.

Commire, Anne, Ed. *Something about the Author*. Gale Research, beginning in 1971.

Commire, Anne, Ed. *Yesterday's Authors of Books for Children*. Gale Research, 1977. Lives of authors who died before 1961.

de Montreville, Doris, and Elizabeth D. Crawford, Eds. *Fourth Book for Junior Authors and Illustrators*. Wilson, 1978.

de Montreville, Doris, and Donna Hill, Eds. *Third Book of Junior Authors*. Wilson, 1972.

Drew, Bernard A. *The 100 Most Popular Young Adult Authors: Biographical Sketches and Bibliographies*. Libraries Unlimited, 1996.

Estes, Glenn E., Ed. *American Writers for Children Since 1960: Fiction. Dictionary of Literary Biography*, Vol. 52. Gale Research, 1986.

Estes, Glenn E., Ed. *American Writers for Children Since 1960: Poets, Illustrators, and Nonfiction Authors. Dictionary of Literary Biography*, Vol. 61. Gale Research, 1987.

Fuller, Muriel, Ed. *More Junior Authors*. Wilson, 1963.

Gallo, Donald R., Ed. *Authors Insights: Turning Teenagers into Readers and Writers*. Boynton/Cook, 1992.

Gallo, Donald R., Ed. *Speaking for Ourselves: Autobiographical Sketches by Notable Authors of Books for Young Adults*. NCTE, 1990. In this and a 1993 sequel, nearly two hundred YA authors introduce themselves.

Helbig, Alethea K., and Agnes Regan Perkins, Eds. *Dictionary of American Children's Fiction. 1960–1984*. Greenwood, 1986.

Helbig, Alethea K., and Agnes Regan Perkins, Eds. *Dictionary of British Children's Fiction*. Greenwood, 1989.

Hipple, Ted, Ed. *Writers for Young Adults*. 3 Vols. Scribner, 1997. Vol. 4, 2000.

Holtze, Sally Holmes, Ed. *Fifth Book of Junior Authors and Illustrators*. Wilson, 1987.

Kirkpatrick, D. L., Ed. *Twentieth-Century Children's Writers*, 3rd ed. Macmillan, 1990.

Kunitz, Stanley J., and Howard Haycraft, Eds. *The Junior Book of Authors*, 2nd rev. ed. Wilson, 1951.

Pendergast, Tom, and Sara Pendergast, Eds. *The St. James Guide to Young Adult Writers*. St. James, 1999.

Rees, David. *The Marble in the Water: Essays on Contemporary Writers of Fiction for Children and Young Adults*. Horn Book, 1980.

Rees, David. *Painted Desert, Green Shade: Essays on Contemporary Writers of Fiction for Children and Young Adults*. Horn Book, 1984.

Rees, David. *What Do Draculas Do? Essays on Contemporary Writers of Fiction for Children and Young Adults*. Scarecrow, 1990.

Rockman, Connie C., Ed. *Eighth Book of Junior Authors and Illustrators*. Wilson, 2000.

Roginski, Jim. *Behind the Covers: Interviews with Authors and Illustrators of Books for Children and Young Adults*. Libraries Unlimited, 1985. Vol. 2, 1989.

Sarkissian, Adele, Ed. *Writers for Young Adults: Biographies Master Index*. Gale Research, 1984.

Townsend, John Rowe. *A Sense of Story: Essays on Contemporary Writers for Children*. Lippincott, 1971.

History of Young Adult Literature

Avery, Gillian. *Behold the Child: American Children and Their Books, 1621–1922*. Bodley House, 1994.

Barnhouse, Rebecca. *The Middle Ages in Literature for Youth: A Guide and Resource Book*. Scarecrow, 2004.

Berg, Rebecca L. *The Great Depression in Literature for Youth, A Geographical Study of Families and Young Lives: A Guide and Resource Book*. Scarecrow, 2004.

Billman, Carol. *The Secret of the Stratemeyer Syndicate: Nancy Drew, the Hardy Boys, and the Million Dollar Fiction Factory*. Ungar, 1986.

Cadogan, Mary, and Patricia Craig. *You're a Brick, Angela! A New Look at Girls' Fiction from 1839 to 1975*. Gollancz, 1976. Delightful, funny, and rich.

Campbell, Patricia. *Sex Education Books for Young Adults, 1892–1979*. Bowker, 1979. Accurate and funny. Most of us can only envy Campbell's prose.

Campbell, Patricia. *Two Pioneers of Young Adult Library Service*. Scarecrow, 1999. On Mabel Williams and Margaret A. Edwards.

Carrier, Esther Jane. *Fiction in Public Libraries, 1876–1900*. Scarecrow, 1965.

Carrier, Esther Jane. *Fiction in Public Libraries, 1900–1950*. Libraries Unlimited, 1985.

Cart, Michael. *From Romance to Realism: 50 Years of Growth and Change in Young Adult Literature*. Harper, 1996, now thoroughly revised and published by the American Library Association, 2011.

Collins, Max Allan. *The History of Mystery*. Collector's Press, 2001.

Crowe, Chris. *More Than a Game: Sports Literature for Young Adults*. Scarecrow, 2004.

Darling, Richard. *The Rise of Children's Book Reviewing in America: 1865–1881*. Bowker, 1968. A seminal book.

Deane, Paul. *Mirrors of American Culture: Children's Fiction Series in the Twentieth Century*. Scarecrow, 1991.

Dyer, Carolyn Stewart, and Nancy Tillman Romalov, Eds. *Rediscovering Nancy Drew*. University of Iowa Press, 1995. Papers from the 1993 Nancy Drew Conference.

Egoff, Sheila. *Worlds Within: Children's Fantasy from the Middle Ages*. ALA, 1988.

Erisman, Fred. *Boys' Books, Boys' Dreams, and the Mystique of Flight*. Texas Christian Press, 2006.

Foster, Shirley, and Judy Simmons, Eds. *What Katy Read: Feminist Re-Readings of "Classic" Stories for Girls*. University of Iowa Press, 1995.

Girls' Series Books: A Checklist of Hardback Books Published 1900–1975. Children's Literature Research Collection, University of Minnesota Library, 1978. Basic for any study of early girls' books. Much like Hudson's work (see Hudson).

Gorham, Deborah. *The Victorian Girl and the Feminine Ideal*. Indiana University Press, 1982.

Griswold, Jerry. *Audacious Kids: Coming of Age in America's Classic Children's Books*. Oxford University Press, 1992.

Howarth, Patrick. *Play Up and Play the Game: The Heroes of Popular Fiction*. Eyre Methuen, 1973.

Hudson, Harry K. *A Bibliography of Hard-Cover Boys' Books*, rev. ed. Data Print, 1977. Basic for any study of early boys' books—and great fun to skim through.

Inness, Sherrie A., Ed. *Nancy Drew and Company: Culture, Gender, and Girls' Series*. Bowling Green State University Popular Press, 1999.

Johnson, Deidre. *Edward Stratemeyer and the Stratemeyer Syndicate*. Twayne, 1993. Anyone working on early young adult literature owes a debt to Johnson.

Johnson, Deidre, Ed. *Stratemeyer Pseudonyms and Series Books: An Annotated Checklist of Stratemeyer and Stratemeyer Syndicate Publications*. Greenwood, 1982.

Jones, Daryl. *The Dime Novel Western*. Bowling Green State University Popular Press, 1978.

Kensinger, Faye Riter. *Children of the Series and How They Grew*. Bowling Green State University Popular Press, 1987.

McFarlane, Leslie. *Ghost of the Hardy Boys: An Autobiography of Leslie McFarlane*. Two Continents, 1976.

Mason, Bobbie Ann. *The Girl Sleuth: A Feminist Guide*. Feminist Press, 1975. Delightful and perceptive.

Meigs, Cornelia, H. S. Commager, A. Eaton, E. Nesbitt, and R. H. Viguers. *A Critical History of Children's Literature*, rev. ed. Macmillan, 1969. Encyclopedic and often most helpful.

Nilolajeva, Neva, Ed. *Aspects and Issues in the History of Children's Literature*. Greenwood, 1995.

Oriad, Michael. *Dreaming of Heroes: American Sports Fiction 1868–1980*. Nelson-Hall, 1982.

Perry, Phyllis J. *Teaching Fantasy Novels: From* The Hobbit *to Harry Potter and the Goblet of Fire*. Teachers Ideas Press, 2003.

Reynolds, Kimberley. *Girls Only? Gender and Popular Children's Fiction in Britain, 1880–1910*. Temple University Press, 1990.

Salmon, Edward. *Juvenile Literature as It Is*. Drane, 1888. Old and significant.

Sloane, William. *Children's Books in England and America in the Seventeenth Century*. Columbia University Press, 1955.

Stonely, Peter. *Consumerism and American Girls' Fiction, 1860–1940*. Cambridge University Press, 2003.

Sullivan, C. W. III. *Welsh Myth in Modern Fiction*. Greenwood, 1989.

Photo Acknowledgments

Cover: University of Central Oklahoma

p. v Photo by Bruce Matsunaga

p. 3, 15, 16, 20, 33, 41, 42, 44, 45, 46, 47, 51, 54, 59, 62, 69, 77 (top), 93, 94, 100, 104, 108, 126, 130, 135, 138, 148, 162, 163, 164, 175, 185, 190, 200, 202, 209, 236, 239, 249, 258, 264, 285, 290, 291, 294 (top), 294 (bottom), 302, 305, 306, 314, 316, 322, 323, 325 (top), 325 (bottom), 344, 355, 356, 380, 393, 398, 405, 414, 420 Photos by A. P. Nilsen

p. 115, 231, 268, 402 Photos by Don L. F. Nilsen

p. 5 Courtesy of Enoch Pratt Free Library

p. 7 Courtesy of Penguin Group

p. 14 Courtesy of Macmillan Children's Publishing Group

p. 49 Courtesy of the Tempe Historical Museum

p. 52 Courtesy of Alleen Pace Nilsen

p. 57 Courtesy of Constance Cormier

p. 58 Photo by Don L. F. Nilsen, courtesy of NCTE

p. 61 Photo by Sigrid Estrada, courtesy of Judy Blume

p. 72 Photo by Don L. F. Nilsen, courtesy of Mary J. Wong

p. 77 (bottom) Photo by Don L. F. Nilsen

p. 84 Photo by Bruce Matsunaga, courtesy of Meredith DeCosta-Smith

p. 86 and 87 Photos by A. P. Nilsen, courtesy of Art Valdespino

p. 88 Photo by A. P. Nilsen, courtesy of Cynthia S. Nicholson

p. 90 Photo courtesy of Marlinda White Kaulaity

p. 107 Courtesy of HarperCollins

p. 122 Photo by Patrick Walsh

p. 139 Photo by Maria Andreotti, courtesy of HarperCollins

p. 140 Photo by Bob Henderson, Henderson Photography, Inc.

p. 145 Photo by Marian Wood Kolisch

p. 146 © Irene Graham 2004

p. 152 Photo courtesy of Alaya Swann

p. 157 Photo by Press Association Images, courtesy of School Library Journal

p. 178 Photo by Andrew Brilliant, courtesy of Clarion Books

p. 187 Photo courtesy of Myrlin Hepworth

p. 193 Photo courtesy of Alberto Rios

p. 215 Photo courtesy of Paul Zindel

Authors, Critics, and Commentators Index

Subject Index

Films
    fantasy, science fiction, dystopias,
        176–177
    Vietnam War, 274
    young adults, 2
First-person shooter games, 222
Flat world, 92, 96, 97
Fool and the trickster, 349–350
Free reading, 342–343
Freedom and Discipline in English, 55
Friendship, 108–110, 348

Gallows humor, 216
Gangsta rap, 186
Gays and lesbians, 307–312
Glogging, 76
Glogster, 76
Glossary of literary terms, 427–433
Google Docs, 76, 78
Google Sites, 75
Gothic fantasy, 152–155
Graphic novels, 219–221, 399
Guided reading, 342
Guys Read, 390

Heroes, 349
High-low books, 339
Hip hop, 186
Historical fiction, 257–282
Historical overview
    censorship, 418–423
    YA literature, 39–66
History and YA literature, 446–447
Holocaust, 279
Homosexuality, 307–312
Honor list, 15–28
Horn Book Magazine, 437
Human body, 133–135
Human relations, 359–361
Humor/humorous stories, 205–218
    age of reader, 205–206
    from chills to giggles, 206–207
    dead-pan presentation, 218
    double entendre, 216
    ethnic-based humor, 207–208
    exaggeration, 216
    gallows humor, 216
    incongruity/incongruity resolution, 216
    irony, 216–217
    outstanding authors, 209–214
    parody, 217
    props, 217
    role reversal, 217
    sarcasm, 217–218
    satire, 218
    surprise, 218
    teaching literary humor, 208
    understatement, 218
    wordplay, 218
Humorous and lighthearted fantasy, 155–158

Iambic pentameter, 197
Illustrations, 350–353
Incongruity/incongruity resolution, 216
Individualized reading, 342
Information books, 285–288, 294–295
Internationally acclaimed books, 95
Internet. *See* Digital literacies
Internment of Japanese Americans,
    279–280
Intertextuality, 337

Irony, 216–217
ISTE NETS, 70–71

Japanese Americans, internment, 279–280
*Journal of Adolescent and Adult Literacy
    (JAAL)*, 437
Journalistic fiction, 291
Journey stories, 103–108, 345–346
Junex versus the Senex archetype, 346–347

Kirkus Reviews, 437

Lesbians, 307–312
Library/librarians
    displays, 324–326
    matching books with readers, 322–324
    programs, 326
    Tuccillo's advice, 320–321
Literary appreciation, 8–15
    aesthetic appreciation, 13–15
    finding oneself in a story, 12
    learning to read, 11
    losing oneself in a story, 11–12
    overview (table), 9
    pleasure and profit, 10
    venturing beyond themselves, 13
Literary fools, 349–350
Literary journalism, 291
Literary journeys/figurative quests,
    103–108
Literary nonfiction, 290–292
Literary terms, defined, 427–433
Literature circles, 384–387
Love and friendship, 108–110
Lover, 348–349
Low-rider literacy, 83
Lucky seven list of activities, 396

Mabinogion, 167–168
Magical realism, 137–142
Magician, 350
Manga, 79
Margaret A. Edwards Award winners, 6
    Anderson, Laurie Halse, 402
    Block, Francesca Lia, 139
    Blume, Judy, 61
    Card, Orson Scott, 140
    Cooper, Susan, 224
    Cormier, Robert, 57
    Crutcher, Chris, 240
    Duncan, Lois, 253
    Garden, Nancy, 311
    Hinton, S. E., 7
    Kerr, M. E., 354
    Le Guin, Ursula K., 145
    L'Engle, Madeleine, 14
    Lipsyte, Robert, 241
    Lowry, Lois, 178
    McCaffrey, Anne, 146–147
    Murphy, Jim, 284
    Myers, Walter Dean, 275
    Paulsen, Gary, 231
    Peck, Richard, 271
    Pratchett, Terry, 158–159
    Voigt, Cynthia, 107
    Woodson, Jacqueline, 386
    Zindel, Paul, 215
Memoirs, 302–303
Mental illness, 359–361
Merlyn's Pen, 390
Michael L. Printz Award, 17

Mountain climbing, 233–235
Movie Maker, 79
Movies. *See* Films
Multicultural texts, 86–87, 130–133,
    356–357
Music, 290–291
MyOn, 78
Mysteries, 245–256
Myth-based fantasy, 158–161

Names and naming, 353–357
Names of African Americans, 88–89
National Defense Education Act (NDEA),
    55, 294
Native American literature, 202
Native American teens, 90–91
NETS, 70–71
New journalism, 290
New literacies, 80–97
Ning site, 76, 85
Nonfiction adventures, 233–236
Nonfiction books, 283–318
    biographical books, 296–304
    emotional and physical health,
        304–313
    evaluation of, 292–293
    information books, 285–288, 294–295
    literary nonfiction, 290–292
    outstanding authors, 313–318
    sex, 305–312
    storytelling, 289
    supporting/extending school curriculum,
        295–296
Nonfiction novel, 290

Orphan, 347
Outstanding articles and books,
    439–447

Palpatory literacy, 83
Parents, 358–359
Parody, 217
PBWorksBasicEdition, 75
Pedagogical articles, 328
Peer groups, 125–127
Physical body, 133–135
Physical education teachers, 340
Picture books, 371–376
Pirate stories, 232–233
Play scripts, 204
Plays (drama), 199–205
Poetic license, 198–199
Poetry, 183–199
    contests, 184–185
    hip hop, 186
    poetic license, 198–199
    schemes, 198
    sensual imagery, 197
    teaching, 195–196
    tropes, 198
Poetry 180, 190–193
Poetry slams, 184–185
Police procedurals, 246–247
Portable display, 325
Pregnancy, 134
Prezi, 76
Private detective, 246
Problem novels, 115–120, 121, 124, 125
Props (as humor), 217
Publication opportunities, 390
Publishers Weekly, 437

Title Index

Abbreviations for publishers have been used in this index, as follows: American Library Association = ALA; Coward McCann = Coward; Farrar, Straus and Giroux = Farrar; Harcourt Brace, Jovanovich = Harcourt; HarperCollins = Harper; Houghton Mifflin = Houghton; International Reading Association = IRA; Little, Brown = Little; Lothrop, Lee, and Shepard = Lothrop; National Council of Teachers of English = NCTE; Penguin/Putnam = Penguin; Random House = Random; and Simon & Schuster = S&S. Nat. has also been used for National and U. for University.

First Blood by David Morrell (Evans, 1972), 349

First Freedoms: A Documentary History of the First Amendment Rights in America by Charles C. Haynes, Sam Chaltain, and Susan M. Glisson (Oxford U. Press, 2006), 406

First Part Last, The by Angela Johnson (S&S, 2003), 24

First People: An Illustrated History of American Indians by David C. King (DK, 2008), 286

Fiske Guide to Colleges, The by Edward B. Fiske (Random, yearly), 296

Five Flavors of Dumb by Anony John (Dial, 2010), 121

Fixer, The by Bernard Malamud (Farrar, 1966), 421

Fledgling, The by Jane Langton (Harper, 1994), 149

Flesh and Blood So Cheap: The Triangle Fire in its Legacy by Albert Marrin (Knopf, 2011), 286

Flight by Sherman Alexie (Grove, 2007), 90

Flipped by Wendelin Van Draanen (Knopf, 2003), 337

Fools Crow by James Welch (Viking, 1986), 91

For Teens Only: Quotes, Notes, and Advice You Can Use by Carol Weston (HarperTrophy, 2003), 287

For This Land edited by Vine Deloria, Jr. (Routledge, 1998), 101

Foreign Exchange: A Mystery in Poems by Mel Glenn (Harper, 1999), 192

Forever by Judy Blume (Bradbury, 1975), 60, 61, 407

Forever by Maggie Stiefvater (Scholastic, 2011), 37

Forever in Blue: The Fourth Summer of the Sisterhood by Ann Brashares (Delacorte, 2007), 111

Forgotten Beasts of Eld by Patricia McKillip (Atheneum, 1974), 149

Forgotten Language, The by Erich Fromm (Holt, 1951), 14

Formal Feeling, A by Zibby Oneal (Viking, 1982), 28

Fort Mose: And the Story of the Man Who Built the First Free Black Settlement in Colonial America by Glennette Tilley Turner (Abrams, 2010), 298

Fortune's Bones: The Manumission Requiem by Marilyn Nelson (Front Street, 2004), 192

Foundling by D. M. Cornish (Putnam, 2006), 151

Foundling's Tale, The: Part Three: Factotum by D. M. Cornish (Putnam, 2010), 151

Four Past Midnight by Stephen King (Viking, 1990), 165

Fourth R, The: Conflicts Over Religion in America's Public Schools by Joan DelFattore (Yale University Press, 2004), 406

Frankenstein: Or, The Modern Prometheus by Mary Wollstonecraft Shelley (1818), 175, 206, 377

Franklin Delano Roosevelt by Russell Freedman (Clarion, 1990), 315

Franny and Zooey: Two Novellas by J. D. Salinger (Little, 1961), 114

Freak Show by James St. James (Dutton, 2007), 127, 310

Frederick Douglass: A Noble Life by David Alder (Holiday House, 2010), 300

Free Speech for Me—But Not for Thee: How the American Left and Right Relentlessly Censor Each Other by Nat Hentoff (Harper, 1992), 425

Freedom and Discipline in English: The Report on the Commission on English (New York Examination Board, 1965), 55

Freedom for the Thought that We Hate: A Biography of the First Amendment by Anthony Lewis (Basic Books, 2008), 406, 426

Freedom Riders: John Lewis and Jim Zwerg on the Front Lines of the Civil Rights Movement by Ann Bausum (Nat. Geographic, 2006), 298

Frenchtown Summer by Robert Cornier (Delacorte, 1999), 25

Frenzy, The by Francesca Lia Block (Harper, 2010), 139

Fresh Takes on Teaching Literary Elements: How to Teach What Really Matters about Character, Setting, Point of View, and Theme by Michael W. Smith and Jeffrey D. Wilhelm (NCTE, 2010), 366

Friction by E. R. Frank (S&S, 2003), 127

Frida: Viva la Vida! by Carmen T. Bernier-Grand (Marshall Cavendish, 2007), 192

Friendly Persuasion by Jessamyn West (Harcourt, 1956), 113

Frog and Toad Are Friends by Arnold Lobel (Harper, 1979), 348

From Digital Natives to Digital Wisdom: Hopeful Essays for 21st Century Learning by Marc Pensky (Corwin, 2012), 80

From the Notebooks of Melanin Sun by Jacqueline Woodson (Scholastic, 1995), 386

Frontier Wolf by Rosemary Sutcliff (Dutton, 1980), 272

Frozen Secrets: Antarctica Revealed by Sally M. Walker (Carolrhoda, 2010), 286

Frumious Bandersnatch, The by Ed McBain (S&S, 2004), 247

Future Shock by Alvin Tofler (Pan Books, 1972), 289

Game, The by Diana Wynne Jones (Penguin, 2007), 161

Gangs by Richard Swift (Groundwork Guide, 2011), 288

Gathering Blue by Lois Lowry (Houghton, 2000), 178

Gentlehands by M. E. Kerr (Harper, 1978), 354, 368

George Gershwin: American Composer by Catherine Reef (Morgan Reynolds, 2000), 318

Getting Away with Murder: The True Story of the Emmett Till Case by Chris Crowe (Phyllis Fogelman, 2003), 263

Getting the Knack: 20 Poetry Writing Exercises by Stephen Dunning and William Stafford (NCTE, 1992), 389

Ghost Belonged to Me, The and Sequels by Richard Peck (Delacorte, 1975, 1977, 1983, 1986), 271

Ghost Canoe by Will Hobbs (Harper, 1996), 229

Ghost Girl: A Blue Ridge Mountain Story by Delia Ray (Clarion, 2003), 136

Ghost Medicine by Andrew Smith (Feiwel, 2008), 254

Ghost World by Daniel Clowes (Fantagraphics, 2001), 221

Ghosts of Everest: The Search for Mallory and Irvine by Jochen Hemmleb, Larry A. Johnson, and Eric Simonson (The Mountaineers, 1999), 234

Ghosts of War by Ryan Smithson (Harper, 2009), 299

Gift from Zeus: Sixteen Favorite Myth, A by Jeanne Steig (Harper, 2001), 203

Gifts by Ursula K. Le Guin (Harcourt, 2004), 145

Gilda Joyce: Psychic Investigator by Jennifer Allison (Dutton, 2005), 210

Gingerbread by Rachel Cohn (S&S, 2002), 105

Girl Goddess # 9 by Francesca Lia Block (Harper, 1996), 369

Girl Named Disaster, A by Nancy Farmer (Orchard, 1996), 26, 232, 355

Girl with a Pearl Earring by Tracy Chevalier (Dutton, 1999), 265, 266

Girlsource: A Book by and for Young Women about Relationships, Rights, Futures, Bodies, Minds, and Souls by GirlSource Editorial Team (Ten Speed Press, 2003), 305

Give Me Death: A Novel of Patrick Henry's Family by Ann Rinaldi (Harcourt, 2003), 270, 277

Giver, The by Lois Lowry (Houghton, 1993), 26, 63, 178, 180, 338, 377, 406, 408, 417

Giving Tree, The by Shel Silverstein (Harper, 1964), 338

Glass by Ellen Hopkins (McElderry, 2007), 118, 190, 423

Glory of Unicorns, A edited by Bruce Coville (Scholastic, 1998), 149

Gnat Stokes and the Foggy Bottom Swamp Queen by Sally M. Keehn (Philomel, 2005), 157

Go and Come Back by Joan Abelove (D. K. Ink, 1998), 25

Go Ask Alice by Anonymous (Prentice Hall, 1971), 56, 60, 399, 407, 421

Go, Team, Go! by John Tunis (Morrow, 1954), 43

Goats, The by Brock Cole (Farrar, 1987), 27

Go-Between, The by L. P. Hartley (Dufour, 1978, NYRB Classics, 2002), 261

God Bless You, Mr. Rosewater, or Pearls before Swine by Kurt Vonnegut, Jr. (Holt, 1965), 174

God Is Not One: The Eight Rival Religions that Run the World by Stephen Prothero (Harper, 2011), 101

Godless by Pete Hautman (S&S, 2004), 24, 34, 113, 124

Going Bovine by Libba Bray (Delacorte, 2009), 23, 32, 141

Going on Sixteen by John F. Cavanna (Ryerson, 1946), 51

Going Postal by Terry Pratchett (Harper, 2004), 159

Gold Rush Women by Claire Rudolf Murphy and Jane G. Haigh (Alaska Northwest, 1997), 302

Golden Compass, The by Philip Pullman (Knopf, 1996), 13, 26, 37, 63, 153

Golem's Eye, The by Jonathan Stroud (Hyperion, 2004), 157

Rat Life by Ted Arnold (Penguin, 2007), 251

Ratha's Creature by Clare Bell (Atheneum, 1985), 149

Rationales for Teaching Young Adult Literature edited by Louann Reid with James Hayes Neufeld (Heinemann, 1999), 406

Rats by Paul Zindel (Hyperion, 2000), 138

Rats Saw God by Rob Thomas (S&S, 1996), 26

Readicide: How Schools Are Kililng Reading and What You Can Do about It by Kelly Gallagher (Stenhouse, 2009), 367

Reading Ladders: Leading Students from Where They Are to Where We Would Like Them to Be by Teri Lesesne (Heineman, 2010), 367

Ready Player One by Ernest Cline (Crown, 2011), 225

Real Revolution, The: The Global Story of American Independence by Marc Aronson (Clarion, 2005), 314

Reality Check by Peter Abrahams (Harper, 2009), 251

Rebecca of Sunnybrook Farm by Kate Douglas Wiggin (1904), 42, 47

Reckless by Cornelia Funke (Little, 2010), 151

Red Badge of Courage, The by Stephen Crane (1895), 364, 418

Red Glass by Laura Resau (Delacorte, 2007), 362

Red Hot Salsa: Bilingual Poems on Being Young and Latino in the United States by Lori M. Carlson (Holt, 2005), 191

Red Pyramid, The: Kane Chronicles by Rick Riordan (Hyperion, 2010), 160

Reef of Death by Paul Zindel (HarperTeen, 1998), 138

Reflections on a Gift of Watermelon Pickle edited by Stephen Dunning and others (Scott, Foresman, 1967, reissued, 1994), 199

Religious Literacy: What Every American Needs to Know and Doesn't by Stephen Prothero (Harper, 2007), 101

Remembering the Good Times by Richard Peck (Delacorte, 1985), 28, 271

Republic, The by Plato (380 BC), 406, 426

Requiem: Poems of the Terezin Ghetto by Paul B. Janezko (Candlewick, 2011), 191

Reservation Blues by Sherman Alexie (Grand Central Publishing, 1996), 90

Return of Sherlock Holmes, The by Arthur Conan Doyle (1905), 248

Revolution by Jennifer Donnelly (Delacorte, 2010), 19, 22, 30, 267, 268

Revolver by Marcus Sedgewick (Roaring Brook, 2010), 22, 31, 238

Richard III by William Shakespeare (1591), 364

Riders of the Purple Sage, The by Zane Grey (1912), 237

Rights of the Reader, The by Daniel Pennac and Sarah Adams (Candlewick, 2008), 367

Ring Around Her Finger by James Summers (1957), 43

Ring of Endless Light, A by Madeleine L'Engle (Farrar, 1980), 14, 114

Ring of Solomon: A Bartemaeus Novel by Jonathan Stroud (Hyperion, 2010), 171

River, The by Gary Paulsen (Doubleday, 1991), 231

Road of the Dead, The by Kevin Brooks (Scholastic, 2006), 83, 252

Road to Many a Wonder, The by David Wagoner (Farrar, 1974), 237

Road to Memphis, The by Mildred D. Taylor (Dial, 1990), 272

Robe, The by Lloyd Douglas (Houghton, 1942), 113

Robert Cormier: A New Casebook by Adrienne E. Gavin (Palgrave MacMillan, 2012), 57

Robert Cormier: Daring to Disturb the Universe by Patty Campbell (Delacorte, 2006), 57

Robocalypse: A Novel by Daniel H. Wilson (Doubleday, 2011), 225

Roderick Rules (Diary of a Wimpy Kid #2) by Jeff Kinney (Amulet, 2008), 210

Rodzina by Karen Cushman (Clarion, 2003), 266

Roll of Thunder, Hear My Cry by Mildred D. Taylor (Dial, 1976), 272, 368, 377

Romeo and Juliet by William Shakespeare (1562), 348

Romeo's Ex: Rosaline's Story by Lisa Fiedler (Holt, 2006), 261

Roots by Alex Haley (Doubleday, 1976), 53, 289

Roots and Blues: A Celebration by Arnold Adoff (Clarion, 2011), 291

Ropemaker, The by Peter Dickinson (Delacorte, 2001), 168

Rose and the Beast Fairy Tales, The: Fairy Tales Retold by Francesca Lia Block (Harper, 2001), 139

Rose Daughter by Robin McKinley (Greenwillow, 1997), 168

Roses and Bones: Myths, Tales, and Secrets by Francesca Lia Block (Harper, 2010), 139

Rules of Survival, The by Nancy Werlin (Penguin, 2006), 23

Run Softly, Go Fast by Barbara Wersba (Atheneum, 1970), 59, 60

Run, Shelley, Run by Gertrude Samuels (Crowell, 1974), 60

Runner, The by Cynthia Voigt (Atheneum, 1985), 107

Running Dream, The by Wendelin Van Draanen (Knopf, 2011), 124

Running Loose by Chris Crutcher (Greenwillow, 1983), 110, 240

Running with the Reservoir Pups (Eddie and the Gang with No Name) by Colin Bateman (Delacorte, 2005), 362

Sacajawea (Lewis and Clark Expedition) by Joseph Bruchac (Scholastic, 2001), 315

Sacred Doorways: A Beginner's Guide to Icons by Lynette Martin (Paraclete Press, 2002), 101

Sacrifice by Kathleen Benner Dubie (S&S, 2005), 259

Safe at Second by Scott Johnson (Putnam, 1999), 25

Salvage the Bones by Jesmyn Ward (Bloomsbury, 2011), 225

Same God, Different Churches by Katie Meier (Tommy Nelson Publishers, 2005), 101

Sandman by Neil Gaiman (Vertigo, 1993), 221

Sapphique by Catherine Fisher (Dial, 2010), 173

Savage Summit: The True Stories of the First Five Women Who Climbed K2, The World's Most Feared Mountain by Jennifer Jordan (Morrow, 2005), 234

Saving Francesca by Melina Marchetta (Knopf, 2004), 119, 128

Saving the Buffalo by Albert Marrin (Scholastic, 2006), 317

Scary Stories 3: More Tales to Chill Your Bones by Alvin Schwartz (Harper, 1991), 161, 207

Scary Stories to Tell in the Dark by Alvin Schwartz (Lippincott, 1981), 161, 203, 207, 375, 396

Scat by Carl Hiassen (Knopf, 2009), 254

Schindler's List by Thomas Keneally (S&S, 1982), 289

Scorch Trials, The by James Dashner (Delacorte, 2010), 152

Scorpio Races, The by Maggie Stiefvater (Scholastic, 2011), 22, 171

Scorpions by Walter Dean Myers (Harper, 1988), 27, 275

Scott of the Antarctic by David Crane (Knopf, 2006), 234

Scrapbook of Frankie Pratt: A Novel in Pictures, The by Caroline Preston (HarperCollins, 2011), 225

Screwtape Letters, The by C. S. Lewis (Barbour, 1992), 216

Sea Gulls Woke Me, The by Mary Stolz (Harper, 1951), 51

Sea of Trolls, The by Nancy Farmer (S&S, 2004), 157

Second Summer of the Sisterhood, The by Anne Brashares (Delacorte, 2003), 111

Secondary School Literacy: What Research Reveals for Classroom Practice edited by Leslie S. Rush, A. Jonathan Eakle, and Allen Berger (NCTE, 2007), 81

Secret Diary of Adrian Mole, Aged 13 3/4, The by Sue Townsend (1982, reissued Harper, 2003), 211

Secret Garden, The by Frances Hodgson Burnett (Bantam, 1987), 112

Secret Knowledge of Grownups, The by David Wisniewski (Harper, 1998), 376

Secret under My Skin by Janet McNaughton (Harper, 2005), 173

Secrets from the Rocks: Dinosaur Hunting with Roy Chapman Andrews by Albert Marrin (Dutton, 2002), 317

Secrets in the Fire by Henning Menkell translated by Anne Connie Stuksrud (Annick, 2003), 95

Secrets of the Shopping Mall by Richard Peck (Delacorte, 1979), 271

Secrets of the Sphinx by James Cross Giblin (Scholastic, 2004), 316

Seedfolks by Paul Fleischman (Harper, 1997), 132

Seeing the Blue Between: Advice and Inspiration for Young Poets compiled by Paul B. Janeczko (Candlewick, 2002), 389

Seek by Paul Fleischman (Cricket, 2001), 25, 129

Sending of Dragons, A by Jane Yolen (Delacorte, 1987), 149

Separate Peace, A by John Knowles (Macmillan, 1961), 54, 132, 329, 348

70,000 to One by Quentin Reynolds (Random, 1946), 51

Seventeenth Summer by Maureen Daly (1942), 43, 51

Sex Education by Jenny Davis (Orchard, 1988), 27